EXTREMIST GROUPS

Information

for Students

EXTREMIST GROUPS

Information for Students

for Students

VOLUME 1: A-K

THOMSON

GALE

Detroit • New York • San Francisco • San Diego • New Haven, Conn. • Waterville, Maine • London • Munich

EXTREMIST GROUPS: INFORMATION FOR STUDENTS: VOLUME 1

Produced by Thomson Gale Editorial and Production Staff

This publication is a creative work fully protected by all applicable copyright laws, as well as by misappropriation, trade secret, unfair competition, and other applicable laws. The authors and editors of this work have added value to the underlying factual material herein through one or more of the following: unique and original selection, coordination, expression, arrangement, and classification of the information.

For permission to use material from the product, submit your request via the Web at http://www.gale-edit.com/permissions, or you may download our Permissions Request form and submit your request by fax or mail to:

Permissions Department
Thomson Gale
27500 Drake Rd.
Farmington Hills, MI 48331-3535
Permissions Hotline:
248-699-8006 or 800-877-4253, ext. 8006
Fax 248-699-8074 or 800-762-4058

Since this page cannot legibly accommodate all copyright notices, the acknowledgments constitute an extension of the copyright notice.

While every effort has been made to secure permission to reprint material and to ensure the reliability of the information presented in this publication, Thomson Gale neither guarantees the accuracy of the data contained herein nor assumes any responsibility for errors, omissions or discrepancies. Thomson Gale accepts no payment for listing; and inclusion in the publication of any organization, agency, institution, publication, service, or individual does not imply endorsement of the editors or publisher. Errors brought to the attention of the publisher and verified to the satisfaction of the publisher will be corrected in future editions.

LIBRARY OF CONGRESS CATALOGING-IN-PUBLICATION DATA

Extremist groups : information for students.
   p. cm.
   Includes bibliographical references and index.
   ISBN 1-4144-0345-3 (hardcover : alk. paper)
   1. Radicals–Encyclopedias. 2. Radicalism–Encyclopedias. 3. Terrorists–Encyclopedias.
4. Terrorism–Encyclopedias.

   HN90.R3.E975 2006
   322.4'203–dc22
                                             2005035599

British Library Cataloguing-in-Publication Data
A catalogue record for this book is available from the British Library.
ISBN 1-4144-1119-7 (vol. 1)

This title is also available as an e-book.
ISBN 1414404832
Contact your Thomson Gale sales representative for ordering information.

Printed in the United States of America
10 9 8 7 6 5 4 3 2 1

Table of Contents

VOLUME 2

Introduction

Extremist Groups: Information for Students is designed to provide key facts and insight into the history, philosophy, and motivations driving 150 extremist organizations. Although some groups are included for historical perspective, the vast majority are active in some form today. The groups profiled range from local political activist and special-interest groups to international terrorist organizations.

What constitutes extremism is usually contentious and often a matter of cultural or political perspective. Some groups actually admit and embrace their extremism as justifiable toward accomplishment of their agenda or goals. Others work hard to present themselves as more mainstream or "activist" groups. Although many extremist attitudes and acts are seemingly indefensible to a large segment of society, it is also fair to note that the charge of "extremism" is an often-used label applied by opponents in order to marginalize or dismiss an organization's philosophical goals.

Consider the similarities and differences in the use of the word "extremists" in the following quotes:

> What is objectionable, what is dangerous about extremists, is not that they are extreme, but that they are intolerant. The evil is not what they say about their cause, but what they say about their opponents. *Robert F. Kennedy*

> The question is not whether we will be extremists, but what kind of extremists we will be ... The nation and the world are in dire need of creative extremists. *Martin Luther King, Jr.*

Clearly these contrasting uses show that the problems of defining extremism dwarf those encountered with other problematic definitions related to "terrorism" or "hate groups," and can at times mimic those encountered for "activist" or "radical groups". For example, all terrorist groups are extremist groups, but the reverse is certainly not true. The vast majority of extremist groups are not terrorist groups. Even if some members engage in violence, most groups can not be easily categorized as terrorist groups because the violent actions associated with them are often those of a disturbed individual or smaller subgroup working under the same philosophical umbrella.

Accordingly, without an accepted scholarly or even popular definition of "extremism" the editors faced difficult choices. Violence or advocacy of violence was always qualifying, but another criteria applied to the selection of non-terrorist, nonviolent groups was whether the group's tactics were not those generally endorsed or used by the majority of groups with similar goals. Some groups operate so far outside the pale of generally accepted morality, ethics, and historical fact that their inclusion as extremist groups was warranted simply based upon rhetoric. Groups that engaged in the loftier types of positive change extremism, were not, conversely, included.

With literally thousands of potential candidate groups, the editorial focus narrowed to including those groups that could best represent the broad spectrum and global diversity of agendas and tactics. The editors, additionally, sought to provide an overview of the variety of responses to extremist groups and the efforts of government and civilian efforts to quash or counter these groups.

Extremist Groups: Information for Students seeks to give readers the basic tools and information to form their own judgments regarding the groups and philosophies examined herein. In an era where news, fact, "spin," and opinion often too easily commingle, *Extremist Groups: Information for Students* should provide a foundation for further critical reading. By offering global perspectives from an international staff of researchers, we intend that *Extremist Groups: Information for Students* will challenge

readers—not necessarily to agree with all the definitions, labels, and assertions contained herein, but rather to form their own opinions about what constitutes extremism.

ADVISORS AND CONTRIBUTORS

While compiling this volume, the editors relied upon the expertise and contributions of an experienced and internationally distributed research staff composed of multilingual scholars, researchers, journalists, and writers. In the vast majority of cases, researchers, writers, and advisors were based in the countries or regions in which the extremist groups listed in this book principally operate.

The editors gratefully acknowledge and extend deep thanks to the editors, imaging, and permissions teams at Thomson Gale for their patience and counsel in handling both content and publishing issues related to this project.

The Editors
Paris
December, 2005

About the Book

Each entry in *Extremist Groups: Information For Students* contains the following six elements:

Overview: Provides a brief overview of the subject of the entry.

History: Provides the background and history of the group, including its origins and the individuals associated with the development and organization of the group.

Philosophy and Tactics: Provides an overview of the philosophy of the group and how that philosophy is implemented by the group to bring about change.

Other Perspectives: Provides an overview of reactions to the group by governments, individuals, or other groups.

Summary: Provides a brief summary of the groups' leaders, governing philosophy, and actions.

Sources: Provides a list of sources consulted or cited within the entry.

The first page of each entry includes quick "at a glance" information about the basics of the organization, such as its leaders, the year it was established, and the estimated size of the group. In addition, most entries feature sidebars with supplemental information, including short biographies of the group's leadership, key events in the history of the group, and primary source excerpts about the group and its activities. Photographs showing members of the group or the results of the group's activities are found in most entries.

When the only verifiable or attributable source of information for an entry comes from documents or information provided by a governmental organization (e.g., the U.S. Department of State), the editors endeavored to carefully note when the language used and perspective offered was that of a governmental organization.

Acknowledgements

The editors wish to thank the copyright holders of the excerpted criticism included in this volume and the permissions managers of many book and magazine publishing companies for assisting us in securing reproduction rights. We are also grateful to the staffs of the Detroit Public Library, the Library of Congress, the University of Detroit Mercy Library, Wayne State University Purdy/Kresge Library Complex, and the University of Michigan Libraries for making their resources available to us. Following is a list of the copyright holders who have granted us permission to reproduce material in this volume of EGIS. Every effort has been made to trace copyright, but if omissions have been made, please let us know.

Copyrighted excerpts were reproduced from the following periodicals:

BBC News, October 30, 1998; April 23, 1999; May 2, 2000; March 31, 2001; May 7, 2002; June 22, 2002; December 8, 2002; December 18, 2002; December 8, 2003; June 11, 2004; August 13, 2004; December 27, 2004; January 4, 2005; June 18, 2005; July 7, 2005; September 16, 2005; September 26, 2005. © BBC MMV. All reproduced by permission from BBC News at bbcnews.com.-*New York Times,* September 25, 2005. Copyright 2005 The Associated Press. All rights reserved. Reprinted with permission of the Associated Press./ March 11, 1986; November 29, 1987; December 8, 1988; June 27, 1993; December 17, 1993; June 16, 2002; February 5, 2004; March 11, 2005; September 2, 2005. Copyright © 1986, 1987, 1988, 1993, 2002, 2004, 2005 by The New York Times Co. All reprinted by permission.-Southern Poverty Law Center, summer, 1998; fall, 1998; summer, 1999; fall, 2000; summer, 2001; fall, 2001; winter, 2002; fall, 2002; winter, 2003; fall, 2003; spring, 2004; summer, 2004; summer, 2005. © Copyright 1998, 1999, 2000, 2001, 2002, 2003, 2004, 2005 Southern Poverty Law Center. All reproduced by permission.

Photographs and illustrations were received from the following sources:

Activists from both sides of the abortion issue on the steps of the federal courthouse, New York, New York, July 16, 1992, photograph. AP/Wide World Photos.-African National Congress supporter takes cover from gunfire alongside South African National Defense Force members, Umlazi township, South Africa, February 25, 1996, photograph by Joao Silva. AP/Wide World Photos.-Afrikaner Resistance Movement members lie dead in Mafikeng street, Mmabatho, South Africa, March 11, 1994, photograph by David Brauchli. AP/Wide World Photos.-Afrikaner Resistance Movement protestors and police in a chaotic clash, Ventersdorp, Transvaal, South

Africa, 1991, photograph. © Ian Berry/Magnum Photos.-Akhil Bharatiya Vidyarthi Parishad members during a rally opposing Sonia Gandhi becoming India's first foreign-born prime minister, Bombay, India, May 17, 2004, photograph. AP/Wide World Photos.-Al Aqsa Martyrs Brigades shoot in the air during a rally, Nablus, August 5, 2004, photograph by Nasser Ishtayeh. AP/Wide World Photos.-Al Jamaa Islamiye members demonstrate in support of Osama bin Laden, Tripoli, Lebanon, October 12, 2001, photograph. Courtney Kealy/Getty Images.-Al-Gamaa al-Islamiyya's twelve leaders, Cairo, June 21, 2002, photograph. AP/Wide World Photos.-Al-Ghozi, Fathur Rohman, suspected Indonesian terrorist, Mainla, Philippines, January 19, 2002, photograph by Ed Wray. AP/Wide World Photos.-Al-Masri, Sheikh Abu Hamza, speaks at the 2nd Conference of the Islamic Revival Movement, London, February 26, 1999, photograph. Gerry Penny/AFP/Getty Images.-Animal rights protester is held down by Arkansas police during a demonstration, October 29, 2001, photograph by Danny Johnston. AP/Wide World Photos.-Animal rights protestor outside the gates of a Huntingdon Life Sciences laboratory, Eye, Suffolk, UK, photograph. Philippe Hays/Peter Arnold, Inc.-Anti-abortion activists demonstration, Washington, D. C., January 22, 2003, photograph. AP/Wide World Photos.-Anti-fur activists graffiti, photograph. Robert Gumpert/Alamy.-Arafat, Yasser, mural liberating his people, Jericho, 1995, photograph. © Abbas/Magnum Photos.-Armed Palestinians kneel in prayer, Gaza City, 2004, photograph. © Abbas/Magnum Photos.-Aryan Nation march, Idaho, 1998, photograph. © Donovan Wylie/Magnum Photos.-Aryan National Alliance members, Coeur d'Alene, Idaho, October 23, 2000, photograph by Tom Davenport. AP/Wide World Photos.-Aryan Nations members with Christian Identity Minister Johnathan Williams, Alabama, September 18, 2004, photograph. David S. Holloway/Getty Images.-Aryan Republican Army, photograph. AP/Wide World Photos.-Assad, Bashar, Syrian President meets with the leaders of ten Damascus-based Palestinian radical organizations, September 10, 2005, photograph. Sana/EPA/Landov.-Azhar, Maulana Massod, leader of the Pakistani Jaish-e-Mohammad terrorist group, Islamabad, Pakistan, August 26, 2001, photograph. Mian Khursheed/Reuters/Landov.-Barboza, Esteban, a rondero, Huantam, Ayacucho, Peru, July 25, 2003, photograph by Martin Mejia. AP/Wide World Photos.-Bari, Judi, photograph by Paul Sakuma. AP/Wide World Photos.-Begin, Menahem, leader of the Irgun Party, Tel-Aviv, Israel, November, 1950, photograph. © Robert Capa © 2001 Cornell Capa/Magnum Photos.-bin Laden, Osama, Al-Qaida leader, with his deputy Ayman al-Zawahri, September 10, 2003, photograph. AP/Wide World Photos.-Black, Don, Ku Klux Klan grand wizard, New Orleans, Louisiana, May 14, 1981, photograph. AP/Wide World Photos.-Bo Gritz, James, Randy Weaver, and William Goehler, Freemen organization supporters, Brussett, Montana, April, 1996, photograph by James Woodcock. AP/Wide World Photos.-Bodies of policemen killed in an ambush by Shining Path guerrillas, Huallaga valley, Tingo Maria, Peru, February 20, 2005, photograph by EPENSA. AP/Wide World Photos.-British National Party street rally, Bethnal Green, London, photograph. David Hoffman Photo Library/Alamy.-Carabinieri police officer patrols Venice courthouse, near Rialto bridge where a bomb exploded, August 9, 2001, photograph by Francesco Proietti. AP/Wide World Photos.-Carette, Pierre, leader of the Combatant Communist Cells, Leuven, Belgium, February 25, 2003, photograph. Oliver Hoslet/AFP/Getty Images.-Civilian patriots patrol their village to protect it against the extremist Armed Islamic Group, Oran, Algeria, 2001, photograph. © Paolo Pellegrin/Magnum Photos.-Communist rebels march during a meeting between government officials and New People's Army, Surigao del Sur, Philippines, January 6, 2004, photograph by Froilan Gallardo. AP/Wide World Photos.

Commuter train, after a bomb exploded near the town of El Affroune, February 24, 1998, photograph. AP/Wide World Photos.-Convicted Palestinian terrorist awaiting an interview with the press, 1969, photograph. © Micha Bar Am/Magnum Photos.-Cow being sacrificed as part of an Ashura ritual, Tehran, Iran, 1997, photograph. © Abbas/Magnum Photos.-Czech riot policemen clash with drunken skinheads, Kozolupy, photograph by Jiri Bervida/CTK. AP/Wide World Photos.-Department store goes up in flames from a bomb planted by the Irish Republican Army, Londonderry, Northern Ireland, January 4, 1972, photograph. AP/Wide World Photos.-Duke,

David, Ku Klux Klan leader, London, 1978, photograph. AP/Wide World Photos.-Duke, David, president of the National Association for the Advancement of White People, August 19, 1980, photograph. © Bettman/Corbis.-Earth First protester, California, 1989, photograph. Jeremy Hogan/Alamy.-East Timorese listen to a speech during the first day of the Revolutionary Front for an Independent East Timor National Congress, Dili, East Timor, May 15, 2000, photograph by Joel Rubin. AP/Wide World Photos.-East Timorese militia patrol with their weapons, Liquica, April, 1999, photograph. AP/Wide World Photos.-Edward Street, after a massive car bomb exploded, Portadown, Northern Ireland, February 24, 1998, photograph by Paul McErlane. AP/Wide World Photos.-Egyptian movie poster defaced by Islamic fundamentalist extremists, 1984, photograph. © Micha Bar Am/Magnum Photos.-Egyptian soldiers tend to wounded after members of the Al Jihad movement opened fire during a military parade, Cairo, Egypt, October 6, 1981, photograph. AP/Wide World Photos.-Etzion, Yehuda head of the Jewish terrorist underground movement, photograph. © Gueorgui Pinkhassov/Magnum Photos.-Fatah Hawks, the military wing of Yasser Arafat's PLO faction, march through the occupied Gaza Strip, Gaza City, Palestine, March 14, 1994, photograph by Jerome Delay. AP/Wide World Photos.-Fatah movement gunman, with a gunman from the Islamic group Hamas face Israeli forces, Bethlehem, October 20, 2001, photograph by Lefteris Pitarakis. AP/Wide World Photos.-Fatah Revolutionary Council training camp run by the Abu Nidal Organization, photograph. © Alain Nogues/Corbis Sygma.-Fatah Youth Organization, Gaza City, January 1, 2001, photograph by Murad Sezer. AP/Wide World Photos.-FBI agents sift through debris of burned down home of Robert J. Matthew, the founder of the neo-Nazi group known as The Order, Whidbey Island, Washington, December, 1984, photograph by Tim Klass. AP/Wide World Photos.-Female guerrillas display traditional Kurdish garb and deadly accessories, Northern Iraq, August 1, 1991, photograph by Burhan Ozbilisi. AP/Wide World Photos.-Filipino Muslim peers through a window prior to a mass funeral of alleged Abu Sayyaf detainees, March 16, 2005, Taguig, Philippines, photograph by Bullit Marquez. AP/Wide World Photos.-Filipino Muslims lower one of

the bodies of alleged Abu Sayyaf detainees into a common grave, Taguig, Philippines, March 16, 2005, photograph by Bullit Marquez. AP/Wide World Photos.-Fire fighters emerge after cleaning toxic gas-contaminated train cars, Tokyo, March 21, 1995, photograph. AP/Wide World Photos.-Fire inspectors examine damage to McDonald's restaurant, after a suspected arson attack from the Animal Liberation Front, Merksem, Belgium, August 12, 1999, photograph by Yves Logghe. AP/Wide World Photos.-Firefighters and police pull an Earth First protester to safety, Missoula, Montana, June 19, 2002, photograph by Tom Bauer. AP/Wide World Photos.-Firemen examine the wreckage of a Civil Guard patrol vehicle, after an ETA bomb exploded, Spain, August 20, 2000, photograph by EFE, Javier Belver. AP/Wide World Photos.-Firey cross at a Ku Klux Klan meeting, photograph. © Hulton-Deutsch Collection/Corbis.-Fiumicino Airport, after Palestinian guerrillas engaged in a gunfight with police before hijacking a jetliner, Rome, December 17, 1973, photograph. AP/Wide World Photos. -Fujimori, Alberto, then Peruvian President, passing the bodies of two Tupac Amaru rebels who were killed in the storming of Japanese ambassador's residence, Lima, April 23, 1997, photograph. AP/Wide World Photos.-Funeral of an 18 year old Catholic girl, Ulster, Northern Ireland, 1997, photograph. © Abbas/Magnum Photos.-Funeral of Bobby Sands, Belfast, Northern Ireland, 1981, photograph. © Peter Marlow/Magnum Photos.-Funeral of the Israeli athletes who were taken hostage by Palestinian terrorists during the 1972 Munich Olympics, photograph. © Micha Bar Am/Magnum Photos.-German neo-Nazis pass by the Brandenburg Gate, Berlin, March 12, 2000, photograph by Herbert Knosowski. AP/Wide World Photos.-Goehler, Bill, Freemen supporter, Jordan, Montana, April 19, 1996, photograph by Bob Zellar. AP/Wide World Photos.-Gonzales, Dan, vice chairman of the League of the South, during the controversy over the fate of Terry Schiavo, Florida, March 22, 2005, photograph. © Winston Luzier/Reuters/Corbis.-Greenpeace activists sail alongside other boats, photograph by Joerg Sarbach. AP/Wide World Photos.-Guynan, Dave, British National Party candidate, Sunderland, England, April 29, 2003, photograph by Will Walker. AP/Wide World Photos.-Hakim, Abu Haris Abdul, photograph by B. K. Bangash. AP/Wide World

Photos.-Hale, Rev. Matthew, leader of the World Church of the Creator with members of the Ku Klux Klan, October 26, 2002, Fayetteville, West Virginia, photograph. AP/Wide World Photos.-HAMAS suicide bomb attack in downtown Jerusalem, March 3, 1996, photograph by Eyal Warshavsky. AP/Wide World Photos.

Hannan, Mufti Mohammad Abdul, believed key leader of the Harkat-ul-Jihad-al-Islam/Bangladesh organization, October 1, 2005, photograph. Abir Abdullah/EPA/Landov.-Haradinaj, Ramush, former leader in the Kosovo Liberation Army, March 9, 2005, photograph. Reuters/Landov.-Harkat-Ul-Jehadi Islami suspected militants jump out of a police truck, Lakhanpur, India, June 30, 2003, photograph by Channi Anand. AP/Wide World Photos.-Harshman, Greg, of the Spokane Regional Intelligence Unit, uses the internet to track and monitor Web sites, like that of Rev. Matthew Hale, founder of the World Church of the Creator, December 9, 1999, photograph by Jeff T. Green. AP/Wide World Photos.-Hekmatyar, Gulbuddin, Afghan warlord, confers with Ustad Abdul Rab Rasul Sayaf an Afghan guerrilla leader, Peshawar, January 17, 1987, photograph. Dimitri Kochko/AFP/Getty Images.-Hertford College boat house, after fire bombed by The Animal Liberation Front, Oxford, England, August 25, 2005, photograph by Kirsty Wigglesworth. AP/Wide World Photos.-Hezbollah guerrillas, Chebaa Farms region, Lebanon, April 10, 2002, photograph by Hezbollah Military Media/HO. AP/Wide World Photos.-Hezbollah militia member, Lebanon, April 14, 1996, photograph. AP/Wide World Photos.-Hideouts of Al-Qaida-linked militants along the Afghan border, South Waziristan, Pakistan, photograph. AP/Wide World Photos.-Hill, Paul, photograph by Mark Foley. AP/Wide World Photos.-Hooded man reads the IRA's Easter Message at a rally, Crossmaglen, Northern Ireland, April 7, 1996, photograph. AP/Wide World Photos.-Horien, Adrian, one of four demonstrators from the militant Army of God anti-abortion group, photograph by David Duprey. AP/Wide World Photos.-Indian Border Security Force personnel escort Sajad Bhat suspected district leader of the Jaish-e-Mohammed, Srinagar, January 3, 2005, photograph. Fayaz Kabli/Reuters/Landov.-Indian man prepares to jump to his death as Hindu extremists demand that the Babu Jammid

mosque be destroyed, 1990, photograph. Network Photographers/Alamy.-Indonesian anti-riot troops beat a student protester during an anti-government protest, Jakarta, August 23, 1999, photograph by Ramli. AP/Wide World Photos.-Indonesian boy wearing a t-shirt featuring a portrait of Osama bin Laden, 2004, photograph. © Abbas/Magnum Photos.-Iranian women demonstrate in support of the Mujahedin-e Khalq Organization, Tehran, Iran, October 28, 2002, photograph. Reuters/Landov.-Irish Republican Army graffiti, West Belfast, Northern Ireland, March 5, 2001, photograph by Peter Morrison. AP/Wide World Photos.-Islamic Jihad member holds up a Holy Koran and a grenade during a rally, Gaza City, Gaza Strip, February 21, 2003, photograph by Brennan Linsley. AP/Wide World Photos. -Islamic Jihad members display weapons during prayers, photograph. Spencer Platt/Getty Images.-Islamic Jihad militant during the funeral processions of Hazem Rahim, a local Islamic Jihad commander and Abdulraof Abu Asse, Gaza City, July 23, 2004, photograph by Adel Hana. AP/Wide World Photos.-Israeli soldiers try to stop young Jewish settler extremists from entering the Kfar Darom settlement, Gush Katif, Gaza Strip, photograph. © Paolo Pellegin/Magnum Photos.-Izzedine Al-Qassam Brigades fighter, Jebaliya, Gaza Strip, October 11, 1994, photograph by Jerome Delay. AP/Wide World Photos.-Janjalani, Khaddafi, and Radulan Sahiron sit with fellow Abu Sayyaf rebels inside their jungle hideout in the Sulu province, Philippines, July 16, 2000, photograph. AP/Wide World Photos.-Jewish Defensive League hate graffiti on an Arab home, Hebron, West Bank, 2003, photograph. © Larry Towell/Magnum Photos.-Jewish settler fires on a crowd of Palestinians, Hebron, December 3, 1993, photograph by Jerome Delay. AP/Wide World Photos.-Jewish settler hate graffiti in a Muslim cemetery, Hebron, West Bank, 2003, photograph. © Larry Towell/Magnum Photos.-Kach Party symbol with graffiti in a burned-out Palestinian home, Hebron, 2003, photograph. © Larry Towell/Magnum Photos.-Kahane, Rabbi Meir, at a Jewish Defense League protest, photograph. © Bettmann/Corbis.-Khaled, Leila, a member of the Popular Front for the Liberation of Palestine, Amman, Jordan, 1970, photograph by Hagop Toranian. AP/Wide World Photos.-King Fahd Mosque, target of a bombing plot by the chairman and another member of the militant Jewish Defense League, Culver City, California, December 12, 2001, photograph by Damian Dovarganes. AP/Wide World Photos.-Kosovar Albanians march, Malisevo, Kosovo, March 16, 2004, photograph. Valdrin Xhemaj/EPA/Landov.-Ku Klux Klan female members, North Carolina, 1964, photograph. Charles Moore/Black Star/Alamy.-Ku Klux Klan member, Greensburg, Pennsylvania, August 16, 1997, photograph by Gary Tramontina. AP/Wide World Photos.-Lebron, Lolita, with three other women shortly after they opened fire from the visitors gallery of the U.S. House of Representatives, Washington, D. C., March 1, 1954, photograph. AP/Wide World Photos.-Leonardo da Vinci Airport, after a terrorist attack by seven Abu Nidal gunmen, Rome, Italy, December 27, 1985, photograph. AP/Wide World Photos.-Londonderry riots, Northern Ireland, 1985, photograph. © Stuart Franklin/Magnum Photos.-Loyalist Volunteer Force announcing their ceasefire in Portadown, Belfast, Northern Ireland, May 15, 1998, photograph. AP/Wide World Photos.-Maaroufi, Tarek ben Habib, co-founder of the Tunisian Combatant Group, Brussels, Belgium, September 13, 2004, photograph. Thierry Roge/Reuters/Landov.-Mahameed, Khaled, Israeli Arab lawyer, Nazareth, May 24, 2005, photograph by Eitan Hess-Ashkenazi. AP/Wide World Photos.-Malcolm X, photograph. © Corbis-Bettmann.-Man training for the Kosovo Liberation Army, Drenica, 1999, photograph. © Corbis Sygma.-McDermott, Bill, white supremacist, with two friends, Dubuque, Iowa, 1991, photograph. William F. Campbell/Time Life Pictures/Getty Images.-McLaren, Richard, self-styled ambassador of the Republic of Texas group, Texas, March 6, 1997, photograph by Ron Heflin. AP/Wide World Photos.-Means, Russell, 1970, photograph. AP/Wide World Photos.

Metzger, Tom, leader of the White Aryan Resistance group, Coeur d' Alene, Idaho, September 5, 2000, photograph. AP/Wide World Photos.-Michigan Militia members set fire to a United Nations flag, Lansing, Michigan, October, 24, 1995, photograph. AP/Wide World Photos.-Morales, William, bomb maker for the terrorist group FALN, 1983, photograph. AP/Wide World Photos.-Moro, Aldo, Italian Premier, body found 55 days after he was kidnapped in a Red Brigade ambush, May 9, 1978, photograph. AP/Wide World

Photos.-Mother Teresa, on a tour of Trilokpuri, a Sikh section of Delhi, photograph. AP/Wide World Photos.-Mourners carry the coffin of Israeli Arab George Khoury, March 21, 2004, photograph. Menahem Kahana/AFP/Getty.-Movimento dos Sem Terra group camp out in front of the INCRA Agrarian Reform Government Agency, Rio de Janeiro Plaza, March 20, 1998, photograph by Renzo Gostoli. AP/Wide World Photos.-Muhammed, Elijah, leader of the Nation of Islam, Chicago, Illinois, February 26, 1966, photograph. AP/Wide World Photos.-Mujahedin-e Kahlq members pass through a U. S. checkpoint, Dayala, Iraq, May 12, 2003, photograph. Roberto Schmidt/AFP/Getty Images.-National Alliance members demonstrate against U. S. support for Israel, Washington, D.C., August 24, 2002, photograph. AP/Wide World Photos.-National Bolshevik Party militants march in front of St. Basil Church, Moscow, 1998, photograph. © Abbas/Magnum Photos.-National Liberation Army, Santa Ana, November 1, 1997, photograph. AP/Wide World Photos.-Nazi storm troopers, Luitpold Arena, Nuremberg, Germany, September 20, 1936, photograph. AP/Wide World Photos.-Neo-Nazis and white supremacists celebrate at NordicFest, Kentucky, 2001, photograph. © Jonas Bendiksen/Magnum Photos.-Neo-Nazis and white supremacists watch a burning swastika at NordicFest, Kentucky, 2001, photograph. © Jonas Bendiksen/Magnum Photos.-Neo-Nazis, Skinheads and Ku Klux Klansmen march in Pulaski, Tennessee, 1989, photograph. © Leonard Freed/Magnum Photos.-New Black Panther members and white-hooded Ku Klux Klansmen, Jasper, Texas, June 27, 1998, photograph by Pat Sullivan. AP/Wide World Photos.-Nicholls, Karen, abortion-rights activist shields herself from anti-abortion leader Rev. Flip Benham, Wichita, Kansas, July 14, 2001, photograph. AP/Wide World Photos.-Ocalan, Abdullah, Beirut, 1998, photograph by Jamal Saidi. Archive Photos/Getty Images.-Ocean Warrior flagship of marine conservation group Sea Shepherd, Port of Miami, July 11, 2001, photograph. AP/Wide World Photos.-Officers clear the scene after a bomb exploded under a police car, Sanguesa, Spain, May 30, 2003, photograph. © Reuters/Corbis.-Okamoto, Kozo, member of the Japanese Red Army group, photograph. © Micha Bar Am/Magnum Photos.-Palestinian gunman wears a slogan that reads, "martyr Abu Ali Mustafa brigade,

Popular Front for the Liberation of Palestine," photograph by Rick Bowmer. AP/Wide World Photos.-Palestinian militant during a march of the al-Aqsa Martyrs Brigades, Gaza City, August 14, 2002, photograph. © Reuters/ Corbis.-Palestinian militant fires at an Israeli armored helicopter, Gaza, photograph. © Abbas/Magnum Photos.-Peace Wall that separates Catholics from Protestants, Ulster, Belfast, 1997, photograph. © Abbas/Magnum Photos.-People Against Gangsterism And Drugs lead members to return fire during clashes with the police, Hannover Park, Cape Town, South Africa, August 11, 1996, photograph by Sasa Kralj. AP/Wide World Photos.-People for the Ethical Treatment of Animals protest the Canadian governments go-ahead for a seal hunt, Washington, April 6, 2005, photograph by Stephen J. Boitano. AP/Wide World Photos.-Philippines National Police Regional Mobile Group patrol the outskirts of a petroleum company, Manila, Philippines, March 16, 2000, photograph. Luis Liwanag/Getty Images.-Plainclothes police officers carry the dead body of a businessman believed kidnapped by the Turkish Hezbollah, Istanbul, Turkey, January 19, 2000, photograph. AP/Wide World Photos.-Police officer looks at the damage after the Shiv Sena party allegedly set fire to the hospital, Thane, India, August 27, 2001, photograph. AP/Wide World Photos.-Police officer reads graffiti in a Lashkar-e-Jhangvi hideout, Quetta, Pakistan, February 18, 2005, photograph. AP/Wide World Photos.-Police officers cordon off the McDonald's restaurant, after a bomb exploded, Brittany, France, April 19, 2000, photograph by Franck Prevel. AP/Wide World Photos.-Police officers examine a hole in the wall, after a bomb explosion, Madrid, Spain, March 13, 1998, photograph by Paul White. AP/ Wide World Photos.-Police officers hold back photographers following a bomb blast at the Marriott Hotel linked to the Jemaah Islamiyah terror group, Jakarta, Indonesia, August 5, 2003, photograph by Achmad Ibrahim. AP/ Wide World Photos.-Police officers remove the bodies of victims of a shooting, which includes Maulana Azam Tariq, the one-time leader of Sipah-e-Sahaba, Islamabad, Pakistan, October 6, 2003, photograph. AP/Wide World Photos.-Policeman guard members of the Russian National Union, Moscow, May 12, 1998, photograph. AP/Wide World Photos.-Policeman inspects a guitar during a search operation, Gauhati, India, April 2, 2005, photograph. AP/ Wide World Photos.-Popular Front for the Liberation of Palestine members during a demonstration, Nablus, October 13, 2001, photograph by Nasser Isstayeh. AP/Wide World Photos.-Poster against imprisonment of militant members of the Red Army Faction, photograph. © Raymond Depardon/Magnum Photos.-Posters of religious leaders and martyrs in Beirut, Lebanon, photograph. © Paolo Pellegrin/Magnum Photos.-Pro-choice demonstrators, photograph. Leonard Lessin/Peter Arnold, Inc.-Protest against the Neo-Nazi party, West Germany, 1965, photograph. © Leonard Freed/Magnum Photos.-Provisional Irish Republican Army mural, West Belfast, Northern Ireland, March 8, 2001, photograph by Peter Morrison. AP/Wide World Photos.- Pulver, Bruce, climbs a fire ladder to photograph newly-constructed homes destroyed by ELF arsonists, photograph. AP/Wide World Photos.-Rahman, Sheikh Omar Abdel, spiritual leader of Jamaa Islamiyya, New York, June, 1993, photograph. Mark D. Phillips/AFP/ Getty Images.-Railway workers and police examine debris of a destroyed train at Atocha railway station, Madrid, Spain, March 11, 2004, photograph by Anja Niedringhaus. AP/Wide World Photos.-Raviv, Avishai, leader of the militant right-wing group Eyal, Tel Aviv Magistrates Court, November 8, 1995, photograph by Nati Harnik. AP/Wide World Photos.-Rayen, Nizar, one of the leaders of HAMAS, Gaza City, photograph. © Abbas/ Magnum Photos.-Rebel soldiers look over lime covered bodies believed to be victims of the Interahamwe during recent battles, Goma, Congo, September 15, 1998, photograph by Jean-Marc Bouju. AP/Wide World Photos.- Regener, Michael, and his lawyer wait for the sentence of the German Federal Supreme Court, Karlsruhe, Germany, March 10, 2005, photograph by Thomas Kienzle. AP/Wide World Photos.-Republic of Texas members, Robert "White Eagle" Otto, Gregg Paulson, and their leader Richard McLaren, Fort Davis, Texas, July 10, 1997, photograph. AP/Wide World Photos.-Rescue worker helps a casualty to an ambulance after an explosion ripped through the Admiral Duncan Pub, Soho, London, April 30, 1999, photograph by David Thomson. AP/ Wide World Photos.-Restaurant damaged by a blast inside two movie theaters, New Delhi,

India, May 22, 2005, photograph by Press Trust of India. AP/Wide World Photos.

Revolutionary Armed Forces of Colombia march during a military practice, La Macarena, Colombia, August 6, 2001, photograph by Zoe Selsky. AP/Wide World Photos.-Revolutionary Armed Forces of Colombia, San Vicente Del Caguan, Colombia, photograph by Ariana Cubillos. AP/Wide World Photos.-Revolutionary Peoples Liberation Party-Front members demonstrate in Istanbul, Turkey, May 1996, photograph. Mustafa Ozer/AFP/Getty Images.-Revolutionary Peoples Liberation Party-Front members march during May Day celebrations, Ankara, Turkey, May 1, 2004, photograph by Burhan Ozbilici. AP/Wide World Photos.-Revolutionary United Front soldier lies dead after a clash with Nigerian peace-keeping soldiers, Sierra Leone, June 11, 1997, photograph by Enric Marti. AP/Wide World Photos.-Reward handout for the capture of leaders of the Abu Sayyaf Islamist extremist group, circulated by the U.S. embassy, Manila, May, 2000, photograph. AP/Wide World Photos.-Right-wing militants fight with anti-fascists during a demonstration, Lyon, France, November 14, 2004, photograph. Jean Philippe-Ksiazek/AFP/Getty Images.-Rockwell, George Lincoln, leader of the American Nazi Party, Montgomery, Alabama, May 23, 1961, photograph. AP/Wide World Photos.-Royal Ulster Constabulary officers examine the Mahon Hotel after Sunday nights bomb attack, believed to have been planted by an Irish Republican Army splinter group, the Continuity IRA, Irvinestown, Northern Ireland, February 7, 2000, photograph by Peter Morrison. AP/Wide World Photos.-Saichi, Amari, No. 2 leader of the Salafist Group for Call and Combat, photograph. AP/Wide World Photos.-Saifi, Amari, the No. 2 of the Salafist Group for Call and Combat group, photograph. AP/Wide World Photos.-Sakar, Anwar, member of the Islamic Jihad movement who became a suicide bomber, photograph. © Abbas/Magnum Photos.-Sankoh, Foday, leader of the Revolutionary United Front, visits troops at camp in Port Loko, Sierra Leone, December, 1999, photograph by Teun Voeten. © Teun Voeten. Reproduced by permission.-Shigenobu, Fusako, founder of the Lebanon-based faction of Japanese Red Army, Tokyo station, Tokyo, Japan, photograph. © AFP/Corbis.-Singh, Danilo, and Rolando Marcello suspected leaders of the Alex Boncayao Brigade, July 17, 2001, photograph. Joel Nito/AFP/Getty Images.-Skinhead supporter of the rightwing German National Democratic Party, NPD, Verden, Germany, April 2, 2005, photograph by Joerg Sarbach. AP/Wide World Photos.-South Carolina Council of Conservative Citizens protest state Senate Bill 61, Columbia, South Carolina, January 30, 1999, photograph by Kim Truett. AP/Wide World Photos.-Spanish fireman, Madrid, January 21, 2000, photograph by Dani Duch/La Vanguardia. AP/Wide World Photos.-Supporter of Puerto Rican nationalist leader Filiberto Ojeda Rios, photograph by Andres Leighton. AP/Wide World Photos.-Supporter of Rabbi Meir Kahane demonstrates on the anniversary of his death, 1995, photograph. © Abbas/Magnum Photos.-Taliban supporters protest during the Pakistani Independence Day Parade, Manhattan, New York City, August 25, 2002, photograph. © Thomas Dworzak/Magnum Photos.-Tamil Tigers march on the road to Thopigila Camp, Sri Lanka, March 4, 2004, photograph by Julia Drapkin. AP/Wide World Photos.-Tamil Tigers women suicide squad members join in the celebration of "Heroes Day," Mullathivu, Sri Lanka, November 27, 2002, photograph by Gemunu Amarasinghe. AP/Wide World Photos.-Tareq, Abu, brother of Abdel Karim As-Saadi, leader of Asbat al-Ansar, Ain el-Helweh refugee camp, Lebanon, photograph. Mahmoud Zayat/AFP/Getty Images.-Tavistock Square, damage from bus bombing, London, August 7, 2005, photograph. Dominic Burke/Alamy.-Teenaged skinheads walk through the gates of Auschwitz, the former Nazi death camp, April 6, 1996, photograph. AP/Wide World Photos.-Terreblanche, Eugene, leader of the Afrikaner Resistance Movement, Western Transvaal, South Africa, 1994, photograph. © Ian Berry/Magnum Photos.-Terry, Randall, founder of Operation Rescue, during a demonstration in Lafayette Park, August 1, 2001, photograph by Stephen J. Boitano. AP/Wide World Photos.-Three Afghan Mujahidin, "holy warriors" stand on a mountain in Pakistan near the Afghan border, photograph. © Steve McCurry/Magnum Photos.-Tokyo Subway passengers affected by sarin gas planted by the Aum Shinri Kyo cults, 1995, photograph by Chikumo Chiaki. AP/Wide World Photos.-Truck burned by rebels of the Revolutionary Armed Forces of Colombia, Los Chorros, January 19, 2004, photograph. AP/Wide World Photos.-Truck with a hand-painted portrait of Osama bin Laden, Indonesia, 2004, photograph. © Abbas/Magnum Photos.-Tupac Amaru rebels show victory sign from roof top of the Japanese ambassador's residence, Lima, Peru, photograph by Kiyohiro Oku-Sankei Shimbum. AP/Wide World Photos.-U. S. flag flies upside down outside a church occupied by members of the American Indian Movement, on the site of the 1890 massacre at Wounded Knee, South Dakota, March 3, 1973, photograph by Jim Mone. AP/Wide World Photos.

Ugandan soldier walks past a charred body after a massacre believed to be committed by the Lord's Resistance Army, Barlonyo camp, Uganda, February 23, 2004, photograph by Karel Prinsloo. AP/Wide World Photos.-Ulster Freedom Fighters, Belfast, Northern Ireland, December 8, 1999, photograph by Peter Morrison. AP/Wide World Photos.-Ulster Volunteer Force marching band, Crumlin Road, Belfast, July 12, 2002, photograph. AP/Wide World Photos.-United Nuwaubian Nation of Moors compound, Eatonton, Georgia, January 22, 2003, photograph by Mark Niesse. AP/Wide World Photos.-Vishwa Hindu Parishad and Shiv Sena activists obstruct train tracks, Bombay, India, September 26, 2002, photograph. AP/Wide World Photos.-Voice of Citizens Together member asking that pre-natal care be denied to illegal immigrants, June 11, 1996, photograph by Damian Dovarganes.

AP/Wide World Photos.-Watson, Captain Paul, Sea Shepherd Conservation Society founder, with Makah Indian Elder Jeff Ides, Monaco, October 20, 1997, photograph. AP/Wide World Photos.-Weapons and paraphernalia seized from the terrorist group November 17, photograph. AP/Wide World Photos.-White separatist demonstrator is sprayed with mace by a counter-protestor during a National Alliance rally, Washington, D. C., August 24, 2002, photograph. AP/Wide World Photos.-Wilson, Eddie, Mississippi police lieutenant examines a hunting rifle found in the home of accused sniper Larry Shoemake, photograph. AP/Wide World Photos.-Woman shouts during a protest against the Basque separatist group, Madrid, February 23, 2000, photograph. AP/Wide World Photos.-World Trade Center, hijacked airplane preparing to crash into the south tower, photograph by Carmen Taylor. AP/Wide World Photos. -Yagan, Bedri, Dursun Karatas, and Sinan Kukul, founders of Turkeys Revolutionary Peoples Liberation Party-Front, photograph. AFP/Getty Images.-Zapatista National Liberation Army, Subcomandante Marcos, during an exclusive interview in La Realidad, Chiapas, May 18, 1999, photograph by Eduardo Verdugo. AP/Wide World Photos.-Zapatista supporters being searched by Mexican Army soldiers at a checkpoint near, La Realidad, Chiapas, May 7, 1999, photograph by John Moore. AP/Wide World Photos.

17 November Organization

The 17 November Organization (17N or N17) was founded in 1975 as a Marxist-Leninist organization on the belief that a communist revolution in Greece was imminent. The group is called Epanastatiki Organosi 17 Noemvri in Greek, and is also known as the Revolutionary Organization 17 November. The 17N organization took its name after a student protest in 1973 that had been violently ended by the Greek government deployment of army tanks. The group professes an anti-American, anti-capitalism stance and seeks the removal of U.S. bases from Greece, Turkish withdrawal from Cyprus, and Greek withdrawal from both NATO and the EU (European Union). The elusive group evaded capture for nearly thirty years and has claimed responsibility for twenty-three assassinations and numerous bombings, mainly targeting individuals and businesses that they accuse of exploiting Greece and creating a climate of underdevelopment.

The 17N organization has been inactive since 2002 after a failed bombing attempt led to a 17N safe house. That initial raid led to the arrest of eighteen other members of the group, whom the Greek police claimed as the group's core members. In December 2003, following the longest trial in Greek history, all but four of the 17N operatives were convicted of various crimes, including murder, destruction of property, and

LEADERS: Alexandros Giotopolous; Dimitris Koufondinas

USUAL AREA OF OPERATION: Greece

Weapons and paraphernalia seized from the terrorist group November 17 are pictured in this undated handout photo. AP/Wide World Photos. Reproduced by permission.

bank robbery. Although the convictions seemingly put an end to the organization's operations, many governments still consider it an active group.

HISTORY

The history of 17N begins in post-World War II Greece, as the cold war was just beginning. In 1952, Greece joined NATO, a coalition of countries intended to deter Soviet expansion. From 1952 through 1965, Greece developed, with the assistance of the Truman doctrine, a plan that provided financial assistance for development and dissuaded Soviet influences throughout Europe. However, between 1965 and 1967, Greece encountered a series of unstable coalition governments. As a result, in 1967, career Army Colonel George Papadopoulous led a coup and assumed power. Citing the threat of communism, Papadopoulous ruled under the guise of a military junta—or dictatorship. He declared

LEADERSHIP

ALEXANDROS GIOTOPOLOUS

Alexandros Giotopolous is believed by the U.S. State Department to be the founding member and leader of 17N, charges that he has denied. Giotopolous was born in France where he participated in a leftist student revolt in 1968. After moving to Greece, Giotopolous participated in the Popular Revolutionary Resistance protest of the military junta in 1971–1972. The U.S. State Department believes that Giotopolous then traveled to Cuba to be trained in urban warfare. When he returned the Greece, he adopted an alias, Mikhalis Oikonomou. During the 2003 trial, members of 17N identified Giotopolous as the founding member, leader, and gunman in the 1975 assassination of Richard Welch. Giotopolous denies these charges. Giotopolous is currently serving multiple life sentences after being convicted of his activities with 17N.

DIMITRIS KOUFONDINAS

Koufondinas was identified by 17N members as the co-leader of the group. He joined 17N in 1984 and was also identified as the group's recruiter and liaison between gunmen and organization leadership. He confessed to the 2000 assassination of Stephen Saunders. He voluntarily surrendered to police in September 2002 and is currently serving multiple life sentences in connection with his activities with 17N.

---

martial law, suppressed civil liberties, and disbanded political parties. Opponents and suspected communists were either imprisoned or exiled. Due to its geographic proximity to the Soviet Bloc nations, the United States chose to support the junta.

In 1973, in an attempt to legitimize his claim to power, Papadopoulous established a democracy, but assumed the presidency. However, on November 15, 1973, students at the Athens Polytechnic University declared a strike to protest the junta and the U.S. support of the military dictatorship. Initially the strike had little impact, but then the students were joined by workers and other youths and the protesters barricaded themselves into the school. Two days later, on November 17, Papadopoulous ordered the army, including tanks, to end the demonstration. As a result, twenty protesters were killed.

Public outcry against the violent action and internal strife among his cabinet led to the demise of the Papadopoulous regime by the end of November 1973. In July 1974, a constitutional government replaced the junta and Papadopoulous was tried and convicted of treason and insurrection.

The 17N group began its activities the following year, 1975. The group claimed responsibility for the assassination of CIA Station Chief, Richard Welch, on December 23, 1975. The weapon used in this killing, a .45-caliber Colt 1911 semi-automatic weapon, became the trademark and weapon of choice for 17N assassination operations. In a communiqué claiming responsibility for the assassination, 17N declared its goal to bring about the communist revolution. Its ideology, based on the revolutionary left, originated as opposing the prevailing political system. The group identified itself as anti-American due to the U.S. backing of the right-wing junta led by Papadopoulous. In its initial communiqué, the group explained that their name originated from the student protest in 1973.

Since 17N opposed the U.S. military bases in Greece, they felt justified in targeting U.S. service members. On November 15, 1983, 17N struck its next target: U.S. Navy Captain George Tsantes. Following a similar operation as the Welch assassination, the gunmen fired on Tsantes and his driver with a .45-caliber magnum while they were stopped at a traffic light. Both the driver and Tsantes were killed. The next two assassination attempts on U.S. service members were in 1984, and followed the same procedure and weapon choice. However, these attempts resulted only in injuries to the victims.

In addition to assassination attempts, 17N began to use bombings to target U.S., EU, NATO, and Greek establishment targets. The first bombing attempt occurred at the French Cultural Institute on November 24, 1984. The bomb was discovered and defused before it could detonate. However, several other bombings occurred throughout Athens that same day. The 17N organization used remote-detonated explosives throughout the 1980s to target busses carrying U.S. military personnel and in the assassination attempt of U.S. Drug Enforcement Agency Agent George Carros. In addition, in 1988 the group claimed responsibility for bombs placed under vehicles intended for Turkish diplomats. Although two bombs exploded, no one was injured. On June 28, 1988, the group claimed responsibility for the assassination of U.S. military attaché, Captain William Nordeen. Moving away from their traditional assassination method, the group detonated a car packed with explosives when Nordeen drove by.

On June 10, 1990, 17N initiated its use of improvised rocket attacks. Targeting the offices of Proctor and Gamble in Athens, the group hit the office in protest of the Greek government's action to sell certain state firms to multinational corporations like Proctor and Gamble. In addition to striking the Proctor and Gamble offices, the group has targeted several other multinational firms: American Life Insurance Company (Alico), Nationalen Nederlanden, IBM, Seimens, McDonald's, General Motors, Chase Manhattan Bank, Midland Bank, and Banque National de Paris.

In 1991, the group voiced its opposition to the Persian Gulf War by hitting coalition targets within Greece. The first occurred on January 21, 1991, as a bomb exploded at the French military attaché residence in Athens. Days later, the British-based Barclays Bank was the target of an explosives attack. On the same day, two Citibank offices were also hit. Continued attacks occurred in Athens on January 28, 1991, with an anti-tank missile fired into an American Express office and a rocket grenade attack on the British Petroleum offices in the city. On March 12, 1991, 17N detonated a remote-controlled bomb that killed a U.S. Air Force sergeant. The group claimed responsibility for the assassination as retaliation for the Iraqi dead from the Persian Gulf War. In 1998 following the U.S. bombing of Iraq, 17N once again retaliated for the action by targeting U.S. interests in Greece.

By 2000, 17N claimed responsibility for twenty-three assassinations, including U.S., British, Turkish, and Greek targets, and 146 armed attacks. On June 8, 2000, British

Brigadier Stephen Saunders was shot with a .45-caliber pistol. The next day, 17N claimed responsibility for the assassination and called it retaliation for the NATO, United States, and EU "bombardments" in Yugoslavia. This assassination brought international pressure on Greece to stop 17N before the coming Summer Olympics in 2004.

The last known operation by 17N was a failed bombing on June 29, 2002. A bomb prematurely detonated injuring Savvas Xiros, a member of 17N. This was the first arrest of a 17N member in the organization's twenty-seven-year history. After searching his apartment, police found 17N paraphernalia, as well as documents that led to the arrest of eighteen other 17N members and the discovery of weapons caches throughout Greece. On September 5, 2002, the police claimed that all 17N's core members were arrested after Dimitris Koufodinas surrendered to police.

In December 2003, after a year-long trial, fifteen of the nineteen members were convicted for their activities with 17N. Five of the members, including Alexandros Giotopoulos and Dimitris Koufondinas, were initially given the death penalty. However those sentences were commuted to multiple life sentences. Since the failed attack in June 2002, the 17N organization has been inactive.

PHILOSOPHY AND TACTICS

The 17N organization was founded on the Marxist-Leninist ideology of communism. According to the MIPT Terrorism Knowledge Database, the group is considered "fanatically" nationalistic and that members "believe all the groups that they target are responsible for the underdevelopment and exploitation of Greece."

The group sought to expel outside influences in Greece. Among their identified goals were the closure of U.S. bases and the withdrawal of Turkish military from Cyprus. In addition, the group claimed to be anti-Greek establishment, anti-capitalism and anti-colonialism, and sought the withdrawal of Greece from NATO and the EU.

In order to accomplish these goals, the group launched a campaign of assassinations and bombings. Assassinations were the first

KEY EVENTS

1973: Twenty student protesters were killed by army tanks at Athens Polytechnic University.

1975: 17N's first assassination: CIA Station Chief Richard Welch.

1984: The French Cultural Institute serves as the organization's first bombing attempt.

1990: The group fires first rocket attack into Proctor and Gamble offices in Athens.

1991: In retaliation for the Persian Gulf War, 17N targets Citibank and Barclay's bank offices.

1991: The group attacks German Lowenbrau and demands $43 billion in reparations from the German government for World War II.

1998: U.S. interests are targeted in protest of bombing of Iraq.

2000: Assassination of Stephen Saunders leads to international pressure on Greece to stop 17N before the 2004 Summer Olympic games.

2002: First arrest of a 17N member leads to the arrest of eighteen more members and the discovery of weapons cache.

2004: Fifteen members of 17N convicted of activities, rendering the group inactive.

---

form of attack, starting in 1975. Targets for assassination ranged from U.S., British, French, and Turkish diplomats to U.S. military service members and Greek industrialists. Bombings, in the form of remote-detonated explosives and improvised rockets, began in the 1980s and were also, at times, used for assassination attempts. Generally, the targets were U.S. or EU multinational corporation offices. In order to pay for their activities, the group undertook bank robberies and attempted to present itself as a modern-day Robin Hood.

OTHER PERSPECTIVES

Although 17N has been inactive since the 2003 arrest of nineteen of its members, some believe that the group still operates. In an October 2003 press briefing, Assistant Secretary of State for Public Affairs Richard Boucher explained that 17N would remain on the U.S. terrorist watch-list until the organization had been inactive for at least two years. Others within the U.S. government question why it took almost thirty years for anyone to be arrested for a 17N attack. In a *New York Times* article, Anthee Carassava writes that within Greece, "decades of sloppy work by an underfunded police force and a lack of political will" are the causes for the delay in stopping the group's activities. The writer quotes L. Paul Bremer as saying, "There may have been affinities between the radical leftist terrorists and the political elite that emerged after the military junta." In addition, other U.S. government officials believe that ties existed between 17N and PASOK (Pan-Hellenic Socialist Movement), the governing socialist party in 2005. Following the arrests and convictions, the group's activities ceased. However, there is speculation, as cited in the MIPT Terrorism Knowledge Database, that the remaining members of 17N have formed a new organization.

SUMMARY

The 17N organization operated for nearly thirty years without a single arrest. Some in the U.S. government attribute this to the lack of political will by the PASOK party. However in 2003, after the 2000 assassination of Stephen Saunders and with the mounting international pressure to ensure the safety of the 2004 Olympics, nineteen members of 17N were arrested and tried for the group's decades of assassinations and bombings. The group claimed responsibility for most of its assassinations and even used a trademark weapon, making it easy for the police to tie the crimes together. Claiming Marxist-Leninist ideology, the group sought to expel European, American, and Turkish influences in Greece.

In December 2003, fourteen members of the group were convicted and sentenced for their operations. This has, for the most part, brought

---

PRIMARY SOURCE

17 November a.k.a. Epanastatiki Organosi 17 Noemvri

DESCRIPTION

17 November is a radical leftist group established in 1975 and named for the student uprising in Greece in November 1973 that protested the ruling military junta. 17 November is an anti-Greek establishment, anti-United States, anti-Turkey, and anti-NATO group that seeks the ouster of US bases from Greece, the removal of Turkish military forces from Cyprus, and the severing of Greece's ties to NATO and the European Union (EU).

ACTIVITIES

Initial attacks were assassinations of senior US officials and Greek public figures. They began using bombings in the 1980s. Since 1990, 17 November has expanded its targets to include EU facilities and foreign firms investing in Greece and has added improvised rocket attacks to its methods. It supported itself largely through bank robberies. A failed 17 November bombing attempt in June 2002 at the Port of Piraeus in Athens, coupled with robust detective work, led to the arrest of 19 members—the first 17 November operatives ever arrested. In December 2003, a Greek court convicted 15 members—five of whom were given multiple life terms—of hundreds of crimes. Four other alleged members were acquitted for lack of evidence. In September 2004, several jailed members serving life sentences began hunger strikes to attain better prison conditions.

STRENGTH

Unknown but presumed to be small.

LOCATION/AREA OF OPERATION

Athens, Greece.

EXTERNAL AID

Unknown.

Source: U.S. Department of State. *Country Reports on Terrorism.* Washington, D.C., 2004.

---

an end to the 17N activities. However, within a week of the 2003 17N arrests, an anonymous communiqué from 17N claimed that the group was still active. The letter demanded the release of the 17N members, or (the letter claimed) the remaining 17N members would initiate hostage taking. The hostage taking never occurred and the U.S. State Department speculates that the remaining members of 17N have been absorbed into a new group called "Revolutionary Struggle."

SOURCES

Periodicals

Davenport, Coral M. "Elusive Terrorist Group Takes a Hit Finally." *Christian Science Monitor.* July 5, 2005.

Carassave, Anthee. "Arrest Destroys Noble Image of Guerilla Group in Greece." *New York Times.* July 29, 2005.

Web sites

CNN.com/World. "Last Key N17 Member Surrenders." < http://archives.cnn.com/2002/WORLD/europe/09/05/ greece..surrender/ > (accessed September 14, 2005).

FAS Intelligence Resource Program. "Revolutionary Organization 17 November." < http://www.fas.org/irp/ world/para/17_nov.htm > (accessed July 29, 2005).

International Policy Institute for Counter-Terrorism. "Revolutionary Organization 17 November." < http:// www.ict.org.il/organizations/orgattack.cfm?orgid = 38 > (accessed July 29, 2005).

MIPT Terrorism Knowledge Database. "Revolutionary Organization 17 November." < http://www.tkb.org/ Group.jsp?groupID = 101 > (accessed September 14, 2005).

Abu Nidal Organization (ANO)

OVERVIEW

The Abu Nidal Organization (also known as the Fatah Revolutionary Council; Black June; the Arab Revolutionary Brigades; the Revolutionary Organization of Socialist Muslims) was a Palestinian terror organization that was responsible for up to 900 killings between 1973 and 1991.

LEADER: Sabri al-Banna (Abu Nidal)

YEAR ESTABLISHED OR BECAME ACTIVE: 1973

USUAL AREA OF OPERATION: Middle East (terror activities were carried out in in more than 20 countries throughout the region and Europe)

U.S. TERRORIST EXCLUSION LIST DESIGNEE: The U.S. Department of State declared the ANO a terrorist organization in 1997

HISTORY

The roots of the Abu Nidal Organization (ANO) lie with the radicalization of Palestinian politics in the late 1960s, and further back to the 1948 settlement that led to the creation of the state of Israel. In every sense, however, they revolve around the life and times of its founder and defining influence, Sabri al-Banna (universally known as *Abu Nidal*, which translates from the Arabic as "father of the struggle"), and understanding his life and struggles offer an insight into the motivations of the cult that he built around him.

Al-Banna had been born to a prosperous family in the town of Jaffa in 1937, but his upbringing was scarred by rejection and fraternal prejudice. His father was a wealthy orange merchant with a large home and family. As an old man, he had taken a second wife, a 16-year-old Alawite maid, who bore a twelfth child,

7

Eighteen people were killed and 120 wounded after a terrorist attack at Rome's Leonardo da Vinci Airport, on Dec. 27, 1985. The simultaneous attacks on El Al ticket desks at the Rome and Vienna airports were carried out by seven Abu Nidal gunmen. AP/Wide World Photos. *Reproduced by permission.*

KEY EVENTS

1971: Abu Nidal denounces Fatah leadership at Third Annual Congress.

1973: Hostage-taking at Saudi embassy in Paris.

1976: Launches Iraqi-sponsored guerilla raids on Syria.

1982: Assassination attempt on Israeli London Ambassador Shlomo Argov precipitates Israeli invasion of Lebanon.

1983: Saddam Hussein expels Abu Nidal Organization, which takes up residence in Syria.

1985: Abu Nidal relocates to Libya and is hosted by Colonel el-Qaddaffi.

1985: Gun attacks on Vienna and Rome airports.

1988: Lockerbie bombing.

1991: Assassination of Fatah deputy, Abu Ilyad.

2002: Abu Nidal found shot dead in his Baghdad home.

Sabri. Repulsed by her impoverished origins, the rest of the family rejected the youngest son, and when the father died in 1945, they turned his mother out of the house.

Three years later, the prosperous middle-class existence of the al-Bannas was also brought to an abrupt halt during the First Arab–Israeli war. Forced to flee their home, they ended up living in dire poverty in a Gaza refugee camp. Neglected and unloved as a child, forced to live as a hungry and impoverished refugee, the series of humiliations suffered by young Sabri al-Banna forged a vengeful and embittered personality, with, it would emerge, a psychotic, misogynistic streak.

As a teenager, he became attracted to Ba'athism and moved to Egypt where he studied engineering, but emigrated to the Gulf before completing his studies. In the Saudi capital, Riyadh, he enjoyed relative success in business, but like many of his contemporaries became increasingly politicized. He founded the Palestine Secret Organization and adopted the alias "Abu Nidal." Following the Six Day War in 1967, the Saudi authorities tortured then expelled Nidal, who moved to Jordan.

It was in Amman that Nidal became more closely involved with the Palestinian cause, allying himself with Yasser Arafat's Fatah movement. He founded a trading company called Impex, which increasingly became a front for Fatah, with members meeting at its offices, and money laundered through its bank accounts. According to his biographer, Patrick Seale, Nidal never forged a reputation as a guerilla during this period of paramilitary foment, locking himself in his office during gun battles.

Palestinian terrorists at an Abu Nidal training camp. © *Corbis*

Nevertheless, he established a solid reputation within Fatah for his organizational aptitude and was appointed Fatah representative to Sudan in 1968, then to Iraq two years later. When King Hussein of Jordan purged his country of the increasingly disruptive Palestinian *fedayeen* (fighters), Palestinian politics in general and Nidal in particular became even more radicalized. The PLO split between comparative moderates (such as Arafat, who continued to tread a political-military line and broach the possibility of a "national authority" on a partial map of Palestine as a first step to a negotiated settlement) and outright extremists (such as George Habash and Fatah's Black September faction, that used hijackings and murders to make their rejectionist case).

Within Fatah, Nidal emerged as the leader of a leftist alliance against Arafat, aligning himself with Abu Dawud, a brutal commander who would mastermind the Black September Munich Olympic attacks in 1972. At Fatah's third congress in Damascus in December 1971, Nidal called for Arafat to be overthrown as an "enemy" of the Palestinian people and demanded brutal revenge against King Hussein.

Provided shelter by the Iraqi government, that found a common cause with his rejectionism and with a group of loyal and impressionable followers, Nidal soon began launching terrorist attacks.

His first operation bore the hallmark of future missions, carried out as it was not against the declared "enemy" of Israel, but against rival Arabs. On September 5, 1973, five gunmen seized the Saudi embassy in Paris, taking 13 hostages and threatening to blow up the compound unless Abu Dawud, who had been arrested in Jordan that February for a plot to kill King Hussein, was released. Following PLO-brokered negotiations (and an alleged $12 million bribe to King Hussein from the Emir of Kuwait), Dawud was released and the crisis ended.

Possibly because he was so reliant on the patronage of sympathetic regimes, Abu Nidal

A crowd mourns at the funeral of eleven Israeli athletes who were taken hostage by Palestinian terrorists during the 1972 Munich Olympic Games. © *Micha Bar Am | Magnum Photos*

emerged as a terrorist for hire. In June 1976, Syria's President Hafez al-Assad had sent his army into Lebanon, newly racked by civil war, to fight the Palestinian guerrillas operating from refugee camps across the country. This effectively put Syria in the Israeli camp and marked an act of Arab heresy akin to King Hussein's Black September purge five years earlier. Saddam Hussein, an ambitious general in the Iraqi army who was increasingly operating as *de facto* president of his country, thought he could boost his own prestige throughout the Arab world by bringing Assad down. On Saddam's behalf, and operating under the name "Black June," Abu Nidal sent raiders into Syria to carry out guerilla activities.

At the same time, Abu Nidal continued to follow his own path toward Palestinian redemption. Following the Saudi embassy hostage taking, senior PLO figures had flown to Iraq to reason with Nidal that such acts were damaging the Palestinian cause. Such appeals had little effect on Nidal, if anything hardening his

resolve. He was not unique in his rejectionism: Arafat had many Palestinian and Arab enemies, though what set Nidal apart was not his opposition, but that he actually set about killing opponents. By the late 1970s, his attacks were directed almost exclusively against Arafat's "capitulationists." These included the PLO's London representative, Said Hammami, who had been engaged in high-level clandestine negotiations with Israeli "doves" and a moderate Egyptian newspaper editor. Although Abu Nidal was vigorously opposed to moderate Palestinian factions, his indiscriminate brutality served to indelibly frame the PLO as a terrorist organization.

Abu Nidal also launched intermittent attacks at Israeli and Jewish targets overseas. These included the murder of the Israeli commercial attaché in Brussels on July 25, 1980, and a hand grenade attack on a synagogue in Antwerp two days later, which killed a child and injured 20 others. What was most marked about the Abu Nidal Organization was its ability to emerge and carry out attacks almost any-where. As well as in Belgium and England, the group would inflict its crimes on more than 20 countries during the 1980s. Not until al-Qaeda two decades later would the tentacles of a terror-ist group spread so far.

In 1983, Saddam Hussein, now Iraqi President and seeking to portray himself as a regional strongman and protector of Western interests in the face of Ayatollah Khomeini's Iran, dispensed of Abu Nidal in an attempt to show its most respectable face; the ANO took refuge in Syria. Damascus sponsored his organi-zation to kill Jordanian diplomats as a way of derailing peace overtures to Israel, but showing a remarkable sense of provoking historically sig-nificant episodes of an epicedian brand, Nidal had already gone one step further.

On June 3, 1982, three Abu Nidal agents attempted to assassinate the Israeli Ambassador to London, Shlomo Argov, shooting him through the head, but not killing him. This was the Middle East's answer to Franz Ferdinand's assassination in Sarajevo, and triggered a cycle of events that would set any Arab–Israeli peace settlement back a decade. Wrongly claiming it was an act ordered by the PLO, Israel launched Operation Peace for Galilee three days later, invading Lebanon to flush it out. In this sense, Nidal saw through his extremist convictions.

Abu Nidal took his freelance terrorist organization to Libya in 1985, a country that would serve, as one commentator noted wryly, as "his most congenial home" (Syria formally expelled him in 1987). He struck an instant personal rapport with Colonel el-Qaddaffi, who placed him in effective control of Libyan intelligence, and, like Syria and Iraq before him, sponsored his organization to carry out an array of attacks that surpassed even Abu Nidal's previous reputation for terror. These included the hijacking of an Egyptair flight in Malta in November 1985 (58 of the 91 passen-gers died after Egyptian commandoes stormed the plane) and machine gun attacks at Rome and Vienna Airports in December 1985 (which were apparently carried out as a reprisal for the Italian and Austrian governments' moves to recognize the PLO). Abu Nidal also paid its respects to its Libyan hosts by targeting Qaddaffi opponents in exile.

Following the U.S. bombing of Beirut in April 1986, el-Qaddafi gave Abu Nidal *carte*

Two injured victims lie on the floor of Rome's Fiumicino Airport after Palestinian guerrillas engaged police in a gunfight before hijacking a plane. AP/Wide World Photo. Reproduced by permission.

blanche to wage his extremist activities on Western targets. Among the attacks was a hijacking of a Pan Am jet in Karachi; a machine gun attack in an Istanbul synagogue; and an assault on the Greek cruise ship, the City of Poros, which killed nine and left 98 injured.

The apogee of Abu Nidal's activities came in December 1988 when Pan Am flight 103 was blown up over Lockerbie, Scotland, killing 270 people. The attack, for which a Libyan security official was convicted, was almost certainly orchestrated by the Palestinian. In 2002, a former Nidal colleague, Atef Abu Bakr, told *al-Hayat* newspaper that Nidal had confided: "I will tell you something very important and serious. The reports which link the Lockerbie act to others are false reports. We are behind what happened."

The zenith of Abu Nidal's terror also marked the start of its decline. Still with a paramilitary militia of around 1,500 and a personal wealth

LEADERSHIP

SABRI AL-BANNA (ABU NIDAL)

Whether Abu Nidal's cruelty was rooted in his deeply unhappy childhood—first as an outcast in his own family, then as a poverty-stricken refugee—is often the starting point of assessments of his life and psyche. Certainly, his boyhood shared similar characteristics to those of other demagogues, such as Stalin and Saddam Hussein. However, too little is known about Abu Nidal, and his name attracts too much rumor to make a definitive judgment.

Nevertheless, torture and execution were certainly a peculiar penchant of Nidal's, particularly as his terrorist excesses saw him increasingly marginalized by his Libyan hosts in the late 1980s. Horrific accounts of victims being buried alive have emerged, likewise accounts of mass purges, notably in November 1987, when he ordered the execution of 170 members.

Part of the success of the ANO came because of the brutal allegiance demanded by Abu Nidal himself and the frequent purges he carried out. New recruits were required to spend several days writing out their life stories, including the names and addresses of family members, friends, and other associates. As a periodic test of loyalty, members would be required to rewrite this information, which was then compared to the original. Discrepancies were taken as evidence that the original had been an invention and that the member was a spy. Such an accusation would be met with torture and often execution.

One continued rumor and line of speculation that was explored by his biographer, Patrick Seale, is that Abu Nidal was a delinquent Mossad agent. Given Israel's proclivity towards such clandestine activity and Abu Nidal's habit of accepting the orders and dollars of his former enemies, such a scenario is not inconceivable; given his inveterate hatred of Israel and a lack of anything approaching hard evidence, it nevertheless remains unlikely.

garnered through his business activities and extortion valued at $400 million, he continued to exert some influence, but this mostly manifested itself in brutal purges of his corps. In February 1991, after many attempts, he killed the Fatah second-in-command Abu Iyad in Tunis. This would be his last significant act.

Faced with the outrage of the West, el-Qaddaffi placed him under house arrest. From here the trail of hard facts goes cold. It seems as if el-Qaddaffi exiled Abu Nidal in the late 1990s, but the circumstances remain shrouded in mystery. Nidal turned up in Iraq: how, when, or why is unknown. Iraqi officials maintained he entered the country illegally; more likely, Nidal bought his way into a country crushed by an economic embargo.

Either way, the fact that Abu Nidal and his last remaining paramilitary corps were in Iraq remained unknown until August 2002 when his death at the age of 65 was announced. Iraqi officials said he committed suicide following a raid on his compound by intelligence agents. Subsequent accounts nevertheless stated that it is unclear whether he killed himself or was killed by someone else.

PHILOSOPHY AND TACTICS

Because of its many guises, homes, and patrons, Abu Nidal has never propagated a continued struggle for any particular cause other than the pursuit of terror in a general sense. Abu Nidal originally broke away from the Fatah movement with his circle of followers in the early 1970s because they disliked the comparatively moderate line taken by its leadership towards King Hussein and the state of Israel. As they saw it, anything other than seeking the death of both was a betrayal of the Palestinian cause. However, this never emerged in a coherent philosophy or manifesto, nor did it tactically. Besides the assassination attempt on Shlomo

PRIMARY SOURCE

Abu Nidal Organization (ANO) a.k.a.
Fatah Revolutionary Council, Arab
Revolutionary Brigades, Black
September, Revolutionary Organization
of Socialist Muslims

DESCRIPTION

The ANO international terrorist organization was founded by Sabri al-Banna (a.k.a. Abu Nidal) after splitting from the PLO in 1974. The group's previous known structure consisted of various functional committees, including political, military, and financial. In November 2002 Abu Nidal died in Baghdad; the new leadership of the organization remains unclear.

ACTIVITIES

The ANO has carried out terrorist attacks in 20 countries, killing or injuring almost 900 persons. Targets include the United States, the United Kingdom, France, Israel, moderate Palestinians, the PLO, and various Arab countries. Major attacks included the Rome and Vienna airports in 1985, the Neve Shalom synagogue in Istanbul, the hijacking of Pan Am Flight 73 in Karachi in 1986, and the City of Poros day-excursion ship attack in Greece in 1988. The ANO is suspected of assassinating PLO deputy chief Abu Iyad and PLO security chief Abu Hul in Tunis in 1991. The ANO assassinated a Jordanian diplomat in Lebanon in 1994 and has been linked to the killing of the PLO representative there. The group has not staged a major attack against Western targets since the late 1980s.

STRENGTH

Few hundred plus limited overseas support structure.

LOCATION/AREA OF OPERATION

Al-Banna relocated to Iraq in December 1998 where the group maintained a presence until Operation Iraqi Freedom, but its current status in country is unknown. Known members have an operational presence in Lebanon, including in several Palestinian refugee camps. Authorities shut down the ANO's operations in Libya and Egypt in 1999. The group has demonstrated the ability to operate over a wide area, including the Middle East, Asia, and Europe. However, financial problems and internal disorganization have greatly reduced the group's activities and its ability to maintain cohesive terrorist capability.

EXTERNAL AID

The ANO received considerable support, including safe haven, training, logistical assistance, and financial aid from Iraq, Libya, and Syria (until 1987), in addition to close support for selected operations.

Source: U.S. Department of State. *Country Reports on Terrorism*. Washington, D.C., 2004.

Argov in 1982, Abu Nidal never committed a significant attack against an Israeli target. While its attacks on Western targets accounted for much of its notoriety, an estimated 70% of its outrages were carried out on fellow Arabs, either at the behest of sponsor governments or because of Abu Nidal's own personal grievances.

Instead, Abu Nidal Organization, partly because of the necessity of sating the demands of host regimes, partly because of the massive financial incentives, and arguably because of its founder's penchant for bloodletting, emerged as a kind of freelance terrorist group. It carried out assassinations, extortion, hijackings, and kidnappings, sometimes in pursuit of its own aims, but often on the instructions of others.

OTHER PERSPECTIVES

David Hirst, who reported from the Middle East for the *Guardian* between 1963 and 2001, saw the full spectrum of Abu Nidal's notorious life and times: "All Palestinian resistance leaders took a *nom de guerre*," he wrote after Abu Nidal's death from an apparent suicide in 2002. "Like Yasser Arafat's Abu Ammar, most were just names. Others embodied an idea. But the man who, at the outset of his career, so grandly styled himself Abu Nidal, or 'father of struggle,' came, by the end of it, to be regarded by most of his compatriots as the antithesis of all the name stood for, the begetter of all that was most treacherous and destructive of the cause he had seemingly espoused more passionately than anyone else....His genius lay in his ability to secure one patron after another—even two, possibly three, mutually hostile ones at once—for the gruesome favours he performed in that underworld of middle eastern conflict of which, in his heyday, he was the undisputed, monstrous king. The patrons were Arab—Iraq, Syria, Libya—but, almost incredibly, they may well have been Israeli too.

"[I]t was Israel's policy to destroy the PLO, to fix it indelibly in the international mind as the terrorist organisation it had never wholly been (and was so less and less). No one helped this strategy like Abu Nidal. Even though the PLO was his victim, that made little difference to international opinion unschooled in the niceties of intra-Palestinian politics; it seemed only to bear out what Israel said about the essentially murderous nature of the whole gang.... Whether he was literally Israel's man or not, one thing is sure: no terrorist ... rendered Israel greater services," concluded Hirst.

Time magazine pondered whether the final act of Abu Nidal's murderous existence was a renewed employment under his old boss, Saddam Hussein: "Exquisitely rare is the news item that can induce a satisfied smile in both Ariel Sharon and Yasser Arafat," remarked Tony Karon. "But both men have reason to cheer the passing of Abu Nidal, the Palestinian terrorist mastermind who, depending on who you believe, either killed himself or was shot dead this week in Baghdad. That's because in a 20-year career that began in 1974, Nidal's organization killed or wounded some 900 people in 20 different countries, making enemies both Arab and Israeli."

SUMMARY

Abu Nidal's death in 2002 apparently marked the end for one of the most infamous criminal gangs in modern history. Whether the ANO has an apostle willing to take up the freelance terrorism of its founder and defining influence remains to be seen.

SOURCES

Books

Savigh, Yezid. *Armed Struggle and the Search for State: The Palestinian National Movement, 1949–1993*. Oxford: OUP, 1999.

Seale, Patrick. *Assad of Syria: The Struggle For the Middle East*. Los Angeles: University of California Press, 1989.

Seale, Patrick. *Abu Nidal: A Gun For Hire*. New York: Random House, 1992.

Periodicals

Hirst, David. "Abu Nidal". *Guardian* August 20, 2002.

Karon, Tony. "Person of the Week: Abu Nidal". *Time* August 23, 2002.

SEE ALSO

Palestinian Liberation Organization (PLO)

Abu Sayyaf Group (ASG)

OVERVIEW

Abu Sayyaf Group (ASG) is a militant organization that is based in the Philippines. Its mission is thought to be the establishment of a separate Islamic state in Mindanao, an island situated in the southern Philippines. Abu Sayyaf literally means "bearer of the sword" in Arabic. Abu Sayyaf Group is also known as Al-Harakat Al-Islamiyyah.

The group claims that it was formed in the early 1990s after it split from Moro National Liberation Front. It was reportedly headed by Abdurajak Abubakar Janjalani. Allegedly, ASG has links with a number of terrorist organizations around the world, including Osama bin Laden's Al-Qaeda, as well as with Razmi Yousef, who was found guilty of the 1993 World Trade Center bombings in New York. The U.S. Department of State has formally listed Abu Sayyaf a terrorist organization since 1997.

ALTERNATE NAME: Al-Harakar Al-Islamiyyah (Bearer of the Sword)

LEADERS: Abdurajak Abubakar Janjalani; Khadaffy Abubakar Janjalani

ESTABLISHED: 1991

AREA OF OPERATION: Mainly operates in the southern part of the Philippines; allegedly operates in Malaysia as well

STRENGTH: Several hundred (estimated)

HISTORY

According to U.S. government statistics, Muslims form about four percent of the total population in the Philippines and are predominantly centralized in the south. Since the 1970s, the Moro National Liberation Front (MNLF), an Islamic separatist group, has been allegedly

Filipino Muslims inter one of the bodies of alleged Abu Sayyaf detainees in a common grave at a cemetery south of Manila, Philippines on March 16, 2005. AP/Wide World Photos. Reproduced by permission.

KEY EVENTS

1991: The group reportedly began its operations with the bombing of a ship in Zamboanga, the Philippines, killing several Christian missionaries.

1995: An attack on the predominantly Christian town of Ipil in coastal Mindanao, the Philippines, left more than 50 people dead.

1998: Founder and leader of ASG, Abdurajak Abubakar Janjalani, died in a combat with the Philippine Army.

2000: ASG came into the international limelight because of its alleged involvement in the kidnapping and subsequent release of foreign tourists in Malaysia after the delivery of a huge ransom.

2001: ASG allegedly kidnapped three U.S. citizens and 17 Filipinos from a tourist resort in Palawan, the Philippines.

2004: ASG reportedly bombed a passenger ferry in the Philippines, killing more than 100.

2005: ASG claimed responsibility for bombings at public places in three cities in the Philippines.

fighting for a separate Muslim state in Mindanao. Between the years 1986 and 1996, the MNLF negotiated with the Philippines government for a separate state. Eventually in 1996, Nur Misuari, the leader of MNLF, reportedly signed a peace agreement with the government in exchange for their separate state. However, terrorism experts report that some extremist MNLF members split from the group during the negotiation process and created their own unit, the Abu Sayyaf Group, in 1991. The group was formed under the leadership of Abdurajak Abubakar Janjalani, and was allegedly a more fundamentalist faction of the original MNLF.

The ASG is reportedly based in the Basilam Province of the Philippines and carries out its operations in that area, as well as in the neighboring provinces of Sulu and Tawi-Tawi (in the Sulu Archipelago region) located in the southern part of the Philippines. The group also allegedly operates on the Zamboanga peninsula, and has links in Manila, the capital city of the Philippines.

Terrorism experts and monitor groups allege that the group started its terrorist activities in August 1991, with the bombing of a ship in the harbor in Zamboanga, and a grenade attack on Christian missionaries that reportedly claimed the lives of two women. The group began a continuous series of bombings and kidnappings that were reportedly targeted at the domestic level. Between 1991 and 1993, the ASG was thought to be involved in several grenade attacks and bombings at public places in the Philippines. After the death of the group leader Abdurajak Abubakar Janjalani in 1998, during a clash with the Philippine Army, the group seemingly split into several factions. After 1998, experts claim that the group forfeited its Islamic fundamentalist ideology and became involved in illicit money-making schemes by asking for huge ransoms for kidnapped hostages.

MGA KIDNAPPER!
MGA MAMAMATAY-TAO!

Abu Sabaya

Hamsiraji Sali

Khadafi Janjalani

Abu Solaiman

Isnilon Hapilon

PREMYO PARA SA IMPORMASYON
HANGGAN $5,000,000

The U.S. Government is offering a reward of up to $5,000,000 for information leading to the arrest or conviction of the terrorists responsible for the kidnapping of Martin and Gracia Burnham, and the kidnapping and murder of Guillermo Sobero. If you have any information about any individuals committing acts of international terrorism against U.S. persons or property, please contact the U.S. Embassy.

PREMYO PARA SA KATARUNGAN
www.rewardsforjustice.net

1-800-10-739-2737 (MANILA)   1-800-877-3927 (USA)

Kung Cell phone ang gagamitin ay tumawag lamang sa 02-526-9832/9833/9834

LAHAT NG IMPORMASYON NA MATATANGAP NAMIN AY ITUTURING SIKRETO

A flyer handed out by the U.S. embassy in Manila announcing the $5 million reward the U.S. would offer for the capture Abu Sayyaf leaders. The Muslim extremist group kidnapped two Americans and killed another on Basilan Island in the southern Philippines. AP/Wide World Photos. Reproduced by permission.

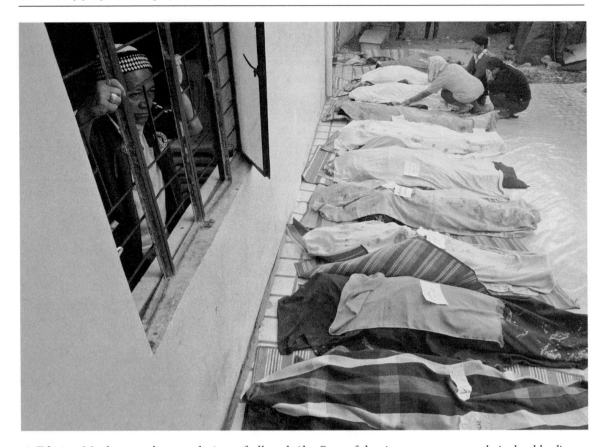

A Filipino Muslim watches as relatives of alleged Abu Sayyaf detainees mourn over their dead bodies. Twenty-two detainees were killed after a siege inside a detention cell in a failed jailbreak attempt. AP/Wide World Photos. Reproduced by permission.

In April 2000, the ASG earned worldwide notoriety after it allegedly attacked a Malaysian diving resort near Borneo. Suspected ASG members kidnapped 10 western tourists, 11 resort workers, as well as several journalists and intermediaries and, after receiving a huge amount of ransom payments, most of the hostages were released.

In May 2001 the group allegedly attacked the Dos Palmas Resort near the Philippine island of Palawan. Around 20 people were held as hostages, including three Americans. The resort kidnappings initiated an intense attempt by the Philippine government to take on the ASG. According to the official Philippine Army records, at least 100 ASG fighters were killed in encounters between July and November 2001.

After the September 11 attacks, the U.S. government increased its efforts against terrorist organizations all over the world, including the ASG. U.S. Department of State published reports stated that in October 2001, with the express intention of eradicating the ASG, the United States sent about two dozen military advisers to the Philippines. Furthermore the reports mentioned that the United States was considering increasing its financial aid to the Philippine military, along with additional weapons assistance, to combat terrorism in the region.

In February 2004, the ASG claimed responsibility for the bombing on the SuperFerry 14, sailing from Manila to Bacolod and Davao. This attack reportedly claimed the lives of more than 100 passengers. As of 2004, the Philippine authorities have asserted that the Abu Sayyaf Group is resurfacing with a vengeance and is allegedly shifting its focus again on its original ideology—to establish an Islamic rule in the southern Philippines.

Abu Sayyaf leaders Khaddafi Janjalani, second from left, and Radulan Sahiron, third from left, sit with fellow Abu Sayyaf members inside their clandestine jungle retreat in the Sulu province of the southern Philippines on July 16, 2000. AP/Wide World Photos. Reproduced by permission.

PHILOSOPHY AND TACTICS

The ASG was reportedly formed by Abdurajak Abubakar Janjalani with an aim to create a separate Muslim state in the southern Philippines. During the initial years of its operations, experts report that ASG was a more fundamentalist and aggressive faction of the Moro National Liberation Front (MNLF). Various studies on extremist groups also mention that some ASG leaders fought in Afghanistan during the Soviet war and were students and supporters of radical Islamic teachings. Janjalani, an Afghan war veteran, allegedly had close links with many other Islamic radical leaders (the group is suspected by the officials to have strong links with Al-Qaeda). It is alleged that the group was initially funded by Al-Qaeda, but as of 2005 it is largely self-financed through ransom and extortion money that the group has received as

well as by the support from Islamic extremists in the Middle East.

Counterterrorism analysts have observed that the group has time and again kidnapped foreigners and subsequently negotiated for their release in exchange for ransom. In 1993, it was alleged that ASG gunmen kidnapped Charles Walton, a 61-year-old language researcher at the U.S.-based Summer Institute of Linguistics and freed him after keeping him hostage for twenty-three days. In 1994, ASG militants were also accused of kidnapping three Spanish nuns and a Spanish priest, on separate occasions, and in 1998, two Hong Kong men, a Malaysian national, and a Taiwanese citizen were kidnapped. Later in 2000, the group allegedly kidnapped several tourists from a resort in Malaysia and released the hostages after payment of a hefty ransom.

The group has also been accused by the Philippine authorities for seeking out minorities,

LEADERSHIP

ABDURAJAK ABUBAKAR JANJALANI

Abdurajak Abubakar Janjalani was the founder of ASG and also led the group until his death in 1998, which according to the Philippine Army was a result of an encounter with the military in the village of Lamitan in Basilam Island of the Philippines. Janjalani was a former Islamic scholar who allegedly studied in Libya and Saudi Arabia, and also took part in the Afghan-Soviet war in the 1980s. Terrorism experts claim that he met and worked with Osama bin Laden during that time.

In 1990, Janjalani returned to the village of Tabuk in the Philippines, where he founded ASG. He reportedly established connections with a budding movement advocating strict Islamic fundamentalism, which was started by the religious leader, Ustadz Wahab Akbar. It is considered that these connections led to the formation of ASG as a fundamentalist disintegrated faction of the Muslim separatist group, the Moro National Liberation Front (MNLF).

It is alleged that the group was initially funded by Mohammed Jamal Khalifa, who is Osama bin Laden's brother-in-law.

KHADAFFY ABUBAKAR JANJALANI

Terrorism analysts state that after Abdurajak Abubakar Janjalani was killed in 1998, a power struggle took place in the group, but eventually his younger brother Khadaffy Abubakar Janjalani took control of the group and arose as the new leader. He also reportedly goes by the alias of Abu Muktar and Khadafi Montanio.

Media agencies reported that Khadaffy Janjalani was killed in an air strike in November 2004 in Datu Piang, the Philippines. His body has never been recovered, and his death has not been confirmed. There have been rumors claiming that he is alive and clandestinely living either in the Philippines or escaped to Malaysia.

---

such as Christians, and has been allegedly involved in various incidents involving shootouts and bombing of Christian-dominated towns. In 1995, several ASG members were allegedly involved in a shootout in a town of mostly Christians that killed more than 50 civilians and soldiers. The Philippine authorities also suspected the ASG of plotting to assassinate Pope John Paul II during his visit to the Philippines.

Terrorism experts charge the ASG with carrying out terrorist activities like bombings, assassinations, kidnappings, and extortion from business companies and rich industrialists to pursue its goals. Government officials have alleged that several ASG members are trained to be experts in long-range shooting in diverse weather conditions. As mentioned before, they also claim that several ASG militants have received extensive military training at Al-Qaeda camps in Afghanistan. Intelligence officials report that the ASG has wide support in the southern Philippines, especially in the provinces

of Sulu and Basilan. Also, the rough topography of that area makes it difficult for the armed forces to invade successfully. Additionally, the ASG is allegedly divided into multiple factions, with each faction operating autonomously, which also highly complicates the job for the Philippine military.

Though the basic aim of ASG remains the formation of a Muslim state in the southern Philippines, according to published intelligence reports, they deviated from their objectives to other criminal activities, such as kidnappings and bombings. Authorities claim that the ASG resorted to kidnappings, extortions, and robberies as the lure of money has made them digress from their goal of establishing Islamic rule over the Philippines. Media agencies and government authorities have reported that this greediness for money by ASG militants, as well as their random and targeted acts of terror against civilians, has cost them the support of native Muslims, who no longer sympathize with

PRIMARY SOURCE

Abu Sayyaf Men Sentenced to Death

Seventeen suspected members of the Islamic rebel group Abu Sayyaf have been sentenced to death in the Philippines. The men—four of whom were tried in absentia—were found guilty of kidnapping four people on the southern island of Basilan three years ago.

This is the first wide-scale conviction of suspected Abu Sayyaf rebels.

One of the smallest of the Muslim rebel groups in the Philippines, Abu Sayyaf is notorious for taking hostages.

The 17 defendants were convicted of kidnapping three nurses and a general hospital worker in June 2001.

Only 13 of the accused were in court. The other four, who escaped from a detention centre in April, were sentenced in absentia.

Separate trial

The court heard that the rebels had raided a hospital in the town of Lamitan to get medicine, and had taken hostages when the building was surrounded by Philippine government soldiers.

The month before, Abu Sayyaf militants are also said to have kidnapped 20 Philippine and American tourists from a beach resort.

Two of the nurses were freed after months of captivity, whilst the hospital worker managed to escape.

The third nurse and an American hostage were killed in a military rescue operation in July 2002.

The militants had earlier beheaded another American.

A separate trial in Manila is dealing with the abduction and deaths of the Americans.

Aileen Marie Gutierrez, a state prosecutor, said the decision to sentence the 17 men to death showed that "justice still works" in the Philippines.

"This is a strong signal that government is determined to wipe out terrorism in the south," she told Reuters news agency.

Abu Sayyaf, which is said to have links with al-Qaeda, has been weakened in recent years.

But the rebels remain active, despite frequent operations by Philippine troops trained and advised by elite U.S. soldiers.

Source: BBC News, 2004

---

the organization. Terrorism experts indicate that the strategies and operations of the group often depend on the whims of the individual leader. Experts also suggest that there is a lack of discipline among the group members.

However, some intelligence experts are of the opinion that with the recent bombing of the passenger ferry in February, 2005, responsibility for which is claimed by ASG, the group is possibly coming back to its original objectives. Media reports speculate that the group is returning to its Islamic fundamentalist ideology and is using the familiar weapons of terror, such as bombing and assassination, to achieve its ultimate goal of establishing an independent Islamic state in the southern Philippines. Authorities dealing with terrorism in the Philippines report that there is

new evidence that indicates that the group is evolving into a stronger version of its original self. Studies have shown that the ASG is setting up an assassination squad known as *Fisabillilah*, or the Path of God. Several terrorists laden with explosives, and allegedly members of the ASG, were captured by the Philippine authorities in 2004.

Intelligence reports assert that the ASG continues to plan terrorist attacks in the Philippines, including bombings, kidnappings, assassinations, and terrorist actions against civilians and U.S. interests, to foster its political, religious, and ideological objectives. Philippine government officials claim that the ASG is the most aggressive faction of MNLF.

PRIMARY SOURCE
Abu Sayyaf Group (ASG)

DESCRIPTION

The ASG is primarily a small, violent Muslim terrorist group operating in the southern Philippines. Some ASG leaders allegedly fought in Afghanistan during the Soviet war and are students and proponents of radical Islamic teachings. The group split from the much larger Moro National Liberation Front in the early 1990s under the leadership of Abdurajak Abubakar Janjalani, who was killed in a clash with Philippine police in December 1998. His younger brother, Khadaffy Janjalani, replaced him as the nominal leader of the group and appears to have consolidated power.

ACTIVITIES

The ASG engages in kidnappings for ransom, bombings, beheadings, assassinations, and extortion. The group's stated goal is to promote an independent Islamic state in western Mindanao and the Sulu Archipelago (areas in the southern Philippines heavily populated by Muslims) but the ASG has primarily used terror for financial profit. Recent bombings may herald a return to a more radical, politicized agenda, at least among certain factions. The group's first large-scale action was a raid on the town of Ipil in Mindanao in April 1995. In April of 2000, an ASG faction kidnapped 21 persons, including 10 Western tourists, from a resort in Malaysia. On May 27, 2001, the ASG kidnapped three US citizens and 17 Filipinos from a tourist resort in Palawan, Philippines. Several of the hostages, including US citizen Guillermo Sobero, were murdered. During a Philippine military hostage rescue operation on June 7, 2002, US hostage Gracia Burnham was rescued, but her husband Martin Burnham and Filipina Deborah Yap were killed. Philippine authorities say that the ASG had a role in the bombing near a Philippine military base in Zamboanga in October 2002 that killed a US serviceman. In February 2004, Khadaffy Janjalani's faction bombed SuperFerry 14 in Manila Bay, killing approximately 132, and in March, Philippine authorities arrested an ASG cell whose bombing targets included the US Embassy in Manila.

STRENGTH

Estimated to have 200 to 500 members.

LOCATION/AREA OF OPERATION

The ASG was founded in Basilan Province and operates there and in the neighboring provinces of Sulu and Tawi-Tawi in the Sulu Archipelago. The group also operates on the Zamboanga peninsula, and members occasionally travel to Manila. In mid-2003, the group started operating in the major city of Cotobato and on the coast of Sultan Kudarat on Mindanao. The group expanded its operational reach to Malaysia in 2000 when it abducted foreigners from a tourist resort.

EXTERNAL AID

Largely self-financing through ransom and extortion; has received support from Islamic extremists in the Middle East and may receive support from regional terrorist groups. Libya publicly paid millions of dollars for the release of the foreign hostages seized from Malaysia in 2000.

Source: U.S. Department of State. *Country Reports on Terrorism*. Washington, D.C., 2004.

OTHER PERSPECTIVES

Abu Sayyaf has been blamed by the Philippine government for several acts of terror conducted at various places in the country, including bombings and kidnappings.

National Security Adviser to the Philippines, Norberto Gonzales, commented on the bombing of a passenger ferry in 2004 that killed more than 100 people: "Because of the nature of the wreck, half-submerged in the bay, it will be difficult for investigators to prove 100% that it was Abu

Sayyaf. But the overwhelming evidence points that way, and I'm certain they were the ones behind the attack."

In February 2005, Abu Sayyaf allegedly set off simultaneous bombs across three cities in the Philippines. In a phone call to the local radio station, an Abu Sayyaf spokesman claimed responsibility for the attack and said, "Our latest operations—planned and executed with precision by the gallant warriors of Islam—is our continuing response to the Philippine government's atrocities committed against Muslims everywhere." Philippine President Arroyo retaliated by saying, "More than ever, we must not pull back but move forward to wipe out the remnants of the Abu Sayyaf." She further stated, "The evil of terrorism has only one aim. It is to rule with absolute power and absolute force."

A joint statement issued in May 2003 by President Bush of the United States and President Gloria Macapagal-Arroyo of the Philippines reaffirmed their commitment to destroy the Abu Sayyaf Group once and for all. Toward that end, both leaders agreed to hold another joint military activity in the near term, in which the United States will provide support to ongoing Armed Forces of the Philippine-led operations against the ASG. In a speech during the Joint Session of Congress in the Philippines, Mr. Bush remarked, "My government and your government pursue a common objective: We will bring Abu Sayyaf to justice. And we will continue to work together, along with our friends in Southeast Asia, to dismantle Jamaah Islamiya—the terrorist network, as well as other groups that traffic in violence and chaos. As we fight the terrorists, we're also determined to end conflicts that spread hopelessness and feed terror."

SUMMARY

The U.S. Department of State formally designated Abu Sayyaf a terrorist organization in 1997, which allowed the government to freeze any assets the group had in the United States.

Following the September 11 attacks, the United States sent about 650 troops with the objective of training and advising Philippine soldiers to confront the Abu Sayyaf militants armed with the knowledge of latest warfare techniques and technological know-how. (That mission ended in July 2002.)

The ASG has reportedly expressed displeasure toward the Arroyo administration and has continued to conduct various terrorist attacks throughout the Philippines with the aim of toppling the government. Filipino officials claim that the ASG has made significant links to the deadliest Southeast Asian terrorist group, Jemaah Islamiya (JI), along with Al-Qaeda.

SOURCES

Web sites

ABC Asia Pacific. "Cause and Effect—Profiles of Terrorist Groups." < http://abcasiapacific.com/cause/network/sayyaf.htm > (accessed September 14, 2005).

Federation of American Scientists. "Abu Sayyaf Group (ASG)." < http://www.fas.org/irp/world/para/asg.htm > (accessed September 14, 2005).

Public Broadcasting Service (PBS). "Profile: Abu Sayyaf." < http://www.pbs.org/newshour/terrorism/international/abu_sayyaf.html > (accessed September 14, 2005).

South Asia Analysis Group. "ABU SAYYAF: The Cause for the Return of U.S. Troops to Philippines?" < http://www.saag.org/papers5/paper417.html > (accessed September 14, 2005).

MIPT Terrorism Knowledge Base. "Terrorist Group Profile: Abu Sayyaf Group." < http://www.tkb.org/Group.jsp?groupID=204 > (accessed September 14, 2005).

Council on Foreign Relations. "AbuSayyaf Group—Philippines, Islamist Separatists." < http://cfrterrorism.org/groups/abusayyaf.html > (accessed September 14, 2005).

The U.S. Embassy at Manila. "U.S., Philippine Presidents Announce Boost to Bilateral Ties." < http://usembassy.state.gov/posts/rp1/wwwhr006.html > (accessed September 14, 2005).

Office of the Press Secretary, Malacanang, Philippines. "President George W. Bush's Speech during the Joint Session of Congress." < http://www.ops.gov.ph/pgwbvisit2003/speeches.htm > (accessed September 14, 2005).

African National Congress

LEADER: Nelson Mandela

USUAL AREA OF OPERATION: South Africa

OVERVIEW

The African National Congress (ANC) was founded in 1912 under the name the South African Native National Congress. On January 8, 1912, hundreds of South Africa's educated elite converged in Bloemfontein to create a national organization that would protest racial discrimination and demand equality under the law. The membership of the organization identified itself as being moderate. While pressing for racial equality, the ANC also openly supported British rule in South Africa. Blacks in South Africa struggled under legislation that hampered rights in the workplace and restricted the areas where they could live. The ANC has evolved from what was considered to be an extremist organization under the discredited apartheid system to a mainstream governing group in South Africa. Nelson Mandela has become one of the world's most widely respected figures.

In 1923, the group renamed itself as the ANC and identified its primary goal of ensuring racial equality to blacks in South Africa. In 1943, a splinter organization was created by members in the ANC who felt the group was too passive in its resistance while racial discrimination moved closer toward apartheid. This group, the Congress Youth League (CYL), engaged in strikes, rallies, and demonstrations. Eventually, the CYL rejoined the ANC and several of its members assumed leadership roles in the ANC,

African National Congress supporters and South African Defense Force members take cover on February 25, 1996, during a stand-off with the rival Inkatha Freedom Party outside Durban, South Africa.

AP/Wide World Photos. Reproduced by permission.

including Nelson Mandela. The ANC continued to expand in the 1950s, and as a result was banned by the government and many of its leadership were imprisoned.

In 1961, the ANC established a military wing called *Umkhonto we Sizwe* (spear of the nation) to begin an armed struggle against the policies of the South African government. The group targeted government facilities and not people directly. However, by 1964, police investigations of the group led to raids and arrests, which ended Umkhonto. Although the militant wing had been eradicated, the ANC continued its resistance to apartheid and was implicated in incidents during the 1980s, targeting multinational corporations operating in South Africa. In 1990, the ANC was legalized, which ended its violent operations. Following its legalization and with the leadership of Nelson Mandela, the ANC continued its struggle to end apartheid. By 1994, apartheid officially ended, paving the way for the ANC to gain control of the newly democratically

elected government and for Nelson Mandela to become president. Mandela served as president until 1999 when his deputy in the ANC, Thabo Mbeki was elected to the presidency.

HISTORY

The presence of gold and diamonds in South Africa has created a history of struggle between colonial powers, thus creating the environment for racial discrimination. In the 1880s, the Dutch, who were the first to settle in South Africa, struggled with the British ruling government. This struggle was exacerbated by the group attempting to establish its own South African national identity called Afrikaners. The Afrikaners argued that they possessed a unique identity rooted in their belief that they were a distinct group with their own fatherland in South Africa. After a bloody three-year conflict, the ruling British government sought to increase the number of English speakers in

LEADERSHIP

NELSON MANDELA

Nelson Mandela is the most widely recognized leader of the ANC. He joined the organization as a young man, and in 1943 served as a leader of the Congress Youth Leaders to mobilize protests against racial discrimination. In 1961, Mandela participated in the formation of Umkhonto we Sizwe. Believing that guerilla warfare was the next step, Mandela traveled throughout Africa to obtain financial support and training for militants. Mandela was arrested upon his return and sentenced to five years for leaving the country without a permit and inciting people. In 1964, Mandela was given a life sentence for treason for his activities with the ANC. In 1990, Mandela was released from prison and assumed leadership of the ANC. He worked with the reformation movement to create a new government in South Africa. In 1994, he was elected president and served until 1999.

South Africa by encouraging large numbers of Britons to emigrate.

During this period, Alfred Milner, British high commissioner in South Africa, expressed in the report by the South African Native Affairs Commission (SANAC) the belief that blacks and whites could never be recognized as equals. However, the three-year war with the Afrikaners was under the cause of abhorring the racially discriminating policies supported by the Afrikaners. As a result, the British received support from the black Africans during the conflict. Therefore, after the war, the SANAC was established to develop a "native policy." Educated African elite testified before the commission, denouncing institutionalized discrimination. However, the commission concluded that territorial separations, as well as separate voter's criteria should be established. The commission also asserted that there should be no political equality between the races.

In the agreement created to form the Union of South Africa in 1910, the question of suffrage for blacks was left to the self-governing colonies to decide. The Cape and Natal colonies used property ownership to qualify a black person for voting rights, while the Orange River Colony and Transvaal denied the vote to all blacks. This was one of the first pieces of legislation that marked the institutionalization of racial discrimination. Three additional legislations were key in creating the environment from which the ANC would emerge to protest. The Native Labour Regulation Act (No. 15), passed in 1911, established that it was a criminal offense for Africans, but not for whites, to break labor contracts. In addition, the Mines and Works Act (No. 12), also passed in 1911, restricted the Africans to semi-skilled and unskilled labor in the mines while allowing the whites to monopolize the skilled-labor jobs. Finally, the most important act in establishing a culture of racial inequalities was the impetus for the conference where the ANC was developed. The Natives Land Act (No. 27) passed in 1913 and divided South Africa into regions where either blacks or whites could own land. Although blacks made up two-thirds of the population, they were restricted to merely 7.5 percent of the land. In addition, the act made it illegal for blacks to reside outside of their relegated lands, unless they were employed by whites.

While the Natives Land Act was being debated, hundreds of South African elites met in Bloemfontein and established the South African Native National Congress. On January 12, 1912, the organization was established and its goals identified. The congress was composed of moderates such as the founding president John L. Dube, a minister and school teacher. The group acknowledged that British rule had been beneficial to South African development in creating the rule of law, promoting education, and introducing Christianity. As a result, the group sought reformation to the British policies as opposed to ending British rule. The group identified its goals as seeking an end to racial discrimination and creating equal treatment of the races under the law. In 1914, the congress sent a delegation to London to protest the Natives Land Act, where the colonial secretary expressed the inability to help. Again, in 1919, the congress sent a delegation who met with Prime Minister Lloyd George. However, the prime minister determined that the issue needed to be solved by the South African government.

By 1923, the congress had renamed itself the African National Congress and continued its moderate push for racial equality. However, during the next decade the ANC would lose much of its influence due to leadership problems and the group's passive stance. In the 1940s, a group of young leaders revived the ANC. This group included Nelson Mandela, Walter Sisulo, Olvier Tambo, and Anton Lembede. In 1943, this group of leaders established the Congress Youth League (CYL) as a way to mobilize mass protests against inequality. As apartheid was being institutionalized in 1948, the ANC adopted the CYL leaders and established a campaign of defiance. As ANC membership grew in the 1950s, so did the government's reaction. The defiance campaigns led by the ANC included rallies, demonstrations, and strikes. The government responded to the campaign by arresting demonstrators and banning leaders under the Suppression of Communism Act.

By 1961, the ANC had been banned and began to operate as an underground organization. In 1961, the militant wing of the ANC, Umkhonto we Sizwe, began to target attacks on police stations and power plants. Umkhonto carefully organized the attacks in order to avoid taking human lives. Its first activities occurred in 1961 with the targeting of government buildings in Johannesburg, Port Elizabeth, and Durban. By 1964, Umkhonto leaders were arrested and, along with the previously arrested Nelson Mandela, were tried for treason. The arrests, as well as an orchestrated police effort, succeeded in eradicating Unkhonto's activities. However, the violent protests of the ANC would continue.

Umkhonto and the ANC sought to economically and politically disrupt the country by targeting power plants, interfering with rail and telecommunications, and striking government buildings and symbols of apartheid. In 1982, limpet mines were used to attack the Mkuze oil depot, owned by Mobile Oil Company. In 1983, another limpet mine was used in an attack on the Ciskei Consulate. The next year saw several attacks of sabotage claimed by the ANC. In April, the ANC targeted an oil storage facility in Transvaal, causing five fuel tanks to be destroyed and several others damaged by fires. Several days later, the ANC detonated a bomb at the Transkei Consulate in Bloemfontein. In May

KEY EVENTS

1912: South African Native National Congress formed to protest the Natives Land Act and to call for racial equality.

1914: Delegation sent to Britain is met by colonial secretary who refuses to help.

1919: Subsequent delegation sent to Britain meets with Prime Minister Lloyd George who advises the issue of equality must be solved by the South African government.

1943: Congress Youth Leaders diverge from ANC to mobilize mass protests.

1948: ANC adopts CYL leadership and organization.

1961: Umkhonto manifesto is released in conjunction with the first act of violence against the South African government. The ANC is banned and moves its operations underground.

1964: ANC leaders are arrested and tried for treason and police activities eradicate Umkhonto. However, violence against the government continues.

1990: ANC is legalized and Nelson Mandela is released from prison.

1994: Apartheid is officially ended in South Africa and multiracial elections give the ANC the majority of votes.

1984, the ANC launched a rocket attack against an oil refinery in Durban. During the attack, four ANC operatives were killed, three civilians were killed, and two police officers were injured. Also in May, the ANC struck a gold mine in Johannesburg.

By April 1985, the ANC threatened to expand operations against multinational corporations operating in South Africa. The group used explosive devices to strike the offices of the mining businesses in Johannesburg. Businesses continued to be a target of the ANC and in

PRIMARY SOURCE
Tutu: 'Tyranny' of ANC

TRUTH AND RECONCILIATION

Archbishop Desmond Tutu says the African National Congress has done itself tremendous damage by trying to stop the publication of the Truth Commission report.

In the 3,500-page report, the ANC is held responsible for deaths and injuries during its time as an exiled movement trying to overthrow apartheid.

The chairman of South Africa's Truth and Reconciliation Commission, Archbishop Tutu says the ANC has damaged its international reputation, and he is concerned by a party with such a large government majority acting to try to stop its electorate from having access to information.

Reporting from Johannesburg, the BBC's Africa Correspondent, Jane Standley, says the respected Nobel peace prize winner's criticisms of the ANC will hit hard: she says that the criticisms are clearly meant for the younger generation of ANC leaders, who have been very hostile to the Commission's findings against them.

Archbishop Tutu is seen as a figure of morality and tolerance across the world.

He accused the ANC of tyranny in its last-minute bid to get a court order blocking findings that the party was responsible for gross violations of human rights in its fight against apartheid.

"The fact that they are the majority party in government does not give them privileges. I did not fight against people who thought they were God to replace them by others," Archbishop Tutu told journalists in Pretoria.

THABO MBEKI: COMMISSION SHOULD HAVE LISTENED TO ANC.

But the South African Deputy President and ANC President, Thabo Mbeki, criticised the commission for not heeding the ANC's objections to the report.

"This does not help the process for which the TRC was established," Mr Mbeki told reporters.

South Africa will hold its second all race elections next year and Thabo Mbeki is expected to become president as Nelson Mandela retires from politics.

The report, which calls for a national summit in 1999 on its recommendations, will "reawaken many of the difficult and troubling emotions that the hearings themselves brought," according to President Nelson Mandela.

September of 1988, the ANC exploded a bomb in the parking lot of a Holiday Inn in East London. In October 1989, the British Petroleum Oil Company offices in Cape Town became a target as simultaneous explosions occurred. The blasts were in response to the British decision against economic sanctions of South Africa.

The 1990s brought an increased movement, both national and international, toward the dismantling of apartheid. In 1990, the president of South Africa announced that Nelson Mandela—who was serving a life sentence for his activities with the ANC—would be released

and that the ANC would no longer be banned. These two actions began the process by which the ANC ended its violent activities by 1992. ANC exiles began to return to South Africa and the group faced opposition toward its reconciliatory attitude. As South Africa dismantled its policies of apartheid, Nelson Mandela and the ANC worked with the reformers to create a new government. On April 26, 1994, the first multiracial election occurred in South Africa, and the ANC won 62.2 percent of the vote. As a result, Nelson Mandela was elected unanimously as president on May 9, 1994. The ANC has remained in power since 1994.

Desmond Tutu's deputy, Alex Borraine, warned that reconciliation would take "a generation at least."

MANDELA WANTS FULL DISCLOSURE

The Truth Commission recommends that individuals who are found accountable for human rights violations, and who chose not to apply for amnesty, could face prosecution.

Former President PW Botha, Home Affairs Minister Mangosuthu Buthelezi, and Winnie Mandela are among those who stand accused.

The ruling African National Congress is also blamed.

But it is the system of apartheid, condemned as a crime against humanity, which receives the harshest criticism from the TRC's report, which was presented to President Mandela on Thursday by commission chairman Archbishop Tutu.

And President Nelson Mandela publicly asked that the report should be published with everything in it, including the allegations against the ANC.

He is known to have argued in cabinet for full disclosure.

The Truth and Reconciliation Commission, after hearing testimony from over 21,000 victims of apartheid, completed its work on 31 July 1998, except for ongoing amnesty investigations, which will continue until next June.

MORE LEGAL CHALLENGES

The handing over of the report was overshadowed by another legal bid to delay publication—by former President FW de Klerk.

Mr de Klerk won a temporary interdict preventing the publication of material linking him to state-sponsored bombings in the 1980s.

The report holds him accountable for killings during his time in office, a period when anti-apartheid resistance was met with increasingly brutal suppression.

Sections of the TRC document, which suggest that Mr de Klerk knew about the bombing plans but failed to report them, have been suppressed until the case is heard again in March.

Chief Buthelezi. Leader of the Inkatha Freedom Party and Winnie Madikizela-Mandela, former wife of the president, have also been implicated in apartheid-era murders.

The report speaks of the former regime and the strategies which supported it as "supporting the notion that the apartheid system was a crime against humanity."

Source: BBC News, 1998

PHILOSOPHY AND TACTICS

In his 1964 speech, "I am prepared to die," Nelson Mandela identifies the philosophy of the ANC as well as the philosophy of Umkhonto. He explained that the primary goal of the ANC since its inception was African nationalism. He characterized this nationalism as "freedom and fulfillment for the African people in their own land." He cited the Freedom charter, which calls for a redistribution of land and a nationalization of mines and banks under an economy of private enterprise.

The ANC began as a lawful way to voice opposition against government policies that marginalized blacks. It spent fifty years peacefully protesting the government actions and promoting a non-racial democracy. In 1956, after ANC leaders had been arrested, the South African courts determined that the ANC did not have a policy of violence. However, by 1960, the leadership of the ANC resolved that their peaceful protests had resulted only in increased repression. After a 1960 massacre occurring in Sharpeville, the ANC was declared unlawful. Its leadership decided that its interests and the interests of blacks were not represented in the government. As a result, the group refused to dissolve.

As police violence against blacks escalated, violent protests escalated in response. The leadership of the ANC believed that a civil war was inevitable and sought to create "controlled violence" to avoid such a conflict. The group began with operations of sabotage. It believed that creating an economic disruption through the targeting of multinational corporations and government facilities would force voters to reevaluate their positions. The group targeted power plants, sought the disrupt rail and telecommunications, and attacked government buildings. Attacks were planned in a way that would spare human fatalities. As the acts of sabotage were carried out, the ANC began to prepare for its next level of conflict—guerilla warfare. Other African states were enlisted to help finance and train militants.

As the ANC reclaimed its political standing in the 1990s, the group reasserted its original ideology of racial equality under the law.

OTHER PERSPECTIVES

Because of the ANC's long history, many groups have held opposing perspectives. While apartheid was policy in South Africa, the government considered the ANC to be a disruptive force. As the ANC embarked on its policy of violence, the group was labeled as a communist organization by both the government and other organizations. In 1971, the Afrikaner Resistance Movement declared its stance against the ANC, calling the group communists. This opposition to the ANC cited the Marxist influences on the policies and agendas of the ANC, as well as the close ties the group held with the Communist Party in South Africa. The ANC and the Communist Party promoted the same primary goal—the removal of white supremacy in South Africa. The ANC asserted that in order to offer an equal footing to blacks, banks and mines should be nationalized. This closely resembled the Communist Party's goal to have a state run on the principles of Marxism.

As apartheid came to an end and the ANC developed into a political party, the group was accused of corruption, misconduct, the misuse of private funds by party leaders, and with a lack of accountability. In 1996, the cabinet minister in charge of health was discovered to have lied to parliament regarding a public affairs program that had been mishandled. The result was a four million dollar program that had not submitted to a proper bidding process. Instead, the contract was awarded to a good friend of the cabinet minister. However, when these charges were discussed by the media, the ANC shifted the blame to a group wanting to oust the minister. In another example, the former wife to Nelson Mandela, in 1996, was under charges of extortion and misuse of private funds. However, the ANC was seen as slow to responding or punishing those found of wrongdoing. In the *New York Times* article "South African Scandal over 'Sarafina' spotlights corruption in the ANC," Suzanne Daley expresses the view of critics of the ANC by stating, "The party often prizes loyalty over honesty and closes ranks around the accused while slurring the accusers." The ANC does not have a viable opposition political party and, as a result, remains in power.

SUMMARY

In 1912, South Africa was in the midst of policy changes that affected the lives and livelihood of blacks. Legislation was passed that created an environment that would eventually lead to the government-advocated policy of apartheid. One such act, the Native Land Act, was the impetus for a group of educated elites to meet and form an organization to oppose the legislation and push for racial equality. As a result the African National Congress was created. The congress began as a moderate political organization that sought to peacefully bring about change. However, as violence toward blacks continued, and the policies of apartheid expanded, the ANC moved toward a policy of violence after 50 years of peaceful protests. Under the militant wing called Umkhonto we Sizwe, the ANC sought to create economic disruptions by scaring foreign investment. The group targeted utilities, rail and telecommunications, government buildings, and any symbol of apartheid. The group was banned and Umkhonto was eradicated, but the ANC moved its operations underground and continued to hit targets in what it called, "controlled violence." By 1990, the ANC had been restored as a legal organization, ANC leader Nelson Mandela was released from prison, and the policies of apartheid began to be dismantled. In 1994, the first multiracial election was held in South Africa, and the ANC became the ruling party and has remained in power ever since.

SOURCES

Periodicals

Byrnes, Rita M. "A Country Study: South Africa." *Library of Congress, Federal Research Division.* May 1996.

Daley, Suzanne. "South African Scandal over 'Sarafina' Spotlights Corruption in the ANC." *New York Times.* October 8, 1996.

Henrard, Kristin. "Post-apartheid South Africa: Transformation and Reconciliation." *World Affairs.* Vol. 6 No. 1 (July 1, 2003).

Web sites

African National Congress. "I am Prepared to Die: Nelson Mandela's Statement." < http://www.anc. org.za/ancdocs/history/rivonia.html > (accessed October 11, 2005).

MIPT Terrorism Knowledge Base. "African National Congress." < http://www.tkb.org/Group.jsp?groupID = 305 > (accessed October 11, 2005).

SEE ALSO

Afrikaner Resistance Movement

Afrikaner Resistance Movement

LEADER: Eugene Terreblanche

USUAL AREA OF OPERATION: South Africa

OVERVIEW

The Afrikaner Resistance Movement was formed in 1973 in South Africa in response to the growing anti-apartheid sentiment that was threatening the white supremacy that had ruled the country. Rooted in Afrikaner nationalism, *Afrikaner Weerstandsbeweging*, or the Afrikaner Resistance Movement (AWB), sought to disrupt the movement toward inclusion of blacks in the South African government. The group, led by Eugene Terreblanche, operated campaigns of intimidation and explosives attacks during the 1980s and 1990s.

HISTORY

The first permanent European settlement in South Africa occurred in 1652 as the Dutch settled at the Cape of Good Hope. The Dutch presence would grow in the next decades and successfully quell the attempt by Africans to expel the settlers. European powers encouraged emigration to South Africa by offering free land to those willing to settle there. The Boer, as the migrant farmers of French, Dutch, and German heritage came to be known, facilitated the expansion of settlements by seizing control of land occupied by Africans. Meanwhile, the

Three members of the Afrikaner Resistance Movement lie dead after a shootout in a Mafikeng street in Mmabatho on March 11, 1994. AP/Wide World Photos. Reproduced by permission.

European powers struggled for positions of power over the settlements. By 1814, the British had gained control. As the colony began to industrialize, relations between the British and the Dutch-speaking Boers became contentious. In addition, the discovery of gold brought an increase of English-speaking immigrants. The Afrikaner movement enveloped the Boers as the Dutch-speakers sought to promote their national identity. S. J. du Toit, a Dutch Reformed minister, published two works supporting the belief that Afrikaners were a separate group of people with their own connection to their fatherland in South Africa, a newspaper *Die Afrikaanse Patriot* (The Afrikaner Patriot), and a book, *Die Geskiedenis van ons Land in die Taal van ons Volk* (The History of Our Land in the Language of Our People). Eventually, the British and Afrikaner differences developed into the South African War (1899–1902). Although the British were successful in the war, the Afrikaner movement was galvanized.

Afrikaners set up their own schools and celebrated their distinct language.

In 1914, Europe was at war. As a British dominion, the leadership in South Africa entered the war on the side of the British and to the protest of the Afrikaners. During this time, J. B. M. Hertzog formed the National Party of South Africa. Hertzog promoted Afrikaner nationalism and a policy of mutual-aid—Afrikaners helping Afrikaners. As the policy of segregation developed into the policy of apartheid, the Afrikaner national movement also grew.

However, by the 1980s, the political climate moved toward dismantling apartheid. The government of P.W. Botha was considering a plan that would grant the constitutionally protected right to vote to the Asian and mixed-race minorities. The founding members of the AWB believed that this was the first step toward communism, black rule, and the demise of the Afrikaner national

Afrikaner Resistance Movement leader Eugene Terreblanche rallies his party in 1994 in the Western Transvaal, South Africa. © *Ian Berry | Magnum Photos*

KEY EVENTS

1973: Seven like-minded Afrikaners meet and create the AWB in Heidelberg, Transvaal, with the goal to protect the Afrikaner national identity and promote white supremacy.

1994: The AWB attempts to disrupt elections by detonating bombs in Pretoria and Johannesburg, killing more than 20 people.

1994: Three AWB militants are killed after entering the region of Bophuthatswana.

1998: Terreblanche accepts responsibility, as leader of the AWB, for the 1994 bombings that killed more than 20 people.

2001: Terreblanche is jailed for the 1996 attempted murder of a black security guard.

2004: Terreblanche is released from jail and promises to develop the AWB into a political party that can serve as the voice of the right wing in South Africa.

---

identity. As a result, resistance organizations emerged to retain white supremacy in South Africa. The Afrikaner Resistance Movement (AWB) became prominent during this time. The group was formed in Heidelberg, Transvaal, and eventually moved its headquarters to the farming town of Ventersdorp, west of Johannesburg. The AWB developed cells of operation among the Afrikaner farmers who resided in the north, as well as a few urban community cells. The group claimed to be a cultural organization intent on the survival of the Afrikaner national identity, while wearing paramilitary uniforms and carrying side arms.

In 1994, the AWB sought to disrupt the election process and was determined to see the African National Congress—a black political organization led by Nelson Mandela—be destroyed. As a result, AWB members detonated bombs in many urban locations, including

an attack on the Johannesburg airport. These bombings killed more than 20 people. In addition, the group sought to disrupt constitutional negotiations by driving an armored vehicle through the doors of the building where the negotiations were taking place. The most publicized activity occurred in the nominally independent Bophuthatswana. The AWB entered the region in paramilitary fashion, wearing khaki uniforms and brandishing their flag—which bears a resemblance to the Nazi flag. However, the AWB was met by Bophuthatswana police, a meeting that left three AWB militants dead.

In 2001, the leader of the AWB, Eugene Terreblanche, was sentenced to five years in prison for a 1996 attack on a black man. After serving three years of his sentence, Terreblanche was released. Still clinging to his self-appointed role of protector of the Afrikaners, Terreblanche asserted that the AWB would move toward politics to become the voice of the right wing.

Police and rightwing AWB extremists clash in 1991 protests in Transvaal (Gauteng) South Africa. Both sides use teargas and batons resulting in chaos. Here one dog bites an AWB protestor and another bites a policeman. © *Ian Berry | Magnum Photos*

PHILOSOPHY AND TACTICS

The AWB is described as a white supremacy, neo-Nazi organization. During the early 1990s as South Africa moved toward a multiracial democracy, the AWB warned of a "holy war." The AWB belief in their rights to the land is rooted in their understanding of the colonial experience in South Africa. Terreblanche stated, "Most overseas people do not understand our history. They think we stole the land from the blacks. Well, that's not true. What happened is, the white people moved from the south to the north. The Transvaal was vast and open and lonely, with more or less no blacks. We built the cities; we worked and developed the mines. The blacks were here for centuries. They walked on diamonds and didn't even pick them up, because they didn't realize the value of what they had. Now they want our mines. Well, we want our land back. It's as simple as that." The

AWB views the granting of racial equality under the law tantamount to the introduction of communism and the end of the Afrikaner nation.

In order to protect their believed claim to the land, the AWB embarked on intimidation campaigns and beatings. In 1994, the group expanded their tactic to include detonating bombs in urban locations in an attempt to disrupt the multiracial elections. Currently, much of the AWB activities surround the speeches given by the group's leader, Eugene Terreblanche.

OTHER PERSPECTIVES

During the 1980s and 1990s, the AWB were viewed as a voice against the African National Congress. However, since the 1994 election, the AWB has slowly lost its membership. Much of the impressions of the AWB are based on the

PRIMARY SOURCE

Terreblanche's 'Return to the Future'

As a theatrical performance it had everything—except perhaps an audience.

Eugene Terreblanche was welcomed back to freedom by maybe two dozen die-hard supporters, with icons of the Afrikaner Resistance Movement's past.

The old flag of apartheid South Africa, the khaki uniforms, the swastika logo on a flag with a red background—throwbacks to a time when the white right commanded support and instilled fear in black South Africa.

But times have moved on—there were just two trumpeters struggling to hit the right notes, and the Terreblanche stiff-arm salute was welcomed by few, as he made his way forward to mount the black horse provided for the occasion.

The large crowd assembled in the conservative town of Potchefstroom had merely come to see the spectacle and have a good gawp at a piece of South African history. And they were not disappointed.

IRONIC WELCOME

Armed with riding whip he took up the reins of his favourite horse, Attila, and with two outriders paraded through the streets waving at the rather bemused passers by and a few more smiling supporters who may perhaps share his ideas, but no longer have the stomach to shout them from the rooftops.

But the parade was probably not what he was expecting—it was not khaki-clad fans who ran alongside chanting and cheering, but black South Africans singing liberation songs amid choruses of "viva democracy."

It was a strange scene, with one of the most notorious champions of right-wing supremacy lauded by his black fellow-countrymen, but this is sometimes a strange country.

"It's a warning," one of the cheerleaders told me. "We are letting him know that the South Africa he's come back to is a different South Africa."

So they were mocking him in a scene of support from a group of people no longer afraid by his outdated ideology.

Back in the 1980s, the Afrikaner Resistance Movement, or AWB as it was known, had influence as it battled to prevent apartheid's racist era from coming to an end—they even planted bombs in an effort to disrupt the first democratic elections.

'DEEPLY CHANGED'

A white Afrikaner state, and the preservation of Afrikaans language and culture was what

---

group's leader, Eugene Terreblanche. Terreblanche is seen as "[walking] a tightrope between racist menace and national joke." Although the AWB is viewed as "still virulently racist, the AWB has mostly become a beer-drinking club for Afrikaners who still want to wear uniforms and complain about black rule." The group is considered largely benign, the national police commissioner, Jackie Selebi stated, "They don't have the potential to overthrow the state, but we take any threat to peace seriously."

The group targeted its opposition toward the African National Congress (ANC)—a black political organization that operated since 1912 and participated in violence between 1970 and the end of apartheid in 1994. The ANC promoted a policy of constitutionally guaranteed racial equality. In order to create this change, the ANC advocated the Marxist-inspired nationalization of banks and mines. These mines had been operated by white settlers and Afrikaners since the discovery of gold and diamonds in South Africa.

SUMMARY

In 1973, in Heidleburg, Transvaal, a group of Afrikaners met. The group formed an Afrikaner nationalist organization called Afrikaner Weestandsbeweging, or the Afrikaner

they were fighting for. But times have moved on—the far right collected just a sprinkling of votes in this year's election.

And scandals surrounding Eugene Terreblanche had eroded his support base even before he was sent to prison—first for badly beating a petrol station attendant and setting his dog on him and then for attempting to murder a black security guard—a man so badly injured that he suffered brain damage in the attack.

But looking his 60 years, his white beard attached to a smaller frame than the man that went into an almost entirely black prison three years ago, he announced to the assembled media that he had changed and found God.

"I believe I am deeply changed in the knowledge that I am only man, and my creator, Jesus Christ, the father, the son and the holy spirit, will give me the right commands to live my life as an honourable citizen who also knows his duty to his Boer folk," he said.

He answered questions about his future and the future of the AWB with talk of flower beds and roses, of peace and of passion for the land.

None of it really made much sense— whether that was a changed man, or just for the media's benefit is another matter.

'BOER NATION'

If his views have changed, his few supporters might be disappointed—the current chairman of the AWB re-affirmed their policies and approach.

"We are not racist," said Andries Versagie, "but we are purely the Boer nation and we do not have space in our midst for any other nation apart from the Boer people.

"The Xhosa people and the Zulu people do not have any white people as members of their nation and they are not seen as racists, I don't understand why we are."

There just is not the support for the far right in South Africa any more—there are a few who still demand a white homeland, and other disgruntled Afrikaners frustrated by the new democracy, but few left with the will to pursue such far-right ideology.

Eugene Terreblanche may well now drift into obscurity, and into a past where many believe he belongs.

Alastair Leithead

Source: BBC News, 2004

Resistance Movement. The group sought to protest the movement in South Africa toward a multiracial democracy. In particular, the group viewed the proposed constitutionally granted right to vote to minority races as the first steps toward communism, black rule, and the end of the Afrikaner national identity. The AWB believes that the Afrikaners are a distinct group in South Africa with a unique national identity. The AWB sought to protect that heritage.

During the 1980s and 1990s, as the South African government moved toward an end to the policy of apartheid, racially motivated violence increased. The AWB asserted that if the policies of apartheid were successfully

dismantled, the group would embark on a "holy war." As a result, the AWB began by launching a campaign of intimidation. The group followed this by detonating bombs in urban locations, including the Johannesburg airport. The AWB also marched into the region Bophuthatswana. However, the group was met by Bophuthatswana police, resulting in the deaths of three AWB militants.

In 1994, the first multiracial elections occurred despite the AWB actions to derail the process, such as detonating bombs in Pretoria and Johannesburg. These attacks caused the deaths of more than 20 people. The election resulted in the rise to power of the ANC—the political black organization led by Nelson

LEADERSHIP

EUGENE TERREBLANCHE

Eugene Terreblanche is the most prominent leader of the AWB. Terreblanche travels flanked by members of his inner circle called the "Iron Guard." He often emerges from his Ventersdorp farm to give speeches promoting the promises of the AWB to oppose the black government in South Africa. In 1998, Terreblanche took responsibility, as the leader of the AWB, for the 1994 bombings in which more than 20 people died. In 2001, Terreblanche was sentenced to five years in jail for the attempted murder of a black security guard. He served three years and was released. Upon his release, he resumed control of a member-diminished AWB.

Mandela. As the ANC rose to power, the AWB began to lose its membership. By 1998, the leader of the AWB, Eugene Terreblanche, took responsibility for the deaths occurring in Pretoria and Johannesburg. In 2001, Terreblanche was sentenced to five years in jail for the 1996 beating of a black man. He was released three years later and greeted by a group of 20 supporters. Upon his release, Terrblanche suggested that the AWB would move toward becoming a political organization and the voice of the extreme right wing in South Africa.

SOURCES

Periodicals

Byrnes, Rita M. "A Country Study: South Africa." *Library of Congress, Federal Research Division.* May 1996.

Hawthorne, Peter. "No Laughing Matter. A Shadowy Group of Racist Afrikaners Is Plotting to Bring Down the Government." *Time International.* October 21, 2001.

Ryan, Michael. "Up Front: Hope Meets Hatred in South Africa." *People.* April 9, 1990.

"World: South Africa, The Wind Rises in Welkom in Defense of Apartheid." *Time.* May 28, 1990.

Web sites

BBC News Online. "Profile: Eugene Terreblanche." < http://news.bbc.co.uk/2/hi/africa/3797797.stm > (accessed October 10, 2005).

BBC News Online. "South Africa's Terreblanche Freed from Jail." < http://news.bbc.co.uk/2/hi/africa/3796467.stm > (accessed October 10, 2005).

Audio and Visual Media

National Public Radio, Morning Edition. "Soldiers Sent to Bophuthatswana to Protect Embassy." March 11, 1994.

Al-Aqsa Martyrs Brigade

OVERVIEW

The al-Aqsa Martyrs Brigade is a largely secular Palestinian nationalist militia group that emerged following the start of the second intifada in October 2000. It has strong links to the Fatah movement, formerly led by the late Yasser Arafat, and has carried out numerous suicide bombings and shootings on Israeli military targets and civilians.

HISTORY

On September 28, 2000, Ariel Sharon, leader of Israel's main right-wing opposition party, Likud, surrounded by an entourage of flag-waving political cronies and accompanied by hundreds of Israeli riot police, marched up to the Haram al-Sharif, the site of the gold Dome of the Rock that is the third holiest shrine in Islam. This deliberately provocative act was designed to show Israeli sovereignty over Muslim holy sites in East Jerusalem, and strengthen Sharon's position within his own party.

Sharon, a figure universally despised by Palestinians for his complicity in the Sabra and Shatila massacre two decades earlier, caused outrage. "This is a dangerous process conducted by Sharon against Islamic sacred places," Yasser Arafat told Palestinian television. As he came

LEADER: Marwan Barghouti

KEY EVENTS

2000: Likud leader Ariel Sharon's visit to Temple Mount prompts rioting that leads to the al-Aqsa intifada.

2001: The Palestinian Brigade of the Martyrs of al-Aqsa, claim responsibility for its first killing, conversely of one of Yasser Arafat's close allies: the Palestinian television chief, Hisham Mikki.

2001: Al-Aqsa Martyrs take responsibility for a number of attacks on West Bank settlements.

2002: Al-Aqsa bomber, Wafa Idris, is the first female to carry out a suicide attack.

2002: Fatah Secretary General Marwan Barghouti arrested for the "murder of hundreds of Israelis" as alleged leader of al-Aqsa Martyrs. He denies the charge.

2003: In bloodiest al-Aqsa attack two suicide bombers kill 23 and injure more than 100 in a Tel Aviv suburb.

2003: BBC journalists learn that the Palestinian Authority was paying $50,000 a month to the al-Aqsa Martyrs.

2004: Palestinian Prime Minister Ahmed Queri says that al-Aqsa is part of the Fatah movement.

2005: Al-Aqsa indicate willingness to agree a truce.

A Palestinian militant wears a belt lined with explosives during an al-Aqsa Martyrs Brigades march in Gaza City on August 14, 2002. Reuters/Corbis

down 45 minutes later, a trail of fury had erupted. Palestinians threw whatever missiles came to hand at Israeli forces; riot police retaliated with tear gas and rubber bullets, and shot one protester in the face.

The following day, Palestinians, leaving the al-Aqsa Mosque in Jerusalem after Friday prayers, broke out into a riot, attacking Jews praying at the Western Wall under Temple Mount. Israeli police opened fire, killing five Palestinians and injuring 200. Over the following days, the teetering peace process instigated by the Oslo Accords seven years earlier, which had very nearly reached a conclusion that summer at Camp David, all but broke down as the worst violence between Israelis and Palestinians in the country's history broke out. This soon became recognized as the second *intifada* (uprising), or the al-Aqsa Intifada.

In the emergent chaos of this uprising, Israeli Defense Forces (IDF) attracted worldwide condemnation for the brutality with which they suppressed rioting, often because they drew in innocent bystanders and, particularly, children. Nowhere, however, was this anger more palpable than in Israel's occupied territories. The armed wings of a number of Palestinian groups moved into action, launching defensive actions to protect its populations, launching guerilla attacks against Israeli military targets and, increasingly, attacks on Israeli citizens.

At the forefront of attacks on Israeli civilians was Hamas, the radical jihadist organization. Islamic Jihad, an offshoot of Hezbollah, was also involved in a number of incidents. On the other hand, Yasser Arafat's Fatah movement largely maintained its traditional distance from attacks on Israeli civilians and tried to uphold its image as comparative moderates.

A masked Al-Aqsa Martyrs Brigade activist speaks on August 5, 2004, during a rally marking the 40th day of the murder of the group's leader, Nayef Abu Sharkh. AP/Wide World Photos. Reproduced by permission.

But as anger increased among the Palestinian population some began to see Hamas, and their suicide bombings, rather than Fatah, as the true "protector" of the Palestinian people.

Unpalatable though they may seem, suicide bombings enjoy broad support among Palestinians. Members of Fatah Tamzin, its armed wing, had been involved in many confrontations with the IDF in late 2000 and early 2001, and were also implicated in a number of civilian shootings in mid 2001. Some of these were attributed to the Martyrs of al-Aqsa, which security analysts claimed was a secular nationalist militia with links to Fatah. When it started paramilitary activity is unknown. On January 18, 2001, the Palestinian Brigades of the Martyrs of al-Aqsa claimed responsibility for a killing for the first time, but this was of one of Yasser Arafat's close allies: the Palestinian television chief, Hisham Mikki, who was killed at a Gaza beachfront hotel. In the summer of 2001, the Israeli

government accused the same group of a number of attacks on West Bank settlements.

It was only in late 2001 that a definite pattern of violence linked to this group emerged. On December 12, gunmen opened fire on a bus of ultra-orthodox settlers traveling to the West Bank settlement of Emmanuel, killing eight and injuring 30. "This is in response to the recent killings by the Israelis in the West Bank and Gaza Strip," said an anonymous telephone caller speaking to *Reuters* news agency. At the end of January 2002, Wafa Idris, a 28-year-old paramedic, became the first female suicide bomber in an attack that killed one and wounded 100. Once more, the al-Aqsa Martyrs claimed responsibility.

From there on, the attacks assumed an even more deadly direction. An al-Aqsa suicide bomber killed 11 at Beir Ysirael in Jerusalem on March 2, 2002; three were killed and 86 injured in a suicide bombing in central Jerusalem on

Mourners carry the coffin of Israeli Arab George Khoury, 20, at the Mount Zion Christian cemetery in Jerusalem. Khoury was killed by Al-Aqsa Martyr's Brigade members on March 19, 2004, when he was mistaken for a Jewish settler. Menahem Kahana | AFP | Getty

March 21; two were killed and 29 injured by another female suicide bomber on March 29; six were killed and 104 injured in a suicide bomb attack on the market at Jaffa; a suicide bomber at a Jerusalem bus stop killed seven and injured 50 on June 19. And so the appalling list of violence against Israeli civilians went on through the rest of 2002, 2003, and into 2005, as the al-Aqsa Martyrs Brigade vied with Hamas to be the most insidious and deadly of Palestinian terror organizations.

There were questions as to whether or not this emergent extremist group was part of Yasser Arafat's Fatah movement. Certainly if it was not, it managed to boost his prestige at a time when the Palestinians accused him of inertia in the face of Israeli repression, and when Hamas was starting to gain preeminence through its militancy. Most analysts, however, were left in no doubt that the al-Aqsa Martyrs Brigade was linked to Fatah, and many of those involved in suicide bombings were either Fatah members or closely linked to the organization. For instance,

the three brothers of Wafa Idris were all Fatah members.

Arafat himself may not have directly led the organization, but he was certainly titular head. Asked by a PBS Frontline team if Arafat was in charge of the Brigade in March 2002, Jihad Ja'Arie, a Brigade leader, told the reporters: "Most naturally, the President, the brother, the leader—'Abu Amar' [Arafat's nom de guerre]—is the president of the state of Palestine and the head of the National Liberation Movement [Fatah], he is the one who makes the first and last decisions on all matters relating to the Palestinian street. We always abide by his decisions and also we abide by all the agreements entered into by the Palestinian Authority. We always abide by the decisions of the political leadership. . . . "

In November 2003, BBC journalists learned that the Palestinian Authority—led by Arafat—was paying $50,000 a month to al-Aqsa. Palestinian ministers claimed that the money was an attempt to wean the gunmen away from

LEADERSHIP

MARWAN BARGHOUTI

Before his arrest in April 2002 as the alleged head of the al-Aqsa Martyrs, Marwan Barghouti was the rising star of the Fatah political movement and earmarked as a potential successor to Yasser Arafat as head of the PLO. At 43, he was relatively youthful and also untainted by accusations of corruption: both were a direct contrast to many in the Palestinian political hierarchy. While admired for his uncompromising calls to fight the Israeli occupation, he was seen by Israelis as a possible negotiating partner and had continually backed the stuttering peace process. He is also a fluent Hebrew and English speaker.

He served as General Secretary of Fatah prior to his arrest, and was in charge of the movement's operations in the West Bank, the area where it holds the most influence. It is unclear why Israel chose to target Barghouti, who had a reputation as a moderate and was one of the first Palestinian leaders to return from exile in 1994. However, from the onset of the al-Aqsa intifada in September 2000,

Barghouti was forced into hiding in the Palestinian stronghold of Ramallah, fearing his arrest or assassination.

The troubled trial process, in which Barghouti and his defense witnesses refused to recognize the Israeli court and offer evidence, failed to shed much further light on his alleged crimes. He was acquitted of 21 of the 26 counts of murder with which he had been charged. It has been speculated that because of his knowledge of Hebrew, he had emerged on Israeli TV as the "voice of the intifada," and Prime Minister Ariel Sharon sought to make an example of the next most prominent figure to Yasser Arafat. It has also been suggested that by sidelining the Palestinians "voice of moderation," Sharon's government sought to confront the PLO in a purely military confrontation. Given the inherent hawkishness of the Israeli Prime Minister, that is not an inconceivable prospect; nor, however, given the many murky links between Fatah and the al-Aqsa Martyrs, is it conceivable that Barghouti was actually guilty of the crimes with which he was accused.

---

suicide bombings and that the policy of paying the money had not been instigated by Arafat, although it was carried out with his knowledge and agreement. In any case, it was argued, the amounts of money given out (up to $250 each) were too small to buy weaponry.

In June 2004, the Palestinian Prime Minister, Ahmed Queri told *Asharq al-Awsat*, a hitherto obscure London-based Muslim newspaper, "We have clearly declared that the Aqsa Martyrs Brigade are part of Fatah. We are committed to them and Fatah bears full responsibility for the group." These comments, which were seized upon by the right-wing *Jerusalem Post*, have never been verified.

To the Israeli government, however, there was no doubt that the al-Aqsa Martyrs were part of the Fatah movement. In a report prepared by a team headed by Israel's Minister of Parliamentary Affairs, it argued that, "Arafat

was personally involved in the planning and execution of terror attacks. He encouraged them ideologically, authorized them financially and personally headed the Fatah Al Aqsa Brigades organization." As evidence, Israeli intelligence presented several documents found in Arafat's headquarters in Ramallah, which included a request for financial aid outlying operations, propaganda, and arms purchases, as well as other documents signed by the group and addressed to Arafat and other high Palestinian officials. All the documents were signed by al-Aqsa Martyrs Brigade that referred to itself as part of Fatah.

In April 2002, Israel arrested Fatah's West Bank leader, Marwan Barghouti, a man widely expected to emerge as Yasser Arafat's eventual successor. They accused him of being the leader of the al-Aqsa Martyrs Brigade and, according to the Israeli Prime Minister, Ariel Sharon, the

---

PRIMARY SOURCE

Israelis Kill Palestinian Militant Linked to Tel Aviv Bombing

Israeli soldiers on Thursday tracked down and killed an armed Palestinian militant who Israeli military officials said had helped orchestrate a recent suicide bombing and was planning further attacks. Palestinians criticized the action, saying it could jeopardize the fragile truce.

Israeli military officials said the militant, Muhammad Abu Khazneh, was a member of Islamic Jihad, which claimed responsibility for the bombing deaths of five Israelis at a Tel Aviv nightclub on Feb. 25. It was the deadliest single attack since the truce was announced Feb. 8.

Overall, the number of killings has dropped significantly since Prime Minister Ariel Sharon and the Palestinian leader, Mahmoud Abbas, called for an end to violence. The two-week period between Thursday's incident and the Tel Aviv bombing was one of the longest without a killing on either side since the fighting erupted in September 2000.

But shooting exchanges still break out almost daily, and the Israelis and Palestinians have been making little progress in negotiations, with both sides expressing frustrations.

In Thursday's operation, Israeli forces surrounded the home where Mr. Khazneh was hiding in the village of Nazlat al Awasta, near Jenin in the West Bank. Using a loudspeaker, the troops called for everyone to come out, and all of them did—except for Mr. Khazneh. The soldiers then sent a trained dog inside to look for him, the military said.

Mr. Khazneh shot and killed the dog, and then fired on troops, according to the military. Soldiers returned fire and tossed grenades inside, later demolishing the house.

When the truce was announced last month, Israel pledged not to carry out operations in Palestinian areas unless facing attack. Military officials said Mr. Khazneh was a target because he was directly involved in the Tel Aviv bombing and was planning additional attacks.

Nafez Azzam, an Islamic Jihad leader in the Gaza Strip, told The Associated Press that the

---

man behind the "murder of hundreds of Israelis." He was eventually tried for the murder of 26 Israelis and found guilty on five counts in May 2004. He maintains his innocence. Amnesty International criticized the trial process because of the use of torture.

In 2003, the Israeli government placed Arafat's compound in Ramallah under siege, bombarding it with shell fire. In September, its cabinet passed a resolution ambiguously calling for the "removal" of Arafat. Ostensibly, it was passed as a reprisal for the continued suicide bombings, although it was widely assumed that that was a convenient cover for the Israeli government to rid itself of its most ubiquitous opponent. As Arafat's biographer, Danny Rubenstein, put it, it was "a license to kill Arafat." It was abandoned the following month after U.S. pressure.

Arafat's death in November 2004, coupled with the efforts of Mahmoud Abbas, his successor as PLO leader, has seen a marked decline in the activities of all Palestinian militant groups, including the al-Aqsa Martyrs Brigade. This has been heightened by the removal of illegal Israeli settlements from Gaza. In January 2005, al-Aqsa spokesman, Abu Mohammed, indicated that his organization would accept a truce, but added: "We think that all the factions, including Hamas and Islamic Jihad, believe that this cease-fire must be mutual."

PHILOSOPHY AND TACTICS

The al-Aqsa Martyrs Brigade are ostensibly a secular Palestinian nationalist paramilitary forces seeking to force Israel into a final political

killing "does not encourage us to continue the state of calmness that currently exists on the ground."

In another development on Thursday, about 20 Palestinian gunmen linked to Mr. Abbas's political movement, Fatah, stormed a large Fatah meeting in the West Bank city of Ramallah.

The gunmen smashed windows and chairs and ordered hundreds of Fatah members out of the hall. As the crowd moved outside, the gunmen fired shots in the air. No one was hurt, but the meeting was called off.

The gunmen, who belong to Al Aqsa Martyrs Brigade, an armed faction of Fatah, said they felt that they were being marginalized by the Fatah leadership.

The episode reflected the problems Mr. Abbas faces in his movement, which has dominated Palestinian politics for decades.

Meanwhile, Islamic Jihad and other armed factions have agreed in principle to a temporary halt in attacks, though compliance has been less than complete. The factions plan to discuss the truce in talks set to begin March 15 in Cairo.

Mr. Abbas plans to attend, and said he hoped the meeting would produce a stronger and more lasting truce. "There are no radical differences, and the Cairo dialogue should crown efforts that are under way," he told reporters in Gaza City.

But he also criticized the Israeli raid, saying it would make it more difficult for the Palestinian leadership to prevent, or at least limit, attacks from the Palestinian side.

"Quiet is required from us," Mr. Abbas said. "At the same time, it is also required from the Israelis, and the Israelis must not carry out these actions."

Greg Myre

Source: New York Times, 2005

settlement and to drive Israeli forces out of Palestinian areas. Whether this encompasses the entire state of Israel or merely the occupied territories (i.e., Gaza and the West Bank) is unclear; however, in the context of the al-Aqsa intifada, it is seemingly the latter. Although Fatah is essentially set up on non-religious lines, Islamic fundamentalist rhetoric has flourished since 2000, and Fatah can be seen as answering a call of jihad that has seemingly come from everyone from clerics to otherwise secular politicians, like the late Yasser Arafat. In particular, the reasoning behind a "Martyrdom" (i.e., a suicide mission) is usually couched in religious terms.

Operating primarily in the West Bank, but also in Israel and Gaza, the al-Aqsa Martyrs progressed from attacks on Israeli military installations and isolated shootings on the West Bank's illegal settlements, to massive suicide bombing missions in Israel itself. The goal was seemingly to disrupt Israeli civil and economic life as much as possible.

OTHER PERSPECTIVES

"Israel, its supporters and apologists around the world, have sought, somewhat successfully, to demonize and vilify the suicide bombings and with them the entire Palestinian struggle for freedom and justice," wrote Khaled Amayreh in *Al Ahram Weekly* in 2003. "This demonisation became especially intense and acquired a strong momentum after the 11 September terrorist attacks in the US. Gruesome televised images enabled Israeli spin-doctors to de-contextualize the bombings by distracting attention from root-

PRIMARY SOURCE

Al-Aqsa Martyrs Brigade (al-Aqsa)

A.K.A. AL-AQSA MARTYRS BATTALION

DESCRIPTION

The al-Aqsa Martyrs Brigade consists of an unknown number of small cells of terrorists associated with the Palestinian Fatah organization. Al-Aqsa emerged at the outset of the 2000 Palestinian intifadah to attack Israeli targets with the aim of driving the Israeli military and settlers from the West Bank, Gaza Strip, and Jerusalem, and to establish a Palestinian state.

ACTIVITIES

Al-Aqsa has carried out shootings and suicide operations against Israeli civilians and military personnel in Israel and the Palestinian territories, rocket and mortar attacks against Israel and Israeli settlements from the Gaza Strip, and the killing of Palestinians suspected of collaborating with Israel. Al-Aqsa has killed a number of US citizens, the majority of them dual US-Israeli citizens, in its attacks. In January 2002, al-Aqsa was the first Palestinian terrorist group to use a female suicide bomber.

STRENGTH

Unknown.

LOCATION/AREA OF OPERATION

Al-Aqsa operates in Israel, the West Bank, and Gaza Strip, and has only claimed attacks inside these three areas. It may have followers in Palestinian refugee camps in southern Lebanon.

EXTERNAL AID

In the last year, numerous public accusations suggest Iran and Hizballah are providing support to al-Aqsa elements, but the extent of external influence on al-Aqsa as a whole is not clear.

Source: U.S. Department of State. *Country Reports on Terrorism.* Washington, D.C., 2004.

---

causes, namely Israel's treatment of the Palestinians.

"Thus, Israeli officials and propagandists told the world that Palestinians were blowing themselves up because they hated Jews so much that they were willing to kill themselves to vent their feelings. The world was also told that the suicide bombings were rooted in Islam, which glorified martyrdom and death for the sake of God. This [is a] scandalous distortion of reality...

"For their part, the Palestinians argued that the suicide bombings were only a reaction to Israeli oppression of the Palestinian people. Indeed, virtually all Palestinian leaders argued that Israel, under the leadership of Ariel Sharon, a war criminal by any standard, was only offering the Palestinians the choice between dying as non-combatants, or killing themselves as suicide bombers in the streets of Israel. Palestinians have long argued that Israeli oppression has reached genocidal proportions, so much so that life for the vast bulk of Palestinians has become a

virtual hell. In this situation, death as a martyr becomes not only inevitable, but desirable as well, if only to escape extreme suffering and persecution."

Alan Dershowitz, Professor of Law at Harvard and author of *Why Terrorism Works*, wrote in an article published in the *Jerusalem Post* and the *Guardian* that suicide bombing was the result of those in authority misusing their power, not the result of oppression or desperation. "As suicide bombings increase," he wrote. "[M]ore and more people have come to believe that this tactic is a result of desperation. They see a direct link between oppression, occupation, poverty and humiliation on the one hand, and a willingness to blow oneself up for the cause on the other. It follows from this that the remedy for suicide bombing is to address its root cause—namely, our oppression of the terrorists.... But the underlying premise is false: there is no such link. Suicide bombing is a tactic that is selected by privileged, educated people because it has proven successful. Some of the suicide bombers themselves defy the stereotype of the impoverished victims driven to desperate measures. Remember the 9/11 bombers, several of whom were university students and none of whom was oppressed by the US [?]"

" ... The bombers accept death because they have been incited by imams preaching 'Kill the infidels.' Sheikh Muhammad Sayed Tantawi, the leading Islamic scholar at the elite al-Azhar University in Cairo, has declared that martyrdom operations—i.e., suicide bombings—are the highest form of jihad. ... The time has come to address the real root cause of suicide bombing: incitement by certain religious and political leaders who are creating a culture of death and exploiting the ambiguous teachings of an important religion. Islamist young people are in love with death, claim some imams; but it is these leaders who are arranging the marriages between the children and the bomb belts."

SUMMARY

The al-Aqsa Martyrs Brigade emerged so that Yasser Arafat could claim among his own people that he had matched the brutality of Hamas during the second intifada. Although politically expedient in the short term, the use of the al-Aqsa Martyrs merely served to bring the chaos of this perennial struggle to a new level of horror.

SOURCES

Web sites

Amnesty International "Report into al-Aqsa Intifada." < http://www.stoptorture.org.il/eng/images/uploaded/publications/43.pdf > (accessed October 21, 2005).

Brickman. "The Involvement of Arafat, PA Senior Officials and Apparatuses in Terrorism against Israel, Corruption and Crime." < http://www.brickman.dircon.co.uk/naveh.html > (accessed October 21, 2005).

freebarghouti.org. "Supporters of Marwan Barghouti." < http://www.freebarghouti.org/index.html > (accessed October 21, 2005).

Observer. "Equality in Death." < http://observer.guardian.co.uk/magazine/story/0,11913,1200794,00.html > (accessed October 21, 2005).

SEE ALSO

HAMAS

Hezbollah

Al-Fuqra

LEADER: Sheikh Mubarik Ali Jilani Hashemi

YEAR ESTABLISHED OR BECAME ACTIVE: 1980 (claimed by group)

ESTIMATED SIZE: 3,000 members

USUAL AREA OF OPERATION: Canada, United States, Pakistan, the Caribbean, Europe, and the Ivory Coast

OVERVIEW

Al-Fuqra (also called Jamaat ul-Faqra), a Pakistani-based Muslim extremist sect, was formed by Sheikh Mubarik Ali Jilani Hashemi (commonly called Sheikh Jilani). The group, which terrorizes primarily with murders and fire-bombings, operates in Canada and the United States, but also is present in Pakistan, the Caribbean, Europe, and the Ivory Coast. The name al-Fuqra is derived from Arabic for *al-fuqara*, meaning "the impoverished."

According to a Federal Bureau of Investigation (FBI) report, as stated in the article "Al-Fuqra," by the National Memorial Institute for the Prevention of Terrorism (MIPT) Terrorism Knowledge Base, the group is actively pursuing its enemies, which include the governments of the United States, Canada, and Israel, along with the Hindus, Hare Krishnas, Jewish Defense League, and Nation of Islam. U.S. law enforcement officials are relatively certain that al-Fuqra headquarters is located in Hancock, New York.

HISTORY

During a first visit to the United States, Sheikh Jilani, a radical Pakistani cleric, found enthusiastic supporters for his new group inside an

African-American mosque when he preached about the better life offered through Islam. The sect was subsequently formed in Brooklyn, New York, in 1980 by Sheikh Jilani, who asserts he is a direct descendant of the Prophet Muhammad.

Sheikh Jilani formed Al-Fuqra in order to purify the Islamic religion—primarily through violence—after perceiving it to be contaminated due to western culture. After his recruiting drive, which involved many recruits from intercity areas and prisons, Sheikh Jilani initiated most followers into the international Islamist movement, specifically to fight in the holy war against the Soviet Union's occupation of Afghanistan.

According to the 1993 article "Al-Fuqra: Holy Warriors of Terrorism." by the Anti-Defamation League (ADL), the U.S. Bureau of Alcohol, Tobacco, and Firearms (ATF) have linked sect members, from 1980–1993, to 16 criminal and terrorist activities in the United States and Canada. During this time, Al-Fuqra, unlike many terrorist groups, did not publicly claim responsibility for its violent acts.

The earliest verified attack by Al-Fuqra members, according to the earlier reported ADL article, occurred in 1979 when attacks were made on a Hare Krishna temple in San Diego, California, an Islamic Cultural Center in Tempe, Arizona, and a Shi'ite Iranian mosque in Queens, New York.

However, its existence was first formally verified by the ATF in 1983 when Al-Fuqra began a series of attacks that it called its Jihad Council for North America. The primary verification occurred at the arrest (and later conviction) of Stephen Paster, a leading Al-Fuqra member. Law enforcement officials found materials inside Paster's home to build pipe bombs. A later raid found handguns, semi-automatic pistols, and plans for electronic bombing mechanisms.

By the early 1990s, ample evidence had been collected by several state and federal U.S. law enforcement agencies, but primarily by the ATF, that Al-Fuqra had developed from a loosely based organization that bombed with crude explosives to a sophisticated network of organized cells whose members committed acts of fraud, violence, and murder using technologically advanced devices.

The group came under additional investigation when it was accused in U.S. Congressional

KEY EVENTS

1979: First verified attack occurred that was committed by Al-Fuqra members.

1980: Al-Fuqra was founded by Sheikh Mubarak Ali Jilani Hashemi in Brooklyn, New York.

1983: The group's existence was verified by U.S. law enforcement officials.

1984: Firebombing attacks occurred at Hare Krishna temples in Denver and Philadelphia and at Hindu and Sikh religious institutions in Seattle.

1985: Attack occurred on a Laotian temple in Rockford, Illinois.

1988: The sect killed a doctor in Augusta, Georgia.

1990: Al-Fuqra members murdered Rashad Khalifa, leader of the Islamic Center in Tucson, Arizona.

1993: Al-Fuqra comes under intense investigation for planning the bombing of the World Trade Center.

2001: Al-Fuqra is linked to Richard Reid (the Shoe Bomber).

2002: Al-Fuqra is linked to the kidnapping of reporter Daniel Pearl.

testimony, as reported in the 2001 article "Jamaat ul-Fuqra" by the South Asia Terrorism Portal, of planning the February 1993 bombing of the World Trade Center in New York City. One Al-Fuqra member, Clement Rodney Hampton-el, was convicted of the crime. The group was also implicated in the abduction of *Wall Street Journal* reporter Daniel Pearl (after Pearl attempted to meet with Sheikh Khalifa in Karachi, Pakistan, in January 2002) and linked with Richard Reid (the "Shoe Bomber," who was convicted of using explosives in the attempted destruction of a Paris–to–Miami aircraft in December 2001).

PRIMARY SOURCE

Specter of Terror; Clinton Administration Has No Plans to Arrest Sheik Now

With the help of a confidential informer operating inside a suspected bombing ring, Federal agents recorded many private conversations of Sheik Omar Abdel Rahman, the fiery Egyptian cleric who has been blamed for inspiring terrorism in Egypt and the United States. But after reviewing those recordings the Clinton Administration does not plan for now to arrest Mr. Abdel Rahman, law-enforcement officials said yesterday.

The decision comes as law-enforcement and Administration officials debate how to proceed with Mr. Abdel Rahman. Senior officials in New York and Washington said the tapes did not reveal enough information to justify an arrest. But others said enough evidence could have been marshaled, but there was a desire to allow Mr. Abdel Rahman to remain free because the Government gains important intelligence about Muslim radicals by watching the people attracted to him as he works from his mosque in Jersey City.

Federal officials continued to gather evidence yesterday, raiding a large, wooded compound with a shooting range in Perry County, Pa., about 35 miles west of Harrisburg, where some of the suspects used the target range and practiced military tactics. The Sunday Patriot-News of Harrisburg said eight F.B.I and United States Navy cars pulled into the compound shortly after noon. A team of Navy divers spent about five hours scouring a small pond, the paper said. F.B.I. officials would not say what they were looking for or whether they found anything.

The owner of the compound, Kelvin Smith, who said he worked for the United State Department of the Interior, told The Patriot-News he had cooperated fully with the agents. He said he did not know any of the suspects.

A decision to hold off action on Mr. Abdel Rahman for now was endorsed by Attorney General Janet Reno, officials said.

The informant who helped break up a major bomb plot last week was a close aide to Mr. Abdel Rahman and worked as a translator and bodyguard for him. It is unclear whether he

PHILOSOPHY AND TACTICS

Al-Fuqra members refer to themselves as "Soldiers of Allah," although earlier they called themselves "Muhammad Commandos." Its ideology is based on the belief that all peoples (both Muslims and non-Muslims) are enemies if they do not follow Islam as dictated by the Koran. A paper written by Sheikh Jilani (found during a 1991 raid by the Colorado Attorney General's Office) instructed Al-Fuqra members to engage in *Jihad* (holy war) against Muslim persecutors.

Its philosophy requires violence against any person, organization, and country with whom it disagrees. For example, during the 1980s, the sect participated in the Afghan war against the Soviet Union. In the 1990s and 2000s, Al-Fuqra members concentrated on terrorism against the United States, which included attacks against Jewish leaders, Hindu religious buildings, and U.S. and Canadian businesses. Its Pakistani activities were centered near the border of the Kashmir province of India where it aided Muslim separatists.

The sect is organized into cells; each is assigned a geographic location. Because U.S. and Canadian criminal activities of Al-Fuqra are especially strong in certain areas, it is conjectured, according to analysts at the MIPT Terrorism Knowledge Base, that these cells are centered around Brooklyn (New York), Baltimore (Maryland), Philadelphia (Pennsylvania), Tucson (Arizona), Portland (Oregon), Colorado (specifically in Denver and Colorado Springs), and Toronto (Canada).

Various Al-Fuqra compounds are located in remote U.S. and Canadian locations. Seven such compounds, according to law

got the tapes through a hidden body recorder or on the telephone, or whether certain locations were set up for audio surveillance. Six of the eight men arrested on Thursday in a plot to bomb the United Nations, the Federal Building and two tunnels were followers of Mr. Abdel Rahman. The man described by law-enforcement officials as the ring leader of the bomb plot also worked as a translator for Mr. Abdel Rahman.

New details, meanwhile, continued to emerge about the eight arrested suspects and at least three confederates known to investigators and about the enigmatic informer working for the Federal Bureau of Investigation who was credited with exposing the plot. Ties to Radical Group.

One suspect, Clement Rodney Hampton-El, was described by New York City police detectives as having worked closely with a radical Black Muslim group called al-Fuqra. The detectives said Mr. Hampton-El is viewed as a religious leader among Black Muslims in Brooklyn

and gave his blessing to violent crimes, from bank robberies to murders.

Investigators said that they were aware of at least three other men who took part in the plot to varying degrees but that the men were not being sought or arrested at this time. The question of whether to charge the Egyptian cleric in the wake of last week's foiled plot has been hotly debated in meetings of law-enforcement officials in New York and Washington, officials said.

Mr. Abdel Rahman is wanted in Egypt for inciting a riot that left hundreds dead in Cairo four years ago. But Egyptian Government officials have made it clear that they do not really want the political trouble that would be touched off among his followers by extraditing Mr. Abdel Rahman back to Cairo. It is not known how the Egyptian Government would view a decision by the United States to arrest Mr. Abdel Rahman and to try him for crimes here.

Ralph Blumenthal

Source: New York Times, 1993

---

enforcement authorities, are located in the Catskill Mountains of New York, Combermere (Canada), Commerce (Georgia), Dover (Tennessee), north-central South Carolina, western Virginia, and Tulare County (California). The compounds isolate members from western society so members dedicate their lives to the Islamic faith and the Al-Fuqra political agenda. U.S. government officials contend that al-Fuqra also maintains a presence in other U.S. states.

In order to preserve the organization's structural core, different cell members never contact each other directly. Contact is usually made through telephone calls at prearranged times. The use of safe houses, figurehead organizations (such as Muslims of the Americas, Quranic Open University, and Professional Security International), aliases, and other cover-up techniques are regularly used. Sheikh Jilani and

other members regularly deny the existence of the organization.

OTHER PERSPECTIVES

Muslims generally describe Al-Fuqra as an organization that performs helpful Islamic activities such as countering drug dealers, cleaning the community, and performing neighborhood watch patrols.

Supporters of Al-Fuqra declare that Sheikh Jilani has regularly told his followers that a Jewish plot to control the world is being formulated and in order to survive they must leave large cities and move into remote areas. These followers are simply following their leader's advice. In a similar line of thinking, members of Muslims of the

Americas, when presented with accusations that Al-Fuqra is a terrorist organization, counter with statements that declare these accusations are only Jewish propaganda to unjustly target Muslims. Guns found by police in the possession of Al-Fuqra members are said to be used only for defensive protection against enemies.

On the other hand, Al-Fuqra members have frequently been convicted of U.S. and Canadian crimes, including conspiracy to commit murder, fire-bombing, racketeering, forgery, smuggling, and fraud. It has been reported that members are currently suspects in over 10 unsolved assassinations and over a dozen fire-bombings in the United States between 1979 and 1990.

U.S. law enforcement officials have collected evidence over the years showing that members of Al-Fuqra use dangerous equipment and materials. For example, during a police raid in Colorado Springs, as reported by the South Asia Terrorism Portal, 30 pounds of explosives (pipe bombs and components), armaments (handguns and semi-automatic firearms), military manuals, bomb-making instructions, plans of proposed targets (oil and gas installations and electric facilities), and Al-Fuqra publications ("Guerrilla Warfare") were found inside property owned by Al-Fuqra members.

Many newspapers in states where Al-Fuqra own compounds have reported on illegal activities by Al-Fuqra members. Among them, *The Rocky Mountain News* in Denver reported in 2002 that Sheikh Jilani was linked to the kidnapping of journalist Daniel Pearl, along with a wide range of illegal activities throughout Colorado.

In Virginia, ATF officials found that members of Muslims of the Americas were illegally buying guns for Al-Fuqua. Later, ATF agent Tom Gallagher described on July 1, 2002 in the article "Militant Muslims Seek Virginia Base" in *The Washington Times* that al-Fuqra is a "violent, black Muslim extremist sect that acts out jihads against perceived enemies."

Susan Fenger, a former chief criminal investigator, said within the article "Muslim Terrorists Convicted on Firearms Charges in the U.S." from the *The Roanoke Times* on December 1, 2001, that the group shows a peaceful side to the public but, in reality, it is set up to defraud various U.S. government agencies.

SUMMARY

In the early 2000s, U.S. intelligence experts reported that al-Fuqra was found to be a splinter group of Jaish-e-Mohammed (Army of Mohammed), an Islamic extremist group based in Pakistan, along with having direct contact to Al-Qaeda, an international network of Islamist organizations headed by Osama bin Laden and Ayman al-Zawahiri.

At this time, Al-Fuqra was thought by these experts to possess about 3,000 members, many militarily trained in Pakistan and living in rural compounds in 19 U.S. states, the Caribbean, and Europe. Within the United States, Al-Fuqra members are suspected of at least 13 fire bombings and 17 murders, as well as various cases of theft and fraud.

Sheikh Jilani left the United States for Lahore, Pakistan, after the 1993 World Trade Center bombing. As of 2004, Sheikh Jilani, who remains the Al-Fuqra leader, continues under investigation by the U.S. government for his alleged links to Al-Qaeda, ties to Pakistan's Interservice Intelligence Agency, and laundering of money between the United States and Pakistan.

SOURCES

Periodicals

Brennan, Charlie. "Al-Fuqra Tied To Colorado Crimes: Leader Owned Land In Buena Vista; Followers Convicted In Bombing Of Krishna Temple." *The Rocky Mountain News.* February 12, 2002.

McCaffery, Jen. "Muslim Terrorists Convicted on Firearms Charges in the U.S." *The Roanoke Times.* December 1, 2001.

Sale, Richard. "Pakistan ISI Link to Pearl Kidnap Probed." *United Press International.* January 29, 2002.

Seper, Jerry, and Steve Miller. "Militant Muslims Seek Virginia Base." *The Washington Times.* July 1, 2002.

Thomas, Jo, and Ralph Blumenthal. "Rural Muslims Draw New, Unwanted Attention." *The New York Times.* January 3, 2002.

Web sites

Anti-Defamation League. "Al-Fuqra: Holy Warriors of Terrorism." < http://www.adl.org/extremism/moa/ al-fuqra.pdf > (September 21, 2005).

Anti-Defamation League. "Muslims of the Americas: In Their Own Words." < http://www.adl.org/extremism/moa/default.asp > (September 21, 2005).

MIPT Terrorism Knowledge Base, National Memorial Institute for the Prevention of Terrorism. "Terrorist Group Profile: Al-Fuqra." < http://www.tkb.org/Group.jsp?groupID = 3426 > (September 21, 2005).

South Asia Terrorism Portal. "Jamaat ul-Fuqra." < http://www.satp.org/satporgtp/countries/pakistan/terroristoutfits/jamaat-ul-fuqra.htm > (September 21, 2005).

Al-Gama'a al-Islamiyya

ALTERNATE NAME: Islamic Group

LEADER: Omar Abdel Rahman

YEAR ESTABLISHED OR BECAME ACTIVE: 1977

ESTIMATED SIZE: Less than five hundred members

USUAL AREA OF OPERATION: Egypt and Afghanistan

OVERVIEW

Al-Gama'a al-Islamiyya is an extremist Islamic group operating in Egypt. The group's purpose is to overthrow the government of Egypt and replace it with an Islamic state. The group has been operating since 1970. From 1970–1990, the group's acts of violence were directed at targets considered to be threats to Muslims, including the Egyptian government. During the 1990s, the group began to target tourists in Egypt, with their largest attack involving the death of fifty-eight tourists in Luxor.

Al-Gama'a al-Islamiyya is also known as Jamaa Islamiyya, Jamaat al Islamiya, Gamaat Islamiya, Islamic Group, IG, and al-Gama'at.

HISTORY

Al-Gama'a al-Islamiyya has been operating in Egypt since 1970. It originated as a set of separate cells linked through contact by the leaders of each cell. Most of the cells formed when members of the Muslim Brotherhood were released from prison by Egyptian President Anwar al-Sadat.

The Muslim Brotherhood is a nonviolent group that has been operating in Egypt since 1928. By the end of the 1940s, the Muslim Brotherhood was thought to have more than a

A 1984 Egyptian movie poster that has been defaced by Islamic extremists. © *Micha Bar Am / Magnum Photos*

million members. This made it a major political force in Egypt. While the group as a whole kept their nonviolent stance, some members carried out acts of terrorism and violence. In 1954, a member of the Muslim Brotherhood was accused of an assassination attempt on President Gamal Abd al-Nasser. In response to concerns about the intentions of the group, thousands of members of the Muslim Brotherhood were arrested and held in prisons and concentration camps, including being tortured. This led some members of the group to argue that the government of Egypt was anti-Muslim, with violent action needed to overthrow the government. In 1970, Anwar al-Sadat became the president of Egypt and began releasing former members of the Muslim Brotherhood. Some of the former members of the Muslim Brotherhood were now convinced that a violent response was needed. These members formed cells in various parts of southern Egypt, with the organization named Al-Gama'a al-Islamiyya.

The purpose of Al-Gama'a al-Islamiyya is to overthrow the government of Egypt and install an Islamic State. Prior to the 1990s, Al-Gama'a al-Islamiyya's attacks were focused on groups within Egypt perceived to be opponents of Islam, especially members of the Egyptian government. These perceived opponents included Egyptian government officials, Egyptian security forces, and Coptic Christians. Attacks were carried out mainly in the south of Egypt, where Al-Gama'a al-Islamiyya had a stronger hold.

In the 1990s, Al-Gama'a al-Islamiyya began targeting tourists and foreigners in Egypt, as well as continuing to engage in violent acts against government targets.

In 1995, Al-Gama'a al-Islamiyya claimed responsibility for an assassination attempt on Egyptian President Hosni Mubarak. In November 1995, Al-Gama'a al-Islamiyya claimed responsibility for a car bomb attack on the Egyptian embassy in Pakistan, which killed 16 people. On April 28, 1996, a shooting at the Europa Hotel in Cairo killed eighteen people.

In 1997, Al-Gama'a al-Islamiyya issued a ceasefire. A senior member of the group, Rifa'i

Sheikh Omar Abdel Rahman (right), the blind spiritual leader of Egypt's largest Islamic extremist group Jamaa Islamiyya is led to his New York apartment building in June 1993. Mark D. Phillips/AFP/Getty Images.

Taha Musa, did not agree with the ceasefire and led a split from the group. Musa became leader of a new faction of the group wanting to continue violent action. Mustafa Hamza led the other faction of the group and continued to support the ceasefire.

It was the faction of Al-Gama'a al-Islamiyya led by Musa that was suspected of conducting an attack on the Temple of Hatshepsut in Luxor. In this attack, six men opened fire on tourists as they exited a tour bus. The attack caused the death of fifty-eight tourists and four Egyptians. Al-Gama'a al-Islamiyya claimed responsibility for the attack and stated that they intended to take hostages for the purpose of forcing the release of their spiritual leader, Sheik Omar Abdel Rahman, from prison in the United States.

The faction of Al-Gama'a al-Islamiyya led by Musa is also suspected of having links with Osama Bin Laden and al-Qaeda, with bin Laden suspected of financing the attacks, and a senior member of al-Qaeda, Dr. Ayman al-Zawahiri, suspected of helping to organize the attacks.

In March 1999, Al-Gama'a al-Islamiyya issued another ceasefire, but this was later broken in June 2000. Then, in March 2002, the group stated that the use of violence was misguided and declared that they would not act in violence.

In the next year, the Egyptian government began to release hundreds of members of Al-Gama'a al-Islamiyya from prison.

PHILOSOPHY AND TACTICS

The actions of Al-Gama'a al-Islamiyya show two differing philosophies and goals. The first is a philosophy based on attacking the Egyptian government and other individuals considered enemies of Islam. The second is based on attacking tourists. This second philosophy indirectly attacks the Egyptian government because of the

Leaders of Egypt's most bloody and ruthless extremist group, al-Gamaa al-Islamiyya, or the Islamic Group, sit around a conference table in Cairo on June 21, 2002. AP/*Wide World Photos*

negative impact on the tourist industry and because of the potential backlash on the people of Egypt.

The first philosophy or goal was the focus of Al-Gama'a al-Islamiyya in the years from its original formation in 1970 until 1990. The tactics in these years were to act violently directly against individuals and groups considered to be enemies of Islam, including the Egyptian government. This led to a range of attacks on security forces, government officials, and Coptic Christians. This also included a number of attacks on Egyptian embassies. These actions continued in the 1990s and included an unsuccessful attempt to assassinate the Egyptian Information Minister Safw Cairo in April 1993 and an unsuccessful assassination attempt on Egyptian Prime Minister Hosni Mubarak. Al-Gama'a al-Islamiyya claimed responsibility for both attempted assassinations. In another incident, a suicide bomber targeted the Egyptian embassy in Pakistan. The incident killed sixteen and injured dozens more. Both Al-Gama'a al-Islamiyya and the International Justice Group claimed responsibility for the attack. This led to speculation that Al-Gama'a al-Islamiyya was

operating as part of a network of Islamic extremist groups.

The second philosophy based on attacking tourists began in the early 1990s and became increasingly prominent throughout the decade. The first of these types of attacks occurred on February 4, 1993, when a bomb was thrown at a tour bus containing South Korean visitors. Al-Gama'a al-Islamiyya claimed responsibility for the attack. On February 19, 1994, two tourists and two Egyptians were wounded when members of Al-Gama'a al-Islamiyya fired on a passenger train. Al-Gama'a al-Islamiyya claimed responsibility for a bomb explosion on a train several days later. The explosion injured six foreign tourists and five Egyptians. In March 1994, Al-Gama'a al-Islamiyya claimed responsibility for shooting at a Nile cruise ship, an incident that injured one tourist. In September 1994, three people were killed and two injured when a member of Al-Gama'a al-Islamiyya opened fire in a tourist area in the town of Hurghada, Egypt. Another incident involving firing on a train occurred in November 1995, with Al-Gama'a al-Islamiyya claiming responsibility for the attack. On April 28, 1996, four members of

Al-Gama'a al-Islamiyya (Islamic Group) members wave hands and banners in support of Osama bin Laden outside the Al Mansouri Mosque in Tripoli, Lebanon on October 12, 2001. Courtney Kealy / Getty Images

Al-Gama'a al-Islamiyya opened fire on Greek tourists outside the Europa Hotel in Cairo. The incident killed eighteen Greek tourists and injured fourteen more.

The largest terrorist attack took place at Luxor in Egypt, when members of Al-Gama'a al-Islamiyya opened fire on tourists visiting the Hatshepsut Temple. The incident killed fifty-eight tourists and four Egyptians. Al-Gama'a al-Islamiyya claimed responsibility for the attack.

These attacks in the 1990s show a significant change in the group's tactics, with the specific focus on attacking tourists. This is considered a way for the group to attack the Egyptian government indirectly, by endangering the tourism industry, an important source of income for Egypt. At the same time, concern about a decline in the tourist industry may cause people to question the Egyptian government and possibly lose faith in the government. In turn, this may assist Al-Gama'a al-Islamiyya by undermining the

government and gaining support for the installation of an Islamic state.

While the two different tactics serve the same overall purpose, sources suggest that the change represents a split within Al-Gama'a al-Islamiyya. There are two likely scenarios. The first scenario is that some members of Al-Gama'a al-Islamiyya began operating independently of the main group in the 1990s, with the spate of attacks on tourists in the early 1990s a result of actions carried out by these renegade members. The second scenario is that Al-Gama'a al-Islamiyya agreed to this strategy as a whole, but that some members of the group questioned the violence throughout the 1990s. In either case, it is known that the group issued a ceasefire in 1997 and that this caused a split. Several months later, the Luxor shootings occurred. It has since been found that the Luxor shootings were organized with assistance from al-Qaeda, including funding from Osama bin Laden. This shows a link between Al-Gama'a al-Islamiyya and al-Qaeda; the link is

LEADERSHIP

OMAR ABDEL RAHMAN

Omar Abdel Rahman, also known as the Blind Sheik, is the spiritual leader of Al-Gama'a al-Islamiyya. Rahman was born in Egypt and lost his eyesight during childhood as a result of diabetes. Rahman studied Islam at the university and later became a Muslim cleric. He developed close links with the Egyptian Islamic *Jihad* (holy war) and Al-Gama'a al-Islamiyya and became the leader of Al-Gama'a al-Islamiyya during the 1980s.

Omar Abdel Rahman was accused by American authorities of being involved in the 1993 World Trade Center bombing. He was not charged, but the accusation caused the FBI to begin investigating. In 1995, he was found guilty of conspiring to bomb various New York City landmarks, including the United Nations building, FBI offices, and several bridges and tunnels. In October 1995, he was sentenced to life in prison.

Although he is incarcerated in the United States, Rahman is still considered Al-Gama'a al-Islamiyya's spiritual leader.

between the split factions of the group led by Musa.

OTHER PERSPECTIVES

While Human Rights Watch does not support the terrorist actions of Al-Gama'a al-Islamiyya, it does have concerns that individuals suspected of being members of the group are not having their human rights upheld. Human Rights Watch describes how the Egyptian government introduced laws in the 1990s, allowing security forces greater powers of arrest. These laws included terms that individuals could be arrested and held without charge on the basis that they were considered a threat to public order and

KEY EVENTS

1970: The Al-Gama'a al-Islamiyya group began to form as former members of the Muslim Brotherhood were released from prison.

Between 1970 and 1990: Members of Al-Gama'a al-Islamiyya carried out various attacks against groups in Egypt considered opponents to Islam.

1990s: Al-Gama'a al-Islamiyya changed its tactics and began targeting tourists and foreigners in Egypt; trains, cruise ships, buses, and tourist areas were the targets of a number of attacks.

1995: Al-Gama'a al-Islamiyya claimed responsibility for an assassination attempt on Egyptian President Hosni Mubarak.

1995: Al-Gama'a al-Islamiyya claimed responsibility for a car bomb attack on the Egyptian embassy in Pakistan that killed sixteen people.

1996: Al-Gama'a al-Islamiyya claimed responsibility for a shooting at the Europe Hotel in Cairo that killed eighteen people.

1997: Al-Gama'a al-Islamiyya issued a ceasefire, causing a split in the group. Rifa'i Taha Musa rejected the ceasefire and became the leader of a faction dedicated to continuing violent action.

1997: Six members of Al-Gama'a al-Islamiyya opened fire on tourists in Luxor, killing fifty-eight people.

2002: Al-Gama'a al-Islamiyya stated that the use of violence was misguided and declared that they would no longer act in violence.

national security. In addition, the new laws allowed civilians to be referred to a military court. Human Rights Watch describes the arrests of hundreds of individuals who were suspected of being either members or supporters of groups, including Al-Gama'a al-Islamiyya, and the trials of some of these individuals by military

PRIMARY SOURCE
Massacre in Luxor

Friends and relatives of tourists killed in a massacre at a tourist attraction have visited Egypt to find out more about the murders.

A total of 58 holidaymakers and four Egyptians were gunned down on the steps of the temple of Hatshepshut in Luxor five years ago.

Three generations of a family from Ripponden, near Halifax—five-year-old Shaunnah Turner, her air hostess mother Karina, 24, and grandmother Joan Turner—lost their lives.

The militants responsible for the massacre were leading members of Egypt's largest Islamist group, Al-Gama'a al-Islamiyya, and had trained at Osama bin Laden's camps in Afghanistan.

Luxor memorial

Also killed were three other Britons, 36 Swiss tourists, and four Japanese honeymoon couples.

Jean Dawson and John Laycock, relatives of the Turner family, were accompanied on their trip to Egypt by a team from the BBC's Correspondent programme.

Mrs. Dawson said: "I've met some very lovely Egyptian people. Just ordinary people that are very kind, very warm. It seems a world away from the terrorists that did the massacre."

The families have been told a memorial to the victims will be constructed in Luxor.

Source: BBC News, 2002

---

courts. Human Rights Watch suggests that the arrests and trials are being carried out to repress individuals who are attempting only to exercise basic freedom of expression and freedom of association. Overall, the view of Human Rights Watch contends that the Egyptian government is unfairly attempting to repress Muslim groups from exercising their basic freedoms.

A report by the BBC raised questions about the ability of the Egyptian government to ensure the safety of tourists within Egypt. This report was completed following the Luxor shootings and noted that the Egyptian authorities had played down terrorist attacks on tourists. The report went on to say that the attack undermined the government's claim that terrorism within Egypt has been defeated. The article showed that the actions of Al-Gama'a al-Islamiyya at Luxor had a negative impact on tourism and on the people of Egypt.

there has been a major decline in the actions of the group. There has also been a major decline in the number of members of the group.

In March 2002, the group reinstated a cease-fire, declaring that they would not act in violence. This was followed by the release of hundreds of members of Al-Gama'a al-Islamiyya from prison. This action by the Egyptian government suggests that Al-Gama'a al-Islamiyya no longer poses a major threat in Egypt. However, it is still suspected that there are some extremist members intent on continuing their goal of installing an Islamic state in Egypt. There are also concerns that some members of Al-Gama'a al-Islamiyya have formed alliances with al-Qaeda, with this move altering their objectives and making them part of a larger terrorist cause.

SUMMARY

Since the Luxor attacks and a series of arrests and trials of Al-Gama'a al-Islamiyya members,

SOURCES

Books

Kepel, Gilles. *Muslim Extremism in Egypt*. Los Angeles: University of California Press, 2003.

PRIMARY SOURCE

Gama'a al-Islamiyya (IG) a.k.a. Islamic Group, al-Gama'at

DESCRIPTION

The IG, Egypt's largest militant group, has been active since the late 1970s, and is a loosely organized network. It has an external wing with supporters in several countries. The group's issuance of a cease-fire in 1997 led to a split into two factions: one, led by Mustafa Hamza, supported the cease-fire; the other, led by Rifa'i Taha Musa, called for a return to armed operations. The IG issued another ceasefire in March 1999, but its spiritual leader, Shaykh Umar Abd al-Rahman, sentenced to life in prison in January 1996 for his involvement in the 1993 World Trade Center bombing and incarcerated in the United States, rescinded his support for the cease-fire in June 2000. IG has not conducted an attack inside Egypt since the Luxor attack in 1997, which killed 58 tourists and four Egyptians and wounded dozens more. In February 1998, a senior member signed Usama Bin Ladin's fatwa calling for attacks against the United States.

In early 2001, Taha Musa published a book in which he attempted to justify terrorist attacks that would cause mass casualties. Taha Musa disappeared several months thereafter, and there is no information as to his current whereabouts. In March 2002, members of the group's historic leadership in Egypt declared use of violence misguided and renounced its future use, prompting denunciations by much of the leadership abroad. The Egyptian Government continues to release IG members from prison, including approximately 900 in 2003; likewise, most of the 700 persons released in 2004 at the end of the Muslim holy month of Ramadan were IG members.

For IG members still dedicated to violent jihad, their primary goal is to overthrow the Egyptian Government and replace it with an Islamic state. Disaffected IG members, such as those inspired by Taha Musa or Abd al-Rahman, may be interested in carrying out attacks against US interests.

ACTIVITIES

IG conducted armed attacks against Egyptian security and other Government officials, Coptic Christians, and Egyptian opponents of Islamic extremism before the cease-fire. After the 1997 cease-fire, the faction led by Taha Musa launched attacks on tourists in Egypt, most notably the attack in November 1997 at Luxor. IG also claimed responsibility for the attempt in June 1995 to assassinate Egyptian President Hosni Mubarak in Addis Ababa, Ethiopia.

STRENGTH

Unknown. At its peak IG probably commanded several thousand hard-core members and a like number of sympathizers. The 1999 cease-fire, security crackdowns following the attack in Luxor in 1997 and, more recently, security efforts following September 11 probably have resulted in a substantial decrease in the group's numbers.

LOCATION/AREA OF OPERATION

Operates mainly in the al-Minya, Asyut, Qina, and Sohaj Governorates of southern Egypt. Also appears to have support in Cairo, Alexandria, and other urban locations, particularly among unemployed graduates and students. Has a worldwide presence, including in the United Kingdom, Afghanistan, Yemen, and various locations in Europe.

EXTERNAL AID

Unknown. There is some evidence that Usama bin Ladin and Afghan militant groups support the organization. IG also may obtain some funding through various Islamic non-governmental organizations (NGOs).

Source: U.S. Department of State. *Country Reports on Terrorism.* Washington, D.C., 2004.

Periodicals

Smith, Barbara. "Heaven or Hell?: Terrorism Hurts Revenue from Tourism." *The Economist*. no. 350 (1999): 14–15.

Web sites

BBC News. "Egypt: The New Spectre of Terror." < http://news.bbc.co.uk/1/hi/world/analysis/ 32048.stm > (accessed September 21, 2005).

Human Rights Watch. "Egypt: Human Rights Background." < http://www.hrw.org/backgrounder/ mena/egypt-bck-1001.htm > (accessed September 21, 2005).

SEE ALSO

Al-Qaeda

Al-Ittihad al-Islami (AIAI)

Terrorism experts are of the opinion that Somalia's biggest Islamic extremist organization, Al-Ittihad al-Islami, rose to power after the fall of Muhammad Siad Barre regime. Al-Ittihad al-Islami (AIAI) is also known as Islamic Union or Somali Islamic Union and operates in many parts of the East African country.

Reportedly, the principal goal of Al-Ittihad al-Islami is to create an Islamic state in Somalia. Moreover, it also allegedly aims to liberate the Ogaden region of Ethiopia that the group claims is a part of Somalia and was unlawfully confiscated from the country during its colonialist period.

ALTERNATE NAME: Islamic Union

LEADER: Hassan Abdullah Hersi al-Turki

YEAR ESTABLISHED OR BECAME ACTIVE: 1990s

ESTIMATED SIZE: 2,000

USUAL AREA OF OPERATION: Somalia, with limited presence in the Ogaden region of Ethiopia and suspected but unproven existence in other countries of East Africa, particularly Kenya

HISTORY

Experts often disagree on the actual period of the formation of AIAI. Some report that the AIAI was conceived after the 1991 crisis involving Siad Barre's ousting, whereas others are of the opinion that it was formed nearly a decade before the Barre crisis. According to these experts, AIAI was reportedly formed in 1983 as a result of the merger between Al-Jamaa Al-Islamiya (Islamic Association, headed by Sheikh Mohamed Eissa, and based in the southern region of Somalia) and Wahdat Al-Shabab

LEADERSHIP

HASSAN ABDULLAH HERSI AL-TURKI

U.S. Government authorities claim that the AIAI has several factions and each faction reportedly has its own leader. AIAI is "factionalized" and "decentralized," according to intelligence reports. Hassan Abdullah Hersi al-Turki is allegedly a prominent leader of one of the main factions of AIAI. On June 3, 2004, the U.S. Department of State categorically blocked his assets in the United States and barred most transactions with him. Hassan Turki allegedly has close contacts with Al-Qaeda and has provided support for the acts of terrorism. Some reports also suggest that Mohamed Ali is the leader of the Togdheer faction based in Somaliland.

Al-Islam (Unity of Islamic Youth, commanded by Sheikh Ali-Warsame, and based in the northern region of the country). However, the majority of terrorism analysts tend to believe that AIAI was formed during the 1990s after the fall of the Barre regime.

Initially, AIAI allegedly focused its activities on influencing the Somalia population by encouraging them to support the take over of the Ogaden region of Ethiopia. Reportedly, this strategy was employed by the AIAI to intensify their power on their home territory. Monitor groups have observed that the majority of the group's preliminary activities, usually attacks on the Ethiopian government, focused on forcing the Ethiopian government to surrender control over Ogaden.

As thought by many anti-terrorism experts, during most of the 1990s AIAI was involved in similar terrorist attacks throughout Ethiopia. However, the Ethiopian military put up a fierce fight against these terrorist attacks that led to major financial and operational losses in the AIAI. Ethiopian government officials speculate that AIAI subsequently abandoned most of its

original goals and allied itself with other terrorist organizations, such as al-Qaeda, and received extensive military training in several of al-Qaeda's bases in Afghanistan. AIAI also aimed many of its operations against the United States and its establishments in the region. U.S. government authorities and counter-terrorism experts have blamed Al-Ittihad al-Islami for gunning down two American helicopters and causing the deaths of 18 U.S. soldiers in 1993.

It was reported by the media and news agencies that the group allegedly carried out a series of bombings in the Ethiopian capital of Addis Ababa in 1996 and 1997. However, 1996–1997, the Ethiopian armed forces attacked and killed several AIAI members, which allegedly resulted in weakening the AIAI power in Somalia. Again, in 1998, the U.S. State Department blamed the AIAI militia for the kidnapping of six Red Cross workers and two pilots in Somalia. Authorities also speculate that the group was involved in several attacks in November 2002 on Israelis in Kenya, including a rocket attack on an Israeli airliner.

After the September 11, 2001, attacks in the United States, the Bush administration demanded that the assets of AIAI be frozen and has placed AIAI on its Terrorist Exclusion List. Experts report that the organization has reduced its size and scope and is currently maintaining a low profile by engaging in small-scale terrorist activities.

PHILOSOPHY AND TACTICS

The AIAI is thought to be formed as a radical Islamic organization whose purpose is spreading the Islamic ideology in Somalia, and also to liberate the state of Ogaden from Ethiopia. U.S. intelligence agencies allege that the activities of AIAI are not just limited to Somalia, but that its mission is to establish a unified Islamic state in the Horn of Africa, which refers to the eastern African peninsula containing Somalia, Djibouti, Ethiopia, and Eritrea. Sometimes, Sudan and Kenya are also included.

After the fall of the Barre dictatorship, Somalia was reportedly in utter chaos. The AIAI allegedly took advantage of this situation and actively engaged in several terrorist activities. At the time, the AIAI had appealed to the common people as well as the provisional

KEY EVENTS

1990s: The AIAI attained notoriety on the terrorism scene of Somalia.

1993: Al-Ittihad al-Islami was accused by U.S. government for bringing down two American helicopters, which ensued into a battle that claimed the lives of 18 U.S. soldiers.

1996–1997: The group was allegedly responsible for the serial bombings in public places in Addis and Ababa. During the same period, Ethiopian authorities allegedly attacked and killed hundreds of AIAI militia in a fierce battle.

1998: The group was blamed for the kidnapping of several relief workers working for the Red Cross in Somalia.

2001: U.S. Department of State listed AIAI in the Terrorist Exclusion List.

2004: The group was allegedly involved in the attack on several relief aid workers in Somaliland.

government. Terrorism experts report that AIAI aimed to spread their fundamentalist Islamic ideology throughout the country and to gain the confidence of the general population, AIAI members supported various social causes, such as the establishment of schools, orphanages, and religious courts.

Since the government of Somalia was seemingly unstable, this allegedly led to the establishment of a so-called parallel government by the AIAI, which had won the hearts of the common people and succeeded in spreading its ideology. It is claimed by many government authorities that, at the time, AIAI actually developed its power base and spread its fundamentalist ideology under the mask of social and humanitarian services.

In the past, some of the tactics employed by AIAI members included kidnapping, bombing,

and shootings. For instance, in 1993, AIAI members were suspected to be behind the killing of eighteen elite U.S. rangers in the Somalian capital of Mogadishu. The AIAI members allegedly gunned down two U.S. helicopters, which claimed the lives of many American soldiers. The U.S. Department of State has also accused the AIAI of a past history of participating in insurgent-style attacks against Ethiopian forces as well as other Somali factions.

Intelligence reports claim that AIAI maintains its own armed force and is responsible for carrying out its operations in many parts of Somalia and Ethiopia. It is alleged that AIAI is a multinational force with political aims going beyond the borders of Somalia, and it is in fact a part of international terrorist movements. AIAI is also accused of having international links with al-Qaeda and its leader, Osama bin Laden. U.S. defense officials have alleged that the members of extreme AIAI factions and al-Qaeda share similar radical ideologies.

However, as of 2005, evidence suggests that AIAI has weakened over the years and has reportedly changed its tactics. The authorities speculate that most prominent members of AIAI now teach in schools and religious institutions with the purpose of recruiting young Islamic students. Government officials also reason that AIAI is involved in trade activities in Somalia. Al Barakaat, Somalia's largest commercial venture, was accused by officials of providing funding to AIAI. It is alleged that the group receives the majority of its funds from Middle East financiers and western Africa, and it is suspected that some AIAI members received training in Afghanistan in the past. According to some published reports, the group has received weapons in the past through Sudan and Eritrea. Experts state that most of these funds are spent on social causes such as establishing schools and orphanages.

OTHER PERSPECTIVES

According to a report published for the Congressional Research Center in 2002, the influence and strength of Al-Ittihad al-Islami is in dispute. The report mentioned, "Many Somali watchers believe that Al-Ittihad's strength is highly exaggerated and that information about its alleged links with international terrorist

PRIMARY SOURCE
Mombasa nightclub attacked

A popular night club in the Kenyan port of Mombasa has been destroyed in an arson attack.

Nobody was hurt in the blaze which police said was caused by a number of petrol bombs thrown into the building at 0600 local time.

The European-owned Tembo disco was popular with tourists.

German manager, Walter Reif told AFP news agency that no-one was hurt in the incident.

"I'm not so sure who did it. Some unexploded Molotov cocktails have been recovered," he added.

On Tuesday, a Kenyan restaurant manager became the 11th Kenyan to die in the attack on the Paradise Hotel.

Lead investigator into the attack, William Lang'at, told AFP news agency that Wema Mutisya, 34, died from his injuries.

INVESTIGATION

Investigators say the bomb which destroyed the hotel was built in the flat of the key suspect, Saleh Ali Saleh Nabhan, who is believed by police to have owned the vehicle used in the attack.

Mr Nabhan's wife Fatuma, and brother are now reported to have been released on bail by a Mombasa court after being detained by police at the weekend.

Last week police released computer-generated images of two men they suspect carried out the failed simultaneous attack in Mombasa on an Israeli airliner.

The police also announced a $6,000 reward for information leading to the arrest of each man.

A statement dated 6 December, purportedly from the al-Qaeda network, claimed responsibility for the twin attacks and threatened more attacks on Israeli and U.S. targets.

But U.S. and Israeli officials have said al-Ittihad al-Islami, a Somali-based group with links to al-Qaeda, could be responsible.

If Mr Nabhan is hiding in Somalia, investigators believe it will be difficult to find him.

Somalia has not had a central government for more than a decade, and there are no law-enforcement agencies that could help track him down.

Source: BBC News, 2002

---

organizations is unreliable." The report further stated, "There is no reliable information or pattern of behavior to suggest that Al-Ittihad has an international agenda."

According to a report published by a United Nations panel in 2003, "Somalia has served as a transit point for international terrorists but its local militant groups appear to be less of a terrorist threat than feared." The report also claimed, "While the panel has found ample evidence that AIAI continues to operate in Somalia, it appears to have few formal links with al-Qaeda, and has a largely local agenda, which includes unification with other Somali-majority areas in neighboring states."

A report published by the Counter Terrorism Division of the FBI mentions that, "at various times from about 1992 until about 1993, Osama bin Laden, working together with members of the *fatwa* (a religious or judicial sentence pronounced by an Islamic religious leader) committee of al-Qaeda, disseminated fatwas to other members and associates of al-Qaeda which directed that the United States forces stationed in the Horn of Africa, including Somalia, should be attacked." The report went on to state that bin Laden has claimed responsibility for the deaths of 18 U.S. servicemen killed in "Operation Restore Hope" in Somalia in 1994.

PRIMARY SOURCE
Al-Ittihad al-Islami (AIAI)

DESCRIPTION

AIAI rose to prominence in the Horn of Africa in the early 1990s, following the downfall of the Siad Barre regime and the subsequent collapse of the Somali nation state into anarchy. AIAI was not internally cohesive and suffered divisions between factions supporting moderate Islam and more puritanical Islamic ideology. Following military defeats in 1996 and 1997, AIAI evolved into a loose network of highly compartmentalized cells, factions, and individuals with no central control or coordination. AIAI elements pursue a variety of agendas ranging from social services and education to insurgency activities in the Ogaden. Some AIAI-associated sheikhs espouse a radical fundamentalist version of Islam, with particular emphasis on a strict adherence to Sharia (Islamic law), a view often at odds with Somali emphasis on clan identity. A small number of AIAI-associated individuals have provided logistical support to and maintain ties with al-Qaeda; however, the network's central focus remains the establishment of an Islamic government in Somalia.

ACTIVITIES

Elements of AIAI may have been responsible for the kidnapping and murder of relief workers in Somalia and Somaliland in 2003 and 2004, and during the late 1990s. Factions of AIAI may also have been responsible for a series of bomb attacks in public places in Addis Ababa in 1996 and 1997. Most AIAI factions have recently concentrated on broadening their religious base, renewed emphasis on building businesses, and undertaking "hearts and minds" actions, such as sponsoring orphanages and schools and providing security that uses an Islamic legal structure in the areas where it is active.

STRENGTH

The actual membership strength is unknown.

LOCATION/AREA OF OPERATIONS

Primarily in Somalia, with a presence in the Ogaden region of Ethiopia, Kenya, and possibly Djibouti.

EXTERNAL AID

Receives funds from Middle East financiers and Somali diaspora communities in Europe, North America, and the Arabian Peninsula.

Source: U.S. Department of State. *Country Reports on Terrorism*. Washington, D.C., 2004.

SUMMARY

After the military defeat at the hands of Ethiopian armed forces, the AIAI stronghold allegedly dispersed into many smaller groups. As of 2005, little is known about the strength and prominent members of AIAI or the extent of their links with other terrorist organizations, including al-Qaeda.

An FBI counterterrorism report from March 2003 alleged that AIAI and al-Qaeda members were being trained for scuba diving to prepare them for attacks from the sea from ships that are passing around the Horn of Africa.

Officials worry that the AIAI seems to be highly capable of such attacks and, since they keep a low profile, it is very difficult to gauge their capability.

SOURCES

Web sites

CNN.com. "Islamic Group Suspected in Kenya Attacks." < http://cnnstudentnews.cnn.com/2002/WORLD/africa/11/29/somali.group/ > (accessed September 21, 2005).

Center for Defense Information. "In the Spotlight: Al-Ittihad al-Islami (AIAI)." < http://www.cdi.org/

program/document.cfm?DocumentID=3026&from_page=../index.cfm > (accessed September 21, 2005).

Federal Bureau of Investigation. "Testimony of J. T. Caruso, Acting Assistant Director, CounterTerrorism Division, FBI." < http://www.fbi.gov/congress/congress01/caruso121801.htm > (accessed September 21, 2005).

The Somaliland Times. "Terrorists Use Somalia As Hub." < http://www.somalilandtimes.net/2003/63/6304.htm > (accessed September 21, 2005).

U.S. Department of State, Department Of Defense Background Briefing. "Terrorist Threat in Horn of Africa." < http://www.state.gov/s/ct/rls/rm/8801.htm > (accessed August 9,2005).

Al-Jama'a al-Islamiyyah al-Muqatilah bi-Libya

LEADER: Anas Sebai
USUAL AREA OF OPERATION: Libya

OVERVIEW

Since 1995, the members of al-Jam'a al-Islamiyyah al-Muqatilah bi-Libya, or Libyan Islamic Fighting Group (LIFG), have conducted an ongoing, low-intensity conflict with Libyan leader Muammar el-Qaddafi. The LIFG believes that the Qaddafi government is un-Islamic and, therefore, the group is pledged to bring about its demise. The group, also known as the Fighting Islamic Group, the Libyan Islamic Group, and the Libyan Fighting Group, seeks to reach its goals of an Islamic state in Libya through assassination attempts, constant clashes with regime security forces, and alliances with organizations such as al-Qaeda.

HISTORY

The LIFG seeks to turn Libya back to the Islamist state that exercised power in the region since the nineteenth century. Muammar el-Qaddafi seized power from the government of King Idris in 1969. The king derived his power from the Sanusi Order, whose founder Sayyid Muhammad bin Ali al-Sanusi dedicated himself and his followers to energize and spread Islam in light of the European infiltration into Arab lands during the nineteenth century. Sanusi, an Algerian, and the order were banned from Egypt

LEADERSHIP

ANAS SEBAI

LIFG is headed by Anas Sebai, who is also a key figure in al-Qaeda. Omar Rashed serves as the spokesperson for LIFG. He voices the groups disdain for Qaddafi. He also criticizes Israel and voices support for international jihad.

and unable to return to Algeria, which remained under French rule. The order then relocated in Libya, a region marked by tribal conflicts and disparate provinces. Using Islam as their authority, the order mediated disputes among tribes and developed cohesion between the provinces. When the Italians entered Libya in 1911, they were unable to create a stronghold due to the influence of the Sanusi. By the close of World War II, the order had successfully used religion to define the country's politics. The group gained its legitimacy through religion and its role in the resistance of colonialism. However, an emerging middle class (due to the discovery of oil), as well as the absence of an economic program of development, corruption within the power structure, and failure to adequately distribute the wealth from the oil, led to the collapse of the Idris monarch and the Sanusi order in Libya.

In 1969, armed with the knowledge that Libya was unified by and founded on Islam, Muammar Qaddafi sought alliances with the Islamic clergy, called *ulama*, to legitimize his claim to power. Qaddafi spoke in mosques and consulted with religions leaders in the first years of his rule. Members of the ulama were awarded prominent roles in the education and legal sectors of government.

In 1973, Qaddafi published a new course for Libya and the restructuring of its society in his *Green Book*. Modeling the Maoist Chinese Cultural Revolution, Qaddafi sought to eradicate the influences held by the traditional institutions, which included religious leaders. His goal was a state based on egalitarianism, socialism, Arabism, and anti-imperialism. Qaddafi, believing that progress in the revolution was hampered by civil liberties and legalities, sought to erode the influence held by clerics. He attacked traditionalists and mosques. The ulama responded by criticizing Qaddafi's actions and the ideas promoted in the *Green Book*. Qaddafi asserted that his ideas were a more progressive interpretation of Islam. This conflict created religion as the opposition to Qaddafi's regime.

Anyone who dared to speak out against Qaddafi's interpretation of Islam was brutalized. In 1981, the most prominent case of this occurred as Salafi preacher, Muhammad al-Bashti, was tortured and killed by Libyan security forces after voicing opposition. This oppression at home led militants to join the *mujahideen* (fighters) fighting against the Soviet Union in Afghanistan. At the close of that conflict, these Libyans scattered. Some returned home, while others joined with Osama bin Laden in Sudan.

After decades of poor economic development, Qaddafi began to liberalize Libya in the 1990s. During this time, Libyans who had fought in Afghanistan against the Soviet Union returned to the dismal economic prospects. In September 1995, fierce fighting erupted between security forces and Islamist guerillas in Benghazi. After weeks of fighting, the LIFG announced its formation and two main goals: The destruction of Qaddafi's regime to be replaced by an Islamic state, and the success of the continued international *jihad* (holy war).

PHILOSOPHY AND TACTICS

Much of the LIFG is considered a mystery. The group was founded with the central goal to overthrow Qaddafi's regime and replace it with an Islamist state in Libya. It looks to the tradition of Islam in Libya, including the clerics Qaddafi originally used to legitimize his own government. Beginning as a group of veterans returning from fighting the Soviet Union in Afghanistan, the group honed its skills in training camps set up in Sudan by Osama bin Laden to train his own militants. Between 1995 and 1998, the group focused its operations within Libya and against Qaddafi. Using guerilla warfare tactics,

KEY EVENTS

1969: Qaddafi seized power from the religious leadership of the Sanusi order.

1973: Qaddafi issues the *Green Book* and seeks to create a Maoist-modeled state based on egalitarianism, socialism, Arabism, and anti-imperialism.

1980s: Libyan Islamic militants escape Qaddafi's oppression and fight in Afghanistan.

1994: First Islamist operative working to topple Qaddafi's government is arrested.

1995: Weeks of armed clashes between Libyan security forces and Islamists lead to the official declaration of the objectives of the LIFG.

1996: Failed assassination attempt on Qaddafi leaves several of his bodyguards dead.

1996: Islamist detainees escape and flee under pursuit by security forces. Fighting between the two groups closes the border with Egypt for several days.

1996: LIFG kill eight policemen in Derna. Qaddafi's security forces respond with an air and ground attack on LIFG mountain bases.

1996: LIFG operative throws a grenade at Qaddafi during a visit to the town of Brak. He escapes uninjured.

1997: LIFG leader, Salah Fathi bin Salman (a.k.a. Abu Abd al-Rahman Hattab), is killed in combat with Libyan security forces.

1998: Qaddafi's security forces launch sweep of hideouts and bases, apprehending sympathizers and operatives.

the group sought conflicts with the Libyan security forces. After officially declaring itself and its goals in 1995, the group launched a series of attacks on security forces in 1996, including several assassination attempts. The last attempt occurred in August 1998 with an attack on

Qaddafi's motorcade. Although all of the assassination attempts have failed, many of the attempts have come quite close to taking Qaddafi's life. Many of the attempts appeared to have assistance from Qaddafi's own security forces. In September and November 1996, two failed military coups also suggested cooperation between military and Islamists. After a 1998 sweep, much of the LIFG was either exiled or imprisoned. By 1999, operations slowed to a low-intensity insurgency. There is still considered to be a clandestine operation within Libya, however, most have left the country to support other Islamic jihad organizations. With their forces weakened within the state, the group began to foster deeper alliances with Osama bin Laden and the al-Qaeda network. It vocally supports international jihad and has smuggled weapons into the country to aid in its struggle. The LIFG operates by obtaining funds from private entities and Islamic non-governmental organizations. The group is also suspected as one of several organizations that supplied materials for the May 2003 suicide bombing in Casablanca.

OTHER PERSPECTIVES

In an article written for the Center for Contemporary Conflict, Christopher Boucek asserts that Islamic opposition to Qaddafi is fragmented and, although it had demonstrated that it can occasionally ally with the military, the groups lacks the strength to topple Qaddafi's regime. Boucek writes, "The strict exclusiveness an Islamic regime may bring would likely run against the fabric of Libyan society." Boucek suggests that Qaddafi himself could bring down his regime because, "30 years of Qaddafi's repressive regime has exhausted much of the public." Qaddafi has made strides to legitimize its government within the international community so that it can obtain economic assistance. By providing post-9/11 intelligence against al-Qaeda, Qaddafi allied with the United States against Osama bin Laden and the al-Qaeda network. The United States did not place the LIFG on the terrorist watch-list until 2004 when its ties to al-Qaeda were identified. Former CIA director George Tenet testified to the Senate Select Committee on Intelligence that, "one of the most immediate threats is from smaller Sunni

PRIMARY SOURCE
Libyan Islamic Fighting Group (LIFG)

DESCRIPTION

The Libyan Islamic Fighting Group (LIFG) emerged in the early 1990s among Libyans who had fought against Soviet forces in Afghanistan and against the Qadhafi regime in Libya. The LIFG declared the Government of Libyan leader Muammar Qaddafi un-Islamic and pledged to overthrow it. Some members maintain a strictly anti-Qadhafi focus and organize against Libyan Government interests, but others are aligned with Usama Bin Ladin and believed to be part of al-Qa'ida's leadership structure or active in the international terrorist network.

ACTIVITIES

Libyans associated with the LIFG are part of the broader international jihadist movement. The LIFG is one of the groups believed to have planned the Casablanca suicide bombings in May 2003. The LIFG claimed responsibility for a failed assassination attempt against Qadhafi in 1996 and engaged Libyan security forces in armed clashes during the 1990s. It continues to target Libyan interests and may engage in sporadic clashes with Libyan security forces.

STRENGTH

Not known, but probably has several hundred active members or supporters.

LOCATION/AREA OF OPERATION

Probably maintains a clandestine presence in Libya, but since the late 1990s many members have fled to various Asian, Persian Gulf, African, and European countries, particularly the United Kingdom.

EXTERNAL AID

Not known. May obtain some funding through private donations, various Islamic non-governmental organizations, and criminal acts.

Source: U.S. Department of State. *Country Reports on Terrorism.* Washington, D.C., 2004.

extremist groups that have benefited from al-Qaeda links. They include ... the Libyan Islamic Fighting Group."

SUMMARY

As one of the few North African countries to repel European expansionism, Libya has a long tradition of Islamic rule. Qaddafi came into power as the result of poorly managed wealth from the discovery of oil and corruption within the government. Initially, he attempted to mobilize the clerics and give them power over the education and legal systems. By 1973, however, he supplanted their power in order to create a new state founded on his interpretation of Islam. His highly repressive activities led to the departure of many militant Islamists, who chose to fight the Soviet Union in Afghanistan. Some of those militants would later train with Osama bin Laden in Sudan in preparation for their armed conflict with Qaddafi's forces. By 1995, the LIFG had officially declared itself and its goal to replace Qaddafi's regime with an Islamic state. The group clashed with security forces for several years until a massive sweep in 1998 tapered their activities. The LIFG shifted its focus, then, to aid other militant Islamists, such as al-Qaeda.

SOURCES

Web sites

American Forces Information Service. "Tenent Briefs Senate on Terror Threats." < http://www.globalsecurity.org/intell/library/news/2004/intell-040224-afps01.htm > (accessed October 18, 2005).

Center for Contemporary Conflicts. "Libya's Return to the Fold?" < http://www.ccc.nps.navy.mil/si/2004/mar/boucekMar04.asp > (accessed October 18, 2005).

The Jamestown Foundation. "The Libyan Islamic Fighting Group (LIFG)." < http://www.jamestown.org/publications_details.php?volume_id = 411&issue_id = 3275&article_id = 2369477 > (accessed October 18, 2005).

Middle East Policy Council Journal. "Qadhafi's Libya and the Prospect of Islamic Succession." < http://www.mepc.org/public_asp/journal_vol7/0002_takey-h.asp > (accessed October 18, 2005).

The National Post. "Al-Qaeda Targets Gaddafi." < http://209.157.64.200/focus/f-news/1046103/posts > (accessed October 18, 2005).

MIPT Terrorism Knowledge Database. "The Libyan Islamic Fighting Group (LIFG)." < http://www.tkb.org/Group.jsp?groupID = 4400 > (October 18, 2005).

SEE ALSO

Al-Qaeda

Al-Jihad

ALTERNATE NAMES: Egyptian Islamic Jihad, Jihad Group, Talaa'al al-Fateh (Vanguards of Conquest)

LEADER: Ayman al-Zawahiri

YEAR ESTABLISHED OR BECAME ACTIVE: 1981

ESTIMATED SIZE: Several hundred

USUAL AREA OF OPERATION: Egypt; Afghanistan; Sudan; Somalia; Pakistan

U.S. TERRORIST EXCLUSION DESIGNEE: The U.S. Department of State declared al-Jihad to be a terrorist organization in October 1997

Al-Jihad (also known as Egyptian Islamic Jihad; Jihad Group; Talaa'al al-Fateh—the Vanguards of Conquest) is an Egyptian Islamist extremist group dedicated to the overthrow of the Egyptian government and its replacement with an Islamic state. It has been implicated in a wide range of atrocities, from the 1981 assassination of the Egyptian President, Anwar Sadat, to the massacre of 58 foreign tourists in Luxor in 1997. Many of its key members have been forced into exile, most notably its former leader, Ayman al-Zawahiri, who is Osama bin Laden's deputy. In June 2001, the group apparently merged with al-Qaeda.

HISTORY

Throughout the 1970s, Egypt's President Anwar Sadat enjoyed and endured a contrary relationship with various Muslim organizations existing within his country. His predecessor, Gamal Abdel Nasser, had generally suppressed such groups, in order to pursue a secular brand of pan-Arabism; but following his death in 1970, and facing the competing demands of pan-Arabism and radical socialism, Sadat had sought to widen his basis of support and legitimacy by embracing the previously suppressed

Egyptian soldiers aid wounded victims after an attack by religious extremist group Al-Jihad on the reviewing platform that killed Egyptian President Anwar Sadat in Cairo on October 6, 1981. AP/Wide World Photos. Reproduced by permission.

Muslim Brotherhood. In 1971, thousands of Brotherhood members and other Islamists were released from prison, and in subsequent years restrictions on meeting, publications, and other rights of association were lessened.

Sadat's relationship with Islamists nevertheless remained testy as economic dislocation and, in particular, the Camp David Accords of September 1978 (which afforded recognition of and peace with Israel) led to popular dissatisfaction. A number of radical Islamic groups emerged in this period, some obscure, some claiming up to 5,000 members.

Despite harsh measures eventually taken by the Egyptian government to curtail or limit such groups, rather than being weakened, they proliferated. The most dangerous of these appeared in the late 1970s, and was known as al-Jihad, or the Jihad organization. It comprised three militant groups initially formed in a coalition, but from June 1981, it merged into one organization. The group sought to bring down the Sadat regime, to introduce Islamic rule, and to return to the Caliphate (an Islamic state ruled by a spiritual leader; Caliph is the successor to the prophet Muhammad) as the central principle of the Islamic state.

Al-Jihad was strongly influenced by the teachings of the young Muslim thinker, Muhammad Abdel Salam Faraj, who taught that Jihad was the "missing" commandment and the sixth pillar of Islam.

On October 6, 1981, al-Jihad carried out one of the most daring assassinations in modern history. While President Sadat was watching the celebrations marking the eighth anniversary of the Yom Kippur War, a detachment of four soldiers who were al-Jihad members opened fire on him and his party and followed through with grenades. Sadat was killed with 20 others, including four American dignitaries.

The Egyptian authorities moved quickly to stop any uprising and brutally suppressed rioting in the following week. Over subsequent months and years, they set about imprisoning, torturing, and executing al-Jihad members. Faraj was executed for his part in the

A poster depicting Anwar Sakar. Sakar, a young member of the Islamic Jihad movement, became a suicide bomber and killed 20 Israeli soldiers at a Beit Lid bus stop. © *Abbas | Magnum Photos*

LEADERSHIP

AYMAN AL-ZAWAHIRI

Ayman al-Zawahiri was born to an affluent and well-connected Cairo family in 1951. He came from a background of anti-colonial agitation: his paternal grandfather was a renowned scholar and resister of British rule, while his maternal grandfather had been the first Secretary of the Arab League.

Al-Zawahiri trained as a doctor, but become radicalized as a student and joined ranks with the emergent Islamist groups in the 1970s. By the time of the Sadat assassination, he was part of the al-Jihad hierarchy, allegedly meeting with Sadat's killers the night before his death. On his way to the airport to escape to Pakistan, he was arrested, brutally tortured, but not found guilty of anything other than illegal possession of a firearm. When he was released from prison in 1984, al-Zawahiri went into exile first in Saudi Arabia, before joining up with Jihadis in Afghanistan, then Sudan.

It was in Sudan that Al-Zawahiri joined forces with Osama bin Laden, and by the mid 1990s, his role and al-Jihad's mission was becoming blurred with that of al-Qaeda. Al-Zawahiri has been accused of masterminding the U.S. embassy bombings and even of being the operational mastermind behind the 9/11 attacks. He has also been described as bin Laden's doctor, spiritual advisor, deputy, or a combination of the three.

Al-Zawahiri's family were reportedly killed in the U.S. bombing of Afghanistan in 2001. He is still at large and usually appears in bin Laden's infrequent broadcasts.

assassination in April 1982. Under this pressure, the group split into two factions, one led by Ayman al-Zawahiri, retaining the name al-Jihad, and the other by Abdel Omar Rahman, called al-Gama'a al-Islamiyah.

Al-Zawahiri, a doctor from a prominent Cairo family, had been one of the principle architects of Sadat's killing, even allegedly meeting the assassins the night before the murder. Nevertheless, the judicial authorities could not find him guilty of anything more than illegal possession of a gun, and after three years in jail, he was released and left Egypt, initially for Saudi Arabia.

From there, he made several trips to Afghanistan to partake in the war against the Soviets. Further radicalized, he began to reassemble al-Jihad from the so-called Afghan Arab armies, comprised of men who had come to

Afghanistan from other Gulf States seeking martyrdom in the war. He trained and formed cells of Jihadis, which he sent back to Egypt.

In Egypt, al-Jihad centered its operations on attacks on high-level government officials. In 1993, the group carried out two assassination

Members of Islamic Jihad display guns during prayers prior to a 2005 demonstration in Gaza city. Spencer
Platt | Getty Images

attempts, one on Egyptian Interior Minister Hassan al-Alfi in August, and the other against Prime Minister Atef Sedky in November.

During the late 1980s and through the 1990s, Egypt was experiencing a large-scale Islamic insurgency, instigated by al-Gama'a al-Islamiyya, which carried out brutal attacks on intellectuals, police officers, Western tourists and businessmen, and, most often, Coptic Christian civilians. Between 1,200 and as many as 10,000 people died in this "silent" war. The full extent of al-Jihad's involvement in this bloodletting is unknown, but is has been accused of holding close ties to al-Gama'a and supplying arms through its cells in other parts of the Middle East.

On November 17, 1997, six insurgents armed with automatic firearms and knives attacked a group of tourists at Deir al-Bahrir, an archeological site and one of Egypt's most popular visitor destinations. In total, they killed 58 Westerners and four Egyptians, beheading and disemboweling some of their victims. Al-Zawahiri's al-Jihad faction, Talaa'al al-Fateh

(the Vanguards of Conquest) claimed responsibility for the attack, which decimated Egypt's tourist industry and plunged the country headlong into economic depression.

Increasingly, however, al-Jihad was becoming noted for attacks outside Egypt, including a suicide truck bomb attack on the Egyptian Embassy in Islamabad, Pakistan, which killed 15 people in November 1995. Moreover, since its leader al-Zawahiri had become increasingly synonymous with an emergent group, al-Qaeda, which was bringing terrorist notoriety to a different level, al-Jihad was linked to a number of attacks for which it may or may not have been responsible.

In 1998, possibly because of al-Zawahiri's relationship with bin Laden, al-Jihad is believed to have been behind the U.S. embassy bombings in Nairobi, Kenya, and in Dar es Salaam, Tanzania, as well as for an unsuccessful attack on the American Embassy in Albania. Al-Jihad is also suspected in the October 2000 bombing of the U.S.S. *Cole* in Aden, and the group has been

KEY EVENTS

1981: Al-Jihad is formally constituted out of a preexisting coalition of three Islamist groups influenced by Muhammad Abdel Salam Faraj.

1981: Al-Jihad assassinates Egyptian President Anwar Sadat.

1982: Faraj executed.

1993: Al-Jihad carries out two assassination attempts, one on Egyptian Interior Minister Hassan al-Alfi, and the other on Prime Minister Atef Sedky.

1997: Luxor massacre kills 58 Western tourists and four Egyptians.

1998: Al-Jihad implicated in U.S. Embassy bombings in Tanzania and Kenya.

2001: Al-Jihad and al-Qaeda apparently merge.

directly implicated in the September 11, 2001, attacks on the World Trade Center and the Pentagon.

Whether these accusations are based merely on the complicity of al-Zawahiri and those who follow him, or whether these attacks were actually carried out in the name of al-Jihad is another matter. Certainly al-Zawahiri's relationship with al-Qaeda had blurred the outlook and identity of the two groups. In 1998, he was the second of five signatories to bin Laden's notorious *fatwa* (struggle) calling for attacks against U.S. civilians. Three years later, in June 2001, al-Jihad and al-Qaeda reportedly merged. The U.S. Department of State nevertheless continues to list al-Jihad as a separate entity in its designated foreign terrorist organizations.

PHILOSOPHY AND TACTICS

Al-Jihad is an Egyptian Islamist extremist group dedicated to the overthrow of the Egyptian government and its replacement with an Islamic state. Its members are influenced by the work of the young Islamic thinker, Muhammad Abdel Salam Faraj, who was a member until his execution in April 1982. In his book published in 1980, Faraj advocated an Islamic Caliphate as an alternative to the secular regime in place. This, however, could not happen without Jihad, which, he believed, was the missing commandment, or "sixth pillar" of Islam. Faraj used historical analogy and his interpretation of the Quran to legitimize his work. He was also critical of other groups, such as the Muslim Brotherhood, for integrating with non-Islamic minorities.

This call for Jihad in Egypt manifested itself in spectacular fashion a year later, when al-Jihad members killed the Egyptian president. This was supposed to inspire revolution, but the Egyptian authorities were quick to crack down on the fledgling rebellion.

Over the following decade, the ranks of al-Jihad were decimated by arrests, executions, and exiles. The group carried out a policy of targeting senior Egyptian politicians, but this later spread to attacks on Westerners. As its leader in exile, Ayman al-Zawahiri moved closer to Osama bin Laden and al-Qaeda, its ambitions and tactics moved correspondingly onto a more global basis. The almost wholesale exile or incarceration of al-Jihad's leading members suggests that its hopes for an Egyptian-based uprising remain on hold.

OTHER PERSPECTIVES

"Why was Sadat assassinated?" asked Youssef Aboul-Enein in *Military Review*, seeing that this could offer an insight into what motivated an al-Jihad member, Abdul-Salam Abdul-Al. "Abdul-Al, an officer in Egyptian Air Defense, was 28 years old in 1981. During his interrogation, he said he thought Egyptian society was in a state of *munkar* (decadence). He saw Sadat as the manifestation of Islamic regression and decided he had to kill him. He discussed how he became aware of Egyptian society's obsession with consumerism, the consumption of alcohol, and an accumulation of interest. He said women who took to the hijab were scorned and that religious scholars who preached the truth were jailed. Abdul-Al was happy with the results of the 1979 Iranian revolution, where the mullahs toppled the American-supported Shah. However, he felt that

PRIMARY SOURCE

Egypt Executes 3 in a Plot to Kill Mubarak

The Government hanged three Muslim militants today for plotting to assassinate President Hosni Mubarak and trying to topple the Government.

The men, who were silent and wearing the red training suits for prisoners on death row, were executed starting at 8 A.M., according to a spokesman for the military prosecution.

Amnesty International had urged Mr. Mubarak to commute the sentences, which it called "the most extreme form of cruel and inhuman punishment." The group has also criticized the authorities for trying civilians in special military courts.

A military spokesman who insisted on anonymity said: "Each hanging took about half an hour. These men have to hang because they are terrorists. They want to get rid of the Government. They kill civilians and explode bombs."

The hangings, which lasted for an hour and a half, were part of a crackdown that has executed 23 militants, the largest number of political criminals executed here in this century. Thirty-eight men have been sentenced to death since late last year, when Mr. Mubarak began transferring the cases to military courts. Nine are fugitives, and six are awaiting execution.

The spokesman said two of those executed today, Ahmed Muhammed Hammouda and Hisham Taha Selim, were members of Organization 19, a group that was on trial in Alexandria for conspiring to kill Mr. Mubarak and overthrow the Government.

The third militant, Yihya Shahrour, was accused of belonging to the Vanguards of Conquest group. The Government said that group was a revival of Al-Jihad, which assassinated President Anwar el-Sadat in 1981. Mr. Shahrour was among 33 defendants in a separate case in Alexandria involving charges of re-forming Al-Jihad and conspiring to bring down the Government.

Al-Jihad is trying to penetrate the armed forces, Mr. Mubarak's power base, Western diplomats said.

Defense lawyers and militant leaders say at least eight army officers and cadets were among four groups of Jihad members on trial in military courts. The militants, headed by the underground Islamic Group and Al-Jihad, have focused on Government officials, police and prison officers, Christians and foreign tourists in their drive to create a strict Islamic state.

The attacks on visitors have hurt tourism. More than 216 people have been killed and 620 wounded in the violence.

Source: New York Times, December 17, 1993

---

the Shi'ite revolution needed a Sunni counterweight and argued that Ayatollah Ruhollah Khomeini was discrediting the Islamic faith. The creation of an Islamic government in Egypt would balance the religious influence of Iran. He translated Abd al-Halim bin Taymiyyah's thirteenth-century writings, which stated that the Tartars had declared themselves Muslims and pledged to rule with Islamic law but, instead, applied their own indigenous Yasiq laws. They built mosques and Islamic schools while also suppressing Islamic thought."

Redel Halal, assistant editor of the Egyptian newspaper, *Al Ahram Weekly*, believed that the roots of Egypt's Islamist revival came with the discrediting of pan-Arabism during the Six Day War. "Nasser's brand of Arab nationalism, based on independence and statist modernization, suffered a resounding defeat in the 1967 War with Israel, provoking the emergence of the Islamists and their concept of a jihad, or struggle, to demolish what they thought of as an illegitimate and corrupt system and a 'return' to Islam," he wrote, adding that the repercussions live on. "Consequently, Egyptian society today is once again polarised between Islamisation and Westernisation."

"The Egyptians Ahmed Zewail and Ayman El-Zawahri are symptoms of this polarisation,

PRIMARY SOURCE

Al-Jihad (AJ) a.k.a. Jihad Group, Egyptian Islamic Jihad, EIJ

DESCRIPTION

This Egyptian Islamic extremist group merged with Usama Bin Ladin's al-Qa'ida organization in 2001. Usama Bin Ladin's deputy, Ayman al-Zawahiri, was the former head of AJ. Active since the 1970s, AJ's primary goal has been the overthrow of the Egyptian Government and the establishment of an Islamic state. The group's primary targets, historically, have been high-level Egyptian Government officials as well as US and Israeli interests in Egypt and abroad. Regular Egyptian crackdowns on extremists, including on AJ, have greatly reduced AJ capabilities in Egypt.

ACTIVITIES

The original AJ was responsible for the 1981 assassination of Egyptian President Anwar Sadat. It claimed responsibility for the attempted assassinations of Interior Minister Hassan al-Alfi in August 1993 and Prime Minister Atef Sedky in November 1993. AJ has not conducted an attack inside Egypt since 1993 and has never successfully targeted foreign tourists there. The group was responsible for the Egyptian Embassy bombing in Islamabad in 1995 and a disrupted plot against the US Embassy in Albania in 1998.

STRENGTH

Unknown, but probably has several hundred hard-core members inside and outside of Egypt.

LOCATION/AREA OF OPERATION

Historically AJ operated in the Cairo area. Most AJ members today are outside Egypt in countries such as Afghanistan, Pakistan, Lebanon, the United Kingdom, and Yemen. AJ activities have been centered outside Egypt for several years under the auspices of al-Qa'ida.

EXTERNAL AID

Unknown. Since 1998 AJ received most of its funding from al-Qa'ida, and these close ties culminated in the eventual merger of the groups. Some funding may come from various Islamic non-governmental organizations, cover businesses, and criminal acts.

Source: U.S. Department of State. *Country Reports on Terrorism.* Washington, D.C., 2004.

the former having been awarded the Nobel Prize in Chemistry and the latter being Osama bin Laden's right-hand man. In 1967, Zewail left Egypt for the U.S. to study, overcoming every barrier and succeeding at the University of California, Berkeley...However, in the same year that Zewail left Egypt for America and for his scientific successes, El-Zawahri was arrested, at the age of 16, for being a member of the outlawed Muslim Brotherhood. Later, he joined Al-Jihad group, a secretive militant Islamist organisation blamed for the assassination of Egyptian President Anwar El-Sadat in 1981. Later still, El-Zawahri headed for Afghanistan, where he established a faction of the Egyptian Islamic Jihad group, before becoming second in command after bin Laden of the International Front for Fighting Jews and Crusaders in 1998, a group that aims to kill Americans and destroy U.S. interests worldwide. Obviously, Islam means very different things for Zewail and El-Zawahri."

SUMMARY

In its current incarnation, al-Jihad is quite different from the organization that emerged prior to the assassination of Anwar Sadat in 1981. Its role and existence is currently blurred by that of its leader, Ayman al-Zawahiri who, as Osama bin Laden's closest lieutenant, has switched his focus, and arguably that of al-Jihad, from Egyptian-based Jihad to Islamic insurrection on a more global scale.

SOURCES

Books

Burke, Jason. *Al-Qaeda*. New York: Penguin, 2004.

Periodicals

"Egypt Executes 3 in a Plot to Kill Mubarak."*New York Times*. December 17, 1993.

Wright, Lawrence. "The Man Behind Bin Laden: How an Egyptian Doctor Became a Master of Terror." *The New Yorker*. September 16, 2002.

Aboul, Youssef. "Why was Sadat Assasinated?"*Military Review*. July—August, 2004.

Web sites

Islamist Watch. "Jihad: The Absent Obligation." < http://www.islamistwatch.org/texts/faraj/obligation/oblig.html > (accessed October 10, 2005).

Federal Bureau of Investigation. "Wanted Poster for al-Zawahiri." < http://www.fbi.gov/mostwant/terrorists/teralzawahiri.htm > (accessed October 10, 2005).

SEE ALSO

Al-Gama'a al-Islamiyya

Al-Qaeda

LEADER: Osama bin Laden

YEAR ESTABLISHED OR BECAME ACTIVE: 1988

ESTIMATED SIZE: Thought to number in the thousands worldwide

USUAL AREA OF OPERATION: Al-Qaeda cells are thought to be currently operational in as many as 50 countries

OVERVIEW

Al-Qaeda (also known as Al-Qaida) was established from a core group of foreigners who came to fight in the Afghani *jihad* (holy war) against the Soviet invasion and occupation in the 1980s. Al-Qaeda today operates as a global network of independent terrorist cells. The group is working to drive Western forces from all traditionally Muslim lands, with a special emphasis on forcing the United States and its allies to withdraw from Saudi Arabia, Afghanistan, and Iraq.

HISTORY

Al-Qaeda (Arabic for "the base") was established in 1988, when Osama bin Laden, Mohamed Atef, and others began compiling a database to document the movements of Arab fighters from all over the Middle East who were coming to aid the *mujahedeen* (warriors in a jihad) in their fight against the Soviet Union. Al-Qaeda's original purpose may have been humanitarian: to provide information to families of jihadists who were inquiring about the fate and whereabouts of their relatives, and to channel money and supplies from international supporters to the resistance.

Abu Haris Abdul Hakim, an Arabic-speaking guerrilla, claims responsibility on behalf of the al-Qaeda terrorist netwok for suicide bombings in Saudi Arabia and Morocco. AP/*Wide World Photos. Reproduced by permission.*

From at least 1989, al-Qaeda has also organized, sponsored, and supported terrorist training camps in Afghanistan for Islamic jihadists from around the world. Graduates of these camps and their own recruiting and support networks within their countries of origin form the loose global network of Islamic extremists and terrorists that are grouped under the umbrella of al-Qaeda.

In 1991, under intense scrutiny for his vocal opposition to the policies of the Saudi government, bin Laden fled Saudi Arabia, ultimately establishing a new base of operations in Sudan. Not coincidentally, in 1992, the first terror attacks attributed to al-Qaeda began to occur, starting in Somalia and South Yemen (today the Republic of Yemen). In 1993, the World Trade Center was bombed by a veteran of bin Laden's training camps. In 1995, truck-bombers linked to bin Laden carried out the first attack in Saudi

Arabia itself. At various times, bin Laden has continued to deny direct involvement in each of these attacks, characterizing his role as that of instigator and enthusiastic supporter.

In 1996, bin Laden published his own "Declaration of War" against the United States, beginning a phase of active dialogue with Western and Arab journalists that would last for several years and culminate in a late 1998 on-camera interview in the mountains of Afghanistan with ABC's John Miller.

The salient points that emerged from this dialogue are as follows:

- Bin Laden sees the United States as an occupying army in Saudi Arabia, and the Saudi government as having committed an unspeakable sacrilege in hosting the U.S. forces.

- Bin Laden asserts that the first Gulf War and the subsequent economic sanctions against

Three police officers patrol Tavistock Square, the area where a bus was bombed on August 7, 2005 in a series of London transit attacks. © *Dominic Burke | Alamy*

Iraq are but the latest acts of aggression in the centuries-old crusader-Zionist campaign to subjugate and plunder Muslim lands.

• Bin Laden and other Islamist extremists argue that every faithful Muslim is obligated to participate in a defensive jihad against the U.S. forces occupying the Arabian Peninsula. This *fatwa* (religious ruling), also known as the 1996 "Declaration of War," was extended in February 1998 to include killing all American citizens, wherever they could be found.

• Al-Qaeda leaders assert that secular Arab governments should also be targeted, but Muslims should first concentrate on driving the United States from the region. In doing so, the jihadists will have "cut off the head of the snake," rendering the rest of the secularist powers easier to deal with.

Within months of the issuance of the 1998 fatwa, the jihad began in earnest. In August, synchronized bomb attacks on the U.S. embassies in Tanzania and Kenya killed hundreds and

injured thousands. In November, a U.S. federal grand jury indicted bin Laden and al-Qaeda for the attacks.

In October 2000, two suicide bombers on a raft attacked the U.S.S. Cole in Yemen, killing 17 sailors. U.S. officials immediately suspected al-Qaeda involvement, ultimately indicting bin Laden and his organization.

On September 11, 2001, al-Qaeda operatives flew hijacked planes into the World Trade Center in New York City and the Pentagon, killing approximately 3,000 people in the single largest act of terror in U.S. history. Arial footage of the second plane hitting the towers was broadcast in real time across the globe by all the major U.S. news networks, searing the event into the consciousness of a generation of viewers. Bin Laden would eventually claim direct responsibility for the attacks in October 2004.

The U.S. government quickly concluded that al-Qaeda was responsible for the September 11th attacks and decided to strike back. Al-Qaeda was known to have a number of bases in

An Indonesian boy wears a T-shirt depicting Osama bin Laden, leader of the terror network Al-Qaeda. © *Abbas | Magnum Photos*

KEY EVENTS

1992: Bombings targeting U.S. troops in Aden and Yemen.

1993: Al-Qaeda claims to have downed U.S. helicopters in Somalia.

1993: Ramzi Yousef and Khalid Sheik Mohammed plot to destroy multiple airplanes over mid-Pacific. The plot is foiled. The extent of their al-Qaeda linkage at the time is uncertain.

1994: Islamic dissident Osama Bin Laden is stripped of his Saudi nationality.

1998: Bombing of U.S. embassies in Nairobi, Kenya, and Dar es Salaam, Tanzania.

2000: Bombing of the U.S.S. Cole

September 11, 2001: Al-Qaeda mounts simultaneous attacks on New York and Washington, D.C.

2001: Richard Reid (also known as the shoe bomber), a self-proclaimed bin Laden loyalist, fails in his attempt to a destroy a transatlantic flight by lighting explosives hidden in his shoes.

2003: A group claiming to be affiliated with al-Qaeda begin insurgent attack against U.S.-lead coalition force in Iraq.

2004: A group claiming to be affiliated with al-Qaeda bombs commuter trains in Madrid.

2005: A group claiming to be affiliated with al-Qaeda bombs subway cars and a bus in London.

2005: Western analysts assert al-Qaeda is responsible for deadly bombing in Sharm el-Sheikh in Egypt.

Afghanistan, where the Islaimic fundamentalist government known as the Taliban was friendly to al-Qaeda's cause. In October 2001, the United States launched an attack on Afghanistan with the support of numerous other nations and the anti-Taliban Northern Alliance within Afghanistan. By March 2002, they had largely succeeded in destroying al-Qaeda's strongholds and driving the Taliban out of power. Bin Laden and most of his close aides, however, evaded capture. And long after large-scale fighting ceased, supporters of the Taliban and al-Qaeda continued to launch small-scale attacks against Afghanistan's new government and the U.S. troops in the region.

In April 2003, the United States and its allies invaded Iraq, quickly subduing the Iraqi regular forces and capturing Iraqi dictator Saddam Hussein in a matter of months. Low-level fighting remained a constant for years thereafter, however, sometimes flaring up into sizable military operations. Iraqis unhappy with the U.S. invasion and the new government were joined by fighters from across the region as they fought U.S. and allied forces with guerilla tactics and launched numerous terrorist attacks against civilians. Al-Qaeda operatives claimed

A commercial plane heads toward one of the World Trade Center towers in New York City on September 11, 2001. Hijackers with knives flew two airliners into both World Trade Center towers, each of which was 110-stories high. (AP Photo/Carmen Taylor)

responsibility for a series of suicide bombing attacks. In June 2004, Abu Musab al-Zarqawi, a key figure in the fighting, beheaded an American civilian contractor on videotape and posted it on an al-Qaeda web site. In October, al-Zarqawi announced that he had sworn *bayat*, a personal oath of fealty, to bin Laden and that his group would now be known as al-Qaeda in Iraq.

Today, al-Qaeda has become something very much like a franchise, with localized cells claiming responsibility for lethal attacks in Madrid, Saudi Arabia, and London. These cells are thought to sometimes receive financial and logistical support from the top al-Qaeda circle that revolves around bin Laden (known to the CIA as Al-Qaeda Central), though not

LEADERSHIP

OSAMA BIN LADEN (USAMA BIN LADEN)

Born in Riyadh, Saudi Arabia, in 1957, Osama bin Laden is the youngest son of a multi-millionaire construction mogul and his fourth and youngest wife.

Bin Laden's radicalism can be traced to his university days at King Abdul-Aziz University in Jeddah, where he was exposed to the teachings of Shaykh Azzam. In 1979, bin Laden joined the Afghanistan resistance to the Soviet invasion, using his family's money to aid the Afghani fighters.

Bin Laden's participation eventually evolved from financier to combat commander. By this time, bin Laden had formed al-Qaeda, which began as an organization to channel money and supplies from international supporters to the resistance.

In 1989, bin Laden returned to Saudi Arabia to find that he had become famous as a leader of the resistance in Afghanistan. The Saudi public had strongly supported the resistance and followed the events of the conflict closely.

Bin Laden's radicalism and his popularity put him in conflict with the Saudi government. His passport was restricted, preventing him from leaving Saudi Arabia again. The Saudis were concerned that he would use his connections to open another front for terror.

King Fahd allowed the United States and its allies to occupy the Saudi kingdom as a staging grounds for the first Gulf War. Claiming that his religious sensibilities were offended, bin Laden was transformed by that event into an implacable foe of both the Saudi government and the U. S.

Today, bin Laden is considered to be the most dangerous terrorist in the world. The U.S. government charges that he is directly responsible for the 1998 bombings of U.S. embassies in Kenya and Tanzania, the attack on the U.S.S. Cole in October 2000, and the September 11, 2001, attacks on the World Trade Center and the Pentagon.

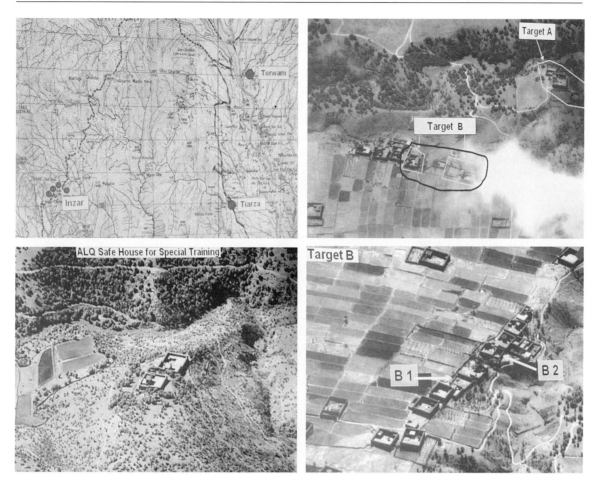

Combined satellite images show al-Qaeda-linked hideouts along the Afghan border in South Waziristan, Pakistan. AP/Wide World Photos. Reproduced by permission.

operational direction. Indeed, the Western intelligence community asserts that Al-Qaeda Central's ability to direct and mount large-scale attacks has been significantly degraded in recent years by the killing and/or capture of a number of key leaders, including Mohamed Atef, Abu Zubaydah, Abd al-Rahim al-Nashiri, and Khalid Sheikh Mohammed. Those that have not been killed or captured are hindered by the relentless pursuit of western governments.

The threat from localized al-Qaeda cells in western cities and moderate Arab states, however, remains very high. The March 11, 2004 train bombings in Madrid; the July 7, 2005, attacks on the London transit system; and the synchronized bombing of an Egyptian resort on July 23, 2005 are all thought to be the result of groups within the al-Qaeda network.

PHILOSOPHY AND TACTICS

Bin Laden has been very clear about the philosophy and objectives of al-Qaeda, beginning with the publication of his 1996 fatwa and continuing to the present day. He carefully casts his conflict with the United States and its allies in theological terms, invoking the memory of the crusades. As proof of what he calls a crusader-Zionist conspiracy, he points to the plight of Muslims in Palestine, Lebanon, and Africa, and to the conditions created in Iraq by UN sanctions. His stated objective is to drive Western forces out of all traditional Muslim lands, beginning with Saudi Arabia.

Bin Laden intends to achieve this goal by globalizing al-Qaeda as a movement, calling on all the world's Muslims to participate in a jihad to return the Middle East to fundamentalist

PRIMARY SOURCE

Terrorist Known Before 9/11, More Say

A Defense Department inquiry has found three more people who recall seeing an intelligence briefing slide that identified the ringleader of the Sept. 11 attacks a year before the hijackings and terrorist strikes, Pentagon and military officials said Thursday.

But the officials said investigators who reviewed thousands of documents and electronic files from a secret counterterrorism planning unit had not found the chart itself, or any evidence the chart ever existed.

The officials acknowledged that documents and electronic files created by the unit, known as Able Danger, were destroyed under standing orders that limit the military's use of intelligence gathered about people in the United States.

At a Pentagon briefing on Thursday, four intelligence or military officials said investigators had interviewed 80 people who served directly with Able Danger, a team organized to write a counterterrorism campaign plan, or were closely associated with it.

Of those 80, 5 in all now say they saw the chart, including Capt. Scott J. Phillpott of the Navy and Lt. Col. Anthony Shaffer of the Army, whose recent comments first brought attention to Able Danger.

At the briefing, the officials said that four of the five recalled seeing a picture of Mohamed Atta, the member of Al Qaeda who planned and carried out the attacks, while one said the chart contained only Mr. Atta's name.

The officials stressed that their inquiry was continuing, and that they still could not definitively prove or disprove whether the unit identified Mr. Atta—and, perhaps, other members of the hijacking team—before the Sept. 11, 2001, attacks.

The witnesses "are credible people," said Pat Downs, a senior policy analyst for the under secretary of defense for intelligence. But investigators "can't find the document," Ms. Downs said.

Another official who described the inquiry, Cmdr. Christopher Chope of the United States Special Operations Command, said there was no evidence that the destruction of Able Danger documents had been anything other than a routine application of privacy regulations.

Commander Chope also said there was no evidence that military lawyers issued orders preventing Able Danger personnel from sharing data they had gathered with the Federal Bureau of Investigation, as Colonel Shaffer has said.

Thom Shanker

Source: New York Times, September 2, 2005

Islamic rule and by inflicting mass casualties upon U.S. troops and U.S. citizens. His experiences in Afghanistan and Somalia have convinced him that the so-called superpowers are nothing more than "paper tigers" that are unwilling to sustain significant casualties in the service of achieving their military objectives.

At the time of the 1998 fatwa, al-Qaeda was a loose network of extremists led by a *shura*, or consultative council of senior operatives, with bin Laden as their *emir*, or prince. Their tactic of choice is the painstakingly planned and patiently executed series of synchronized suicide attacks used so effectively in East Africa and in the 2001 attacks on the Pentagon and the World Trade Center in New York City. Bin Laden has a self-proclaimed passion for martyrdom, and he has been very successful in inducing young Arab men to give their lives in the service of his cause. Al-Qaeda attacks are meticulously planned, well-funded, nearly impossible to defend against in open societies, and lethal.

Besides hoping to instill terror and amass large numbers of casualties, bin Laden has said that al-Qaeda attacks are designed to weaken the economy of the target country.

Osama bin Laden, leader of the terrorist group al-Qaeda, walks behind his deputy Ayman al-Zawahri in this undated video tape released on Sept. 10, 2003. This footage, the first video image of bin Laden to be released in nearly two years, was aired by the Arabic satellite channel Al-Jazeera on the eve of the second anniversary of the September 11 attacks. AP/Wide World Photos. Reproduced by permission.

This early version of al-Qaeda, or Al-Qaeda Central, however, is thought to have been decimated by the capture and killing of many of its top leaders in the years since September 2001. The surviving leaders are hindered by the relentless pursuit of Western governments that are intent on their destruction and they are thought to be no longer capable of conducting major, long-range, coordinated attacks.

Today's al-Qaeda has devolved into a global movement, a decentralized web of localized, independent cells that are only loosely connected to Al-Qaeda Central. These receive little more than inspiration from bin Laden, though some cells in the Middle East and Europe are thought to receive financial and logistical support. These localized al-Qaeda franchises have claimed responsibility for major bombings in Iraq, Madrid, London, and Egypt.

Even though this loosely connected version of al-Qaeda has less resources for mounting major, long-range operations, in one sense this shift represents the accomplishment of one of bin Laden's most important goals. From his earliest statements to the world press, he has sought to inspire a global movement of homegrown Islamist jihadists who would rise up to wreak havoc in their native countries. He describes himself as instigator.

In some respects, the new al-Qaeda represents an even more formidable challenge to Western governments than the old organization. With the old al-Qaeda, there was a central hierarchy that could be targeted and a network that could be traced. Now there are isolated, self-started cells whose capture or destruction has little effect on the global movement.

PRIMARY SOURCE
Al-Qa'ida

DESCRIPTION

Al-Qa'ida was established by Usama Bin Ladin in 1988 with Arabs who fought in Afghanistan against the Soviet Union. Helped finance, recruit, transport, and train Sunni Islamic extremists for the Afghan resistance. Goal is to unite Muslims to fight the United States as a means of defeating Israel, overthrowing regimes it deems "non-Islamic," and expelling Westerners and non-Muslims from Muslim countries. Eventual goal would be establishment of a pan-Islamic caliphate throughout the world. Issued statement in February 1998 under the banner of "The World Islamic Front for Jihad Against the Jews and Crusaders" saying it was the duty of all Muslims to kill US citizens, civilian and military, and their allies everywhere. Merged with al-Jihad (Egyptian Islamic Jihad) in June 2001, renaming itself "Qa'idat al-Jihad." Merged with Abu Mus'ab al-Zarqawi's organization in Iraq in late 2004, with al-Zarqawi's group changing its name to "Qa'idat al-Jihad fi Bilad al-Rafidayn" (al-Qa'ida in the Land of the Two Rivers).

ACTIVITIES

In 2004, the Saudi-based al-Qa'ida network and associated extremists launched at least 11 attacks, killing over 60 people, including six Americans, and wounding more than 225 in Saudi Arabia. Focused on targets associated with US and Western presence and Saudi security forces in Riyadh, Yanbu, Jeddah, and Dhahran. Attacks consisted of vehicle bombs, infantry assaults, kidnappings, targeted shootings, bombings, and beheadings. Other al-Qa'ida networks have been involved in attacks in Afghanistan and Iraq.

In 2003, carried out the assault and bombing on May 12 of three expatriate housing complexes in Riyadh, Saudi Arabia, that killed 30 and injured 216. Backed attacks on May 16 in Casablanca, Morocco, of a Jewish center, restaurant, nightclub, and hotel that killed 33 and injured 101. Probably supported the bombing of the J.W. Marriott Hotel in Jakarta, Indonesia, on August 5, that killed 12 and injured 149. Responsible for the assault and bombing on November 9 of a housing complex in Riyadh, Saudi Arabia, that killed 17 and injured 122. The suicide bombers and others associated with the bombings of two synagogues in Istanbul, Turkey, on November 15 that killed 20 and injured 300 and the bombings in Istanbul of the British Consulate and HSBC Bank on November 20 that resulted in 41 dead and 555 injured had strong links to al-Qa'ida. Conducted two assassination attempts against Pakistani President Musharraf in December 2003. Was involved in some attacks in Afghanistan and Iraq.

In 2002, carried out bombing on November 28 of a hotel in Mombasa, Kenya, killing 15 and injuring 40. Probably supported a nightclub bombing in Bali, Indonesia, on October 12 by Jemaah Islamiya that killed more than 200. Responsible for an attack on US military personnel in Kuwait on October 8 that killed one US soldier and injured another. Directed a suicide attack on the tanker M/V Limburg off the coast of Yemen on October 6 that killed one and injured four. Carried out a firebombing of a synagogue in Tunisia on April 11 that killed

The 2004 Madrid bombings were a turning point in the world's understanding of this new development. In the wake of the attacks, counterterrorism forces looked for links to Al-Qaeda Central. They quickly found there were none. Instead, the plan for the attack was put together in a mere eight weeks, using bombs constructed by the leader of the cell, who had links to veteran jihadists trained in Afghanistan. There were apparently no orders issued from bin Laden's group.

Instead of a network, the structure of the global movement has been described as a web of influence that is much more difficult to track

19 and injured 22. On September 11, 2001, 19 al-Qa'ida suicide attackers hijacked and crashed four US commercial jets—two into the World Trade Center in New York City, one into the Pentagon near Washington, DC, and a fourth into a field in Shanksville, Pennsylvania—leaving nearly 3,000 individuals dead or missing. Directed the attack on the USS Cole in the port of Aden, Yemen, on October 12, 2000, killing 17 US Navy sailors and injuring another 39.

Conducted the bombings in August 1998 of the US Embassies in Nairobi, Kenya, and Dar es Salaam, Tanzania, that killed at least 301 individuals and injured more than 5,000 others. Claims to have shot down US helicopters and killed US servicemen in Somalia in 1993 and to have conducted three bombings that targeted US troops in Aden, Yemen, in December 1992.

Al-Qa'ida is linked to the following plans that were disrupted or not carried out: to bomb in mid-air a dozen US trans-Pacific flights in 1995, and to set off a bomb at Los Angeles International Airport in 1999. Also plotted to carry out terrorist operations against US and Israeli tourists visiting Jordan for millennial celebrations in late 1999 (Jordanian authorities thwarted the planned attacks and put 28 suspects on trial). In December 2001, suspected al-Qa'ida associate Richard Colvin Reid attempted to ignite a shoe bomb on a trans-Atlantic flight from Paris to Miami. Attempted to shoot down an Israeli chartered plane with a surface-to-air missile as it departed the Mombasa, Kenya, airport in November 2002.

STRENGTH

Al-Qa'ida's organizational strength is difficult to determine in the aftermath of extensive counterterrorist efforts since 9/11. However, the group probably has several thousand extremists and associates worldwide inspired by the group's ideology. The arrest and deaths of mid-level and senior al-Qa'ida operatives have disrupted some communication, financial, and facilitation nodes and interrupted some terrorist plots. Al-Qa'ida also serves as a focal point or umbrella organization for a worldwide network that includes many Sunni Islamic extremist groups, including some members of Gama'a al-Islamiyya, the Islamic Movement of Uzbekistan, and the Harakat ul-Mujahidin.

LOCATION/AREA OF OPERATION

Al-Qa'ida has cells worldwide and is reinforced by its ties to Sunni extremist networks. It was based in Afghanistan until Coalition forces removed the Taliban from power in late 2001. Al-Qa'ida has dispersed in small groups across South Asia, Southeast Asia, the Middle East and Africa, and probably will attempt to carry out future attacks against US interests.

EXTERNAL AID

Al-Qa'ida maintains moneymaking front businesses, solicits donations from like-minded supporters, and illicitly siphons funds from donations to Muslim charitable organizations. US and international efforts to block al-Qa'ida funding have hampered the group's ability to obtain money.

Source: U.S. Department of State. *Country Reports on Terrorism.* Washington, D.C., 2004.

and disrupt. Indeed, the Western intelligence community presumes that the death or capture of bin Laden himself would have little effect on this web.

Some analysts and political groups argue that the war in Iraq has created a new breeding and training ground for Sunni extremists worldwide. Abu Musab al-Zarqawi has created a new, smaller al-Qaeda splinter group in Iraq, whose penchant for suicide attacks, mass casualties, civilian targets, and the execution of those viewed as collaborators closely mirrors the tactics of the original al-Qaeda. The jihadists who survive the war in Iraq will leave with invaluable

Spanish railway workers and police inspect the remains of a wrecked train at Madrid's Atocha railway station. Three Madrid stations reeled from explosions on March 11, 2004. The bombs killed more than 190 rush-hour commuters and wounded over 1,240 in Spain's worst ever terrorist attack. AP/Wide World Photos. Reproduced by permission.

experience in urban guerrilla warfare, potent tools that can be used to destructive effect in their own countries.

Some argue that in the event of bin Laden's death, al-Zarqawi will become the new *de facto* leader of the global jihadist movement, despite the fact that Al-Qaeda Central has its own plan of succession, with Ayman al-Zawahiri designated to assume leadership upon bin Laden's death. In such a scenario, as the leadership shifts to al-Zarqawi, the base of operations will shift to Iraq. Alternately, other extremist groups like the Indonesian-based Jemaah Islamiya could assume the mantle of the primary Islamic terror group.

OTHER PERSPECTIVES

Most Muslims denounce bin Laden as an extremist and al-Qaeda as a terrorist organization, but to Islamist extremists worldwide, bin Laden is a hero of almost messianic proportion. Bin Laden's legend continues to grow, even as he is forced deeper and deeper underground to evade international pursuit.

There are signs that support for bin Laden and al-Qaeda is waning. A recent poll conducted by the Pew Research Center for the People & the Press found that support for bin Laden is shrinking in the Middle East, especially in those Arab nations that have themselves been the target of terror attacks. In Lebanon, for example, support for al-Qaeda's fight has dropped from 73% down to 39%. Similar drops were seen in Jordan, and smaller drops in Pakistan, Indonesia, and Morocco. The trend is even more dramatic among Muslims living in Western Europe. The Islamic Commission of Spain has gone so far as to issue a fatwa against bin Laden himself, denouncing him as apostate and calling on other Muslim clerics to do the same.

SUMMARY

Since its beginnings in Afghanistan in 1988, al-Qaeda has evolved from an organized, hierarchical network capable of major long-range operations in 2001 to a shadowy global web of independent cells that receive inspiration and little else from bin Laden and his organization in 2005. The Western intelligence community believes that the original leaders of al-Qaeda are mostly dead, captured, or in hiding, and that the organization as it existed in 2001 has been significantly degraded, unable to provide operational direction to its remaining cells.

Al-Qaeda the movement, however, is alive and well, with independent, self-starting cells carrying out lethal attacks in Madrid, London, Egypt, and especially in war-torn Iraq. Western observers fear that the conflict there is creating a new generation of Islamists from across the region: younger, more sophisticated, with tested experience in urban terror operations.

SOURCES

Books

Cook, David. *Understanding Jihad.* Berkeley: University of California Press, 2005.

Jacquard, Roland. *In the Name of Osama bin Laden: Global Terrorism and the bin Laden Brotherhood, Revised and Updated Edition.* Durham, NC : Duke University Press, 2002.

Moore, Robin. *The Hunt for bin Laden.* New York: Random House, Inc., 2003.

Periodicals

Shanker, Tom. "Terrorists Known Before 9/11, More Say." *New York Times.* September 2, 2005.

Web sites

CNN.com. "Special Report, War Against Terror: Osama bin Laden." < http://www.cnn.com/SPECIALS/2001/trade.center/binladen.section.html > (accessed September 22, 2005).

MSNBC.com. "Poll Finds Muslim Support for bin Laden Waning." < http://www.msnbc.msn.com/id/8569229/ > (accessed September 22, 2005).

MSNBC.com. "U.N. Seeks First Political Definition of Terrorism." < http://www.msnbc.msn.com/id/8676132/ > (accessed September 22, 2005).

PBS.org. "Inside al-Qaeda." < http://www.pbs.org/wgbh/pages/frontline/shows/network/alqaeda/ > (accessed September 22, 2005).

SEE ALSO

Jemaah Islamiya (JI)

Alex Boncayao Brigade (ABB)

ALTERNATE NAME: Revolutionary Proletarian Army-Alex Boncayao Brigade (RPA-ABB)

LEADERS: Felimon Lagman; Nilo de la Cruz

YEAR ESTABLISHED OR BECAME ACTIVE: 1984

ESTIMATED SIZE: 500 members

USUAL AREA OF OPERATION: The Philippines, particularly the islands of Luzon, Negros, and the Visayas

U.S. TERRORIST EXCLUSION LIST DESIGNEE: The U.S. Department of State declared the ABB as a terrorist organization on December 11, 2001

OVERVIEW

The Alex Boncayao Brigade (ABB), which was formed in 1984, began as an outgrowth of an extremist group called the New People's Army (NPA). The New People's Army is the armed faction of the Communist Party of the Philippines' Marxist-Leninist Group; it had its inception in 1969. The ABB has been closely aligned with the Revolutionary Proletarian Army (RPA) of the Philippines, and a political group called the Filipino Workers Party.

The Alex Boncayao Brigade operates from the Philippines, and the largest membership concentrations are located on the islands of Luzon, Negros, and the Visayas. The United States added the ABB to its Terrorist Exclusion list in December of 2001.

HISTORY

The Communist Party of the Philippines (CPP), which was started by a Filipino revolutionary theorist named Jose Maria Sison during the 1960s, was the parent organization from which the New People's Army and the Alex Boncayao Brigade evolved. The New People's Army, the militarist segment of the Communist Party of the Philippines Marxist-Leninist Group, became progressively more powerful and, by the early

Suspected Alex Boncayao Brigade extremist group leaders Danilo Singh, left, and Rolando Marcello, right, are arrested on July 17, 2001. The two were found with guns and documents outlining a plan to create "civil disturbance." Joel Nito/AFP/Getty Images.

1980s, had set up a rival government situated in the southern islands of the Philippines.

The philosophy of the New People's Army, the immediate predecessor of the Alex Boncayao Brigade, was that the most effective means of fomenting, and then winning, a revolution was through the united efforts of peasants and workers, expressed through the use of jungle-based guerilla warfare. This modus operandi was in keeping with the Marxist-Leninist ideals of worker-peasant alliances, and was the strategy that was in place from the inception of the New People's Army in 1969 until a faction of the NPA called the Manila-Rizal Committee expressed progressively stronger opposition to these tactics during the early part of the 1980s. The Manila-Rizal Committee, led by Felimon Lagman, espoused the belief that urban terrorism was the most appropriate means to the achievement of the group's goals.

In 1984, Felimon Popoy Lagman reorganized the Manila-Rizal Committee, which he then named The Alex Boncayao Brigade after a comrade who had been murdered in the 1970s. The ABB's dedicated aim was to take its terrorist tactics to the streets of the cities of the Philippines, declaring urban war against capitalism and the government. Although there was escalating friction between the leadership of ABB, the New People's Army, and that of the

Communist Party of the Philippines, Lagman effectively maintained an uneasy alliance with them throughout the 1980s.

At the start of the 1990s, the central structure of the CPP began to implode in the face of intense internal disagreement regarding strategic approach. This was catalyzed by disagreement over the ABB's very high-profile use of assassination as a means of achieving its political aims. As a result, Sison and his inner circle of followers repeatedly attempted to eliminate the most incendiary and extremist members of the CPP. Ultimately, this led to an unbreechable rift between Lagman's ABB and the New People's Army in 1993. After that point, the CPP markedly diminished in political power.

Through the early and middle portion of the 1990s, the ABB barely managed to survive as a result of internal struggles brought about both by government infiltration and its own systemic fragmentation. By the later 1990s, Lagman had lost considerable control of the ABB; he had also been arrested more than once for his political and terrorist activities. In 1997, Nilo de la Cruz, commander of a rival faction of the ABB, wrested control of the Alex Boncayao Brigade from Lagman.

De la Cruz reconstituted the faltering ABB, and consolidated it with the Revolutionary Proletarian Army of Arturo Tabara. Lagman's followers gradually either joined de la Cruz or drifted into other extremist groups. Lagman turned away from revolutionary warfare and became a labor union organizer. In 2000, Lagman issued a public statement in which he denigrated de la Cruz's tactics as being too conciliatory, and expressed his continuing support of the CPP. He went on to state that he believed that the ABB had been "hijacked" by Nilo de la Cruz. A single gunman assassinated Lagman two months later; this was deemed to be an act of reprisal for his negative statements about de la Cruz and the ABB.

Shortly after it was organized in 1984, the ABB chose Manila as its first base of extremist operations. In expression of Lagman's conviction that urban warfare constituted the shortest route to a successful revolution, the ABB shifted from rural and jungle-style guerilla tactics and began to utilize political assassinations along with terrorist acts in order to make its ideological presence known. The initial focus of ABB attention was on police officers, which is credited

In response to bombings and threats by the Alex Boncayao Brigade, armed members of the Philippines Regional Mobile Group patrol the perimeter of a petroleum company in Manila on March 16, 2000.
Luis Liwanag/Getty Images.

with the murder of nearly 200 of them by 1993. The ABB signature murder included hanging a list of purported transgressions around the necks of the slain police officers. Early in this series of murders (1984), the ABB claimed responsibility for the assassination of the senior police general Tomas Karingal. They also reported murdering U.S. Army Colonel James Rowe, a counterinsurgency operations advisor to the Philippine Army, in 1989.

The ABB acquires most of its funding through extortion and intimidation of wealthy residents and local business owners. This serves a dual purpose: it increases the available financial resources, and creates an atmosphere of anxiety and fear among the populace. The ABB has referred to these payments as "revolutionary taxes" or "protection payments." Those who refuse either to pay or to be intimidated are beaten or killed and publicly labeled "anti-worker." There have also been a small number

of ransom-based kidnappings attributed to the Alex Boncayao Brigade.

PHILOSOPHY AND TACTICS

At the outset, the goal of the Alex Boncayao Brigade was revolution, and ultimately overthrow of the populist government. The ideological roots of the ABB lay in the political dogma of the CPP-ML, and the original philosophy was to unite the working class and the peasantry in an uprising that would overthrow the government and establish Marxist-Leninist Communist rule. The early tactics for achieving those aims lay in the use of guerilla-style jungle combat. When the ABB, under the leadership of Felimon Lagman, separated from the NPA, the tactics began to change, moving from the rural and primitive areas to the cities and commercial areas. As is quite common among terrorists and extremist

LEADERSHIP

FELIMON LAGMAN

Felimon (Popoy) Lagman was an early leader of the ABB, having been a prominent member of the New People's Army in the 1980s. Felimon Lagman was the leader of an NPA faction called the Manila-Rizal Committee, which evolved into the urban terrorist organization that came to be known as the Alex Boncayao Brigade. The ABB broke away from other extremist factions in 1991, with Lagman at the epicenter of leadership.

NILO DE LA CRUZ

By the late 1990s, Lagman lost control of the ABB to Nilo de la Cruz. When de la Cruz gained control of the Alex Boncayao Brigade in the late 1990s, he sought to merge it with another extremist organization, the Revolutionary Proletarian Army. Currently, the group is known as the Revolutionary Proletarian Army-Alex Boncayao Brigade.

groups, Lagman's ABB utilized visible fear-evoking tactics: they openly assassinated police officers, military, and government personnel, and publicly claimed responsibility for their actions. They utilized kidnapping, threats, intimidation, and violence as means of ensuring financial viability.

In the late 1990s, when Lagman was ousted and Nilo de la Cruz assumed leadership of the group and united it with the RPA, the philosophy and tactics of the Alex Boncayao Brigade (eventually called the RPA-ABB) again shifted, and moved more into alignment with the earlier philosophical goals of revolution and uniting of the peasants with the working class population in an effort to achieve common aims. Much of the RPA-ABB activity remained concentrated in urban areas, but the focus changed to something akin to a terrorist version of public protest: offices and government agency buildings were symbolically attacked and damaged in protest

of unfair conditions, such as rising gasoline or oil prices, for workers and the common citizenry.

At the beginning of the twenty-first century, the RPA-ABB, together with its political ally, the *Rebolusyonaryong Partido ng Manggagawa–Pilipinas* (RPM-P) publicly announced its intention to achieve peace with the Philippine government, headed by President Joseph Estrada. Nilo de la Cruz, together with the leader of the RPA, Arturo Tabara, engaged in peaceful negotiations with both the President and the National Commander Carapali Lualhati. The result of those discussions was a December 2000 truce with the Philippine military.

The truce did not prevent the group from continued political activism/terrorist acts aimed at prevention of Philippine entry into western-style globalization, however. During the year 2000, the ABB claimed responsibility for attacks on the Manila/Makati offices of Citibank, Shell Oil, Petron, and the U.S. Department of Energy. The ongoing use of the terrorist tactics of bombings and attacks on public buildings was the catalyst for the ABB's inclusion in the U.S. Department of State Terrorist Exclusion List in 2001.

OTHER PERSPECTIVES

Johnna Villaviray, a senior reporter for the *Manila Times*, reported on December 26, 2003, that Nilo de la Cruz had shifted from terrorist activities as leader of the ABB to organizing the labor forces of the Philippines into trade unions. Villaviray reported that de la Cruz had turned his political energies toward the creation of a "multisectoral grassroots political party," the goal of which is to permit inclusion of labor, peasant, and youth leaders as party-list members of Congress, which Villaviray reported had historically been dominated by traditional politicians, powerful landlords, and businessmen.

On February 6, 2004, the Centers for Defense Information reported that the ABB could either have become so fragmented and disenfranchised as to be limited to street gang-type activity, or far more likely, it could have reinvented itself as a paramilitary group that may be functioning in the service of the Philippine government.

KEY EVENTS

1998: Three days after oil price increases, a bomb exploded at the Petron Oil Corporation Offices in Makati. The ABB claimed responsibility. There were no reported injuries or fatalities.

1999: Ten members of the ABB fired a grenade at the Pilipinas Shell Petroleum Corporation headquarters in Makati. The ABB claimed responsibility for this act, and stated that it was part of a siege on oil companies that would continue until the government implemented a peace agreement engineered with the ABB. There were no reported injuries or fatalities.

2000: The Makati offices of Shell and Petron were bombed. The office of the Department of Energy in Fort Bonifacio in Makati was attacked with automatic weapons and a rocket-launched grenade. The ABB claimed responsibility for all of these events, and stated that they were in response to impending increases in gasoline prices. There were no reported injuries or fatalities.

SUMMARY

The Alex Boncayao Brigade began in 1984 as a paramilitary extremist faction of the Communist Party of the Philippines Marxist-Leninist Group. The activities of the ABB were aimed at revolution and overthrow of the current government, in service of the Communist Party. The early ABB utilized techniques of jungle-style guerilla warfare, designed, in Leninist fashion, to unite the peasantry with the working classes against the perceived common enemy of the proletariat government. Under the leadership of Felimon Lagman, the Alex Boncayao Brigade separated from the New People's Army and markedly changed activity level and style, moving from rural guerilla tactics to urban terrorism, using highly visible and inflammatory techniques of assassination, kidnapping, and extortion, aimed at creating a climate of fear and intimidation as means to the same political ends (revolution and overthrow of the government). When Nilo de la Cruz replaced Lagman, the ABB dramatically altered trajectory, and its tactics changed from street-level urban warfare to something akin to political activist terrorism, aimed more at anti-globalization and the broadening of the people's governmental voice. Although the RPA-ABB is categorized by the United States as a terrorist group, it appears to be functioning almost as a Philippine government paramilitary group currently, and any violent activity has been reported to consist primarily of factional in-fighting.

SOURCES

Web sites

Center for Defense Information. "In the Spotlight: Alex Boncayao Brigade (ABB)." < http://www.cdi.org/friendlyversion/printversion.cfm?documentID = 2052& from_page = ../program/document.cfm > (accessed September 15, 2005).

MIPT Terrorism Knowledge Base. "Alex Boncayao Brigade (ABB)." < http://www.tkb.org/Group.jsp?group ID = 3011 > (accessed September 15, 2005).

The Manila Times Internet Edition SPECIAL REPORT. "Struggle Continues for Rebels." < http://www.manila-times.net/others/special/2003/dec/26/20031226spe1.html > (accessed September 15, 2005).

GlobalSecurity.org. "Alex Boncayao Brigade (ABB)." < http://www.globalsecurity.org/military/world/para/abb.htm > (accessed September 15, 2005).

Allied Democratic Forces (ADF)

The Allied Democratic Forces is a rebel organization operating against the Ugandan government that reportedly emerged in late 1996. Most of the members of the Allied Democratic Forces (ADF) are former members of the now-defunct National Army for the Liberation of Uganda (NALU), Islamic fundamentalists from the Salaf Tabliq group, fighters from the Democratic Republic of Congo (DRC), and Hutu militants from Rwanda.

The ADF gained great notoriety between 1996 and 1999 and was considered by most terrorism experts as one of the best-organized terrorist forces that had ever operated in Uganda. The group is also known as the Alliance of Democratic Forces, and Uganda Allied Democratic Forces.

On December 5, 2001, then-U.S. Secretary of State Colin L. Powell designated 39 groups, including the Allied Democratic Forces, as Terrorist Exclusion List (TEL) organizations under section 212 of the Immigration and Nationality Act.

HISTORY

The Allied Democratic Forces claims to have started its operations in 1996 as a small group

LEADER: Jamil Mukulu

YEAR ESTABLISHED OR BECAME ACTIVE: 1989 (claimed by group); reportedly started operations in 1996

ESTIMATED SIZE: A few hundred members

USUAL AREA OF OPERATION: Western Uganda, eastern Congo (DRC)

LEADERSHIP

JAMIL MUKULU

Various published reports state that the ADF had several prominent leaders. That said, most of these reports assert that Jamil Mukulu, a former Catholic, was a key figure in the formation of ADF, and also the self-proclaimed leader of the outfit. Reports further suggest that Abdullah Yusuf Kabanda, in the 1990s, acted as the chairman of the organization. The position of army commander is held by Henry Birungi.

Very little information is available about Jamil Mukulu, except that he is a former Catholic turned Islamic extremist belonging to the Tabliq sect. There are reports that lead to the conclusion that he belonged to the Tabliq Youth Movement and was imprisoned for his radical activities in 1989.

In early 2005, intelligence reports suggested that Jamil Mukulu distributed taped footage of Islamic teachings through which he encouraged Muslims all over the world to join their hands together to fight against the Ugandan government. The Ugandan government has made several unsuccessful attempts to obtain an international warrant for Mukulu.

with its base on the slopes of Mt. Ruwenzori located on the border between Congo and Uganda; it expanded its operations over the years. The major area of operation for the ADF was reportedly western Uganda and eastern Congo. The outfit is an extension of the National Army for the Liberation of Uganda (NALU).

Founded in 1988, the NALU reportedly consisted of ex-commanders of the Idi Amin regime in Uganda. NALU was formed to express opposition against the Ugandan government led by President Yoweri Museveni since 1986. Reports indicate that NALU opposed the presence of foreign nationals in Uganda as well as the setting up of refugee camps for Rwandans in Uganda. NALU's active period lasted from 1988–1998. Researchers point out that after this period most of the NALU members were associated with the ADF. During its operational period, NALU was allegedly involved in a series of terrorist attacks against civilians. Ugandan authorities indicate that the ADF was eventually formed as a coalition of a group of terrorists with similar ideology—to oppose the Ugandan government led by President Museveni, and to establish an Islamic state of Uganda.

Apart from the NALU, the ADF, as thought by monitor groups and analysts, also has roots in the Islamic Tabliq Youth Movement. This organization also aimed to establish Islamic rule in Uganda, and gained prominence in the early 1980s. The organization allegedly split in 1989, and Jamil Mukulu, a prominent Islamic leader of this movement, started his own organization—the ADF. Additionally, the group also included ex-commanders of the Idi Amin army. One of Idi Amin's sons, Taban Amin, is believed to have served as chief-of-staff of the ADF in 1998.

During its initial period of operation, ADF reportedly launched several attacks from its bases located in DRC. News reports suggest that most of the terrorist activities conducted by the ADF were against local civilian populations. Members of the ADF, drove them from their homes and farms and robbed them. Analysts assert that unlike other terrorist outfits, the ADF did not create an atmosphere of terror immediately after its conception in 1996. In fact, as reported, the organization was involved only in occasional strikes against the government, which did not cause much concern to the authorities. However, in 1997 the ADF was allegedly involved in a surprise attack on Ugandan Army personnel at Mpondwe, near the Ugandan-Congo border. This was followed by a series of attacks on civilians and military staff that were blamed on the ADF by the Ugandan authorities.

According to Uganda Peoples Defense Force (UPDF), in 1997, 600 ADF revolutionaries occupied the town of Kasese, Uganda, which was later rescued by UPDF personnel. The Ugandan government blamed ADF for several bombings that took place in the Ugandan capital city of Kampala in 1998. In the same year, the ADF allegedly carried out its deadliest terror attack thus far—setting ablaze a college dormitory and murdering close to 80 students, and abducting 80 more. This was followed by the abduction of more than 100 school children, along with several fatal attacks on civilians. The NALU, closely affiliated with the ADF, claimed responsibility of bombing three buses in August 1998 that resulted in the death of 30 people.

In 1999, the Ugandan armed forces known as Uganda Peoples Defense Force (UPDF) successfully destroyed several bases of the AFD and managed to restrain their operational supply. The ADF reportedly fought back fiercely against this armed assault, with battles lasting until the government forces finally prevailed in 2001, capturing the ADF s headquarters.

Subsequently, later in the same year, the Ugandan government overthrew the ADF headquarters located on the border of DRC and Uganda. The war in the DRC was also dying down in intensity, making it more difficult for the ADF to strike from the border. ADF activity subsequent to 2001 has been light, and they are believed to have been reduced to a small faction operating in some areas of DRC.

As of 2004 Western intelligence agencies and monitor groups asserted that the ADF is inoperative. In 2004, the United States removed ADF from its list of designated terrorist organizations, claiming that the organization is inoperative. However, Ugandan officials claimed in 2005 that the self-proclaimed ADF leader, Jamil Mukulu, distributed tapes in which he declared war on non-Muslims and Muslims who did not participate in the *Jihad* (holy war) against the Ugandan government. Mukulu also reportedly expressed displeasure over the ADF members who surrendered to the army.

As of 2005, Ugandan officials estimate that thousands of ADF members are active in the eastern region of Congo. The officials also claim that the group has amassed significant funds to recruit new members. On the other hand, counterarguments put forward by the United Nations state that the active militants in Uganda do not necessarily belong to the ADF. These may be merely other groups claiming to be ADF.

KEY EVENTS

1996: Operating out of a base in Congo, the ADF makes its first reported attack on a Ugandan target in November 1996.

1998: The deadliest attack attributed to the ADF occurs when ADF militants set a locked dormitory of Kichwamba Technical College in Kabarole district of Uganda on fire, killing 80 students. An additional 80 students are abducted.

1999: Ugandan government officials indicate that the ADF was involved in a series of terrorist attacks on Ugandan targets leading to the murder of at least 350 civilians and the abduction of more than 200 children.

2001: Chief-of-staff of the Ugandan Army, James Kazini, states that the army has captured ADF Commander Abdallah Yusef Kabanda's headquarters at Kanombyo, on the Ugandan–DRC border.

2005: After years of virtual inactivity, Ugandan authorities indicate that there is evidence that the ADF is resurfacing.

PHILOSOPHY AND TACTICS

The ADF has Islamic extremist ideology. It denounces other religions, regarding them as anti-Islam. Experts claim that the ADF ideology is similar to the doctrine followed by other Islamic fundamentalists, including Al-Qaeda.

Most of the prominent members of the ADF purportedly have strong Islamist ties. The ADF initially claimed that Muslims were sidelined in Uganda and that it was their duty to take the matters in their own hands. However, experts argue that the ADF was not clear on its Islamic ideology, and it attacked only with the purpose of terrorizing civilians. Military personnel, in the past, have been often quoted saying that the ADF is a "rebel without a cause." Ugandan authorities also believe that the organization

PRIMARY SOURCE

More Aid Workers Leave Western Uganda

More international aid agencies have withdrawn from western Uganda's Bundibugyo district because of increased attacks by rebels of the Allied Democratic Forces ADF.

A spokesman in Uganda for the United Nations food agency Michael Jones said it was waiting to see how the situation developed.

The agency the World Food Programme was in the process of delivering two-hundred tonnes of food for distribution when it halted operations.

The move came after rebels entered Bundibugyo town on Monday night and began shooting, killing at least two civilians and wounding an unknown number of others. The French agency, *Medecins sans Frontieres*, has also pulled out of the area; another agency, Actionaid, withdrew last month because of the deteriorating security situation. The ADF rebels have been active in western Uganda for about two-and-half years; at least eighty people have died in ADF raids in the past three months.

Source: BBC News, 1999

---

probably carried out terror acts for revenge on civilians who refused to aid the ADF.

Military sources have been quoted saying that there were two main reasons for the ADF for choosing western Uganda as their operation sector. The first reason is that the lush Ruwenzori mountain ranges were favorable for their clandestine operations. Secondly, the proximity to Congo would make it easy for them to take advantage of the preexisting clashes among the minorities of that region. The ADF also allegedly forced the natives of that region to guide them through the mountains. As mentioned earlier, the organization is thought to have taken a majority of its members from the mostly inoperative National Army for the Liberation of Uganda (NALU), and moved its bases to Congo. Reportedly, large numbers of recruits were also Congo nationals who were promised money and education in return for their support.

Ugandan intelligence reports mention that the ADF used pamphlets and mobile radio to spread their messages to the general population to rebel against the government. Additionally, the reports also state that ADF used guerrilla warfare tactics such as hit-and-run operations. That said, most analysts assert that the ADF's preferred method of terrorizing was the use of terrorist bombs placed in public buses and taxis or in busy shopping areas in Ugandan towns and cities, including the capital city of Kampala.

It is believed that ADF members generally operated in small groups rather than in large numbers. In 1997 and 1998, it was thought by Ugandan intelligence that the ADF strengthened their activities in western and southwestern Uganda by attacking civilian targets, including trading centers, private homes, and businesses. ADF was the primary suspect behind several murders and abductions that took place during that period. The ADF also allegedly planted land mines at multiple locations in cities as well as rural areas, military camps, and government authority bases.

Ugandan government officials and independent monitor groups believe that, the ADF, while operational, received financial assistance from various Islamic extremist organizations based in Saudi Arabia, Pakistan, and Afghanistan—especially from a Sudan-based militant organization known as the National Islamic Front. This organization, operational as of 2005, aims to establish a supreme Islamic rule in Sudan as well as its neighbors, including Uganda. Assistance in the form of supplies, training, and money was also allegedly provided by the Sudanese government, as well as by groups belonging to the Rwandan Hutu tribe.

OTHER PERSPECTIVES

A published statement signed in 1998, allegedly by a prominent ADF member, Frank Kithasamba, emphasized that the ADF is determined to "crack down" on all those individuals who were responsible for the death of ADF members. The statement also asked locals "to keep their eyes open" for authorities, especially from the government, who have selfish motives.

In December 1999, ADF spokesperson Rogers Kabanda (a.k.a Ali Bwambale Mulima) told the Independent Monitor that the attacks on the Ugandan government and civilians proved "the power of ADF" and also demonstrated "its intentions to fight against the government forces."

In October 2001, in a statement delivered to the United Nations, Fred Beyendeza, the Ugandan ambassador to the UN said, "Uganda and its people had been suffering from terrorist activities since more than 15 years, majority of which were carried out by the fundamentalist Lord's Resistance Army (LRA)—in the northern parts of Uganda, and the Allied Democratic Forces (ADF) in south-western Uganda." Mr. Beyendeza further implicated Sudan as an ally of both the LRA and ADF.

In a report published in 2005, James Mugira, Uganda's Acting Chief of Military Intelligence, is quoted saying, "the long absence of a central government in the DRC had given the ADF time to regroup there." He also claims that the ADF had received funding, operational training, and weapons from "foreign Islamic fundamentalist groups in Muslim countries." Mugira stated that Jamil Mukulu, the leader of ADF, is considered by his government to be as dangerous as Osama bin Laden.

SUMMARY

The Allied Democratic Forces had a fundamentalist Islamic ideology. However, analysts emphasize that the methodologies employed by ADF members did not attest to their Islamic claim. Terrorism experts have often mentioned that the ADF terror activities, including murders and kidnapping, were undertaken only to spread fear. In 2001, after an attack on the ADF headquarters by the Ugandan army, the group reportedly started disintegrating. Subsequently, authorities were quoted saying that the ADF was no longer active.

However, in 2005 there were reported claims by the Ugandan authorities that the ADF had resurfaced. The validity of these reports, though, has been questioned by most of western intelligence, the United Nations, monitor groups, as well as antiterrorism experts.

SOURCES

Periodicals

Nantulya, Paul. "Exclusion, Identity and Armed Conflict: A Historical Survey of the Politics of Confrontation in Uganda with Specific Reference to the Independence Era."

Web sites

African Terrorism Bulletin. "Renewed Threat from Defeated Ugandan Rebel Group?" < http://www.iss.org.za/Pubs/Newsletters/Terrorism/0305.htm > (accessed September 22, 2005).

GlobalSecurity.org. "Allied Democratic Forces: National Army for the Liberation of Uganda (NALU)." < http://www.globalsecurity.org/military/world/para/adf.htm > (accessed September 22, 2005).

Institute for Security Studies. "Uganda." < http://www.iss.co.za/AF/profiles/Uganda/SecInfo.html > (accessed September 22, 2005).

Institute for War and Peace Reporting. "New Danger from Ugandan Rebel Group?" < http://www.reliefweb.int/rw/RWB.NSF/db900SID/RMOI-6D53DW?OpenDocument > (accessed September 22, 2005).

MIPT Terrorism Knowledge Base. "National Army for the Liberation of Uganda (NALU)." < http://www.tkb.org/Group.jsp?groupID=3515 > (accessed September 22, 2005).

SEE ALSO

Lords Resistance Army (LRA)

American Border Patrol

LEADER: Glenn Spencer

YEAR ESTABLISHED OR BECAME ACTIVE: 1992

ESTIMATED SIZE: Unknown, though some reports suggest the number to be less than 50

USUAL AREA OF OPERATION: California, Arizona (border counties)

Many Americans are concerned about the flow of illegal immigrants across the border with Mexico into the southwestern United States, especially those who live in that region of the country. American Border Patrol (ABP) is one of a number of groups that believe private citizens are justified in taking the law into their own hands and capturing illegal immigrants themselves. The focus of ABP's efforts appears to be on propaganda and supporting the efforts of other vigilante groups that patrol regions near Mexico rather than engaging in its own patrols. It maintains a website, broadcasts radio programs, and engages in border surveillance.

The ABP was officially founded by Glenn Spencer after he moved from California to Arizona in 2000. However, Spencer already had a history as a leader of anti-immigration groups with essentially the same goals as American Border Patrol. Although Spencer maintains that these groups—American Patrol and Voices of Citizens Together—are separate organizations, they can also be seen as the same organization operating under different names, and indeed they are often used interchangeably by the media.

HISTORY

Glen Spencer claims to have formed the anti-immigration extremist group Voices of Citizens

A member of the California anti-immigration group Voice of Citizens Together protests pre-natal care for illegal immigrants while pointing to a helicopter carrying President Clinton, who was in the area to address local college students.

AP/Wide World Photos. Reproduced by permission.

KEY EVENTS

1992: Voices of Citizens Together is founded in California by Glenn Spencer.

1994: VCT supports the passage of the controversial Proposition 187.

2000: Glenn Spencer moves to Arizona and renames his group American Border Patrol.

---

prominent activists of Latin American heritage, parents as well as teachers, who thought that the proposition was unjust. The VCT and other groups concerned about the growing population of ethnically Latin American illegal immigrants in California supported the proposition. They were successful, in that Proposition 187 was passed by the people and became law in 1994. However it was immediately challenged in court, where it was found to be unconstitutional. The appeals process dragged on for years, ending in 1998 when Gray Davis, and opponent of Proposition 187 was elected governor. Spencer and his supporters believe that Proposition 187 was constitutional and that Davis betrayed the will of the people of California by not appealing the case to the Supreme Court.

Angered by the fate of Proposition 187, VCT stepped up its efforts and campaign against Mexican immigrants. In 1998, VCT claimed that it was growing faster than ever. According to VCT proclamations, the organization, as of the early 2000s, received the patronage of a huge number of citizens. The group also claimed that, at the time, more than 3,000 people subscribed to the American Patrol newsletter. Other analysts, such as the Southern Poverty Law Center, believe that the group was in decline and that this is why Spencer decided to relocate to Cochise County, Arizona in 2002 and establish a "new" group with much the same goals as the VCT, the American Border Patrol. Arizona experienced a rise in illegal immigration in the early 2000s and many other anti-immigration groups were active in the area. Since Spencer's arrival in Arizona the ABP

Together (VCT), the group that would become ABP, in California in 1992. The VCT and its associated radio programs and newletters (called American Patrol) first came to the attention of the media with its promotion of California's controversial Proposition 187. Proposition 187 was designed to enhance the powers of California law enforcement agents to capture illegal immmigrants and to deny public benefits, such as education and medical care, to people who could not prove they were legal residents of the United States. The proposition targeted students of Latin American descent in particular.

A number of individuals of Latin American ethnicity raised an objection to Proposition 187 and carried out rallies on the streets of California contesting the proposition. According to media reports, they were joined in their cause by

PRIMARY SOURCE

Anti-Immigrant Extremism: Immigration Activist Shoots Up Woman's Garage

"We're not kooks," Glenn Spencer assured Southeast Arizona residents last fall after he moved the headquarters of his anti-immigration hate group, American Patrol, from Southern California to the troubled Arizona border county of Cochise.

But in early August, Spencer became the third anti-immigration activist on the border to land in legal trouble this year.

After a neighbor reported hearing two shots fired and a weapon cocked outside her home, local officers drove out and found that bullets had been fired into the woman's garage door. Spencer, claiming that he opened fire after hearing suspicious noises outside, was arrested on three felony counts of disorderly conduct with a weapon, one felony count of endangerment and one count of misdemeanor criminal damage. A few days earlier, following a series of death threats against Spencer, his home headquarters had been burglarized, Spencer claimed.

Though it's been highly controversial in Cochise County, American Border Patrol, the spinoff group Spencer founded, continues its work of "lighting up" the border, videotaping illegal immigrants and broadcasting the images of what Spencer has called a "Mexican invasion" over its Web site.

Meanwhile, Jack Foote, a Texan who leads the paramilitary outfit Ranch Rescue, is battling a lawsuit filed by six migrants who say members of Foote's group held them at gunpoint and beat one of them with the butt-end of a gun. "These two trespassers were treated with the utmost of kindness and respect," Foote has insisted.

Chris Simcox, the rabble-rousing newspaper publisher who organized the Civil Homeland Defense militia last fall in Arizona, pleaded not guilty on Aug. 21 to three misdemeanor weapons charges. Simcox, whose trial date has not been set, was nabbed while carrying a firearm on National Park Service land, and he also is charged with lying to a ranger about the gun.

Simcox, who issues calls to arms in his tiny local paper, the Tombstone Tumbleweed, said he had innocently stumbled into an area of the park that was not marked as federal land.

Source: Southern Poverty Law Center, 2003

---

has continued to lobby for stronger enforcement of anti-immigration laws and to warn those who will listen about the perils of illegal immigration. It also operates drone aircraft that it uses to document illegal border crossings.

PHILOSOPHY AND TACTICS

The self-proclaimed leader of the VCT/American Patrol, Glenn Spencer has often expressed his strong sentiments against the existing anti-immigration laws in the United States, as well as against the government's stance on this issue. Glenn Spencer and other members of the ABP and its related groups have allegedly organized a number of operations—some of them violent in nature—to stop illegal immigration.

The ABP maintains a web site in which anti-immigration (and more specifically, anti-Mexican) views are expressed. The organization's radio program, American Patrol, routinely airs interviews of anti-immigrant individuals with racist mindsets. The organization, allegedly, strongly supports the viewpoints and philosophies of several extremist organizations with similar ideologies, including members of the racially prejudiced Council of Conservative Citizens. Glenn Spencer claims that he supports (and is supported by) the Jewish extremist organization, Jewish Defense League.

The ABP encourages fellow anti-immigration extremists to report illegal Mexican immigrants and take photographs (or video) of illegal trespassing they witness. In 2000, the American Patrol allegedly sent leaflets to various anti-

LEADERSHIP

GLEN SPENCER

Glen Spencer is the self-proclaimed leader of American Border Patrol and the related organizations American Patrol and Voices of Citizens Together. Based on his writings and public statements, Spencer believes that illegal immigration across the southern border of the United States is part of a concerted effort by the Mexican government to undermine law and order in preparation for a *reconquista* (reconquest) of the southwestern United States.

immigration organizations throughout United States to join the group to deter illegal Mexican immigration on the Arizona border with Mexico. Glenn Spencer has also written letters to Congressmen and to various publications defending his stance and his organization. At one point Spencer sent every member of the United States Congress a copy of his videotape, "Bonds of Our Nation," that allegedly supports his claim that the Mexican government and Mexican Americans are planning a takeover of the Southwest region of the United States.

American Border Patrol (ABP) allegedly receives a major portion of its funding through donations made to the organization by like-minded anti-immigration proponents. ABP is a tax-exempt organization.

OTHER PERSPECTIVES

According to published reports from the U.S. government and other organizations, as of 2005, "organized hate groups like the Ku Klux Klan have historically terrorized blacks and Jews in the Southeast. But the recent influx of Latin American immigrants to the region has given hate groups 'such as the VCT' a new target, and officials say new immigrants (especially illegal immigrants) are increasingly targets

of hate crimes." Additionally, these reports mention that it is difficult to find actual statistical information on the hate crimes perpetrated on illegal immigrants, as most of them prefer not to go to the law authorities because of their undocumented status in the United States.

SUMMARY

American Border Patrol, the latest in a series of anti-immigration groups headed by Glenn Spencer, continues to advocate tougher border enforcement, if necessary by private citizens. It documents and publicizes the illegal immigration from Latin America that, in its view, constitutes a grave and deliberate threat to the United States. While it has not publicly engaged in such patrols itself, the group calls for the support of those who do and works to document illegal obrder crossings. ABP supports reportedly assert that they are nationalistic and have a pro-American attitude, rather than an anti-immigrant attitude. However, human rights organizations believe that the American Patrol is not tolerant of individuals belonging to Latin American ethnicity and is highly racist in its approach.

SOURCES

Web sites

Southern Poverty Law Center. "Intelligence Report: Anti-Immigration Groups." < http://www.splcenter.org/intel/intelreport/article.jsp?sid = 175 > (accessed September 24, 2005).

The Ontario Institute for Studies in Education of the University of Toronto (OISE/UT). "History of Education: Selected Moments of the 20th Century." < http:// fcis.oise.utoronto.ca/~daniel_schugurensky/assignment1/1994stretz.html > (accessed September 24, 2005).

La Voz de Aztlan Communications Network. "Information on Jewish Defense League Terrorist Glenn Spencer of American Border Patrol." < http://www.aztlan.net/spencerterror.htm > (accessed September 24, 2005).

Journal of American History. "Migration, Emergent Ethnicity, and the 'Third Space': The Shifting Politics of Nationalism in Greater Mexico." < http://www.indiana.edu/~jah/mexico/dgutierrez.html > (accessed September 24, 2005).

American Coalition of Life Activists

LEADERS: Andrew Burnett; David Crane

YEAR ESTABLISHED OR BECAME ACTIVE: 1994

USUAL AREA OF OPERATION: Portland, Oregon

NOT A U.S. TERRORIST EXCLUSION LIST DESIGNEE

AFFILIATED GROUPS: Operation Rescue; Advocates for Life; Pro-life Action Movement

OVERVIEW

The American Coalition of Life Activists (ACLA), based in Portland, Oregon, is best known for a series of court cases that stretched from 1999 through 2003, in which ACLA was sued by a group of physicians who perform abortions. The physicians sued ACLA for publishing "wanted" posters of abortion providers, and a web site called the "Nuremberg Files," in which more than 200 abortion providers' photos, home addresses, and telephone numbers were prominently displayed. The case traveled through the U.S. Ninth Circuit Court of Appeals in 2001 and 2002, and the U.S. Supreme Court was asked to hear the case, though they declined in 2003.

In the end, the original 1999 Oregon court ruling, which awarded $107 million to the physicians and declared the posters and web site to be speech not protected by the First Amendment, was upheld.

The group, which split from Operation Rescue, approves of the use of violence in the fight against legal abortion, and considers the murder of abortion providers to be "justifiable homicide."

HISTORY

The American Coalition of Life Activists (ACLA), founded in 1994, formed as an offshoot

Anti-abortion activist Paul Hill, right, as he approaches a female passerby on February 28, 1994, outside the judicial center in Pensacola, Florida. Hill was later convicted of killing a physician who performed abortions as part of his practice. AP/Wide World Photos

of the anti-choice/pro-life organization, Operation Rescue. Identifying themselves as "pro-life," the founders and the group state that violence and murder are acceptable means to securing their end: the abolition of legal abortion in the United States.

Throughout its history, ACLA has called the murders of abortion providers "justifiable homicide." ACLA considers Paul Hill a "hero"; in 1994 Hill murdered Dr. John Britton and his unarmed escort, James Barrett, at a Pensacola, Florida, clinic.

LEADERSHIP

ANDREW BURNETT

Andrew Burnett is the publisher of *Life Advocate*, founder of Advocates for Life Ministries, and one of the founders of the American Coalition of Life Activists. According to public profiles, Burnett attended Multnomah Bible College in Portland, Oregon, where he received a Bachelor's Degree in 1976, and a Master's Degree in 1978, both in Religious Studies. In 1984, he became an anti-choice/pro-life activist, reportedly, after viewing a documentary on abortion. In 1985, he formed Advocates for Life, in 1987 he helped to form the high-profile group Operation Rescue, and in 1994 he helped to create ACLA, an offshoot of Operation Rescue that condoned the use of violence and murder as a means to ending legal abortion.

Life Advocate is considered to be the primary anti-choice/pro-life publication in the movement, and is one of the most vocal publications in supporting the use of violence in ending legal abortion in the United States. With articles that openly condone the murder of abortion providers in promoting the pro-life cause, *Life Advocate* and Burnett's primary organization, Advocates for Life Ministries, have gained national attention for holding and advocating violence as a tactic. Burnett was named as an individual defendant in the *Planned Parenthood of the Columbia/Willamette Inc. v. American Coalition of Life Activists* case.

In 1995, a group of physicians sued ACLA and other pro-choice groups for creating wanted posters of various abortion providers, medical doctors who performed abortions at clinics that included Planned Parenthood sites. Two pro-life organizations and 14 individuals were named as defendants in the *Planned Parenthood of the Columbia/Willamette Inc. v. American Coalition of Life Activists* case. The wanted posters included personal information about the doctors, offered rewards for helping to induce doctors to stop performing abortions and for helping to close clinics. In 1996, Neal Horsley, a leader in the American Coalition of Life Activists, also created a web site called the Nuremberg Files. This web site listed information on more than 200 doctors who performed abortions, including home addresses, telephone numbers, and personal details. The physicians who sued ACLA and others claimed that the web site and posters constituted "harassment, intimidation and threats of violence in order to cause violent acts and to drive plaintiffs out of business." On the Nuremberg Files web site, abortion providers who had been killed were depicted with a line through their poster, while those wounded were shaded gray. The web site explicitly explained the meanings of these symbols.

ACLA and the other groups, as defendants, claimed that the posters and the web site were protected under the First Amendment, as free speech. The ACLA claimed that the posters did not directly advocate violence; none of the writings told people to harm any single person, nor did they make explicit threats to the doctors.

The plaintiffs used the Freedom of Access to Clinic Entrances Act (FACE), which criminalizes the use of force or threat of force against anyone seeking an abortion in a clinic or with abortion providers, and the Racketeer Influenced and Corrupt Organizations (RICO) law as the legal basis for their arguments against ACLA's activities. In 1999, an Oregon court sided with the physicians, awarding them more than $107 million in damages. ACLA immediately filed an appeal, which reached the U.S. Ninth Circuit Court of Appeals in 2001. Three judges on the Ninth Circuit heard the case, and reversed the lower court's decision. The judges looked back at *NAACP v. Claiborne Hardware Co.*, 458 U.S. 886 (1982). In this case, the NAACP organized a boycott of white-owned stores, and organizers wrote down the names of black patrons who crossed the boycott lines to shop in the white-owned stores. These names were announced at rallies, and some violent acts were later experienced by those whose names had been announced. One of the boycott organizers, Charles Evers, threatened at a public rally that, "If we catch any of you going in any of them racist stores, we're gonna break your damn neck."

In its ruling, the Supreme Court found that Evers did not directly incite violence against those black patrons, although the collection of their names and public announcements did lead to some violent acts against them. In its 2001 decision handed down by a three-judge panel, the Ninth Circuit Court of Appeals used the Supreme Court's ruling in *NAACP v. Claiborne Hardware Co.* to make a conclusion.

> Defendants can only be held liable if they "authorized, ratified, or directly threatened" violence. If defendants threatened to commit violent acts, by working alone or with others, then their statements could properly support the verdict. But if their statements merely encouraged unrelated terrorists, then their words are protected by the First Amendment.

The lower court ruling in favor of the physicians and the $107 million judgment were reversed. The physicians appealed and, in 2002, the entire United States Ninth Circuit Court of Appeals (11 members) sat *en banc* (in full) to hear the case.

In a reversal of its own three-judge panel's decision, the Ninth Circuit Court's 2002 decision stated that, in fact, the speech did constitute a threat to the abortion providers. In their judgment, the court reaffirmed the original 1999 court ruling.

> ACLA was aware that a "wanted"-type poster would likely be interpreted as a serious threat of death or bodily harm by a doctor in the reproductive health services community who was identified on one, given the previous pattern of "WANTED" posters identifying a specific physician followed by that physician's murder. The same is true of the posting about these physicians on that part of the "Nuremberg Files" where lines were drawn through the names of doctors who provided abortion services and who had been killed or wounded. We are independently satisfied that to this limited extent, ACLA's conduct amounted to a true threat and is not protected speech.

The American Coalition of Life Activists appealed the 2002 decision to the United States Supreme Court. In 2003, the Supreme Court declined to hear the case; the 2002 decision from the United States Ninth Circuit Court of Appeals stood. ACLA is still bound by the court's decision and cannot publish the Nuremberg Files online or in print.

KEY EVENTS

1996: ACLA creates the Nurenberg Files web site.

1999: Lost a lawsuit against physicians after two reviews by the United States Ninth Circuit Court of Appeals.

PHILOSOPHY AND TACTICS

ACLA clearly states that its goal is to stop legal abortion. The group does not shy away from the use of force, intimidation, or violence in achieving this end.

The primary reason for the creation of ACLA was the issue of violence; while other anti-choice/pro-life organizations declared their disapproval of the use of violence, and even murder, in the cause to make abortion illegal, ACLA was created expressly as an organization that condoned violence. The "Nuremburg Files," developed as a strategy in the summer of 1996, offered a reward "for information leading to arrest, conviction and revocation of license to practice medicine."

David Crane, ACLA's national director at the time, announced that the purpose of the files "will be to gather all available information on abortionists and their accomplices for the day when they may be formally charged and tried at Nuremberg-type trials for their crimes. The information in these files will be specifically that kind of evidence admissible in a court of law."

Crane and Andrew Burnett, ACLA's founder, both laid out the main purposes for ACLA: to use publicity to identify abortion providers and to gather information about them, and to help local groups close abortion clinics. ACLA offered a $500 reward to individuals and groups that convinced abortion providers to stop performing abortions, a $1,000 reward to those who helped to close an abortion clinic, and $5,000 for information leading to the arrest of an abortion provider, or information leading to the revocation of an abortion provider's medical license.

PRIMARY SOURCE

Hit List or Free Speech?

A key decision on what constitutes a "true threat" is revisited in the wake of the September terror attacks.

In one of the highest-profile cases of 2001, the United States Court of Appeals for the 9th Circuit reversed a multi-million dollar jury verdict in the "Nuremberg Files" litigation—an action claiming that pro-life activists used WANTED-style posters, Internet hit lists, and other forms of protest to create a climate of fear and danger for abortion providers.

Legal scholars were not surprised by the court's decision—the jury's verdict had been controversial on First Amendment grounds. What did catch some scholars off-guard was the court's recent decision to withdraw its first opinion and order the case reargued.

The rehearing order came more than six months after the original decision, but a mere three weeks after the Sept. 11 attacks—and that timing may not have been coincidental.

The Nuremberg Files litigation began in 1995, when abortion providers sued the American Coalition of Life Activists (ACLA), Advocates for Life Ministries and 14 individuals for engaging in "harassment, intimidation and threats of violence in order to cause violent acts and to drive plaintiffs out of business."

ACLA and the other defendants argued that the First Amendment shielded them from liability.

But the court did not buy the First Amendment argument in its entirety, leaving the jury to decide whether ACLA's free speech rights extended to certain posters and a website known as "The Nuremberg Files."

The site, created by Neal Horsley using information provided by ACLA, included a list of approximately 200 doctors under the heading "ABORTIONISTS: the shooters."

Many names were linked to photographs and detailed identifying information. Perhaps the most chilling feature of the site was the legend explaining the significance of certain typefaces: "Grayed-out Name (wounded); Strikethrough (fatality)." Although neither contained explicit exhortations to violence, the jury determined that both the posters and the website—quite ominous in context—constituted "true threats," a characterization that stripped them of all First Amendment protection.

The jury awarded the plaintiffs $107 million in damages, and the court enjoined the posters and imposed substantial limitations on what could be published on the website.

The group also highlighted Paul Hill's role in the murder of a doctor who performed abortions and his escort. Andrew Burnett has been photographed holding a sign that states: "Free Paul Hill! JAIL Abortionists." Unlike other anti-choice/pro-life groups, ACLA explicitly addressed the use of violence as a viable tactic in fighting to end legal abortion in the United States. ACLA has honored people such as Michael Bray, the author of a book that defends the use of assassination of abortion providers, and John Salvi III, who killed two clinic employees and wounded five people in Brookline, Massachusetts, in 1997.

OTHER PERSPECTIVES

The United States Ninth Circuit Court of Appeals decision was a narrow 6–5 in favor of the plaintiffs. In his dissenting opinion, Circuit Judge Alex Kozinski stated that "a true threat warns of violence or other harm that the speaker controls." He further elaborated.

The record reveals one instance where an individual—Paul Hill, who is not a defendant in this case—participated in the preparation of the poster depicting a physician, Dr. Britton, and then murdered him. All others who helped to make

The Court Reconsiders

Horsley, the website's creator, has never paid the slightest bit of attention to the injunction, declaring that nothing short of his arrest would stop him. "This court case won't shut me up," he said.

As a result, the only interruptions in the availability of the "Nuremberg Files" have resulted from decisions by private Internet Service Providers to discontinue Horsley's service. As of this January, the site was fully functional and included a long list of names.

In March 2001, the 9th Circuit threw out the damages award and vacated the injunction. The court held that neither the posters nor the website constituted "true threats" because they had not "authorized, ratified, or directly threatened acts of violence."

The court viewed the posters and website as indistinguishable from the constitutionally protected comments of an NAACP activist—warning "that boycott breakers would be 'disciplined' and . . . that the sheriff could not protect them at night"—at the heart of a famous Supreme Court opinion.

Noting that "[e]xtreme rhetoric and violent action have marked many political movements in American history," the 9th Circuit concluded that if the NAACP activist's "speech was protected by the First Amendment, then ACLA's

speech is also protected." Planned Parenthood immediately asked the court to reconsider, but six months elapsed without a word from the court. On Oct. 3, the 9th Circuit withdrew its prior opinion and ordered the case reargued before a larger panel of judges.

Several judges at the Dec. 11 rehearing appeared skeptical of the plaintiffs' argument that the posters and Web site constituted threats. As one judge pointedly asked: "Who was going to do what to whom?" The court has no timetable for deciding the case.

It is hard to ignore the possibility that the decision to rehear the case was motivated, at least in part, by the terrorist attacks on the World Trade Center and the Pentagon.

The last few months have witnessed a sea change in criminal procedure: secret tribunals from which even elected representatives are excluded, a drastic curtailment of the attorney-client privilege, suspicionless interrogation and racial profiling.

In the wake of Sept. 11, courts may be less inclined to afford First Amendment protection to speech that intentionally "encourage[s] unrelated terrorists," or makes "it easier for any would-be terrorists to carry out their gruesome mission."

Source: Southern Poverty Law Center, 2002

---

that poster, as well as those who prepared the other posters, did not resort to violence. There is therefore no pattern showing that people who prepare wanted-type posters then engage in physical violence. To the extent the posters indicate a pattern, it is that almost all people engaged in poster-making were nonviolent.

Although reaction among anti-choice/pro-life organizations to the court's decision was largely negative, many mainstream organizations such as Operation Rescue, Feminists for Life, and Democrats for Life continue to reject the concept of "justifiable homicide" and

condemn the use of violence and murder in the effort to end legal abortion in the United States.

SUMMARY

Neal Horsley's Nuremberg Files web site, which was at the center of the trials and the judicial decisions, had a message posted on its index page.

"The Web Sites Above Have Been Censored. The List of Abortionists On This Web Site and the Live Cameras Posted Outside Butchertoriums across the Nation Have Been

Removed By the Federal Government of the USA Because It Deterred People From Aborting Unborn Babies, Thereby Depriving Satan of the Daily Allotment of Dead Babies Committed to Him by the Federal Government. Your Continuing Support of the Federal Government Made This Possible."

In the fall of 1997, ACLA disbanded, although the court cases continued until 2003. As of this writing, they are no longer an organization, though their leaders and membership are active in other groups, such as Advocates for Life Ministries and Operation Rescue.

Andrew Barnett continues to lead Advocates for Life Ministries, and is the current publisher of *Life Advocate* magazine.

SOURCES

Books

Mason, Carol. *Killing for Life: The Apocalyptic Narrative of Pro-Life Politics*. NY: Cornell University Press, 2002.

Web sites

American Civil Liberties Union. "Planned Parenthood of the Columbia/Willamette Inc. v. American Coalition of Life Activists." 1999 decision. < http://www.aclu.org/ReproductiveRights/ReproductiveRights.cfm?ID = 13583 &c = 227 > (accessed July 27, 2005).

U.S. Court of Appeals for the Ninth Circuit. "Planned Parenthood of the Columbia/Willamette Inc. v. American Coalition of Life Activists." 2001 decision. < http://www.ce9.uscourts.gov/web/newopinions.nsf/0/1b21cad7a2e437d988256a1d006a03a1?OpenDocument > (accessed July 27, 2005).

U.S. Court of Appeals for the Ninth Circuit. "Planned Parenthood of the Columbia/Willamette Inc. v. American Coalition of Life Activists." 2002 decision. < http://www.ca9.uscourts.gov/ca9/newopinions.nsf/0F569EF00290007188256BC0005876E6/$file/9935320 ebcorrected.pdf?openelement > (accessed September 22, 2005).

SEE ALSO

Operation Rescue

American Indian Movement

LEADERS: George Mitchell, Dennis Banks, and Clyde Bellecourt

YEAR ESTABLISHED OR BECAME ACTIVE: 1968

USUAL AREA OF OPERATION: United States

OVERVIEW

The American Indian Movement (AIM) was founded in Minneapolis, Minnesota, during the summer of 1968, when community activists George Mitchell, Dennis Banks, and Clyde Bellecourt organized a meeting attended by about 200 Native Americans from the surrounding area. Actor Russell Means later became a prominent leader in the group. The stated goal of AIM is to foster spiritual and cultural revival among native peoples in the hope of attaining native sovereignty and the re-establishment of the treaty system for dealing with the "colonialist" governments of North and South America.

The first actions of the group focused on documenting cases of police brutality, using police scanners and CB radios to arrive at the scene of arrests of Native Americans. Inspired by the 1969 occupation of Alcatraz Island, the group began to look beyond its original focus on urban Native American issues, and progressed to more radical and ambitious methods. Their major actions include the forceful takeover of the Bureau of Indian Affairs in 1972, followed swiftly by the dramatic, 71-day siege that came to be known as Wounded Knee II. In recent years, the group has broken into factions, each claiming to represent the true spirit of AIM, with a western faction led by Russell Means and a Minnesota faction led by Clyde Bellecourt.

A U.S. flag flies upside down outside an American Indian Movement (AIM) church. The church was erected on the site of the 1890 massacre at Wounded Knee, South Dakota. AP/Wide World Photos. Reproduced by permission.

HISTORY

The American Indian Movement emerged from social tumult of the late 1960s in Minneapolis, Minnesota, founded by activists who were determined to improve the lives of urban Native Americans. In the summer of 1968, George Mitchell, Dennis Banks, and Clyde Bellecourt organized a meeting to discuss the issues facing the Native American community of Minneapolis. Among the problems addressed were poverty, substandard housing, the highest unemployment rate of any ethnic group, and police brutality. The approximately 200 attendees founded a group called the Concerned Indians of America. The name was changed shortly afterwards to the American Indian Movement to avoid reference to the acronym commonly used for the Central Intelligence Agency.

The earliest actions of the group involved the founding of the Minneapolis AIM Patrol, that used CB radios and police scanners to arrive at the scene of police investigations involving Native Americans, in order to document instances of police brutality. These AIM patrols continue to the present day.

Were it not the turbulent decade of the 1960s, with civil upheaval and social protest sweeping across the country in waves, AIM might have stayed an urban movement focused on local issues. Within a year of AIM's founding, however, "Red Power" burst onto the national consciousness with the dramatic occupation of Alcatraz Island by San Francisco-area Native American activists. Inspired by the success and the boldness of the action, native youth from all over the country flocked to join in the protest, including members of AIM. Citing an 1868 treaty that said Indians could use any part of federal territory that was not being used by the government, the activists managed to hold on to the occupation for 19 months, and garnered much publicity for their cause before the government finally forced them off the island.

In 1972, AIM leaders in Colorado joined with other groups to organize what became the Trail of Broken Treaties caravan to Washington D.C. The plan was to attract publicity generated by the last days of the upcoming presidential campaign to draw attention to Native American issues. Native American activist from across the country formed a caravan and traveled from Denver to Washington to present Richard Nixon and the government with their platform of demands, which they called the 20 Points. When the caravan arrived at its destination, the activists found little in the way of accommodations, as hundreds more activists arrived over the course of a few days in early November. The activists claimed that the government had reneged on its promise to provide accommodations; the government blamed the situation on poor planning by the organizers of the caravan. At any rate, the immediate result was that a group of AIM members stormed the Bureau of Indian Affairs offices, overwhelming security, and occupying the office for six days.

The most dramatic confrontation with federal authorities, however, came in 1973 when AIM activists led members of the Lakota Sioux tribe from the Pine Ridge reservation in a

Russell Means, an American Indian Movement leader, stands in front of a statue of Massasoit and speaks to a crowd in 1970. AP/Wide World Photos

KEY EVENTS

1969: 1969 occupation of Alcatraz Island by Native American activists.

1972: AIM leaders in Colorado joined with other groups to organize what became the Trail of Broken Treaties caravan to Washington D.C.

1973: AIM activists led members of the Lakota Sioux tribe in a siege that came to be known as Wounded Knee II.

takeover and occupation of the site of the 1890 Wounded Knee Massacre. Pine Ridge residents had been engaged in an ongoing internal political struggle pitting the traditionalists of the tribe against the more assimilated members. The traditionalists voted to impeach Dick Wilson, the government-backed head of the tribal administration, only to encounter federal resistance and brutal oppression by Wilson's supporters. They turned to AIM for help, and found the activists more than willing to take up their cause. Group lore has it that it was the Lakota women who goaded the men into seizing the Wounded Knee site as a way to fight back and dramatize their plight. The siege that came to be known as Wounded Knee II lasted from February 27 until May 8, resulting in the deaths of two activists and one FBI agent and the arrest of nearly 1,200 people. Under the intense glare of the national media that drew relentless parallels to the 1890 massacre, the siege ended with a ·negotiated ceasefire and the activists abandoning the site. Meanwhile, the conflict between the traditionalists and the assimilators raged on in Pine Ridge and in the larger Native American community.

Though AIM participated in other actions, most notably the Longest Walk protest march from San Francisco to Washington D.C., the influence of the group began to decline by the mid 1970s. This decline is thought to be at least partially due to the FBI's infamous operation COINTELPRO, in which dissenting groups with anti-government leanings were "neutralized" through the same ruthless counterintelligence tactics employed against hostile governments.

Today, AIM is a splintered shadow of its former self, with two factions engaged in a war of rhetoric that seems to be another reflection of the struggle between the traditionalists and the assimilators. One faction, based in Colorado and loosely organized around University of Colorado professor Ward Churchill and actor Russell Means, plays the traditionalist role; another, led by one of AIM's founding fathers, Clyde Bellecourt, is incorporated under the laws of the United States, has returned to its early urban focus, and points to its legislative accomplishments and its history of establishing native schools and social programs.

PHILOSOPHY AND TACTICS

At the heart of AIM is the idea of Indian sovereignty and cultural revival. In its heyday, the group inspired many young men and women to

PRIMARY SOURCE

In Court, AIM Members Are Depicted as Killers

The former companion of a leader in the American Indian Movement clutched a single feather as she took the witness stand in a federal court here on Wednesday and tearfully depicted the movement's leaders as murderous.

In a full but silent courtroom, the witness, Ka-Mook Nichols, said leaders of the militant Indian civil-rights group known as AIM had orchestrated the death of one of its own members, Anna Mae Pictou Aquash, nearly three decades ago. And Ms. Nichols implicated Leonard Peltier, AIM's best-known member, in the earlier killing of two federal agents, crimes for which Mr. Peltier has been sent to prison for life.

Mr. Peltier, who has always maintained his innocence, has an international following among those who believe he was framed by federal authorities seeking revenge.

The trial, in its second day, will determine the fate of Arlo Looking Cloud, a former low-level AIM member charged with killing Ms. Pictou Aquash, another AIM member. But the testimony here stretched far beyond this case, presenting a sweeping and frightening look at violence and suspicion inside the militant movement that drew national attention to southwest South Dakota in the 1970s.

"You would think the American Indian Movement was on trial," Vernon Bellecourt, a spokesman for the movement, said angrily from his seat in the front row of the gallery, which has been full of people who remember those volatile clashes between Indians and federal authorities: AIM sympathizers, residents from the Pine Ridge Reservation where the occupation of Wounded Knee took place, and federal agents, now mostly retired.

Mr. Bellecourt denied all accusations against the movement, and said the latest revelations were merely another effort by the federal authorities to hide their own wrongdoing. "It's virtually impossible," he said, "for an Indian to receive a fair trial in South Dakota."

Ms. Nichols, who had an 18-year relationship and four children with Dennis Banks, a leader of AIM from its earliest days in the late 1960s, told jurors how she joined the movement as a high school student living on Pine Ridge and never confided all she had seen until now because she supported the group's goals—treaty recognition, self-determination for Indians, a return to traditional ways.

"At the time I was committed to the movement and I believed in what the movement stood for," said Ms. Nichols, now 48. "I never talked to anybody about anything."

But on Wednesday, Ms. Nichols described details of the group's wanderings around the country—those fleeing the authorities, building bombs and planning their next moves. She also told how AIM leaders worried that their own members might be spying for the authorities.

She testified that the leaders, including Mr. Banks and Mr. Peltier, strongly suspected Ms. Pictou Aquash, a Micmac Indian who left Canada to join the movement, might be a federal informer. At an AIM convention in June 1975, Ms. Nichols said, leaders openly discussed that possibility.

Mr. Peltier once put a gun to Ms. Pictou Aquash's head, Ms. Nichols testified, and

---

reclaim their traditions and ethnic pride. The group's spirituality is infused with a warrior ethic and a determination to restore dignity to the Native American people.

The group's own materials speak proudly of its history of "forceful action." In seizing BIA headquarters and in sustaining the occupation of Wounded Knee, AIM has used force in pursuit of its goals, but has never been wantonly violent. In their words, AIM is "Pledged to fight White Man's injustice to Indians, his oppression, persecution, discrimination and malfeasance in the handling of Indian Affairs. No area in North America is too remote when trouble impends for

demanded to know if she was a spy. Another time, he talked about giving her truth serum, Ms. Nichols testified. All this made Ms. Pictou Aquash angry and fearful, she said. "I knew she was scared of Dennis and Leonard at that point."

Months later, on Feb. 24, 1976, Ms. Pictou Aquash's decomposing body was found in a ravine on Pine Ridge. She had been shot in the head, but the authorities said they could not identify her for several weeks. The day the body was found, however, Mr. Banks called Ms. Nichols and said Ms. Pictou Aquash had been turned up dead, Ms. Nichols testified.

"From the day he called me, I started believing it was the American Indian Movement that has something to do with it," she said.

Mr. Banks, who has been separated from Ms. Nichols since 1989, was traveling and could not be reached for comment on Wednesday. But Mr. Peltier's lawyer, Barry A. Bachrach, said his client considered Ms. Nichols' testimony utterly false.

"He has no idea why she's saying this," Mr. Bachrach said in a phone interview. "Anna Mae was not afraid of AIM or Leonard. Ka-Mook is doing nothing but parroting government testimony."

Mr. Looking Cloud's lawyer, Tim Rensch, suggested that Ms. Nichols might be seeking revenge on her former companion, Mr. Banks, because he had once had an affair with Ms. Pictou Aquash. He also suggested that she might be in it for money—the government has paid her $42,000, partly for moving expenses to protect her from AIM members—or even planning to write a book.

But on Wednesday, Ms. Nichols said she simply was telling the truth on behalf of a dear friend, Ms. Pictou Aquash. One reason, she said, that AIM leaders might have feared the possibility of spying so much was that Ms. Pictou Aquash had witnessed sensitive information.

She said that she had been riding in a motor home with Ms. Pictou Aquash, Mr. Peltier and others one day in 1975 when Mr. Peltier began boasting about shooting the federal agents at Pine Ridge.

Ms. Nichols testified that Mr. Peltier made a gun with his fingers and said that one agent had begged "for his life, but I shot him anyway."

Mr. Peltier, in a federal prison in Leavenworth, Kan., denies all connection to the killings and to any boasting. "Why is she doing this?" Mr. Bachrach said. "Leonard is baffled."

The defendant in this trial, Mr. Looking Cloud, seemed almost an afterthought on Wednesday. In opening statements, his lawyer, Mr. Rensch, acknowledged that Mr. Looking Cloud had been there with other AIM members when Ms. Pictou Aquash was killed, but that he had not participated or known what was coming.

Wearing glasses, with a braid running down his back, Mr. Looking Cloud, 50, looked small and hunched at the defense table. His lawyer said he quit AIM after what happened to Ms. Pictou Aquash, and wound up drinking too much, living on the streets of Denver.

Monica Davey

Source: New York Times, 2004

Indians. AIM shall be there to help the Native People regain human rights and achieve restitutions and restorations."

Besides being forceful, AIM actions have also been obviously calculated for optimal dramatic effect. The Trail of Broken Treaties was specifically planned around the expectation of media coverage. The Wounded Knee site was specifically chosen for its symbolic value. For their part, the national media was understandably eager to cover the colorful defenders of an oppressed tradition; they made excellent copy. AIM has had no shortage of charismatic, photogenic leaders who look great on film,

Russell Means and perhaps Ward Churchill being the preeminent examples.

Be that as it may, the movement proved to be no match for the resources of the federal government; the FBI used such techniques as infiltration and "snitch-jacketing" (planting misinformation to the effect that a particular key group member was a government informant) to exploit the community's historically divisive nature, exacerbating the infighting and tribal corruption that ultimately put the movement into decline.

In recent years, the Minnesota faction has tempered its traditional rhetoric with a willingness to use the U.S. legal system for its purposes, to good effect. A legal corporate entity, the AIM Grand Governing Council has filed successful suits against the U.S. government, established schools and job programs, and has generally assumed the role of a Native American civil rights organization. Most recently, Bellecourt has founded the National Coalition on Racism in Sports and the Media (NCRSM) to organize against the use of Native American images and names in professional and collegiate sports. Though its mission might have once seemed quixotic, NCRSM has recently made important inroads toward accomplishing its goals. In the end, it may be that by working within the legal system and using its assets wisely, the modern Minnesota AIM may accomplish more than the more radicalized 1970s AIM could ever have hoped to achieve with its "forceful actions."

In contrast, Autonomous AIM styles itself as an uncompromising native liberation movement and as the real keepers of AIM spirituality and Native American heritage. Completely decentralized, Autonomous AIM's interests and mission are the local issues of the chapters. In Colorado, where Autonomous Aim originated, these have centered on organizing against Denver Columbus Day celebrations.

OTHER PERSPECTIVES

National AIM was incorporated by the Bellecourt brothers in 1993, who wasted no time in issuing a September press release announcing that "...only those chapters which have been duly authorized and chartered by the National Office should be recognized in the future as legitimate representatives of the American Indian Movement. Questions in this regard can be resolved by calling the National Office."

In response, 60 representatives of 19 state chapters met in New Mexico in December 1993 and issued the Edgewood Declaration, defining themselves as a confederacy of autonomous chapters and renouncing any national authority claimed by the Bellecourts' organization. According to Means, the Declaration did not represent the forming of a new group, but rather a reaffirmation of the principles that had governed AIM since 1975, when a national meeting of AIM members from throughout the United States had decided to abolish national offices and suspend the practice of electing national leaders and spokespersons.

These dueling proclamations were the culmination of a contentious war of rhetoric that had been raging for years. The precise origins of the conflict between the factions are difficult to ascertain. Accounts of the events that led up to the Edgewood Declaration are only to be found in the group's own materials; it has been well established that the leaders of both sides of the struggle are no strangers to historical exaggeration and self-serving embellishment.

It appears that the fight began as a dispute over the leadership of the Colorado AIM chapter. The chapter had been established by Vernon Bellecourt and Joe Locust in 1970. By 1972, Bellecourt had returned to the national offices in Minnesota, and the chapter steadily grew inactive and lost membership over the next decade. In 1983, Locust recruited Glenn Morris and Ward Churchill, a fiery rhetorician and professor of Ethnic Studies at the University of Colorado, to help revitalize the chapter. Membership grew over the next 10 years, and the chapter was successful putting together a coalition to organize a massive protest against the Columbian Quincentennary in 1992. The event was hailed as a great victory for Colorado AIM, and drew lots of national press. Almost immediately, the mutual recriminations began on both sides, with Vernon Bellecourt holding a press conference where he maintained that Morris and Churchill had been expelled from AIM. In response, Means, Churchill, and their supporters met in Edgewood, Colorado, to formulate the Declaration that formally severed any remaining ties with the newly incorporated National AIM Grand Governing Council. Today, more than a decade later, the war of rhetoric continues with no signs of abating.

SUMMARY

The American Indian Movement emerged out of the tumultuous decade of the 1960s, when a group of local activists led by George Mitchell, Dennis Banks, Clyde Bellecourt, and others began meeting to discuss the problems faced by Native Americans in urban Minnesota. The group began by organizing local patrols to document and/or to prevent instances of police brutality in and around Minneapolis. Within a year of its founding, the group was inspired by the occupation of Alcatraz by San Francisco-area activists. A group of Minnesota AIM members visited the occupiers, returning to Minnesota with a bigger vision for the movement and a new national agenda.

Numerous actions modeled after the Alcatraz occupation followed, culminating with the 1973 takeover and occupation of the Catholic Church and museum that had been erected at the site of the 1890 Wounded Knee Massacre. The ensuing siege by federal authorities lasted for 71 days, under the full glare of the largely sympathetic national media. Wounded Knee II became the celebrated cause of the political left, drawing celebrity advocates such as Marlon Brando, who famously used the broadcast of the Oscars that year to denounce the federal government's handling of the situation.

In the ensuing years after Wounded Knee, the FBI managed to infiltrate, prosecute, and basically degrade the movement into a shadow of its former self. Today, AIM is split into two factions, each claiming to represent the authentic spirit of the original movement, one based in Colorado and the other, led by the Bellecourts, based in Minnesota. The Minnesota faction is incorporated under the laws of the state of Minnesota and the United States, and has established an impressive history of legislative and social accomplishments.

SOURCES

Books
Matthiessen, Peter. *In The Spirit of Crazy Horse.* New York: Viking Press, 1983.

Periodicals
Davey, Monica. "In Court, AIM Members are Depicted as Killers." *New York Times.* February 5, 2004.

Web sites
PBS.org. "Alcatraz Is Not an Island." < http:// www.pbs.org/itvs/alcatrazisnotanisland/activism.html > (accessed October 15, 2005).

MSNBC.com. "Time & again—Wounded Knee—Siege of 1973." < http://msnbc.com/onair/msnbc/Time and Again/ archive/wknee/1973.asp > (accessed October 15, 2005).

American Nazi Party

LEADER: George Lincoln Rockwell

YEAR ESTABLISHED OR BECAME ACTIVE: 1958

ESTIMATED SIZE: 100–250

USUAL AREA OF OPERATION: United States: chiefly Virginia; Washington, D.C.; Dallas; Chicago; Los Angeles; and San Francisco

OVERVIEW

The American Nazi Party, founded in 1958 as the Union of Free Enterprise National Socialists by the late George Lincoln Rockwell, sought domination of the world by white Christians. In imitation of its ancestor, the National Socialist Party of Germany headed by Adolf Hitler, the American Nazis were virulently anti-Semitic and racist. They chiefly worked for the extermination of Jews, but also supported the removal of African Americans from the United States and the end of the United Nations, as well as the supremacy of men over women.

When the group changed its primary focus from anti-Semitism to civil rights opposition, Rockwell changed its name to the National Socialist White People's Party. Never especially large, the Party effectively died with the assassination of Rockwell by another Nazi in 1967.

HISTORY

The American Nazis, a paramilitary organization, formed in 1958 as part of a right-wing reaction to the cold war between the United States and the Soviet Union. Fearful of communist world domination, Rockwell and his supporters saw conservatism as only a weak reaction to communism. They believed that fascism was the true

George Lincoln Rockwell, center, and his American Nazi Party followers stop to fill the gas tank of their "hate bus" in Montgomery, Alabama, on their way to Mobile on May 23, 1961. AP/Wide World Photos

opposite of communism and that the only way to defeat the "Red Menace" coming from the Soviet Union was to embrace fascism. As Rockwell stated, the American Nazis believed themselves to be the shock troops of Americanism and the vanguard of a right-wing revival.

The theme of patriotism runs through most of the utterances and publications of the American Nazis. Rockwell and his followers emphatically stated that they were not Germans and were not emulating the Germans. Although they wore swastikas, they strictly prohibited the wearing of German Nazi uniforms or insignia, did not "goose-step," and did not use German titles. They stressed that they were Americans and that many of the original members of the American Nazi Party had served in the United States Armed Forces. However, as noted in the

Official Stormtrooper's Manual, Rockwell typically signed his name under the salutation, "Heil Hitler!," referred to his young male supporters as "storm troopers," and stated his admiration for the Germans and the principles of National Socialism.

The U.S. government regarded the Nazis with suspicion. In 1960, at about the same time that Rockwell was being drummed out of the Navy for his Nazi beliefs, the House Un-American Activities Committee placed the American Nazi Party on the "to be watched list" as a subversive organization. Rockwell did not have any better luck with foreign governments. He joined British Nazi Colin Jordan in forming the World Union of National Socialists (WUNS) in July 1962. Rockwell hoped to set up a system of Nazi parties in the United States, Great Britain, Germany,

LEADERSHIP

GEORGE LINCOLN ROCKWELL

Rockwell was born in Bloomington, Illinois, on March 9, 1918, the oldest of three children of George "Doc" Rockwell, a successful vaudeville comedian and Claire Schade, a dancer. Rockwell's parents divorced when he was six. He attended Hebron Academy in Maine and spent three years at Brown University in Rhode Island. With the American entrance into World War II, Rockwell joined the Navy to serve as a fighter pilot in the South Atlantic and Pacific. After the war, he studied commercial art. He then bounced from job to job working as a sign painter, cartoonist, salesman, and founder of a magazine for servicemen's wives. He married twice and divorced twice. When the Korean War began, Rockwell was recalled to service in 1950. During this tour of duty, Rockwell formed his pro-Nazi views. A Navy board would revoke his commander's commission and discharge him in 1960 from the Naval Reserves for being a Nazi.

Rockwell attempted to form a worldwide Nazi movement, but he succeeded only in getting banned from Great Britain when he conferred with British fascists. A man with a quick temper and sharp tongue, Rockwell clashed often with others. John Patier, once the fourth ranking officer in the American Nazi Party, was expelled from the Nazis in April 1967. Officially, Patier, a swarthy Greek American, was banned for fomenting dissension between fair-skinned and dark-skinned Nazis. However, Patier, had also threatened Rockwell's leadership of the group by promoting civil rights counter-protests. On August 26, 1967, Patier fired his Mauser semi-automatic revolver from the rooftop of a one-story laundry, sending two shots through the windshield of Rockwell's car as the Nazi leader backed out of a parking space at a shopping center. Rockwell staggered out of the car with fatal wounds to his chest and head. He died at the scene.

Austria, France, Ireland, and Belgium. However, he was seized by Scotland Yard in August 1962 and expelled from Britain. (British villagers, showing a distinct lack of support for Nazi principles and alerted to the presence of Rockwell by the London newspapers, raided the camp where the Nazis had been staying in the hope of catching the American leader, but just missed him.) WUNS never became established.

More talk than action, the American Nazi Party never had more than 100–250 active members scattered across the country. Headquartered in Arlington, Virginia, the American Nazi home base consisted of a townhouse for the use of Rockwell and a handful of young men who slept in barracks within the home. Rockwell enjoyed the title of commander and his always-armed storm troopers spent much of their time participating in drills. In the early 1960s, the tiny Virginia group included New Yorker Daniel Burros, a rabid anti-Semite who fantasized about torturing Jews with piano wires attached

to electric batteries. Burros turned out to be a troubled Jew who committed suicide in 1965 after exposure as a Nazi by the *New York Times*. The Nazis were never especially well-funded, partly because the troops had trouble finding employment and partly because the quick-tempered Rockwell had the habit of antagonizing financial backers with his sharp tongue.

In 1966, Rockwell shifted the primary focus of the Nazis away from anti-Semitism to anti-black activities. He changed the name of the group to the National Socialist White People's Party. The changes reflected pressure within the Nazi Party to embrace the new "White Power" movement that had risen in response to civil rights gains. The shift was not much of a stretch. The Nazis had always insisted that the various races differed in intelligence and creative ability. Firm believers in the separation of the races, they proposed that a new nation be established in Africa and that black migration be encouraged. Rockwell organized a "white guard" to oppose

KEY EVENTS

1960: American Nazi Party was placed on the "to be watched" list by the House Un-American Activities Commission as a subversive organization.

1966: Nazis shifted their focus from anti-Semitism to opposition to civil rights for African Americans.

1967: George Rockwell murdered by fellow Nazi.

civil rights marches and led a counter-protest in Chicago that prompted his arrest for disorderly conduct.

With the shift in strategy, the American Nazi Party seemed poised to capitalize on the intense racial conflict of the 1960s. The white guard units attracted quite a bit of favorable notice from white supremacists. However, Rockwell's death in 1967 prevented the organization from becoming a major partner in the rising White Power movement. Matt Koehl assumed leadership of the Nazis after Rockwell's death. Koehl declared that the white supremacy movement could not be stopped by the bullets that killed Rockwell. However, Rockwell's group could not survive without him and collapsed within a year of his murder.

PHILOSOPHY AND TACTICS

Although notably anti-Semitic and racist, the American Nazi Party viewed itself primarily as an anti-communist organization. Rockwell, in the *Official Stormtrooper's Manual*, declared that the American Nazi Party was not any different, fundamentally, from the original concepts of the Republican and Democratic Parties in that it sought to create a wholesome social, economic, and political organization by lawful means. In an interview with a psychiatrist after

an arrest for disorderly conduct, he declared that he was not against Jews, but communists, and that most Jews were communists and those that were not communists were active in covering them up. Claiming that most non-Jewish Americans hated communism, race-mixing, and moral subversion as much as the Nazis, he repeatedly tried to paint the organization as an all-American one.

Rockwell's definition of "wholesome" included genocide. Expecting the Nazis to come to power in the early 1970s, he proclaimed in 1962 that "Jews are already talking about smelling the gas," a reference to the Nazi-run gas chambers that killed millions of Jews during the Holocaust in World War II. An anonymous Nazi Party member further declared in the mid 1960s that "We are not going to stop the world's master crooks, the Jews, and their nigger-communist army by any fancy-pants education or prayers or anything else except legal force—trials and convictions and the gas chamber." The Nazis advocated the use of eugenics to guide the sterilization of lesser races, chiefly blacks, and to promote the reproduction of the "best human stock," that of the white race.

Despite Rockwell's grandiose proclamations, the American Nazi Party never resembled a well-oiled political machine. Too small to stage mass demonstrations, the Nazis generally selected targets with the aim of getting publicity. In their first act, they picketed the White House with anti-Semitic signs because such an event made a good photo opportunity for the press. In May 1961, to protest the Freedom Riders trying to integrate public transportation in the South, Rockwell organized a "Hate Bus." The Nazis painted the bus with anti-black and anti-Jewish slogans and took the same route as the Freedom Riders, until they were turned back in New Orleans. Whenever a play or movie on any controversial subject opened, the Nazi picketed the opening with their signs and uniforms with the objective of gaining press attention. For the opening of the Jewish-themed film *Exodus* in 1961, they became involved in a near riot. Some of Nazi tactics amounted to no more than petty vandalism, such as defacing the property of Jewish organizations with swastika stickers. Members were convicted of assault, disorderly conduct, and unlawful possession of weapons, among other charges.

PRIMARY SOURCE

'Lone Wolves': Despite Tough Talk, Curtis Tells All

White supremacist Alex Curtis, indicted last November on federal hate crime charges, promised never to cooperate with the government. The American Nazi Party, for one, hoped Curtis' legal battle would become the "FIRST time that the Racialists PRESENT A UNITED FRONT AGAINST THE SYSTEM."

Curtis was famous, after all, for his essay on how to answer all law enforcement questions with just five words: "I have nothing to say."

But Curtis crumbled. In March, he pleaded guilty to three conspiracy charges, admitting that he had harassed U.S. Rep. Bob Filner with racist messages and put a snakeskin through his mailbox, defaced two San Diego County synagogues and the homes and offices of local civil rights activists with racist graffiti, and left a dummy grenade for La Mesa, Calif., Mayor Art Madrid.

In exchange for a sentencing recommendation of three years (he had faced 10 or more), Curtis agreed to apologize for the crimes and to refrain from promoting racism for three years after his release.

He also promised during that period not to associate with any of a list of 138 "known" white supremacists—including White Aryan Resistance founder Tom Metzger, a vigorous ally who had raised money for Curtis' legal defense.

Curtis, who used his *Nationalist Observer* on-line newsletter to promote "lone wolf" violence against the government, allegedly was part of a small cell of racist activists in custody on related charges. One pleaded guilty and has been sentenced to a year in prison; two others await trial.

Metzger, while lamenting the "misplaced respect given to Mr. Curtis by his many supporters," seemed resigned to accept the plea bargain.

"Nothing shocks me anymore," he wrote to readers of his own newsletter. "I never promised you a rose garden."

Source: Southern Poverty Law Center, 2001

Whenever Rockwell spoke, Nazi storm troopers would stand around in uniforms and swastika armbands in the hope of provoking a confrontation that would garner publicity. Rockwell had his troopers wear the swastika symbol to attract attention and because it was the symbol of the white race. He claimed that the Party had to organize along military lines to defend itself from persecution by political opponents. Before a talk, Rockwell would notify the local police to ensure protection as well as to draw crowds and the press. Often, he would call the Anti-Defamation League, a Jewish defense group, so that the Jews would have time to prepare a protest. Rockwell knew that Jewish hecklers would mean more publicity.

Heavily dependent on Rockwell, the Nazis did not develop a new philosophy or new tactics after his death. Without their charismatic leader, the group could not function.

OTHER PERSPECTIVES

The American Nazi Party found no supporters in the mainstream media or in academia. Roger Raba, in his work on Nazi literature, reported that the Anti-Defamation League declared the Party to be "a political nonentity and certainly no meaningful menace," but nevertheless a symbol of evil that needed to be totally rejected. In response, Rockwell argued in the *Official Stormtrooper's Manual* that "because the American Nazi Party recognizes the vicious subversive and parasitic nature of many Jews and does not fear to tell the truth about this dangerous subject, the Party is brutally and unfairly persecuted by almost every social and governmental organization in America."

SUMMARY

A product of the anti-communist hysteria of the mid-twentieth century, the American Nazi Party also formed part of the nascent White Power movement. Always a very small organization, the Nazis were too dependent upon Rockwell to survive the death of their leader. Within a year after Rockwell's 1967 assassination, the organization virtually ceased to exist. Its members drifted into other white supremacist groups, particularly Aryan Nations and the Ku Klux Klan.

SOURCES

Books

American Nazi Party. *Official Stormtrooper's Manual.* Arlington, VA: American Nazi Party, 1962.

Rosenthal, A. M., and Arthur Gelb. *One More Victim.* New York: The New American Library, 1967.

Periodicals

Graham, Fred P. "Rockwell's Nazis Lost Without Him." *New York Times.* April 8, 1968, p. 21.

SEE ALSO

Aryan Nations

Ku Klux Klan

Americans for Self-Determination

LEADER: Jeff Anderson
YEAR ESTABLISHED OR BECAME ACTIVE: 1995

OVERVIEW

Americans for Self-Determination (ASD), based in Falls Church, Virginia, advocates racial separatism: the complete separation of all races into distinct, sovereign sections of the United States. Using the Tenth Amendment to the Constitution of the United States as its political justification for such decentralization, ASD's brand of racial separatist thought, a subset of white supremacy, argues for the complete separation of races, with none dominant over the other.

The group's leader, Jeff Anderson, predicts a future race war, invoking Yugoslavia's experience in the 1990s as an example of extreme racism and violence. ASD argues that separating the races is an answer to ending racism.

HISTORY

Founded in 1995 by Jeff Anderson, Americans for Self-Determination states that "a just and peaceful racial separation must come about if America is to survive the 21st century, and it is ASD's mission to see that it does." Arguing that "racial separatism and reparations will be the new civil rights movement in the 21st century," the group believes that racial separatism, rather than direct white supremacy, is the answer to racial tension and issues in the United States.

LEADERSHIP

JEFF ANDERSON

Little is known about Jeff Anderson, the founder of Americans for Self-Determination. In a 1997 interview with the publication "Spartacus," published on National Anarchist Online, Anderson described himself as having been raised in Minneapolis, Minnesota. He claims to have studied sociology at the University of Minnesota, and later studied law and theology, although he gives no further detail.

In the interview, he claims that the idea for ASD came to him in 1990, while working in Washington, D.C., as a political activist for conservative groups.

By partitioning the country into various states—white, black, Hispanic, multicultural, "rainbow"—ASD and its leader argue that racial tensions will decrease, leading to greater harmony.

PHILOSOPHY AND TACTICS

Americans for Self-Determination addresses racial separatism with a plan of action (ASD Plan) that calls for the development of separate spheres for each race. By creating states in the United States for specific races—states for blacks, states for whites, states for Hispanics, and states for "rainbow", and states for those persons who are in interracial relationships, or those who wish to live among people of a different race—ASD argues that racial tensions will decrease.

According to ASD, the mechanism by which this plan can be implemented is two-fold: the end of racial preferences and economic incentives. First, in white states, racial preference programs such as affirmative-action would be eliminated. ASD states that this would be a disincentive for

non-whites, and that they would naturally begin to move to other areas.

Whites would then use economic incentives and "buy out" the land and houses owned by non-whites in white states. There would be no economic incentives for black persons who prefer to remain in white states, or for white persons preferring to stay in black states.

ASD gives special consideration to the following groups as well: Hispanics, Native Americans, Asians, Hawaiians, people of Middle Eastern descent, and "other groups" such as feminists and homosexuals. ASD notes that, in the Southwest, "Politically, many Hispanics call for a reconquest—*reconquista*—of the region, through violence if necessary." The Southwest and Florida (by virtue of its strong Cuban population in the southern tip of the state) would be candidates for separate Hispanic states under ASD's plan.

Native Americans, under the ASD Plan, get scant attention, with a short paragraph about the current reservation system and the conclusion that, "As provisions are made to accommodate other groups, a just solution to the need for Native American sovereignty will doubtlessly present itself."

Asians are considered to be fairly well assimilated with Americans of European descent by ASD, and the Plan notes that the states of Washington and Oregon, along with part of Canada, might be prospects for a future state. The author of the Plan also states that, "Clearly, there should be no transfer of wealth from whites to Asians, in spite of certain nineteenth-century unpleasantries, because Asians are on average more prosperous, and are fortunate to be here." Hawaii, because of its sizeable Asian population, is considered fairly easy to separate, but the Plan spends considerable time discussing the issue of Middle Easterners.

The Plan distinguishes between Middle Easterners who have assimilated into white society, and those who are religious Muslims. According the ASD, "The problem is that Islamic culture is fundamentally incompatible with Western culture. For Islam, coexistence with non-Islamic social and political institutions is not possible. Western-style democracy, with its separation of church and state, and individual freedoms, is not acceptable." Because of this, and issues surrounding the World Trade Center and Pentagon attacks in 2001, religious Muslims should have their own "enclaves," according to ASD, and these persons "complicate the racial and ethnic situation in America."

In a section of the Plan labeled "Other Groups," ASD cites the Amish as an example of a separatist group that coexists peacefully with other groups. ASD further believes that just as the Amish live as they choose, "radical feminists may want Amazon colonies, with no men allowed. Gays often congregate in gay neighborhoods. Why not make those areas official with clearly delineated boundaries and local gay government and police forces?" Through separation, both racially and socially, ASD believes that "[g]enuine diversity would make our country a rich and colorful garden of contrasts."

To date, the group's tactics have largely included information gathering and disseminating, with little in the way of direct action. In terms of activism, according to reports on both the Americans for Self-Determination web site and the Stormfront White Nationalist Community web site, on December 19, 2000, pro-white and racial separatists held a press conference at the National Press Club. The event was covered live on C-SPAN, and Jeff Anderson was a speaker. This is the only notation of Mr. Anderson's involvement as a representative of ASD in any political arena.

There is no call for political action, political violence, or any other sort of direct movement on the part of members in the group.

OTHER PERSPECTIVES

Groups such as the Anti-Defamation League and the Southern Poverty Law Center note Americans for Self-Determination among lists of hate groups on the World Wide Web, but do not highlight ASD and its actions or leaderships in any of either organization's special reports on hate groups, white supremacists, or racial separatism.

SUMMARY

Jeff Anderson and Americans for Self-Determination appear to have stopped their work in the fall of 2003. Dispatches from the group's web site end with a September/October 2003 update, and the group does not appear in press articles or web commentary after autumn 2003. The ASD Plan remains a major component of their web site and other writings on the Internet, but there appears to be little action on the part of the membership or leaders.

SOURCES

Books

Gardell, Mattias. *Gods of the Blood: The Pagan Revival and White Separatism.* NC: Duke University Press, 2003.

Web sites

Southern Poverty Law Center. "Appeasing the Beast." < http://www.splcenter.org/intel/intelreport/article.jsp? aid = 66 > (accessed September 25, 2005).

Animal Liberation Front (ALF)

OVERVIEW

The Animal Liberation Front (ALF) was founded in England in 1976 by animal activist Ronnie Lee, who had become increasingly dissatisfied with the purely legal tactics employed by British hunt sabotage groups. According to its published credo, the ALF "carries out direct action against animal abuse in the form of rescuing animals and causing financial loss to animal exploiters, usually through the damage and destruction of property." The tactics employed by Lee and his cohorts were so effective and generated so much publicity that the movement quickly expanded and became international in scope, with active cells in twenty countries.

While the United States has become a primary front for ALF actions in recent years, even animal liberation movement historians themselves cannot agree on the precise date and manner in which the ALF migrated to the United States. Although the FBI charges that ALF actions in the United States began as early as the late 1970s, the first widely publicized direct action by U.S. activists was a 1982 raid on a Howard University animal research lab. The ALF made the FBI's domestic terrorism list in 1987 with a multimillion dollar arson at a veterinary lab in California. The group remains very active in the United States today, claiming responsibility for thirteen separate major direct illegal actions in the first eight months of 2005.

LEADER: Ronnie Lee

YEAR ESTABLISHED OR BECAME ACTIVE: 1976

USUAL AREA OF OPERATION: Active cells in twenty countries

The Animal Liberation Front (ALF) claimed responsibilty for fire bombing this Hertford College boathouse on July 4, 2005. The group cited animal research at Oxford's new biomedical building as the reason for the attack. AP/Wide World Photos. Reproduced by permission.

HISTORY

The beginnings of the Animal Liberation Front can be traced to the militant Hunt Saboteurs Association (HSA), founded in England in 1962 and still in operation today. The HSA was created to oppose the sport of foxhunting, and has historically engaged in only legal direct actions. Typical tactics employed by the HSA involve distracting the hounds, spreading false scents, and otherwise disrupting hunts by setting off smoke bombs or blocking roads.

In 1972, two members of the Luton HSA chapter, Ronnie Lee and Cliff Goodman, having grown increasingly impatient with the HSA's strictures, formed the Band of Mercy, taking the name from a nineteenth century anti-vivisectionist group. The Band of Mercy took a more militant approach to the fight against hunting, destroying hunters' vehicles, boats, and other equipment.

Within a year of its founding, the Band of Mercy broadened its targets to include animal research and meat production facilities. In 1974,

Lee and Goodman were arrested while trying to firebomb the Oxford Laboratory Animal Colonies in Bicester and sentenced to three years in prison. Goodman ultimately renounced his radicalism and became an informant, while Lee became even more radical.

Upon his release in 1976, Lee formed a new, even more militant group from the remaining members of the Band of Mercy and a few new recruits. Although the Animal Liberation Front began with as few as thirty members, it carried out ten actions against vivisection targets in the remaining months of that year alone.

In 1977, the ALF carried out fourteen more attacks, the most successful in terms of economic impact against the Condiltox lab in North London, which soon afterwards went out of business. British authorities responded with a crackdown, capturing and jailing half of a dozen of the most active members, including Lee, in late 1977 and early 1978. It was at about that same time that ALF activity began occurring in the United States.

Fire inspectors stand amid the damaged remains of a McDonald's restaurant in Merksem, Belgium on August 12, 1999. Police suspected it was an arson attack from the Animal Liberation Front (ALF), which had claimed responsibility for nine attacks against McDonald's and other fast-food chains.

AP/Wide World Photos. Reproduced by permission.

The details of how this migration occurred are sketchy at best. From the beginning, the ALF had received a lot of press in England, and so it is possible that sympathetic activists in the United States independently decided to act on the ALF credo. One account, Ingrid Newkirk's *Free the Animals: The Amazing True Story of the Animal Liberation Front*, claims a much more direct link between the activists in the two countries. According to Newkirk, a woman with the pseudonym Valerie became radicalized after observing experimentation on primates at the Institute for Behavioral Research in Maryland, subsequently traveled to the UK, and was ultimately trained in guerilla tactics by the original ALF. By this account, Valerie led

the first U.S. ALF action in late 1982, a raid on an animal lab at Howard University.

The FBI, however, traces the beginnings of ALF activity in the United States to earlier dates in the late 1970s. In 1977, activists freed two dolphins from a research facility in Hawaii. In 1979, activists freed some animals from New York Medical Center. However it began, the ALF would soon become very active, focusing its early efforts on attacking animal research facilities at major universities across the United States. During the first few years of activity, activists conducted illegal actions at Howard University, Bethesda Naval Research Institute, the University of California, the University of Oregon, the University of Pennsylvania, Texas Tech University, and other research institutions.

In 1984, the activists scored a major coup when ALF operatives broke into the University of Pennsylvania's Head Injury Laboratory, causing $60,000 worth of damage. Much more importantly, the activists managed to steal sixty hours of videotape documenting the research program. The ALF promptly turned the footage over to the People for the Ethical Treatment of Animals (PETA). PETA, in turn, used their considerable resources to edit the stolen video and produce the film, *Unnecessary Fuss*, featuring shocking footage of researchers using press-like machines to fracture the skulls of living primates. The film was a huge public relations victory for the ALF and PETA, and led directly to the closure of the lab.

Encouraged by the public outcry, the two groups repeated the tactic, with the ALF raiding the City of Hope National Medical Center in Los Angeles and documenting the conditions in the animal labs, and PETA using the documentation in a polished, effective media campaign. The public was again stirred to outrage, leading to government investigations of the facility that ultimately found serious violations of the federal Animal Welfare Act. The City of Hope lost more than a million dollars in National Institutes of Health funding, and the offending studies were stopped.

In the same year, UK activists began experimenting with a new method of inflicting economic damage on perceived animal exploiters by contaminating their retail products, forcing costly recalls and considerable loss of revenue. The first of these contamination actions came in July 1984, when the ALF contaminated supplies of Sunsilk shampoo with bleach, forcing a recall. Similar attacks continued throughout the year, with threats of contamination in beef, turkey, and even candy. In November, the group claimed to have contaminated supplies of Mars bars, a claim that later proved to be a hoax, though the economic impact to the parent company was the same as if it had been true.

At this point, ALF actions in the United States began a gradual shift away from animal rescue and toward an emphasis on destruction of property and arson. This trend culminated in 1987, when activists set fire to a veterinary lab at the University of California at Davis, causing millions of dollars in damage and landing them on the FBI's domestic terrorism list.

In February 1992, Rod Coronado and other ALF activists set fire to laboratories at Michigan State University. Coronado was apprehended, charged, and ultimately convicted for his part in the raids and sentenced to fifty-seven months in prison in 1995. In the years since, the ALF has continued to engage in high-profile attacks, including arson attacks on the fur industry in 1996 and well-publicized releases of thousands of minks from fur farms in Oregon in 1997 and Washington in 2003.

Today, the ALF is alive and well, with active cells in over twenty countries, and claims of responsibility for destructive actions on a near weekly basis in the United States alone. At the same time, public sympathy for the animal rights movement is at an all-time high, with groups like PETA attracting the financial support and public endorsements of high-profile celebrities from across the United States and Britain.

PHILOSOPHY AND TACTICS

Organized efforts to draw attention to and protect animals from human cruelty first emerged in England in the early 1900s, and were formalized with the establishment of the Royal Society for the Prevention of Cruelty to Animals in 1824. By the end of the century, similar groups had been established in the United States. Since that time, these groups have worked within the legal system, lobbying government to enact animal protection laws, most recently the Animal Welfare Act of 1970.

KEY EVENTS

1976: Animal Liberation Front began in England with as few as thirty members; it carried out ten actions against vivisection targets.

1977: ALF carried out fourteen attacks.

1978: ALF activity began occurring in the United States.

During the 1970s, the animal welfare movement was transformed by the publication of philosophical works such as Pete Singer's hugely influential *Animal Liberation* in 1975. Though Singer, currently a professor of ethics at Princeton, did not argue for existence of animal "rights" per se, he arrived at many of the same positions held by later animal rights thinkers through utilitarian analysis.

Specifically, Singer argued against what he called "speciesism," which he defined as discrimination against beings on the basis of their non-human status. Singer's book led to the transformation of the mainstream animal welfare movement to the animal rights movement, and the establishment of new groups specifically organized around the notion of animal rights. The largest and most influential of these groups, PETA, was founded in 1982, the same year as the first documented ALF action in the United States.

Against the backdrop of this emerging animal rights zeitgeist, the ALF was born. Although the ALF has a founder, a history, professional spokesmen, and a large support group, the ALF as an organizational entity does not exist. What does exist are a mission statement, credo, and guidelines for direct action that are published throughout the world on supporters' web sites, along with reports of completed actions.

Anyone may claim responsibility for an action in the name of the ALF if it meets the ALF published guidelines, which are as follows:

- To liberate animals from places of abuse, i.e., laboratories, factory farms, fur farms, etc., and place them in good homes where they may live out their natural lives, free from suffering.

- To inflict economic damage to those who profit from the misery and exploitation of animals.

- To reveal the horror and atrocities committed against animals behind locked doors, by performing non-violent direct actions and liberations.

- To take all necessary precautions against harming any animal, human and non-human.

By virtue of the shadowy, clandestine nature of its existence, the ALF has proven to be nearly impossible to infiltrate and stop. Though prominent members of the UK ALF were captured and jailed during the 1970s, for example, the impetus simply shifted to the United States for a time, and illegal actions continued unabated.

The ALF accomplishes its sophisticated public relations, fundraising, and support functions though alliances with legal groups. PETA has been observed to work very closely with the ALF, using its considerable financial resources to fund the publication of materials stolen in ALF raids and posting completed ALF actions on its web site. By the simple tactic of disclaiming direct knowledge of any illegal activity or direct association with the ALF, PETA remains within the law. Another legal organization, the Animal Liberation Front Supporters Group (ALFSG), exists to provide financial and emotional support to those activists who are apprehended and jailed for ALF actions. Working together, these organizations form a potent force arrayed against the interests and industries they deem exploitative to animals. Stopping them would require a rewriting of the laws that govern free speech in the UK and the United States.

Operationally, ALF tactics are as sophisticated and as hard to defend against as its support structure. With very few exceptions, ALF actions take place at night, usually over a weekend when staffing at the target facility is at its lowest point. ALF actions show evidence of careful reconnaissance before the actual attack, with apparent foreknowledge of security measures, staff schedules, and detailed knowledge of any onsite activities that may have public relations potential. Law enforcement professionals believe that ALF members frequently spend months infiltrating (sometimes by joining the staff) prospective targets before undertaking action.

In the thirty years since its inception, actions undertaken in the name of the ALF have become increasingly destructive. During the early years, the most common ALF actions involved simple vandalism and/or the rescue (i.e., theft) of laboratory and farm animals. By the time the ALF had spread to the United States, destruction of property actions came to the forefront, and arson became the tactic of choice. Today, ALF affiliated web sites host training manuals for the would-be revolutionary, complete with instructions for improvising simple but destructive incendiary explosive devices. The typical action today involves the destruction of property worth hundreds of thousands of dollars, with some actions involving multimillion dollar losses for the targeted facility. ALF actions are never merely symbolic, but rather are specifically designed to inflict economic damage on the targeted concern.

Despite the mandate against causing harm to human beings, ALF activists have engaged in increasingly threatening and violent rhetoric over the years. Whenever isolated incidents of violence have occurred, ALF spokesmen have refused to condemn the perpetrators. ALF founder Ronnie Lee set the tone for future public statements in this regard when he wrote, "Animal liberation is a fierce struggle that demands total commitment. There will be injuries and possibly deaths on both sides. That is sad but certain."

In 2001, when Huntingdon Life Sciences director Brian Cass was attacked and severely beaten outside his home, UK ALF spokesperson Robin Webb commented: "The Animal Liberation Front has always had a policy of not harming life, but while it would not condone what took place, it understands the anger and frustration that leads people to take this kind of action." The ALFSG continues to list the assailant, David Blenkinsop, as one of its "prisoners of conscience."

OTHER PERSPECTIVES

The steady growth and legislative accomplishments of legal animal welfare organizations since their origins in the early nineteenth century

PRIMARY SOURCE

From Push to Shove: Radical Environmental and Animal-rights Groups Have Always Drawn the Line at Targeting Humans. Not Anymore.

A Chicago insurance executive might seem like one of the last people who'd be opening a letter with this succinctly chilling message: "You have been targeted for terrorist attack."

But that's what happened last year, when a top official at Marsh USA Inc. was informed that he and his company's employees had landed in the crosshairs of an extremist animal rights group. The reason? Marsh provides insurance for one of the world's biggest animal testing labs.

"If you bail out now," the letter advised, "you, your business, and your family will be spared great hassle and humility."

That letter—and the harassment campaign that followed, after Marsh declined to "bail out"—was another shot fired by Stop Huntingdon Animal Cruelty (SHAC).

This British-born group, now firmly established in the United States, is waging war on anyone involved with Huntingdon Life Sciences, which tests drugs on approximately 70,000 rats, dogs, monkeys and other animals each year. In the process, SHAC is rewriting the rules by which even the most radical eco-activists have traditionally operated.

In the past, even the edgiest American eco-warriors drew the line at targeting humans. They trumpeted underground activists' attacks on businesses and laboratories perceived as abusing animals or the environment—the FBI reports more than 600 incidents, causing $43 million in damage, since 1996.

But spokespeople for the two most active groups in the U.S., the Animal Liberation Front (ALF) and the Earth Liberation Front (ELF), have always been quick to claim that their underground cells have never injured or killed any people.

Since 1999, however, members of both groups have been involved with SHAC's campaign to harass employees of Huntingdon—and even distantly related business associates like Marsh—with frankly terroristic tactics similar to those of anti-abortion extremists.

Employees have had their homes vandalized with spray-painted "Puppy killer"and "We'll be back" notices. They have faced a mounting number of death threats, fire bombings and violent assaults. They've had their names, addresses and personal information posted on Web sites and posters, declaring them "wanted for collaboration with animal torture."

---

are testament to the human tendency to feel compassion for animals. Indeed, few people are not moved to a sense of moral outrage by accounts of animal cruelty. Couple this natural tendency with the well-reasoned arguments of thoughtful, articulate philosophers like Pete Singer and Steven Best and there is a potent force for social change.

The animal rights movement grows larger every day, drawing members from every segment of society. Observers of this trend have long been accustomed to the phalanx of animal rights supporters from the political left, with Hollywood celebrity endorsements a fixed staple of PETA's well orchestrated media

campaigns. But when someone with the sterling conservative credentials of a Matthew Scully, former speechwriter for George W. Bush and contributing editor to the *National Review*, writes a bestselling book calling for the abolition of factory farming and "canned" hunts, a sea change is in the air.

There can no longer be any doubt that the notion of animals possessing rights is entering the mainstream. Best and Singer hold prestigious positions in the philosophy departments of major research universities, the very sorts of institutions that have been the historically favored targets of the ALF. Steven Best

When cowed companies began responding to the harassment by pulling away from Huntington, many radical environmentalists cheered—even when SHAC's actions clearly went over the "nonviolent" line.

Still, the ELF and ALF insist that they remain dedicated to what their spokespeople describe as nonviolent "economic sabotage," such as tree-spiking and arson. They vigorously deny the label that increasingly sticks to them: "eco-terrorist."

Spokespeople continue to chant the public-relations mantra that the ALF's David Barbarash invoked again on National Public Radio this January: "There has never been a single case where any action has resulted in injury or death."

SHAC's escalating violence is not unique. North America's most active and widespread eco-radicals—the ELF and ALF took credit for 137 "direct actions" in 2001 alone—have clearly taken a turn toward the more extreme European model of activism. The rhetoric has begun to change along with the action.

Reached by the Intelligence Report, SHAC-USA's Kevin Jonas—a former ALF spokesman—was unusually frank about the lengths to which the new breed of activists will go.

"When push comes to shove," Jonas said, "we're ready to push, kick, shove, bite, do whatever to win."

Connections between the ALF and ELF run deep. From the start, they made pledges of solidarity, and they clearly shared a coterie of hard-line activists. They were also structured similarly, with a handful of activists designated as spokespeople who would announce and encourage "direct actions."

Essentially, anyone who carried out one of these actions—whether or not they were acquainted with the groups' aboveground spokespeople—became, in effect, a member.

The structure is remarkably similar to that of the so-called Army of God, a violent anti-abortion "group" that is "joined" by simply carrying out an attack and claiming credit. Although there is no real "membership," these groups can appear large because every attack undertaken in their name generates significant publicity.

Source: Southern Poverty Law Center, 2002

especially has been increasingly vocal in his support for militant action to liberate animals, and is at the forefront in the fight to counter public perceptions of the ALF as a terrorist organization in the wake of the FBI's placement of the group on the domestic terrorism list.

For its part, the U.S. government is not shrinking from the effort to combat the ALF. In 1992, Congress passed the Animal Enterprise Protection Act, making it a federal crime to disrupt the functioning of an animal enterprise, legislation that was obviously directly aimed at increasing the government's ability to prosecute ALF activists. In 2004, the U.S. Senate Judiciary Committee held hearings in a prelude to strengthening and broadening the scope of the act to cover threats and intimidation of persons employed in the animal enterprise industry. According to the FBI, the ALF's strictures against causing harm to human beings are merely a facade. The same militants that make up the ALF, the government charges, are also members of more violent groups like the Animal Rights Militia (ARM). According to this view, activists simply wait until the outcome of an illegal action, such as a firebombing, is known. If no humans are harmed, the action is claimed in the name of the ALF. If the action causes harm or would be perceived by the public as recklessly endangering human life, then it is claimed in the name of the more militant group.

SUMMARY

Founded in England by the militant activist Ronnie Lee in 1976, the ALF has grown to an international movement, with cells claiming responsibility for illegal actions in more than twenty countries. Dedicated to the liberation of all animals by any means necessary, the ALF's stated goal is to inflict economic damage on all enterprises that profit from the exploitation of animals through illegal acts of sabotage, vandalism, and arson. During the thirty years of the ALF's existence, the United States has become a major focus of militant action, with activists claiming responsibility for increasingly destructive attacks on animal enterprises on an almost weekly basis.

Law enforcement efforts to stop the ALF are made more difficult by the fact that the ALF has no central organizing structure, and no formal membership. In fact, the ALF exists only as a set of guidelines specifying the types of actions that can be claimed in the name of the ALF. These guidelines are published around the world on supporters' web sites. Anyone can claim responsibility for an illegal action in the name of the ALF.

The ALF's agenda and mission are served by other groups that stay within the law. The Animal Liberation Front Supporters Group (ALFSG) exists to provide financial and emotional support to militants who are jailed for ALF actions. The ALF press office exists to provide public relations functions for the militants, and PETA has been observed to work closely with ALF militants as well, producing media campaigns based on materials and information resources stolen by militants during ALF raids.

SOURCES

Books

Singer, Peter. *Animal Liberation*, third edition. New York: HarperCollins, 2002.

Scully, Matthew. *Dominion: The Power of Man, the Suffering of Animals, and the Call to Mercy.* New York: St. Martin's Press, 2002.

Periodicals

Southern Poverty Law Center. "From Push to Shove." *Intelligence Report.* Fall, 2002.

Web sites

BBC News. "Animal Rights, Terror Tactics." < http://news.bbc.co.uk/1/hi/uk/902751.stm > (accessed September 14, 2005).

Anti-Imperialist Territorial Nuclei (NTA)

The Anti-Imperialist Territorial Nuclei (NTA, or in the Italian language, *Nuclei Territoriali Antimperialisti*) is a group of Marxist-Leninist terrorists headquartered in the northeastern region of Friuli-Venezia Giulia in Italy. The group operates primarily out of the Friuli-Venezia Giulia region, along with the northeastern Italian region of Veneto and the north-central region of Emilia-Romagna. The NTA has been known to extend its violence further south into central Italy. Some of its aliases include Anti-Imperialist Territorial Nuclei for the Construction of the Fighting Communist Party, Anti-Imperialist Territorial Nuclei-Combatant Communist Party, and Anti-Imperialist Territorial Units.

The NTA uses as its logo an encircled five-point star, which is based on the symbol of the historically well-known terrorist group Red Brigades (BR). As stated in the Federation of American Scientists (FAS) article, which is dated May 21, 2004, and entitled "Anti-Imperialist Territorial Nuclei (NTA)," the group is dedicated to developing an "anti-imperialist fighting front." The ideology of the NTA is based on the objective of class struggle; that is, it intends to eventually replace the present Italian government with one based on the rule of the working class (or proletariat). NTA members primarily bomb Italian political and commercial buildings and related materials and symbols of value, but

LEADER(S): Unknown

YEAR ESTABLISHED OR BECAME ACTIVE: 1995

ESTIMATED SIZE: Approximately twenty

USUAL AREA OF OPERATION: Italy (primarily the northeastern part of Italy and near U.S. military bases in the northern part of the country)

A Carabinieri police officer stands guard near a Venice courthouse where a bomb went off just a few hours before an outdoor food market was scheduled to open on August 9, 2001. AP/Wide World Photos. Reproduced by permission.

since 2002 made plans to attack and murder people within the Italian government and the commercial sector, both in Italy and within the region of the European Union (EU).

HISTORY

The left-wing extremist group NTA was first organized in 1995 in the Friuli-Venezia Giulia region of northeastern Italy. The NTA was initially formed to mirror the famed Marxist-Leninist terrorist Red Brigades. By taking on the symbolism, language, ideology, and other important characteristics of the Red Brigades, leaders of the NTA hoped to eventually combine with its successor group, the Red Brigades-Combatant Communist Party (BR-PCC, sometimes also called the New Red Brigades).

According to the article "Anti-Imperialist Territorial Nuclei for the Construction of the Fighting Communist Party" (which was last updated June–July 2005) by the National Memorial Institute for the Prevention of Terrorism (MIPT), the date of the group's first attack is unknown. Thus, for the four years between 1995 and 1999, its scattered actions were just being noticed by Italian police officials.

By the year 1999, however, the NTA was well known by Italian law enforcement officials to be actively spreading its violence in northern Italy. For instance, during the North American Treaty Organization (NATO) intervention in Kosovo, NTA members threw gasoline bombs at the Rome and Venice headquarters of the Democrats of the Left, which at that time was the controlling party of the Italian government. The violence by the NTA was done to protest NATO's military and later peacekeeping actions in Kosovo after the extremist Albanian group, the Kosovo Liberation Army (KLA), took violent actions against the Serbian government with the purpose to make Kosovo an independent state.

On September 15, 2000, the NTA conducted its first coordinated attack when two separate NTA groups planted and detonated bombs at the Institute for Foreign Trade and at the office of the Central European Initiative, both in Trieste, Italy. The group declared itself responsible for both attacks. Then, on August 9, 2001, the NTA successfully bombed the Venice Law Courts/Tribunal Building, also publicly claiming responsibility for the incident. However, on January 8, 2002, its raid on the Rivolto Military Air Base was stopped when police officers prevented four NTA members from gaining access to the base.

The Center for Defense Information (CDI), in its article "In the Spotlight: The Nuclei Territoriali Antimperialisti (NTA)" (March 3, 2005), states that in January 2002 Italian law enforcement agencies acquired leaflets NTA leaflets that identified officials of the Italian government that NTA members were targeting for assassination. The specific four government sectors whose members were targets included Federalism, Jobs and Pensions, Justice Reform, and Privatizations. This public announcement was the first indication received by Italian law enforcement officials that the NTA had changed its policy of targeting only property to one that targeted both property and personnel.

Then in 2002, the CDI reported that many terrorism experts were under the opinion that even though the NTA had been trying for years to merge with the BR-CCP, little had been accomplished over the previous seven years. CDI researchers stated that there was no visible link between the three major leftist Italian extremist groups: the NTA, BR-PCC, and NIPR (Revolutionary Proletarian Initiative Nuclei). The CDI report further declared that a future consolidation was unlikely to occur.

On the other hand, in the same CDI report, its researchers had found other experts who contended that these three left-wing extremist groups had already merged together. With such differing opinions, researchers from the CDI concluded that, along with information gathered from Italian government and law enforcement agencies, the three groups were at times joining forces with respect to their individual operations but were most likely not in a position in the near future to formally merge together or even to jointly plan attacks of any major significance.

In 2003, the NTA claimed responsibility for three arson attacks against U.S. Army vehicles and personnel at the Aviano and Ederle military bases in Italy.

Throughout its existence, the majority of NTA activities were limited to small-scale attacks against government buildings, properties, and symbols in Italy and the European Union, along with U.S. air bases in both regions. According to the article "Anti-Imperialist Territorial Nuclei (NTA) a.k.a. Anti-Imperialist Territorial Units" (which was written between January 2004 and August 2005) by the Overseas Security Advisory Council (OSAC, which is under the direction of the U.S. Department of State), there has been no reported activity by the group since January 2004, at which time the arrest of its founder and leader occurred. (The leader's name had not been released to the public as of November 2005.)

According to the MIPT article, there have been no known attacks by the NTA in 2005. As of 2005, as reported within the CDI article, no known convictions or arrests have ever been made of any members of the NTA. In addition, there is no known information that supports the contention that the NPT is provided outside financial or material assistance in carrying out its terrorist activities.

KEY EVENTS

1995: NTA is formed.

1999: During the NATO intervention in Kosovo, NTA members bomb the Venice and Rome headquarters of the then-ruling party, Democrats of the Left.

2000: NTA makes its first coordinated attack on the Institute for Foreign Trade and on the Central European Initiative, both in Triest.

2001: NTA bombs the Venice Law Courts/Tribunal Building.

2002: NTA's raid on the Rivolto Military Air Base is prevented by police.

2002: Italian law enforcement officials acquire NTA leaflets identifying officials in the Italian government as assassination targets.

2003: NTA claims responsibility for three attacks against U.S. Army vehicles and personnel at military bases in Italy.

2004: The NTA's leader is reportedly arrested.

PHILOSOPHY AND TACTICS

The goals and ideology of the NTA are to change Italy into a proletarian state (that is, one ruled by working class people with a Marxist economic system). Since the group is primarily a communistic/socialistic-type group, it is against the philosophy of free-market capitalism, especially the political and economic policies (what it calls imperialism) of the North Atlantic Treaty Organization (NATO) and the United States. It also denounces and condemns Italy's economic, foreign relations, and labor policies. In addition, the leaders of the NTA are opposed to the country of Israel and its Jewish citizens.

Much of the philosophy, propaganda, and symbolism of the NTA have been directly derived from the older terrorist group, the Red

Brigades. The historically well-known left-wing terrorist organization Red Brigades worked under a Marxist-Leninist ideology in Italy during the 1970s and early 1980s. Like the NTA, the Red Brigades also attempted to overthrow the Italian democratic government in order to replace it with its own governmental system. The currently operating offshoot of the Red Brigades is called the Red Brigades-Combatant Communist Party (BR-CCP) or simply the New Red Brigades. The NTA has been frequently linked to the BR-CCP.

To achieve its goals the NTA has bombed or otherwise attacked various Italian governmental and political sites, as well as U.S., NATO, and European Union targets in Italy. The NTA has also threatened Italian leaders with assassination. The NTA often plants pamphlets or group paraphenalia at the scenes of its attacks in order to claim responsibility for them and increase their visibility.

The NTA is thought to be interested in uniting Italy's various left-wing extremist organizations into a single group, including such ally organizations as the New Red Brigades and the NIPR. According to the MIPT article, leaders of the NTA have devoted much effort and spent large amounts of money on activities to merge its group with other left-wing extremist groups in Italy. CDI researchers believe that the NTA hope to join forces with the BR-PCC in order to create a stronger, larger, and more technically advanced extremist group. With such an alliance, CDI officials contend that the NIPR would also merge with the NTA/BR-PCC because it is already allied with the BR-PCC. In theory a single, larger, group would be better able to carry out the NTA's goals of attacking (and eventually overthrowing) the Italian government and U.S. and European Union interests in Italy.

The MIPT believes that the NTA is part of a cohesive network of Marxist-Leninist groups in Italy. Other experts contend that the NPT acts alone or in a loose alliance with other similar groups. However organized—either as an individual group or part of a larger group—the NTP has cooperated with other Italian extremist groups over the years. These coordinated efforts have resulted in increased violence, including murders and assassinations of high-ranking officials.

OTHER PERSPECTIVES

Because it models itself after the Red Brigades, most extremist group and terrorism experts view the philosophy of the NTA as being very similar to the classical form of communism that was practiced after the Russian Revolution of 1917—rather than the modern version of communism that is seen in the twenty-first century.

In fact, according to the CDI article, the NTA does not promote any new or relevant issues that are currently popular in Italy. The Italian chief public prosecutor Guido Papalia, according to the MIPT article, reiterated this belief when he stated that the NTA had not in the past nor does it currently (as of 2005) recognize modern-day protests such as extreme-leftist arguments against expanding globalization and the practices of the European Union.

SUMMARY

Since it was formed in 1995, the NTA has been carrying out minor terrorist attacks, especially in the Friuli-Venezia Giulia (or Tri-Veneto) region in northeastern Italy. The rate of violent activities by the NTA has steadily increased nearly every year of its existence. When it was discovered in 2002 that leaders of the NTA were changing their tactics to include the killing of people rather than just the destruction of property, Italian government officials were concerned that the group would step up its terrorist activities. However, little increase in terror activities was actually seen.

Experts at the CDI have concluded, as of early 2005, that the threat from NTA members to the Italian government, its European interests, and to U.S. and European Union interests is "fairly limited." The CDI further concluded that such a limited threat to the Italian government and to Italy in general will most likely remain in the future unless the NTA merges with the Red Brigades-Combatant Communist Party.

As of 2005, several experts within organizations that track the activities of the NTA have given its membership a range from one to 20, but the majority of reports hold its members at the higher number. It is currently unclear if the NTA has merged or intends to merge in the near future with the BR-PCC or with other leftist extremist

PRIMARY SOURCE

Anti-Imperialist Territorial Nuclei (NTA) a.k.a. Anti-Imperialist Territorial Units

DESCRIPTION

The NTA is a clandestine leftist extremist group that first appeared in Italy's Friuli region in 1995. Adopted the class struggle ideology of the Red Brigades of the 1970s and 1980s and a similar logo—an encircled five-point star—for their declarations. Seeks the formation of an "anti-imperialist fighting front" with other Italian leftist terrorist groups, including Revolutionary Proletarian Initiative Nuclei and the New Red Brigades. Opposes what it perceives as US and NATO imperialism and condemns Italy's foreign and labor polices. In a leaflet dated January 2002, NTA identified experts in four Italian Government sectors—federalism, privatizations, justice reform, and jobs and pensions—as potential targets.

ACTIVITIES

To date, NTA has conducted attacks only against property. During the NATO intervention in Kosovo in 1999, NTA members threw gasoline bombs at the Venice and Rome headquarters of the then-ruling party, Democrats of the Left. NTA claimed responsibility for a bomb attack in September 2000 against the Central European Initiative office in Trieste and a bomb attack in August 2001 against the Venice Tribunal building. In January 2002, police thwarted an attempt by four NTA members to enter the Rivolto Military Air Base. In 2003, NTA claimed responsibility for the arson attacks against three vehicles belonging to US troops serving at the Ederle and Aviano bases in Italy. There has been no reported activity by the group since the arrest in January 2004 of NTA's founder and leader.

STRENGTH

Accounts vary from one to approximately 20 members.

LOCATION/AREA OF OPERATION

Primarily northeastern Italy and near US military installations in northern Italy.

EXTERNAL AID

None evident.

Source: U.S. Department of State. *Country Reports on Terrorism.* Washington, D.C., 2004.

---

groups in Italy. However, its limited activities tend to show that it has not merged with such groups.

SOURCES

Periodicals

"Italian Northeast Seen as Fertile Recruitment Ground for Terrorism." *BBC.* March 24, 2002.

Web sites

Federation of American Scientists. "Anti-Imperialist Territorial Nuclei (NTA)." < http://www.fas.org/irp/world/para/nta.htm > (accessed August 1, 2005).

MIPT Terrorism Knowledge Base, National Memorial Institute for the Prevention of Terrorism (MIPT). "Anti-Imperialist Territorial Nuclei for the Construction of the Fighting Communist Party." < http://tkb.org/Group.jsp?groupID = 16 > (accessed August 1, 2005).

Overseas Security Advisory Council (OSAC). "Anti-Imperialist Territorial Nuclei (NTA) a.k.a. Anti-Imperialist Territorial Units." < http://www.ds-osac.org/Groups/group.cfm?contentID = 1306 > (accessed September 25, 2005).

SEE ALSO

Red Brigades (Br)

Kosovo Liberation Army (KLA)

Arkan's Tigers (or Serbian Volunteer Guard)

ALTERNATE NAME: Serbian Volunteer Guard
LEADER: Zeljko Raznatovic (Arkan)
YEAR ESTABLISHED OR BECAME ACTIVE: 1990
USUAL AREA OF OPERATION: Former Yugoslavia

OVERVIEW

The Serbian Volunteer Guard (SDG/ SSJ) was a semiofficial militia active in the Yugoslavian Civil War. Led by Zeljko Raznatovic (better known as Arkan), the group was accused of a number of incidents of ethnic cleansing in Croatia and Bosnia-Herzegovina, and was later implicated in the Kosovan war. The SDG has also been implicated in extortion, gun-running, political executions, and smuggling.

HISTORY

Besides the Holocaust against Europe's Jewish population, of all the regions involved in World War II, the people of Yugoslavia were struck most brutally by ethnic conflict and civil war. More than one million Yugoslavs died in the war, mostly at the hands of other Yugoslavs.

Following Axis occupation in 1941, the Nazis installed Croatian fascists, called the Ustasha, to control their own state, and later Bosnia. With a force that left even some Nazis shocked, the Ustasha carried out a program of genocide and forced religious conversion against Croatia and Bosnia's Serb population. The Serbs responded with the creation of a force known as the Chetniks—a loose alliance of Serb nationalists and royalists—seeking the

LEADERSHIP

ZELJKO RAŽNATOVIC (ARKAN)

Zeljko Ražnatovic was born into a Yugoslav military family—his father was a senior air officer in the air force—in Slovenia, in 1952. A teenage delinquent, his father got him involved with the Yugoslavian internal security service, the Ubda, with whom he retained a connection while embarking on a lucrative criminal career in exile. Across northern Europe in the latter 1970s, Ražnatovic was involved in a series of bank robberies and in other violent crimes, linked to Yugoslav crime families in Frankfurt, Norway, and the Benelux countries. It was during this period that he picked up the *nom de guerre*, Arkan. He was caught often, but had a remarkable habit of escaping jail—in the Netherlands and Germany—and evading arrest—in Sweden and Italy. This is often attributed to his involvement with Ubda. In return, he is believed to have carried out a number of assassinations for Tito.

He returned to Belgrade in 1986 a rich man, and developed extensive business interests, some legitimate—he owned Belgrade's best cake shop—others patently not. His involvement with Red Star Belgrade's "Ultra" fans brought him close to extreme Serb nationalist hooligans, from whom he could pick recruits for his criminal gang, and from 1990–1991, a paramilitary force—the Serbian Volunteer Guard (SDG) or, more commonly, the Tigers.

While helping Serb authorities in destabilizing Croatia in the fall of 1990, he was arrested for illegal possession of weapons, but Slobodan Milosevic bought his freedom—for one million German marks—and he returned to Belgrade six months later, boasting he would soon "be back in Zagreb to open a cake shop on Republic Square."

The deal showed how closely Arkan was involved with the Milosevic government, and he soon returned to Croatia to do the Serb government's bidding: providing brutality when called upon, but distant enough to provide the cover of deniability. At the same time, Arkan courted publicity, mixing with Western journalists and even allowing an embedded photographer to follow his militia. To ethnic Croats and later to Bosnian Muslims and Kosovans, he was feared like no other; to the West, his implication in atrocities, such as that at Vukavor, saw him despised; but to Serb nationalists, he was an adored figure, a glamorous hero that was loved and lionized. In 1995, he married Ceca, Yugoslavia's most famous pop star, in a lavish ceremony broadcast on national television.

The Dayton Accords required the dissolution of the SDG, but Arkan retained many of his key Tigers to operate his increasingly criminalized business empire. Many of the rest remained semi-dormant, but his ability to pick his paramilitary force for the Kosovo conflict showed that Dayton had barely been observed in letter and not at all in spirit.

His business interests and forays into politics made him almost as many enemies among fellow Serbs as his paramilitary activities had done among Croats, and the now former Yugoslavia's Muslims. Following his assassination in January 2000, it was perhaps unsurprising that no one knew the perpetrator's motive as he had so many enemies. It could have been a rival criminal or politician, or a foreign government, Croatian or from beyond.

---

creation of a Greater Serbia. Like the Ustasha, they waged a brutal genocidal campaign, but largely against Bosnia's Croat and Muslim populations, who they viewed as Ustasha collaborators. A third force, the communist Partisans, led by Josip Broz (better known as Tito), was predominantly Serb, but included a large number of Muslims, Croats, and Slovenians (Tito was half Croat, half Slovenian). The Partisans fought a two-fronted campaign against the Axis forces and the Chetniks, both of which they eventually crushed.

From the remnants of the Kingdom of Yugoslavia, Tito formed modern Yugoslavia (comprising a federation of six republics, including Slovenia, Croatia, Bosnia, Serbia, Montenegro, and Macedonia, and two autonomous regions within Serbia: Vojvodina and Kosovo), which he led until his death in 1980. It seemed an unlikely federation, but he suppressed ethnic nationalism and the hatreds carried over from World War II with a policy he called "brotherhood and unity."

When Tito died in 1980, however, Yugoslavia started to come apart. The key figure in the breakup and the hostilities that followed was the Serbian politician, Slobodan Milosevic. He encouraged, and later exploited, Serb nationalism within Serbia and among Serb minorities in other republics as a way of extending his influence. Although, like Tito, a communist, Milosevic exploited the sense of "victimhood" among Yugoslavia's Serbs. He also stripped Kosovo and Vojvodina of their autonomy, taking control of their votes in the rotating presidency that had replaced Tito's rule.

Deeply suspicious of Milosevic's growing power and the impact of his nationalism, Slovenia and Croatia seceded from the Yugoslav federation in 1991. Bosnia was to follow in 1992. Yet, the rumblings of discontent across the Balkans had long been anticipated in Serbia's capital Belgrade, and militias—along the lines of those that had made up Chetnik forces in World War II—had begun to form, often with the support of the Serbian federal government.

What would emerge as the most notorious of these—the Serbian Volunteer Guard, or Tigers—was formed towards the end of 1990 by Zeljko Ražnatovic (Arkan), a Slovenian-born Serb and career criminal. Born into a military family, Arkan had been a delinquent adolescent, turning his energies to theft and football hooliganism. It is believed that his father, a senior officer in the Yugoslav air force, put him in touch with the state security police, the Ubda, as a way of keeping him from trouble. With Ubda's alleged collaboration, Arkan became an international bank robber in the latter half of the 1970s, even escaping from German and Dutch jails. In return for Ubda's apparent support, he carried out assassinations of Tito's enemies abroad.

When he returned to Yugoslavia a rich man in the 1980s, Arkan took control of a series of businesses in Belgrade. His Ubda connection did not end there, however, and they arranged for him—reverting to his adolescent pastime of football hooliganism—to take control of the youth brigades of Red Star Belgrade. As well as being a notoriously violent gang of hooligans, these were among Serbia's most virulent nationalists, and because of their preeminence in European soccer (they would win the European Champions Cup in 1991), arguably the most exposed to the outside world.

In 1990, under the orders of an Interior Ministry chief, Radovan Stojcic (known as Bazda), Arkan's detachment of football hooligans began receiving arms training, in case Belgrade came under attack. They were a well-equipped irregular detachment, which, after Croatia's secession in 1991, became essential to Serb forces seeking to provide the sizeable Serb minority in Croatia with its own little state. Serb forces brutally cleansed parts of eastern Croatia of ethnic Croat civilians. Indeed, as fighting escalated, Arkan's "Tigers" became increasingly important to Milosevic. They could be called upon whenever Belgrade required actions of extreme brutality, but their tentative links with the Milosevic regime afforded the Yugoslav President the option of deniability.

At the heart of the battle in the early stages of the war with Croatia was the prosperous town of Vukavor, near the border with Serbia. This was virtually razed to the ground after a three-month siege in the fall of 1991 and, in November 1991, as it was about to fall to Serb forces, three hundred of the town's remaining Croats took sanctuary in its hospital, where they waited until a deal for their safe passage out of Vukavor was brokered by the Croatian and Serb sides. Yet before this could happen, SDG forces intervened and bussed the patients—mainly Croats—to a deserted field and massacred them. In 1997, the War Crimes Tribunal in the Hague indicted Arkan for leading this massacre.

The Vukavor massacre gained Arkan instant recognition in both the crumbling edifice of Yugoslavia and abroad. In Croatia, and later Bosnia and Kosovo, it meant that when rumors of Arkan's Tigers imminent arrival circulated in villages and towns, the populations would flee *en masse*, fearing for their lives. On the occasions that the Tigers did turn up, they would loot and burn what was left them. To Serbs, by contrast, he was a hero, afforded celebrity status, which was cemented in 1995 when he married the country's most famous pop star, Ceca—an event that was shown on national television.

Internationally, however, the Tigers' actions—coupled with those of other militias, and rogue divisions of the regular Yugoslav Army, such as that led by General Ratko Mladic—led to the dissipation of any political or historical sympathy for Belgrade.

Croatian forces nevertheless fought back, also expelling Serb citizens and becoming implicated in atrocities, in a struggle that would last until 1995.

When Bosnia declared independence in 1992, a conflict there would play out along similar lines. Here, Arkan's troops committed their most heinous crimes. Sweeping across eastern Bosnia, they pillaged towns, villages, and communities, raping, beating, torturing, and killing their victims. Horrific remnants of their crimes would be left—a victim with their eyes gouged out left in the middle of a street in Bielijina (scene of one of the Tigers' most notorious attacks in April 1992), or mutilated Bosnian Muslim bodies left floating in the Drina at the town of Visegrad—as "calling cards," increasing already high levels of panic among the Bosnian Muslim population. Despite international condemnation, Arkan, who spoke fluent English, courted Western journalists and even allowed an American photographer, Ron Haviv, to become "embedded" with the Tigers. Haviv captured many of their atrocities on film.

Under the Dayton Accords, which brought an end to the Bosnian conflict, the SDG were formally disbanded, but in reality remained only semi-dormant, so that they could be called upon in times of a "national emergency." Arkan retained many as his own personal bodyguards as he built on his extensive business operations. He even indulged his old passion for football, buying Obilic, a minor Belgrade team, which was transformed—with his wealth—into Yugoslav national champions, and entered the European Champions League.

Arkan also attempted to enter politics, which brought a public distance with Milosevic, although secretly they apparently remained close. When war broke out in the Serb province of Kosovo in 1998–1999, Arkan urged his men to join the regular army, but in reality they were involved in many of the attacks on Muslim villages that marked an upsurge in the fighting. Arkan based himself in Pristina's main hotel (which he also owned) where he was believed to direct many of the Tigers' operations.

Immediately prior to the NATO bombing of Yugoslavia in March 1999, the UN War Crimes Tribunal made public Arkan's indictment, although he continued to deny the accusations waged against him.

Milosevic was himself indicted in May that year, which increased the pressure on Arkan. In the months that followed, he allegedly ordered the murders of several allies from the Yugoslavian wars, each with the potential to testify that Milosevic had personally sponsored the crimes of which he was accused.

On January 15, 2000, Arkan was assassinated in the lobby of the Intercontinental Hotel in Belgrade. It was initially assumed that his killing had been ordered by foreign agents or rival gangsters. It is since believed that his killing followed a wider pattern of deaths and was carried out on Milosevic's instructions. Whether this was to protect him against Arkan's testimony at the War Crimes Tribunal, or to boost the interests of his son, Marko, who himself had extensive underground interest, remains unclear.

His widow, Ceca, remains a prominent figure in Serbian society, and it is believed that the remnants of the Tigers continue to run the late warlord's underworld interests.

PHILOSOPHY AND TACTICS

The SDG was an extreme Serb nationalist paramilitary organization, which believed in the creation of a Greater Serbia. This ideology calls for the unity of all Serb people—defined by language and belief in Orthodox Christianity—into a single nation state. Its second tenet was a kind of pan-south Slavism, which foresees the acceptance of Serb nationalism and rule over the Balkans.

In some respects, this was a Serb tilt on Yugoslav nationalism, but in practice manifested itself as xenophobia of the worst kind. The SDG were the modern successors of the Chetniks, extreme nationalists who believed that only the ethnic cleansing of "their" lands could see the creation of a workable Greater Serbia.

The SDG's influence was perhaps exaggerated by the nature of its crimes and the charismatic, publicity-seeking presence of its leader, prostitution, and latterly, people-smuggling. Even after Arkan's death, the SDG has retained an important position in the Serbian underworld.

KEY EVENTS

1990–1991: SDG formed from criminal gangs associated with Red Star Belgrade football club

1991: Arkan released after six months in Croatian custody, following a Serb bribe of one million German marks.

1991: SDG emerge as most powerful paramilitary unit in eastern Slavonija (area around Serbo-Croat border).

1991: Vukavor massacre.

1992: Tigers assault on Bosnian town of Bielijina marks entry into Bosnian war.

1995: Dayton Accords call for the dissolution of the SDG.

1998–1999: SDG implicated in disturbances that lead to Kosovo war.

1999: Arkan indicted for war crimes.

2000: Arkan assassinated in Belgrade hotel lobby.

Arkan. It could provoke terror and the evacuation of a dozen villages (and thus successfully ethnically cleanse them) merely by spreading rumor of its intended arrival in a district. This was because of the savagery of the attacks it was involved in, which included not just murder, but torture, rape and mutilation.

Arkan, for his part, was publicity-conscious in the extreme, both among fellow Serbs and to the Western media, which he courted relentlessly. Seldom would the latter report his crimes favourably, but among many Serbs he was seen as a hero and celebrity, a position he cemented with his marriage to Ceca in 1995.

Following the Dayton Accords, which called for its dissolution despite its part in the Kosovo war, the SDG became part of Arkan's criminal empire. Its activities expanded to extortion, smuggling, gun running, assassinations,

OTHER PERSPECTIVES

Arkan's violent death in January 2000 prompted a flurry of speculation, but as of 2005, the answers are no clearer than the speculation that immediately followed his killing.

"Even a brief look at Arkan's life—from bank robber and arms dealer to leadership of one of Serbia's most notorious paramilitary groups—reveals a long list of those who could have wanted him dead," argued Joe Havely in a January 2000 BBC online report. "Consequently conspiracy theories about who was behind the killing are rife. The list of those mentioned in connection with Arkan's death range from Yugoslav President Slobodan Milosevic to rival gangsters, arms dealers, drug smugglers and even Serbian soccer chiefs, angered that Arkan had apparently used his position as the head of Obilic football club to engage in match fixing." Havely also speculated that "Bosnian Muslims, Croats or members of the Kosovo Liberation Army had put a price on his head, or that associates of his superstar 'turbo-folk' singing wife, Ceca, may have been involved."

Nevertheless, Havely wrote, "By far the most popular theory is that Arkan was killed because he knew too much, and possibly because he was about to hand over evidence to international prosecutors implicating President Milosevic in war crimes."

Ultimately, as concluded in *The Observer*: "Few in Belgrade are confident that the authorities will ever truthfully get to the bottom of Arkan's murder."

SUMMARY

The SDG has virtually disappeared from the headlines since the end of Yugoslavia's decade-long civil war. Moreover, the targeted killings of many of its leaders mean it is likely to escape justice in the war crimes tribunal in The Hague. As it struggles towards democracy,

Serbia remains beset by underworld intrigue and Arkan's successors are said to retain a stronghold.

SOURCES

Books

Glenny, Misha. *The Balkans 1804—1999: Nationalism, War and the Great Powers.* London and New York: Granta, 2000.

Periodicals

Calabres, Massimo. "My Tea with Arkan the Henchman." *Time.* April 12, 1999.

Web sites

Havely. Joe. *BBC News Online.* "Arkan Murder Mystery." < http://news.bbc.co.uk/1/hi/world/europe/ > (accessed September 5, 2005).

Human Rights Watch. "Bosnia and Hercegovina Unfinished Business: The Return of Refugees and Displaced Persons to Bijeljin." < http://www.hrw.org/reports/2000/bosnia/index.htm#TopOfPage > (accessed October 17, 2005).

Armed Islamic Group (GIA)

LEADER: Antar Zouabri (longest serving)
YEAR ESTABLISHED OR BECAME ACTIVE: 1992
ESTIMATED SIZE: Less than a hundred
USUAL AREA OF OPERATION: Algeria, France

OVERVIEW

The Armed Islamic Group works with the aim of establishing an Islamic state in Algeria. The organization is known as the *Groupe Islamique Arme* (GIA) in French. Mansour Meliani reportedly started the GIA in 1992, after the Algerian military government did not recognize the victory of the Islamic Salvation Front (FIS) party in the December 1991 elections.

Although GIA's leadership has frequently changed since its inception, the group, as thought by analysts, has operated primarily against eliminating those who it perceives as working in tandem with the government. Algerian government officials state that civilians and entities that do not abide by the group's philosophy are targeted. Citing the violent nature of GIA, several countries, including the United States, Algeria, and France, have declared it as a terrorist organization.

HISTORY

Mansour Meliani claimed to create the GIA in July 1992 after leaving the Islamic Armed Movement (MIA). Soon after its creation, however, Meliani was arrested, reportedly leading to the breakup of the group. In 1993, Abdelhak Layada revived the GIA with a focus on the

Eighteen people were killed and 25 injured when a commuter train near Algiers exploded on February 24, 1998. No person or group claimed responsibility, but the region has often been a target of the militant Armed Islamic Group. AP/Wide World Photos. Reproduced by permission.

ideology of Omar El-Eulmi, an Islamic fundamentalist. Due to internal disagreements the group's leadership changed frequently until Cherif Gousmi became its leader in March 1994.

The GIA engaged in a variety of violent activities throughout Algeria, including bombings, kidnappings, and murders. They are thought to be responsible for thousands of deaths during the 1990s. The GIA was especially active in a region to the south of Algiers, the capital of Algeria. The GIA referred to this region as the "liberated zone," which in 1997–1998 came to be known as the "triangle of death" because of the bloodbath that occurred in the region.

In November 1993, the GIA declared a *fatwa* (declaration of war) against prominent leaders of the FIS. These leaders included Abderrezak Redjam, exiled and United States-based Anwar Haddam, Said Makhloufi, and Mohammed Said. Interestingly, as claimed by experts, these same leaders subsequently joined

the GIA. In August 1994, the group reportedly declared an independent Islamic Algerian government, appointing Cherif Gousmi as the commander, Haddam as the foreign minister, Makhloufi as the interior minister, and Mohammed Said as the government head. Reports suggest that this declaration, however, suffered a massive blow when Makhloufi withdrew from GIA and Haddam claimed never to have had any association with it.

After Gousmi, Djamel Zitouni (alias Abou Aberrahmane Amine) became GIA's new leader. He continued with the group's activities in Algeria and expanded them into France. In December 1994, GIA members hijacked Air France flight 8969. This led to a 54-hour negotiation session that ended with a French anti-terrorist squad storming the plane and killing the hijackers. By then, the terrorists had also killed three hostages. In 1995, according to French government officials, the group attempted several bombings in France.

In cooperation with Algerian anti-terrorist forces (GIS), civilians patrol their village to prevent Armed Islamic Group (GIA) attacks. © Paolo Pellegrin/ Magnum Photos

LEADERSHIP

ANTAR ZOUABRI

The leadership of GIA changes frequently. Some experts also say that GIA appoints multiple leaders at the same time. In spite of the often-changing leadership, Antar Zouabri is reportedly the longest-serving commander, from 1996–2002. He was also allegedly the most ruthless leader, responsible for killing many civilians, including children. The mass murders, especially in the regions of Rais and Bentalha, occurred during Zouabri's reign. Zouabri died at the age of 31, supposedly while fighting with government forces, in 2002.

Abou Tourab took over as the leader after his death. Though not much is known about the group's activities as of 2005, the Algerian Ministry of the Interior confirmed Abou Tourab's death in July 2004, at the hands of his own associates. The Ministry also claims to have arrested GIA's next leader, Nourredine Boudiafi, but the government has been tight-lipped about giving any further details.

The GIA attempted to keep Algerians from voting in the 1995 national elections through intimidation, proclaiming "one vote, one bullet." Monitor groups, however, argue that after the elections internal disagreements within the group grew rapidly. FIS leaders who had switched loyalties to GIA were supposedly eliminated and, toward the latter part of 1995, other GIA members seemingly refused to acknowledge Zitouni as their leader. Reports claim that some of them even formed separate groups.

Islamic League for Preaching and Combat (GSPC), an offshoot of GIA under the leadership of Ali Benhadjar, is believed to have killed Zitouni in July 1996. Antar Zouabri took over leadership of the GIA. He would maintain control of the GIA until 2002, and under his leadership, Algerian authorities allege that GIA carried out even more terrorist operations and killings.

The GIA is the primary suspect for the August 1997 massacre at Rais village, located south of Algiers. The villagers had initially supported the GIA and other Islamic fundamentalists by regularly providing them food and money. They, however, stopped doing so toward the middle of 1997. The massacre is thought to have been carried out in response to discontinuation of the villagers' support.

In Rais, though officially 98 people were reportedly killed and 120 injured, witnesses and medical personnel estimated 200 killed and approximately double that number wounded. Survivor accounts report a group of terrorists storming into the village around 1:00 a.m. and continuing with violence till 6:00 a.m. Everyone, including men, women, pregnant women, children, and even animals were reportedly executed.

PRIMARY SOURCE
Armed Islamic Group (GIA)

DESCRIPTION

An Islamist extremist group, the GIA aims to overthrow the Algerian regime and replace it with a fundamentalist Islamic state. The GIA began its violent activity in 1992 after the military government suspended legislative elections in anticipation of an overwhelming victory by the Islamic Salvation Front, the largest Islamic opposition party.

ACTIVITIES

The GIA has engaged in attacks against civilians and government workers. Starting in 1992, the GIA conducted a terrorist campaign of civilian massacres, sometimes wiping out entire villages in its area of operation, and killing tens of thousands of Algerians. GIA's brutal attacks on civilians alienated them from the Algerian populace. Since announcing its campaign against foreigners living in Algeria in 1992, the GIA has killed more than 100 expatriate men and women, mostly Europeans, in the country. Many of the GIA's members have joined other Islamist groups or been killed or captured by the Algerian Government. The GIA's most recent significant attacks were in August, 2001.

STRENGTH

Precise numbers are unknown, but probably fewer than 100.

LOCATION/AREA OF OPERATION

Algeria, Sahel (i.e. northern Mali, northern Mauritania, and northern Niger), and Europe.

EXTERNAL AID

The GIA has members in Europe that provide funding.

Source: U.S. Department of State. *Country Reports on Terrorism*. Washington, D.C., 2004.

In September 1997 another massacre took place at Bentalha, a small town south of Algiers and only a short distance away from the village of Rais. The GIA is also thought to be responsible for this attack. Equipped with a variety of weapons, the members of GIA came to the town and allegedly killed everyone in sight. News reports also state various incidents of robbery. According to Amnesty International, 200 people were killed in this attack.

Zouabri was reportedly killed in a February 2002 encounter with Algerian forces. Abou Tourab (alias Rachid Oukali) was named the next GIA leader after Zouabri. Tourab's main aim as the GIA leader is thought to be that of advancing the group's activities until Algeria became an Islamic state. However, not much is known about him or other leaders subsequent to Zouabri. By the late 1990s the GIA appears to have become lost active. The huge number of deaths blamed on the GIA had gained it much notoriety but cost the group local support. Also, many of its members took advantage of a pardon offered in 1999, gave up fighting, and attempted to return to normal life.

PHILOSOPHY AND TACTICS

The GIA claims that its mission is to replace the democratically chosen government in Algeria with an Islamic state. It is a non-secular group that views all opposing individuals and organizations as anti-Islam. Beyond its aim of establishing an Islamic government in Algeria, the GIA has not come out with any other political agenda. Experts state that the group is also against the government and people of France, Algeria's former colonial ruler.

As part of their tactics and propagation of ideology, the GIA is alleged by Algerian government officials to have killed thousands in numerous acts of terror. According to the Islamic fundamentalists who are members of this organization, everyone with or supporting

KEY EVENTS

1993: GIA kidnapped three French diplomats in Algiers; the group reportedly claimed responsibility for the kidnapping after a few days, killed a police officer who tried to avert the kidnapping; later, the GIA released all the kidnapped diplomats unharmed.

1993: Attacked the construction site of a hydro-electric project in Tamezguida, Algeria, abducting 14 Croatian workers, of which 12 workers were allegedly killed, while the remaining two Croatians escaped with some injuries.

1994: Attacked a French residential area in Algiers, killing five French embassy officers and injuring one.

1994: Hijacked Air France flight 8969 going from Algiers to Paris.

1997: Alleged massacre of the Rais village.

1997: Alleged massacre of Bentalha.

1999: GIA declared *jihad* (holy war) against France.

2002: Antar Zouabri, the longest-serving leader of GIA, reportedly killed while fighting the government forces.

2003: The Algerian government's antiterrorist units captured Abou Tourab (successor to Zouabri).

the Algerian government harbor anti-Islamic sentiments and, therefore, are a target. In the GIA's view, artists, scholars, teachers, academicians, musicians, sports enthusiasts, women moving around without a veil, and all foreigners working in Algeria, including officers working in embassies, are potential targets.

According to the GIA, children killed as part of their operations are considered to be martyrs who end up giving their lives to a "noble" cause. The GIA has resorted to car bombings and assassinations as part of their strategy. The group, reportedly, kills people by slitting their throats. Other violent activities the group resorts to are hijackings and massacres of civilians.

Most members of the group are thought to be Berbers (native North Africans) based primarily in the Atlas Mountains (in northern Algeria). Anti-terrorism experts state that an extremely high rate of unemployment in the region drives young Algerian men to join the GIA and other similar groups. Additionally, Afghans who have been trained in the numerous training camps of Afghanistan are thought to comprise a significant portion of the group.

According to news reports, the GIA might be in some way connected to al-Qaeda, Osama bin Laden's terrorist network. There is, however, no proof of the existence or the extent of this connection. The link, if it exists, is thought to be limited in nature. Some news agencies suggest that the GIA may have connections with *Al Hayat*, a Saudi newspaper published from Beirut, Paris, and London.

In the past, to generate funds, the GIA allegedly imposed taxes on the people of the villages that group members lived in, robbed banks, and raided villages. In addition, they are also reported to acquire money from the governments of Sudan and Iran, and from Algerian nationals living abroad, especially in Western Europe. To equip themselves for their activities, they purportedly stole arms and ammunition from police stations, as well as from police and military men who died in the encounters with them.

Since the late 1990s and early in the 2000s, the GIA is thought to have lost its edge, while other militant groups have emerged as potential threats to the government of Algeria. The government has also claimed to disrupt several smaller cells of the GIA. The International Institute for Strategic Studies estimates the strength of the GIA to be in the hundreds. However, according to published reports from the U.S. Department of State, as of 2005, the GIA is estimated to have less than 100 members.

OTHER PERSPECTIVES

Although the Algerian government claim that the GIA is responsible for most of the terrorist attacks Algeria suffered in the 1990s, they have rarely made public statements against the group.

PRIMARY SOURCE

Algeria Reveals Rebel Crackdown

The leader of a radical Islamic rebel group in Algeria has been arrested and his deputy has been killed, the Interior Ministry has said.

Security services detained Nourredine Boudiafi, head of the Armed Islamic Group (GIA), in the eastern Algiers suburb of Bab Ezzouar in November.

His deputy, Chaabane Younes, was killed in Chlef, 210km (160 miles) west of Algiers, the ministry added.

The GIA has already been weakened by internal rivalries, the statement said.

The ministry statement did not give precise details of Mr Boudiafi's arrest or of the killing of Mr Younes.

But it said his arrest followed the killing of Mr Boudiafi's predecessor, Rachid Ouakali, alias Abu Tourab, in July by his own men so that Mr Boudiafi could take over.

WANING POWER

The GIA was the most radical of Algeria's armed Islamic movements, says the BBC's Mohamed Arezki Himeur in Algiers.

It has been behind the majority of attacks and assassinations targeting intellectuals, journalists and foreigners.

The group was also responsible for the bloody hijacking of an Air France airbus in December 1994 at Algiers airport, and a series of civilian massacres in several parts of the country during the 1990s.

But its power started to wane at the end of the 1990s following the death of leader Djamel Zitouni by Islamic rivals in an ambush, says our correspondent.

The battle for the leadership led to internal divisions and rivalries that sparked the establishment of other armed groups.

The Salafist group, GSPC—considered today to be the most important armed Islamic movement—was born in 1998 out of the wrangling of the GIA.

Source: BBC News, 2005

However, as reported by CNN in 1997, after the Rais massacre, the then-prime minister of Algeria, while referring to the GIA, stated that "Algerians were being killed each day in remote communities." The report also states that soon after launching a manhunt against the group, a statement issued by the government read, "The state will continue to struggle without mercy against the barbarous criminals until their eradication."

That said, news reports from CNN, Associated Press, and Amnesty International (among others) claim that survivors and dissident military officers have questioned the many killings credited to the GIA. Accounts from these survivors quite often point toward complete destruction of entire villages, at times in spite of military camps being in the vicinity. According to most of these reports, while the GIA is clearly

responsible for carrying out several of the many documented killing episodes, the government and associated paramilitary setups also carried out some of these bloodsheds in the GIA style to generate opposition against the group.

A survivor account given to Amnesty International in 1997 states, " 'The army and the security forces were right there; they heard and saw everything and did nothing, and they let the terrorists leave.... They waited for the terrorists to finish their dirty task and then they let them leave. What does this mean to you?' "

SUMMARY

The GIA was most active during the 1990s when it reportedly carried out massive bombings, hijackings, kidnappings, and killings of civilians. In the decade-long violence that the GIA unleashed, thousands of people have been reported killed, and many properties have been destroyed.

Toward the end of 1990s, GIA became extremely notorious for its anti-civilian activities, seemingly losing local support. At the time, the then-elected Algerian President Abdelaziz Bouteflika started a massive campaign against such militants and their organizations. He also offered pardon to members of these groups, including those of the GIA. Consequently, in accordance with the 1999 amnesty law and concord agreements, which the GIA reportedly rejected, several of its members gave up the life of a terrorist, entered the mainstream, and started living like other people. Due to this, the group is no longer considered as active as it was and many of its members are thought to be based in the United States and other places outside Algeria.

SOURCES

Periodicals

"Algeria reveals rebel crackdown." *BBC News (UK edition)*. January 4, 2005.

Web sites

CNN.com. "Islamic Terrorists Slaughter Algerian Villagers." < http://edition.cnn.com/WORLD/9708/29/ algeria.new/ > (accessed September 25, 2005).

Associated Press. "Hundreds of Villagers Killed in Algeria's Worst Massacre." < http://www.southcoasttoday. com/daily/08-97/08-30-97/a03wn016.htm > (accessed September 25, 2005).

Amnesty International. "Algeria: A Human Rights Crisis: Civilians Caught in a Spiral of Violence." < http://web.amnesty.org/library/Index/ > (accessed July 28, 2005).

Human Rights Watch Group. "Algeria: Human Rights Development." < http://www.hrw.org/worldreport99/ mideast/algeria.html > (accessed September 25, 2005).

Army for the Liberation of Rwanda

OVERVIEW

The Army for the Liberation of Rwanda (ALIR; also known as Democratic Forces for the Liberation of Rwanda, FDLR) is an irregular force representing the 1994 amalgamation of Rwanda's Former Armed Forces (FAR) and the Interahamwe, a Hutu civilian militia. Both groups are held largely responsible for the deaths of 937,000 Tutsi and other regime opponents in Rwanda's 1994 genocide. The group in 2005, mostly in exile in the Democratic Republic of Congo, seeks to replace Rwanda's Tutsi-dominated government with Hutu control and possibly complete the genocide.

ALTERNATE NAME: Democratic Forces for the Liberation of Rwanda

LEADER: Tharcisse Renzaho

YEAR ESTABLISHED OR BECAME ACTIVE: 1994

USUAL AREA OF OPERATION: Rwanda; Democratic Republic of Congo; Uganda

HISTORY

Rwanda's 1994 genocide was one of the defining events of the twentieth century, ending the illusion that genocide belonged to the past. Just as shocking as the deaths of nearly one million Tutsis and moderate Hutus, was the intensity of the killings—most were carried out within a period of just 100 days—and the complicity of the United Nations, France and the United States, each of which ignored warnings about the massacres and/or refused to intervene.

The genocide owed its origins to a post-colonial power struggle, but it is initially difficult

Rebel soldiers regard 12 lime-covered bodies on September 15, 1998, in Goma, Congo. Congo rebels maintain the people were victims of the Interahamwe, a group responsible for the 1994 Rwandan genocide in which more than 500,000 people were murdered. AP/Wide World Photos. Reproduced by permission.

to fathom given the inherent similarities between Hutu and Tutsi peoples. As Human Rights Watch's definitive and exhaustive report on the killings "Leave None to Tell The Story" makes clear: "For centuries they had shared a single language, a common history, the same ideas and cultural practices. They lived next to one another, attended the same schools and churches, worked in the same offices, and drank in the same bars. A considerable number of Rwandans were of mixed parentage, the offspring of Hutu-Tutsi marriages."

Rwanda was one of the few African nations to follow its historical borders. The kingdom of Rwanda had been controlled by a Tutsi royal family, but Hutus had also held places in the nobility. Despite holding power, Tutsis historically made up a minority within the country, albeit a significant one, accounting for between a sixth and a fifth of Rwanda's population.

The country was governed by German, then Belgian, colonial overlords, but the Tutsis were favored, particularly by the Belgians, who heightened racial divisions with a divide and rule policy. By giving the Tutsis some of the scraps of colonial rule, they could control the Hutu majority, but they accentuated divisions by getting the Tutsis to do their bidding for them. They gave credence to the writings of the nineteenth-century anthropologist, John Hanning Speke, who believed that Tutsis had "nobler," more "naturally" aristocratic features than the "coarse" and "bestial" Hutus. The view of the first bishop of Rwanda, Leon Classe, was typical. He warned in 1930 that any attempt to replace Tutsi chiefs with "uncouth" Hutus "would lead the entire state directly into anarchy," adding "we have no chiefs who are better qualified, more active, more capable of appreciating progress...than the Tutsi."

After World War II, Rwanda was placed under UN trusteeship, although the Belgians essentially remained power-brokers until 1959 when free elections brought the Hutu Nationalist Party of the Hutu Emancipation Movement

PRIMARY SOURCE

Democratic Forces for the Liberation of Rwanda (FDLR) a.k.a. Army for the Liberation of Rwanda (ALIR), Ex-FAR/Interahamwe

DESCRIPTION

The Democratic Forces for the Liberation of Rwanda (FDLR) in 2001 supplanted the Army for the Liberation of Rwanda (ALIR), which is the armed branch of the PALIR, or the Party for the Liberation of Rwanda. ALIR was formed from the merger of the Armed Forces of Rwanda (FAR), the army of the ethnic Hutu-dominated Rwandan regime that orchestrated the genocide of 500,000 or more Tutsis and regime opponents in 1994, and Interahamwe, the civilian militia force that carried out much of the killing, after the two groups were forced from Rwanda into the Democratic Republic of Congo (DRC—then Zaire) that year. Though directly descended from those who organized and carried out the genocide, identified FDLR leaders are not thought to have played a role in the killing. They have worked to build bridges to other opponents of the Kigali regime, including ethnic Tutsis.

ACTIVITIES

ALIR sought to topple Rwanda's Tutsi-dominated Government, reinstitute Hutu domination, and, possibly, complete the genocide. In 1996, a message—allegedly from the ALIR—threatened to kill the US ambassador to Rwanda and other US citizens. In 1999, ALIR guerrillas critical of US-UK support for the Rwandan regime kidnapped and killed eight foreign tourists, including two US citizens, in a game park on the Democratic Republic of Congo-Uganda border. Three suspects in the attack are in US custody awaiting trial. In the 1998–2002 Congolese war, the ALIR/FDLR was allied with Kinshasa against the Rwandan invaders. FDLR's political wing mainly has sought to topple the Kigali regime via an alliance with Tutsi regime opponents. It established the ADRN Igihango alliance in 2002, but it has not resonated politically in Rwanda.

STRENGTH

Exact strength is unknown, but several thousand FDLR guerrillas operate in the eastern DRC close to the Rwandan border. In 2003, the United Nations, with Rwandan assistance, repatriated close to 1,500 FDLR combatants from the DRC. The senior FDLR military commander returned to Rwanda in November 2003 and has been working with Kigali to encourage the return of his comrades.

LOCATION/AREA OF OPERATION

Mostly in the eastern Democratic Republic of the Congo.

EXTERNAL SUPPORT

The Government of the Democratic Republic of the Congo provided training, arms, and supplies to ALIR forces to combat Rwandan armed forces that invaded the DRC in 1998. Kinshasa halted that support in 2002, though allegations persist of continued support from several local Congolese warlords and militias (including the Mai Mai).

Source: U.S. Department of State. *Country Reports on Terrorism.* Washington, D.C., 2004.

(PARMEHUTU) to power. Racial tensions built up over the preceding half century were played out during the elections, with some 20,000 Tutsis killed and a further 200,000 fleeing the country. PARMEHUTU established one-party rule until 1973 when a military coup brought Juvenal Habyarimana to power, but he too relied on Hutu nationalism for his power base. Pogroms carried out against the Tutsi minority in 1964 and 1974 killed large numbers.

By the 1980s, up to half a million Tutsis lived in exile, many in refugee camps in neighboring Uganda. In their own right, they were a powerful force, fighting alongside Ugandans to depose Uganda's dictator, Milton Obote, in 1985. A Tutsi-dominated Rwandese Patriotic Front

(RPF) was established in 1985 under the leadership of Paul Kagame, with the aim of bringing out their right to return and as a force to bring recognition of Tutsi rights.

The RPF invaded Rwanda from their Ugandan base in October 1990, plunging the country into a 22-month-long civil war. President Habyarimana played out the conflict as a Tutsi attempt to enslave the Hutu race; Hutu nationalism escalated, racial tensions increased. Peace was nevertheless agreed in August 1992, with accords signed 12 months later that gave a timetable for power-sharing.

Tensions, however, remained high, and Hutus, with government backing, began to organize into a militia, called the Interahamwe. By 1994, this was 30,000 strong and heavily armed.

On April 6, 1994 the jet carrying President Habyarimana was shot down. Who carried out this attack remains a mystery. It has been suggested that it was probably Hutu extremists close to Habyarimana concerned at moves to share power with the RPF. Either way, the attack was blamed on Tutsis. The following morning, the moderate Hutu Prime Minister, Agathe Uwilingiyimana, along with the 10 Belgian UN troops protecting her, was murdered by the Presidential Guard.

The murders seemed to provide the signal for the onset of an extraordinary period of killing by the FAR and Interahamwe militia. From that point until the start of July, the army and militia embarked upon a massacre that would claim 937,000 lives. Most victims were Tutsis, but some moderate Hutus were killed too (the term "moderate" encompassed those who backed power-sharing on a political level, or merely those—and their families—who refused the exhortations to join the bloodletting in the towns and villages of Rwanda). The orgy of violence seemed even more horrific given the Hutu weapon of choice—the machete—and the torture, rape, and mutilation that often accompanied killings.

The UN (UNAMIR) force in Rwanda appealed to its Security Council for reinforcements, but was rebuffed. Many have since laid the blame at the door of U.S. President Clinton, who sought to avoid a repeat of U.S. peacekeeping failings in Somalia a year earlier. Kofi Annan, the UN's future Secretary General, but then undersecretary for peacekeeping operations, insisted on his organization's "impartiality," even

KEY EVENTS

1994: Murder of Rwandan President Habyarimana is the pretext for Rwanda's Armed Forces (FAR) and the Hutu Interahamwe militia to embark on an extraordinary murder spree of Tutsi and moderate Hutus. The genocide lasts 100 days.

1994: Rwandese Patriotic Front repel the genocide and force the army and militia into neighboring Zaire. ALIR formed.

1994–2000: Border raids launched by ALIR (later Democratic Republic of Congo) against Tutsis in Rwanda, and also against Zairian Tutsis.

1999: Murder of eight tourists in Uganda.

in the face of genocide. Indeed, the frustrated and impotent UNAMIR force was depleted to just 260 men after the withdrawal of Belgian troops following the murder of 10 of its men with Uwilingiyimana. Even when the UN belatedly sent reinforcements, their deployment was delayed further by wrangling over cost.

Indeed, it was only RPF forces that repelled the genocide. Its battalion based in Kigali came under immediate attack following the presidential assassination, but fought its way out to the north of the country where it was joined by RPF forces previously based in Uganda and Tanzania. Over May and June 1994, it battled FRA and Interahamwe forces, with the massacres going on concurrently, until, at the start of July it exacted victory with two million Hutu refugees and defeated soldiers and militiamen fleeing to Burundi, Tanzania, Uganda, and Zaire.

It was in Zaire that the Army for the Liberation of Rwanda (ALIR) formed from the remnants of FRA and Interahamwe forces. Essentially, it was a broken force at first—albeit one consisting of upwards of 30,000 men—with its downtrodden members living in appalling conditions in the refugee camps of Zaire. However, the ALIR soon began initiating raids against Zairian Tutsis and across the border into Rwanda. In 1996, it also issued a death threat to the U.S. Ambassador to Rwanda and other U.S. citizens. The motivation behind this was seemingly the fact that the United States had been among the first countries to recognize the RPF government.

In November 1996, the increasingly embattled Tutsi population of the South Kivu Province of Zaire was expelled on the threat of death. They erupted into rebellion, which spread across Zaire, and joined Laurent Kabila's Alliance of Democratic Forces for the Liberation of Zaire (AFDL), which was also given support by the Rwandan and Ugandan governments. This became known as the "First Congo War," and although ALIR fought against AFDL forces, theirs was a small role. In July 1997, Kabila succeeded in defeating the forces of Zairian President Mobuto Sese-Seko.

Once in power, however, Kabila soon changed tack—wary of Rwandan presence within the new Democratic Republic of Congo (DRC)—and, in August 1998, ordered all ethnic Tutsis from his government and all Rwandan and Ugandan officials out of the DRC.

Rwanda and Uganda then turned on their former ally, invading almost immediately. This marked the onset of four years of war, which would prove more bloody and horrific than even the Rwandan genocide.

During its course, Kabila provided extensive support to the ALIR, which not only fought with his forces, but continued to direct assaults on Tutsi populations on each side of the Rwandan/DRC border. They also carried out its threat against U.S. citizens when it orchestrated the kidnapping and murder of eight foreign tourists, including two Americans, in a Ugandan nature reserve in 1999.

Under the terms of the treaty that brought an end to the Second Congo War in 2002, the ALIR were meant to disband in exchange for a Rwandan exit from the DRC. Officially, Congolese support was ended, although the U.S. Department of State has published allegations that the ALIR receives backing from a number of Congolese warlords.

LEADERSHIP

THARCISSE RENZAHO

Tharcisse Renzaho was Prefect (Mayor) of Kigali prior to the genocide, and held control over the city's police force. Yet far from using his position to prevent the genocide, it has been alleged that he was zealous in coordinating the planning of the slaughter in the city, and served as a colonel in the KAR forces. The International Criminal Tribunal for Rwanda indictment against him accuses him of having "de jure and de facto control over the armed forces who were under his authority, whom he could order to commit or to refrain from committing unlawful acts, and whom he could discipline or punish for unlawful acts or omissions."

Following the genocide, he fled to Zaire where he was among the most active of the Hutu genocide suspects in exile, serving as a divisional commander of ALIR until 1996. He was arrested by DRC officials in September 2002, and handed over to the International Criminal Tribunal for Rwanda. He currently awaits trial.

PHILOSOPHY AND TACTICS

The ALIR's avowed aim is to topple the Rwandan government of Paul Kagame and return Hutu power to the country. An assumed aim is that they also wish to finish the 1994 genocide.

However, because it has fought in so many conflicts and in so many guises, pinning down the tactics of the ALIR is rather more difficult.

During the Rwandan massacre, Rwanda's Former Armed Forces (FAR) and the Interahamwe organized the killing by manning road blocks, cutting off villages, and exhorting the Hutu population to turn on their neighbors. Arms, widely spread leading up to the massacre, were used with savage frequency. They also turned on moderate Hutus who refused to comply with the bloodletting.

As the ALIR, they have fought much as a conventional army, either carrying out raids on Tutsi villages or in fighting Rwandan forces in the DRC.

Their "conventional" terrorist attacks on Westerners have been limited, but its most notorious attack, on holidaymakers in Uganda, was carefully targeted. This was a revenge attack for Ugandan involvement in the RPF invasions of Rwanda and the DRC. Uganda, which is heavily reliant on tourist dollars, found its holiday industry decimated in the wake of the attacks.

OTHER PERSPECTIVES

"The memory of Rwanda sits like a tumour leaking poison in the back of my head," wrote the former *Reuters* correspondent Aidan Hartley in his memoir of *Africa, the Zanzibar Chest*. Hartley, who had seen virtually every war, famine, and natural disaster suffered by Africa during the late 1980s and 1990s struggled to comprehend what he had witnessed. "History is supposed to explain why events happened as they did. But how do you account for the evil we saw in the green hills of that nation in 1994, where one day we saw a mother with an infant tied to her back gleefully using a machete to hack up another woman also carrying an infant?"

Speaking of his motives for writing an account of the Rwandan massacre, *We Wish to Inform You That Tomorrow We Will Be Killed With Our Families*, the journalist Philip Gourevitch told students at the University of Berkeley that: "The story had been bothering me ... People were murdered at a rate that exceeded by three times the speed the extermination of Jews during the Holocaust. It happened in our time, in front of our noses, somewhat before our cameras. And it vanished very quickly. As soon as the blood was dry, the story disappeared from the newspapers. Nobody really had explained it. When one read the papers it didn't seem to me to make much sense. It was described as anarchy and chaos, which struck me as implausible simply because in order to kill at that clip requires organization, it requires method, it requires mobilization. It requires the opposite of anarchy and chaos. Mass destruction is not

arbitrary, it doesn't just come about willy-nilly ... I felt the story was being told wrong, and casually and cavalierly, and that in some basic way a great calamity had happened which we were quite content to be ignorant of."

SUMMARY

The remnants of the ALIR are difficult to pin down, existing as they do in a country—the Democratic Republic of Congo—that is neither their own, nor effectively governed by its leaders. It is possible that it does exist as a unified, albeit diminishing force, seeking to overthrow Rwanda's Tutsi rulers and also evade the attentions of the International Criminal Tribunal for Rwanda. All intelligence suggests, however, that it has been separated into units and absorbed under the command of Congo's many warlords. It may still carry out acts of terrorism against Tutsi and other foreign nationals, but as time progresses it seems an increasingly dormant force.

SOURCES

Books

Courtemanche, Gils. *A Sunday at the Pool in Kigali*. Edinburgh: Canongate Books, 2004.

Dailaire, Romeo. *Shake Hands With the Devil*. New York: Arrow, 1995.

Gourevitch, Philip. *We Wish to Inform You That Tomorrow We Will Be Killed With Our Families*. London: Picador, 2000.

Web sites

Human Rights Watch. "Leave None to Tell the Story." < http://www.hrw.org/reports/1999/rwanda/ > (accessed October 12, 2005).

African Studies Quarterly. "Conventional Wisdom and Rwanda's Genocide." < http://web.africa.ufl.edu/asq/v1/3/10.htm > (accessed October 12, 2005).

Army of God

LEADERS: Currently, Chaplain Pastor Michael Bray; past leaders: Don Benny Anderson, Neal Horsley, James Kopp, and Eric Robert Rudolph

YEAR ESTABLISHED OR BECAME ACTIVE: 1982

ESTIMATED SIZE: Unknown

USUAL AREA OF OPERATION: United States

OVERVIEW

The Army of God is an underground American religious extremist group, the stated mission of which is to utilize violence in order to stop medical clinics, and the staff members working in them, from performing abortions—which they refer to as "baby-killing." In addition to that directive, the Army of God has in recent years taken on the mantle of attacking gay men and lesbians in an effort to put a stop to what they consider the "homosexual agenda," utilizing similar methods to those they have employed at abortion clinics.

Currently, Pastor Michael Bray is the Chaplain of the Army of God. Among his official duties is the hosting of the yearly White Rose Banquet in honor of "soldiers" incarcerated for antiabortion (and possibly, anti-homosexual) violence. He is the author of a book entitled *A Time To Kill*, in which he quotes from the Bible as a means of justifying the use of lethal violence in order to permanently stop people from performing abortions.

HISTORY

The Army of God was organized in 1982, with the express purpose of stopping the performance of abortions, using whatever means are

Adrian Horien, a member of the militant Army of God anti-abortion group, shows his support of James Kopp. Kopp is an anti-abortion activist convicted of shooting Dr. Barnett Slepian, an obstetrician who performed abortions as part of his practice. AP/Wide World Photos. Reproduced by permission.

KEY EVENTS

1973: *Roe v. Wade* legalizes abortion in the United States.

1982: First act of terrorism claimed by the Army of God: kidnapping of doctor and wife at abortion clinic.

1996: Eric Robert Rudolph was charged with the bombing of Olympic park in Atlanta.

1997: Bombings of a gay/lesbian bar in Atlanta.

1997, 1998: Bombings of abortion clinics in Atlanta.

1998: James Kopp was convicted in the shooting death of Dr. Barnett Slepian; Kopp also claims responsibility for at least six similar shootings between 1994 and 1997.

2001: Clayton Waagner claims responsibility for sending more than 550 anthrax threat letters to abortion clinics; on the Army of God web site, he also posted his intent to kill at least 42 specific abortion clinic staff members.

2003: Eric Rudolph was arrested after more than five years of living as a fugitive and charged with the Atlanta bombings.

2005: Eric Rudolph was tried and sentenced in 2005 to life in prison with no possibility of parole in exchange for information leading to the recovery of unexploded dynamite and bombs.

necessary in order to do so. The *Army Manual* explicitly states that this is a "real" army, with the stated mission of choosing violent means both to permanently end the ability of medical personnel to perform abortions and to draw media attention to their opposition to women's right to choose to have abortions.

The Army of God manual is quite explicit in its descriptions of methodology for how to prevent persons from being able to enter abortion clinics and how to construct, obtain, or utilize butyric acid, bombs, and arson as violent means of shutting down clinics. Several members have been arrested, tried, and convicted for these types of activities, as well as for the shooting deaths of clinic staff. It is explicitly stated in the manual that violence is the preferred means to

the desired end, and there are references to "execution" of abortion clinic staff.

In the early 1980s, a group of fundamentalist protestors repeatedly mobbed an abortion clinic in Granite City, Illinois. In 1982, the clinic's medical director, Dr. Hector Zevallos, and his wife were kidnapped and held in an abandoned ammunitions bunker for eight days by a group of men calling themselves the Army of God. The group vowed that they would kill the couple unless Dr. Zavallos pledged to permanently stop the performance of abortions. He agreed to do so; he and his wife were released. Three men were eventually convicted of the

LEADERSHIP

Don Benny Anderson kidnapped an Illinois abortion provider and his wife in 1982. This was the first crime officially linked to the Army of God.

Neal Horsley's Nuremberg Files web site, reported to function as a "hit list" for the Army of God, contains the names, personal data, and photographs of abortion providers. Horsley is also a secessionist, and is Webmaster for the separatist group Republic of Texas (RoT).

James C. Kopp received a second-degree murder conviction for the death of Dr. Barnett Slepian, and was sentenced to 25 years in state prison. Prior to joining the Army of God, Kopp was active in several other antiabortion groups, including the Lambs of Christ. As of early 2005, Kopp is awaiting federal trial in Dr. Slepian's death.

Eric Robert Rudolph, the confessed Atlanta club, clinic, and Olympic Park bomber, successfully eluded capture for five years before his arrest in May 2003. In summer 2005, Rudolph entered into a plea bargain agreement in which he received several life sentences with no possibility of parole—rather than a death sentence—in exchange for revealing the whereabouts of large quantities of undetonated explosives.

Donald Spitz has been Webmaster of the official Army of God web site, on which he posted running correspondence from Clayton Waagner during the time that Waagner was a fugitive. Spitz was the "spiritual advisor" to former Presbyterian minister Paul Hill prior to Hill's execution for the murder of a physician and his bodyguard outside an abortion clinic.

Clayton Waagner escaped from prison and was a fugitive for a year before his re-arrest in December 2001. He admitted to, and was convicted for, sending in excess of 550 anthrax threat letters to abortion clinics across the United States. Many of the letters purportedly sent by Waagner were signed by the Army of God. Waagner served as his own attorney at trial; he was convicted by a federal jury, in December 2003, on 51 of 53 charges, and is currently serving time in a federal penitentiary.

Michael Bray is the current Chaplain of the Army of God, and he hosts the annual White Rose Banquet in honor of those members of the Army of God who are serving prison time for antiabortion violence. He is the author of a book entitled *A Time To Kill*, in which he utilizes biblical quotes as a means of justifying the use of lethal violence against abortion providers. Bray has been convicted of, and has served time for, bombing abortion clinics.

---

kidnapping; one of them was Army of God leader Don Benny Anderson, who stated that he had been told by God that he had a mission to "wage war on abortion." Anderson was sentenced to 30 years in prison for the kidnapping; he also received a second 30-year sentence for arson involving two Florida abortion clinics.

In 1984, a Norfolk, Virginia, women's medical clinic was firebombed and the acronym "AoG" was written on a wall. Also in 1984, an abortion clinic outside of Washington, D.C., was firebombed, and a man purporting to represent the Army of God contacted media to claim that the group was responsible for the firebombs.

In 1993, Rachelle Shannon of Oregon shot an abortion clinic doctor in Wichita, Kansas. Shannon claimed membership in the Army of God, and stated that her act was a means of "enforcing God's will." Area police found an Army of God manual buried in Shannon's backyard, and reported that it was filled with quotes from the Bible, along with detailed instructions for assembling incendiary devices (bombs), and dogma stating that those who perform abortions must be killed. The manual was reported by the police to state that the local members of the Army of God are not told of the identities of other members, in order to make certain that "the Feds will never stop us."

PRIMARY SOURCE

One More Enemy: The Army of God Web Site, a Long-time Cheerleader for the Murderers of Abortion Doctors, Now Is Taking on Blacks

The Rev. Donald Spitz has never been a pleasant man. Considered a wild-eyed extremist even among his colleagues on the radical anti-abortion scene, the head of Pro-Life Virginia and long-time principal of the Army of God Web site (www.armyofgod.com) applauds the murderers of physicians, clinic workers and secretaries.

He rails against "filthy faggots" and "lesbos." Islam is "Satanic," Arabs are "Rag-Heads," and Muslims "should not be allowed to live in the United States." New York City is a "sex perverted cesspool" that richly deserved Sept. 11.

But there is one type of vicious group hatred Don Spitz has always denied—the "false accusations of racism" against blacks "put out by desperate babykilling abortionists." If a black man accepts Christ, "then that man is my brother."

Well, maybe. And maybe not.

This summer, on the Web site long run by Spitz, a remarkable series of headlines began to appear under "Current News Stories for Christians." To almost anyone but Spitz, these racy one-liners reflect the crudest kind of racism.

"African-American on bike randomly shoots people," screams one link to a legitimate news story. "83 Year old White Woman beaten to death by three African-Americans," says another. "African-American Killed her," a third reads under photos of the principals, "because she was White and her parents 'didn't allow her to have sex with a black man.'" And the list goes on:

- "NAACP calls for the murder of Police Officers."

- "Black robbers mug chancellor's [white] wife."

- "White woman carjacked, raped and executed by African-Americans."

And a longer headline accompanied by a photograph of an attractive white woman: "White Rebekah Hanson marries African-American Kashard Brown, then White Rebekah Hanson murdered by her African-American husband Kashard Brown."

A little further down the list, another headline is limited to a single quote: "Let's rape these White Girls, kill them and throw 'em off the bridge!"

These eye-catching headlines are published on the Army of God Web site that Spitz has run for years. The Army of God is a loosely connected collection of people who have carried out violent attacks on abortion clinics, doctors and other clinic workers.

Although there is no evidence to suggest a formally structured group, scores of violent criminals, saying they were called to their work directly by God, have described themselves as "members" of this self-appointed army.

In January 1996, a women's clinic in Atlanta was bombed, using a "dirty bomb stuffed with rusty nails and bits of metal to act as shrapnel; in February of the same year, a gay and lesbian nightclub was also bombed in that city. After the nightclub bombing, a handwritten, unsigned letter was sent to the Reuters news agency, claiming that the bombs were the work of "units of the Army of God." It also stated that any person involved in any way with the performance of abortions, "may become victims of retribution." Regarding the bombing of the gay and lesbian nightclub, the letter stated, "We will target sodomites, their organizations, and all those who push their agenda."

The letter also threatened both the U.S. government and the United Nations, as it stated, "We declare and will wage total war on the ungodly communist regime in New York and your legislative-bureaucratic lackeys in Washington. It is you who are responsible and preside over the murder of children and issue the

Spitz, who does not have a record of criminal violence, claimed that he had not personally written the headlines—but he saw little problem with the person who supposedly did.

Those two guys in Texas, he told the *Intelligence Report* in a reference to the truck-dragging murder of James Byrd Jr., "no one had a problem making race the issue there. So I don't know why this would be considered a racial issue."

The news stories "have a racial component" and the headlines merely reflect that, he said. They are "not making a dialogue or a commentary," Spitz added.

Spitz, 56, said he had recently turned over day-to-day control of the site, temporarily, to a man he refused to name—a man who goes by the pseudonym of Ehud Gera. (Ehud, son of Gera, is a left-handed character in the Bible's Book of Judges who uses stealth and a dagger to murder Eglon, king of Moab, and then goes on to lead the Israelites to victory over the 10,000-man army of Moab.)

Spitz may not direct the site. But the Web site directs correspondents to write "Gera" at a Chesapeake, Va., postal box held for years by Spitz and his wife. Spitz, who has lived in Chesapeake for many years, described "Gera" only as an ally.

Spitz has courted controversy for years. He was kicked out of Operation Rescue after the first murder of an abortion doctor in 1993. A Pentecostal minister without a congregation, he has cheered such murders as "righteous," posted "war criminal" posters of doctors, and been arrested at clinics.

According to *Wrath of Angels*, a book on the abortion wars by James Risen and Judy Thomas, authorities found his name and unlisted phone number in the possession of John Salvi after Salvi murdered two clinic workers and wounded five others in 1994.

Salvi was caught after he carried out the murders in the Boston area and then traveled more than 500 miles to fire a barrage of shots at the Hillcrest Clinic in Norfolk, Va.—a clinic that was routinely picketed by Donald Spitz. Spitz later held a "prayer vigil" outside Salvi's jail cell, shouting, "We love you, John Salvi!"

Last year, Spitz was contacted by Clayton Waagner, who was then a fugitive who boasted of mailing some fake anthrax threats to abortion clinics. Many of Waagner's threats were signed "Army of God, Virginia Dare chapter." Dare was the first white child born in America, and is often romanticized by white supremacists.

For his part, Spitz insisted that he harbors no racial animosity—indeed, he said, "I know more black people than I know white people." The headlines on the Web site, the reverend explained, merely reflect "black-on-white racism."

Source: Southern Poverty Law Center, 2002

policy of ungodly perversion that's destroying our people . . . Death to the New World Order."

The letter was turned over to the FBI for processing and analysis, and was eventually given to the American media for widespread national distribution in an effort to identify the author(s). The Army of God responded to the media statements, in which terrorist acts against clinics and nightclubs were referred to as cowardly, by stating that they are engaged in a war against abortionists and against the government of the United States. They reported that the only cowardice in their acts was in not immediately claiming responsibility for them. They concluded that their acts are terrorist in nature, but not cowardly in that they have openly declared war and assumed responsibility for their actions.

PHILOSOPHY AND TACTICS

The Army of God maintains numerous web sites that prominently feature the manifestos of each webmaster, along with myriad biblical citations denouncing people who perform abortions, and extolling the virtues of committing acts of lethal violence in order to put a permanent stop to the performance of abortions. Most of the web sites also contain dozens of color photographs of aborted fetuses that have been given biblical names and are identified by gender and date of "death."

Members of the Army of God state that there has been an undeclared war in the United States since *Roe v. Wade*, in 1973, which "effectively declared war against the children of God." The media has repeatedly referred to the act of bombing abortion clinics and gay and lesbian bars as cowardly; the Army of God responds by stating that they commit terrorist acts in the name of an undeclared war against the United States and against abortionists. They contend their acts are necessary in order to "defend God's children." In reference to their web site photographs of aborted fetuses, they state: "The people in those pictures have been slaughtered because our government, in the name of we the people, has declared war against them."

They feel that their mission is to end legalized abortion in the United States, by whatever means necessary. Their motivation is a religious one, fueled by a strong belief in the rights of the unborn. Their dogma is that life is created by God, and that an unborn fetus has as much right to exist as any other living, breathing human. In fact, their terrorist actions have indicated that the unborn have more right to life than the already independently living, as the Army of God is explicit in its plans to kill (and has murdered) those who perform abortions in order to prevent them from being able to continue doing so. They have been quite clear, in repeated public statements, that their intent is to obliterate abortion clinics and to kill those who perform abortions. The Army of God has stated that it will continue to carry out acts of terrorism against abortion clinics and health care workers until all laws legalizing abortion are repealed.

Since the terrorist acts that occurred in the United States on September 11, 2001, the Army of God has been linked, in and by the media—both popular press and Army of God web sites, to Muslim extremist groups—not in terms of any actual association, but in terms of the use of religious and political dogma to justify violence against persons and against governments. Since the start of the twenty-first century, the Army of God has also espoused progressively more inflammatory anti-homosexual sentiment, suggesting that they are broadening their base of potential targets beyond the abortion industry to homosexuals.

OTHER PERSPECTIVES

The Army of God declared a new "war" when it openly lauded the Saudi Arabian government for the public execution by beheading of three accused gay men on January 1, 2002. As the Army of God has historically been known for its use and endorsement of violence as a means of achieving its stated aims, the anti-homosexual rhetoric has aroused considerable concern among gay and lesbian human rights organizations. Additional red flags have been raised by the Army of God web sites' professed sense of solidarity with right-wing Muslim extremist groups as a result of the terrorist activities on September 11, 2001. There have been linkages, again, both within the popular media and echoed on the Army of God web sites, to other extremist militarist Middle Eastern groups in the use of anthrax threats in the letters sent by accused Army of God antiabortion activist Clayton Waagner. Reputed members of the Army of God have been quoted in the media as having expressed enthusiasm for the use of chemical and biological weapons in acts of terror.

Historically, the pro-choice and women's rights movements have expressed concern that the federal government has failed to take significant action to protect the rights of those who are involved in the legal practice of abortions, and to keep them safe from the violent acts of antiabortionists. The post-9/11 War on Terror has focused more attention on within-country terrorist groups and their activities, making it more difficult for antiabortion and other extremist groups to commit violent acts. This increased vigilance was publicly evidenced by the arrests and convictions of Eric Robert Rudolph and Clayton Waagner, and has served to force extremist groups such as the Army of God to move further underground. In 2002, Michael Bray, the chaplain of the Army of God, decided to call off the annual White Rose Banquet and annual protest near the White House on the anniversary of *Roe v. Wade* in favor of private meetings as a means of avoiding public scrutiny. However, as the group became more silent on the issue of antiabortion violence, it has become increasingly more vocal in its condemnation of nontraditional lifestyles. Michael Bray has expressed a hope that the beheading of homosexuals in Saudi Arabia may engender talk of theocracy in the United States. He used the Army of God web site as a means of fomenting anti-homosexual sentiment and attempting to link doctors who perform abortions, homosexuals, traitors, adulterers, witches, and kidnappers as groups that deserved to be targeted and killed in the name of "justice." Lorri L. Jean, of the National Gay and Lesbian Task Force, states, "I think this is a blatant call for people to murder gays and lesbians, among others. It's the logical extension of radical fundamentalism and religious intolerance."

Although it is atypical for an ultraconservative, far-right religious fundamentalist group to align itself with anything related to Islam, Chip Berlet, of Massachusetts Political Research Associates believes that Bray and the Army of God's support of the Saudi Arabian acts against homosexuals is because "They can side with a religion they disapprove of against a scapegoat they both loathe and demonize." Insurgent groups like the Army of God, Berlet says, view their ideological enemies as "a three-headed monster—of liberalism, feminism (which includes abortion), and the gay and lesbian civil rights movement. And the monster doesn't die until you cut off all three."

SUMMARY

The Army of God had its ideological beginnings at the moment that abortion was legalized in the United States. It had both philosophical and practical success in that the group claimed to be responsible for considerable destruction of abortion clinics, abortion practitioners were seriously injured or killed, and an atmosphere of fear and suspicion grew at the clinic sites. At the start of the twenty-first century, there has been political movement aimed at lobbying for the repeal of women's rights to have abortions, and clinics where abortions are performed have become veritable high-security facilities.

As the War on Terror has been mounted in the United States, it has become progressively more difficult for extremist groups to successfully launch attacks against medical facilities—so the group appears to have either gone underground until the political climate is more favorable for renewed acts of violence, quietly put energy and enthusiasm into ultraconservative political movements, or shifted tactics and taken on the cause of hate crimes against homosexuals. Perhaps the group has lost momentum and is no longer active, but perhaps not . . .

SOURCES

Web sites

CNN.com/U.S. "Army of God Letters Support Accused Bomber Eric Rudolph." < http://archives.cnn.com/2002/US/03/18/army.god.letters/index.html > (accessed September 25, 2005).

FOXNews.com—U.S. & World. "Abortion Doctor's Murderer Dies by Lethal Injection." < http://www.foxnews.com/story/0,2933,96286,00.html > (accessed September 25, 2005).

CBS NEWS.com/U.S. "'Army of God' Anthrax Threats." < http://www.cbsnews.com/stories/2001/11/09/national/main317573.shtml > (accessed September 25, 2005).

CNN.com/U.S. "Atlanta Olympic Bombing Suspect Arrested." < http://www.cnn.com/2003/US/05/31/rudolph.main/ > (accessed September 25, 2005).

Salon.com. "Brand New War for the Army of God? Parts 1 and 2." < http://www.salon.com/news/feature/2002/02/19/gays/index_np.html > (accessed September 25, 2005).

SEE ALSO

Republic of Texas

Aryan Nations

LEADER: Richard Butler
USUAL AREA OF OPERATION: United States

OVERVIEW

The Aryan Nations, based in Hayden Park, Idaho, acts as a paramilitary hate group and is one of America's most predominant and active white supremacist and anti-Semitic organizations. The group incorporates ideals both of Christian Identity, which predicates its ideologies of hatred of other religions and ethnicities on Christian theology, as well as some aspects of neo-Nazism. The group strongly advocates the establishment of a white state with the exclusion of all other races.

The group is involved with active recruitment of members and allies itself with numerous other hate and extremist organizations, and numerous splinter entities have been produced from within the ranks of the Aryan Nations. Some of these splinter groups have been actively involved in violence, even while this is not the official mode of operation for the organization.

HISTORY

The Aryan Nations was founded in the mid 1970s under the leadership of Richard Butler, an adherent to the teachings of Christian Identity, who had served in the U.S. armed forces in World War II. Butler set up a compound as a base for the organization in a rural

Aryan Nation members march in Idaho in 1998. © *Donovan Wylie | Magnum Photos*

area of Idaho and began setting up conferences and recruitment sessions. The organization in its early years began to train recruits in paramilitary activities as well as tactics of urban terrorism and guerilla warfare.

The compound was designed to offer people who shared the ideologies of Christian Identity and white supremacists with a site away from the easy grasp of law enforcement or the media. The Aryan Nations proudly reached out to other groups, including the Ku Klux Klan and other neo-Nazi groups, to unite in embracing their common worldviews and ambitions to create a white state.

The Aryan Nations made a concerted effort in its early years to reach out to young people through a variety of youth activities. In the early 1980s, an Aryan Nations Academy was established. The birthday of Adolf Hitler each April served as the occasion for large youth conferences. The Aryan Nations also cultivated the creation of several white power bands with names like Bound for Glory and Christian Identity Skins.

Beginning in 1979, Butler made a concerted effort toward recruitment in the nation's prison

system. The group wrote letters to inmates and was involved with the distribution of materials among the prisoners. This activity intensified in the late 1980s when several of the leaders of the organization were imprisoned as a result of federal prosecutions.

In 1987, the activities of the Aryan Nations were expanded into a new center in Utah as well as on the radio with the introduction of a weekly broadcast entitled "The Aryan Nations Hour." The show only lasted for a few weeks because of death threats and advertisers canceling. Yet, the organization continued to grow into the 1990s with offices opening in more than a dozen states.

Over the course of the 1990s, even with its growth, the Aryan Nations experienced considerable internal disarray with several leading members leaving the group to found new white supremacist organizations. By 1997, the group had grown to include 18 state offices with funds largely originating from member fees and some donations from outside backers.

A video still produced by an organization that calls itself the Aryan Republican Army is displayed at a Philadelphia news conference on January 30, 1997. AP/Wide World Photos. Reproduced by permission.

In 1994, the Aryan Nations was able to attract its largest audience to the annual Aryan youth festival held on the occasion of Hitler's birthday. The occasion welcomed the participation of many of the leaders of the different neo-Nazi and hate movements in North America. Even while continuing to avoid directly advocating violence, several incidents made the Aryan Nations the target for considerable public and media outrage. On August 10,1998, Buford Furrow, who had been involved with the organization as a guard, opened fire at a Jewish community center in Los Angeles, California. He wounded five people and later killed a Filipino postal worker while fleeing police. After surrendering to the FBI, Furrow said that the shooting spree was intended as a wakeup call to America to kill Jews.

In September 2000, the Aryan Nations and Richard Butler were required by a jury to pay $6.3 million to a mother and son who had been assaulted and shot at while seated in their car outside of the Aryan Nations compound. The decision bankrupted the organization, but through private funding, Butler was able to reopen under the name of the Aryan National Alliance.

In recent years, the Aryan Nations has been able to continue their publicity efforts, aided by the internet and, despite continuing internal tensions, the group has remained intact. With Butler's death in 2004, considerable questions have emerged regarding the future of the organization.

Throughout their existence, the Aryan Nations has been opposed by groups like the Anti-Defamation League, the National Association for the Advancement of Colored People (NAACP), and the Southern Poverty Law Center, as well as by numerous efforts by local, state, and federal law enforcement to limit the activities of the organization.

Members of the Aryan National Alliance, formerly known as Aryan Nations, give fascist salutes after marching through Coeur d'Alene, Idaho on October 28, 2000. Aryan Nations leader Richard Butler and two dozen supporters paraded through the downtown area where they were shouted at by protesters. AP/ *Wide World Photos. Reproduced by permission.*

PHILOSOPHY AND TACTICS

The ideologies of the Aryan Nations find their origins in the philosophies of Christian Identity and neo-Nazism. Christian Identity in the United States is most often connected with the teachings of Wesley Swift, a former Ku Klux Klan organizer from California who was one of the mentors of Richard Butler. Swift, who founded the Church of Jesus Christ–Christian in 1946, openly called for genocide to be carried out against Jews. Today, the United States today contains several hundred chapters of Christian Identity groups, with the Aryan Nations having become one of the most organized and vocal.

The central belief of Christian Identity espouses that the white people are the chosen people and only they have hope for salvation. Most Christian Identity believers adhere to a fundamentalist and literal interpretation of biblical sources. According to this ideology, God created a second race referred to as "Mud People," who were the ancestors of all modern day peoples of color. Christian Identity teaches that these races were created by God to serve as the servants of white people and are soulless, are not truly human and have no value in God's eyes. The third race, the Jews, was created by Satan, and they are only involved in trying to destroy the Aryan race.

The Aryan Nations accepted these philosophies in developing an ideology that advocated a strong anti-Jewish as well as anti-governmental stance. The Aryan Nations see the Jewish people as a virus that is designed to destroy the Aryan culture and race. The official Aryan Nations' "Declaration of Independence" refers to the United States as the "Zionist-occupied

LEADERSHIP

RICHARD BUTLER

Known within the Aryan Nations as "Reverend," Richard Butler founded and led the organization from its creation in the mid 1970s until his death in 2004. Born in 1918 in Colorado, Butler had joined the U.S. army in World War II, an experience that shaped his conception regarding American society and his beliefs that the government was not looking out for the best interests of the country.

Following the war, he worked as an engineer and in that capacity he was introduced to William Potter Gale, a retired colonel who had served as an aide to General Douglas MacArthur, one of the U.S. military leaders on the Pacific front in World War II. Gale was a paramilitary leader and a founder of the Posse Comitatus, an antigovernment group. Through the teachings of Gale, Butler came to embrace the ideologies of Christian Identity and, in the mid 1960s, he had assumed the position as the

National Director of the Christian Defense League, an organization involved with popularizing Christian Identity.

In 1971, when the founder of the Christian Defense League died, Butler moved his operations to northern Idaho with the stated goal of forming a national racial state. From that time until his death, Butler became one of the most active leaders in the United States in supporting the fundamentals of Christian Identity, paramilitarism, and neo-Nazism as well as a devout respect for Adolf Hitler, whom Butler believed to be the second greatest figure in history behind Jesus Christ.

With Butler's death in 2004, the group, which had faced numerous internal struggles over leadership, was left in a state of confusion over its future and over who would assume the position that Butler had held since the group's founding.

---

government of the United States of America" and established that the goal of all followers of the Aryan Nations should be to be of any connection or commitment to the United States.

In keeping with their anti-Semitic philosophy, the Aryan Nations believes that Jews are not only an inferior race, but also deserve to destroyed as the natural enemies of the Aryan race.

In hopes of beginning the effort towards the development of a white racist homeland, the Aryan Nations established their compound in the rural community of Hayden Lake, Idaho, which Butler designed to become the international headquarters of the white race. In the summers, the compound would host festivals for white supremacists under the banner of World Congress of Aryan Nations. The compound consisted of a 20-acre ranch that was patrolled by armed guards and dogs.

The outreach successes of the Aryan Nations are connected with the extensive

network that the group has formed with other white supremacist organizations. The group has formed alliances with the two major factions of hate groups in the United States, which were formed after the breakup of the American Nazi Party in the 1960s. The first was the Christian Defense League, which is based on Christian Identity philosophies, and the other was the National Alliance, which is based primarily on pro-Nazi ideologies with the goal of replicating the Nazi party influence in the United States. Despite these varying philosophies, Richard Butler made an effort to reach out to both of these groups as well as the various other splinter groups.

While the base of operations is in Idaho with extensions around the United States, the Aryan Nations made considerable inroads in Canada as well, beginning in the early 1980s. The leader of Canada's Aryan Nations, Terry Long from Alberta, was ordained by Richard Butler and is now said to be in hiding from the authorities. As in the United States, the

KEY EVENTS

1971: Reverend Richard Butler moves his congregation to Hayden Lake, Idaho, to begin efforts to set up a racist national state.

1983: Followers of the Aryan Nations formed The Silent Brotherhood, also known popularly as The Order, and set out to over throw the United States government and establish an Aryan homeland in the Pacific Northwest.

1998: Former guard of the Aryan Nations, Bufford Furrow, opened fire on a Los Angeles Jewish community center injuring four people and later killing a Filipino-American postal worker.

Canadian factions of the Aryan Nations have experienced growth primarily by allying with similar extremist groups. Most prominently, the pro-Hitler and neo-Nazi group, the Aryan Resistance Group (ARM), is based out of Mission, British Columbia, with an extensive history of involvement with violence and crime, and is a regular attendee of Aryan Nations conferences.

The Aryan Nations network in Canada is involved with the publication of a periodical on Christian Identity thought and news entitled *Winston's Journal*. The journal has denied the existence of the Holocaust, as well as referring to the Jews as satanic. In 1994, the journal declared their "Man of the Year" to be Paul Hill, a Christian fundamentalist who had been convicted for murdering an abortion doctor in Pensacola, Florida.

At the Aryan Nations youth festival held in 1994, many of the leaders of the numerous hate groups in attendance called for a new strategy they labeled "Leaderless Resistance." Actively advocating violence, the approach promoted the creation of numerous smaller groups of terrorists whose job it would be to go out and commit criminal acts and violence. The aim of these attacks would be to provoke society to recognize the influence of the white power movement and lead to the creation of a white racial state. Through this new strategy, which was never really clarified in terms of practice, the umbrella groups of leadership like the Aryan Nations would exercise less control, and smaller factions would be created with the purpose of carrying out more violent attacks aimed at provoking society.

The Aryan Nations have throughout their history acted on a local level with limited tools for recruitment. After selecting communities that they view as a source of new recruits, the Aryan Nations often begins by placing leaflets on cars with racist and anti-Semitic content. The group most often targets areas with high traffic of the young and most impressionable segments of society like schoolyards, sporting facilities, and public restrooms. The targets for recruitment will be almost exclusively young whites beginning at the high school age who, given their relatively young age, are able to be easily molded to carry out the directives of the group's leadership.

In recent years, the Aryan Nations have come to rely heavily on the Internet both for recruitment purposes as well as a tool to inform the world of their ideologies. The official Aryan Nations web site includes an application for new members, an online catalog of books with themes relevant to the philosophies of the organization, and an extensive list of links to other hate groups. The site prominently features a section it calls "Public Notices," providing information regarding current events and activities being organized or sponsored by local Aryan Nations groups.

OTHER PERSPECTIVES

Recent events both in the United States and around the world have changed the perception of the Aryan Nations and other hate groups as only threats to society. Now they are being increasingly looked at as terrorist groups and even as allies with international terrorists. The Aryan Nations and other Christian Identity groups, despite their approach to minorities and people of color in specific, have come out in support of some of the actions of Islamic terrorists. For that reason, these white power

PRIMARY SOURCE

Youth Action Corps: Led by a 15-year-old, the neo-Nazi Aryan Nations' Long-defunct Youth Organization Seems to Be Coming Back to Life

Hoping to secure the next generation of neo-Nazi leaders, the Idaho-based Aryan Nations has made energetic efforts throughout its history to recruit 14- to 20-year-olds for its Aryan Nations Youth Action Corps (ANYAC).

But convincing white youth to see Jews as "the literal children of Satan" and view people of color as "muds" has not proven easy, and the last active ANYAC contingent died out in 1999.

Logan Brown is out to change all that. In January, the 15-year-old organized a Southern California chapter of ANYAC that is now six members strong. He's also put up two ANYAC Web sites to attract kids from elsewhere in the U.S.

Logan believes that most teenagers are "brainwashed by the media—the Disney Channel, MTV with their multiculturalism, Jewish traditions, black traditions. It's unmoral. A cesspool." By contrast, he believes he's working for the betterment of the future—the white future.

But don't get him wrong. "I'm not the stereotypical racist," he insists. "You know, I'm not a redneck. I don't generally get picked on by minorities at my school."

There aren't many minorities around to pick on him. Like many youthful newcomers to white supremacy, Logan is growing up in a predominantly white, middle-class milieu—the mountain community of Lake Arrowhead, Calif.

Logan and his "racially aware" ANYAC allies attend predominantly white Rim of the World High School. "We do get a select number of blacks that are bused here," Logan says. "Gangsters or thugs, or whatever they want to call themselves."

MASQUERADING AS MAINSTREAM

To make their politics look more palatable, Logan and his comrades have also started a campus group called the Council of Concerned Students.

"Inside the school we're being conservative" rather than extremist, Logan says, "so we won't be prosecuted [sic] or attacked." But the real purpose is to woo prospective neo-Nazis.

"I'm using [the group] as a way to get the word out about ANYAC," Logan says.

In lieu of racial violence, the council's chosen weapon has been circulating petitions. "Basically, you know, we don't want to take drastic action like stereotypical maniac racists," Logan explains.

The first petition called for the banning of gay pride T-shirts; Logan says wearing the shirts is "vulgar—shoving it in my face," and he claims

groups are being considered by society and law enforcement with a renewed attempt to limit their activities.

In statements put out by the Aryan Nations, they have declared Islam to be their ally as a result of the standards of morality espoused by the Muslim religion. The Aryan Nations specifically points to what they claim to be the efforts of Islam to uproot the Jews from society. As a result of these statements, Aryan Nations is increasingly being labeled by its opponents as a terrorist group, although the central organization has not yet been directly connected with any specific terrorist act.

Groups like the Anti-Defamation League and the Southern Poverty Law Center have approached the activities of the Aryan Nations with direct action to shut them down. Most notably was the 2000 lawsuit that bankrupted the organization. These groups also work with law enforcement to encourage them to crack down on branches of the Aryan Nations by exposing any dissemination of hate literature. These groups work with state and federal government to develop laws that make the activities of hate and extremist groups illegal and to severely limit their activities. They are principally involved with informational

150 students have signed on. (School administrators would not comment.)

Logan and his buddies have also started a petition to ban the display of Jewish symbols at Rim of the World High. Logan casts it as a simple matter of fairness. "They can wear their Star of David, but I can't wear my swastika?"

Logan hopes to inspire other kids to follow his path into neo-Nazism. He says his "traditional" upbringing made for an easy segue into white power. "I basically had some of the roots of a racialist," he says, "anti-immigration, anti-drug, et cetera."

After joining the racist Skinhead movement at age 12, Logan "grew out of that" pretty quickly. Then he picked up *White Power*. Published in 1967 by George Lincoln Rockwell, the founding father of American neo-Nazism, *White Power* explores the racial "mongrelization" of the U.S.

"That was a real eye-opener," Logan says. "Say it's the 1920s when everything was white and beautiful. We were a white, civilized nation."

After imbibing Rockwell's views, Logan sought something more spiritual—and found it in the Aryan Nations' anti-Semitic theology, Christian Identity.

"Jews are basically the literal children of Satan," he says, echoing fundamental Identity tenets. "They can go back to their country. They don't belong here."

Same goes for people of color. "Africans can go back to Africa," he says. "I mean, technically they are not citizens." Mexicans, he says, "are illegals anyway. Immigration is only for pure white immigration—that's what our forefathers meant."

THINKING BIG

Logan's extremism has come with a cost. He says his family doesn't "support me whatsoever"—especially his stepmother. "She's just close-minded," he says. His older brother doesn't like Logan's activism, either.

"[He] raided my room and stuff like that," Logan complains. "He's just a middle-class white boy trying to fit in with the black crowd."

Logan vows he won't follow the path of the last youngster to lead ANYAC, Shaun Winkler. Winkler's activism began with peaceful activities like distributing fliers—but as he rose up the ranks of national leadership in the Aryan Nations, he became more violent.

This April, Winkler, now 25, was convicted on charges stemming from a confrontation with

(continued on next page)

efforts to counter the materials that are put out by the hate groups and believe that the most effective way of combating hate and extremism is through educational and publicity efforts.

Both the Anti-Defamation League and the Southern Poverty Law Center have used mass media to highlight the activities of the Aryan Nations and, because of their resources and access to influential personalities and government officials, the actions of these groups have achieved considerable successes in curtailing the continued growth of groups like the Aryan Nations.

SUMMARY

The Aryan Nations has steadily grown in membership despite their internal struggles and considerable opposition from tolerance organizations and law enforcement. Throughout their existence, the organization has thrived by reaching out to similar hate groups and adhering to the ideologies of Christian Identity and neo-Nazism.

While the Aryan Nations group itself has not been directly involved with many acts of violence, splinter groups as well as past members

PRIMARY SOURCE

Youth Action Corps: Led by a 15-year-old, the neo-Nazi Aryan Nations' Long-defunct Youth Organization Seems to Be Coming Back to Life (continued)

another Nations member and his children; following an outburst during his trial, Winkler now faces charges of resisting arrest and battery on a police officer.

Logan says he'll remain nonviolent—unless violent methods are needed to create a white homeland. "I just want what's best for our people," he says.

Logan's ANYAC chapter has been busy recently—holding a fund-raising concert in honor of Hitler's birthday, celebrating the prison release of former Klan leader David Duke—but his plans stretch way beyond Rim of the World High.

His Web sites and frequent postings on white-power message boards helped inspire a new ANYAC chapter in Illinois. Logan says he's also recruited members in Arkansas, Maryland, and several other states.

Meanwhile, he's mapping out a plan to restore the grown-up Aryan Nations to its

former prominence among neo-Nazi groups. Posting on an Aryan Nations forum, Logan lamented the loss of the group's Idaho headquarters and, with a teenager's enthusiasm, urged members to rise up.

"It is time to rebuild and show these filthy Jews we mean business," he wrote. "I purpose [sic] to set up a fund to raise enough money to rebuild HQ bigger and better than ever!"

That might have to wait, Logan admits, until he finishes college, gets his Ph.D. in history, attends law school and becomes a district attorney.

"Then I'd like to go to Idaho and take over," he says, pausing to correct himself, "or help the Nations."

Nia Hightower

Source: Southern Poverty Law Center, 2004

---

of the organization have carried out several attacks against minority targets, and Aryan Nations leaders have not shied away from supporting violence. The growth of the Internet has been embraced by the Aryan Nations as an additional tool for recruitment and the group continues to recruit through local activity carried out by its branches across the United States as well as in Canada.

While the structure of the group remains largely uncertain as a result of the death of its founder Richard Butler in 2004, as well as financial instabilities brought on by lawsuits, the Aryan Nations' name continues to be associated with the leading hate groups in North America, and its rise from the 1970s and into the twenty-first century indicated the potential for the continuing growth of hate-inspired extremist groups.

SOURCES

Web sites

The Southern Poverty Law Center. "Intelligence Project; Monitoring Hate and Extremist Activity." < http://www.splcenter.org/intel/intpro.jsp >   (accessed September 25, 2005).

The Anti-Defamation League. "Fighting Anti-Semitism, Bigotry and Extremism." < http://www.adl.org/ > (accessed September 25, 2005).

Rick A. Ross Institute. "Christian Identity." < http://www.rickross.com/groups/christian_identity.html > (accessed September 25, 2005).

SEE ALSO

Ku Klux Klan

Posse Comitatus

Asbat al-Ansar

OVERVIEW

Asbat al-Ansar (Usbat al-Ansar) was formed in 1985 in the refugee camp, Ayn al-Hilwah (also spelled Ain il-Hilweh), as a splinter faction from one of the Muslim groups that fought in the Lebanese civil war. The group adheres to the Sunni sect of Islam and seeks to overthrow the Lebanese government and replace it with an Islamic state. The group also seeks to purge the country of Western influences and anything it perceives as anti-Islam. Asbat al-Ansar believes that its goal to create a fundamentalist Islamic state justifies violence, even against civilians and other Muslims. Membership in the Asbat al-Ansar is largely Palestinian, leading to conflicts with other groups in the refugee camp such as the Fatah movement founded by Yasser Arafat. As such, the group is virulently against the peace with Israel and seeks to derail the peace process occurring between Israel and its Arab neighbors.

The name *Asbat al-Ansar* is translated to mean "League of Followers" or "Partisan League." Its early attacks were lower-level bombings of targets considered to be "un-Muslim," such as churches, nightclubs, casinos, and bars. However, many of the members of Asbat al-Ansar have been either trained in al-Qaeda camps or are veterans from the Afghan-Soviet war. In either case, the ties to al-Qaeda and Osama bin Laden are apparent. This alliance

LEADER: Abu Muhjen

USUAL AREA OF OPERATION: Lebanon

Abu Tareq, whose brother is the leader of Islamic Palestinian group Asbat al-Ansar, attends a 2001 demonstration that marks the first anniversary of the Palestinian uprising against Israel. Mahmoud Zayat | AFP |
Getty Images

caused the United States to list Asbat al-Ansar as one of the first 11 groups identified as a terrorist organization after the attacks on the United States of September 11, 2001.

HISTORY

Lebanon was once a haven for political cooperation. It was structured to reflect its population as identified in a 1932 census. This National Pact provided for representation of each of the parties in the country: by custom, the president would be a Maronite (or Christian), the Prime Minister would be a Sunni Muslim, and the speaker of the Chamber of Deputies would be a Shi'ite Muslim. By mid 1975, the government no longer accurately represented the population and thus set the stage for civil war as sectarian militias and external regimes clamored for power. The first events of the civil war occurred in 1975, with

an assassination attempt on Pierre Gemayel, who had been the founder of the Phalange party, a Maronite (and Christian) paramilitary youth organization. The party gained support and power through the 1960s with its hope for a Lebanon made distinct from its Arab and Muslim neighbors through the embracing of Western influences. Phalangists believe Palestinians were the would-be assassins of Pierre Gemayel, and retaliated by killing 26 Palestinian passengers riding a bus across a Christian neighborhood. These were Palestinian refugees who had resided in the southern outskirts of west Beirut since the first Arab-Israeli War in 1949. The conflict, however, was deeper than Muslim versus Christian. By 1991, the civil war had ended, but the country had to rebuild many of its institutions. The political structure was rebuilt under the Ta'if Accord and a system more representative of the population was established, in particular by providing Muslims more access in the political process.

LEADERSHIP

HISHAM SHREIDI

Hisham Shreidi founded Asbat al-Ansar in 1985 to rival the Fatah movement, which was then led by Yasser Arafat. Shreidi was assassinated in 1991 by Fatah operatives.

ABU MUHJEN

Abu Muhjen, also known as Ahmed Abdul Karin al Saadi, is the current leader of Asbat al-Ansar. Muhjen is believed to be residing in the Ayn al-Hilwah refugee camp and directing operations from there. He was convicted in abstentia on three separate occasions for the assassination of Sheikh Nizar al Halabi, the former leader of the Islamic Charity Projects Association, or the Ahbash Movement.

Granting Muslims greater involvement in the political system did little to appease those wishing to create an Islamic state and purge Lebanon of anything of Western influence. Many of these dissidents were refugees residing in camps in the southern region of the country. Palestinians who fled the Arab-Israeli wars in 1948 and 1967 resided in these refugee camps. However, the Arab League accords have resolved that the refugee camps are not under the direction of the Lebanese government. The camps are, in fact, autonomous units. This has led to a power struggle for leadership of the various camps between groups like Asbat al-Ansar, Fatah, and Hezbollah. These power struggles have created violence inside the camps.

Asbat al-Ansar was created in 1985 by Hisham Shreidi in one of these refugee camps, called Ayn al-Hilwa. Shreidi was assassinated by Fatah in 1991. The group was a splinter faction from a Muslim group that fought during the Lebanese civil war. Many of its first activities occurred in the early 1990s. The attacks were considered low-level targeting of un-Islamic sites, such as churches, bars, and

casinos. The group was also linked to a series of murders against rival Palestinian and Islamic groups that also operate in southern Lebanon. One such attack was the assassination of rival Sunni cleric, Sheikh Nazar Halibi, the former leader of the Islamic Charity Projects Association, or Ahbash Movement. Asbat al-Ansar leader, Abu Mahjan, was later convicted of the assassination. By 1999, the group had begun to seek larger targets. It then successfully bombed a customs building and killed four judges.

Although many of Asbat al-Ansar's operatives are Palestinians, the group has been well trained in guerilla warfare. Many of the members fought in Afghanistan during the war with the Soviet Union. Others were trained in al-Qaeda training camps. This connection became more apparent as al-Qaeda and Osama bin Laden provided funding for additional attacks. In 2000, Asbat al-Ansar operative, Abu Kharab, fired rocket-propelled grenades into the Russian Embassy in Beirut to show solidarity with the Chechen rebels. The attack injured seven and killed one before Kharab was then shot to death himself. In 2001, Jordanian and Lebanese intelligence services foiled a plot to similarly attack the Jordanian, U.S. and British embassies in Beirut. Also in 2001, Asbat al-Ansar became one of the first organizations designated for sanctions on grounds of supporting al-Qaeda by U.S. presidential Executive Order 13224.

In 2003, Asbat al-Ansar continued to move toward its goal of an Islamic state while struggling for power within the refugee camp. Ibn al-Shahid, an Asbat al-Ansar operative, was charged with attempted car-bombings at fast-food restaurants in 2002, and targeting a McDonald's restaurant in 2003. In addition, the group participated in rocket attacks on a TV building in Beirut. At the same time, violent clashes in Ayn al-Hilwa pitted Asbat al-Ansar against the Fatah movement. By the end of the violence, eight people had been killed and 25 were wounded.

In 2004, much of the activities of Asbat al-Ansar surrounded the struggle for power within the Ayn al-Hilwa refugee camp. The group did, however, vocalize its condemnation for the U.S. presence in Iraq. In communiqués, the group exhorted Iraqi insurgents to kill U.S. personnel and to avenge the deaths of Hamas leaders, Abdul Aziz Ratisi and Sheikh Ahmen Yassin,

KEY EVENTS

1985: Asbat al-Ansar is formed in the Ayn al-Hilwah refugee camp near Sidon in Southern Lebanon. The group was a splinter faction from Muslim forces that fought during Lebanon's civil war.

1990s: The group engages in low-level attacks on non-Islamic or western targets such as churches, bars, casinos, and nightclubs.

1991: Founder of Asbat al-Ansar, Hisham Shreidi, is assassinated by Fatah operatives.

1996: Leader of Asbat al-Ansar, Abu Mahjan, assassinates rival Sunni leader, Sheikh Nizar al Halabi.

1999: The group launches bombing attack on customs building and kills four judges.

2000: Asbat al-Ansar operative, Abu Kharab, fires rocket propelled grenades into the Russian embassy in Beirut to show solidarity with Chechen rebels. He injures seven and kills one before he is shot to death by Lebanese police.

2001: Jordanian and Lebanese intelligence services foil a plot to attack Jordanian, U.S., and British embassies in Lebanon.

2001: Asbat al-Ansar is designated as a terrorist organization by President George W. Bush's Executive Order 13224 due to ties with al-Qaeda.

2003: Ibn al-Shahid is charged with the attempted car bombing of several fast-food restaurants, including a McDonald's restaurant in Beirut.

2003: Violent clashes between Asbat al-Ansar and Fatah erupt within the Ayn al-Hilwah refugee camp.

2003: Members of Asbat al-Ansar launch rocket propelled grenade attacks on a TV building in Beirut.

2004: Italian, Lebanese, and Syrian intelligence services stop a plot to attack the Italian embassy, Ukrainian consulate, and Lebanese government offices.

2004: Asbat al-Ansar voices vocal condemnation of U.S. presence in Iraq and urges insurgents to kill U.S. personnel.

2004: Mahir al-Sa'di, an operative in Asbat al-Ansar, is sentenced in abstentia for the assassination plot against former U.S. ambassador to Lebanon David Satterfield.

---

who were both assassinated during Israeli attacks on Gaza city. Also in 2004, Asbat al-Ansar operative Mahir al-Sa'di, was sentenced in abstentia for a plot to assassinate the former U.S. ambassador to Lebanon, David Satterfield. In another example of the alliance between Asbat al-Ansar and al-Qaeda, al-Sa'di worked along side Abu Muhammad al-Masri who headed the al-Qaeda movement in the Ayn al-Hilwa refugee camp.

PHILOSOPHY AND TACTICS

Asbat al-Ansar is a Sunni Muslim group with a salafist tradition. Salafists believe in a strict interpretation of Islam. The Islamic state that the group wishes to create in Lebanon would adhere to the strict interpretation of Islam. As part of the tradition, the group employs a "defensive jihad" to fight perceived attacks on Islam. As such, the group seeks to purge any Western influences or anything deemed un-Islamic from Lebanon. To reach these objectives, the group has employed the tactics of assassinations, or attempted assassinations, and rocket-propelled grenade attacks on specific sites, such as foreign embassies, fast-food restaurants, churches, and nightclubs.

In addition, Asbat al-Ansar is virulently opposed to the presence of an Israeli state in the Middle East. As a result, the group has struggled for power within the Ayn al-Hilwah refugee camp with other Palestinian organizations.

PRIMARY SOURCE
Asbat al-Ansar

DESCRIPTION

Asbat al-Ansar, the League of the Followers or Partisans' League, is a Lebanon-based Sunni extremist group, composed primarily of Palestinians with links to Usama Bin Ladin's al-Qa'ida organization and other Sunni extremist groups. The group follows an extremist interpretation of Islam that justifies violence against civilian targets to achieve political ends. Some of the group's goals include overthrowing the Lebanese Government and thwarting perceived anti-Islamic and pro-Western influences in the country.

ACTIVITIES

Asbat al-Ansar has carried out multiple terrorist attacks in Lebanon since it first emerged in the early 1990s. The group assassinated Lebanese religious leaders and bombed nightclubs, theaters, and liquor stores in the mid-1990s. The group raised its operational profile in 2000 with two attacks against Lebanese and international targets. It was involved in clashes in northern Lebanon in December 1999 and carried out a rocket-propelled grenade attack on the Russian Embassy in Beirut in January 2000. Asbat al-Ansar's leader, Abu Muhjin, remains at large despite being sentenced to death in absentia for the 1994 murder of a Muslim cleric.

Suspected Asbat al-Ansar elements were responsible for an attempt in April 2003 to use a car bomb against a McDonald's in a Beirut suburb. By October, Lebanese security forces arrested Ibn al-Shahid, who is believed to be associated with Asbat al-Ansar, and charged him with masterminding the bombing of three fast food restaurants in 2002 and the attempted attack on a McDonald's in 2003. Asbat forces were involved in other violence in Lebanon in 2003, including clashes with members of Yassir Arafat's Fatah movement in the 'Ayn al-Hilwah refugee camp and a rocket attack in June on the Future TV building in Beirut.

In 2004, no successful terrorist attacks were attributed to Asbat al-Ansar. However, in September, operatives with links to the group were believed to be involved in a planned terrorist operation targeting the Italian Embassy, the Ukrainian Consulate General, and Lebanese Government offices. The plot, which reportedly also involved other Lebanese Sunni extremists, was thwarted by Italian, Lebanese, and Syrian security agencies. In 2004, Asbat al-Ansar remained vocal in its condemnation of the United States' presence in Iraq, and in April the group urged Iraqi insurgents to kill US and other hostages to avenge the death of HAMAS leaders Abdul Aziz Rantisi and Sheikh Ahmed Yassin. In October, Mahir al-Sa'di, a member of Asbat al-Ansar, was sentenced in absentia to life imprisonment for plotting to assassinate former US Ambassador to Lebanon David Satterfield in 2000. Until his death in March 2003, al-Sa'di worked in cooperation with Abu Muhammad al-Masri, the head of al-Qa'ida at the 'Ayn al-Hilwah refugee camp, where fighting has occurred between Asbat al-Ansar and Fatah elements.

STRENGTH

The group commands about 300 fighters in Lebanon.

LOCATION/AREA OF OPERATION

The group's primary base of operations is the Ayn al-Hilwah Palestinian refugee camp near Sidon in southern Lebanon.

EXTERNAL AID

Probably receives money through international Sunni extremist networks and possibly Usama Bin Ladin's al-Qa'ida network.

Source: U.S. Department of State. *Country Reports on Terrorism*. Washington, D.C., 2004.

Members of Asbat al-Ansar adopt the belief that by giving in to the two-state agreement in the Oslo Accords, Yasser Arafat began chiseling away at regaining the territory once known as the British Mandate Palestine. By negotiating with Israel, Asbat al-Ansar and other like-minded groups labeled Arafat an "infidel" and have sought to dismantle the power structure led by the Palestinian Liberation Organization and Fatah. Within this struggle, the group engages in assassinations and intimidation campaigns targeting supporters of Fatah.

OTHER PERSPECTIVES

The residents of the Lebanese refugee camps fled their homes during the Arab-Israeli wars of 1948 and 1967. Asbat al-Ansar had struggled with other Palestinian organizations such as Fatah for power. The Center for Defense Information asserts that, "Asbat al-Ansar is thus a leading authority over a crowd of disenfranchised, largely radicalized Palestinians operating under the protection of the Arab world (though not a particular state) and responsible to no one." As a result, the group works toward marginalizing those groups that would allow a Palestinian state. Fatah is considered such a group since the organization was founded by Yasser Arafat and it was Arafat who signed the two-state agreement in the Oslo Accords. The Center for Defense Information states, "It seems likely that the militants of Asbat al-Ansar will continue to prevent such a peace agreement from coming about. Furthermore, with a supply of funds from Osama bin Laden and other international Sunni extremist networks, and under the continued protection of the Palestinian refugee camps in Lebanon, Asbat al-Ansar will be difficult to eradicate. Lebanon, for its part, had done little to curb the violence within the camp, or the alliances fostered with other organizations such as al-Qaeda." Jonathan Schanzer of the Washington Institute for Near East Policy believes that since Asbat al-Ansar is the Lebanese faction of al-Qaeda, more should be done to destroy it or the consequences could be devastating to the Western world. He writes, "Lebanon, however, allows this group to grow by ignoring it. If this continues, Asbat al-Ansar may come to pose a greater threat. Indeed, it could become a launch pad for other al-Qaeda attacks in the future."

SUMMARY

Asbat al-Ansar was formed in 1985 as a splinter organization from one of the Muslim groups that fought during the Lebanese civil war. Its expressed goal is the creation of an Islamic state in Lebanon. Other goals it seeks to achieve are the removal of Western influences from the Middle East and the destruction of Israel. When Asbat al-Ansar began, it employed low-level attacks on un-Islamic sites such as churches, nightclubs, casinos, and bars. However, as it developed ties with Osama bin Laden and al-Qaeda, the group attempted to instigate larger attacks. One successful attack occurred in 2000 when operatives from the group launched rocket-propelled grenades into the Russian Embassy in Beirut to demonstrate solidarity with Chechen rebels. Much of the recent violence, however, is the result of a power struggle occurring within the refugee camp where the group operates. Asbat al-Ansar and Fatah have exchanged assassinations of leaders and intimidation campaigns on members in an effort to gain control of the refugee camp. The struggle goes deeper than that, however. Members of Asbat al-Ansar believe that by negotiating with Israel, Yasser Arafat—who founded Fatah—betrayed the Palestinian people. As such, Asbat al-Ansar seeks to lead the movement to destroy Israel and purge Western influences from the region. This conflict, however, has led to internal struggle within Asbat al-Ansar. In 2001, the son of the founder of Asbat al-Ansar broke away from the group with approximately 250 guerilla supporters. This breakaway faction is known as *Jama'at al-Nur*, or Association of the Enlightened.

SOURCES

Periodicals

Shanzer, Jonathan. "Lurking in Lebanon." *Washington Institute for Near East Policy*. June 4, 2003.

Trindle, Giles. "Splinterned Loyalties Shattered Lives." *Middle East*. February 1, 2003.

Web sites

Center for Defense Information. "In the Spotlight: Asbat al-Ansar." < http://www.cdi.org/terrorism/asbat.cfm > (accessed October 15, 2005).

CIA Government Factbook. "Tunisia." < http://www.cia.gov/cia/publications/factbook/geos/ts.html > (accessed October 15, 2005).

Foreign and Commonwealth Office. "Asbat al-Ansar." < http://www.fco.gov.uk/servlet/Front?pagename = OpenMarket/Xcelerate/ShowPage&c = Page&cid = 1049909003789 > (accessed October 15, 2005).

Middle East Intelligence Bulletin. "Intelligence Briefs: Lebanon." < http://www.meib.org/articles/0110_lb.htm#lb1 > (accessed October 15, 2005).

Overseas Security Advisory Council. "Asbat al-Ansar." < http://www.ds-osac.org/Groups/group.cfm?contentID = 1275 > (accessed October 15, 2005).

U.S. State Department. "Patterns of Global Terrorism." < http://www.state.gov/s/ct/rls/pgtrpt/2003/31638.htm > (accessed October 15, 2005).

SEE ALSO

Fatah Revolutionary Council

Hezbollah

Aum Supreme Truth (AUM)

ALTERNATE NAME: Aleph, formerly Aum Shinrikyo

LEADER: Asahara Shoko

YEAR ESTABLISHED OR BECAME ACTIVE: 1987

ESTIMATED SIZE: Two thousand in Japan; a similar number of followers live in Russia, where it has been outlawed

USUAL AREA OF OPERATION: Japan; Russia; United States, United Kingdom

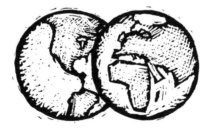

Aum Shinrikyo (now known as Aleph) is an apocalyptic Japanese religious cult. Their belief that world salvation could only come through the destruction of most of the planet's population reached its horrifying denouement in 1995 when its members carried out a deadly nerve gas attack on the Tokyo subway system, killing 12 and injuring thousands more. Despite being on the U.S. Department of State's list of terrorist organizations, it continues to operate under the name "Aleph."

HISTORY

Aum Shinrikyo's path from obscure religious cult to brutal terrorist group occurred over a decade, but its journey is telling of the dangers that can be posed by powerful and devout religious sects.

It was founded in 1987 by Asahara Shoko (born Chizuo Matsumoto; Asahara is his "holy" name), a blind herbalist and acupuncturist. Asahara had become devoutly religious when, as a 22-year-old a decade earlier, he had moved to Tokyo to study. He began to follow Agonshu, a new religion only created in 1969, which taught that people should strive to realize enlightenment

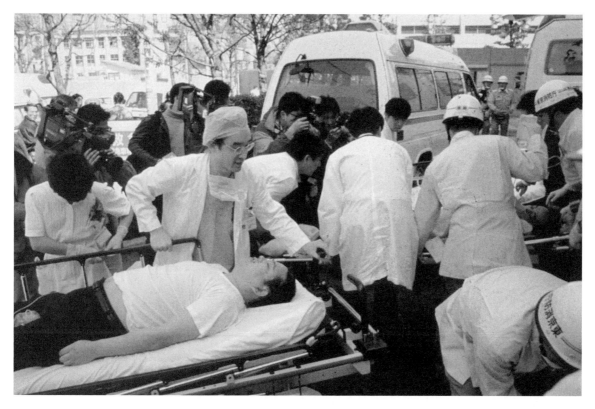

Subway passengers harmed by sarin gas circulated through central Tokyo stations are brought into St. Luke's International Hospital on March 20, 1995. AP/Wide World Photos. Reproduced by permission.

in this life and that "bad karma" could be relieved by meditation.

Later, as a yoga instructor, he began to attract a following as a spiritualist and meditation guru. Yet, it was only in 1987 that he completed his "spiritual journey" and formed his own cult, which occurred following a trip to India when Asahara claimed to have received enlightenment. On his return to Japan, he changed his name and created Aum Shinrikyo. *Aum* is Sanskrit for "the powers of destruction and creation of the universe" and *Shinrikyo* means the "teaching of the supreme truth." The group's aim—as its name suggested—was to teach the truth about the creation and destruction of the universe.

Asahara Shoko's new cult soon acquired a following that numbered a couple of thousand. It attracted followers from across the spectrum of Japanese society, particularly, it seemed, those who felt alienated from the increasing materialism in a nation that was then approaching the peak of its economic power. Devotees

were expected to live an ascetic life, eschewing material goods, giving their possessions to the cult and living in communes. In August 1989, following a legal dispute with the Tokyo authorities, Aum was finally granted legal status allowing members benefits such as tax privileges, the right to own property as an organization, and, perhaps crucially, a degree of protection from state or external interference in its workings.

Nevertheless, unfavorable accusations began to play out in the Japanese press during the summer of 1989 when the prominent newspaper, the *Sunday Mainichi*, published a seven-part series on the group. This included claims that members were involuntarily separated from their families and that children received no schooling, as well as accusations of mind control techniques, including sleep and food deprivation and "blood initiations." The newspaper also suggested sizable "donations" were, essentially, extorted from members. Aum responded by threatening to sue the editors of the *Sunday*

Firefighters emerge from Tokyo's Kodemmacho subway station after cleaning cars that were contaminated by gas in an attack by the Aum Shinri Kyo cult on March 12, 1995. AP/Wide World Photos. *Reproduced by permission.*

Mainichi, but the newspaper received more than 200 letters of support from former members who also expressed similar grievances.

The *Sunday Mainchi* stories also cast light on an ongoing legal case initiated by the Yokohomo-based lawyer, Sakamoto Tsutsumi. Tsutsumi was taking forward an action against Aum on behalf of parents separated from their children. As part of his investigations, Sakamoto had discovered that a bizarre claim made by

LEADERSHIP

ASAHARA SHOKO

Asahara Shoko (born Chizuo Matsumoto) is Aum's founder and spiritual leader. The blind former herbalist and acupuncturist was born in 1955 and claimed to be a religious guru following a trip to India in 1986, in which he reached a state of "enlightenment." His supporters claim he is a charismatic preacher and a deity, an image that apparently belies the popular portrayal of Asahara as a slovenly, long-haired madman.

His bizarre claims to hold supernatural powers because his blood contained "unique" DNA code, and his belief that the world would be ravaged by nuclear war in 1999 have seen him mocked; and the violent crimes carried out under his orders have seen him despised.

While others masterminded the sarin attacks of 1994 and 1995, it was Asahara who gave the initial instructions, and followers who have confessed involvement in other crimes have claimed they were acting under his direct orders. In February 2004, he was sentenced to death, a verdict that—at the time of writing—is still pending appeal and likely to do so for quite some time: Asahara is currently in a state of "permanent meditation" and refusing to cooperate with Japan's judicial authorities. His family, on the other hand, claimed in June 2005 that he is mentally ill and should be transferred from prison to a hospital.

Asahara—that tests conducted at Kyoto University showed that his blood contained unique DNA, thus proving some special spiritual powers—was a complete fabrication and that no such tests had taken place.

Tsutsumi's investigation would, however, come to an abrupt end in November 1989 when he disappeared from his home with his wife and 14-month-old son. Blood at the scene pointed to a violent ending, possibly at the hands of Aum. However, no bodies were found until September 1995 when police were finally able to pin the disappearance on several of the cult members. Tsutsumi and his wife had been beaten and strangled to death, their baby drugged and smothered, teeth smashed out to obfuscate any investigation, and the bodies buried in three separate mountain locations.

In the midst of Aum's rising notoriety in 1989, Asahara decided that political action was necessary to save the world and so launched *Shinrito* (Supreme Truth Party) as a way of publicizing his teachings and offering salvation to a larger audience. Asahara was apparently convinced that each of the 25 candidates he put forward would win—but they lost miserably and became something of a national joke.

This further ostracized Aum from Japanese society and marked the onset of a major ideological shift. From seeking to prevent an apocalypse, Aum saw it as inevitable (even if it would have to be at their instigation) and began to prepare and protect its members—who would be chosen to survive and lead the post-Armageddon world to salvation—from the forthcoming "judgment day." Aum's leadership began to intensify the austerity of its members' existences, also beginning the construction of nuclear bunkers and communes. This increased introversion strengthened Aum's hierarchical structure, and the power of its leaders.

Secretly, on Asahara's orders, a team of members was set up to develop chemical weapons. Tsuchiya Masami, who possessed a Master's degree in Organic Chemistry, was placed in charge of chemical weapons research in March 1993, and by the end of the year had succeeded in producing the deadly nerve gas, sarin.

On June 27, 1994, a sarin attack took place in a residential area of the central city of Matsumoto. Seven people died and hundreds were injured. It was revealed in a subsequent court case that Asahara had ordered the attack—carried out by refrigerated trucks equipped with spraying mechanisms—to be conducted in the vicinity of three judges set to hear a case against Aum members. The attack succeeded in injuring the men.

Asahara's delusions of grandeur increased following the attacks. He established his own "government" in opposition to the Japanese government to promote his so called "imperial aspirations."

Not until January 1995, however, would police make the link between the Matsumoto attack and Aum. This was in spite of a major gas leak at the Aum commune just two weeks after the attack, in which Aum numbers were reportedly seen running from a building on the site wearing gas masks.

Police were, nevertheless, slow to make arrests. On March 19, 1995, they raided the Aum headquarters in Osaka and arrested three members for the alleged abduction of a member.

A day later, and seemingly fearing that the noose was tightening on the organization, ten Aum members in the midst of Tokyo's rush hour released packets containing liquid sarin onto trains in its underground system. The packages containing the poison were wrapped in newspaper and punctured by umbrella tips. Each contained around one liter of sarin: less than 1 milliliter can kill a person if administered through the skin. As a liquid, it is less potent, but the vapor caused by the leaked sarin was still devastating: twelve people died, and 5,500 more were seriously injured by the attacks.

Further violence followed as police cracked down on Aum, arresting two hundred of its members. On March 30, 1995, there was an attempt to assassinate the chief of the national police agency, and further gas attacks followed on trains in the Tokyo–Yokohama area. Plans were uncovered that Aum planned and intended to disperse seventy tons of sarin throughout Japan—enough to kill 36 million people—and that a former Russian military helicopter had been acquired.

Police took several weeks of searching Kamikuishiki, the village where Aum is located, to uncover Asahara, who was found meditating in the company of several comatose followers (who had been drugged), and a haul of cash and gold bars. He was eventually indicted for murder in relation to the Tokyo and Matsumoto attacks, as well as for the kidnapping and murder of Tsutsumi and his family and several other deaths and assaults. The lengthy police investigation also revealed that thirty-three Aum followers were believed to have been killed in the seven years leading to March 1995.

KEY EVENTS

1987: Formed by Shoko Asahara as Aum Shinrikyo.

1989: Revelations about the cult's darker side in the Japanese press.

1989: Kidnapping and murder of Yokohomo-based lawyer, Sakamoto Tsutsumi, and his family.

1994: Sarin attack on Japanese city of Matsumoto kills seven.

1995: Sarin attacks on Tokyo underground kill twelve and injure 5,500.

2000: Aum Shinrikyo relaunches as Aleph.

1996–2004: Trial proceedings against Asahara culminate in his death sentence in February 2004; sentence currently pending appeal.

Asahara was sentenced to death by hanging by a Tokyo court in February 2004 after a trial process lasting eight years. He appealed the verdict before the Japanese Supreme Court, but the case has stalled because of Asahara's refusal—or inability—to communicate with the authorities. Eleven other Aum members have been sentenced to death pending appeal.

Aum's membership base was decimated following the attacks, and although it was declared a terrorist organization by the U.S. Department of State, it was, conversely, never declared illegal in Japan. In 2000, the organization regrouped under the leadership of Fumihiro Joyu and changed its name to Aleph (aleph being the first letter of the Hebrew alphabet, meaning to start anew). Despite apologizing for the sarin attacks and setting up a compensation fund for its victims, the group has never revoked its ties to Asahara.

PHILOSOPHY AND TACTICS

The aims of Aum Shinrikyo and the reasons they carried out such horrific attacks in 1994 and

PRIMARY SOURCE
Japanese Cult Leader Sentenced to Death

A former leader of the Aum Shinrikyo, or Supreme Truth Cult, has been sentenced to death in Japan for his involvement in a series of murders, including the 1995 sarin gas attack on the Tokyo underground.

Tomomitsu Niimi, "home affairs minister" of the cult, was found guilty in seven murder cases and two attempted murder cases that took place between 1989 and 1995.

At the beginning of his trial in 1996, Niimi refused to enter pleas and pledged eternal loyalty to Aum guru Shoko Asahara, who is accused of masterminding the attack on the underground.

Niimi is since reported to have admitted to all the charges against him, except the one relating to the sarin gas attack, which killed 12 people and left thousands ill.

'FOLLOWING ORDERS'
He allegedly said he was following Mr. Asahara's orders and should not be sentenced to death.

Mr. Asahara is still on trial for the attack on the underground.

Niimi was also found guilty of helping to organise the killing of lawyer Tsutsuni

Sakamoto and his wife and son. Mr. Sakamoto was one of the first to question the group's activities.

Has about 1,000 lay followers and 650 followers in cult communes. Predicted an apocalypse that only cult members would survive. Thought to raise most funds from computer software business it runs.

Prosecutors have demanded the death penalty for 11 cult members. Eight have been sentenced, but some have appealed and none of the sentences have been carried out.

Niimi is also expected to appeal the verdict.

Lawyers for Mr. Asahara—whose real name is Chizuo Matsumoto—are not expected to end their submissions until next year.

Aum Shinrikyo has since changed its name to Aleph and claims to have renounced violence.

But Japanese security agencies announced last month that they were renewing their three-year surveillance of the cult as they believe it remains a threat.

Source: BBC News, 2002

1995 remain muddied by the contradictory statements and subsequent silence of its leader Asahara Shoko. If one takes the sarin attacks to their most far-fetched potential, they may have triggered off the doomsday scenario to which he seemed to aspire. *Destroying The World To Save It*, one of many books on Aum, contains the essence of Asahara's apocalyptic beliefs.

Aum Shinrikyo's more benign teachings were based on strands of Hinduism and Buddhism, but it seemed to have no theological basis, nor manifesto, and its core beliefs have evolved substantially over the organization's relatively short life. Activities include yoga, meditation, and breathing exercises, and Aum's members lead Spartan lives far removed from

the hustle and bustle of Japanese society. It has been argued that this austerity—by marginalizing members from the outside world—increases Aum's leaders' control over its followers and that this dominance has been one of the keys to Aum's relative success in attracting and retaining followers.

OTHER PERSPECTIVES

Robert Jay Lifton, a Professor of Psychiatry and Psychology at The City University of New York, has termed the control of Aum's leaders over its members as "ideological totalism." This essentially means, he writes, that "everything

PRIMARY SOURCE
Aum Shinrikyo (Aum) a.k.a. Aum Supreme Truth, Aleph

DESCRIPTION

A cult established in 1987 by Shoko Asahara, the Aum aimed to take over Japan and then the world. Approved as a religious entity in 1989 under Japanese law, the group ran candidates in a Japanese parliamentary election in 1990. Over time, the cult began to emphasize the imminence of the end of the world and stated that the United States would initiate Armageddon by starting World War III with Japan. The Japanese Government revoked its recognition of the Aum as a religious organization in October 1995, but in 1997 a Government panel decided not to invoke the Anti-Subversive Law against the group, which would have outlawed it. A 1999 law continues to give the Japanese Government authorization to maintain police surveillance of the group due to concerns that the Aum might launch future terrorist attacks. Under the leadership of Fumihiro Joyu, the Aum changed its name to Aleph in January 2000 and tried to distance itself from the violent and apocalyptic teachings of its founder. However, in late 2003, Joyu stepped down, pressured by members who wanted to return fully to the worship of Asahara.

ACTIVITIES

On March 20, 1995, Aum members simultaneously released the chemical nerve agent sarin on several Tokyo subway trains, killing 12 persons and injuring up to 1,500. The group was responsible for other mysterious events involving chemical incidents in Japan in 1994. Its efforts to conduct attacks using biological agents have been unsuccessful. Japanese police arrested Asahara in May 1995, and authorities sentenced him in February 2004 to death for his role in the attacks of 1995. Since 1997, the cult has continued to recruit new members, engage in commercial enterprise, and acquire property, although it scaled back these activities significantly in 2001 in response to public outcry. In July 2001, Russian authorities arrested a group of Russian Aum followers who had planned to set off bombs near the Imperial Palace in Tokyo as part of an operation to free Asahara from jail and smuggle him to Russia.

STRENGTH

The Aum's current membership in Japan is estimated to be about 1,650 persons. At the time of the Tokyo subway attack, the group claimed to have 9,000 members in Japan and as many as 40,000 worldwide.

LOCATION/AREA OF OPERATION

The Aum's principal membership is located in Japan, but a residual branch comprising about 300 followers has surfaced in Russia.

EXTERNAL AID

None.

Source: U.S. Department of State. *Country Reports on Terrorism.* Washington, D.C., 2004.

---

had to be experienced on an all-or-nothing basis. A number of psychological patterns characterize such an environment. Most basic is milieu control, in which all communication, including even an individual's inner communication, is monopolized and orchestrated, so that reality becomes the group's exclusive possession. Aum's closed subculture of guru and renunciants lent itself to an all-encompassing form of milieu control, though no such control can ever be complete or foolproof."

Professor Catherine Wessinger of Loyola University in New Orleans agrees that Aum members were cowed by its leaders and possibly coerced into carrying out acts of violence. Yet, she ultimately believes that the assaults came about because of the failings of Japan's law enforcement agencies. "The Japanese new religion known as Aum Shinrikyo stands in contrast to Jonestown and the Branch Davidians," she wrote in her history of religious cults, *How the Millennium Comes Violently: From Jonestown to*

Heaven's Gate, "because Aum devotees detained, coerced, tortured, and killed people, and pursued the development of weapons of mass destruction in a national context in which the activities of religious organizations were not scrutinized by law enforcement agents. Aum's guru, Shoko Asahara, and his devotees saw themselves as belonging to a persecuted religious organization, but the activities of their cultural opponents were miniscule compared to the violence perpetrated by Aum devotees. Aum leaders were anxious to block investigation of Aum Shinrikyo because of crimes that members had committed before serious cultural opposition had developed. In terms of financial resources and violence against members and outsiders, Aum Shinrikyo makes Jim Jones's Jonestown and David Koresh's Mount Carmel Center appear small-scale."

SUMMARY

Because of the scandal and outrage created by the sarin attacks and possibly because of the passing of the millennium (and the deadline for Asahara's apocalyptic prophesies), Aum Shinrikyo has regrouped under the name Aleph and apologized for its past violence. However, it has not denounced Asahara, whom it still regards as its spiritual leader.

Despite being regarded as a terrorist organization elsewhere in the world, its main area of operation—Japan—refuses to outlaw Aum, because its government "cannot prove" that it is an imminent threat to security. It has nevertheless placed Aleph under extended surveillance.

Its membership now numbers a couple of thousand members and it adopts more the characteristics of a conventional religious cult. Nevertheless, it maintains relatively extensive business interests, including a publishing group, record company, yoga training center, computer manufacturers, and software developers.

SOURCES

Books

Lifton, Robert Jay. *Destroying the World to Save It: Aum Shinrikyo, Apocalyptic Violence, and the New Global Terrorism.* New York: Owl Books, 2000.

Reader, Ian. *Religious Violence in Contemporary Japan: Case of Aum Shinrikyo.* Honolulu: University of Hawaii Press, 2000.

Wessinger, Catherine. *How the Millennium Comes Violently: From Jonestown to Heaven's Gate.* New York: Chatham House Publishers, 2000.

Web sites

Apologetics Index. "Aum Shinrikyo." <http://www.apologeticsindex.org/a06.html> (accessed October 10, 2005).

Basque Fatherland and Liberty (ETA)

ALTERNATE NAME ETA

LEADER: Arnaldo Otegi

YEAR ESTABLISHED OR BECAME ACTIVE: 1959

ESTIMATED SIZE: Unknown

USUAL AREA OF OPERATION: Spain; southwest France

U.S. TERRORIST EXCLUSION LIST DESIGNEE: The U.S. Department of State declared ETA to be a terrorist organization in October 1997

Euskadi Ta Askatasuna (ETA, Basque Fatherland and Liberty) is a Basque separatist organization, which has waged a long-running campaign of violence to gain the secession of the Basque parts of Spain and France, and to create an independent Basque state.

HISTORY

ETA was founded in the 1950s as a student discussion group, which evolved by the late 1950s into a direct-action resistance organization. However, its socialist and, above all, Basque nationalist roots lie at least two decades further back.

Spain, in the 1950s was still under the control of its fascist dictator General Francisco Franco, who, for a variety of reasons, had survived the fate of his former stalemates—Adolf Hitler and Benito Mussolini—to continue leading Spain in the post-war era (and would continue doing so until 1975). Franco had risen to power in the late 1930s after crushing the democratically elected socialist government of the Spanish Second Republic in the Spanish Civil War. Spain's Second Republic had extolled a benevolent kind of socialism (e.g., small-scale land redistribution and wide-scale literacy

A woman protests against the ETA in Madrid on February 23, 2000. The demonstration took place after a Basque socialist politician was killed in a car bomb attack in Vitoria. AP/Wide World Photos

ETA emerged as a student discussion group at the University of Deusto in the Basque city of Bilbao in 1953. It was an offshoot of the youth group of the PNV (the foremost Basque nationalist party in the Second Republic and leading party in the Basque government in exile in France, but suppressed by Franco) and originally called *Ekin* (to get busy). The emergence of a student "talking shop" to discuss ideas of Basque nationhood and identity less than two decades after the Spanish Civil War was at once daring, but also a signal of defiance at the suppression of Basque identity in Franco's Spain.

The group reconstituted itself as ETA in 1959, and articulated the view that Basque nationality is defined by language, rather than ethnicity or religion as other Basque nationalists had traditionally tended to do. Its leaders also extolled a brand of socialism, which has remained a part of its identity in the years since. In 1965, this evolved into a Marxist-Leninist position, although this was later modified in the 1980s.

In its early life, ETA, probably by necessity, remained largely in the shadows, confining itself to the hanging of Basque flags—forbidden by Franco—and the destruction of Spanish symbols and other infrastructure. When it turned to more overt violence remains the subject of some debate, and while several died as a result of ETA sabotage attacks in the early 1960s, it seems unlikely that these were intentional. Certainly, the first ETA assassination to attract widespread notoriety came in August 1968, when ETA members killed Meliton Manzanas, a secret police chief in the Basque city of San Sebastian. Manzanas was a notorious figure who oversaw the torture of prisoners during interrogations and had been a Gestapo collaborator in France's Vichy regime. Six ETA members would be sentenced to death for the killing, but quite whether this was a political attack on the Franco regime or merely a reprisal for the killing by Spanish police of Xabi Etxebarrieta, an ETA militant, remains the subject of some conjecture.

Five years later, however, ETA, secured worldwide fame by assassinating Franco's anointed successor, the Spanish Prime Minister, Admiral Luis Carrero Blanco, in Madrid. The daring attack—a ton of explosives had been buried under a Madrid side street and detonated as Blanco's car drove over it, catapulting the

programs as opposed to the often brutal revolutionary Marxist-Leninism undertaken in the USSR at that time) and afforded large degrees of autonomy to the linguistically and ethnically unique areas of Catalonia and the Basque Country.

Franco characterized his fight for Spain both during and after the Spanish Civil War (1936–1939) by brutally cracking down on socialists and those who sought self-determination. His most notorious assault on Basques was, in many ways, the defining moment of the Spanish Civil War when he ordered the bombing of the town of Guernica, which was destroyed in four hours of air raids. Not only was this the first large-scale civilian bombing in history (later immortalized in Pablo Picasso's painting of the same name), but Guernica was a deeply symbolic place for the Basques. Franco had intended the bombing to crush the Basque national spirit. However, in many Basque minds, Guernica represented an historic breaking point with the rest of Spain represented not just by Franco and government from Madrid, but linguistically and nationalistically. This would hold deep significance in later years.

Officials clear the scene after an explosion under a police car May 30, 2003 in Sanguesa in northern Spain.
Reuters/Corbis

vehicle over a church and against the roof of a five-story apartment building before it crashed onto the street below—had followed a crackdown on Basque separatists and coincided with the start of a trial of ten leading Franco opponents.

Far from securing universal notoriety, however, ETA's attack was even praised by some Spanish liberals, and for breaking the Francoist plan for succession. When Franco died in November 1975, rather than one of his political allies succeeding him as head of state, this role returned to the monarchy, to King Juan Carlos. He then transferred control of Spain back to a democratically elected Parliament after elections in June 1977.

During this period of transition towards democracy, Spain in general and ETA in particular experienced profound changes. After

Franco's death followed an amnesty of former political prisoners, including many from ETA's ranks, some of whom had been engaged in violence. At this point, ETA split into two discernable groups: the majority into ETA political-military, ETA(pm), and a minority into ETA military, ETA(m). The former abandoned violence, accepted Spain's new constitutional democracy, with limited self-government for the Basque country (and Catalonia), and integrated into the political party Euskadiko Ezkerra.

ETA(m), which would soon become known simply as ETA, adopted a more radical approach and refused to recognize Spain's new constitutional democracy. Like the IRA, to which it is often compared, nothing less than full independence was deemed acceptable. Spain's first years of democracy marked ETA's

Firefighters inspect a wrecked Civil Guard patrol vehicle after an ETA bomb exploded, killing officers Irene Fernandez Pereda and Jose Angel de Jesus Encinas in northern Spain on August 20, 2000. AP/Wide *World Photos. Reproduced by permission.*

most violent period, in which they claimed more than two hundred lives. Some of these attacks were made on former ETA members who had turned to democracy in post-Francoist Spain, most notoriously the murder of Maria Dolores Katarain, a former director of ETA whom they accused of "desertion" after she abandoned their armed struggle.

By the mid 1980s, ETA had adopted many of the tactics favored by violent paramilitary groups, including car bombings or attacks targeted at shopping areas. Usually they would be preceded by a warning—the intention being to disrupt rather than to maim—but often this would be misplaced or given too late. A series of atrocities, such as an attack on a Barcelona shopping center that killed twenty-one and injured forty-five in June 1987, provoked outage and heightened the Spanish government's resolve against ETA.

Between 1983 and 1987, officials within Spain's center-left PSOE government sponsored a so-called "dirty war" against Basque extremists. Carried out by *Grupos Antiterroristas de Liberación* (GAL, Antiterrorists Groups of Freedom), they operated largely from the French side of the border, targeting ETA leaders and militants and murdering twenty-three people, around a third of whom had no terrorist connections.

According to Paddy Woodworth in *Dirty Wars, Clean Hands: ETA, the GAL and Spanish Democracy*, a GAL operation, in October 1983 bore the imprint of later missions. GAL kidnapped two young ETA members, Joxean Lasa and Joxe Zabala, in Bayonne, took them to an abandoned palace belonging to a PSOE leader, Julen Elgorriaga, in San Sebastian, where they were tortured by members of the Civil Guard for several weeks. They were

Spanish firefighters put out flames from a vehicle that suspected ETA separatists drove to escape after detonating a car bomb in Madrid on January 21, 2000. The explosion killed Colonel Pedro Antonio Blanco Garcia and injured several others.
(*AP Photo/Dani Duch/La Vanguardia*)

then stuffed into the boot of a car, and driven 800 kilometers to Alicante, taken to a lonely desert spot, and shot in the back of the head and buried in quicklime.

The scandal created by GAL's activities (the Spanish Interior Minister Jose Barrionuevo was jailed in 1998 for sanctioning the "dirty war" and the Prime Minister, Felipe Gonzalez, was implicated, too) effectively saved ETA by the outrage caused among Spain's Basque population. This did not necessarily manifest itself in violent ways—*Gesto por la Paz* (Association for Peace in the Basque Country), which was founded in 1986, organized silent demonstrations following either ETA or GAL killings—but it cast attention on the issue of Basque separatism and prompted political talks between Basque political parties and the Spanish government in early 1988. ETA called a ceasefire, but when negotiations broke down, it soon returned to violence.

In 1992, ETA's three top leaders, Francisco Mujika Germendia, Jose Luis Alvarez Santacristnia, and Jose Maria Arregi Erostarbe—respectively, its military, political, and logistical leaders—were arrested in the French Basque town of Bidart. This briefly weakened ETA and saw a switch in tactics to a so-called street struggle. Essentially, it was an organized campaign of vandalism often carried out by minors. When further peace talks broke down in 1995, however, ETA soon returned to more overt violence, which included a failed car bombing directed at Jose Maria Aznar, the leader of *Partido Popular* (PP, Popular Party), Spain's largest conservative political party, and an abortive assassination attempt on King Juan Carlos.

Further outrage came in September 1997 when ETA kidnapped Miguel Angel Blanco, a low-ranking PP activist, and threatened to kill him unless the Spanish government's policy of dispersing ETA prisoners in jails across Spain ended. Six million people demonstrated to demand Blanco's release, but when the Spanish government refused to switch its policy, Blanco was shot in the head and dumped near the town of Pamplona. His execution prompted further furious protests against ETA.

Increasingly, the extremism of ETA meant it was becoming marginalized within its own heartlands. While most Spanish Basques favored greater autonomy, be it in a federal Spain or as an independent nation state, few backed the violent means ETA saw as a necessity. There was also a decline in patience at its unyielding obstinance in political talks, which it usually ducked out of when things were not going in its favor.

In March 2003, the Spanish government finally lost patience with ETA and banned Batasuna, ETA's political wing, and increased the security operation on its former members and those of ETA. This prompted yet another upsurge in violence.

On March 1, 2004, leading up to Spain's general elections, ETA left a massive truck bomb near Madrid, with the potential to cause a massacre had it not been for the intervention of police. Ten days later, on March 11, a series of bombs left on commuter trains in Madrid killed 192 people. The attacks were widely blamed on ETA at first, but it quickly turned out to be the work of al-Qaeda.

LEADERSHIP

KEY EVENTS

ARNALDO OTEGI

Born in 1958, Arnaldo Otegi was leader of the now-outlawed political wing of ETA, Batasuna, and is currently a member of the Basque regional parliament. It was largely for his refusal to denounce violence carried out by ETA that led the then-Spanish Prime Minister Jose Maria Aznar to outlaw Batasuna in 2003, although Otegi acts as *de facto* head, and when he makes his frequent appearances in the Spanish media, it is assumed that he speaks for Batasuna and, in turn, ETA.

Moves towards a negotiated settlement with ETA have stalled in part because of the Spanish government's continued attempts to silence Otegi. As well as banning his political party in 2003, he was jailed for fifteen months for "extolling terrorism" in 2004 (later reversed on appeal), and he was arrested in May 2005 for membership in ETA.

Nevertheless, his pledge in November 2004 to "take the conflict off the streets and bring it to the negotiating table," although initially viewed with skepticism, seems to have been taken seriously, and paved the way for secret peace negotiations during the summer of 2005.

Spain was left shocked by the Madrid bombings, and it seemingly marked the end of any sort of toleration—no matter how thin it may have been—for extremism. Perhaps taking its lead from the national mood, ETA went quiet for the following six months, although it resumed its bombing campaign, albeit on a smaller scale, toward the end of 2004.

At the same time, however, there have been moves toward reaching a sort of political settlement. Arnaldo Otegi, Batasuna's leader, pledged in November 2004 that he would "take the conflict off the streets and bring it to the negotiating table." That same month, a letter from six jailed Basque terrorists—including its former leader,

1959: Founded out of the remnants of a student discussion group.

1968: Assassination of secret police chief, Meliton Manzanas.

1973: ETA murders Spanish Prime Minister and Franco's anointed successor as head of state, Admiral Luis Carrero Blanco.

1977–1978: Split between ETA(pm), which backs constitutional democracy, and ETA(m) which favors violent methods.

1983–1987: Government-backed GAL declares "dirty war" on ETA.

1997: Kidnapping and murder of political activist, Miguel Angel Blanco, prompts massive demonstrations against ETA.

2004: Madrid train bombings by al-Qaeda just a week after an ETA bomb plot was uncovered prompt huge mood shift among Spanish population.

2005: Secret talks between ETA and Spanish government prompt hopes of a political settlement.

Mugica Garmendia—urged ETA to abandon its campaign of violence and to back "institutional and mass struggle" for an independent Basque homeland.

In May 2005, the Spanish government stated its willingness to enter new talks with Basque separatists on the proviso of an ETA ceasefire, and according to *El Mundo* newspaper, secret talks were staged between ETA and the Spanish government throughout the summer of 2005.

PHILOSOPHY AND TACTICS

ETA is a Basque nationalist organization committed to the creation of an independent state for its people. It has declared its belief that the

PRIMARY SOURCE

Basque Fatherland and Liberty (ETA)
a.k.a. Euzkadi Ta Askatasuna, Batasuna

DESCRIPTION

ETA was founded in 1959 with the aim of establishing an independent homeland based on Marxist principles and encompassing the Spanish Basque provinces of Vizcaya, Guipuzcoa, and Alava, as well as the autonomous region of Navarra and the southwestern French Departments of Labourd, Basse-Navarra, and Soule. Spanish and French counterterrorism initiatives since 2000 have hampered the group's operational capabilities. Spanish police arrested scores of ETA members and accomplices in Spain in 2004, and dozens were apprehended in France, including two key group leaders. These arrests included the capture in October of two key ETA leaders in southwestern France. ETA's political wing, Batasuna, remains banned in Spain. Spanish and French prisons are estimated to hold over 700 ETA members.

ACTIVITIES

Primarily involved in bombings and assassinations of Spanish Government officials, security and military forces, politicians, and judicial figures, but has also targeted journalists and tourist areas. Security service scrutiny and a public outcry after the Islamic extremist train bombing on March 11, 2004, in Madrid limited ETA's capabilities and willingness to inflict casualties. ETA conducted no fatal attacks in 2004, but did mount several low-level bombings in Spanish tourist areas during the summer and 11 bombings in early December, each preceded by a warning call. The group has killed more than 850 persons and injured hundreds of others since it began lethal attacks in the 1960s. ETA finances its activities primarily through extortion and robbery.

STRENGTH

Unknown; hundreds of members plus supporters.

LOCATION/AREA OF OPERATION

Operates primarily in the Basque autonomous regions of northern Spain and southwestern France, but also has attacked Spanish and French interests elsewhere.

EXTERNAL AID

Has received training at various times in the past in Libya, Lebanon, and Nicaragua. Some ETA members allegedly fled to Cuba and Mexico while others reside in South America. ETA members have operated and been arrested in other European countries, including Belgium, The Netherlands, and Germany.

Source: U.S. Department of State. *Country Reports on Terrorism.* Washington, D.C., 2004.

Basque people hold sovereignty over the entire Basque region, which encompasses northeastern Spain and parts of southwestern France. It extols violence as a way of pressuring the Spanish government and people into giving in to its aims.

It has also always extolled a socialist ideology. For a time, this was Marxist-Leninist, but it moderated these views in the 1980s. Nevertheless, the remnants of Batasuna retain many leftist views, and ETA is identified with the Basque National Liberation Movement, a left-wing coalition of political parties, trade unions, and youth groups.

ETA's view of Basque nationalism is defined by language rather than ethnicity or religion. This partly explains why it has been more successful on the Spanish side of the border, where Euskara is more widely spoken, than in the French part of Basque country. While French Basques will commonly define their identity by flying Basque flags, sometimes speaking Euskara, or attending bullfights and Basque-style fiestas, they do so in synch with their French nationality. By contrast, Basques on the Spanish side of the border go in for the same cultural trappings, but will commonly define themselves as exclusively Basque. Tellingly,

PRIMARY SOURCE

ETA 'Ends Attacks' on Politicians

The Basque militant group ETA has said it will no longer attack Spanish politicians, in a statement reported by the Basque newspaper, *Gara*.

The group said it has closed its "front" against politicians because of changes in the political climate.

Madrid has offered to negotiate with ETA if it lays down its weapons.

The militants, who are blamed for some 800 deaths in their 40-year fight for an independent Basque nation, say they are ready to talk but not to disarm.

A statement issued by the group on Friday stressed that the right to self-determination would have to be central to any peace process.

PROTESTS

ETA's latest statement, issued on Saturday, said it was waiting for the Spanish and French authorities to "respond positively to the will" it had displayed.

The militants' planned Basque homeland encompasses areas of northern Spain and south-western France.

Over the past two years, it has carried out several small attacks without causing any deaths.

Some 250,000 people marched in Madrid earlier in June to protest at Prime Minister Jose Luis Rodriguez Zapatero's offer to negotiate with the militant separatists.

Source: BBC News, 2005

---

support for an independent Basque nation is barely in issue in France, while polls show around a third of Spanish Basques support the idea, and a further third back greater autonomy.

ETA's tactics have included assassinations, bombings, and kidnappings. It has also involved itself in attacks on drug dealers—a politically popular move on a local level. Its funding has traditionally come from bank robberies, but it has also been accused of kidnapping and extortion.

OTHER PERSPECTIVES

Writing in the *New Statesman*, the Madrid-based journalist John Carlin wrote that he believed extreme Basque and Catalan nationalism would die out within a generation. "Franco ... exercised such a strong centralist grip—he banned the Basque and Catalan languages—that, when the lid came off, nationalist fervour inevitably bubbled over." By contrast, "The people who will be ruling Spain in ten or 20 years, who were born around the time of Franco's death, have not grown up in a climate

of political oppression. Neither have they the inferiority complex of their parents vis-a-vis the British, Germans or French. Basques learn in Basque at school; Catalans in Catalan. They have their own newspapers, TV stations, historical street names. However, young Catalans increasingly use Castilian Spanish in everyday conversation. And young Basques, bludgeoned into learning an abstruse tongue by their political elders, will probably follow. In general, young people are more relaxed about their regional identities, more confident about their status in Europe, less slaves to political passion."

"What do the Basques want now?" asked Luis Núñez Astrain in *The Basques: Their Struggle for Independence*. "Don't they already have a democratic system comparable with that of any other European country? Don't they enjoy a substantial measure of autonomy? So what is the point of their interminable protests, their huge demonstrations, their armed struggle?" The problem, according to Astrain, is the institutions themselves, as they "are complex and confused, and far from making up an entity peculiar to the Basques, they have exactly the opposite effect, of actually preventing the people from achieving unity. It is not that these political institutions do not work but that they exist in excessive numbers. There are too many of them and their functions are too various. What is lacking, in short, are institutions with a unitary function which would make for cohesion and ensure the sovereignty of a country which stands in great need of them." Until this issue is resolved, in other words, a satisfactory political resolution for the Basques will not exist.

SUMMARY

As of 2005, ETA has undergone the longest period in its history without causing death through its violence. Secret negotiations initiated by the Spanish government may bring a political solution to the region, but it is difficult to see where talks can lead to short of full independence. At present, no region in the world enjoys such a high degree of self-government as the Basque Country, and it has its own regional rule, its own police, and even its own tax system. Failing independence, as the Basque people become more integrated within both Spain and the European Union, and continue to lose their appetite for extremism in the post-Madrid bombings era, ETA may become a thing of the past, or, at least reflect the views of an ever-increasing minority.

SOURCES

Books

Núñez Astrain, Luis. *The Basques: Their Struggle for Independence*. Cardiff: Welsh Academic Press, 1997.

Preston, Paul. *A Concise History of the Spanish Civil War*. New York: HarperCollins, 1996.

Woodworth, Paddy. *Dirty Wars, Clean Hands: ETA, the GAL, and Spanish Democracy*. Ireland: Cork University Press, 2001.

Periodicals

Carlin, John. "An Ethical Nation, Full of Bluster: Spaniards Love Europe Because They Hate Each Other. So will the Country Fall Apart?" *New Statesman*. June 16, 2003.

Web sites

Eushal Herria Journal. "Navarre." < http://www.ehj-navarre.org/navarre/na_repression_intro.html > (accessed October 11, 2005).

SEE ALSO

Irish Republican Army

Blood and Honour

OVERVIEW

Blood and Honour is a white-power skinhead organization that uses music to spread its political views. The group is a loosely based network that claims no political affiliations and no leadership. Calling itself a leaderless resistance, the group seeks to recruit and educate youths regarding their worldview of white supremacy through various publications, CDs, and most notably, concerts.

The group was founded by Ian Stuart Donaldson (known as Ian Stuart) in 1987. Stuart, who started as a punk musician, moved more toward the skinhead music movement as his music career progressed. However, his involvement with the skinheads led him to be rejected and unable to play the venues that he played as a punk musician. As such, Stuart found other outlets that were more agreeable to his political ideology. While playing at these underground concerts, Stuart performed an original song called "Blood and Honour." The phrase, once used by members of Hitler's Youth, inspired the name of the organization that would use music to spread its message of white supremacy throughout Central and Western Europe, Australia, and the United States.

HISTORY

Blood and Honour stemmed from the white-supremacy skinhead music movement called

Czech riot policemen wrestle with drunken skinheads at a private rock concert in Kozolupy, some 100 kilometers southwest of Prague, where about 700 skinheads from the Czech Republic, Hungary, Poland, and Germany met. The event was reportedly organized by the international neo-Nazi organization Blood and Honour. AP/Wide World Photos. Reproduced by permission.

"Oi!" Prior to its formation, the National Front, an extreme right-wing nationalist political movement provided venues, recordings, and literature used by the white supremacy movement under the name Rock Against Communism. Under Rock Against Communism, bands, such as Ian Stuart's Skrewdriver, No Remorse, and Brutal Attack, were managed through the organization of the White Noise Club and White Noise Records. The music groups' performances, largely at underground concerts and festivals, began to generate revenues for Rock Against Communism, as well as for the National Front. However, by 1986, the National Front split apart, which ended the White Noise Club. Ian Stuart and other musicians discovered that the White Noise Club had cheated both bands and concertgoers. Ian Stuart's disillusionment with the leadership of the White Noise Club and the National Front

led him to create a new umbrella organization for his music movement called Blood and Honour.

In 1987, Stuart called for a meeting among the skinhead movement leadership with the goal to create a new coalition that would be self-sufficient and independent. By July, the group had officially declared itself and its goals. Believing politics would hinder the progress of the movement, Stuart insisted on no political affiliation. Stuart, and the High Command made up of band members, would direct the group by providing assistance to units in the areas of venue organization, security, and propaganda—to include magazines and Internet operations. As such, July of 1987 saw the inaugural publication of the magazine, *Blood and Honour*.

LEADERSHIP

IAN STUART

Although Blood and Honour advocates a leaderless resistance, Ian Stuart is looked to as the founder of the movement. Stuart was born on April 11, 1958, in Poulton-Le-Fylde, England. He began his musical career with several friends from grammar school. The group, known as Tumbling Dice, mainly played Rolling Stones' songs. After being heavily influence by punk music, Stuart reformed the bank in 1977, and renamed it Skrewdriver. As Stuart began to write more of the band's songs, the group shifted once more toward Oi!, or white-supremacy skinhead music. By mid 1978, the band's ideology, and being labeled as a National Front band, led to it being boycotted from playing venues in London, or being recorded.

By 1980, Stuart had totally transformed Skrewdriver into a skinhead band and developed ties with Rock Against Communism, a music organization with ties to the extreme right-wing National Front. However in 1986, the National Front split under allegations that some within the organization were taking advantage of bands and concert-goers. One year later, Stuart would take the lead in the formation of Blood and Honour.

Stuart would continue to perform his music and meet with others in the skinhead movement, at home and abroad. In doing so, he created the groundwork for the spread of his music and political ideology internationally. In 1993, he died in a car accident, which many of his supporters suspect was caused by the British Security Services.

Most of the present day leadership operates under pseudonyms. An example of this is Max Hammer, who hosts the official Blood and Honour web site.

As followers of Stuart and Blood and Honour established their own bands, including hatecore, racist hardcore punk, and racist metal, the groups began to create an international base. Groups of supporters with active members

KEY EVENTS

1987: The group was founded by Ian Stuart Donaldson (known as Ian Stuart).

2000: The German government banned Blood and Honour from operating within its borders.

numbering 30 or more were granted "division" status and smaller groups were granted "sectional" status. The first division appeared in Australia and the movement then moved throughout Romania, Bulgaria, Slovenia, Serbia, Germany, and the United States. However on September 14, 2000, the German government banned Blood and Honour from operating within its borders.

Recently the group has experienced discord regarding the extent of its political affiliations. Max Hammer, the pseudonym of the official web site host, writes that the Blood and Honour has actually split between the moderates and the militants. According to Hammer, the moderates believe that Blood and Honour is an organization of musicians who can assist the national socialist parties promote their ideology. The moderates favor using the profits generated by the musicians to fund the political movement. The militants, on the other hand, promote a sister organization called "Combat 18" to act as the armed wing of the movement. The militants believe that Blood and Honour, itself, was created as a political power, and resent those who use the movement for fame and fortune.

PHILOSOPHY AND TACTICS

Blood and Honour acts as an umbrella organization to connect small groups of white supremacist skinheads through music, propaganda, and the Internet. The group believes

PRIMARY SOURCE

White Pride Worldwide: The White Power Music Industry Is Helping to Drive the Internationalization of Neo-Nazism

Close to 500 racist Skinheads gathered in a small town outside Atlanta last October for Hammerfest 2000, the largest white power music concert held that year in the United States. While headliner bands Brutal Attack, Hate Crime and Extreme Hatred played furious "hatecore" music, men dove from the stage into a mosh pit of raging, tattooed Skinheads.

Georgia newspapers didn't cover the concert at all, and local authorities didn't show up at the remarkable gathering in Bremen, Ga., either. For neo-Nazi Skinheads, though, the show was world famous.

Hammerfest 2000 drew fans from Austria, Canada, France, Ireland, the Netherlands and Spain, as well as from across the United States. Four bands flew in from Britain for the weekend. The concert culminated months of worldwide networking by sponsors Panzerfaust Records and Resistance Records, the premier neo-Nazi music labels in the U.S.

The growing white power music industry, now valued at millions of dollars in annual sales, is not just the largest source of money and recruits for the Western world's most dynamic racist revolutionaries. It is also astonishingly international.

Thanks largely to the Internet and cheap air fares, racist music has spread over the last quarter-century from Britain to the rest of Europe and on to the United States.

Today, racist compact discs might be recorded in Poland, pressed in the United States and sold via the Net in Sweden. A German neo-Nazi might see his favorite American band at a concert in Switzerland.

In many ways, this remarkably violent music is accomplishing for the radical right what decades of racist theorizing didn't: It has given Skinheads and many other extremists around the world a common language and a unifying ideology—an ideology that replaces old-fashioned, state-based nativism with the concept of "pan-Aryanism."

"In the last decade, white power music has grown from a cottage industry to a multimillion-dollar, worldwide enterprise," says Devin Burghart of the Center for New Community, which has studied this music extensively.

"Along the way, the music scene has created international ties where there were none, and has inspired an ideological pan-Aryanism that has broken down the walls between racist groups."

It has also spawned a culture of violence.

In internecine disputes, neo-Nazis in the music industry have been willing to stomp each other with boots, to beat each other with baseball bats, and to torture each other with hammers. They have hired hit men and burned down buildings. Racist music fans have bombed children and bludgeoned people with iron pipes; they have drowned homosexuals and executed police officers.

In Europe, where such music is generally illegal, governments have started deporting racist aliens, raiding white power CD caches, and banning neo-Nazi music organizations. Such pressure has driven racist music underground even as profit

that music can be a tool for change. It is the expressed goal of Blood and Honour to bring down the rule of their enemy, whom they call, the "Zionist-occupation governments." Upon the destruction of these governments, members of Blood and Honour wish to establish a new order based on their principles of white supremacy. The members of the group fear that the migration of foreigners into their countries is creating a scenario in which whites will be the minority. The group attempts to subjugate others by promoting the belief that other ethnic groups are physically and intellectually inferior. Their propaganda includes guides to organization as well as leaflets on holocaust denial.

Blood and Honour seeks to use white power music to attract and set in motion young people

margins have shot up—and increasingly, it has made the United States, with its unusual First Amendment protections of even neo-Nazi speech, a haven for the racist music business.

PICKING UP TEETH

The violence begins with the music. "You kill all the niggers and you gas all the Jews," George Burdi sang with his band Rahowa, short for Racial Holy War. "Kill a gypsy and a commie too. You just killed a kike, don't it feel right?"

"Goodness gracious, Third Reich."

And it is contagious. "The concerts were crazy," recalls Burdi, a former neo-Nazi who now says he has left the movement. "Friends would beat each other up and then laugh about it afterwards, with their eyes swollen shut and their noses broken and picking their teeth up off the ground."

Such blind anger might not appear conducive to starting a moneymaking business or even building up an extremist political organization. But the foundations are there and growing.

Internet-based "radio" shows stream racist music around the world at all hours of the day. In the U.S., racist music from 123 domestic bands and 229 foreign ones is available on-line from more than 40 distributors, according to the Center for New Community.

The leading U.S. label, Resistance Records (started by Burdi in 1993), reportedly expected to sell 70,000 CDs last year, meaning more than $1 million in potential gross revenue. Industry profits go to political neo-Nazi groups like the National Alliance and Hammerskin Nation.

The anger and violence that characterize racist Skinhead groups like the Hammerskin Nation may actually help the cause. "All too often we turn [our anger] against ourselves," writes Resistance owner William Pierce, who heads up the National Alliance, America's premier neo-Nazi organization.

"We need to give a proper direction to that anger . . . [Resistance Records will distribute] music of defiance and rage against the enemies of our people. . . . It will be the music of the great, cleansing revolution which is coming."

'RUNNING THE SHOW'

If white power music is big business in the United States, it is even bigger in Europe (where it is largely illegal)—and especially in Eastern Europe. Interpol estimated in 1999 that the European neo-Nazi music industry was worth $3.4 million a year, and it has only grown since then.

With the cost of producing a CD little more than $2, Interpol said profit margins were better than for selling hashish.

In Poland, some racist bands sell as many as 30,000 albums, comparable to successful local pop bands. In that country of 39 million people, there are 15,000 individuals intimately involved in the racist Skinhead scene, according to Rafal Pankowski of the Polish anti-fascist group Never Again.

Though there is no reliable count of the American racist Skinhead scene, it is at most a

(continued on next page)

within their cause. The group uses concerts, rallies, and the Internet to link like-minded people and to promote their publications. The group also promotes a leaderless resistance, believing that it will result in more personal initiative. Some within the group advocate the use of violence, believing that they are at war. Ian Stuart, himself, was imprisoned during the mid 1980s for assaulting a black woman.

Propaganda guides include field manuals and links to the militant wing of the movement.

OTHER PERSPECTIVES

Blood and Honour and Oi! music are identified by the Anti-Defamation League as the recruitment machine used by racist skinheads. The

PRIMARY SOURCE

White Pride Worldwide: The White Power Music Industry Is Helping to Drive the Internationalization of Neo-Nazism (continued)

fraction of that size—in a country with seven times as many people.

In Germany, before the neo-Nazi music organization Blood & Honour was banned last year, there were about 180 white power concerts a year—or one every other day—according to Antifaschistische INFO-Blatt (AIB), a German anti-fascist organizations. In Sweden, a 1997 survey showed that 12% of young people aged 12 to 19 listened to white power music "sometimes" or "often."

Racist music is found in every one of Europe's 30 countries, but it is especially widespread in the Czech Republic, Germany, Hungary, Poland, Serbia and Slovakia, among others.

Perhaps most frightening is that racist Skinhead culture, which has always sought the extreme, has even come to seem normal in places. In Germany, where the neofascist National Democratic Party (NPD) has openly sold white power music for election funds, racist Skins boastfully call some neighborhoods "National Liberated Zones"—no-go areas for any foreigners, blacks or Jews who want to avoid a beating or worse.

"White power music has reached far beyond the hard core of the neo-Nazi movement," said a representative of the German anti-fascist AIB, who asked not to be identified for fear of reprisals. "In some places, neo-Nazis are running the show."

After moving from Britain two years ago, the largest, best-organized and most influential European white power music organization is now headed by Erik Blücher of Helsingborg, Sweden. Blood & Honour (B&H) publishes magazines, organizes concerts, distributes music, and has links to neo-Nazi political parties throughout Europe.

The primary B&H label, Ragnarock Records, is run by Blücher from Sweden, but there are at least 10 other labels associated with B&H, according to Stieg Larsson of the Swedish anti-fascist group Expo.

An American branch of B&H was active in California and Minnesota in the 1990s, but went dormant several years ago until this spring. Today, it has chapters in California, Georgia, Ohio and Texas.

Trying to maximize distribution, the California chapter now sells a sampler CD of white power music at what it says is cost. Many of the international B&H Web sites are registered on a server in Alaska.

B&H is active in most European countries, but is strongest in the Czech Republic, Hungary, Switzerland and throughout Scandinavia. The group had a large presence in Germany until it was banned last fall, after simultaneous government raids on the homes of 30 members.

Since then, German B&H has organized concerts in the nearby Czech, French, Swiss and Hungarian border regions. German officials said Blood & Honour was guilty of "the poisoning of minds and hearts."

Source: Southern Poverty Law Center, 2001

League expresses that hate music, such as Oi!, has become a significant aspect of the white supremacy movement. By providing a source of income, by attracting young people, and by promulgating a subculture of hate, groups such as Blood and Honour are ensuring the perpetuation of the movement and a rise in the threat of racially motivated violence. *The Economist* asserts that no discourse is possible because,

"when interviewed, they say little, standing arms crossed, fists clenched, eyes burning."

SUMMARY

For close to 20 years, Blood and Honour has been the umbrella organization used to promote the ideology of white supremacy throughout

Europe, Australia, and the United States. Following the model created by founder Ian Stuart, member divisions and sections use concerts and propaganda to attract young people into their groups. Although banned in Germany, groups in Eastern Europe and the United States continue to operate.

SOURCES

Periodicals

"Central Europe's Skinheads: Nasty, Ubiquitous, and Unloved." *The Economist*. March 20, 1999.

Charney, Marc. "Word for Word / The Skinhead International; Some Music, It Turns Out, Inflames the Savage Breast." > *The Economist*. July 2, 1995.

"Germany: Far Right Organization Banned." *U.S. News and World Report*. September 28, 2000.

Web sites

The Anti-Defamation League. "Neo-Nazi Hate Music, A Guide." < http://www.adl.org/main_Extremism/hate_music_in_the_21st_century.htm?Multi_page_sections=-sHeading_1 > (accessed September 26, 2005).

The Anti-Defamation League. "Neo-Nazi Skinheads and Racist Rock: Youth Subculture of Hate." < http://www.adl.org/poisoning_web/racist_rock.asp > (accessed September 26, 2003).

SEE ALSO

Neo-Nazis

Breton Revolutionary Army

LEADER: Christian Georgeault

USUAL AREA OF OPERATION: France; Brittany

The Breton Revolutionary Army, known in French as the *Armée Revolutionnaire Bretton* (ARB), began as the militant wing of the Breton Liberation Front in 1971. The Breton Liberation Front was created to obtain the liberation of the region of Brittany from France. In 1974, the group began its armed resistance to France by targeting a variety of government facilities. Over the next 30 years, the group would be held responsible for over 200 bombings. The group established a political front in 1982 called *Emgann* (combat).

HISTORY

The region of Brittany operated independently under the rule of a duke until 1488. In 1488, France defeated the Duke of Brittany and forced the duke to submit to a treaty with the king. The region remained ruled by the duke until it was incorporated into the Kingdom of France in 1532. After the French Revolution in 1789, Brittany, along with other culturally diverse regions, lost its "privileges" in favor of a one-nation, one-language France.

In the 1960s and 1970s, the region of Brittany began to experience a cultural revival due, in part, to the emergence of immersion

Police officers rope off a McDonald's restaurant where a bomb explosion killed an employee outside Dinan, Brittany, France on April 19, 2000. Authorities suspected the small separatist group Breton Revolutionary Army was responsible for the attack. AP/Wide World Photos. Reproduced by permission.

schools called *Diwans*. These schools fostered the use of the Breton language, and ancient Celtic dialect. In 1963, during this period of cultural revival, the Breton Liberation Front (FLB) formed with the goal of achieving liberation from France. Emerging from the FLB, the Breton Revolutionary Army (ARB) was established in 1971 as the armed branch of the FLB.

The ARB launched more than 200 armed attacks over the next 30 years. These activities generally took the form of explosives at government facilities, such as tax offices and town halls, and resulted in few human casualties. However, two members of the ARB were killed as they attempted to defuse a bomb they had planted. In addition, on April 19, 2000, an explosives attack on a McDonald's restaurant killed an employee.

In 1982, the ARB established the official front of the group called Emgann. This group operates through campaigns of demonstrations and the distribution of literature to promote their goal of self-determination. Two key leaders of the ARB had ties to Emgann. Christian Georgeault is the former general secretary and Gael Roblin is a former spokesperson.

In the 1990s, the group's strategy shifted from a separatist movement to an anti-American and anti-globalization ideology. The ARB joined forces with other nationalist groups such as the Real IRA (Irish Republic Army) and the Basque Fatherland and

LEADERSHIP

CHRISTIAN GEORGEAULT

Christian Georgeault is the former secretary general of Emgann. He is currently serving an eleven-year sentence for his involvement in the April 2000 bombing at the McDonald's restaurant. Gael Roblin, the former spokesperson for Emgann, is also serving a sentence for the April 2000 bombing. Both are awaiting trails on the explosives stolen in 1999.

Freedom (ETA) separatist movement from Spain. In September 1999, ETA and the ARB successfully stole an eight-ton cache of explosives from a quarry in Brittany. These explosives were linked to a string of bombings throughout Brittany.

PHILOSOPHY AND TACTICS

The goal of the ARB, when it began, was autonomy from French rule. It attempted to achieve its mission by planting bombs on specific targets, usually a French government office. The ARB successfully planned the symbolic bombings in the middle of the night so that there would be no casualties. In a *Time* magazine article, Bruce Crumley called the group, "quixotic," with a "quaint reputation" and "folkloric nobility" due to its use of force with no casualties. In the late 1990s, however, the group allied with other organizations whose goals were to separate from their prevailing powers, namely ETA. Together with ETA, the ARB moved into a new arena of operations after stealing an eight-ton cache of explosives. The group shifted their focus from a nationalist and anti-French colonialism to an anti-American, anti-globalization stance. The ARB accepted responsibility for an eighteen-month wave of attacks in an interview given to the Basque separatist newspaper *Gara*. In that article, the ARB stated that it would expand their targets beyond symbolic actions. The

KEY EVENTS

1998: An explosion at a tax office in Matignon leaves little damage and no injuries.

1999: A bomb is defused at a Callac tax office.

1999: Mayenne court is hit by explosives attack.

1999: An overnight bombing at a tax office occurs in Morlaix.

1999: A bomb containing a kilo (2.2 pounds) of dynamite explodes at a Cintegabelle tax office, creating extensive damage to office complex and nearby homes.

1999: Twenty-five sticks of dynamite and a detonator are found and defused at a government-run employment agency called ANPE.

1999: A bomb is found and detonated at an ANPE office in Rennes.

1999: Explosives cause extensive damage to tax office, post office, and town hall; a young boy is injured.

2000: An explosion damages the town hall and police offices in La Baule.

2000: Armed attacks on tax offices occur in the towns of Pontorson and Dol.

2000: Shots are fired into a Gendarmerie recruitment office.

2000: Explosives destroy ground and first floor of the tax office in Argentre-du-Plesis.

2000: Explosives linked to the cache stolen with ETA in September 1999 kill McDonald's restaurant employee in Quevert.

---

bombing at the McDonald's restaurant in April 2000, and the death of the employee, is considered to be the last target struck in that wave of attacks.

Although the members of the ARB maintain their innocence in the bombing at the McDonald's, the bombing coincided with the discovery of another bomb at a Rennes post office. The two both contained explosives that were traced to the cache stolen with ETA.

PRIMARY SOURCE

Five Arrested over McDonald's Bombing

Five suspected Breton activists have been arrested in connection with a fatal bomb attack on a McDonald's outlet in western France last month.

A 27-year-old female McDonald's employee died in the 19 April (2000) attack, which also blew off part of the roof of the building, shattered windows and left a large crater.

Three men and two women were arrested by anti-terrorist police. One was the spokesman of Emgann, a group seen as a front for the Breton Revolutionary Army, known by its French initials ARB.

The ARB issued a statement to the newspaper Journal du Dimanche on Sunday denying it planted the bomb which exploded at the drive-in counter outside the McDonald's at Quevert, near Dinan in northern Brittany.

SECOND ATTACK

However, in the same statement the group said it had bombed another McDonald's restaurant five days before the attack in Quevert.

On Tuesday, Justice Department sources confirmed the claims by the Breton separatists.

This attack—on the restaurant in Pornic, near Nantes—happened on 14 April and went unreported publicly at the time.

Justice sources said the director of the Pornic McDonald's had filed a complaint for break-in and damages, but local police failed to fully investigate because the damages were slight.

They returned to investigate after the ARB claim and found there had been a bomb explosion.

Source: BBC News, 2000

OTHER PERSPECTIVES

For Brittany, wanting independence from France has been a centuries-old struggle. After the centralization of French government with the French revolution, many of Breton customs were close to extinction. Even up until the 1900s, student caught speaking the Breton language in school were beaten. However, in the last several decades, the region has gained much autonomy from France and the cultural revival of the 1960s is flourishing. Festivals celebrating traditional music have grown in popularity and the Breton flag flies next to the French flag at town halls. This cultural revival has, according the Jon Henley of *The Guardian* newspaper, "tended to make the ARB seem absurd."

SUMMARY

In his *Time* magazine article, Bruce Crumley expressed that the ARB "had an innocence that derived from the movement's success in not harming innocents despite scores of symbolic bombings." John Henley from *The Guardian* wrote that the attacks carried out by the ARB, "were mainly harmless and symbolic." As the group allied with ETA and the Real IRA, their strategy changed. The bombing at the McDonald's appeared to be their last target. The political wing of the ARB, Emgann, continues to promote the idea of independence from France.

SOURCES

Web sites

The Guardian. "Breton Separatists on Trial for Attacks." < http://www.guardian.co.uk/france/story/o.html > (accessed July 20, 2005).

MIPT Terrorism Knowledge Base. "Breton Revolutionary Army." < http://www.tkp.org/Group.jsp?groupID = 3548 > (accessed July 20 2005).

Time Magazine Europe. "From Quaint to Bloodthirsty." < http://www.time.com/time/Europe/magazine/ 2000.0501/burgerbomb.html > (accessed July 20, 2005).

British National Party

LEADERS: John Tyndall; Nick Griffin

YEAR ESTABLISHED OR BECAME ACTIVE: 1980 as the New National Front; the BNP from 1982

ESTIMATED SIZE: Unknown

USUAL AREA OF OPERATION: Britain

OVERVIEW

Founded by a former chairman of the National Front, John Tyndall, as the "New National Front" in 1980; the British National Party (BNP), as it became known in 1982, claims to be the United Kingdom's foremost nationalist political party. Its extreme right views and links to violent organizations, notably Combat 18, have resulted in accusations of fascism, claims that it vehemently denies.

Far-right politics has always been a minority interest in Britain, and the British National Party has traditionally punched above its weight, attracting more headlines and votes. It has never been a significant electoral force, collecting in its entire history a mere handful of the 6,000 council seats that become available in the United Kingdom every four years. In national elections, Britain's first "past the post" system precludes the BNP from making a breakthrough; but in any case, they have never polled more than one percent of the national vote.

HISTORY

Extreme right-wing politics has always been an ideology of the minority in Britain. Its most notorious advocate was the former Labour MP and government minister, Oswald Mosley, who

Dave Guynan, Local British National Party (BNP) candidate, greets a potential voter in the Town End Farm area of Sunderland, northern England on April 29. 2003. AP/Wide World Photos. Reproduced by permission.

formed the British Union of Fascists (BUF) in 1932. This followed seismic splits within his former party after its leadership merged into a national government a year earlier, ignoring Mosley's ambitious economic program based on huge investments in public work schemes and empire based on protectionism. An inveterate publicity seeker, Mosley became notorious for his association with Adolf Hitler, and although BUF black shirts were involved in numerous inner-city disturbances, they were never remotely an electoral force.

Following the World War II, former members of the British Union of Fascists took on the name of the British National Party, although this would be a negligible force for years. In 1967, it merged to join the nascent National Front.

Over subsequent years, the National Front waged a noisy campaign against the influx of the so-called "Windrush" generation of West Indian immigrants. Encouraged by the outpourings of the Conservative MP, Enoch Powell, who spoke

of "rivers of blood," it helped instigate a national debate not just on immigration, but on the very future of Britain and "Britishness." Prominent though it was during the 1970s—a period of deep industrial unrest and economic strife—it never came close to gaining an electoral breakthrough, despite claiming 15,000 members. When Margaret Thatcher led a resurgent Conservative Party to power in 1979, it was decimated.

Out of the ashes of this organization, John Tyndall, a National Front leader in the early 1970s, formed the New National Front, which was renamed the British National Party (BNP) in 1982. Tyndall would lead this new political party for seveteen years, a period largely characterized by successive public relations disasters. These ranged from Tyndall's public dedication to Nazi racial ideals, the party's attempts at Holocaust denial, and intermittent violence that accompanied its rallies. Nevertheless, the adage that "some publicity is better than no publicity", may have been true in Tyndall's eyes, and despite faring little better electorally than such marginal political organizations as the

Members of the British National Party rally in a Bethnal Green, London, street. David Hoffman Photo Library / Alamy

KEY EVENTS

1980: Founded by former National Front leader, John Tyndall, as New National Front.

1982: Name changed to British National Party.

1993: Derek Beackton wins council seat in Millwall, the BNP's first electoral success.

1999: Nick Griffin replaces Tyndall as BNP leader.

2001: BNP accused of stirring up tensions ahead of race riots in northern England.

2004: BBC documentary exposes racism within the BNP.

2005: Griffin and several other leading members charged with inciting racial hatred.

British Communist Party and even Screaming Lord Sutch's Monster Raving Loony Party, he was afforded a level of the public exposure that belied his party's electoral stature.

Despite repeated assertions that it was a nationalist, not racist political party, the bad headlines would not go away. Its poor image was typified by an incident in 1990 when Tyndall's deputy, Richard Edmonds, was asked if the BNP was a racist party. He responded: "We are 100 percent racist, yes."

Nevertheless in September 1993, a BNP candidate, Derek Beackton, was returned as a local councilor in Millwall, south of London. Far from representing an electoral breakthrough, this was the BNP's only success under Tyndall, and Beackton lost his seat the following year.

Following a leadership election in 1999, Tyndall was replaced by Nick Griffin, a Cambridge law graduate who had joined the

party only four years earlier. Like Tyndall, Griffin had been a former National Front chairman, but he set out to transform the BNP into a respectable white-collar-friendly political party.

He was helped, to an extent, by a change in the British political climate. As the country underwent its most sustained period of economic prosperity in living memory, electoral concerns shifted from issues like unemployment to the perceived explosion in immigration—with particular emphasis on abuses of the political asylum laws—and closer integration with the European Union. By the time of the 2001 general election, even the Conservative Party's single biggest electoral cause (which failed woefully) was the anti-European card. Griffin took advantage of this mood and mixed the sort of vows made by the so-called party of government with the usual BNP pledges about repatriation and reversal of equal opportunities legislation. This led to an increase in support at local, national, and European elections. As of 2005, the BNP has 24 local councilors, the largest number in its entire history. Nevertheless, this is still only around 0.004 percent of the total number of

LEADERSHIP

JOHN TYNDALL

Born in Exeter in 1934, and brought up in London, John Tyndall started his lifelong association with fascism in his early 20s. Impressed by *Mein Kampf*—an attraction he partially renounced when it become clear that associating with Hitler was electorally disadvantageous—at 22, he briefly joined the League of Empire Loyalists. This marked the start of the path that led through a number of extreme-right groups, many of which he helped to form, including the National Labour Party (until forced by the Labour Party to abandon the name), the National Socialist Movement, the militaristic Spearhead, and the Greater British Movement.

But it was the National Front, which he led in the early 1970s, and the British National Party, which he formed as the New National Front in 1980, that brought him greatest public prominence. Essentially a latter-day Oswald Mosely, he was a rabble-rousing orator, energetic campaigner, and a man never shy of controversy or conflict—be it verbal or physical. He was jailed for a year in 1986 for inciting racial hatred.

His beliefs, which he toned down in public, were of "unashamed white supremacism" and of "real manhood and real womanhood". He sought a Britain from which black people and Asians would be "humanely but compulsorily repatriated" and where able-bodied people would feel the "stiff breeze of compulsion to work"

Replaced as leader by the more elector-friendly Nick Griffin in 1999, Tyndall was twice subsequently expelled from the party he had formed for criticizing the new leadership. Yet, he was always welcomed back, and always remained prominent.

Following the broadcast of a damning BBC undercover documentary about the BNP in 2004, Tyndall, along with 11 other members, was arrested and charged with inciting racial hatred. He died in July 2005 on the eve of the court case.

"He was one of the two or three key players in the post-war era," Gerry Gable, the antifascist campaigner, told the *Guardian* the day after Tyndall died in July 2005. "But essentially he was a loser who never managed to see a realization of his national socialist ideals."

---

councilors in England and Wales. It has no elected politicians beyond that level.

The BNP remains tainted by intimations of fascism. The party is still accused of Holocaust denial and Griffin himself has published a pamphlet claiming a Jewish cabal controls the British media. In 2001 and 2003, the BNP was accused of stirring racial tensions, which directly led to riots in Burnley, Oldham, and Bradford. It is heavily implicated with Combat 18, which started off life as a kind of "storm trooper" wing of the BNP. Also, the Labour Party has repeatedly accused the BNP of using intimidating tactics before elections.

In 2004, an undercover BBC investigation exposed "racist elements" within the party. For instance, Griffin was caught describing Islam

as a "wicked, vicious faith"; one of its members gleefully described assaulting an Asian man in the 2001 Bradford riots; another that he wanted to attack the city's mosques with a rocket launcher; and a BNP council candidate even confessed to pushing dog excrement through the letterbox of an Asian take-out restaurant.

Griffin denounced the documentary as a set-up and claimed that members had been plied with alcohol during filming and that the BBC used selective editing. Nevertheless, police arrested twelve people in the wake of the documentary, including Griffin and John Tyndall. In April 2005, Griffin was charged by police with four offenses of using words or behavior intended or likely to stir up racial hatred.

PRIMARY SOURCE

Extremists Target Students Claim

An academic claims extremists are operating on UK university campuses, threatening national security.

In a report to be published next week Professor Anthony Glees of Brunel University warns that the authorities are "ignoring the problem."

He says the extremists include Islamist Jihadists, animal rights activists and the British National Party.

University leaders have dismissed the report as "largely anecdotal."

But they say they take matters of extremism on campus very seriously.

Education secretary Ruth Kelly yesterday told universities to watch out for extremists.

She said that in the wake of the July terror attacks in London, universities should protect free thinking but inform police of "unacceptable behaviour" by students or staff.

CHANNELS

Professor Glees, of Brunel's centre for intelligence and security studies, told the Today programme on BBC Radio Four: "There is a culture of extremism and terrorism on Britain's campuses.

"It may not be very large in number but you do not need very large numbers of people in order to do terrorism and the university authorities have simply ignored the problem."

Professor Gleeson says the extremists target universities, as well as other places, to recruit people, because societies at universities can be useful channels for them.

For his research, he studied 24 British universities and made case studies of a dozen convicted terrorists who had attended university.

He said there was no reason to believe that any one university was more prone to being targeted by extremists than any other.

PHILOSOPHY AND TACTICS

As probably befits a legitimate political party, the BNP is at once nuanced and cautious in publicly arguing some of the extreme racist arguments linked to its leading members. This is because of its current policy of seeking to engage the political mainstream. For instance, a glance at its web site or manifesto reveals nothing of the denial of the Holocaust or of the violence that is synonymous with the BNP's name; there is also an array of policy ideas unrelated to nationalism. These include everything from organic farming to the reintroduction of national service.

However, there is a hint at racial supremacy, and is at once explicit and unsophisticated in its linkage of Islam to terrorism.

In the BNP's mission statement, it defines its aims as seeking "to secure a future for the indigenous peoples of these islands." Its definition of "indigenous" is at once general and explicit, and describes "the people whose ancestors were the earliest settlers here after the last great Ice Age and which have been complemented by the historic migrations from mainland Europe." The ancestors include "Celts, Anglo-Saxons, Danes, Norse and closely related kindred peoples." Nevertheless, they are not clear whether this includes a recent influx of East Europeans into Britain.

According to its mission statement, the BNP is engaged in "struggle" on three fronts. They see themselves as the "torch bearers" of British culture and view it as their duty to preserve Britain's "rich legacy of tradition, legend [and] myth ... The men and women of the British National Party are motivated by love and admiration of the outpouring of culture, art, literature and the pattern of living through the ages that has left its mark on our very landscape."

They view positive discrimination and legislation aimed at promoting equal opportunities as fundamentally unjust. They claim to work

Universities UK, which represents the vice-chancellors of the country's universities, said it took the issues of extremism on campus and related issues very seriously.

A spokesperson said: "Universities UK has noted the report by Professor Glees.

"It appears to us that the report is based largely on anecdotal evidence and that university authorities were not involved or consulted in its preparation."

INTOLERANCE

"Universities UK is far from complacent on the issue, which is why, together with ECU and SCOP, we are updating our existing guidelines on extremism and intolerance on campus.

"The updated guidance will look at the range of hate crimes and intolerance on campus, with a strategic and practical focus on solutions that promote good relations, and guidance on dealing with situations that can impede good relations."

The Federation of Student Islamic Societies said Professor Glees' comments were unsubstantiated and very damaging.

Faisal Hanjra, from the federation said: "The work that many Islamic societies have played in promoting interfaith relations, campus harmony and cordial mainstream participation has been severely undermined.

"There may be pockets of individuals who are operating on campus but they are not representative and they are insignificant in number. In fact they are often not students at all.

"We are urging all students to be vigilant and to work with university authorities to get this balance between freedom of religious practice and the safeguarding of national security"

Source: BBC News, 2005

---

with "our people in their homes and communities addressing the fundamental issues of civil liberties and reverse discrimination." They add that "increasingly our people are facing denial of service provision, failure to secure business contracts as well as poor job prospects as both reverse discrimination excludes our people from the school room, workplace and boardroom. A key role of the British National Party is to provide legal advice and support to victims of repression and those denied their fundamental civil rights."

Their ultimate aim, however, is political power. They have pledged to "contest and win elections at council, parliamentary, Assembly or European level in order to achieve political power to bring about the changes needed."

In elections at local and national levels, the BNP has stood accused of an array of malpractice that has ranged from assaults on rival candidates and their election teams, to photographing antifascist rivals and disbursing their images on the Internet. Speaking shortly after the 2003 local elections, the Labour MP Martin Salter told the House of Commons: "The BNP do not understand the process of government. They might be very good at getting elected by playing on people's fears and damaging race relations. They might also be very good, as they were the other week, at mobilizing support for a bunch of football hooligans to go rampaging round the streets of Halifax ripping leaflets out of the hands of members of opposition parties. They might also be very good at mobilizing thugs to cause the violence that we saw at the England versus Turkey game, but they are a cancer at the heart of British politics."

OTHER PERSPECTIVES

According to a leading expert on British far-right groups, Nick Ryan, Griffin wants the BNP to follow the example of France's Jean-Marie Le Pen, Austria's Jörg Haider, and Australia's

Pauline Hanson. He is keen to abandon the public emphasis on forced repatriation of "foreigners" (he sees it as "one of the main obstacles to electoral success"), and to switch the campaigning focus to asylum-seekers, Islamic militants, and the threat to British culture from economic integration with the rest of the world.

The social commentator, Andrew Anthony, interviewed Nick Griffin for the *Observer* in 2002. He characterized Griffin's political tactics as typically "bald political analysis, followed by implicit controversy...finished off with an attack on extremism." It was the mission of Griffin, believed Anthony, to make the BNP the apotheosis of normality. Griffin's problem, however, was an inherent misunderstanding of "the diversity of the modern world, because he refuses to grasp its most sacred truth: there is no such thing as normality."

"When he makes the effort," wrote Anthony, "Griffin knows how to play with received opinions and casual assumptions. And he often attempts to disarm his opponents by agreeing with them. For example, he has recognized that he can recruit the liberal's politics of guilt for use in his own politics of hate. So when white bleeding hearts or black radicals accuse white people of being inherently racist, he is in complete accord. 'That's right,' he says, ' that's perfectly natural.' He also argues that it is immoral to import Third World skilled labor because Third World countries are in much greater need of that labor. But he seems unable to maintain this more nuanced stance for long before returning to more instinctive scare tactics. When I ask him about rumors that the BNP are thinking of admitting black members, he replies: 'We can put up with the blacks. The question of Islam is another matter. They convert the lowest

groups wherever they go. As things stand now, we are going to end up with an Islamic republic some time in the future.'"

SUMMARY

Despite the negative headlines attracted by the BBC's 2004 documentary and the court proceedings that, as of 2005, hang over the heads of a number of its leading figures, the BNP currently holds its strongest electoral position in its history. Griffin's attempts to modernize the party have met with some success, although the BNP continues to be tainted by accusations of racism, fascism, and violence. Following the London bombings in July 2005, when Griffin attempted to exploit the acts with an attack on the British Muslim community, his words attracted universal condemnation and derision.

SOURCES

Books

Ryan, Nick. *Homeland: Into a World of Hate*. Edinburgh, Scotland: Mainstream, 2004.

Sykes, Andrew. *The Radical Right in Britain*. New York: Palgrave Macmillan, 2004.

Copesy, Nigel. *Contemporary British Facism: The British National Party and the Quest for Legitimacy*. New York: Palgrave Macmillan, 2004.

SEE ALSO

Combat 18

Christian Identity Movement

OVERVIEW

The Christian Identity Movement (CIM) includes a large collection of autonomous churches and organizations. While the specifics of their beliefs and practices vary, all are characterized by a theology based in British-Israelism (Anglo-Israelism). The biblical account of the twelve tribes of Israel describes an Assyrian invasion in 721 B.C., which scattered ten of the tribes; Christian Identity theology teaches that these scattered Jews eventually made their way to Europe, where they settled and became the ancestors of today's white Europeans. Based on this belief, adherents to this theology teach that the Anglo-Saxon, Celtic, Germanic, and Scandinavian cultures of Europe are the direct racial descendents of the biblical theocracy of Israel, making them the legitimate heirs of the Old Testament promise of Jehovah's protection and provision.

Christian Identity asserts that the European races, specifically the white or Aryan races, constitute the chosen people of God today. Based on this understanding, adherents are often vigorously racist and anti-Semitic (claiming that they are truly God's people, while Jews are not). No formal organizational structure links the various Christian Identity groups, making an accurate census difficult; most experts estimate their numbers at somewhere around 50,000 in the United States. The largest and most visible Christian

YEAR ESTABLISHED OR BECAME ACTIVE: 1946
ESTIMATED SIZE: Less than 50,000 (Estimated)
USUAL AREA OF OPERATION: United States

Aryan Nations members from Georgia, pose with their leader, Christian Identity minister Johnathan Williams, (second from left) after the Aryan Nations-sponsored White Heritage Days Festival held near Scottsboro, Alabama in 2004. David S. Holloway/Getty Images

Identity Movement group today is the Ku Klux Klan, whose roots stretch back to the Reconstruction era group of the same name. Despite a resurgence in the 1960s in response to racial desegregation and the civil rights movement, Klan membership in recent years has fallen to around 5,000.

HISTORY

British-Israelism, the general theology underlying the Christian Identity perspective, is frequently claimed by its adherents to have ancient origins. Historians, however, give this movement a much more recent origin, dating it to the 1700s and the teachings of Richard Brothers, whose 1794 work, *A Revealed Knowledge of the Prophecies*

and Times, described the basic tenets of the movement's beliefs. Reverand John Wilson's 1840 volume, *Our Israelitish Origins*, offered a more detailed exploration of the topic, with explanations based in logical argument and scriptural application. Wilson traveled extensively following the book's publication, speaking and promoting his ideas.

Despite the early work of Brothers and the extensive promotional efforts of Wilson, British-Israelism remained something of a theological curiosity until the late 1800s, when archeological discoveries in the Middle East were claimed to support the theology's account of Jewish migration to ancient Europe. Modern British-Israelism asserts that the direct descendents of Israel now living in Europe are the chosen people of God. The European manifestations of this perspective are largely theological, focusing on questions of national identity and political power and generally avoiding questions of individual status or value. However, the offshoot Christian Identity Movement (CIM) in the United States has focused its attention largely on racial issues.

Wesley Swift was the driving force behind the rise of Christian Identity in the United States. Swift founded the White Identity Church of Jesus Christ–Christian, a 1940s California church in which he developed and disseminated a theology interweaving British-Israelism, militant anti-Semitism, and extreme political perspectives. Swift's preaching was also widely broadcast by radio in the 1950s and 1960s, spreading his beliefs to a wider audience and furthering the movement.

Christian Identity groups have no formal organizational structure linking them together, existing instead as a loose network of churches and groups with similar views and objectives. Among the better-known groups are the Aryan Nations, Jubilee, and White Separatist Banner, as well as Kingdom Identity Ministries, an Arkansas-based outreach ministry of Christian Identity teaching. Numbering about 50,000 members, many of these groups advocate violence against Jews, homosexuals, and others who they portray as threats to the white race and America. They teach that a final cataclysmic battle will pit good against evil, and be followed by God's kingdom on earth, in which whites will be recognized as the true chosen people of God.

PHILOSOPHY AND TACTICS

Christian Identity groups are organized around a fundamental belief that the white European races are direct descendents of biblical Israel. Stemming from this belief, these groups are openly anti-Semitic, portraying Jews as enemies of the true chosen race. Some groups refer to Jews as Zionists, claiming that these Jews are attempting a takeover of the U.S. government or a co-option of its leadership from within. Many Christian Identity leaders openly advocate violence against Jews.

In addition, because Christian Identity adherents claim to base their theology on biblical teaching, some of their members have begun to claim that violence is morally justified when it

KEY EVENTS

1794: Richard Brothers publishes *A Revealed Knowledge of the Prophecies and Times*, the volume that defines the underlying beliefs of the Christian Identity Movement. The book goes largely unnoticed.

1840: The Reverend John Wilson expands on Brothers' work, publishing *Our Israelitish Origins*, and traveling extensively to promote his views regarding British Israelism. Wilson's efforts prove instrumental in the spread of the movement.

1940s: Wesley Swift founds the White Identity Church of Jesus Christ–Christian. He helps launch the movement in California and across North America.

1970s: Groups, including the Aryan Nations, Jubilee, and White Separatist Banner, all belong to the loosely organized Christian Identity Movement. Despite their organizational autonomy, the myriad groups are largely unified by their opposition to non-whites.

punishes those who violate God's law. This rationale has led to attacks on prostitutes, homosexuals, and interracial couples, as well as efforts to destroy abortion clinics and retail outlets that sell pornography. This same line of reasoning has been used to justify both bank robbery and fraud; Christian Identity members claim that banks are committing usury, or the loaning of money at exorbitant rates, which they believe justifies their actions.

Christian Identity provides a glum picture of the future, portraying an end of time conflict in which the white race will battle Jews and other non-whites. The specifics of this battle vary from group to group. Some leaders teach that the United Nations will be used by the Jews in their attempt to create a single worldwide government; others focus on the importance of the chosen white race physically battling evil when it arises in the "End Times," leading them to undertake paramilitary training and to store weapons and supplies for the coming battle. While these specifics differ among groups, Christian Identity believers are consistent in their contention that this ultimate conflict is inevitable, that they will be called on to fight for their cause, and that the final result will be the recognition of the white race as the true chosen people of God. This apocalyptic vision guides their efforts against non-whites.

OTHER PERSPECTIVES

Virtually all mainstream Christian churches and theologians reject the extremist actions of the Christian Identity Movement. In addition, most Christian scholars find little basis for the movement's claims that white Europeans are the direct descendents of Israel. Researchers examining the rise of right-wing radical groups in the United States point to Christian Identity as a pivotal group within the movement. Michael Barkun, an expert on the movement, described it as a key force among extremist groups in America today, portraying it as "the 'glue' of the racist right."

While right-wing factions are often perceived as being unified in purpose, some far-right extremists reject CIM teachings outright. Neo-Nazis, who advocate a return to Nazi or fascist principles, share both Christian Identity's perspective on white supremacy and its hatred for Jews. Yet neo-Nazi groups reject the movement's claims of ancestral links to Israel as absurd. Further, because they reject any ideas based on Hebrew values or teachings, they view Christian Identity's claims of Jewish roots as a mark of shame, rather than pride.

SUMMARY

The Christian Identity Movement is less an organized movement than a group of loosely linked organizations sharing a similar worldview. The groups share claims of Jewish ancestry via European roots (though they are generally anti-Semitic), a belief in a coming battle for control of earth, and the eventual triumph of the white race as the chosen rulers of earth and people of God. They advocate violence as a legitimate tool for advancing the white race. Many of these groups effectively use the Internet to spread their views; however, they do not appear to be growing significantly. Given current concerns about terrorism, the heavy-handed tactics of these and other extremist groups are falling under much closer scrutiny by both the general public and law enforcement agencies.

SOURCES

Books

Barkun, Michael. *Religion and the Racist Right: The Origins of the Christian Identity Movement.* Chapel Hill, NC: University of North Carolina Press, 1997.

Quarles, Chester L. *Christian Identity: The Aryan American Bloodline Religion.* Jefferson, NC: McFarland & Company, 2004.

Web sites

MIPT Terrorism Knowledge Base. "Ku Klux Klan, Key Leader Profile: Berry, Jeff." < http://www.tkb.org/KeyLeader.jsp?memID = 109 > (accessed September 29, 2005).

Religious Tolerance.org. "Christian Identity Movement." < http://www.religioustolerance.org/cr_ident.htm > (accessed September 29, 2005).

SEE ALSO

Ku Klux Klan

Aryan Nations

Neo-Nazis

Christian Patriot Movement

OVERVIEW

The Christian Patriot Movement originated in the mid 1980s in Oregon. Christian Patriot members were united by a set of common beliefs, including a strong antigovernment perspective and opposition to gun control. Most Christian Patriots also believed in a vast conspiracy to establish a world government, sometimes referred to as the "New World Order." Many within the movement were also virulently racist and anti-Semitic, and some predicted that the end of U.S. law and the collapse of the economy would take place on January 1, 2000. The Christian Patriot Movement overlapped extensively in its beliefs with Christian Identity Movement, a racist movement that claims that whites are the physical descendents of biblical Israel, and the militia movement of the 1980s and 1990s. The Christian Patriot Movement began declining in number during the mid 1990s, and have largely disappeared, though some fragments remain intact.

YEAR ESTABLISHED OR BECAME ACTIVE: 1980s

ESTIMATED SIZE: Unknown

USUAL AREA OF OPERATION: United States

HISTORY

The origins of the Christian Patriot Movement are difficult to pinpoint. The name itself originated with the Christian Patriot Association, founded during the 1980s. Some other groups within the movement adopted similar titles:

PRIMARY SOURCE

Murder Trial Starts for Survivalist and Son, Both Accused of Torture

The leader of a survivalist cult and his teen-age son went on trial for murder today, with the prosecutor saying they had committed lurid acts of torture and killing in the name of a vengeful God.

The cult leader, Michael Ryan, a 37-year-old former truck driver, and his son, Dennis, now 16, were arrested in August on a remote farm where the prosecution says Michael Ryan exhorted his followers to hate Jews and prepare for Armageddon.

Defense attorneys do not dispute that a member of the group was killed in early 1985 as the cult prepared for Armageddon, the final apocalyptic battle between the forces of good and evil. But they said in opening arguments that they would question whether witnesses who have testified under plea-bargaining agreements played more extensive roles than they have admitted.

"I'll admit he is a killer," said Rodney Rehm, Dennis Ryan's attorney. He said he would show the boy had grown up "in a loony bin, on a nut farm," and that he was mentally ill.

"If this were not so tragic it would be ludicrous," Mr. Rehm said.

ACTS OF THEFT ALLEGED.

Randall L. Rehmeier, the prosecutor, said he would prove that the group, which had a headquarters on a farm in southeastern Nebraska, had been preying on farmers, stealing machinery and cattle, to finance the stockpiling of ammunition and automatic weapons as they prepared for Armageddon.

Although virulently anti-Semitic, according to the prosecutor's opening arguments, Michael Ryan invoked the name of Yahweh, the ancient Hebrew name for the Deity, when ordering members to commit crimes.

The man who was slain, James Thimm, a 26-year-old member of the cult, was tortured for falling from grace with Yahweh, Mr. Rehmeier said.

Michael Ryan's attorney, Louie M. Ligouri, while saying he would dispute testimony on who committed the crime, also suggested he might argue a defense of insanity.

Mr. Rehm, Dennis Ryan's attorney, attempted to draw a picture of an impressionable son deeply influenced by a corrupt father whom the boy revered.

The cult described by the prosecutor is one of many small groups of far-right extremists that have sprung up across the Middle West, and many have attempted to exploit the current economic problems of agriculture by recruiting debt-burdened farmers. In the case of the Ryan group, according to the prosecutor, the members merely stole the farmers' possessions.

Many of the groups, such as the Aryan Nations, the Posse Comitatus, the Christian Patriots Defense League and the Farmers' Liberation Army, are linked by a common fundamentalist theology that they call Christian

---

The Christian Patriots Defense League, for one, offered education and training designed to help those in the Christian Patriot Movement survive the predicted collapse of civilization. Other groups share Patriot goals, but have dissimilar titles: The Citizens Emergency Defense System is a privately organized and funded militia intended to maintain order in the event of crisis.

The Christian Patriot Movement's history frequently revolves around specific leaders and their actions or statements. In 1992, Louis Beam, an outspoken white supremacist, issued a public call for resistance to the federal government, specifically what he called "leaderless resistance," or small cells of fighters answering to no organized command hierarchy. This idea of small, isolated combat cells was adopted by many within the Patriot movement in the following years; coincidentally, it is also the structure preferred by al-Qaeda and other terrorist organizations.

Identity. Its beliefs include white supremacy, while its theorists voice hatred and contempt for other races and beliefs.

They also offer farmers simplistic reasons for their problems, including conspiracies of "international Jewish bankers."

The Ryan cult first came to light last June 25, when two of its members were arrested and charged with transporting stolen farm equipment. The arrests led to a raid on the farm, where hoards of stolen farm machinery and a cache of thousands of rounds of ammunition and dozens of weapons, including automatic rifles, were seized.

The Nebraska State Patrol and the Federal Bureau of Investigation returned to the farm Aug. 17 and began digging. The next day they unearthed two bodies, which subsequently were identified as those of Mr. Thimm and Luke Stice, 5, son of one of the cult members.

The current trial concerns the death of Mr. Thimm. Michael Ryan is accused of murdering the child and awaits a separate trial in that case.

THE PROSECUTION'S CASE

In early 1984, Mr. Rehmeier said, Michael Ryan and several young men began attending meetings where they heard anti-Semitic tirades of a Wisconsin man, James Wickstrom, who has been identified as the leader of the Posse Comitatus, an anti-tax, anti-government group with violent teachings.

Michael Ryan subsequently led people he met at the meetings in a splinter group that wound up headquartered in rundown buildings on a small farm near Rulo, Neb.

One of those was Mr. Thimm. Others were listed as Richard Stice, Luke's father; James Haverkamp; Tim Haverkamp, his cousin; John David Andreas; two sisters of James Haverkamp; their mother, and 10 children, besides Dennis Ryan.

RYAN CALLED PERSUASIVE

Michael Ryan was a persuasive leader whose commands led at first to thefts, Mr. Rehmeier said, and later to abuse of Luke Stice, to treatment of Mr. Stice and Mr. Thimm as "slaves," and then to the torture, mutilation and slaying of Mr. Thimm.

Tim Haverkamp has pleaded guilty to second-degree murder. James Haverkamp and Mr. Andreas have been charged with assault in the torture and beating of Mr. Thimm. They have said in pretrial testimony that they followed Michael Ryan's orders for fear of Yahweh and of "burning in hell." All are expected to testify.

Mr. Ligouri, Michael Ryan's attorney, said he would prove that all the "accomplices" were untruthful. And, while he said Michael Ryan had been involved in "some of the assaults," the extent of his involvement would be disputed. He described the others' prospective accounts as self-serving.

William Robbins

Source: New York Times, 1986

The year 1992 also witnessed the emergence of James "Bo" Gritz, a former Green Beret and decorated Vietnam veteran who ran for president and called for civilians to create their own militias. Finally, 1992 saw the infamous standoff at Ruby Ridge, Idaho, in which the wife and son of white supremacist Randy Weaver were killed. This incident, along with the Branch Davidian confrontation in Waco the following year, fueled the antigovernment fires of the early Patriot movement.

By 1994, militia groups were springing up across the country, with one group in Michigan claiming more than 6,000 members. In 1995, 2,000 supporters gathered in Meadville, Pennsylvania, to discuss tactics for resisting the coming new world government. In April of that same year, Timothy McVeigh and Terry Nichols blew up a federal office building in Oklahoma City; both

KEY EVENTS

1992: Vietnam veteran James Gritz emerges as a Patriot Movement leader, calling for citizens to form their own militia groups.

1992: The wife and son of white supremacist Randy Weaver are killed in a shoot-out with authorities at Ruby Ridge, Idaho.

1995: Timothy McVeigh and Terry Nichols blow up the federal office building in Oklahoma City. The two are later found to have ties to the militia movement.

1990s: State governments begin tightening laws restricting the use of fraudulent liens, eliminating a major source of Patriot funding.

1999: Officials seize the property of Greater Ministries International, a front group whose pyramid scheme is estimated to have taken in a half billion dollars, much of it ultimately destined for Patriot organizations.

---

men had ties to Patriot and white supremacist ideologies. A report by the Southern Poverty Law Center numbered the Patriot movement at more than 800 groups in 1996, with the number gradually declining thereafter.

From 1995–1998, state governments began taking aggressive steps to limit the use of fraudulent liens, one of the most common tactics of antigovernment organizations. Property liens are easily filed and render a piece of real estate unsellable without court action by the property owner. Many antigovernment groups actively used these fraudulent liens as a harassment tactic against local government officials.

In 1999, federal officials seized the property of Greater Ministries International, a Florida "church" famous for offering money-doubling investment programs. Following an extensive investigation, it was determined that GMI was actually one of the largest pyramid schemes ever operated in the United States, having taken in as much as half a billion dollars. Further, the group's leaders (all currently in prison) allegedly

had ties to the Patriot movement. Church records showed that the group's leaders had planned to buy their own island, along with an extensive arsenal, including sniper rifles, antipersonnel mines, grenade launchers, and explosives.

PHILOSOPHY AND TACTICS

Christian Patriot Movement groups, while fiercely independent, share a common worldview. As a general rule, they believe that the U.S. federal and state governments are corrupt and controlling; their responses range from the benign, such as maintaining antigovernment web sites, to the violent, including assaulting government officials and judges. Patriot groups generally oppose paying federal income tax and sometimes distribute information on how to avoid taxes. In a handful of cases, Patriot groups have purchased real estate, then claimed that the property is no longer part of the United States. In the case of the Republic of Texas, the group claimed that the entire state was in fact a sovereign country, and not subject to U.S. laws.

One of the more peculiar aspects of the movement's antigovernment bent was the extensive pattern of financial fraud perpetrated by Patriot groups during the 1990s. In response to alleged government abuses, numerous Patriot members launched grandiose financial schemes, defrauding individuals and businesses of millions of dollars. Mary Broderick, a Patriot in Colorado, not only passed fake checks (netting herself over a million dollars), she also conducted workshops showing others how to do the same. Broderick's 8,000 phony checks eventually caught up with her; despite her claim that she was an ambassador of the Kingdom of Hawaii, she was sentenced to 16 years in federal prison.

While Christian Patriot groups are unanimous in their contempt for the government, they also believe that things can actually get worse: most Patriot groups are convinced that a mysterious international organization is well along in its plans to take over the United States, probably with the assistance of the United Nations. Donald Beauregard, a militia leader in Florida, shared this belief, and was naturally alarmed by the discovery of a "secret map" showing how the United Nations planned to divide up and rule the United States. Beauregard and his group quickly began publicizing the map and the alleged scheme behind it. In 1998, Beauregard was completing plans to blow up power stations in Florida when he was arrested. He reached a plea agreement in exchange for a five-year sentence.

Despite their stated support for the U.S. Constitution and the Bill of Rights, Christian Patriot groups frequently espouse racist views. While Christian Identity, Neo-Nazis, and other perspectives differ in the details, they are consistent in their position that men and women of Western European descent are superior to other races. Many Patriot groups echo these perspectives, weaving anti-Semitism into their ideology by asserting that Jews are instigators of the UN takeover. In other cases, purported Jewish bankers are cited as justification for financial scams and check fraud. Some Patriot organizations have attempted to set up their own communities for "like-minded" people, generally meaning white Protestants expecting the collapse of the U.S. government.

OTHER PERSPECTIVES

Members of the Christian Patriot group are often associated with other right-wing extremist and white supremacy groups. There are no mainstream groups that share the racially charged rhetoric of the Christian Patriot Movement.

Members of the Christian Patriot Movement assert that the Constitution is a divinely inspired document. They further claim that only the original articles and the Bill of Rights Amendments are valid law, disclaiming all subsequent amendments. The group advocates abandonment of the 13th and 14th amendments, which abolished slavery and granted citizenship and voting rights to African-Americans. They further disavow the 19th amendment, which granted women the right to vote, asserting that only white males are entitled to the full privileges of U.S. citizenship.

Though the Christian Patriot Movement asserts that some mainstream United States judges share their interpretation of the U.S. Constitution, legal scholars widely hold that extremist ideology has no place in modern jurisprudence. Many mainstream legal scholars hold an "originalist" view that gives deference to the original articles of the Constitution and the Bill of Rights, but no mainstream scholar advocates abandonment of any subsequent amendments. Equality of all persons under the law is a firmly entrenched principle of American law.

SUMMARY

The Christian Patriots Movement reached its Zenith during the mid 1990s, offering a synthesis of antigovernment rhetoric, white supremacist ideology, and New World Order conspiracy theories. While the groups' intentionally unstructured form gave local leaders extreme flexibility in pursuing their objectives, it also provided little cohesion among Patriot organizations. Over time, a combination of factors, including legislative changes, growing public concern over Patriot tactics, and the death or imprisonment of Patriot leaders, hastened the Movement's decline.

SOURCES

Books

Barkun, Michael. *Religion and the Racist Right: The Origins of the Christian Identity Movement.* Chapel Hill, NC: The University of North Carolina Press, 1997.

George, John, and Laird Wilcox. *American Extremists: Militias, Supremacists, Klansmen, Communists & Others.* NY: Prometheus Books, 1996.

Web sites

American Religion.com. "The Identity Movement." < http://www.americanreligion.org/cultwtch/identity. html > (accessed September 29, 2005).

Anti-Defamation League. "Patriot Profiles #2: Patriot Purgatory: Bo Gritz and Almost Heaven." < http://www.militia-watchdog.org/gritz.asp > (accessed September 29, 2005).

Anti-Defamation League. "James 'Bo' Gritz." < http://www.adl.org/learn/ext_us/gritz.asp?xpicked = 2&item = 5 > (accessed September 29, 2005).

SEE ALSO

Christian Identity Movement

Republic of Texas

Chukakuha

YEAR ESTABLISHED OR BECAME ACTIVE: 1957
ESTIMATED SIZE: Unknown
USUAL AREA OF OPERATION: Japan

Chukakuha (or Chukaku-Ha) is a Marxist-leftist insurgency group in Japan. The group is also known as the Middle Core Faction, Nucleus Faction, or Zenshinsha.

HISTORY

Chukakuha is a Marxist-leftist group that was initiated in 1957, following a split in the Japanese Communist Party. The group has a political and military wing, and has carried out attacks in Japan against the Japanese government, U.S. military installments in Japan, and the UN.

Chukakuha was originally part of a Trotskyite organization in Japan, with the objective of revolting to implement socialism. Chukakuha, and another group called Kakumaruha, resulted when the Trotskyite organization split in 1963. Chukakuha was most active during the 1960s when the antigovernment movement was at its peak. However, Chukakuha remains the largest of fifty new-left groups currently in the country. The group has held a normal active membership of about two hundred, and has had as many as 3,500 supporters.

In 1974, members of Chukakuha bought a building in Tokyo, posing as a printing company seeking a location for their business. Several months later, their real identity became clear, and police began to monitor the premises. There have been police raids at the location over the last several decades, and nearby residents are angered at the group's continued presence in the neighborhood.

Chukakuha and other leftist groups have protested Tokyo's International Airport and its expansion for many years. In 1985, clashes between police and Chukakuha broke out at the airport, injuring twenty-five police officers. Nineteen leftist activists were arrested and given sentences over the clash.

Three buses were exploded without casualities in 1992 during further resistance toward airport expansion. In 1998, the group was involved with bombing the home of Tadanori Yamaguchi, an airport official in charge of buying more land to increase the number of runways. Yamaguchi was uninjured. In 1998, the group injured one employee when several explosives were set off in the airport. The car of a government official working on a project related to the airport was destroyed by Chukakuha in 2001.

Chukakuha protested Japanese military decisions in 1992. Rockets were fired at the homes of several high-level government officials, including that of Takashi Inoue, the Chairman of the Upper House of Parliament Steering Committee. The committee had approved a law allowing troops to be deployed overseas in Cambodia. The home of the U.S. Consul General in Nishinomiya was also damaged by a Chukakuha mortar attack in 1992. There were no injuries reported.

Chukakuha was responsible for the sabotage and firing of projectiles on railways and subways in Tokyo, and carrying out arson attacks at Shinto shrines in 1992. These attacks were in opposition to the enthronement of Japanese Emperor Akihito.

In 1993, Chukakuha injured a diplomat and slightly damaged the United Nations Technology Center in Osaka, Japan, by setting off a homemade explosive device.

Also in 1993, Chukakuha attempted an offensive against the G-7 summit in Tokyo. However, the group only managed to set off several homemade rockets that landed near the U.S. Army Base Zama.

KEY EVENTS

1963: Chukakuha and Kakumaruha split from Trotskyite organization.

1960s: Chukakuha active in the antigovernment movement.

1974: A building purchased by Chukakuha in a Tokyo neighborhood serves as an official headquarters for the organization.

1985: Clashes occur with police during a Chukakuha protest of the expansion of Tokyo International Airport.

1992: Buses destroyed during a protest of airport expansion.

1992: Chukakuha fires rockets at homes of government officials, protesting sending peacekeeping troops to Cambodia.

1992: Enthronement of Emperor Akihito and his visit to China is protested by Chukakuha.

1992: The home of the U.S. Consul General in Nishinomiya was damaged by a Chukakuha mortar attack.

1993: Chukakuha injured a diplomat during an attack at the United Nations Technology Center in Osaka.

1993: An attempt to attack the G-7 summit in Tokyo by launching homemade rockets aimed at the U.S. Army Base Zama.

1998: The home of an official at the Tokyo International Airport is bombed by Chukakuha.

2001: The car of an official working on an airport-related project is destroyed.

PHILOSOPHY AND TACTICS

Chukakuha is a Marxist group, claiming to support communism for the benefit of the common Japanese citizen. The group claims to do this by fighting against structures, organizations, and processes that it labels "imperialistic." These structures include the imperial system of Japan, a largely symbolic system, certain activities of the Japanese government, activities of the United States, and of the United Nations.

The group has been particularly critical of the U.S.-Japan Security Treaty, transportation projects paid for by the Japanese government, and the dispatch of Japanese forces to Iraq.

One of Chukakuha's largest causes has been resistance toward the international airport in Narita. Their disagreement with the airport began as land was to be taken from Japanese farmers to create room for the rapidly expanding airport. However, the group's resistance toward the airport and projects related to the airport have continued for over twenty years, even after expansion has been completed.

Chukakuha is also active against Japan's involvement in military actions overseas. The group has been against the U.S.-Japan Security Treaty. Chukakuha has protested the sending of Japanese forces to positions throughout Asia, and more recently to Iraq.

Typically, Chukakuha has carried out its activities of sending political messages through legal channels. However, the group often reverts to violent activities. Usually, these attacks specifically target government facilities. The group claims that its violent operations have been designed to garner publicity for its positions on public policy. The group alleges that it attempts to damage or destroy property, not to kill or injure people.

Chukakuha has attempted to align itself with other citizens' groups protesting activities that the government is carrying out. Their hope is to be seen as a more legitimate voice in Japan. The construction of a highway near the headquarters of Chukakuha was protested by residents in the neighborhood. Chukakuha made attempts to coordinate and lead the protests, attempting to be more widely accepted by the community.

The group has also distributed leaflets containing information about the group's motives and philosophy at various universities. This was the case when the group set off explosives to deter the emperor and empress from visiting shrines where the couple was to carry out traditional imperial duties. The group explains that it is unhappy with the religious events associated with the emperor.

OTHER PERSPECTIVES

Chukakuha claims to be working for the rights of the common Japanese citizen. The group says that its main goal is to send political messages that meet this end. However, the question of whether or not the group has been working in the best interest of the people has been posed.

Those living in the neighborhood where Chukakuha bought a building and set up headquarters have called for them to leave the area. They say the group is more of a nuisance than a help. The local citizens claimed to be unhappy with the group when it participated in and coordinated protests against the building of a highway in their neighborhood.

Attempts to draw attention to the issues involved with the expansion of the airport did cause the Japanese government to rethink its strategy for expansion. It is unclear if the approach of Chukakuha to use legal political routes, and only use violence to destroy property and not cause causalities, gives the group more legitimacy.

SUMMARY

Chukakuha has its roots in communism, arising after a split in the Japanese Communist Party in the 1950s. The group was most active in the 1960s, when resistance against government saw its peak. However, the group remains the largest of the radical new-left groups in Japan. The group has been outspoken against Japanese presence in Iraq, and one of its last known attacks was in 2001 against property of a government official working on an airport-related issue.

SOURCES

Periodicals

Japan Economic Newswire. "Chukakuha Claims Series of Attacks." *Kyoto News International Inc.* November 1990.

Japan Economic Newswire. "Nineteen Activists Given Sentences over Airport Clash." *Kyoto News International Inc.* October 1989.

Japan Economic Newswire. "Radical Leader Held over Narita Threats." *Kyoto News International Inc.* September 1989.

Web sites

National Memorial Institute for the Prevention of Terrorism—Terrorism Knowledge Base. "Chukakuha." < http://tkb.org/Group.jsp?groupID = 3578 > (accessed September 27, 2005).

Federation of American Scientists. "Patterns of Global Terrorism: 1992, Asia Overview." < http://www.fas .org/irp/threat/terror_92/asia.html > (accessed September 27, 2005).

International Policy of Counter-Terrorism. "Chukakuh-ha." < http://www.ict.org.il/inter_ter/orgdet.cfm?orgid = 9 > (accessed September 27, 2005).

Anti Terrorism Force Protection 1st Marine Aircraft Wing. "Chukakuh-ha." < http://www.1maw.usmc.mil/ATFP/News/02-3.pdf#search = 'MiddleCore%20Faction' > (accessed September 27, 2005).

Cinchoneros Popular Liberation Movement

YEAR ESTABLISHED OR BECAME ACTIVE: 1980

USUAL AREA OF OPERATION: Honduras

OVERVIEW

The Cinchoneros Popular Liberation Movement (in Spanish, *Movimiento Popular de Liberación Cinchoneros*, MPLC) was a leftist revolutionary group seeking to overthrow the Honduran government in the 1980s and early 1990s.

HISTORY

The Cinchoneros Popular Liberation Movement (Cinchoneros) served as the armed wing of the People's Revolutionary Union, a group that splintered from the Honduran Communist Party in 1980. The Cinchoneros were a Marxist-Leninist revolutionary group whose objective was to overthrow the Honduran government. The Cinchoneros were particularly known for hostage taking. The group demanded political and monetary demands in exchange for the release of its hostages.

An Honduran plane headed to New Orleans was hijacked by five Cinchoneros members in 1981. The plane, with eighty-seven passengers, was flown to Nicaragua. The group threatened to kill the passengers and destroy the plane if sixteen leftists from El Salvador, who were in Honduran prisons, were not released. They also demanded that the government of Honduras take a neutral role in El Salvador's civil war

KEY EVENTS

1980: Cinchoneros acted as the armed wing of the People's Revolutionary Union, which split from the Honduran Communist Party.

1981: Leftist members jailed in Honduras were released per the demands of Cinchoneros members, who threatened to kill the passengers aboard a plane they hijacked.

1982: Honduran Cabinet members and leading businessmen were held hostage for ten days by Cinchoneros members demanding the release of leftist prisoners and the removal of U.S. military advisors.

1988: U.S. military personnel were wounded in a Cinhoneros attack.

1989: Honduran General Gustavo Álvarez Martínez was killed by Cinchoneros forces.

1990s: Cinchoneros activities declined, coinciding with the end to civil wars in neighboring Guatemala, Nicaragua, and El Salvador.

and provide protection for thirty-five leaders of Honduran leftist groups. The Ambassador of Panama in Nicaragua negotiated with the Cinchoneros to have the plane flown to Panama. The Honduran government released the prisoners to Panama, where they applied for political asylum in Cuba. The passengers of the plane were released without harm.

In September 1982, ten Cinchoneros members took 105 people hostage from the Honduras Chamber of Commerce building. Among the hostages were two Cabinet ministers and eighty well-known business leaders. The Cinchoneros demanded the release of sixty leftist activists from Honduras, El Salvador, and other Latin American countries who were held in Honduran jails, or who had disappeared after being held by government forces. They also wanted U.S. military advisors who were based in Honduras to be removed from the country. The Honduran government did not meet the

hostage-taker demands, but did provide the Cinchoneros involved in the incident with safe passage to Cuba, when all of the hostages were released ten days later.

The Cinchoneros were also known to carry out bombings. Between 1983 and 1985, the group bombed the offices of Honduran, Costa Rican, and U.S. airlines and other businesses in the city of San Pedro Sula, 125 miles north of Tegucigalpa, the capital of Honduras.

U.S. military personnel were wounded by a Cinchoneros attack in San Pedro Sula in 1988. The group also killed the former head of the army in Honduras, General Gustavo Álvarez Martínez in 1989.

Cinchoneros-related activities declined in the early 1990s, coinciding with end of civil wars in neighboring El Salvador, Nicaragua, and Guatemala. However, a possible resurgence of activity was suspected in December 2004, when armed militants killed twenty-eight of seventy passengers on a bus in San Pedro Sula. The attackers left a note saying they were Cinchoneros members, and made threats against the President of Honduras, Ricardo Maduro, who vowed to be tough on crime. The message also warned against reinstating the death penalty, which had been pushed for by some governmental candidates.

PHILOSOPHY AND TACTICS

The Cinchoneros claimed to be the protectors and representatives of the poor people of Honduras. The group's name was taken from Serapio Romero, a Honduran peasant leader who was said to be executed in the nineteenth century. Romero's nickname was Cinchonero.

Although the Cinchoneros did carry out visible operations in the country, Honduras never experienced the same level of violence from left-wing revolutionary groups as did the nearby countries of Guatemala, El Salvador, and Nicaragua. The Cinchoneros were considered the largest leftist group operating in Honduras, with only 300 members. However, the Cinchoneros organization was involved with the leftist revolutionary efforts throughout Latin America.

Many Cinchoneros activities were aimed at assisting the leftist groups in the countries surrounding Honduras. They made demands for the release of leftist leaders and members from prison, and were opposed to the interests of the United States in Latin America. Cinchoneros believed U.S. interests were against the left-wing forces.

The Cinchoneros financed many of its operations with bank robberies and kidnappings in which ransoms were demanded. The group also relied on support from the leftist organizations outside of Honduras. A guerrilla organization from El Salvador, the Farabundon Martí National Liberation Front (FMLN), trained Cinchoneros members and participated in joint kidnapping operations with the group. The Sandinista government of Nicaragua gave Cinchoneros fighters safe haven in Nicaragua. The Sandinista government used Cinchoneros forces to assist in fighting against the contras in Nicaragua. Cinchoneros drastically declined upon the end of the civil wars of these neighboring countries.

OTHER PERSPECTIVES

The United States accused Cuba of providing the Cinchoneros with finances, training, weapons, and logistical support during its times of operations. This claim is likely, as Cuba had an interest in the leftist struggles throughout Latin America. The Cinchoneros aided other leftist revolutionary groups throughout the region.

There has been controversy in Honduras over who is to blame for the bus attack that killed 28 people in December 2004. The perpetrators called themselves Cinchoneros rebels. According to media reports, many Hondurans believe this claim. The public believes the attack is part of a recently emerging rebel movement to change the government. The Honduran government claims the Cinchoneros are being used as a scapegoat by the criminal gangsters they say carried out the bus attack. The Cinchoneros had been blamed for at least one previous attack in 1994, when a politician was kidnapped and later released. The government insists the armed criminal gangs who carried out the attack are upset about the crackdown on crime by the government. Political experts have also analyzed the situation. Social science professor Isbela Orellana, from the National Autonomous University of Honduras, has said the conditions for a guerrilla group to launch an attack in Honduras do not exist. Another professor, Anibal Delgado Fiallos,

believes the attack was the work of individuals, not gangs or the Cinchoneros.

SUMMARY

The Cinchoneros were an active leftist group in Honduras during the 1980s and early 1990s. Their objective was to overthrow the Honduran government. Although the group was active, with nearly 300 members, the leftist revolutionary movement was not as strong in Honduras as it was in El Salvador, Nicaragua, and Guatemala. The Cinchoneros did play a role in the armed leftist struggles and civil wars of these neighboring countries. Their trademark was hostage taking, which they used as a means to make political demands, such as the release of leftist prisoners being held in Honduras. The Cinchoneros also spoke out against and targeted American interests in the region, in retaliation for what the group called American support for antirevolutionary forces. The group's activities declined in the early 1990s, as the various civil wars in the region ended. Recent attacks in Honduras have been blamed on the Cinchoneros group, but there is skepticism as to whether the group has become active again.

SOURCES

Books

Anderson, Sean K., Sean Anderson, and Sloan Stephenson. *Historical Dictionary of Terrorism, Second Edition*. Lanham, MD: Scarecrow Press, 2002.

Periodicals

Ottey, Michael A.W. "Many Hondurans Say Guerillas, Not Gangs, Were Behind Massacre." *The Miami Herald*. December 29, 2004.

Thompson, Ginger. "Gunmen Kills 28 on Streets of Honduras; Street Gangs Blamed." *New York Times International*. December 25, 2004.

Web sites

National Memorial Institute for the Prevention of Terrorism—Terrorism Knowledge Base. "Cinchoneros Popular Liberation Movement." < http://www.tkb.org/ Group.jsp?groupID = 3987 > (accessed September 28, 2005).

Resource Center of the Americas.org. "28 Killed in Bus Attack—Weekly News Update on the Americas #778." < http://www.americas.org/item_17213 > (accessed September 28, 2005).

Combat 18

Combat 18 (or C18) is a British neo-Nazi organization founded in the early 1990s as a "strong arm" for the far-right British National Party (BNP). It was created as a response to increasingly violent clashes between BNP supporters and followers of Anti-Fascist Action, a militant left-wing group.

Taking its name from the initials of Adolf Hitler (the "18" in their name is commonly used by neo-Nazi groups, and the A and H being the first and eighth letters of the alphabet), its small following is closely associated with football hooligans and loyalist paramilitaries in Northern Ireland. Tinged with rumors of manipulation by Britain's internal secret security service, MI5, decimated by the arrest of many of its leading members, and also beset by rifts between its leaders, the organization went into sharp decline in the late 1990s. It was nevertheless linked to the London nail bomb attacks in 1999 and race riots in northern England two years later.

HISTORY

It was clashes between British National Party (BNP) members and followers of Anti-Fascist Action in 1991 that precipitated the formation

LEADERS: Charlie Sergeant; Will Browning

YEAR ESTABLISHED OR BECAME ACTIVE: 1991

ESTIMATED SIZE: 200

USUAL AREA OF OPERATION: London, Kent, Essex; northern England

A rescue worker helps an injured victim to an ambulance on April 30, 1999, after an explosion at London's Admiral Duncan pub, a gay meeting place. Police believed the bombing was the third in a series of nail bombs claimed by right-wing extremists. AP/Wide World Photos. Reproduced by permission.

of Combat 18 (C18). While the BNP attempted to take a path toward electoral respectability, C18 operated as its so-called "strong arm," providing security to its meetings and rallies, and engaging in the sort of physical battles with anti-fascist supporters that would otherwise have proven damaging to the BNP's reputation.

At its inception, C18 was comprised of BNP and National Front members, followers of the skinhead music scene (centered around Blood and Honour), and a coalition of football hooligans. English football thugs had a long-standing (and not always deserved) reputation as the black sheep of European soccer hooliganism. Combat 18 brought together thugs associated with West Ham, Millwall, and most notably, Chelsea, whose Headhunter gang was among the most notorious in football. C18 was always

a small organization, never comprising more than 200 followers (it never had formal members), of which possibly half were activists.

As well as being linked to violence that accompanied BNP meetings, C18 waged an organized campaign of terror and intimidation called "Red Watch," which identified and targeted political opponents, ethnic minorities, and police officers. It included a hate campaign against high-profile mixed race couples, including the former Olympic swimmer, Sharon Davies, and her then-husband, Derek Redmond, who received hate mail when they married in 1994. Another target, heavyweight boxer, Frank Bruno, his wife Laura, and his mother Lynette received death threats. High-profile British Jews were also targeted. C18 was also active in firebombing private homes and the offices of progressive

LEADERSHIP

CHARLIE SARGENT

Paul David "Charlie" Sargent founded Combat 18 in 1991 and led it over the subsequent six years. A violent, charismatic, and controversial figure, his leadership was mired by suggestions of personal corruption and profiteering. A dispute in 1997 with his successor, Will Browning, over the proceeds of the Nazi record production company ISD (the twenty or so CDs it had produced were estimated to have reaped profits of £200,000) led to the fatal stabbing by Sargent of Browning-ally, Chris Castle, who Sargent described as "a casualty of war." Sargent was convicted of Castle's murder in 1998.

In a 1996 *Independent on Sunday* interview conducted by Nick Ryan, expert on the British extreme right, Sargent was described as a hard-looking man, well-versed in violence and with plenty to say about "White Revolution." He was an aggressive, intimidating character, and, according to Ryan, had on at least one occasion bitten off an opponent's nose.

Sargent explained to Ryan why it had been necessary for C18 to come into existence: "The reds were going around and they were beating the living daylights out of the right-wing. They were kicking in doors, petrol bombing people, and beating old men black and blue with hammers [a reference to an attack by antifascists on a right-wing meeting in Kensington Library during 1992]. Red Action [an extreme left-wing group] were absolutely battering the Right." he then went on to claim that C18 turned the tables: "We . . . battered 'em wherever we met until there was no [one] left standing."

Yet by the time of Sargent's conviction in 1998, Combat 18 was a movement in disarray. Having already lost the leadership of his organization to Browning, he faced substantial accusations of being a paid informant for the British government.

Following his demise, Sargent's brother, Steve, founded the National Socialist Party, a fascist organization loyal to Combat 18's founder. In 2000, it was revealed that the London nail bomber, David Copeland, was a paid member of this splinter group.

Sargent is currently serving a life sentence for the murder of Castle.

---

organizations, as well as the Communist newspaper, the *Morning Star*.

C18 was also closely associated with the loyalist paramilitary organizations, the Loyalist Volunteer Force (LVF) and the Ulster Defense Association (UDA). Although never actively involved in Northern Ireland's conflict, C18 provided shelter to paramilitaries on the run, most notably the UDA leader, Johnny "Mad Dog" Adair, and the former UDA leader, John White.

The most high-profile assaults linked to C18 came in April 1999. On consecutive Saturdays, nail bombs were left in Brick Lane, the heart of London's Bangladeshi community, and the ethnically diverse inner suburb of Brixton. C18 claimed responsibility. As London braced itself for a successive Saturday attack, the most devastating bomb of all went off on Friday, April 30, in the Admiral Duncan pub in Soho, the heart of London's gay community. Three people were killed, including a pregnant woman, and seventy-nine were seriously hurt. The following morning police arrested a 23-year-old man, David Copeland.

Copeland was found to be a former member of the BNP, and although he was dismissive of C18, calling them a "bunch of yobs" and claiming to have acted alone, he was also found to be a member of the National Socialist Movement, a C18-splinter group loyal to C18's founder, Charlie Sargent.

By the time of Copeland's conviction in 2000, C18 was in disarray. A feud between Sargent and Will Browning (who took over as

KEY EVENTS

1991: Formation as "strong arm" of BNP.

Mid-1990s: Hate campaign against high-profile mixed-race couples.

1997: Split between Will Browning and Charlie Sargent leads to the murder of Browning supporter, Chris Castle.

1998: Conviction of Sargent for murder of Castle.

1998–2000: Widespread arrest of C18 members by Scotland Yard.

2000: London nail bomber, David Copeland, is linked to C18 splinter group, the National Socialist Party.

2001; 2003: C18 implicated in race riots in Oldham, Burnley, and Bradford.

C18 leader in 1997) over the money generated by ISD Records, a Nazi hate music outfit, had crippled the organization. Many of its supporters became disillusioned, dropping out altogether, or defecting to a newly formed Blood and Honour group. The Browning-Sargent feud became murderous in 1997 when Sargent stabbed an ally of Browning to death. He was subsequently charged and convicted of murder.

During this period, dozens of C18 members were also arrested in dawn raids conducted by Scotland Yard, in cooperation with MI5. This apparently served as confirmation of speculation—some of it emanating from C18's own members who had cooperated with the BBC documentary on the subject—that C18 had been thoroughly infiltrated by MI5. Even Sargent was accused of being a paid informant. This was never proven, nor was the suggestion, made by another TV investigation, that C18 had been stage-managed by MI5 from the outset as a vehicle through which intelligence could be gained on neo-Nazis and, in particular, Loyalist paramilitaries in Northern Ireland.

PHILOSOPHY AND TACTICS

Combat 18 members are white supremacists, inspired by German National Socialism. In interviews, leading members have spoken of "white homelands," although this has never been codified in its brief manifesto, nor has the desire to "repatriate" Britain's significant community of first-, second-, and third-generation immigrants.

Its central tenet is a "code of honour" based on the motto of the Nazi SS *Meine Ehre Heisst True* ("My Honour Means I am Loyal"). "Many who call or have called themselves National Socialists since the immolation of Adolf Hitler," reads their Code of Honour, "have either not understood the concept of honour or ignored it. It needs to be stated and repeated as often as possible that unless a person is prepared to strive to be honourable—and to take a real oath on their honour to the Cause and the Leader—then they have no right at all to call or describe themselves as National Socialists. An oath on honour means what it says—to break that oath is dishonourable, a cowardly act, and as such deserves death or everlasting ignominy."

It proclaims that action should only be taken overtly if it is not in contravention of race relations laws or the Public Order Act—legislation enforced by what C18 terms a "Zionist-occupation government" (ZOG). "The most important reason for avoiding overt action," reads its web site, "is that any such action immediately guarantees you an entry in ZOG's intelligence files and all that entails."

According to C18's handbook, covert action can assume three forms: direct, political, and social.

"Direct action involves the disruption and elimination of all that is detrimental to our race and opposed to the cause of National Socialism. Direct action is also the clearest demonstration of National Socialism in action, often involving acts of great courage and heroism. As such, direct action serves to show our Cause in the best possible light, strengthens the bonds between fellow National Socialists and inspires others with the right qualities to join our Cause."

The best method for this, the handbook asserts, is the "lone wolf" tactic: operating alone and speaking to no one of one's plans. The nail bomber, David Copeland, was a notorious example of this.

"Political covert action usually means infiltrating an already existing non-National Socialist group or organization or the setting up of such an organization as a 'front'. The main purpose of this type of action is to recruit members of these organizations for our Cause and to further spread the National Socialist message. The best recruiting grounds for our Cause are existing racial nationalist organisations as they will often contain the raw material needed for the advancement of our Cause."

Finally, " 'social action' involves the subtle propagation of extreme right views over months and years in a workplace. Its manifesto uses the example of a teacher using his or her influence to gently guide his students away from the accepted orthodoxies and encouraging their freedom of thought especially on subjects such as the so-called 'holocaust.' "

Its manifesto also propagates the use of "disruption" in a cumulative way. It does not elaborate on methods, but the aim "is for individuals, gradually and slowly, to increasingly disrupt 'everyday life' and services—to edge the System towards chaos and breakdown by using their employment or influence to this end."

Combat 18, according to its handbook, has one ultimate mission: "to advance the cause of National Socialism. Our long-term aim is to convert all our people to the noble National Socialist way of life. To achieve this however we must work on all levels."

OTHER PERSPECTIVES

Nick Ryan, an expert on far-right groups, spent much time with Combat 18 activists while writing his book, *Homeland*. He characterized a world of hard men who spend as much time and energy fighting and feuding with each other as they do with their enemies. Ryan found their existences squalid and repulsive. Their business was conducted in decrepit pubs and filthy flats with dreams of establishing a rural Aryan commune—the "homeland" of the title—undermined by internal disputes, disorganization, and time in prison. Around them were loners such as the nail bomber, David Copeland. Ryan writes, "That 'race warriors' and Aryan heroes often turn out to be such pathetic losers, mentally ill and unstable, is hardly a glowing testament to the cause."

Graeme Atkinson, an antifascist campaigner and journalist, believes that despite its current weakness, the impact of Combat 18 is still widely felt. "Despite its present weakness and its organizational and political incompetence," he writes; "C18 still has considerable dangerous influence and violent potential. This is why Maxim Brunerie, the author of the failed attempt to assassinate French president Jacques Chirac in July 2002 was in touch with C18. It is also the main reason why equally psychotic nazis in Germany want to use C18's name and copy its activities and style, despite C18 having no proven formal links with the mob raided in northern Germany."

SUMMARY

Divided by the murderous internal feuds in the late 1990s, widely discredited by the links to MI5, and decimated by high-profile arrests, it is widely assumed that Combat 18 is in its death throes. Nevertheless, the members are periodically accused of an array of violence, which has included trouble before an England v. Turkey football match in 2003 and race riots in 2001 and 2003. Moreover, they are strongly linked to European skinheads, who have imitated the group's activities and methods.

SOURCES

Books

Lowles, Nick. *White Riot: The Rise and Violent Fall of Combat 18*. London: Milo Books, 2001.

Ryan, Nick. *Homeland: Into a World of Hate*. Edinburgh, Scotland: Mainstream, 2004.

Sykes, Andrew. *The Radical Right in Britain*. NY: Palgrave Macmillan, 2004.

SEE ALSO

Blood and Honour

British National Party (BNP)

Loyalist Volunteer Force (LVF)

Ulster Defense Association (UDA) / Ulster Freedom Fighters

Combatant Communist Cells

LEADER: Pierre Carrette

YEAR ESTABLISHED OR BECAME ACTIVE: 1984

ESTIMATED SIZE: four known members, including Carrette

USUAL AREA OF OPERATION: Belgium and, on one occasion, France

AFFILIATED ORGANIZATIONS: Direct Action of France and Red Army Faction of West Germany

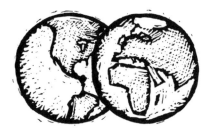

OVERVIEW

The Combatant Communist Cells (CCC) formed in Belgium in the mid 1980s to oppose the North Atlantic Treaty Organization (NATO) alliance and capitalism. It bombed a number of NATO-related targets in 1984 and 1985. More interested in gaining publicity than in taking lives, the CCC targeted property.

The CCC was briefly affiliated with the Red Army Faction (RAF, formerly known as the Baader-Meinhof Gang) in West Germany and Direct Action (DA) of France. Following the 1986 imprisonment of Pierre Carrette, the founder and leader of the CCC, the organization has been inactive.

HISTORY

The CCC is one of a number of anarchistic, left-wing terrorist organizations that appeared in Western Europe in the 1970s and 1980s to combat capitalism and promote communism. Along with the Red Brigades of Italy, Prima Linea of Italy, the RAF, and DA, the CCC appeared to pursue terrorist violence as an end in itself. Although the CCC claimed interest in a military-political struggle that would end American influence in Europe, it made no attempt to construct

Pierre Carette, leader of the Combatant Communist Cells terrorist group, waves to reporters after being released from prison in Leuven, Belgium, on February 25, 2003. Carette was arrested for his role in a series of 1980s bombings, but his life sentence was commuted because he suffers from Crohn disease. Oliver Hoslet/ AFP/Getty Images.

a new political foundation. It limited itself to destruction, terror, and pamphleteering.

The CCC chiefly targeted NATO. Headquartered in Brussels, NATO in the 1980s was a military and diplomatic alliance of twenty-six countries in Europe and North America. Founded in 1949, NATO sought to protect the democratic nations of Europe from an attack by the communist Soviet Union. It was the major European defense against communism and it was dominated by the United States, since American involvement in the alliance was believed to be the best deterrent against Soviet military force.

The CCC emerged in October 1984 with a string of bombings that targeted companies employed in placing U.S. nuclear cruise missiles in Europe. The first day of bombings damaged the offices of Sweda International, a division of the American firm, Litton Industries. Litton conceived and produced guidance systems for the nuclear cruise missiles deployed by the U.S.-dominated NATO. The second day of bombings damaged trucks belonging to a German company that produced materials for the transport of cruise missiles. Subsequent CCC targets included the European headquarters in Brussels of U.S.-based Motorola; a Belgian

branch of the Bank of America; the main office of the Bruxelles Lambert Bank; a state tax office; the headquarters of a metalworking firm; and a branch of the Societe Generale de Banque, Belgium's leading bank, as well as attacks against NATO facilities and the NATO Central Europe Operating Agency in Versailles, France. Some of the explosives used by both the CCC and DA were traced to the same theft in Belgium and it is possible that the CCC worked with DA to attack the French NATO target. The CCC also attacked the Belgian Employers Association building and the central offices of the Belgian police. The group's activities came to an abrupt halt with the arrest of four of its leaders in late 1985.

PHILOSOPHY AND TACTICS

The CCC protested against the Americanization of Europe, capitalism, and Belgian involvement in NATO. According to a statement by the group, it aimed to launch an armed military-political struggle in Belgium, which had shown little interest in communism. The CCC targeted companies that were involved in the NATO program to deploy nuclear missiles in Europe as well as offices of the Liberal and Christian Democrat political parties.

The CCC did not have any state sponsorship, but affiliated with the Red Army Faction (RAF) and Direct Action (DA) in an anti-imperialist armed front to coordinate actions against NATO member governments. Unlike RAF and DA, the CCC picked symbolic and strategic targets for bombings as a means of gaining publicity. Much more of a propaganda group than a gathering of would-be killers, the CCC did not expressly target people. After planting a bomb, the CCC would typically issue a warning either by telephone or by pamphlet about thirty minutes before the scheduled detonation to give people time to evacuate. When two firefighters were killed as an unintended result of a May 1985 bombing attack against the Belgian Employers Association building, the CCC issued a statement blaming police for not warning the victims in time, and bombed a state police administrative center in the early morning hours in retaliation. It typically dropped leaflets around the sites of its attacks to publicize its cause.

LEADERSHIP

PIERRE CARRETTE

Pierre Carrette, leader of the CCC, offered no resistance when he was arrested in a Namur, Belgium, snack bar in December 1985, along with three of his followers. Born in 1952, Carrette was one of the suspects in a June 1979 bomb attack on the car of U.S. General Alexander Haig, who at the time was NATO's Supreme Allied Commander in Europe. In May 1982, Carrette was in a car with a bundle of Direct Action pamphlets and with Nathalie Menigon, a Direct Action leader, when he was involved in an accident and briefly detained by French police. Carrette ran a printing shop in Brussels until he disappeared in October 1984 in the aftermath of the first CCC bombings in Brussels. Carrett's suspected links to terrorism sparked the interest of the Belgian police and the authorities began searching for him. On November 4, 1985, he fired a gun at a security guard during a bomb attack on a bank. Later that same day, he was spotted surveying the damage done to another bank by a CCC bomb.

The three people arrested with Carrette were long known to police. Pascale Vandegeerde, Didier Chevrolet, and Bertrand Sassoie had ties to left-wing political groups; Sassoie had deserted from the Belgian army. The four CCC leaders were convicted on January 14, 1986, for the attempted murder of a security guard in a bank bombing on November 5, 1985. All have since been released from prison, with an unrepentant Carrette raising his clenched fist as he exited jail.

OTHER PERSPECTIVES

The short-lived and small CCC garnered comparatively little attention. In the wake of its first bombing in 1984, Belgian Justice Minister Jean Gol said that the bombs appeared to be the work of amateurs, but the method used to publicize the bombings was more professional. He warned that it was time for Belgium to arm itself against the very real threat of terrorism. An unnamed NATO official subsequently lamented that NATO had become a target. He added that the CCC attacks served as a warning about the alliance's vulnerabilities. With the exception of CCC members, no one publicly spoke in support of the terrorist organization.

SUMMARY

Small and short-lived, the CCC did not have much of an impact. It failed to halt NATO activities in Europe and it did not spark much interest in communism among Belgians. During the years of CCC activity, Belgium deployed forty-eight U.S. cruise missiles under the terms of a NATO agreement. Polls in the 1980s indicated that most Belgians wanted to remain in NATO and they opposed a unilateral move to break previous Belgian commitments to the alliance.

The greatest success of the CCC came when it bombed six Belgian valve pit sections of NATO's oil pipeline system in 1984. The attacks spewed fountains of burning fuel along a 100-mile belt of pipeline running from the French border to the West German border across the southern half of Belgium. The CCC halted NATO's pumping of fuel for three days and drew attention to the vulnerability of NATO's supply lines. However, NATO forces in Belgium had extra fuel supplies, thereby minimizing the impact of the attack. NATO leaders discussed ways to coordinate antiterrorism activities among the countries of the alliance in the wake of this bombing.

The CCC has not been heard from since the 1985 arrests of its leaders. It is probable that the arrests ended the existence of the organization, although there have been periodic rumors that the CCC was attempting to reform. The end of the cold war and the subsequent shift in NATO policy away from anticommunism has undoubtedly weakened procommunist terrorist organizations by removing some of the justification for their existence.

SOURCES

Periodicals

"Communist Terrorists Bomb Police Offices." *United Press International.* May 6, 1985.

"Four Accused of Terror Group Links." *United Press International.* December 16, 1985.

"Group Claims Bombings As Protest of U.S. Missiles." *United Press International.* October 4, 1984.

"Terrorist Bombings Knock Out NATO Supply Lines." *United Press International.* December 12, 1984.

SEE ALSO

Red Brigades

Communist Party of Nepal Maoists (CPN-M)

LEADERS: Pushpan Kamal Dahal
YEAR ESTABLISHED OR BECAME ACTIVE: 1996
ESTIMATED SIZE: More than 5,000
USUAL AREA OF OPERATION: Nepal

The Communist Party of Nepal Maoists (CPN-M) is an extremist organization employing Maoist guerilla war principles. The CPN-M has claimed responsibility for various terrorist activities in Nepal in the late 1990s as well as early 2000s. These terrorist operations are reportedly targeted at government establishments.

As of 2005, the Communist Party of Nepal Maoists has been banned by the government of Nepal.

The Communist Party of Nepal Maoists (CPN-M) broke away from the United People's Front (UPF) political party to form their own organization in 1994. The CPN-M felt that recent political reforms, which had instituted a democracy in Nepal after many years of rule by a monarchy, had not gone far enough. Led by Pushpan Kamal Dahal (also known as Comrade Prachandra) and Baburam Bhattarai, the CPN-M wanted a complete end to the monarchy, the democratic political system, the abolishment of the caste system, and redistribution of wealth along communist lines.

The first known terrorist act carried out by members of the group was on February 13, 1996,

LEADERSHIP

PUSHPAN KAMAL DAHAL

Pushpan Kamal Dahal is thought to be a communist with Maoist ideologies. He was part of the United People's Front when it was formed after 1990. Dahal also served as a parliamentarian until 1994. Analysts state that owing to his radical ideologies, Dahal left the UPF and formed the Communist Party of Nepal-Maoists in 1995.

Dahal is thought to be the mastermind of several terrorist operations carried out by the CPN-M in the late 1990s. Also known as Comrade Prachanda, he reportedly served as General Secretary of CPN-M until 2000. As of 2001, Pushpan Kamal Dahal is wanted by the Nepalese police and is thought to be hiding somewhere in Nepal.

when they destroyed several police stations in northwestern Nepal. The CPN-M's leaders declared this to be the start of the "People's War" in Nepal, with the ultimate goal of seizing control of the country. Over the next several years the CPN-M made a series of similar attacks in isolated areas while gradually gaining strength.

In 2001, the Crown Prince of Nepal killed his entire family, including the king, before committing suicide. The king's brother, Gyanendra, became the new king. Seeking to capitalize on the instability following this massacre, the CPN-M stepped up its attacks, including small-scale bombings in the capital of Katmandu, and a strike against an army post. In November 2001 King Gyanendra ordered the army into battle against the CPN-M for the first time. Previously the government had relied upon the police to battle the group.

Fighting intensified in subsequent years. The Maoists engaged in guerilla tactics, rarely engaging the army head on but often attacking

smaller units by surprise. In the many rural, mountainous areas where the army could not reach effectively, the CPN-M essentially took over. The army and government maintained control over Katmandu and other major cities, but the CPN-M was blamed for a series of bombings within them. Twice in 2004 they shut down traffic into Katmandu by threatening to attack vehicles traveling on the two highways into the city.

By 2005 outside observers believed that as many as 10,000 people had died in the People's War. Analysts felt that the army did not have the ability to defeat the CPN-M in its rural strongholds, and that likewise the CPN-M lacked the strength to capture Nepal's major cities. Citing the need to defeat the CPN-M, King Gyanendra staged a coup in 2005, ending democratic government in all but name. In late 2005 the CPN-M began negotiating with the political parties that were forced out by this coup in an attempt to form a common front against the government.

PHILOSOPHY AND TACTICS

The CPN-M, before it split from the United People's Front, existed as the Maoist wing of the UPF. Owing to ideological differences, leaders of the Maoist wing of UPF formed the CPN-M in 1996. Leaders and members of the CPN-M are thought to be inspired by various communist leaders and movements around the world. These include Chinese leader Mao Tsetung and the extremist guerilla movement of Peru, the *Sendero Luminoso* (Shining Path).

The main objective of the CPN-M is to establish communist power in Nepal through the use of Maoist guerilla war principles. As thought by analysts, to promote their philosophies, the group called for the People's War in Nepal, in 1996. The group had reportedly delivered to the Nepal government a list of demands that recommended various changes in the governing system of the country. These include elimination of an elite class, removal of privatization of companies, and abolition of democracy, among other issues. The People's War is thought by most to be a reaction to the Nepal government's refusal to accept the CPN-M's demands.

KEY EVENTS

1996: The Communist Party of Nepal-Maoists is formed after splitting from its parent, the United People's Front

1996: The first terrorist attack by the CPN-M is reportedly carried out on February 13. Members allegedly attack two police stations and declare "People's War" in Nepal.

2000: The United People's Front is dissolved.

2001: King Gyanendra orders the army in its action to fight the CPN-M.

2004: Insurgency reportedly increases in Nepal.

2005: King Gyanendra suspends the democratic government and assumes power.

When the People's War began in 1996 the CPN-M's tactics centered around attacking the government and symbols of authority in Nepal's many isolated, mountainous regions. By 2005 the CPN-M was in effective control of many such regions and appeared to be trying to govern them along Maoist lines. Outside of these regions, the CPN-M has been suspected in various bombings on government buildings and offices of Nepalese, as well as foreign-owned businesses. In addition, CPN-M targets also include parliamentarians from Nepal and the Prime Minister of Nepal.

According to published reports, the CPN-M has allegedly organized terrorist operations in neighboring India as well. Intelligence officials claim that these attacks were organized in association with local communist groups such as the People's War Group (PWG) and the Maoist Communist Center (MCC) in the Indian states of West Bengal, Bihar, and Uttar Pradesh. As of 2005, proclamations and press releases by the CPN-M threaten to target foreign diplomatic establishments as well.

OTHER PERSPECTIVES

The strategies and tactics of CPN-M have been widely criticized by governments, as well as by terrorism experts around the world. According to Dr. J. Michael Waller, the Walter and Leonore Annenberg Professor of International Communication at the Institute of World Politics and a noted expert on terrorism, a majority of the tactics and ideologies of the CPN-M are borrowed from the Shining Path. In 2003, he commented that Shining Path "was the most violent guerrilla and terrorist organization ever seen in the Americas," and added that "It is precisely Shining Path's tactics that are so revered by Prachanda, [and] Nepal's Maoists."

Human Rights Watch activists have often strongly condemned the activities of CPN-M. However, they are also equally critical of the policies of the Nepalese government. Brad Adams, executive director of Human Rights Watch's Asia division, said in a 2004 statement: "Neither the government nor the Maoists appear particularly concerned with the protection of civilians while they fight this dirty war. If they want to have any legitimacy in Nepal or with the international community, they need to end attacks on civilians."

SUMMARY

As of 2005, the Communist Party of Nepal Maoists is considered to be a highly active group. In early 2005, as prdicted, King Gyanendra assumed ruling power of Nepal, owing to the increase in terrorist acts by CPN-M. Intelligence officials point out that the membership of the CPN-M has increased multifold over the years. With at least 5,000 members, the group is thought to have more than 30,000 followers and supporters in Nepal.

SOURCES

Web sites

CDI Center for Defense Information. "In the Spotlight: Communist Party of Nepal-Maoists (CPN-M)." < http://www.cdi.org/program/document.cfm?documentid=2397& programID=39& from_page=../friendlyversion/print version.cfm > (accessed October 21, 2005).

FrontpageMag.com. "Nepal's Maoist Insurgency." < http://www.frontpagemag.com/Articles/ReadArticle .asp?ID=9090> (accessed October 21, 2005).

Human Rights News. "Nepal: Government Forces, Maoist Rebels Target Civilians." < http://hrw.org/english/ docs/2004/10/07/nepal9452.htm> (accessed October 21, 2005).

MIPT Terrorism Knowledge Base. "Communist Party of Nepal Maoists." < http://www.tkb.org/Group.jsp? groupID=3531 > (accessed October 21, 2005).

Continuity Irish Republican Army (CIRA)

LEADERS: Ruairi O Bradaigh (of political wing, Republican Sinn Fein), Gerry Adams

YEAR ESTABLISHED OR BECAME ACTIVE: 1986 as Republican Sinn Fein; military wing, the Continuity IRA, began activity around 1994

ESTIMATED SIZE: Less than fifty

USUAL AREA OF ACTIVITY: Northern Ireland and the Republic of Ireland

A U.S. TERRORIST EXCLUSION LIST DESIGNEE: The U.S. Department of State declared the CIRA to be a terrorist organization in July 2004

OVERVIEW

The Continuity IRA (CIRA) is the clandestine military wing of the political party Republican Sinn Fein, an Irish nationalist party committed to the removal of British forces from Northern Ireland and to Irish unification. It was formed in 1986 after Sinn Fein-proper's perceived collaboration with British and Irish governments, the legitimacy of which it fails to recognize. The CIRA became active following the provisional IRA's ceasefire with the British government eight years later, in 1994.

HISTORY

The history of the Continuity IRA (CIRA) is intrinsically linked to that of Republican Sinn Fein (RSF), a splinter group from the main part of the Irish nationalist party that formed in October 1986. The cause of the schism was a resolution at Sinn Fein's General Army Convention in favor of ending abstention from the Irish Parliament, the Dáil.

Historically, although it contested in elections in both Dublin and Westminster, Sinn Fein refused to allow its MPs to sit in either the Irish or British parliaments. The refusal to acknowledge the British Parliament may seem easier to understand than that which saw the

Royal Ulster Constabulary officers investigate the scene of a bomb attack at the Mahons Hotel in Irvinestown, Northern Ireland on Feb. 7, 2000. The device is alleged to have been planted by a splinter group of Irish Republican Army, the Continunity IRA. AP/Wide World Photos. Reproduced by permission.

Irish Republic ignored, but the roots were similar: the IRA failed to recognize the 1921 decision of the Irish Free State to grant secession to the six counties that make up Ulster. This was a betrayal of Irish nationalism, they believed, and gave way to civil war in the newly formed Irish Free State.

Long after the IRA had ended in defeat, they maintained an uncompromising commitment to an independent Ireland of thirty-two counties (as opposed to the Irish Republic's twenty-six). Anything less would effectively count for nothing, in their view. Moreover, the IRA and its political backers refused to acknowledge the new Republic or its institutions, claiming up until the 1980s to be the "Provisional Government of the Irish Republic" it had declared in 1918 (and which

was annulled by the Free State's creation three years later).

When Sinn Fein decided to recognize the Irish Republic and participate in the Dáil in 1986, some members disagreed. Two of them, Ruairi O'Bradaigh and Daithi O'Conouill, led other disaffected members to form a new group dedicated to the complete unification of Ireland: Republican Sinn Fein. Two years later at its Ard-Fheis (convention), it stated its support for an armed struggle to bring about its aims. Continuity Irish Republican army was established to carry out this struggle.

This did not manifest itself in any real way until 1994, when the Provisional IRA announced a ceasefire, an act, according to Republican Sinn Fein, of "national treachery." Fearing Republican Sinn Fein's military wing would continue with violence where the Provisionals had left off, Irish *Gardai* (police) launched a series of preemptive raids on Republican Sinn Fein members throughout 1994 and 1995.

Not until July 1996 was the Continuity IRA linked with a major terrorist attack when a 1,200-pound bomb destroyed the Killyhevlin Hotel in Enniskillen, just minutes after it was evacuated. Seventeen people were injured.

Tony Blair's election as British Prime Minister in May 1997 brought a fresh impetus to the search for a political solution to Northern Ireland's troubles. Republican Sinn Fein opposed any political solution that involved the British government and saw it as their "duty" to stand up for their view of Irish nationalism, a cause they believed Sinn Fein had betrayed by engaging with their political enemies. The Continuity IRA was linked to at least eight major car bombings and numerous minor attacks in 1997 and 1998 as it tried to disrupt the peace process. It was a reflection, however, of Republican Sinn Fein and the CIRA's relative lack of manpower and resources that the bombing was not more sustained or effective. In any event, the attacks did nothing to dissuade other nationalist and loyalist parties from reaching political agreement with the British and Irish governments, nor did it cow the populations of the Republic or Northern Ireland into rejecting that agreement when it was put to a referendum in May 1998.

Nevertheless, the CIRA was loosely implicated in the Omagh bombing of August 1998,

LEADERSHIP

RUAIRI O'BRADAIGH

Although Republican Sinn Fein denies any involvement with the Continuity IRA (much in the same way that Sinn Fein-proper denies association with the Provisional IRA), its founder and leader, Ruairi O'Bradaigh, remains entrenched in a tradition of violent Irish nationalism. Born to a middle-class Republican family in Longford, in the Irish Free State in 1932, and trained as a teacher, O'Bradaigh joined the IRA while attending university and was part of a number of daring arms and border raids throughout the 1950s. On several occasions, he was jailed for his activities, but by the early 1960s had risen to be the IRA's chief of staff, a position he twice held.

His unrelenting opposition to the dropping of abstentionism during 1969 and 1970 saw his stature rise even further, and he was elected Sinn Fein President in October 1970, a position he held until 1983 when he was usurped by Gerry Adams.

As Sinn Fein President, O'Bradaigh oversaw the IRA's most bloody period of terror, with numerous atrocities carried out in Ulster, the Republic, and mainland Britain. Unyielding and unbending in his outlook, the likelihood of a political solution in Northern Ireland seemed a remote possibility during this period.

When Adams took over as leader in 1983, he sought to engage in the political process, leading to the end of abstentionism in 1986 and—effectively—the IRA's claims to being Ireland's "provisional" government. In many ways, this marked the onset of Sinn Fein's modernization, but was anathema to a hardliner like O'Bradaigh, who believed in an old-school type of Irish nationalism that seemed more grounded in principle than political reality.

The nascent Republican Sinn Fein fulfilled those ideals and, never a man at ease with political compromise, O'Bradaigh continued to carry out a brand of nationalist ideals on the fringe Irish politics. For the two decades that followed, he retained his hard-line stance, but was an increasingly marginal figure, not up-to-date with the realities of expectations or expectations of modern Ireland.

which killed twenty-nine people. The extent of its involvement in the attack, which was carried out by the Real IRA, remains unclear, but it is believed that they picked out the target. The Real IRA nevertheless claimed responsibility.

Invariably, Republican Sinn Fein rejected the terms of the Good Friday agreement. In turn, the British Northern Ireland Secretary, Mo Mowlam, announced that imprisoned CIRA members would not be subject to the same terms of early release as members of other groups.

In the years that followed the Good Friday agreement, the CIRA continue to be linked to a number of terrorist attacks, most notably several bombings in London in 2000 and 2001. Nevertheless, some of these accusations were probably misplaced and muddled with other IRA factions.

In July 2000, the U.S. Department of State belatedly designated the CIRA as a foreign terrorist organization, a move that made it illegal for Americans to provide support for it. It also estimated that the CIRA had just 50 remaining activists.

PHILOSOPHY AND TACTICS

Republican Sinn Fein and, in turn, the Continuity IRA claimed to be the "true" inheritors of the sort of Irish republicanism that dates back to the old IRA, which fought the War of Independence (1916–1921). In essence, this is the creation of a united Ireland through armed struggle. In this instance, however, the CIRA envisaged the creation of a social democratic state.

Its unyielding refusal to even acknowledge the British or Irish governments is reminiscent of the sort of deeply principled obstinance that led

KEY EVENTS

1986: Republican Sinn Fein created as a protest at Sinn Fein's ending of abstentionism from the Dáil.

1988: Ruairi O'Bradaigh affirms Republican Sinn Fein's commitment to armed struggle with the goal of a socialist democratic Republic of Ireland.

1994: Republican Sinn Fein vigorously opposes the Provisional IRA's ceasefire. Intermittent paramilitary activity linked to the Continuity IRA.

1996: A bombing in Enniskillen marks the first major act of the Continuity IRA; seveteen people injured.

1997–1998: Increased Continuity IRA activity in the run up to the Good Friday agreement, which it opposes.

1998: British Northern Ireland Secretary, Mo Mowlam, announces that Continuity IRA prisoners not eligible for early release under the Good Friday agreement.

2004: CIRA placed on U.S. Department of State list of banned terrorist organizations.

to the Irish Civil War (1922–1923) between Free Staters, who had signed away, in 1921, the largely Protestant Ulster to the British in order to secure the freedom of the Catholic South, and the IRA who refused to accept or believe in an Ireland comprising of anything less than its thirty-two constituent counties.

While this viewpoint might have held a place in the revolutionary foment of early twentieth-century Ireland, it was outmoded by this century's end. Of course, the fact that some still believe in nothing short of a thirty-two-county Ireland and continue to refuse to acknowledge the institutions that brought its partition, led to the formation Republican Sinn Fein and the Continuity IRA, but they were marginalized in their views from the outset. Their belief and propagation of armed struggle in the mid 1980s found little support in a province readying itself for peace after years of violence.

Suspected Continuity IRA activities have included bombings, assassinations, and kidnappings, as well as extortion and robbery. Targets have included British military and police officers, as well as loyalist rivals. In this sense, their actions are little different from other Northern Irish terrorist organizations, however they continue to be marked by their rivals as "amateur" and their intermittent attacks have failed to ignite the insurrection they hope will bring a socialist democratic republic of Ireland.

OTHER PERSPECTIVES

"Most disillusioned republicans have realized that the constitutional people have won the long struggle; others are waiting for the next campaign," wrote Ruth Dudley Edwards in an *Irish Sunday Independent* comment piece in 2003. "There has always been resistance," O'Bradaigh told *The Times*. The CIRA bombs "are indications that militant republicanism is not dead. Maybe you can say that these things are only a token and instead of a flame they are only a spark but so what, it is there. That is the lesson of history." "Until the Brits are out, the bombs will go off. Republican Sinn Fein sees itself as the guardian of true republican principles," as explained in their Eire Nua policy document: "We've gone back to our roots which is the birth of Irish republicanism in the age of enlightenment." "Interesting ideas, shame they emanate from people so rigid they still won't recognize the Dáil and so stupid they can't see that it is peace, not bombs, that will move British troops out."

"The Provos [the Provisional IRA] know their history and the perils associated with it," wrote the former *Daily Mirror* editor, Roy Greenslade, in the *Guardian* in 2001. "At several points when militants, feeling they had achieved all that was possible by violence, then pursued their goals without the gun, there were splits. Each time, the breakaway group carried on the military struggle and claimed to be the true bearers of the soul of Irish nationalism... Provo wits lampooned them as 'the Coca-Colas,' a reference to the drinks company's advertising slogan for 'the real thing,' but their activities have been

PRIMARY SOURCE
Man Accused of Directing Terrorism

The brother-in-law of IRA hunger striker Bobby Sands has become the first person in the Irish Republic to be charged with directing terrorism.

Michael McKevitt, 51, with an address in Blackrock in the border town of County Louth, was remanded in custody on Friday at the non-jury Special Criminal Court in Dublin.

He faces a maximum sentence of life imprisonment if found guilty of the offence—created in legislation passed after the 1998 Omagh bombing.

He is also accused of "belonging to an illegal organisation," named as the Irish Republican Army, or IRA, from 29 August 2000 to March 2001.

Irish law does not distinguish between different wings of Republicanism such as the Real IRA or Continuity IRA.

Two men and a woman arrested at the same time as Mr. McKevitt on Thursday have been released without charge.

HUNGER STRIKER

Mr. McKevitt is accused of directing terrorism between 29 August 1999 and 23 October 2000.

His wife Bernadette is the sister of Bobby Sands who was elected to the U.K. Parliament in 1981 shortly before becoming the first of 10 IRA prisoners to die on hunger strike.

Mr. McKevitt is a member of the hard-line republican 32 County Sovereignty Movement which has been linked with the Real IRA republican paramilitary group.

Members of the lobby group have denied any links with the Real IRA, which carried out the 1998 Omagh bombing in County Tyrone, killing 29 people and injuring more than 200 others.

Both the 32 County Sovereignty Committee and the Real IRA are opposed to mainstream republican involvement in the current Northern Ireland peace process.

Mr. McKevitt spoke only once during the 15-minute hearing on Friday to confirm his name.

He was remanded in custody until 3 April when a bail application is expected to be lodged at the Special Criminal Court.

Source: BBC News, 2001

---

nothing to joke about. By threatening the stability of the Provos, they undermine their claim to speak for all republicans . . . ", as written in the *Guardian*.

SUMMARY

Although the political settlement of Good Friday 1998 has suffered various crises during its short life, few Republicans have become so disillusioned with it that they have switched allegiance to Republican Sinn Fein and its outmoded commitment to armed struggle and staunch refusal to engage with either British or Irish governments. If anything, British and Irish security forces have switched focus from mainstream terrorist organizations, like the IRA, to niche groups, such as the CIRA, that threatened Ulster's awkward peace by their refusal to acknowledge the political settlement reached in 1998. Invariably, this has diminished their effectiveness further; as did the U.S. government's classification of the CIRA as a terrorist organization, which cut off the trickle of funds from American sympathizers.

SOURCES

Books

Maloney, Ed. *Secret History of the IRA*. London: Penguin, 2003.

McKittrick, David, and David McVeigh. *Making Sense of the Troubles*. London: Penguin, 2003.

PRIMARY SOURCE

Continuity Irish Republican Army (CIRA) a.k.a. Continuity Army Council, Republican Sinn Fein

DESCRIPTION

CIRA is a terrorist splinter group formed in the mid-1990s as the clandestine armed wing of Republican Sinn Fein, which split from Sinn Fein in 1986. "Continuity" refers to the group's belief that it is carrying on the original Irish Republican Army's (IRA) goal of forcing the British out of Northern Ireland. CIRA's aliases, Continuity Army Council and Republican Sinn Fein, were also designated as FTOs. CIRA cooperates with the larger Real IRA.

ACTIVITIES

CIRA has been active in Belfast and the border areas of Northern Ireland, where it has carried out bombings, assassinations, kidnappings, hijackings, extortion, and robberies. On occasion, it has provided advance warning to police of its attacks. Targets include British military, Northern Ireland security forces, and Loyalist paramilitary groups. Unlike the Provisional IRA, CIRA is not observing a cease-fire. CIRA has continued its activities with a series of hoax bomb threats, low-level improvised explosive device attacks, kidnapping, intimidation, and so-called "punishment beatings."

STRENGTH

Membership is small, with possibly fewer than fifty hardcore activists. Police counterterrorist operations have reduced the group's strength, but CIRA continues to recruit, train, and plan operations.

LOCATION/AREA OF OPERATION

Northern Ireland, Irish Republic. Does not have an established presence in Great Britain.

EXTERNAL AID

Suspected of receiving funds and arms from sympathizers in the United States. May have acquired arms and material from the Balkans in cooperation with the Real IRA.

Source: U.S. Department of State. *Country Reports on Terrorism*. Washington, D.C., 2004.

Toolid, Kevin. *Rebel Hearts, Journeys in the Republican Movement*. New York: Picador, 1995.

Web sites

CAIN Web Service "Speech by Ruairi O'Bradaigh." < http://cain.ulst.ac.uk/issues/politics/docs/sf/rob021186.htm > (accessed September 28, 2005).

SEE ALSO

Real Irish Republican Army

Provisional Irish Republican Army

Irish Republican Army

Council of Conservative Citizens

LEADER: Gordon Lee Baum

YEAR ESTABLISHED OR BECAME ACTIVE: 1985

ESTIMATED SIZE: 20,000

USUAL AREA OF OPERATION: United States

OVERVIEW

The Council of Conservative Citizens (CCC or CofCC) is a highy conservative political organization and a white supremacist/white separatist group that adheres to a mythical Southern way of life. According to the Anti-Defamation League (ADL), the CCC considers itself a grass-roots organization that solves conservative problems, promotes conservative rights, and coordinates political activities, primarily at the local and state level but also nationally. According to the Southern Poverty Law Center (SPLC) and the International Relations Center (IRC), it claims to be the True Voice of the American Right. Rather than violence—which is common in white supremacist groups—the CCC uses its financial and political influence to elect and influence politicians.

The CCC consists of a national headquarters in St. Louis, Missouri, and numerous local, decentralized chapters, with its two largest chapters located in Missouri and Mississippi. The CCC's founder and national leader is its chief executive officer, Gordon Lee Baum, and its publication is *The Citizens Informer*, with a circulation of about 20,000.

Members of the South Carolina Council of Conservative Citizens protest state Senate Bill 61 on January 30, 1999. The bill called for the removal of the Confederate flag from the State House dome. AP/Wide World *Photos. Reproduced by permission.*

HISTORY

The CCC was founded in Atlanta, Georgia, on March 7, 1985, by Baum and thirty activists from the John Birch Society, former leaders of the Citizens Councils of America (CCA, its predecessor), and members of segregationist political administrations and campaigns. The group was founded due to the men's dissatisfaction with liberal U.S. government programs such as food stamps, quotas, and welfare checks.

The Confederate flag became an effective membership instrument beginning in the early 1990s. Southern conservatives and extremists

PRIMARY SOURCE

Into the Mainstream: George Wallace Jr. Delivers Major Speech to Hate Group

MONTGOMERY, Ala.—Alabama Public Service Commissioner George C. Wallace Jr., whose father famously vowed to defend racial segregation "forever" in a 1963 speech from the steps of the state Capitol, gave the welcoming speech to the national delegates of a white supremacist hate group meeting here on June 3.

The younger Wallace, whose official resumé boasts of an NAACP Freedom Award, opened up the first day of the annual national convention of the Council of Conservative Citizens (CCC), a group whose Web site has referred to blacks as "a retrograde species of humanity." More than 100 delegates heard his speech, which went without any immediate coverage in the Alabama print or broadcast media.

There is little debate that the CCC is a racist group. In fact, the head of the Republican National Committee in 1999 warned party members to avoid the group after the Southern Poverty Law Center published an exposé detailing its racism. The CCC was created from the mailing lists of the old White Citizens Councils, which were set up in the 1950s and 1960s to resist efforts to desegregate Southern schools, and which Thurgood Marshall once described as "the uptown Klan." Recently, it has embraced Holocaust deniers and published anti-Semitic articles on its Web site.

In the audience listening to Wallace were a number of leading white supremacists. They included Don Black, proprietor of Stormfront.org, the most influential hate site on the Internet, and former Alabama grand dragon of the Knights of the Ku Klux Klan; Jamie Kelso, right-hand man and Louisiana roommate of former Klan leader David Duke; Jared Taylor, editor of the neo-eugenicist *American Renaissance* magazine; Ed Fields, an aging white supremacist leader from Georgia; Alabama CCC leader Leonard "Flagpole" Wilson, who got his nickname shouting "Keep Bama white!" from atop a flagpole

were attracted to the group because it aggressively supported the flag as the traditional symbol for Southern heritage. Efforts to eliminate or minimize the flag's visibility were strongly opposed by the CCC. Some of its actions—according to a November 1999 article in the *Augusta Chronicle* (Georgia)—included over a dozen protests at the Georgia state capital over the removal of the Confederate flag from display.

In the mid 1990s, the CCC claimed that it held members in every state, with chapters and affiliates in twenty of the states. Later, in 1999, the CCC numbered about 15,000 members and thirty-three chapters in over twenty states, with 5,000 members in Alabama, Georgia, and Mississippi.

The CCC raised its stature in the white supremacist movement by inviting prominent Southern politicians and white supremacist leaders to speak and participate at its conferences and meetings. Although the CCC was a local organization known primarily in extremist circles, it quickly vaulted itself into the national spotlight in the winter of 1998–1999. Journalists (primarily those with the *Miami Herald* and *The Washington Post*) and researchers (mainly at the SPLC) learned that many conservative federal, state, and local politicians, including U.S. Representative Robert Barr (Republican-Georgia) and U.S. Senator Trent Lott (Republican-Mississippi), had appeared one or more times at CCC events from the late 1980s to the late 1990s.

In fact, the *Washington Post* reported that Lott had been the 1992 keynote speaker at a CCC-Mississippi conference. Paralleling the story, conservative columnist Armstrong Williams said of the political pair: "Lott and Barr gave legitimacy to this racist organization by speaking before them."

Whether or not these politicians knew about the CCC's racist viewpoints, a controversy nevertheless followed. The Chairman of the

during University of Alabama race riots in 1956; and the CCC's national leader, St. Louis personal injury lawyer Gordon Lee Baum.

Wallace could not immediately be reached for comment. Later, he told The Associated Press, "There is nothing hateful about those people I've seen." He said he welcomed the delegates and spoke about his family and conservative values.

This was not Wallace's first flirtation with the CCC, a group that has grown more openly radical and racist in recent years. Wallace, who was Alabama state treasurer between 1986 and 1994 and was elected to the Public Service Commission in 1998, gave speeches to the CCC once in 1998 and twice during 1999.

Also speaking at the most recent convention was John Eidsmoe, a former law school professor and close friend and one-time legal adviser to Roy Moore, the Alabama chief justice ejected from his post for defying federal court orders to remove a Ten Commandments monument from the Supreme Court rotunda. Like Moore, Eidsmoe has suggested that the government "may not act contrary to God's laws."

The elder Wallace, who was governor of Alabama three times in the 1960s and 1970s, was famous for his resistance to desegregation, and he ran for president four times on a racist platform. But after his final defeat, Wallace came home to Alabama and sought to reconcile with civil rights leaders and others whom he had pilloried for most of his political life. In 1982, he was elected governor once more—this time with most black Alabamans behind him. It was never clear whether it was his conscience or political expediency that was behind this transformation.

Source: Southern Poverty Law Center, 2005

Republican National Committee, Jim Nicholson, eventually denounced the CCC and suggested that Republicans resign from the group. A subsequent Congressional resolution to condemn the CCC was considered, but ultimately did not garner sufficient votes to pass.

For some time, the racist CCC was unable to pass itself off as a mainstream politically conservative group. Although much of its power diminished after this event, the CCC still remains politically effective, especially maintaining its strength in Mississippi. For example, CCC members were instrumental in soundly defeating a 2001 referendum to change the Mississippi state flag to include a less noticeable version of the Confederate battle flag. In addition, the CCC assisted in the 2003 gubernatorial election of CCC friend, Republican Haley Barbour of Mississippi.

In 2005, the web site of the CCC claimed to have at least fifty chapters and members in all fifty states, plus the District of Columbia. It describes its Mississippi chapter in Greenwood as its flagship chapter.

PHILOSOPHY AND TACTICS

CCC leadership maintains an ideology that supports the traditional Southern culture involving such principles as restricting non-white immigration, removal of government-sponsored race preference programs, eliminating race-mixing, removal of school integration, and support for the Confederate flag. CCC leaders attempt to disguise their racist policies behind a conservative advocacy policy. For example, the CCC aggressively promotes such mainstream conservative issues as states rights, race relations, and conservative Protestant Christianity, while aggressively opposing such topics as big government and gun control.

Consistent with its beliefs, the CCC regards the society of the United States as an outgrowth

KEY EVENTS

1985: The Council of Conservative Citizens is formed by Gordon Baum as an offshoot of Citizens Councils of America.

1990s: The Confederate battle flag helps to recruit new members; the CCC claims members in every state, with chapters and affiliates in twenty states.

1998–1999: The CCC is nationally exposed to be not a mainstream conservative political group, but instead a white-supremacist organization with connections to prominent politicians.

1999: The CCC claims 15,000 members and thirty-three chapters in over twenty states.

2005: The CCC claims members in all fifty states and the District of Columbia, and at least forty-eight chapters predominantly in the northeastern, southeastern, and central parts of the United States.

LEADERSHIP

GORDON BAUM

Baum is a personal injury attorney in St. Louis, Missouri, who specializes in automobile accidents and workers' compensation claims. He has been a white-power activist throughout his professional career. Baum was the Midwest field director/organizer for the white-segregationist and anti-Semitic CCA until the organization folded after it lost the fight for Southern segregation. In 1985, Baum formed the CCC from the CCA's mailing lists. As of 2005, Baum remains its founder and leader in the position of chief executive officer.

OTHER PERSPECTIVES

Leaders of the SPLC, the ADL, and the National Association for the Advancement of Colored People (NAACP) have frequently accused the CCC of promoting racist ideas, especially between black and white Americans.

Julian Bond, the 1999 NAACP chairman, asked the U.S. Senate to condemn the CCC for its activities of promoting white supremacy while degrading minority groups. According to the ADL, U.S. Representative Robert Wexler, a Florida Democrat, and U.S. Representative Michael Forbes, a New York Republican, introduced a Congressional resolution in response to Bond's statement condemning the racism of the CCC. A modified resolution, proposed by Representative J.C. Watts of Oklahoma failed to pass.

The SPLC issued a report on December 18, 1999, that described the CCC as the "incarnation" of the CCA, which resisted integration and promoted segregation in Southern states during the civil rights movement. Joe Roy, director for the center's Intelligence Project, stated that the CCC has for years tried to disguise itself as a respectable conservative group—while all along holding white supremacist views.

of the European culture. The CCC also claims that the issues it promotes have nothing to do with race. Its leaders, however, admit that they favor white European-Americans, while not advocating nor supporting the repression of non-white races or ethnic groups.

As a result of using the strategy of respectability within the mainstream, many conservative politicians have been attracted to the group over the years. CCC members often use economic pressure to sway politicians and businesspersons toward its viewpoints. For example, in 1999, the North Carolina chapter protested outside a Tyson Foods plant (threatening to boycott its foods) after it supposedly hired illegal immigrants.

Although not all chapters are considered extremist groups, all operate on the premise of bigotry against minorities, especially African Americans. Local leaders focus on such issues as interracial marriage, black-on-white violence, and white Southern culture.

Although CCC leaders maintain the group is not a Southern racist group, investigations into the group's activities throughout its existence show that it regularly associates with other known white-power groups and publishes racist articles. According to the ADL, organizations that have regularly advertised in the CCC's *The Citizens Informer* include the TC Allen Company (which sells racist pamphlets), Heritage Lost Ministries (an Ohio-based racist organization), and *The Resister* (a racist and anti-Semitic journal). The publication regularly voices the superiority of the white race while emphasizing, for example, excessive black violence and Hispanic immigration.

SUMMARY

The CCC continues to attract conservative political leaders to its membership roles and as speakers at its events. As a result, the CCC has been able to recruit members into its organization based on the assumption that it is a conservatively-based political group. With primarily aging members, the CCC began in 1998, according to the SPLC, a campaign to bring in younger members, including the establishment of a youth chapter and an education committee.

The CCC continues to maintain strong ties with white-power groups. As investigated by such groups as the SPLC and the ADL, its policies, records, and public statements prove that it has not attempted to cut its ties with such extremist organizations. Conversely, it has furthered its strategies of advocating what critics contend is a fundamentally racist agenda.

SOURCES

Periodicals

Kefner, John. "Lott, and Shadow of a Pro-White Group." *The New York Times*. January 14, 1999.

Web sites

Anti-Defamation League. "Council of Conservative Citizens: December 21, 1998." < http://www.adl.org/backgrounders/ccc.asp > (accessed October 23, 2005).

A *Anti-Defamation League.* "Extremism in America: Council of Conservative Citizens." < http://www.adl.org/learn/ext_us/CCCitizens.asp?xpicked = 3&item = 12 > (accessed October 23, 2005).

Dennis Roddy, Post-Gazette. "Jared Taylor, a Racist in the Guise of 'Expert,'" < http://www.post-gazette.com/pg/05023/446341.stm > (accessed October 23, 2005).

Heidi Beirich and Bob Moser, Intelligence Report, Southern Poverty Law Center. "Communing with the Council." < http://www.splcenter.org/intel/intelreport/article.jsp?pid = 804 > (accessed October 23, 2005).

Institute for the Study of Academic Racism. "Council of Conservative Citizens." < http://www.ferris.edu/isar/Institut/CCC/homepage.htm > (accessed October 23, 2005).

International Relations Center. "Council of Conservative Citizens." < http://rightweb.irc-online.org/org/cofcc.php > (accessed October 23, 2005).

Southern Poverty Law Center. "The Neo-Confederates." < http://www.splcenter.org/intel/intelreport/article.jsp?-pid = 461 > (accessed October 23, 2005).

Southern Poverty Law Center. "Sharks in the Mainstream." < http://www.splcenter.org/intel/intelreport/article.jsp?aid = 360 > (accessed October 23, 2005).

The Covenant

ALTERNATE NAME: Covenant, Sword, and Arm of the Lord

LEADER: James Ellison

YEAR ESTABLISHED OR BECAME ACTIVE: 1978

ESTIMATED SIZE: 100

USUAL AREA OF OPERATION: United States

OVERVIEW

The Covenant, also known as the Covenant, Sword, and Arm of the Lord (CSA), is a racist, religious, ultra-conservative Christian Identity survivalist group that was founded by James Ellison in 1978. Prior to founding the CSA, Ellison ran a Christian Identity retreat center on his 250-acre property in a town called Elijah, Arkansas, located near the Missouri–Arkansas border. Ellison professed to have had a vision in 1978, in which he "saw" a race war about to overtake the United States. At that point, Ellison decided to turn his former retreat into a paramilitary survivalist training camp dedicated to the ideology of white supremacy and to the principles of Christian Identity.

As an extension of the white supremacist philosophy, the CSA purported to be particularly opposed to Judaism, and promoted acts of anti-Semitism. The group was also opposed to the political underpinnings of the United States, and vowed to overthrow the government. The CSA's first stated objective was the elimination of government workers, beginning with federal agents. Between 1983 and 1985, the CSA committed several violent acts, including an arson attack on a church in Missouri, the firebombing of a synagogue in Indiana, and an attempted bombing of a Chicago gas pipeline. On April 19, 1985, approximately 200 federal officers surrounded the compound in Elijah, and ordered the roughly one hundred residents to surrender. A four-day standoff and negotiations ensued, and the compound eventually surrendered without bloodshed. After the compound was emptied of inhabitants and searched, a significant arsenal was recovered.

HISTORY

James Ellison was a fundamentalist minister from San Antonio, Texas. He reported that he had a religious vision in 1971 in which he was instructed to go to Arkansas to "establish a refuge and take people in." In 1976, he bought 224 acres of land in order to establish his own community. The property had an independent water supply, and was able to generate its own electrical power.

Ellison was a strong proponent of the Christian Identity Movement and ran a religious retreat on his property until he had a vision of an impending race war in 1978. He then founded the Covenant, Sword, and Arm of the Lord, and turned his retreat into a white supremacist, survivalist, Christian Identity paramilitary survivalist training center. Over time, the compound grew to be a "home" for the CSA, with about a hundred full-time residents. The philosophies of the CSA included an overarching belief in Jewish inferiority and encouragement of strongly anti-Semitic behavior, and a professed need to overthrow the United States government by any and all necessary means. The group vowed to begin to carry out this objective by eliminating anyone involved in the workings of the government, particularly federal agents and law enforcement personnel.

The group supported itself by encouraging theft, as well as by selling homemade machine guns, silencers, and explosives at gun shows, which also served as their primary recruiting area. They sought out gun enthusiasts as potential CSA members, and invited them to participate in the Covenant's Endtime Overcomer Survival Training School, whose curriculum contained paramilitary training in the use of various weapons, techniques of urban warfare, wilderness survival, and "Christian" martial arts.

In addition to the manufacture of weapons, explosives, and ammunition, the members of the Covenant wrote and self-published a journal and an assortment of books. The group also developed a book list devoted to racist, white supremacist, anti-Semitic, and survivalist treatises.

Based on the vision by Ellison in late 1978, the members of the CSA believed that the United States was approaching a total economic collapse, which would initiate widespread famine, rioting, and an all-out race war. In an effort to prepare for the coming apocalyptic event, the group stockpiled weapons, munitions, food, and wilderness survival gear. One of the group's leaders, Kerry Noble, stated "We are Christian survivalists who believe in preparing for the ultimate holocaust." The Covenant's publicly disseminated literature advertised that it would "build an Ark for God's people during the coming tribulations" and that "the coming war is a step towards God's government." In an effort to prepare financially for the coming apocalypse, the Covenant members began to steal from department stores, and to commit acts of arson for pay.

In July 1983, a white supremacist leadership (Aryan Nations Congress) meeting was attended by James Ellison, Richard Butler (Aryan Nations leader and head of the Identity Christian Church of Jesus Christ Christian in Hayden Lake, Idaho), Louis Beam (ambassador-at-large for the Aryan Nations), and Robert Miles (leader of the Mountain Church in Cohoctah, Michigan and former grand dragon of the Michigan Knights of the Ku Klux Klan), among others. The group created a manifesto for the destruction and overthrow of the United States government—referred to by the group as the "Zionist-Occupied Government" (ZOG), and developed a plan for the inception of a separate Aryan Nation in the United States. The group planned to implement an elaborate computer linkage system for facilitating communication among the right-wing extremist groups (including the Covenant). The Aryan Nations Congress developed a detailed strategy for carrying out their political and ideological aims, which included the assassination of government employees, federal officials, and practitioners of Judaism, destruction of public utilities (gas, electrical, and water systems), and bombing of federal office buildings. Among the federal buildings listed as a target was the Alfred E. Murrah building, eventually attacked by Timothy McVeigh in April 1995. It was anticipated that these acts of terrorism would set the stage for the revolution that would result in ultimate white power and supremacy in the United States.

After the Congress meeting, the Covenant escalated its terrorist activities, and, in November 1983, admitted to detonating an explosive device along a natural gas pipeline that supplied much of the midwestern United States. Later that same month, the group reported detonating an explosive device on an electrical transmission line at Fort Smith, Arkansas.

The FBI and the Bureau of Alcohol, Tobacco, and Firearms, already investigating the group, stepped up its surveillance through the use of informants. One such informant was Randall Rader, a former deputy of the Covenant, who had shifted over to The Order. The informant gave the FBI some information related to the murder of a woman, through the use of a foot-long knife, by a CSA member. This was consonant with a body that had been found several months earlier, but for whom no suspect had been identified. The informant also told the FBI that the CSA was stockpiling specific types of weapons, booby-trapping the perimeter of the compound, and engaging in paramilitary training activities, among other things.

On April 15, 1985, a Missouri state trooper pulled over a van driven by an Order member named David Tate during a routine traffic patrol. When the trooper called in the license plate number, he discovered that Tate was a neo-Nazi who had a federal arrest warrant out for firearms-related charges. As the trooper approached Tate's vehicle, the suspect rolled out, opened fire on the trooper with a submachine gun, killed him, and left the scene. State police from Missouri and Arkansas, along with FBI SWAT team members, carried out an intensive six-day manhunt for Tate, during which time they learned that he had been en route to the CSA compound, where a number of other members of The Order had also sought refuge. The FBI obtained a warrant to search the Covenant's compound. On April 20, 1985, the FBI and approximately 200 law enforcement officers approached the compound, resulting in a standoff between authorities and CSA members. After some days of negotiations, the Covenant members surrendered and left the compound with no ensuing violence.

After it had been completely evacuated, the compound was searched, resulting in the location of landmines encircling the perimeter, large numbers of illegal weapons and munitions, including twenty-three hand grenades, an Army light antitank weapon, fifteen automatic rifles, and an equal number of silencers, along with the framework for an armored car (under construction). They also discovered some thirty gallons of cyanide; it had been intended as a means of poisoning the city supply for an unspecified location.

Later in 1985, CSA members were charged, and convicted, of the August 1983 arsons of the Metropolitan Community Church in Springfield, Missouri, and the Bloomington, Indiana, Jewish Community Center. At the same time, they were charged with the November 1983 bombing of a natural gas pipeline near Fulton, Arkansas. During the trial for these terrorist acts, it was uncovered that the Covenant had also planned to bomb the federal building in Oklahoma City through the use of rocket launchers.

In 1986, Ellison became a federal informant, and began providing authorities with information regarding the activities of other extremist groups with which he had previously been allied. As a result, in 1988, the United States accused fourteen of the participants at the July 1983 Aryan Nations Congress of sedition. The jury felt that Ellison was not a plausible witness, as he stood to significantly benefit if his testimony resulted in convictions, and the government failed to win the case. In 1988, Ellison successfully petitioned for a reduced sentence, and his term was reduced to five years.

Richard Snell, Ellison's closest associate in the plot to bomb the Murrah building, was tried for the 1983 murders of a Texarkana, Arkansas, pawnbroker (he had believed that the businessman was Jewish) and an Arkansas state trooper (the officer was African American). He was convicted and sentenced to death. While on death row, he was reported to have made numerous comments that there would be some sort of explosion on the day of his execution. He was executed by means of a lethal injection on April 19, 1995, within twelve hours of the bombing of the Murrah Federal Building in Oklahoma City.

KEY EVENTS

1971: James Ellison had a vision in which he was told to go to Arkansas to establish a refuge.

1976: Ellison bought the property that was to house the Covenant.

1978: Ellison has another vision, in which he sees an impending race war. He founds the Covenant, Sword, and Arm of the Lord in this same year.

1983: Aryan Nations Congress meeting.

1983: As a result of the Aryan Nations Congress meeting, the most violent members of each member group are recruited to form The Order, whose mission is to finance the coming war.

1983: CSA attempts to blow up a natural gas pipeline supplying the Midwest region of the United States.

1983: CSA detonates a device attempting to destroy an electrical transmission line in Fort Smith, Arkansas.

1983: The FBI and the Bureau of Alcohol, Tobacco, and Firearms engage in progressively more intense investigation and surveillance of CSA activities.

1985: A state trooper pulls over a van driven by David Tate, a member of The Order en route to the CSA compound. Tate fatally wounds the officer, sparking a massive SWAT team search for Tate. Ultimately, this provides a catalyst for the FBI to obtain a warrant to search the CSA compound.

1985: The FBI surrounds the compound and instructs the CSA to surrender. Several days of negotiation resulted in a peaceful surrender of the compound's inhabitants.

1985: Members of the CSA are charged with, and convicted of, numerous acts of terrorism.

1988: The U.S. government charged fourteen of the participants in the Aryan Nations Congress with sedition. Ellison becomes a federal informant for the case, which is unsuccessfully litigated.

1995: Ellison completes his parole and moves to Elohim City, another armed camp, where he marries the granddaughter of Pastor Millar, the head of the compound. Richard Snell, former close associate of Ellison, is executed by means of a lethal injection on the day that the Murrah Building was bombed.

PHILOSOPHY AND TACTICS

The Covenant, Sword, and Arm of the Lord was a Christian Identity religious fundamentalist white supremacist group whose goal was the overthrow of the U.S. government and the establishment of a separatist Aryan nation. They planned to wage a race war in the country, believing that the economy was about to collapse. The group prepared by engaging in paramilitary and survivalist training, creating and acquiring large quantities of illegal weapons and ammunition, and creating a veritable fortress within the CSA compound. The leadership of the CSA met with the upper echelons of allied Aryan Nations groups in July 1983, and devised an elaborate plan of attack that was to result in

the crippling and overthrow of the ZOG, and establishment of a new order. Between 1983 and 1985, the group engaged in numerous acts of terrorism. In April 1985, the compound was successfully raided by federal and state authorities, resulting in the surrender of CSA members and the closure of the compound. The "Honor Guard" of the CSA was arrested, charged, pled guilty to, and was convicted of terrorist activities. Ellison turned federal informant not long after he began serving his prison sentence, and was able to have his time significantly reduced. He completed his parole in 1995, moved to another armed compound, and married the granddaughter of the leader of Elohim City (the compound). Since the closure of the compound in 1985, along with the convictions of the

CSA members who had been the power behind the organization, the Covenant has not publicly claimed any terrorist acts.

OTHER PERSPECTIVES

The CSA was a Christian Identity extremist group, which is made up of religious right-wing reactionaries. They believe that there were two separate "creations," one for the white Aryan races—British, Germanic-Teutonic, and Scandinavian ancestry—and one for the Jewish race. They believe that Jesus was sent to save the Aryans, and that the Jewish peoples are actually the result of a union between Eve and the serpent (Satan) in the garden of Eden; they are therefore considered to be antichrist peoples. Covenant members believe that the Bible gives them proof of this assertion in Chapter 8 of the Gospel of Saint John. They also assert that non-white peoples lie on the evolutionary continuum about halfway between apes and humans; they are not evil like the Jewish peoples are believed to be, they are simply subhuman.

Identity Christianity is the dominant religion of the ultra-conservative radical right and the white supremacist factions in the United States, and has been gaining in popularity since the last quarter of the twentieth century. It is historically determined to have originated during the seventeenth century in Western Europe.

Identity Christians believe that the human societies are corrupt and that an apocalypse is imminent. The aftermath of the apocalypse will result in the beginning of a new age, peopled by a chosen few who are selected by God to survive the "Endtime" for which the members of the CSA were training.

The Covenant also believes that the American form of government is fatally corrupt and is guilty of robbing citizens of their fundamental rights, hence their desire to overthrow the government, which, as it is bound by secular law, is not relevant to those who believe in the "Divine Order."

SUMMARY

The Covenant was a racist, ultra-conservative, right-wing reactionary, white supremacist,

Identity Christian religious extremist group, formed by former minister James Ellison in 1978 after he claimed to have a series of visions about the coming apocalypse. The group was allied with other Aryan Nations groups, and made a pact with them to create the conditions that were believed to catalyze the toppling of the U.S. government and the hastening of a race war in America. It was expected that this would result in the creation of a separatist Aryan nation within the country. The CSA prepared for these events by the creation of a compound dedicated to preparation and carrying out of the planned terrorist activities.

Between 1983 and 1985, the CSA committed many illegal and violent terrorist acts, while engaging in paramilitary training and preparations for survival of the Endtime. The violence and paramilitary activities, including weapons stockpiling, of the group attracted the attention of the FBI and the Bureau of Alcohol, Tobacco, and Firearms, and an investigation ensued. The murder of a state trooper by an Order member in 1985 galvanized an intensive manhunt resulting in the several-day standoff at the compound between federal and local law enforcement authorities and CSA members. In the end, the CSA members left without bloodshed, the compound was searched, weapons and munitions were seized, and the group was effectively crippled by the resultant trials, convictions, and prison sentences of the membership.

SOURCES

Books

Tucker, Jonathan, editor. *Toxic Terror: Assessing Terrorist Use of Chemical and Biological Weapons (BCSIA Studies in International Security)*. Cambridge, Massachusetts: MIT Press: Bantam, 2000.

Web sites

The Nizkor Project. "Paranoia as Patriotism: Far-Right Influences on the Militia Movement. Covenant, Sword, and Arm of the Lord." < http://www.nizkor.org/hweb/orgs/american/adl/paranoia-as-patriotism/covenant.html > (accessed October 3, 2005).

MIPT Terrorism Knowledge Base. "Group Profile—Covenant, Sword, and Arm of the Lord (CSA)." < http://www.tkb.org/Group.jsp?groupID=3226 > (accessed October 3, 2005).

Domestic Terrorist Group Profiles—MILNET. "Sword and Arm of the Lord (SAL)." < http://www.milnet.com/ domestic/data/sal.htm > (accessed October 3, 2005).

Steven Alan Hassan's Freedom of Mind Center. "About Kerry Noble." < http://www.freedomofmind.com/ resourcecenter/articles/noble.htm > (accessed October 3, 2005).

SEE ALSO

Aryan Nations

Ku Klux Klan

Order, The

Earth First!

LEADER: Dave Foreman

USUAL AREA OF OPERATION: United States; worldwide

Earth First! (EF) is a radical environmentalist organization that defines itself as an anarchist political movement. During its first years, they promoted peaceful protests and educational campaigns on environmental conservation, trying to draw the attention of the press and local communities to the need of protecting forests, rivers, and species from pollution and destruction caused by human activity. They also tried to promote, unsuccessfully, the approval of new biological preserves. However, EF rapidly assumed an extremist attitude as new members and its founders started preaching "direct actions" against mining, logging, agricultural, and oil companies, as well as against bioengineering and pharmaceutical research laboratories. Examples of the most radical actions by EF's activists range from sabotage, destruction of property, hate mail, telephone harassment of employees, arson, physical aggression, tree spiking, and bombing.

EF claims to be a non-hierarchical movement, promoting and supporting, through its journals and a bulletin exclusive for its affiliated members, the formation of local organizations to sponsor a specific local cause, either as Earth First! chapters or with a different name. Therefore, hundreds of Earth First! units are spread through the United States and several other countries. Many other extremist organizations were also the result of EF's spin-offs. Some of them coordinate and

Firefighters and police pull an Earth First demonstrator to safety after he and another protester lowered themselves over the side of a bridge with ropes. The ropes were attached to a logging truck stopped by other protesters on June 19, 2002, in Missoula, Montana. The two were protesting logging in the Bitterroot National Forest. AP/Wide World Photos

carry on legal activities, whereas others promote illegal and even criminal acts. EF's branches may come temporarily into existence as a result of specific projects or as new organizations, such as Bioengineering Action Network, Cold Mountain, Cold Rivers Video Project, Friends of the Wolf,

Two Earth First protesters stand on top of logging equipment near Quaking Aspen, California, in 1989. Jeremy Hogan | Alamy

Direct Action Fund, Direct Action Network, Cascadia Forest Defenders, Earth Liberation Front (ELF), Animal Liberation Front (ALF), etc.

HISTORY

David Foreman, Mike Roselle, Howie Wolke, and Bart Koehler founded Earth First! in the early 1980s. EF history is divided in two phases. The first one (from 1980–1986) was characterized by public protests against logging, hunting, as well as the promotion of an ecological philosophy known as "Deep Ecology." This philosophy, developed by Arne Naess, George Sessions, and Bill Devall, assumes the equal value and significance of all life forms, including humans, in the context of the ecosystem. These ideas led EF to create the slogan "No compromise in defense of Mother Earth!" Another source of inspiration for the EF founders, especially for Dave Foreman,

was the novel *The Monkey Wrench Gang* by Edward Abbey. The novel tells the story of four environmentalists who decide to organize a radical group to sabotage and vandalize human enterprises, which they perceived as disruptive to ecosystems in the American Southwest.

Mike Roselle replaced Foreman as the editor of the *EF Journal* in 1990, inaugurating the second phase of the organization with a much stronger emphasis on the direct-action approach and on decentralized leadership. This loose non-hierarchical approach was aimed at giving EF a new face as a movement rather than an organization, in an attempt to dilute legal responsibility by actions promoted by activists from different chapters or "bioregions." Finally, the Journal's publication started being rotated among several EF bioregions, with a progressive escalation in radicalism, offering tactical information to saboteurs, lists of targets (buildings, equipment, and persons) under article titles such as "Why I Set Fire at Romania Chevrolet" and "Most-Wanted Eco-terrorists: The Biotechnology Industry." In spite of the claims that not even affiliation is needed, they also publish another bulletin exclusive for affiliates.

EF tells its own history as follows: "The idea of Earth First! emerged in a VW bus in the great Southwestern desert in the spring of 1980. Inspired by Rachel Carson's *Silent Spring*, Aldo Leopold's land ethic, and, most of all, Edward Abbey's *Monkey Wrench Gang*, a group of activists, fed up with mainstream environmental organizations, pledged 'No Compromise in Defense of Mother Earth!' Environmental activist Dave Foreman, ex-Yuppie (Youth International Party), Mike Roselle, Wyoming Wilderness Society representatives, Bart Koehler and Howie Wolke, and former Park Ranger Ron Kezar were traveling in Foreman's VW from the Pincate Desert in northern Mexico to Albuquerque. Enraged at the sellout by mainstream enviros during the RARE II (the Forest Service's Roadless Area and Review Evaluation—an ongoing process recently undermined by the Bushies) meetings, the activists envisioned a revolutionary movement to set aside multimillion-acre ecological preserves all across the United States. Suddenly Foreman called out, 'Earth First!' The next thing you know, Wolke says, 'Roselle drew a clenched fist logo, passed it up to the front of the van, and there was Earth First!' "

Judi Bari stands on stage at a 1996 Earth First! rally to protest logging. AP/Wide World Photos

"From the beginning, Earth First! has been an anarchical movement. Really, Earth First! is a tribe existing in autonomous, consensus based groups who oppose the ignorance and destruction of industrial society and share a vision of a free, natural existence. No bureaucracy, no lobbyists, no organizational spokespersons, not even any membership. Earth First! happens when a group of committed activists decide together to stop further destruction of life. Independence Day 1980 marked the inaugural Earth First! Round River Rendezvous..."

They also list with pride the names of eco-activists serving time in jail for crimes such as harassment of Huntingdon Life Sciences (HLS) shareholders; use of explosives to target nuclear facility power lines; sabotage of a dam construction site; damaging equipment at a chicken processing plant and destroying eggs of thousands of chickens; conspiracy to commit arson and possession of incendiary devices to destroy SUVs; attack of the managing director of HLS;

aggravated assault on federal agents; escape; and bank robbery—funneling money stolen from banks to the Zapatista Army of National Liberation—; and property destruction of the homes of multiple HLS affiliates.

PHILOSOPHY AND TACTICS

Earth First! Journal is the main propaganda vehicle of the organization, inviting people to meetings and teaching them how to organize. They regularly publish ongoing activities, new projects, and the agenda of EF meetings. The journal also sets the tone for EF policies and sister-organizations. In its own words, "To avoid co-option, we feel it is necessary to avoid corporate organizational structure so readily embraced by many environmental groups." The implication is that nobody else in EF—besides the perpetrators of a given felony—will be criminally responsible by their acts. This is an

LEADERSHIP

DAVE FOREMAN

Dave Foreman was born in 1947, and first became involved in politics in college during the 1960s, when he founded the New Mexico branch of Young Americans for Freedom, a conservative youth organization that supported the Vietnam War. After graduation in 1968, Foreman started dedicating himself to environmental protection. Between 1973 and 1980, he worked as Southwest Regional Representative for the Wilderness Society, in New Mexico. From the late 1970s until 1980, he was the director and lobbyist of Wilderness Affairs in Washington, D.C., and a board member for the New Mexico chapter of The Nature Conservancy. Disillusioned with the mainstream environmental movement and the outcome of the Second Roadless Area Review and Evaluation (RARE II) by the United States Forest Service, which authorized the opening of thirty-six-million acres of forest for logging in 1979, he quit his job in early 1980 and

founded Earth First! with his friends Mike Roselle, Bart Kohler, and Howie Wolke in April of that same year. He also acted as editor of the *Earth First! Journal* from 1982 until 1988, and published in 1985 the first edition of his book *Ecodefense: A Field Guide to Monkeywrenching*, teaching sabotage techniques. The FBI arrested him in 1990 on charges of conspiracy in the attempt to sabotage a power line that feeds a water pumping station in Arizona. After his release, he stopped acting as spokesman for EF, and in 1991, he co-founded the Wildlands Project with the purpose of establishing protected wilderness areas in the United States. For two years (1995–1997), he was one of the directors of the Sierra Club organization. He co-founded in 1997 the Wilderness Alliance (WA) and in 2003, he and other WA's directors founded the Rewilding Institute to develop and promote conservational strategies in North America.

---

attempt to avoid charges of conspiracy, as illustrated by Foreman's arrest by the FBI in the past. Nevertheless, EF not only sponsors such criminal acts as morally justifiable in its direct-action propaganda but also supports and raises funds for those under prosecution or serving time in prison. Therefore, there is not an EF central headquarters, but there are numerous EF chapters and other organizations under different names. However, as fundraising is necessary, EF also has organized foundations to raise funds such as Earth First! Foundation (later changed to Fund for Wild Nature), Trees Foundation, and the Earth First! Direct Action Fund. These organizations are legal, tax-exempt foundations that ask for contributions in support of EF projects and activities—including from other foundations and entrepreneurs. These foundations then funnel resources to the various EF projects and direct-action performances as well, such as tree sitting, tree spiking, road blockades, sabotage, lawsuits, and saboteurs, legal defense in the courts.

EF followers are provided an ample list of issues to adhere to or fight against, which ranges from dietary changes (stop eating meat) to others also shared by mainstream environmental organizations such as recycling non-organic materials, the use of alternative renewable sources of fuel and energy, protection of ancient forests, and stop whaling. Concerns about genetically modified foods are an issue still in discussion by the scientific community and the public health authorities from many countries. Earth First! agenda however is not open for discussion on this issue and opts for their direct-action doctrine and "monkeywrenching" tracts against biotechnology companies.

Direct-action tactics, such as tree spiking, aims at breaking chain saws, which also works as booby traps that can seriously hurt and maim workers operating such tools. "Ecotage," or monkeywrenching, includes destruction of bulldozers and research laboratories, arson of construction sites and condominiums, planting bombs in dams, cutting power lines, harassment

KEY EVENTS

1989: Mark Davis, Marc Baker, and Dave Foreman were arrested by the FBI. The first two, on charges of attempt to cut power lines, and Foreman on charges of conspiracy.

1990: Judi Bari and Darryll Cherney, two EF activists, were seriously injured when a pipe bomb blows off. The FBI and local police arrested the two of them a few hours after the explosion.

1991: Bari and Cherney started a civil lawsuit against six FBI agents and three Oakland police officers on charges of false arrest, unlawful search and seizure, and violating their civil rights.

2002: The Grand Jury at Oakland Civil Court decided in favor of Cherney and Bari and determined a $4.4 million compensatory award to be paid by the FBI and the Oakland police.

of logging and biotechnology companies' employees and shareholders, hate mail and telephone harassment of employees' families, and physical violence. It also includes civil disobedience actions as tree sitting to gain time for legal suits to advance through the judiciary system, and public protests to obtain ample publicity and to denounce corporate environmental malpractices such as illegal dumping of chemical wastes in soils and rivers.

Earth First! also promotes an annual rendezvous to celebrate their accomplishments and sponsors local workshops at chapters' discretion to debate specific issues and actions. EF also promotes rap music groups sympathetic to the EF cause, books written by extremist environmentalists, and promotes animist religious ceremonies aiming at leading its followers to identify themselves with trees and animals through mystical experiences.

OTHER PERSPECTIVES

In 2002, the FBI defined eco-terrorism as "the use or threatened use of violence of a criminal nature against innocent victims or property by environmentally-oriented sub-national groups for environmental-political reasons, or aimed at an audience beyond the target, often of a symbolic nature."

The U.S. Patriotic Act of 2001 defines domestic terrorism as "acts dangerous to human life that are a violation of the criminal laws of the United States or of any State, and appear to be intended to intimidate or coerce a civilian population; to influence the policy of a government by intimidation or coercion; or to affect the conduct of a government by mass destruction, assassination, or kidnapping . . . ." Under this Act, Earth First!, along with some of its sister-organizations, was considered an eco-terrorist organization due to its extremist actions in violation of the criminal laws of the United States.

The ActivistCash.com is a web site maintained by the Center for Consumer Freedom, an organization that monitors and provides information for individual donors about the funding sources of radical organizations and their activists, through the IRS documentation analysis. Individual contributions are sought by EF among the public, through the EF press in their respective interlinked web sites. The Fund for Wild Nature claims that "The Fund relies on individual contributors like yourself, and your friends. We accept donations of cash, stock or other financial assets."

ActivistCash.com denounces the eco-terrorist character of Earth First! and its spin-offs organizations such as ELF and ALF, highlighting the illegal activities and declarations of several of its members, such as Rodney Coronado, a convicted arsonist, who replaced Dave Foreman for some time as the spokesperson for the organization. According to this source, Coronado had declared in an issue of EF Journal about "the sixty-eighth raid on fur farms since 1995 . . . . There have been nearly that many raids on genetically engineered crops. All the federal agents in the United States will not stop more actions of this sort." ActivistCash.com publishes an extensive report on the EF and other extremist eco-terrorist movements and organization, citing their own respective publications, books, and statements to the press, showing the strong misanthropic feelings of these eco-extremists as well as their bias against mainstream scientific research and governmental environmental policies.

PRIMARY SOURCE
Truth Is Still Elusive In 1990 Pipe Bombing

When the pipe bomb went off in their Subaru wagon in May 1990, Judi Bari and Darryl Cherney were in Oakland, driving from California's North Coast to stir up support for demonstrations to stop the logging of ancient redwood trees.

Almost immediately, they concluded that someone had tried to kill them. They were, after all, rabble-rousing leaders of the Earth First movement, which had clashed repeatedly with loggers by blockading logging trucks, sitting in trees and shouting at rallies. Both had received written death threats and reported them to the police, Ms. Bari just weeks earlier. A year before, a logging truck had rammed her as she sat in a car.

But just hours after the blast, as Ms. Bari lay in a hospital bed with her pelvis crushed, she and Mr. Cherney, who was slightly wounded, were arrested by the Oakland police and the Federal Bureau of Investigation.

The authorities concluded that Ms. Bari and Mr. Cherney had accidentally bombed themselves. They accused the pair of transporting the bomb for use in some act of environmental sabotage.

The charges were dropped six weeks later for lack of evidence. But the furor over what has become known as "the Judi Bari bombing" has raged for the last 12 years, even beyond Ms. Bari's death from cancer in 1997, overshadowing the radical environmental movement as no other incident has.

A federal lawsuit brought by the pair against the F.B.I. and Oakland police ended last week, when a jury found that the authorities had violated their civil rights and awarded $4.4 million to Mr. Cherney, 46, and Ms. Bari's estate.

The decision, however, is unlikely to quell the longstanding debate over who did it, and whether the authorities were justified in assuming that the pair had carried the bomb.

The bombing has also continued to cast a large shadow of controversy over Ms. Bari and Mr. Cherney and environmentalists in general in communities that depend on forests for jobs.

The F.B.I. long insisted that there was ample reason to suspect the pair: Earth First had espoused tactics like sabotaging logging trucks

---

Conversely, the EF and other extremist environmentalist organizations are not in shortage of support from several segments among both the news media, college faculty, and writers. The University of Arizona Press published on its web site the prologue of the book *Coyotes and Town Dogs: Earth First! and the Environmental Movement* by Susan Zakin, wherein she tells about the arrests of Dave Foreman by the FBI in his home on May 30, 1989, and how the FBI had infiltrated an agent in the organization who actually coaxed Peggy Millet and three other activists into cutting a power line near Salome, Arizona. The author suggests that the FBI was in shortage of domestic terrorists in the 1980s, therefore starting to stalk "tough-talking nature lovers like Dave Foreman" because he was an "obvious choice when the agency had to justify its whopping $35 million-a-year counter-terrorism budget."

Zakin also describes a more controversial event that occurred on May 24, 1990, when Judi Bari and Darryl Cherney were severely injured when a bomb planted under the front seats of Judi's car went off, in Oakland, California. The FBI claimed that Bari and Cherney had accidentally set off a bomb that they made themselves, and arrested them. A judge, however, rejected the FBI allegation and the charges were dropped. Bari, who had her pelvis blown apart by the explosion, and Cherney, sued the FBI and the Oakland Police for framing them—a lawsuit that took 12 years to be concluded. Judi Bari died from cancer before the court decision. In 2002, a jury decided that six from the seven defendants have violated the U.S. Constitution's First and Fourth Amendments by arresting the complainants, conducting unlawful searches of their homes, and carrying out a defamatory campaign

or spiking trees to damage saw blades, and the F.B.I. said it had suspected Ms. Bari and Mr. Cherney of downing power lines in Santa Cruz a month before the bombing, though they were never charged.

Even as the possibility that Ms. Bari was the target of someone she knew personally hovered in the background, law enforcement authorities through the years continued to say they had reasons to believe she and Mr. Cherney were transporting a bomb. Ms. Bari, until she died at age 47, and Mr. Cherney, the star witness in the trial, continued to say the F.B.I. framed them, maybe even bombed the car, so that it could blame the Earth Firsters, besmirch their reputations and cast a cloud over the burgeoning radical environmental movement.

Indeed, like Ms. Bari, who was maimed by the bombing, Earth First has never fully recovered from its aftermath. The bombing—and the arrests—have forever since been mentioned in references to the group, along with terms like "fringe" and "marginal."

Ms. Bari and Mr. Cherney, who continued to be strident voices for Earth First and for their vindication in the case, remain controversial figures in California's redwood country. The local weekly newspaper in the North Coast, The Anderson Valley Advertiser, has repeatedly mocked their federal suit and accusations against the authorities as a "scam."

Even the outcome of the trial, which left the large question of who is responsible for the bombing untouched, is unlikely to quiet much of the debate.

In a victory for the environmentalists, the trial exposed contradictions between F.B.I. investigators and the agency's crime laboratory over whether the bomb was under the driver's seat or, as investigators said, behind it, visible to the car's passengers before it detonated.

The Oakland police testified that they based their arrests on the F.B.I.'s findings, and the F.B.I. agents vigorously denied misleading the Oakland police. But both agencies admitted they had amassed intelligence on the couple before the bombing.

Evelyn Nieves

Source: New York Times, 2002

in the press, calling Earth First! a terrorist organization and the two victims of the car bombing of "bombers." The director of the Equal Justice Program at the Howard University School of Law, Nkechi Taifa, said on the occasion of the verdict that, "The jury verdict is yet another indication of what is in store should Ashcroft's plans to loosen the longstanding Levi guidelines become a reality," adding that such guidelines "were implemented to curb FBI abuses uncovered during the Senate investigations of the mid-'70s . . ."

SUMMARY

Earth First!, several autonomous chapters, and its sister-organizations have divided public opinion and fostered the formation of organized centers of opposition against its doctrines and direct-action tactics throughout the last twenty-five years. As new extremist groups as ALF and ELF carry on the violent agenda preached by this organization, Earth First! seems to be trying to change its public image to something closer to a mainstream environmental organization.

SOURCES

Web sites

Activist.com. "At ActivistCash.com, We Follow the Money—for You." < http://www.activistcash.com/aboutUs.cfm> (accessed September 29, 2005).

Activist.com. "Earth First!" < http://www.activistcash.com/organization_overview.cfm/oid/271> (accessed September 29, 2005).

Answers.com. "David Foreman." < http://www.answers .com/topic/david-foreman> (accessed September 29, 2005).

Federal Bureau of Investigation. "The Threat of Eco-Terrorism." < http://www.fbi.gov/congress/congress02/ jarboe021202.htm> (accessed September 29, 2005).

Guardian.com. "$4.4m for Environmentalists Framed by FBI." < http://www.guardian.co.uk/print/0,3858,4431940-103681,00.html > (accessed September 29, 2005).

ReasonOnline. "David Foreman vs. the Cornucopians." < http://www.reason.com/rb/rb082901.html > (accessed September 29, 2005).

The University of Arizona Press. "Coyotes and Town Dogs: Earth First! and the Environmental Movement."

< http://www.uapress.arizona.edu/books/bid1417.htm > (accessed September 29, 2005).

UMN.edu. "The Earth Liberation Front and Environmental Terrorism." < http://www1.umn.edu/dcs/ earthliberationfront3pub.htm > (accessed September 29, 2005).

SEE ALSO

Earth Liberation Front (ELF)

Animal Liberation Front (ALF)

Earth Liberation Front (ELF)

LEADER: Craig Rosebraugh

USUAL AREA OF OPERATION: Worldwide

OVERVIEW

Earth Liberation Front (ELF) is an eco-terrorist (environmental extremist) movement founded in Brighton, United Kingdom, in 1992, as a spin-off from Earth First! ELF has since been involved in numerous cases of arson, bombing, sabotage, vandalism, and tree spiking. Tree spiking consists of the insertion of a long iron nail inside tree trunks to cause chain saws to break when loggers are cutting it. Tree spiking is not only harmful for trees and chain saws, but also causes serious accidents, hurting or maiming workers.

HISTORY

During the First U.K. Earth First! meeting in 1992, in Brighton, England, a group of activists decided that the movement was not radical enough to impact environmental policies. Judy Bari, Earth First!'s leader, felt that Earth First! should adopt a non-violence code and do civil disobedience blockades, while other more aggressive acts (e.g., arson, sabotage, and vandalism) might be done by Earth Liberation Front (ELF). She also mentioned that the England's Earth First!, although sympathizing with the ELF's activities, were not directly engaged in them, and the same should be done by Earth First! elsewhere, including in the United States.

Fire Marshall Bruce Pulver climbs a fire ladder to take pictures of two newly-constructed homes that had been destroyed by ELF extremists. AP/Wide World Photos

Therefore, it seems clear that the Earth Liberation Front (ELF) is a branch of its mother-organization, the Earth First! radical environmentalist organization, being formed to carry out the most violent "direct-action" agenda, while the Earth First! gradually changed its public image into a "more moderate" environmental organization.

ELF's activists have initially dedicated themselves to the sabotage of bulldozers, while its propaganda incited others to join in and start their own cells of radical "direct action." In the mid-1990s, the American ELF cell (or cells) was very active in several regions of the United States, breaking into fur and horse farms, releasing animals, and setting fire to buildings, as well

LEADERSHIP

CRAIG ROSEBRAUGH

Craig Rosebraugh was the spokesperson for the Earth Liberation Front during four years (1997–2001), advocating non-violence to the ELF activists. However, from 2003 on, after getting a master's degree at the Institute for Social Ecology of Goddard College in Vermont, his discourse changed. He published a book in the same year with the title *The Legitimacy of Political Violence*, wherein he defends bloody revolution and the use of a range of tactics, both violent (including armed struggle, bombing, and assassination) and non-violent ones. Rosebraugh has publicly defined non-violent tactics as massive property destruction, online sabotage, physically occupying buildings, and large-scale urban rioting. Other targets he incites activists to attack are the national and international media networks, such as CNN, ABC, CBS, FOX, and NBC, among others. He recommends that these companies should not only have their building and offices physically occupied, but that activists should engage in strategies and tactics that knock the networks off the air. He formed a new organization, Arissa. In Rosebraugh's own words, "The primary goal of Arissa is to create a political and social revolution in the United States of America." Although officially detached from ELF, his violent doctrine was welcomed by some of ELF's activists, resulting in the shooting of a police officer in Red Bluff, California. Rosebraugh did not try to hide his sympathy for the perpetrator in the underground media.

---

as wrecking veterinary offices that provided services to those enterprises. The movement quickly became an umbrella and an excuse for a variety of troublemakers and vandals who could give a "noble face" (as being environmentally concerned) to their personal rage, anti-American feelings, or those in search for a rush of adrenaline.

ELF's disclaimer in its publication states that, "Because the ELF structure is non-hierarchical, there is no centralized organization or leadership. There is also no 'membership' in the Earth Liberation Front.... Individuals who choose to do actions under the banner of E.L.F. do so only driven by their personal conscience. These have been (sic) individual choices, and are not endorsed, encouraged, or approved of by the management, contributors, or readers." In contradiction to the first sentence, they also acknowledge an existing "management." After the fashion of Earth First! propaganda, they also publish a list of activists who have committed arson, property destruction, and vandalism on behalf of environment defense—many of them being prosecuted or already convicted.

The list of felonies committed by ELF's activists is long, starting in 1996. They claimed responsibility for numerous acts. But, in spite of ELF's claims of being a loose, decentralized, and leaderless movement, some militants have acted more directly now and then, either as ELF's spokesperson, webmaster, or recruiter.

PHILOSOPHY AND TACTICS

The main ideology behind the escalation of violence by ELF's cells seems to derive from Rosebraugh's doctrines in favor of a violent revolution against the U.S. government and private enterprises, also targeting wealthy communities and upper-middle-class people, who symbolize the American way of life. Rosebraugh's discourse is full of contradictions becasue he advocates in his writings bloody revolution, murder, rape, and pillage, stating that "terrorism can be okay, can be justified." Nevertheless, he also claims that he respects human life, stating that he struggled to present a non-violent philosophy on behalf of ELF, although he personally questioned "... if there is credibility involved in non-violence at all." A message released by ELF in 2002, containing information about arson and sabotage, also informed that they would no longer hesitate to pick up the gun to implement justice. Another ELF activist, Phillip Dawdy, said during a speech in 2003 that "The threat to the life of the planet is so severe that political violence must be understood as a viable option."

ELF's goal is to inflict the maximum economic damage to those enterprises they consider to be destroying the environment, such as fur

KEY EVENTS

1977: John Hanna, who bombed seven aircraft with homemade napalm bombs at the Salinas airport, was convicted to five years in prison.

2001: Four of ELF's activists were arrested on charges of arson of four new homes in Middle Island and another one under construction in Miller place, and arson conspiracy to set fire to a duck farm and a McDonald's in Miller Place, in New York.

2002: Jacob D.B. Sherman was convicted by the arson attack against Schoppert Logging Company.

2002: Andrew McCrea was arrested on charges of murder of a police officer.

2002: Arson of several Californian auto-dealers stores and vehicles.

2003: Posting on the Internet of instructions on how to build bombs. Vandalism against a mink farm in Washington State, vandalism against McDonald's restaurants, and bomb attack on Chiron Corporation, a pharmaceutical research company.

2004: William Cottrell was convicted for torching a SUV.

2005: Three firebombings of residential construction sites in Sacramento, California.

---

farms, meat packers, construction companies and urban developers, agricultural enterprises, biotechnology companies, leaders of big industries, drivers of SUVs, pharmaceutical laboratories, tourism businesses and resorts, etc.

ELF accuses capitalism of being at the root of all injustice and violence around the world, showing sympathy for the Taliban regime, Zapatista guerrilla, and leftist terrorist groups acting in the United States and in several other countries. They accuse the American people of being shallow, alienated, and selfish, always supportive of governmental policies designed to interfere with the self-determination and sovereignty of other nations, waging wars to achieve economic profit for U.S. corporations without hesitation. They keep a close relationship with another extremist spin-off from the Earth First!, the Liberation Animal Front (ALF) that is dedicated to similar violent actions on behalf of animal rights advocacy. In 2001, an ELF's spokesperson declared to the Associated Press that what kept them going was, "The realization that what the ELF and ALF are doing is correct. The realization that I support underground direct action aimed at destroying the capitalist ideology, and I want it to increase dramatically."

ELF distributes a manual, "The Nighttime Gardening Guide," providing information on how to destroy biotechnology plantations, how to break into greenhouses, laboratories, and buildings, climb fences, sabotage equipment, how to clean from any evidence the crime scene, and how to evade it without being caught.

Constant mobility of activists and a violent discourse through books and underground media seem to be the main assets of ELF. The cells seem to act independently, as small groups that use urban guerrilla tactics to sabotage, bomb, torch, or wreck buildings, crops, etc., during the night. However, investigators suspect of the existence of a small central group that recruits new activists to carry on specific attacks, especially among teenagers and young adults from small communities.

OTHER PERSPECTIVES

Before the Subcommittee on Forests and Forest Health in February 12, 2002, the testimony of James F. Jarboe, Domestic Terrorism Section Chief, Counterterrorism Division, FBI, said, "During the past several years, special interest extremism, as characterized by the Animal Liberation Front (ALF) and the Earth Liberation Front (ELF), has emerged as a serious terrorist threat. Generally, extremist groups engage in much activity that is protected by constitutional guarantees of free speech and assembly. Law enforcement becomes involved when the volatile talk of these groups transgresses into unlawful action. The FBI estimates that the ALF/ELF has committed more than 600 criminal acts in the United States since 1996, resulting in damages in excess of 43 million dollars."

PRIMARY SOURCE

Eco-radicals: Environmental Faction Decides to "Pick up the Gun"

It looked like business as usual for America's eco-radicals when a U.S. Forest Service research station in Irvine, Pa., was torched on Aug. 11.

Certainly, no one familiar with the movement was surprised when the Earth Liberation Front (ELF) claimed responsibility for the $700,000 arson. Like the attack, the press release was standard operating procedure for the ELF, a loose-knit group of individual activists and tiny cells that has claimed responsibility for millions of dollars in damage.

But this communiqué was anything but routine. While the ELF and its sister group, the Animal Liberation Front (ALF), have been tagged by the as America's top "domestic terrorism" threat, their activists have always insisted that the "terrorist" label is wrong.

The two groups openly promote economic sabotage and other "direct actions"—they're blamed for more than million in property damage since—but have consistently cautioned followers to steer clear of harming people. The's manual for new members requires them "to take all necessary precautions to ensure no one is physically injured."

It may be time to rewrite the manual. The Sept. 3 statement claiming the Pennsylvania attack made it clear that some of the ELF's operatives have decided to trade in property attacks for terror.

"[S]egments of this global revolutionary movement are no longer limiting their revolutionary potential by adhering to a flawed, inconsistent 'non-violence' ideology," the communiqué said.

"While innocent life will never be harmed in any action we undertake, where it is necessary, we will no longer hesitate to pick up the gun to implement justice [emphasis added]."

Lest this chilling message be misunderstood, the statement went on: "The diverse efforts of this revolutionary force cannot be contained, and will only continue to intensify as we are brought face to face with the oppressor in inevitable, violent confrontation. We will stand up and fight for our lives against this iniquitous civilization until its reign of **TERROR** is forced to an end—by any means necessary."

This dramatic ideological shift toward violence reflects, at least in part, the potent influence of a British-born group called Stop Huntingdon Animal Cruelty (SHAC). Since it brought its openly terroristic approach to the United States in 1999, members have participated in its campaign of harassment against employees of companies who do business with Huntingdon Life Sciences, one of the world's largest animal-testing firms.

Source: Southern Poverty Law Center, 2002

In May 2004, three years after the firebombing of the University of Washington's Center for Urban Horticulture, a $50,000 reward was posted by the FBI for information leading to the perpetrators. According to investigators, the incendiary devices and arsonists' style were identical to those of an arson at an Oregon tree farm, where the initials "ELF" were left as a signature. Investigators strongly suspect that an ELF cell may be responsible for the arson in Washington. ELF and ALF are considered by the FBI among the most dangerous domestic terrorist groups.

The FBI advised in its 2000–2001 Review that the criminal activities perpetrated by environmental extremists have increased in both frequency and intensity in that period, with the escalation of such practices encompassing arson, bombing, harassment of individuals and businesses, death threats, and hate mail. The Review also said that ELF has targeted laboratories and research facilities, fur farms, horse ranches, meat-processing plants, forest service research centers, and logging companies.

The FBI 2000–2001 Review also cited ELF's self-definition as an "international underground organization consisting of autonomous groups of people who carry out direct action according to E.L.F. guidelines, such as 1), to inflict economic damage to those who profit from the destruction and exploitation of the natural environment; 2), to reveal and educate the public on the atrocities committed against the environment and all the species which cohabitate in it; and 3), to take all the necessary precautions against harming any animal, human and non human."

The Center for Consumer Freedom (CCF) denounces the dangers posed by ELF and other extremist environmentalist groups, and the contradictions between their discourse of respect for all life forms and their violent acts against property and individuals. Moreover, they mention ELF's propaganda and statements to the press, saying that as "global revolutionaries," they must no longer adhere to a "flawed, inconsistent, non-violent ideology." CCF also reported in a 2002 article that the Forest Service Officials have alerted loggers in Montana that the many out-of-state activists in their area were trained in vandalism, arson, and bomb-making, informing the loggers that many of such activists were associated to the Earth Liberation Front. CCF also draws attention to the violent discourse and actions by ELF activists as an indication of the risk of an escalation in violence in the near future.

SUMMARY

Earth Liberation Front activities are currently under intense scrutiny by state and federal agencies, and the increase in arrests and convictions of recent years seems to have exerted an impact on the group's activity. However, terrorist and extremist environmentalist groups tend to support each other in many ways such as sharing information, giving financial support, hiring lawyers, and organizing a network of safe houses for activists.

SOURCES

Web sites

Activist.com. "At ActivistCash.com, We Follow the Money—for You." < http://www.activistcash.com/aboutUs.cfm> (accessed October 21, 2005).

Center for the Defense of Free Enterprise. "Ecoterror Response Network." < http://www.cdfe.org/ern.htm> (accessed October 21, 2005).

Center for the Defense of Free Enterprise. "Earteh Liberation Front." < http://www.cdfe.org/elf.htm> (accessed October 21, 2005).

Center for the Defense of Free Enterprise. "Ecoterrorism Top Stories." < http://www.cdfe.org/top_stories.htm> (accessed September 29, 2005).

Center for the Defense of Free Enterprise. "The Center View: Profiles in Ecoterror Advocacy." < http://www.cdfe.org/rosebraughs%20degree.htm> (accessed October 21, 2005).

Federal Bureau of Investigation. "The Threat of Eco-Terrorism." < http://www.fbi.gov/congress/congress02/jarboe021202.htm> (accessed October 21, 2005).

Fox News Channel. "Fire May Be Connected to 'Eco-Terrorism' Group." < http://www.foxnews.com/printer_friendly_story/0,3566,122902,00.html> (accessed October 21, 2005).

Fox News Channel. "ELF Suspected in California Eco-Terror." < http://www.foxnews.com/printer_friendly_story/0,3566,146927,00.html> (accessed October 21, 2005).

The Fox News Channel. "FBI: Radical-activist Groups Are Major Threat." < http://www.foxnews.com/printer_friendly_story/0,3566,161825,00.html> (accessed October 21, 2005).

Fur Commission USA. "In Their Own Words." < http://www.furcommission.com/debate/words6.htm?FACTNet> (accessed October 21, 2005).

The Pittsburgh Channel. "Group Claims Credit For Irvine, Pa., Lab Fire; < http://www.thepittsburghchannel.com/team4/1775308/detail.html> (accessed October 21, 2005).

Reason Online. "David Foreman vs. the Cornucopians." < http://www.thepittsburghchannel.com/team4/1775308/detail.html> (accessed October 21, 2005).

Seattle Weekly. "Violence and Protest." < http://www.seattleweekly.com/features/0315/news-dawdy.php> (accessed October 21, 2005).

UMN.edu. "The Earth Liberation Front and Environmental Terrorism." < http://www.is.wayne.edu/mrichmon/earth_liberation_front.htm> (accessed October 21, 2005).

SEE ALSO

Animal Liberation Front (ALF)

Earth First!

European Nationalist Fascists

LEADER: Robert Petit

YEAR ESTABLISHED OR BECAME ACTIVE: 1980

ESTIMATED SIZE: Unknown

USUAL AREA OF OPERATION: France

OVERVIEW

The French neo-fascist group, *Faisceaux Nation-aux Europeéns* (FNE), translates into English as European Nationalist Fascists (or in some literature, National Fascists). They have also been called the European National Fasces. Previously, the group was called the Federation for National European Action (*Fédération d'Action Nationale Européene*, FANE).

HISTORY

The primary activity of the European Nationalist Fascists (FNE) was to harass and intimidate Jews, Arabs, Africans, and other religious and ethnic minority groups living in France. Their objective was to force these people to leave France.

Anti-Semitic acts peaked in France in 1980, with 122 reported incidents of arson and other violent crimes, and many more threats directed toward members of minority groups. FNE was created as a reformation of the Federation for National European Action (FANE), immediately after FANE was banned by the French government in September 1980. FANE was forced to dissolve because of its role in promoting two violent anti-Semitic incidents. Members of FANE, which was founded in 1966 by French

Right-wing militants in Lyon, France, fight with anti-fascists at a demonstration by the right-wing youth movement on November 14, 2004. The latter has been against the proposed entry of Turkey into the European Union. Jean Philippe-Ksiazek/AFP/Getty Images

fascists and anti-Semites, were suspects in the bombing of the Rue Copernic Synagogue in Paris. The bombing was later found to be the work of a Palestinian group.

Robert Petit, director of the Vichy regime's Center for the Study of the Jewish Question, was named as the head of FNE. The Vichy regime ran France under Nazi control between 1940 and 1944.

FNE has been closely associated with neo-Nazi groups outside of France. Two groups were particularly influential. The first was a Spanish organization called *Círculo Español de Amigos de Europa* (CEDADE, Spanish Circle of Europe Friends). CEDADE is involved with women's and youth organizations in Spain. It also publishes many periodicals, including one called *Joven Europa* (Young Europe). The second group linked to FNE was *Nouvel Ordre Européen* (NOE, New Order Europe). This group was set up in France, but held meetings throughout Europe, greatly influencing right-wing thought. The

group stopped functioning in 1980. Together, these three groups were called *Notre Europe* (Our Europe).

Following the peak of anti-Semitic activity in 1980, there appeared to be minimal investigation of FNE activities by the French authorities. It was believed in 1980 by French Jewish organizations and the secretary-general of the French Detectives Union that over 150 French national policemen were members of FNE and other neo-fascist groups. There were claims that up to one-third of FNE's membership were police officers.

In more recent times, many members have left FNE to join the right-leaning National Front (FN) political party of Jean-Marie Le Pen, which was formed in 1972 as an attempt to unify the many different far-right groups in France. The FN was politically insignificant until the mid 1980s, when it began earning more votes in major French elections. The FN Party won 35 Parliamentary seats in 1986. In 1994, Le Pen won fifteen percent of the vote in

KEY EVENTS

1966: French fascists and anti-Semites form the fascist group Federation for National European Action (FANE).

1972: Jean-Marie Le Pen forms the National Front (FN) Party to bring together right-wing groups.

1980: Peak in anti-Semitic violence in France.

1980: FANE banned by the French government for promoting violent anti-Semitism.

1980: European Nationalist Fascists (FNE) is formed, led by Robert Petit.

1980: Less investigation into the FNE's activities provided evidence that policemen were members of the group.

1986: The FN Party emerges with thirty-five Parliamentary seats in French elections.

1994: Le Pen wins fifteen percent of the vote in the first round of the presidential election.

2002: Le Pen goes to the second round of the French presidential elections with twenty percent of the vote.

---

the first round of the presidential election. Le Pen went on to the second round of the French presidential elections in 2002, with twenty percent of the vote.

PHILOSOPHY AND TACTICS

Throughout Europe, far-right political parties concentrate on the fears of the public regarding unemployment, rising crime, and loss of cultural identity. These fears are blamed on high levels of immigration, which often leads to the racism and anti-Semitism seen in groups such as FNE.

FNE used violence as one means to illustrate its views on immigration. In addition, the use of propaganda literature to explain its viewpoints was also employed by FNE and other groups.

The numerous neo-Nazi periodicals printed were used as a means of unifying the fascist groups throughout Europe, and a way to reach new recruits.

In previous times, the dictatorships of Hitler, Franco, and Mussolini represented fascism in Europe. These regimes practiced extreme ethnic intolerance, but they also discussed expansion and territorial acquisitions. During the FANE era, and at the beginning of the FNE formation, the use of violence and intimidation to promote racism and anti-Semitism was reminiscent of the approach used by earlier fascists. However, this began to change as extreme-right members realized they could actually influence the political scene through the FN Party.

These neo-fascists began to blend in with the political scene and to relate to the common people through discussions on unemployment, crime, and the loss of social identity, all of which they blamed on ethnic minorities. It was this approach that helped the FN Party emerge as a more influential party.

OTHER PERSPECTIVES

The neo-fascists claim there should be equal rights for all, but the mindset is that people should be in their country of origin to experience these rights. With this line of thought, in France, it is the ethnically French who should have priority. It is argued that Arabs should have rights in their own part of the world, as should all other ethnic groups.

Right-leaning political parties in the middle ground, and in the mainstream, have begun to listen to what the extreme right has to say. This is because the extreme right has steadily gained more influence. Scholar Richard Wolin explained that even when they are not directly incorporated into government agenda, neo-racist ideas of the modern fascists do have an impact on European political discourse. Wolin gave the example of immigration laws enacted in France, in 1993, which made it much more difficult for people born in France of non-French parents to become French citizens. The issue of ethnicity and citizenship has also been a priority for debate in the European Union. Wolin explains that overemphasis on ethnicity, as seen in the 1930s, can result in xenophobia, racism, and persecution.

SUMMARY

The European Nationalist Fascists were never a very large group. However, through its history of FANE, and in the early 1980s, it was thought of as a very potent, neo-Nazi group, with the capability of murdering, intimidating ethnic populations, and destroying property. The growth in popularity of the National Front Party headed by Le Pen has been a result in part of the transition of members of the far right, including FNE, to an organized political party. It appears that FNE has not been active in the last several years. However, it is not clear whether or not the organization has ceased to exist.

SOURCES

Books

Anderson, Sean, and Stephen Sloan. *Historical Dictionary of Terrorism, 2nd Edition.* Lanham, MD: Scarecrow Press, 2002.

Periodicals

Griffin, Roger. "Europe for the Europeans Fascist Myths of The European New Order 1922–1992." *Humanities Research Centre Occasional Paper.* Oxford Brookes University: No. 1 (1994).

Ivaldi, Gilles. "Conservation, Revolution and Protest: A Case Study in the Political Cultures of the French National Front's Members and Sympathizers." *Electoral Studies.* vol. 15, No. 3, pp. MO-362, 1996.

Sheean, Thomas. "Italy: Terror on the Right." *The New York Review of Books.* Volume 27, Number 21 & 22, 1981.

Wolin, Richard. "Mussolini's Ghost; Europe and the Specter of Fascism." *Tikkun.* vol. 9, No. 4, p.13, 1994.

Web sites

BBC News UK Edition. "Profile: Jean-Marie Le Pen." < http://news.bbc.co.uk/1/hi/world/europe/3658399.stm> (accessed September 29, 2005).

SEE ALSO

Neo-Nazis

Fadaeeyan-i Islam

LEADER: Seyyed Mojtaba Navvab-I Safavi
YEAR ESTABLISHED OR BECAME ACTIVE: 1945
USUAL AREA OF OPERATION: Iran

OVERVIEW

Fadaeeyan-i Islam (Society of Devotees of Islam) was an Iranian Islamic group, notorious for its high-profile assassinations. It was primarily active in the late 1940s and early 1950s, but briefly re-emerged as part of the coalition of groups that helped overthrow Reza Shah Pahlavi in 1978. Fadaeeyan-i Islam is sometimes credited with responsibility for the Iranian hostage crisis (1979–1981) and, more recently, groups carrying its name have carried out attacks on Westerners in Iran and Afghanistan.

HISTORY

The establishment of the Society of Fadaeeyan-i Islam was announced in 1945 by a young cleric, Seyyed Mojtaba Navvab-I Safavi, in a statement he had written entitled "Religion and Revenge." In it, Navvab contended that Islam had come under attack, and he promised to "avenge" such attacks.

The young cleric quickly attracted a band of followers, and his group allied themselves with Ayatollah Kashani, the most prominent member of the Iranian clergy to preach about the unity of religion and politics and to make a visible challenge to British colonial rule. Kashani had been exiled in 1946, a decision which Fadaeeyan-i

LEADERSHIP

SEYYED MOJTABA NAVVAB-I SAFAVI

Seyyed Mojtaba Navvab-I Safavi was born to a lower-middle class family in South Tehran in 1924. His father, a cleric-turned lawyer, had been imprisoned by Reza Shah's government for his opposition. But Navvab's own rebelliousness apparently dated to British occupation during World War II. Navvab had been working in Abadan in the petroleum industry when a British worker beat up an Iranian employee. In the wake of the assault, Navvab arranged a strike and demonstration, leading to a confrontation with police. Fearing the consequences, he fled to the Iraqi holy city of Najaf, where he took up religious instruction.

Three and a half years later, in 1945, he returned to Iran and declared his statement of "Religion and Revenge." An attempt on the life of the historian Ahmed Kassravai that same year (his followers would finish off the job a year later) earned him minor fame, and although he was arrested, he was released after pressure from the *Ulama* (Islamic clergy). The nascent Fadaeeyan-i Islam soon earned a reputation as a group of fearless militants, but for the majority of its existence Navvab was in and out of prison. Finally, in January 1955, following an attempt on the life of Prime Minister Hossein Ali, Navvab was arrested and hanged.

Islam loudly protested. The group's activities, however, quickly assumed a more overt political complexion and they campaigned against women not wearing the hijab; attacked shops selling alcohol; and enrolled volunteers to fight Zionist forces in Palestine.

Fadaeeyan-i Islam also began to carry out a series of assassinations against those they believed imperilled Islam within Iran. Its first victim, in March 1946, was the historian Ahmed Kassravai, who had publicly scorned Iran's Shi'ites and intended to revive Iran's pre-

Islamic customs. They also challenged Iran's post-colonial government, which was still dominated by the British, and which threatened to make a number of disadvantageous oil concessions to Britain. In 1949, after a parliamentary election marred by irregularity and fraud had resulted in the re-election of a pro-British government, Fadaeeyan-i Islam assassinated Prime Minister Abd-ol-Hossein Hajir, in an attempt to curtail the proposed concessions. The following year, Fadaeeyan-i Islam was responsible for the assassination of another pro-Western prime minister, General Ali Razm-Ara.

In the wake of this latest killing, Mohammed Mossaddeq of the Iranian National Front, was appointed prime minister. Fadaeeyan initially supported Mossaddeq, who was more circumspect in his relations with the West, but soon came to the conclusion that this distance did not go far enough, nor did his eagerness to implement Islamic laws. He also refused to relent to their demands to release Navvab from jail for his part in the killing of Razm-Ara. In the wake of this falling out, Fadaeeyan apparently plotted to kill Mossaddeq, and failed in an attempt to assassinate his foreign minister, Hossein Fatami.

A U.S.-backed coup in 1953 finally removed Mossaddeq from power, but the inevitable pro-American stance of his successors was not to Fadaeeyan's liking. In 1955, the group attempted to assassinate Prime Minister Hossein Ali, but succeeded only in wounding him. Following this attempt on his life, there followed a huge crackdown on the group's activities, and the majority of its leaders were arrested and executed, including Navvab.

Thereafter, Fadaeeyan-i Islam went into an inexorable decline. Many of its members joined Heyat-ha-I Moetalefe-h Islami (Coalition of Islamic Groups), the loose alliance of opponents to the Shahist regime, led by Ayatollah Ruhollah Khomeini, that teetered between exile or suppression by Iran's brutal secret police.

As the Shah's regime neared collapse in the late 1970s, Fadaeeyan's old followers re-emerged, although their input as an organized group on Iran's 1978 revolution was negligible. The following year, in 1979, Iranian students, calling themselves the Sons of Imam, seized the U.S. embassy in Tehran, and would hold its occupants hostage for 444 days. The hostage crisis has sometimes been blamed on Fadaeeyan-i Islam,

KEY EVENTS

1945: Establishment of the Society of Fadaeeyan-i Islam announced by a young cleric in a statement entitled "Religion and Revenge".

1946: Fadaeeyan assassinate the historian, Ahmed Kassravai.

1949: Fadaeeyan assassinate Iranian Prime Minister Abd-ol-Hossein Hajir.

1950: Fadaeeyan responsible for the assassination of another pro-Western prime minister, General Ali Razm-Ara.

1955: An attempt on the life of Prime Minister Hossein Ali leads to a huge crackdown on the group. Many leading members, including Navvab, executed.

but such an attack was almost certainly beyond the means of the Fadaeeyan at the time, and such suggestions are possibly the result of confused translation (Fadaeeyan can be translated as "one who is prepared to die," as well as referring to a group of radicals, typically guerrillas).

In November 1998, a bus carrying American businessmen and their wives was attacked near Tehran by a mob shouting anti-U.S. slogans and attacking their vehicle with metal bars. A group claiming to be Fadaeeyan-i Islam said it carried out the attack, but whether it had any relation to its forerunner is unclear. Certainly, this seemed to be an isolated incident. In more recent years, groups carrying Fadaeeyan's names have claimed attacks in Afghanistan against so-called U.S. collaborators.

PHILOSOPHY AND TACTICS

The contemporary resonance of Fadaeeyan-i Islam is carried by what it believed, as opposed to what it actually achieved. Its founder, Seyyed Mojtaba Navvab-I Safavi, called on Muslims to

"Rethink about their religion and their surrounding world in order to salvage their thought from the valley of ignorance ... and to try to uncover the shining truth of Islam which is covered by sinister political clouds." In other words, Navvab was making an intrinsic link between politics and Islam: engaging in political action was a way of defending the faith and strengthening the position of Muslims in the face of colonial rule. Muslims were traditionally weak, believed Navvab, because they were politically complacent. Politicians and businessmen also abused Islam for their own benefit by engaging in activities such as the alcohol trade or—worse still—selling out to Western governments.

At the root of this was the perceived indifference of the Ulama (Islamic clergy) to political vice and Iran's social problems. Navvab called for reforms in teaching, the radicalization of religious schools, and even for the purge of non-political Ulama. He believed that Ulama should increase emphasis on the Islamic instruction of "promoting virtue and preventing vice." He believed that this push towards conservatism could be accelerated by political power.

This manifested itself most notably through Fadaeeyan's assassination of top-ranking politicians. There were two intentions: to remove from power men who were allying Iran too closely with Western (and by definition, heretical) interests, and to serve as a warning to others who refused to take their calls for Islamic conservatism seriously. They were also involved in numerous small-scale attacks against proprietors of alcohol stores.

Fadaeeyan-i Islam never set out to be a mass movement, and was inherently undemocratic. It believed that the masses should follow power rather than reason, but also that law, which is against Islam, is illegitimate. Parliament, it believed, should be a body to interpret Islamic principles under the supervision of Ulama.

OTHER PERSPECTIVES

Seyed Mohammad Ali Taghavi is one of the few contemporary academics to take a closer look at the activities of Fadaeeyan-i Islam. He believes that they are "The Prototype of Islamic hardliners in Iran." Writing in *Middle Eastern Studies*, he stated that what set them apart was: "They viewed Islam primarily from a political angle. Their political approach to Islam, together with their courage and sincerity, were the source of Fadaeeyan's achievements on the political scene. The Iranian nationalist movement of the early 1950s owed as much to Fadaeeyan as to other nationalist political and religious leaders of that era. Because of lack of political support, Fadaeeyan could not enjoy the benefits of their actions; and lack of a relatively coherent theoretical approach prevented their having constructive impacts on society. Nevertheless, they provided the next generation of Iranian Muslim devotees with a pattern, which is now followed in a somewhat more articulated form by hardliners in Iran."

In December 2004, the *Economist* reported that the Ulama-dominated political system—as originally envisaged by Fadaeeyan-i Islam—had left Iran in a kind of torpor of "stagnation and depression," from which there was only one escape. "According to some reports, disaffection with the regime even among the clergy is spreading," it was written. "A cleric from an influential religious family, also out of favour with the supreme leader, derides the Council of Guardians for mostly taking 'orders and hints from the powers that be'—a euphemism for Mr Khamenei [the then president]. Most striking of all, sociologists and educators report that religious belief and observance, especially among the young, have slumped since the mullahs took power a quarter of a century ago. Instead of fortifying the people's devotion, the system seems to have switched many people off the spiritual side of life, inspiring a shallow materialism instead . . . "

The *Economist* continued: "Is there a Gorbachev elsewhere among the mullahs? It is an unlikely prospect, but the inner workings of Iran's clerical establishment are mysterious and supremely opaque . . . [However,] the opposition,

at present, is numb. Only if the price of oil, say, halved, and the economy really dived would the anger and frustration well up again and bring people out on the street. And so long as that does not happen, the Iranians are miserably stuck with what they've got."

SUMMARY

Fadaeeyan-i Islam were a small group of Islamic fundamentalists whose political power passed half a century ago, but whose influence lives on today. The ideas articulated by its founder Seyyed Mojtaba Navvab-I Safavi are imprinted on Iran's existing political system, but more widely on Islamic militant groups across the globe. In many ways—by making the link between politics and religion—Fadaeeyan can be seen as forerunners of an array of Islamist insurgents who propagate political violence in defense of their faith.

SOURCES

Books

Kinzer, Stephen. *All the Shah's Men: An American Coup and the Roots of Middle East Terror.* Hoboken, NJ: John Wiley and Sons, 2004 .

Periodicals

Taghavi, Seyed Mohammad Ali. "Fadaeeyan-i Islam: The Prototype of Islamic Hard-liners in Iran." *Middle Eastern Studies.* January 2004.

Web sites

Islamic Republic of Iran Broadcasting. "Navab Safavi's Martyrdom." < http://www.irib.ir/occasions/Navab-e-Safavi/Navab-e-Safavi-En.htm > (accessed October 7, 2005).

Fatah Revolutionary Council

OVERVIEW

Fatah (*Harakat al-Tahrir al-Watani al-Filastini*, translation for Palestinian National Liberation Movement) is one of the oldest, and, largely because of the all-pervasive role in Palestinian politics of its late leader, Yasser Arafat, arguably the preeminent Palestinian political-military organization during the five decades of its existence. Following the death of Arafat in November 2004, it has been beset by an internal power struggle.

ALTERNATE NAME: Fatah

LEADERS: Yasser Arafat; Farouk Kaddoumi

YEAR ESTABLISHED OR BECAME ACTIVE: 1957

ESTIMATED SIZE: More than 10,000

USUAL AREA OF OPERATION: Israeli-occupied territories; Jordan; Syria

HISTORY

Fatah was formed by Palestinian graduates working in Kuwait in 1957 as a Palestinian liberation organization under the leadership of Yasser Arafat, Khalil Wazir, and Salah Khalaf. Initially, they believed that the sort of armed struggle that would lead to the eviction of the French from Algeria in 1962 could be replicated in Palestine.

In its early years, it was little more than a talking shop, and it was not until 1965 that Fatah announced itself to the world with its first cross-border raids from Jordan and Lebanon. The first raid was stopped by the Lebanese authorities; and the group's first

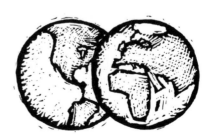

A Palestinian gunman from the Fatah movement, left, and a gunmen from the radical Islamic group Hamas, right, target opposing Israeli forces, in the West Bank town of Bethlehem on October 20, 2001.
AP/Wide World Photos. Reproduced by permission.

"martyr" was killed not by the Israelis, but by Jordanian border guards.

After the Six-Day War in 1967, Fatah moved its operations to Jordan on a wholesale basis, and began operating a guerilla movement in the recently occupied West Bank in an effort to bring about a popular uprising and usurp its new conquerors. Fatah organized guerilla cells to attack Israeli occupiers, but found the Israeli forces too pervasive and West Bankers too shocked by the occupation to collaborate on a wide scale. Again, Fatah initially enjoyed little success, but it soon switched tactics. Instead of working from within the West Bank, it instead started to mount hit and run attacks from outside Israel's new borders. This show of defiance and the relative success of the attacks had a galvanizing effect on the hitherto demoralized population. Moreover, for the first time since Israel's formation two decades earlier, a distinct Palestinian–Israeli conflict opened up as part of the wider Arab–Israeli conflagration.

Things came to a head on March 18, 1968, when an Israeli bus struck a mine left by Palestinian fighters in the south of the country. A doctor and instructor accompanying a party of high school students were killed, and several teenagers injured. It was Fatah's thirty-eighth such operation in barely three months.

Israel decided to strike a reprisal attack at Fatah's headquarters in a refugee camp outside Karameh in Jordan three days later. However, Jordanian intelligence had tipped-off the Palestinians about a likely attack, and they were waiting when Israeli paratroopers landed at dawn. Unexpectedly, Israeli troops came under fierce fire from gunmen, while the main Israeli force faced heavy fire from Jordanian units. What had been planned as an operation to liquidate Fatah's leadership became a pitched battle. In the end, the Israelis destroyed the town, killed 120 Fatah men, and took a similar number prisoner. But, the Israelis had themselves suffered twenty-eight dead before finally

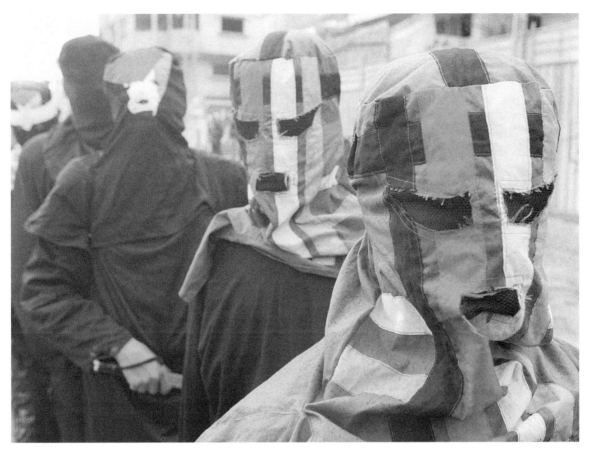

Fatah Hawks march through occupied Gaza territory in Palestine on March 14, 1994. *AP/Wide World Photos.*
Reproduced by permission.

retreating, and worst still, abandoned both casualties and equipment in the field.

Less than a year after the disaster of the 1967 war and in the wake of successive routings by the Israeli Defense Force (IDF), Karameh represented a triumph of sorts, and for the first time removed some of the aura of invincibility that seemed to hang over the IDF. It also transformed Arafat—who had masterminded the Palestinian battle—into an iconic figure, not just within the Palestinian and Arab world, but also across the globe. Suddenly, he found his face on the cover of *Time* magazine.

Although Israel largely stamped down on the emerging rebellion, Fatah enjoyed considerable success in recruiting and deploying the large numbers of Palestinian youths attracted to the cause of Palestinian nationalism. Moreover, it used its expanding popularity to open up a number of proto-state institutions within Jordan,

including a political department, newspapers, and grassroots recruitment networks.

In an effort to try and control the emergent Palestinian liberation movement and boost his own prestige in the Arab world, Egyptian President Gamal Abdul Nasser had backed the formation of the Palestinian Liberation Organization (PLO) in May 1964 in Jerusalem. This was conceived of, and served as, an umbrella for all Palestinian resistance groups, providing political and military coordination when needed, but essentially leaving individual groups free to act as they liked. In July 1968, Fatah joined the PLO. The following year, Yasser Arafat was elected chairman of the PLO executive committee, a position he was to hold for thirty-five years. This made him not just Fatah's preeminent individual, but Palestine's, too.

Fatah's rise and enduring appeal result from the consistent and relatively simple ideology it

Fatah Youth Organization members lift their guns as they march with flags in downtown Gaza City on January 1, 2001, to celebrate the 36th anniversary of Yasser Arafat's Fatah movement. AP/Wide World Photos. *Reproduced by permission.*

propagated and maintained. It was a Palestinian nationalist organization above everything else, and linked its basic message of recovering a Palestinian homeland to historic episodes of Palestinian nationalism, like the 1936–1939 uprising and Karameh, to huge effect. It never tainted itself by pledging and confusing the Palestinian cause with rival doctrines, such as Pan-Arabism, Communism or Ba'athism; and its nationalistic focus tended to cut across class and religious lines. It also maintained the necessity of recovering the Palestinian homeland through an armed struggle. By maintaining this basic, consistent line, and by the ubiquity of its leaders, particularly Arafat, it succeeded in forming a fairly uniform Palestinian political and national identity and helped restore a Palestinian dimension to the Arab–Israeli conflict.

In a way, the late 1960s and early 1970s became the most potent era for Palestinian-led terrorism, with high-profile hijackings, assassinations, and guerilla assaults a seemingly weekly occurrence. With one eye on Arafat's role within the PLO, Fatah tried to distance itself from many of these acts.

The rising number of violent incidents, however, particularly those carried out from Jordan, led the Jordanian ruler, King Hussein, to believe his position was coming under threat. Fearing revolution by Palestinian radicals within his country, on September 16, 1970, Hussein declared military rule, and the Jordanian military killed and expelled thousands of Palestinian militants.

This assault became known as "Black September," and again radicalized Fatah, which was forced to relocate to Lebanon. Although it denied any links, a Fatah offshoot also known as "Black September," emerged determined to take revenge on Hussein. This was a leaderless resistance and also comprised

LEADERSHIP

FAROUK KADDOUMI

Farouk Kaddoumi is among the longest-standing figures within the Fatah movement, having joined the Arafat-led organization as far back as 1960, while working in the United Arab Emirates. He went on to forge a career as a PLO and Fatah bureaucrat, at one time heading the PLO's Political Department in Damascus.

A noted hardliner, in 1983 he led a mutiny attempt against Arafat, later switching sides to be reunited with him. Nevertheless, he resolutely opposed the Oslo Accords, even refusing to leave exile in Tunisia to take up a role in the Palestinian Authority in Gaza. Following Arafat's death in November 2004, Kaddoumi emerged as the surprise victor in the Fatah leadership election. He has indicated a willingness to engage in talks with Israel, but equally pledged to return to an armed struggle if necessary.

---

members of other Palestinian resistance organizations. Its list of attacks—including the assassination of the Jordanian prime minister, the highjacking of a Belgian passenger jet, and an attack on the Saudi embassy in Khartoum (killing U.S. and Belgian diplomatic staff)—was topped for notoriety by the attack on the Olympic village during the 1972 games in Munich, which killed eleven Israeli athletes. When the Israeli government sent out a Mossad death squad to kill its perpetrators, the list of casualties that emerged over the years included a number of individuals with close links to Fatah, including Ali Hassan Salameh, a commander in Arafat's personal security detail.

The Yom Kippur War in 1973 marked a downturn in Palestinian international terror, although the PLO soon became deeply embroiled in the Lebanese civil war. Virtually, the only organization actively carrying out international terrorist attacks was Abu Nidal's group

of followers. Nidal, a deeply paranoid and psychopathic individual, had previously been allied with Arafat at Fatah, but had broken away in 1973 and carried out a hideous range of terrorist attacks, eventually it seemed, almost on a freelance basis. Fatah's acts of "extremism" during the late 1970s and 1980s tended to be limited to attacks on Abu Nidal members or the regimes that sheltered them. The exception came in 1985 when Fatah murdered two Israeli undercover agents in Barcelona.

Arafat, in his dual role as head of the PLO and Fatah, continued to carve out a political niche for the Palestinian cause. But in 1982, like the majority of the Palestinian leadership in exile in Beirut, he was outcast again as a result of Israel's invasion of Lebanon and forced to relocate to Tunisia.

By having to move even further from the heart of the action, Fatah was weakened, but at the same time it reinforced Arafat's conviction that it could not defeat Israel on the battlefield. He renewed moves towards a political solution, heightening the need for internal discipline among Fatah ranks, even at a time when his recognition of Israel on behalf of the PLO (1988) and his removal of paragraphs within the Palestinian Charter calling for the destruction of Israel (1989) caused deep domestic anxiety and opposition to Fatah.

These moves would culminate in the Oslo Accords of 1993, when Arafat renounced terrorism in exchange for the right to form a Palestinian-led administration in Gaza and the West Bank. A year later, Arafat would be made a Nobel Peace laureate.

However, in 1995, partly to crack down on Hamas and Islamic Jihad militants and partly to protect his own position, Arafat formed a new militia, Fatah Tanzim. This was initially involved in the suppression of militants within the Palestinian Authority, following a series of suicide bombings within Israel in 1996 and 1997. Yet when the al-Aqsa Intifada broke out in the fall of 2000, Tanzim stood accused of becoming embroiled in the violence. The Committee for Accuracy in Middle Eastern Reporting in America (CAMERA) accuses Fatah Tanzim of more than a hundred deaths since 2001. (It is worth mentioning that CAMERA is vehemently pro-Israeli, and accuses Fatah Tanzim of killings that different sources have attributed to other groups.)

KEY EVENTS

1957: Formed by Palestinian graduates working in Kuwait.

1967: Fatah moves its operations to Jordan, from where it launches hit and run attacks across the Israeli border.

1968: Battle of Karameh.

1969: Fatah leader, Yasser Arafat, elected head of the PLO.

1970: Fatah expelled from Jordan; Black September movement emerges.

1972: Murders of eleven Israeli athletes at the Munich Olympics by Black September.

1973: Abu Nidal Organization breaks ties with Fatah.

1982: Fatah leadership forced into exile from Lebanon to Tunisia.

1993: Oslo Accords followed by Fatah's return to the occupied territories.

2004: Arafat's death.

2006: HAMAS wins control of Palestinian Authority Parliament.

Another group associated with Fatah is the al-Aqsa Martyrs' Brigade, which carried out a number of suicide attacks against Israeli civilian targets. Although the brigade was neither officially recognized nor openly backed by Yasser Arafat or Fatah, brigade members tended to belong to Fatah. Israel prosecuted Marwan Barghouti, the Fatah leader in the West Bank and potential successor to Arafat, for being the head of the al-Aqsa Martyrs' Brigades, a charge he continues to deny.

PHILOSOPHY AND TACTICS

Fatah is a secular Palestinian organization committed to the recovery of Palestinian homeland on the territory of the state of Israel. It emphasizes its nationalistic strain as its central tenet. As a political party, it propagates a brand of moderate socialism, but has traditionally distanced itself from rival doctrines such as Pan-Arabism, communism, or Ba'athism. Its nationalistic focus has tended to cut across class and religious lines, but its secularism has brought it into conflict with rival Palestinian movements, such as Hamas, founded on religious lines. Although it is regarded as a moderate organization in the scheme of Palestinian politics and recognizes Israel and the need for a political dialogue, it has maintained the "necessity" of recovering the Palestinian homeland through an armed struggle.

Although it started out as a political-military organization and was behind the Palestinian resistance at Karameh, Arafat's preeminence in the PLO and engagement as a political leader saw Fatah largely abandon its military struggle. In a way, this helped breed its success: political discipline bred continuity, and stability led to ubiquity and ascendancy.

Nevertheless, Fatah has continued to be linked to extremism through its armed wing, Fatah Tanzim. Moreover, it has also been hit by accusations that its leaders have maintained links with breakaway militant groups, including Black September, Abu Nidal, and the al-Aqsa Martyrs' Brigade.

OTHER PERSPECTIVES

Profiling Arafat in 1974, *Time* magazine believed it was his single-mindedness and ability to network that catapulted Arafat and his Fatah movement to preeminence. "Arafat has never married," noted *Time*. "Palestine is my wife," he once remarked, and those who know him well agree with the judgment. "It is his complete devotion," says one Palestinian friend, "twenty-four hours a day, thirty days a month, 365 days a year. There is no stop—ever." Says a PLO official: "He is one of the few people I can think of who can fly directly from Riyadh to Moscow and get along well in both places."

The article continues: "Despite his fire-eating anti-Israel rhetoric, Arafat in private is quiet, almost self-effacing. He seldom talks about himself or his past life, largely, it seems, because he wants to avoid creating a personality cult. Within Al Fatah and the PLO, he has no close-knit circle of advisers or a kitchen cabinet. At staff meetings he solicits opinions from everyone, picking and choosing from the advice given him. Compared with Egypt's expansive President Sadat or even with the zealous George Habash, Arafat has little in the way of charisma, but he can inspire devotion nonetheless. In part, that may be because he seems to care genuinely about his fellow Palestinians—in exile."

Writing in the *Guardian* in November 2004, as Arafat lay on his death bed, Ahmad Samih Khalidi, a former Palestinian negotiator and senior associate member of St. Antony's College, Oxford, stated why he believed Arafat was so important not just to Fatah, but the Palestinian people as a whole: "The clichés used to describe him—father of the Palestinian people, symbol of their resistance, supreme decision-maker on their behalf—are well-founded. But Arafat's most important role has been twofold: first, to lead the Palestinian people out of the state of political concussion that befell them after the loss of their homeland in 1948; and then to lay the foundations for a resolution of the conflict with Israel, based on a Palestinian state living alongside Israel."

Kahlidi continued: "Arafat, along with other founder members of the mainstream Palestinian nationalist movement Fatah, played a decisive role in recreating the Palestinians' sense of national identity and reconstructing the shattered remnants of Palestinian political society, pulverised and dispersed as a result of the destruction of their homeland."

Khalidi wrote: "The emergence of Fatah marked the transition of the Palestinian cause from a humanitarian issue of destitute refugees into one of a people who had taken their destiny into their own hands. Fatah soon transformed itself—as it took over the leadership of the Palestine Liberation Organisation in the late 1960s—into the overarching umbrella encompassing all shades of Palestinian opinion, creed and ideology. Indeed, it became synonymous with the Palestinians themselves. Arafat's importance emerges from this sense that he embodies the national spirit not only within Palestine itself, but—crucially—outside Palestine, too, in the larger diaspora where the majority of Palestinians still live."

SUMMARY

A sweeping upset victory by HAMAS backed candidates in the January 2006 elections threw Fatah and the Palestinian political scene into turmoil. HAMAS gained control of Parliament and clashed with Fatah leaders over the control of security forces and foreign policy.

Despite HAMAS gaining political supremacy in Parliament, Palestinian leader Mahmoud Abbas , elected President in January 2005, stated that his government would continue to honor peace agreements with Israel and urged outside nations not to withdraw aid to Palestine. HAMAS control of parliament did not directly threaten Abbas's role as President, but forced him to negotiate with HAMAS to select a new prime minister. Criticism began to grow regarding Fatah leaders' alleged corruption and lack of progress in both domestic and foreign issues.

SOURCES

Books

Aburish, Said. *Arafat: From Defender to Dictator.* London: Bloomsbury, 1998.

Cleveland, William L. *A History of the Modern Middle East.* Nashville, TN: Westview, 2000.

Wallach, Janet. *Arafat: In the Eyes of the Beholder.* New York: Citadel, 2001.

SEE ALSO

Palestinian Liberation Organization (PLO)

Al-Aqsa Martyrs Brigade

Abu Nidal Organization

First of October Anti-fascist Resistance Group

ALTERNATE NAME: GRAPO
LEADER: Manuel Perez Martinez
USUAL AREA OF OPERATION: Spain

OVERVIEW

In 1975, days after Spanish dictator Francisco Franco died, the First of October Anti-Fascist Resistance Group was formed with the goal to overthrow the transitioning Spanish government and replace it with a communist state. The group, called Grupo de Resistencia Anti-Fascista Primero de Octubre (GRAPO; First of October Anti-fascists Resistance Group), was created as the armed wing of the illegal Communist Party of Spain-Reconstituted. GRAPO has spent the last decades after Francisco's death resisting the democratic changes to the Spanish government through assassinations and bombing of government and political targets, leading to the deaths of eighty-two people. In addition to the creation of a communist state, GRAPO is vehemently opposed to the presence of the U.S. military in Spain. As such, the group has targeted U.S. military personnel and bases. The group is opposed to Spanish membership in both the European Union and NATO. Following the September 11, 2001, attacks on the World Trade Center in New York, GRAPO issued a communiqué in support of the action against the United States. In December 2001, the group was designated for sanctions as a terrorist organization by presidential Executive Order 13224. Since 2001, French and Spanish authorities launched a cooperative effort to seek GRAPO

Police officers examine a giant gap in the wall of a Madrid tax office on March 13, 1998, after a bomb explosion. An anonymous caller speaking on behalf of the dormant armed leftist group GRAPO, claimed responsibility for the blast.

AP/Wide World Photos. Reproduced by permission.

operatives throughout Europe. As a result, twenty-two of its members were arrested. One of the operatives detained and charged was Manuel Perez Martinez. Martinez was identified at the time of his arrest as the leader of GRAPO. Since his conviction for criminal conspiracy with terrorist intent, no replacement leader has been named, and the group has been largely inactive.

HISTORY

In 1975, Spain emerged from the authoritarian regime of Generalissimo Francisco Franco. Franco had ruled the country since the end of the Spanish civil war in 1937. Franco had been chosen by a military junta to rule the country as leader of the Nationalist Party, and in 1947 passed the Law of Succession, which named him ruler for life. Franco never formed a formal constitution and was the final authority over all

decisions of state. Blaming the political parties for the chaos that preceded the civil war, Franco outlawed all political parties. The leader moved to create institutions that would maintain his authoritarian system of governing. Those laws, including the Law of Succession, made it possible to create a parliamentary monarchy after his death.

In 1975, Francisco Franco died and his hand-chosen successor assumed power, Juan Carlos Delgado de Codex. By 1976, King Juan Carlos and his prime minister began to make sweeping reforms to the Spanish government, which moved the country toward a democracy. The first free election since the civil war occurred on June 15, 1977. During this time, GRAPO sought to disrupt the transition from an authoritarian state to that of a parliamentary monarchy. The group was founded in 1975 by Juan Carlos Delgado de Codex and declared its goal to be the creation of a Marxist-Leninist state. As the parliamentary monarchy began to take formation in Spain, the group began to seek the overthrow of the Spanish state in order to achieve its political goals.

As the newly emerging Spanish state established foreign relations with Europe and the rest of the world, GRAPO began to strike international targets located within Spain. GRAPO's first action occurred in Madrid on August 2, 1975, as operatives murdered two members of the Spanish Civil Guard. In October 1975, members of GRAPO killed four policemen in Madrid in retaliation for the police execution of two associates of ETA (Basque Fatherland and Liberty) and three of the People's Revolutionary Armed Forces.

In 1977, GRAPO claimed responsibility for an explosion at a German cultural center in Madrid. Another foreign target in Spain was struck by GRAPO in May 1977 as a bomb exploded at the U.S. Information Service and cultural center in Madrid. There were no injuries from the bombing, but it caused extensive damage to the building. In July 1977, a bomb exploded at the French Cultural Institute in Madrid, causing extensive damage to the building and injured two people. The next foreign-based targeting within Spain occurred in February 1979 as a bomb exploded in the basement of the French Embassy in Madrid. In a GRAPO communiqué, the group explained that, "the action is in response to the latest measure adopted by

LEADERSHIP

MANUEL PEREZ MARTINEZ

Manuel Perez Martinez was born in Manila. He was the secretary general of the Communist Party of Spain Reconstituted before assuming the leadership of GRAPO in 1979, after the death of founder Juan Carlos Delgado de Codex. He was arrested in 2000 after a failed attempted robbery of an armored vehicle. He was sentenced to ten years for criminal conspiracy with terrorist intent. Since his detention, no replacement for leadership of GRAPO has been publicly named.

France against Basque refugees in France." Also in 1979, founder Juan Carlos Delgado de Codex was shot and killed during an altercation with police. After Codex's death, Manuel Perez Martinez took control of the group.

GRAPO also targeted foreign businesses in its activities. In April 1979, the group claimed responsibility for an explosion at a Ford Motors showroom in Valencia where thirteen cars were damaged. Another bombing occurred in July 1979 at the newly opened offices of the Banque Nationale de Paris in Madrid; two additional explosive devices were found and detonated by National Police. A GRAPO communiqué expressed that the operation was in retaliation for the deaths, which the group called assassinations, of two leftists in Paris.

The group's activities continued through the next two decades. In June 1995, GRAPO kidnapped Publio Cordon, a businessman. Cordon was never released, even though his family paid the ransom demanded by GRAPO for his return. In 1990, GRAPO embarked on its first international activities by detonating a bomb in a car dealership in Freiburg in the then-German Democratic Republic. In 1998, the group continued its domestic activities by planting three explosive devices at tax offices in Madrid. Two of the devices were set off before being

discovered. Only one device was found and diffused by police. In addition, in April 1998, GRAPO claimed responsibility for two bombs found at the Previasa Insurance agency. One bomb exploded resulting in no injuries; the other bomb was found and diffused by National Police. In June 1998, GRAPO began to target temporary employment agencies. The first attack successfully exploded a bomb at an agency and injured two policemen. In November, a package of explosives was planted at a temporary employment agency in Vigo. The bomb, however, was discovered and diffused before it could detonate. Another bomb exploded at a temporary employment agency in Madrid, destroying the building. In June 1999, GRAPO began to target political opponents by planting a bomb in the women's restroom of the Spanish Socialist Worker's Party. The bomb detonated and caused damage to the building. Another politically motivated attack occurred in March 2000 as a bomb exploded in the Socialists of Catalonia headquarters building in Barcelona. In May 2000, operatives killed two security officers in an attempt to rob an armed truck carrying $2 million dollars. The attempt was unsuccessful and eventually led to the arrest of some GRAPO members. In September 2000, the group once again targeted temporary employment agencies by placing bombs in sites at Valencia, Vigo, and Madrid. Only one of the bombs exploded as a telephone caller representing GRAPO warned the police in time for the other bombs to be diffused. Within days of those attacks, the El Mundo newspaper in Catoalonia was targeted as an explosive device was planted in a trash can outside the building. The next month saw the arrest of seven GRAPO members, including leadership. As a result, GRAPO members shot and killed a police officer.

Of the men arrested in November 2000, many were considered leaders of GRAPO. Manuel Perez Martinez was widely considered the group's leader. Also arrested were Jose Filipe Lopez who was credited with directing GRAPO's central command operations and Fernando Silva Sanda, the head of the military network. In addition to the arrest, a cache of detonators, remote-controlled explosive devices, forged papers, and currency were also seized. Additional arrests were made in 2002, with the capture of twenty-two operatives. By 2004, sweeping arrests throughout Spain and France

KEY EVENTS

1975: GRAPO founded by Juan Carlos Delgado de Cordex as the armed wing of the Communist Party of Spain Reconstituted.

1975: GRAPO operatives kill two members of the Spanish Civil Guard.

1975: Four policemen in Madrid are killed by GRAPO members in retaliation for the police execution of five allies: two Basque operatives and three members of the People's Revolutionary Armed Forces.

1977: GRAPO strikes foreign targets in Spain by planting explosive devices at the USIS Cultural Center, the French Cultural Institute, and the German cultural institute. The German embassy was also damaged in the explosion on the German cultural institute.

1979: Founder Codes dies in a shoot-out with police. Manuel Perez Martinez assumes the leadership of the organization.

1979: Bomb is exploded at Ford Motors showroom in Valencia, damaging thirteen cars.

1979: French targets are hit in retaliation for the deaths of Basque operatives in France: bombs explode in the basement of the French Embassy and at the offices of the Banque Nationale de Paris.

1990: GRAPO undertakes its first international action by planning a bomb at a car dealership in Freiburg, the German Democratic Republic.

1995: GRAPO kidnaps businessman Publio Cordon. Although his family pays the ransom requested, he is never released.

1998: Bombs are placed at Previasa Insurance agency, Madrid tax offices, and temporary employment agencies.

1999: Explosives device is planted and detonates in the Spanish Socialist Worker's Party.

2000: A bomb is exploded at the headquarters of the Party of the Socialists of Catalonia in Barcelona. Another bomb detonates at the office of the electoral census in the National Statistical Institute of Barcelona.

2000: A series of bombs are left at temporary employment agencies, as well as at the *El Mundo* newspaper in Catalonia.

2000: An attempted robbery of an armored vehicle carrying over $2 million in cash leads to the arrest of seven GRAPO members, including leader Manuel Perez Martinez.

2000: In retaliation for the arrest of its members, GRAPO operatives kill a police officer.

2001: GRAPO issues communiqué in support of the attacks on the United States on September 11, 2001.

2002: Twenty-two GRAPO members arrested throughout Spain and France.

2004: An additional twenty-four members of GRAPO arrested, leaving the group with a remaining active base of less than twenty members.

---

had left the group with fewer than thirty active members.

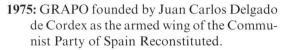

PHILOSOPHY AND TACTICS

The First of October Anti-Fascist Resistance Group seeks to overthrow the Spanish parliamentary monarchy with a self-styled, Marxist-Leninist state. The group also employs Maoist influences of peasant rebellion in its ideology. In addition to the creation of a communist state in

Spain, the group seeks to purge Spain of U.S. influences, which entails the removal of all U.S. military bases and personnel from the state. GRAPO also desires the withdrawal of Spain from NATO. To reach these goals, the group employs the tactics of kidnappings, assassinations, and bombings. GRAPO specifically targets police for killings and targets political and economic sites for bombings. The group has hit French and U.S. businesses, the Madrid Stock Exchange, the Economic Ministry, and Constitutional Courts. The group funds its activities through robberies and kidnappings,

PRIMARY SOURCE

First of October Antifascist Resistance Group (GRAPO) Grupo de Resistencia Anti-Fascista Primero de Octubre

DESCRIPTION

GRAPO was formed in 1975 as the armed wing of the illegal Communist Party of Spain during the Franco era. Advocates the overthrow of the Spanish Government and its replacement with a Marxist-Leninist regime. GRAPO is vehemently anti-American, seeks the removal of all U.S. military forces from Spanish territory, and has conducted and attempted several attacks against US targets since 1977. The group issued a communiqué following the September 11, 2001, attacks in the United States, expressing its satisfaction that "symbols of imperialist power" were decimated and affirming that "the war" has only just begun. Designated under EO 13224 in December 2001.

ACTIVITIES

GRAPO did not mount a successful terrorist operation in 2004, marking the third consecutive year without an attack. The group suffered more setbacks in 2004, with several members and sympathizers arrested and sentences upheld or handed down in April in the appellate case for GRAPO militants arrested in Paris in 2000. GRAPO has killed more than ninety persons and injured more than 200 since its formation. The group's operations traditionally have been designed to cause material damage and gain publicity rather than inflict casualties, but the terrorists have conducted lethal bombings and close-range assassinations.

STRENGTH

Fewer than two dozen activists remain. Police have made periodic large-scale arrests of GRAPO members, crippling the organization and forcing it into lengthy rebuilding periods. In 2002, Spanish and French authorities arrested twenty-two suspected members, including some of the group's reconstituted leadership. More members were arrested throughout 2003 and 2004.

LOCATION/AREA OF OPERATION

Spain.

EXTERNAL AID

None.

Source: U.S. Department of State. *Country Reports on Terrorism.* Washington, D.C., 2004.

---

such as the 1995 kidnapping of businessman Publio Cordon. The group has also developed ties with other organizations such as the German Red Army Faction, the Red Brigades, and Irish Republic terrorists.

OTHER PERSPECTIVES

Since its formation in 1975, GRAPO has operated within Europe. As a result, the group has become sought after by both the Spanish and French governments. In 2001, GRAPO was identified as a terrorist organization by the U.S. through Executive Order 13224. By 2004, much of its membership was imprisoned for their activities with the organization. However, the Center for Defense Information states, "Although GRAPO lacks the popular support of other terrorist organizations in Spain (such as the Basque Fatherland and Liberty, or ETA), it still remains a threat to the Spanish government and the United States." In 2003, the Spanish government outlawed both GRAPO and the Communist Party of Spain–Reconstituted, identifying the two organizations as a single unit for the first time.

SUMMARY

In 1975, Spain emerged from the dictatorship of Generalissimo Francisco Franco and began the process of moving toward a democracy. During this time, Juan Carlos Delgado de Codex formed the First of October Anti-Fascist Resistance Group. The objective of the organization was the creation of a communist state, one that adheres to Marxist-Leninist ideology. As the organization flourished during the last few decades, the group has claimed responsibility for attacks on police, business, and government installations that have resulted in over 200 people injured and the deaths of eighty-two people. By 2004, the majority of its active members had been imprisoned by either French or Spanish authorities. As such, the group's membership is presumed to be less than twenty, rendering it largely inactive.

SOURCES

Web sites

Center for Defense Information. "In the Spotlight: First of October Anti-Fascist Resistance Group." < http:// www.cdi.org/program/document.cfm?DocumentID = 2873&from_page = ../index.cfm > (accessed October 15, 2005).

CNN World Edition Online. "Spanish Terror Suspects Arrested." < http://edition.cnn.com/2000/WORLD/eur-ope/11/09/france.grapo/ > (accessed October 15, 2005).

MIPT: Terror Knowledge Base. "First of October Antifascist Resistance Group." < http://www.tkb.org/ Incident.jsp?incID = 13139 > (accessed October 15, 2005).

Overseas Security Advisory Council. "First of October Antifascist Resistance Group (GRAPO)." < http:// www.ds-osac.org/Groups/group.cfm?contentID = 1312 > (accessed October 15, 2005).

SEE ALSO

Basque Fatherland and Liberty

Freemen

ALTERNATE NAME: Montana Freemen
LEADER: Leroy Schweitzer
USUAL AREA OF OPERATION: Montana

OVERVIEW

The Montana Freemen were an extremist group headquartered on Justus Ranch, a 960-acre farm compound in rural Montana during the 1990s. The group grew out of the 1995 merger of two smaller organizations within the Posse Comitatus movement, which opposes the U.S. government and advocates radical local government. Groups within the movement refuse to recognize any government authority above the local level, normally meaning the local sheriff. Members of these groups frequently refuse to pay income tax or obtain drivers' licenses. While various individuals and groups have occasionally adopted the Freemen moniker, the Montana group is by far the best known.

HISTORY

When land values and crop prices plummeted during the 1980s, Montana farmer Ralph Clark found himself facing financial ruin near the small town of Jordan. Leroy Schweitzer convinced Clark, his brother Emmett, son Edwin, and nephew Richard to join him in a radical group called Freemen. A decade later, with the Clarks owing more than one million dollars in back taxes, Schweitzer and other Freemen leaders engineered the merger of two smaller

William Goehler, right, stands in the back of the room at a town meeting of Freemen supporters in Brussett, Montana. This photograph was taken in April 1996 during the 81-day standoff between the Freemen and the FBI. Standing in the center are Randy Weaver and Bo Gritz, left of Weaver. AP/Wide World Photos

Freemen groups and joined the Clarks on their farm, which they renamed Justus Ranch.

In response to mounting evidence of Freemen fraud, the FBI made plans to arrest the group's leaders. This plan was developed in the wake of disastrous standoffs at Waco and Ruby Ridge, in which numerous people were killed and injured, and government tactics were blamed for the bloodshed. To avoid this outcome, the Montana action was conducted very differently than previous standoffs. First, two major leaders were arrested outside the compound in advance, avoiding a possible scenario in which leaders encouraged members to martyr themselves for their cause.

Second, whereas FBI agents had previously employed military-style clothing and vehicles,

they utilized civilian attire and equipment, hopefully reducing the sense of siege felt by those inside. Also, rather than a visible ring of troops around the ranch, the FBI chose to focus only on limiting access to and from the property. Finally, negotiation and mediation formed the core of government efforts, which included contact with other extremist groups around the country in order to defuse any tension that might be triggered by the standoff. The result of these new tactics was a successful resolution; the remaining Freemen eventually surrendered and left the ranch peacefully.

Following their arrest, the group's leaders were tried, and four, including Leroy Schweitzer and Daniel E. Peterson Jr., were convicted of federal conspiracy and bank fraud for their role

Freemen ally Bill Goehler of Marysville, California, flies the American flag upside down in a signal of distress. He rode to Jordan, Montana, to show his support for the Freemen on April 19, 1996. AP/Wide World *Photos*

in producing more than 3,400 counterfeit checks with a staggering face value of over $15 billion. The trials were marred by frequent disruptions from the Freemen, who often screamed profanities at the judge and threatened to have him arrested. In some cases, Freemen were so unruly that they were removed from the courtroom, and many were eventually forced to watch the proceedings via closed circuit television from a nearby holding cell. Schweitzer himself refused to enter the courtroom for his sentencing, at which he received a term of twenty-two years in prison.

In March 2003, two Freemen sympathizers (age 55 and age 81) posing as federal marshals entered the federal prison in Edgefield, South Carolina, and attempted to free Schweitzer. Both men were arrested and charged with assisting an escape attempt.

PHILOSOPHY AND TACTICS

The Montana Freemen held four basic beliefs. First, all forms of government beyond the local level are illegitimate, meaning that U.S. residents are free to ignore tax bills, drivers' license and car tag laws, and court orders. Second, as sovereign citizens they were not subject to foreclosure, which

LEADERSHIP

LEROY M. SCHWEITZER

Leroy Schweitzer, a former crop-duster and tax evader, became the leader of the Montana Freemen in the mid-1990s. Schweitzer is believed to have gained many of his fraudulent skills at a 1992 seminar taught by Roy Schwasinger, who is considered one of the prime developers of the many get-rich-quick schemes used by the antigovernment Patriot movement. Schweitzer combined these schemes with his own racist teachings as the foundation of the Montana Freemen. He also taught his techniques to an estimated 800 people from various parts of the country, most of whom paid $100 apiece to attend his classes.

Schweitzer was arrested outside his Montana compound in 1996, just prior to an eighty-one-day siege of the group's property. Following the eventual surrender of those inside the Justus Ranch, Schweitzer and others were tried and convicted, with Schweitzer being sentenced to twenty-two years in federal prison.

---

was an immediate threat for Clark. Third, they granted themselves the authority to arrest, try, and sentence local officials for crimes. Fourth, they believed that fraud was a legitimate tool in advancing their cause; based on this belief, the Freemen devised and carried out a variety of financial schemes in order to defraud individuals, companies, and the government of billions of dollars.

In some cases, Freemen wrote fraudulent checks for double the amount due, then demanded refunds of the balance. In others, they produced counterfeit checks and money orders of exceptionally high quality, and the scope of this massive fraud eventually formed the basis of the government's case against them. Running throughout the philosophy of the Freemen was a constant stream of racism, a white supremacist perspective strongly influenced by other extremist groups in the United States.

The Freemen were particularly notorious for their use of liens, which they filed against property owned by various public officials. While these liens, which claimed that the targeted officials owed them money, were clearly frivolous, they served as a powerful harassment tactic, since the targeted individuals had to go to court to have them removed. Further, they served to bog down the court system, indirectly helping the Freemen in their attempts to shut down the government. In response to this tactic, several states have since passed laws restricting the use of frivolous liens.

OTHER PERSPECTIVES

Not surprisingly, the events at Justus Ranch were perceived somewhat differently by individuals who share the Freemen's views. Since antigovernment groups remain active in the United States and on the web, they frequently portray the Montana Freemen as simply the latest in a long string of groups silenced by the vast conspiracy in Washington. These supporters ask why the Montana Freemen were arrested, since their only crime was writing a few hot checks. They also characterize the convicted Freemen as political prisoners, held for their efforts to return control of America to American citizens. Finally, the fact that several hundred people attended Schweitzer's fraud training classes suggests that support for his cause might be fairly widespread.

Most other observers are understandably nervous about organizations that threaten government officials, avoid paying taxes, and stockpile weapons. And while the group's use of hot checks is hardly revolutionary, Mark Pitcavage, the so-called Militia Watchdog for the Anti-Defamation League, described the use of bogus liens as "paper terrorism," a tool that allows radical groups to inexpensively defame and intimidate their enemies.

SUMMARY

The Montana Freemen were the most visible of several Freemen groups advocating the overthrow of the U.S. government. While the Montana group dissolved following their leaders' arrest, others remain active. While some Freemen websites claim more than one million members, the actual number is probably less than 10,000.

KEY EVENTS

1980s: Leroy Schweitzer recruits disgruntled farmer Ralph Clark to join the Freemen, an antigovernment group.

1995: Schweitzer, Daniel Peterson, and other Freemen move in with the Clark family, marking the start of the Montana Freemen group. The group proceeds to file numerous bogus liens against government officials, as well as committing massive fraud and teaching others the same techniques.

1996: FBI agents arrest Schweitzer and Peterson near the group's headquarters at the Justus Ranch. Other members of the group refuse to leave the compound, leading to an eighty-one-day standoff. The remaining members of the group eventually surrender peacefully.

1998: Schweitzer, Peterson, and other group leaders are convicted of fraud.

2003: Two men attempt to break Schweitzer out of federal prison, and are arrested.

SOURCES

Books

Jakes, Dale, Connie Jakes, and Clint Richmond. *False Prophets: The Firsthand Account of a Husband-Wife Team Working for the FBI and Living in Deepest Cover with the Montana Freemen.* Allen Park, MI: Dove Books, 1998.

Web sites

Anti-Defamation League. "Paper Terrorism's Forgotten Victims: The Use of Bogus Liens against Private Individuals and Businesses." < http://www.adl.org/mwd/privlien.asp > (accessed October 18, 2005).

MIPT Terrorism Knowledge Base. "Montana Freemen." < http://www.tkb.org/Group.jsp?groupID = 3406 > (accessed October 18, 2005).

Southern Poverty Law Center. "False Patriots." < http://www.splcenter.org/intel/intelreport/article.jsp?pid = 366 > (accessed October 18, 2005).

SEE ALSO

Posse Comitatus

Fuerzas Armadas Liberación Nacional (FALN)

Fuerzas Armadas Liberación Nacional (FALN), also known as the The Armed Forces of National Liberation, a Puerto Rican organization designed to fight for Puerto Rico's independence from the United States, was founded in 1974. Responsible for a wide range of bombings and attempted political violence, the group operated primarily in the continental United States.

FALN is often mentioned in conjunction with the Popular Boricua Army (*Ejército Popular Boricua*), which goes by the nickname Los Macheteros. Los Macheteros formed within two years of FALN, and by the same leader, but Los Macheteros' activities were centered in Puerto Rico. The two organizations formed a front designed to use political violence to gain Puerto Rican independence. From the mid-1970s until the arrest and conviction of various FALN leaders in the early 1980s, the group was directly responsible for more that 120 separate bombings on the United States' mainland. During their stretch of political violence, FALN was responsible for the deaths of six people, injuries to more than fifty, and caused more than $3 million in damage to property.

ALTERNATE NAME: Armed Forces of National Liberation

LEADERS: Filberto Ojeda Ríos; Oscar Lopez Rivera

USUAL AREA OF OPERATION: Continental United States

William Morales, 37, a bomb maker for the terrorist group FALN, shown jailed in 1983. Mexican authorities eventually released him and allowed him to flee to Cuba. His release drew sharp criticism from the U.S. government, and its ambassador to Mexico, Charles J. Pilliod, was recalled. Morales lost both hands in a bomb explosion in 1979. AP/Wide World Photos. Reproduced by permission.

HISTORY

Puerto Rican independence and its effects on political violence in the United States have a history that begins before the formation of FALN. In 1954, twenty years before FALN was created, the National Party of Puerto Rico attacked the United States House of Representatives during a session on March 1, 1954, spraying the chamber with bullets. In the end there were no deaths, but the incident left five members of Congress injured. There were more than 240 members on the floor of the House at the time of the shooting.

Puerto Rico had been named a commonwealth just two years before the shootings; the

next decades brought questions of political sovereignty, full statehood, and in-between status to the forefront of Puerto Rican politics.

In the 1960s, Puerto Rican independence was not simply a leftist or radical idea, but a topic discussed among mainstream politicians. In 1968, the New Progressive Party (PNP) was founded by Luis A. Ferré, a party that sought greater freedoms for Puerto Rico. The previous year, Filiberto Ojeda Rúos founded Armed Revolutionary Independence Movement (MIRA), the first political organization devoted to serving the cause of Puerto Rican independence. The PNP viewed Puerto Rican independence as a civil rights issue, and the introduction of this hard-left political party fed the development of even more political organizations devoted to fighting for Puerto Rican independence. More radical independence groups, such as the Puerto Rican Socialist Party (PSP), formed in the early 1970s. PSP, a Marxist- and Cuban-friendly party, never achieved prominence in Puerto Rico, but the creation of such a party did gain attention from the mainland United States.

In 1974, Ojeda created FALN, which operated out of New York City. The organization planned and executed a series of bombings with the goal of gaining national attention for the cause of Puerto Rican independence and Puerto Rican sovereignty.

Most of FALN's activities took place between 1974 and 1980. In 1980, eleven FALN members, including then-leader Oscar Lopez Rivera, were arrested for attempting to rob an armored car at Northwestern University in Evanston, Illinois. The FALN members were tried and convicted on charges of sedition and conspiracy, though not for any of the bombings committed by FALN.

In 1999, President Bill Clinton offered clemency to the sixteen imprisoned members of FALN, but only if the prisoners agreed to renounce violence and terrorism. Clinton's offer angered Republicans in Congress, although none of the sixteen FALN members were involved in any of the group's known bomb attacks that resulted in the death or injury of any person. Thirty-five Republicans in Congress, led by Representative Vito Fossella (R–New York), condemned the offer of clemency and accused the president of sending a message to terrorists that the United States

Capitol police place three of four Puerto Rican nationalists under arrest shortly after they opened fire from the visitor's gallery of the U.S. House of Representatives on March 1, 1954. Five members of Congress were injured. Lolita Lebron, one of the nationalists, said, "I want freedom for my country. My country is Puerto Rico." AP/Wide World Photos. Reproduced by permission.

does not take terrorism seriously, "making terrorism more likely and endangering every American."

In addition to angering Republicans in Congress, the U.S. Attorney's office, the FBI, the Federal Bureau of Prisons, and the Fraternal Order of Police all opposed the president's clemency offer. Clinton's offer of clemency also drew opposition from First Lady Hillary Clinton. Mrs. Clinton was running for the United States Senate in New York, and publicly differed with her husband on this issue. In the end, citing executive privilege, Clinton refused to turn over documents related to his decision. On August 11, 1999, President Clinton commuted the sentences of sixteen FALN members.

PHILOSOPHY AND TACTICS

From its inception, FALN used threats of bombings and bombings themselves to coordinate and execute a plan of action designed to bring attention to the pro-independence goals of the organization. With bombings in prominent U.S. cities such as New York, Chicago, and Washington, D.C., FALN captured the public's attention.

With some bombings, the group disseminated a "communiqué to the press, usually the Associated Press. These communiqués explained the purpose of the bombings and reiterated the political organization's demands and goals.

FALN's founder, Filiberto Ojeda Ríos, became intensely involved in Los Macheteros, a

LEADERSHIP

FILIBERTO OJEDA RÍOS

Filiberto Ojeda Ríos founded the first Puerto Rican independence movement, Armed Revolutionary Independence Movement (MIRA), in Puerto Rico in 1967. He fled Puerto Rico in the early 1970s when the group was broken apart by the police. Ojeda moved to New York City and founded FALN in 1974. A musician by trade, he eventually became one of the FBI's Most Wanted fugitives for his part in FALN activities on U.S. soil, which included a string of more than 120 bombings between 1974 and 1983.

In 1976, Ojeda formed Los Macheteros, a political organization that operated solely in Puerto Rico. There was a great deal of fluidity between Los Macheteros and FALN, however. Ojeda is still wanted by the FBI for his alleged role in the theft of $7 million from a Wells Fargo depot in West Hartford, Connecticut. In 1992, he was tried in absentia in the United States, sentenced to fifty-five years in prison, and fined $600,000. His whereabouts are still unknown, although he continues to lead Los Macheteros, and was linked to a string of political violence in Puerto Rico as recently as 1998.

OSCAR LOPEZ RIVERA

Oscar Lopez Rivera, the leader of FALN at the time of his arrest in Evanston, Illinois, in 1980, served as an infantryman in the U.S. army in Vietnam from 1966–1967. He earned a Bronze Star during his service, and upon his return became a community organizer in Chicago. Shortly thereafter, he became involved in the Puerto Rican independence movement. In 1980, he was one of eleven FALN members arrested and convicted of sedition, conspiracy, armed robbery, and lesser charges.

He was granted clemency by President Bill Clinton in 1999.

splinter group formed in 1976 to apply the same tactics as FALN, but on Puerto Rican soil. As FALN's bombings and threats continued on the United States mainland, Los Macheteros' activities increased in frequency on Puerto Rico.

After eleven group members were arrested during an attempted robbery of a Wells Fargo armored car in Illinois in 1980, the group fell apart. Ojeda focused on Los Macheteros in Puerto Rico, engaging in more political violence there. In 1983, Ojeda and other members of Los Macheteros succeeded in a robbery of more than $7 million from a Wells Fargo depot in Connecticut.

The group's use of violence and theft to aid in the pro-independence cause led to isolation from political parties and other mainstream organizations in Puerto Rican society. With a cycle of bombing and communiqués, FALN's tactics spread information about their pro-independence cause, but their robbery attempts led to the arrest of most members of the organization. By the time the majority of the leadership was arrested and convicted on sedition and conspiracy charges, support in Puerto Rico for their cause had diminished even further.

OTHER PERSPECTIVES

The International Committee of the Fourth International, on its World Socialist web site, considered Clinton's offer of clemency and the condition requiring the renunciation of violence and that the prisoners not associate with known fellows "cruel." In a statement about the prisoners, they state: "The jailing of the FALN prisoners is one of the most savage and remorseless acts of repression in recent American history. No evidence was presented linking any of the defendants to specific acts of violence. All were convicted of conspiracy and sedition charges after brief trials in which they refused to participate, on the grounds that they did not recognize the authority of the United States government. The sentences imposed ranged from thirty-five years to a staggering 105 years in prison—for Luis Rosa, a 19-year-old just out of high school."

On the other hand, Senator Orrin Hatch (R–UT) and Congressman Vito Fossella (R–NY) proposed a measure in 2000 that would require the Office of Pardon Attorney in the Justice Department to inform victims or their families of

KEY EVENTS

1974: FALN was founded.

1980: Eleven FALN members arrested and convicted of sedition, conspiracy, armed robbery, and lesser charges.

1983: Last recorded action was in 1983.

1999: Sixteen members granted clemency from prison sentences by President Clinton.

any clemency proceeding or persons being considered for clemency. The measure would also require law enforcement agencies to analyze the effect of a grant of clemency. Opponents of the measure deemed it too restrictive, and stated that it violated the president's executive powers. The measure did not pass, although it had the full backing of law enforcement agencies that did not agree with President Clinton's clemency decision.

SUMMARY

The last known official activity from FALN members took place in 1983. In 1999, when President Bill Clinton vacated the sentences of eleven FALN members (a decision with which First Lady Hillary Clinton, running for the U.S. Senate in the state of New York, disagreed), he required that the FALN members renounce the use of violence.

Since 1999 the group has taken part in no political violence, nor has anyone claiming to represent FALN taken responsibility for any violent acts. As of 1998, fewer than three percent of the population of Puerto Rico supported independence from the United States.

SOURCES

Books

Burnett, Christina Duffy, and Burke Marshall, editors. *Foreign in a Domestic Sense: Puerto Rico, American Expansion, and the Constitution.* Durham, NC: Duke University Press, 2001.

Web sites

MIPT Terrorism Knowledge Base. "Terrorist Group Profile: Armed Forces of National Liberation." < http://www.tkb.org/Group.jsp?groupID = 3229 > (accessed October 18, 2005).

National Institute of Justice. "The American Terrorism Study: Patterns of Behavior, Investigation and Prosecution of American Terrorists." < http://www.ncjrs.org/pdffiles1/nij/grants/193420.pdf > (accessed October 18, 2005).

SEE ALSO

Los Macheteros

German Workers Freedom Party

LEADERS: Friedhelm Busse; Lars Burmeister

YEAR ESTABLISHED OR BECAME ACTIVE: 1979

ESTIMATED SIZE: 400 listed members, dropping to 200 members after its banning

USUAL AREA OF OPERATION: Germany, chiefly the Berlin area

OVERVIEW

The German Workers Freedom Party or the Liberal Workers Party (*Freiheitliche Deutsche Arbeiterpartei*, or FAP) was founded in 1979. It operated mostly in the Berlin area with an estimated four hundred official members. A neo-Nazi group, the FAP declared that, like Adolf Hitler's Nazis, it would exterminate dissidents after seizing power. Members railed against Jews, people of color, and foreigners while greeting one another with a raised right arm and a Heil Hitler salute.

The German government prohibited membership in FAP in 1995 after declaring the group to be unconstitutional, racist, anti-Semitic, and subversive. Despite the ban, the group is still in existence, albeit underground.

HISTORY

The FAP began in 1979. Like other neo-Nazi groups, FAP sprang up in response to Germany's economic woes. It remained small and comparatively inactive for many years. In 1988, FAP gained a dynamic new leader, Friedhelm Busse, who possessed stellar Nazi qualifications and a flair for public speaking. FAP then became one of the most visible fascist groups in Germany.

LEADERSHIP

FRIEDHELM BUSSE

The long-time head of the FAP was Friedhelm Busse. He was born on February 4, 1929, in Bochum das Licht der Welt outside of Munich, Germany. Busse was one of the youngest members of the Hitler Youth during the Third Reich. In the 1950s, he joined the Bund Deutscher Jugend (BDJ), an elite U.S. Central Intelligence Agency-trained paramilitary organization composed largely of ex-Hitler Youth, Wehrmacht, and SS personnel in West Germany. In the event of a Soviet invasion, Busse's group was assigned to go underground and engage in acts of sabotage and resistance. However, instead of focusing on foreign enemies, Busse's group of ex-Nazis drew up a death list that included future Chancellor Willi Brandt and other leading Social Democrats (then West Germany's main opposition party) who were to be executed in the case of a national security emergency. In October 1952, the West German press discovered that American intelligence was backing a neo-Nazi death squad. The scandal resulted in a serious loss of U.S. prestige and the dismantling of the BDJ.

Busse went on to direct several West German neo-Nazi groups. Typical of neo-Nazis, he advocates the overthrow of the democratic German government and denies that the Holocaust occurred. He became the head of FAP in 1988, but received a prison sentence of eight years in 1995 for defying a ban on an earlier pro-Nazi group and having in his possession copies of Adolf Hitler's *Mein Kampf*, which is banned in Germany. Busse then lost the FAP post. Following his release from jail, Busse became involved with the National Democratic Party, the most radical of several German far-right political parties and one that targets immigrants and refugees. Although he is popular with neo-Nazis, especially skinhead youth, observers believe that Busse's headstrong nature and image as an inflexible Nazi will prevent him from uniting and leading Germany's radical right.

Following German unification in 1990, many former East Germans struggled to find a place in the new Germany. They blamed immigrants, particularly Turks, for their problems. Some of these Germans joined right-wing political groups, including FAP. The organization's estimated membership, which ranged from 220–400 in its heyday, does not include thousands of FAP supporters. FAP members may have been involved in an arson attack in Moelin in November 1992 that killed three Turks and led the German government to promise to clamp down on right-wing extremism.

In August 1993, FAP provoked a nationwide outcry when it gathered about 500 right-wing extremists in the southwestern German city of Fulda to celebrate the anniversary of the death of Hitler's former deputy, Rudolf Hess. The demonstration prompted the German government to seek a ban on FAP. As a political party, FAP could only be prohibited by an act of the Federal Constitutional Court, and it took some time for the political machinery to move against FAP. Meanwhile, in 1993, FAP members smashed seventeen gravestones and daubed swastikas and "FAP" on twenty-six other gravestones in a Jewish cemetery in the village of Wriezen, north of Berlin. In 1994, Busse attempted to bring together under one banner different neo-Nazi groups in the state of Baden-Wuerttemberg but the organizational meeting was broken up by a police raid and the arrest of Busse for distributing pro-Nazi materials. In the wake of the Hess celebration, left-wing extremists began targeting FAP members.

Upon its banning by the court on February 24, 1995, German authorities raided the offices and homes of dozens of members. The police confiscated fascist books, flags, and World War II weapons and made many arrests for

KEY EVENTS

1993: FAP provoked a nationwide outcry when it gathered to celebrate the anniversary of the death of Hitler's former deputy, Rudolf Hess.

1993: FAP members smashed seventeen gravestones and daubed swastikas and "FAP" on twenty-six others in a Jewish cemetery.

1995: The German government banned FAP for being unconstitutional, racist, anti-Semitic, and subversive.

violating the constitutional ban on glorifying Nazism. The police also impounded the bank statements of the group and froze FAP accounts. German authorities received some criticism for being slow to act against neo-Nazis. In the case of FAP, some members managed to elude police.

PHILOSOPHY AND TACTICS

FAP aims to restore Nazi rule in Germany. The Nazis, or National Socialists, came to power in 1933 because they promised to end the Depression and put Germans back to work. Led by Adolf Hitler, the Nazis promised political stability and the restoration of Germany's former glory. To achieve these goals, the Nazi state exterminated those people that it regarded as defective or less than human, including the mentally disabled, physically disabled, Jews, homosexuals, and gypsies. The state also eliminated political opponents, especially communists. The Nazis created a hierarchy of nationalities and aimed to force "lesser" people like the Russians and the other Slavs to become slaves for the Aryan master race.

FAP is a neo-Nazi organization. It wants to create a Germany just like the Germany of the Third Reich. Like the Nazis of old, FAP's tactics

are violent. FAP documents indicate that its leaders planned to shoot all enemies after taking power in Germany. FAP members have launched attacks on immigrants, especially Turks. They are responsible for the arson deaths of homeless in hostels. Typical of neo-Nazis, FAP members glorify the virtues of Hitler and deny the existence of the Holocaust. The organization disregards human rights, defames democratic institutions, and is anti-Semitic as well as anti-foreigner.

OTHER PERSPECTIVES

In a 1993 speech to FAP faithful, Busse declared his plans for the nation once neo-Nazis took control of Germany. He stated, "There will be no concentration camps... but rather work camps where enemies of the German people, especially foreigners, will perform useful tasks."

FAP has no apparent supporters in the German government. The official request to ban FAP followed a 1993 report by Interior Minister Manfred Kanther that concluded FAP "rejects liberal democratic order, disparages democratic institutions and fights democratic parties in a way which demonstrates that they should be banned from political life." Chancellor Helmut Kohl said in 1993 that FAP's violence against foreigners "shamed" Germany, that the attacks threatened internal security and that "the state and we all must stand up resolutely against these murderous attacks and this whole outrageous behavior." Berlin mayor Eberhard Diepgen added his voice to the anti-FAP chorus by declaring in 1995 that, "This offspring of the National Socialists has been a burden to the image of German democracy."

SUMMARY

Germany has an abundance of neo-Nazi groups. In 1995, when FAP was banned, twenty-nine openly neo-Nazi groups continued in existence. The banning of FAP simply sent its members into such right-wing extremist organizations as the National List and the National Democratic Party. In 1997, two former FAP members were arrested for attempting to set up a "werewolf" group similar to the Nazi underground organization that battled Allied forces in occupied

Germany in April 1945. One of the men was an unemployed roofer while the other was a casual laborer.

The neo-Nazi organizations grow at a pace with Germany's economic woes. As they did in the 1930s, unemployed and underemployed Germans scapegoat minorities for their troubles. Although opposed by the vast majority of Germans, neo-Nazism has proven impossible to stamp out. FAP apparently continues in existence, though in a severely weakened state. It had an estimated 230 members in 1995, at the time that its current head, Lars Burmeister, was arrested in Norway on a German warrant.

SOURCES

Books

Lee, Martin A. *The Beast Reawakens.* New York: Little, Brown, 1997.

Periodicals

"Germans Outlaw Neo-Nazi Group." *Evening Standard (London)* February 24, 1995.

"Germany Bans Two Neo-Nazi Groups, Police Carry Out Raids." *Deutsche Press-Agentur* February 24, 1995.

"Germany to Ask Court to Ban Neo-Nazi Party." *Agence France Presse* September 15, 1993.

"Jewish Cemetary Desecrated by Neo-Nazis in Eastern Germany." *United Press International* September 8, 1993.

Greenpeace

LEADER: Gerd Leipold

ESTIMATED SIZE: 2.8 million

USUAL AREA OF OPERATION: Worldwide (headquarters in Amsterdam; offices in forty-one countries)

Greenpeace is an international environmental group with offices in forty-one countries worldwide and 2.8 million supporters. Since it was founded in 1971, it has been instrumental in drawing worldwide public attention to a host of environmental concerns, including whaling, global warming, genetic modification of crops, and nuclear testing. Its mission statement disavows violence, but its critics say that its campaigning tactics have teetered over into extremism.

HISTORY

In many ways, Greenpeace can be viewed as an extension of the 1960s' peace and hippy movement. It emerged in Vancouver in 1969 as the "Don't Make a Wave Committee," and consisted of a group of Canadian and American expatriate (many of whom were living in self-imposed exile to dodge the Vietnam draft) political activists and hippies.

Its initial motivation was to "bear witness" to U.S. underground nuclear testing at Amchitka, an island off the west coast of Alaska. Its motivations were a mix of environmental concerns about the fate of the island's sea otters and bald eagles, and a deep-seated aversion to nuclear weapons. A seaborne mission in

Greenpeace activists displaying a protest banner against the French government's planned nuclear tests on the South Pacific island of Mururoa. AP/Wide World Photos. Reproduced by permission.

spring of 1971 on the boat, the Phyllis Cormack, was intercepted before it reached Amchitka, and the nuclear test went ahead. But, the activists had created a flurry of interest. Later on that year, the United States ended nuclear testing on the island.

The Committee renamed itself later in 1971 as a way of uniting interests of its members within its title. According to a possibly apocryphal story on its web site, it was a member called Bill Darnell who came up with the "dynamic" combination of words to bind together the group's concern for the planet and opposition to nuclear arms. "Somebody flashed two fingers as we were leaving the church basement and said 'Peace!'" Bill said. "Let's make it a Green Peace. And we all went Ommmmmmmm." The committee was renamed Greenpeace.

Two intrinsically linked events changed this fledgling organization from a minor Canadian pressure group to the world's biggest environmental organization. In 1972, Greenpeace put out an appeal for sympathetic yacht owners to help them protest against French atmospheric nuclear tests in the Pacific. Over the next twenty-five years, this would be Greenpeace's most ardently fought and famous campaign, helping heap international condemnation on successive French governments.

Answering that call was David McTaggart, a 40-year-old Canadian former entrepreneur, who was traveling the world in his yacht, as he put it, "finding himself." By his own account, he was initially more annoyed by the French government's unilateral decision to close off part of the Pacific to shipping than about the actual issue of nuclear testing, but his subsequent encounters with the French changed all that.

On June 17, 1972, and after seventy days at sea evading the New Zealand and French navies,

LEADERSHIP

GERD LEIPOLD

German-born Gerd Leipold has been International Executive Director of Greenpeace International since June 2001. The role serves as leader and public spokesperson of the entire organization, and he is responsible for leading its campaigns. A long-standing activist, Leipold had held a variety of senior positions within the organization prior to taking up the role. These have included directing Greenpeace's Nuclear Disarmament Campaign and the positions of Executive Director of Greenpeace Germany, Chair of the Board of Greenpeace Nordic, and a board member of Greenpeace Germany and Greenpeace USSR.

Speaking of his sense of mission and where he saw Greenpeace heading, Leipold said in 2003: "There are huge numbers of people on every continent who are committed to the common good, and who are no longer willing to accept the agendas of timid or inept governments or unscrupulous corporations. This global social movement has been described as the 'emerging second superpower' and is made up of millions of people dedicated to environmental protection, human rights and social development. The continued growth of Greenpeace shows that even in economically difficult times people have a vision of a different world. This is our best hope for a better future."

McTaggart succeeded in holding up the tests by sailing his tiny 38-foot ketch, the Vega, within a few miles of the about-to-be detonated bomb, daring the French to kill him. The Vega was eventually rammed and taken in tow by a minesweeper, an action the French tried to pass off as a rescue.

A year later when he repeated the protest, McTaggart's yacht was boarded by French commandos, who gave him a severe beating. McTaggart lost the sight in one of his eyes for several months. The French tried to claim he had had an accident, then released photos of McTaggart dining with French naval officers, suggesting events had been amicable and that McTaggart had somehow staged his injuries. However, graphic photographs on a film taken by a fellow crew member, Anne-Marie Horne, were smuggled out and proved the French had lied. In the controversy that followed, the French abandoned atmospheric testing, but moved its nuclear testing underground.

These two events gave Greenpeace worldwide publicity and McTaggart a sense of mission. Previously a successful businessman and hugely single-minded individual (he was three times Canadian badminton champion), he had seemed to lose his direction when, in his mid 30s, a gas explosion at a ski lodge he owned had seriously injured one of his employees. He had subsequently left his wife and children to embark on his voyage of discovery when he had found his calling.

McTaggart utilized both the publicity he and Greenpeace had gained after the Vega's two missions and his business acumen to transform the Vancouver outfit into a global organization. In his mid 40s, McTaggart set about creating a Greenpeace in Europe, finding like-minded people to set up national organizations. By 1979, Greenpeace was unified across the Atlantic—as Greenpeace—with McTaggart running it. He remained chairman until 1991.

Greenpeace had also found a second hugely popular cause: "Save the Whales." This added to the organization's burgeoning popularity in the mid-1970s. In a series of spectacular protests, Greenpeace activists would chase whaling fleets and interpose themselves between the harpoon of a catcher ship and a fleeing whale. As with the protests against French nuclear testing, film and photographic footage was circulated in the world's media.

As environmental concerns crossed over into mainstream political debate in the 1980s, Greenpeace's protests branched out, though never losing its focus. As McTaggart would later say of its approach: "No campaign should be begun without clear goals; no campaign should be begun unless there is a possibility that it can be won; no campaign should be begun unless you intend to finish it off." Its protests during this time included the destruction of the Amazonian rain forests, pollution

KEY EVENTS

1969: Don't Make A Wave Committee emerges in Vancouver. Their first acts are the blocking of the Canadian border with Alaska to stop nuclear tests and later observance of tests.

1971: Group renamed as Greenpeace.

1972: David McTaggart brings worldwide attention by evading New Zealand and French navies to disrupt nuclear testing in the Pacific.

1973: McTaggart savagely beaten by French commandoes while again disrupting nuclear tests.

1975–1979: McTaggart organizes Greenpeace organizations across Europe. This culminates in the formation of Greenpeace International in 1979.

1985: French Special Forces bomb Rainbow Warrior.

1991: Greenpeace Support peaks at 4.8 million.

2001: Death of David McTaggart in a car crash in Italy.

---

caused by disused oil wells, contamination of the oceans, and global warming. Worldwide support for Greenpeace would peak in 1991 at 4.8 million.

But protests against nuclear testing remained its most potent campaign and source of publicity as well as acting as a constant source of irritation for various governments, particularly the French, who seemed to bear the brunt of Greenpeace's protests. In 1985, as Greenpeace prepared another flotilla to try to avert French nuclear testing at Moruroa atoll, French special forces, acting under the direct orders of President Francois Mitterand, attached two bombs to the hull of the Greenpeace ship, Rainbow Warrior. When the two bombs detonated, they sank the ship, killing a Portuguese photographer, Fernando Pereira.

The bombing of Rainbow Warrior caused international outrage, and the French government went on to pay the New Zealand authorities considerable compensation, as well as offering a formal apology. Yet, some critics of Greenpeace have suggested that the French were right to attack Rainbow Warrior as Greenpeace had itself used illegal methods in some of its protests. This suggested that, for all the worthy causes it backed, Greenpeace was actually using extremism in pursuit of its causes.

Greenpeace has always disavowed violence, although some of its "peaceful" confrontations at sea and interventions in whaling expeditions or nuclear testing have been in contravention of maritime law, or placed other vessels (including its own) in danger. Denmark has used its anti-terrorism laws to prosecute a Greenpeace member, although this was for trespassing rather than placing other people in imminent danger. Indeed its stunts, now, as ever, hold nuisance value rather than anything more insidious. For instance, in 2005, its British Executive Director, Stephen Tindall, chained himself with other activists to an SUV production line. More recently, thirteen members in the U.K. were arrested for leading protests at silos holding genetically modified grain, which Greenpeace claimed were of an "illegal" strain. They were later acquitted of public nuisance crimes.

It would be difficult, moreover, to take all of the criticisms of Greenpeace seriously. Some of Greenpeace's opponents dislike the group's left-wing origins, and others dislike its anti-corporate stance. A typical and well-publicized complaint was a letter published in the New Orleans *Times-Picayune*, republished on the anti-environmentalist web site, *envirotruth.org*, by Dan S. Borné, President of the Louisiana Chemical Association. Mr. Borné pondered whether: "Greenpeace is a tool of state-sponsored eco-terrorism?" The nub of his complaint was that Greenpeace had published a variety of petrochemical worst-case scenarios on the Internet and given details of plants so that activists could protest. A would-be terrorist could not only take inspiration from such a scenario, he believed, but be led—thanks to Greenpeace—to the site of a potential crime.

At the same time, it is worth mentioning that Greenpeace has lost prominent supporters because some members assert that it is not

The 20th anniversary of the bombing of the Greenpeace flagship Rainbow Warrior in Auckland harbour will be marked on 10 July.

The bombing, carried out by French secret service agents, was an attempt to sabotage the 1985 Greenpeace campaign against Pacific Island nuclear testing.

The attack resulted in the sinking of the Rainbow Warrior and the death of crew member Fernando Pereira, a freelance photographer.

The event hurtled Greenpeace into instant global celebrity and ensured that Rainbow Warrior Mark II became an enduring icon of the environmental movement.

DIRECT ACTION

Andy Booth, former Greenpeace UK campaign director, remembers the day well: "At the time, we were planning a direct action against the Drax power station in Yorkshire, as part of our international campaign to stop acid rain.

"We used to sleep in the office during busy periods and it was in the middle of the night here when the news first broke.

"Back then, Greenpeace was a small organisation and everyone knew everyone. We were a close group of people who cared deeply about the deteriorating state of the world and everyone wanted to make a difference.

"We were young, believed right was on our side, and felt almost invincible. The sinking and Fernando's death shook the organisation to its core. It brought home the life and death nature of the campaigns we were waging—but for most of us, it only served to strengthen our resolve."

Captain of the Rainbow Warrior in 1985 was Pete Willcox, who has job-shared the captaincy for over 24 years.

Today, moored for the weekend in the New Zealand fishing port of Nelson, Greenpeace gets a mixed reception from the locals, many of whom are fishermen dependent on their employers' use of bottom-trawling—which Greenpeace wants to ban.

But nothing too scary: "Bared buttocks and paint bombs we can live with," says Mr Willcox.

Asked about the events of 20 years ago, Mr Willcox describes how the noise of the first bomb woke him in his cabin and his immediate thought was a collision at sea—until he remembered they were berthed in Auckland harbour.

"I looked out the porthole, saw the lights on the dock and relaxed. Then the generator stopped, there was a silence followed by the shattering of glass as the water burst in."

radical enough. It has been accused of links to Earth First!, an eco-terrorist group infamous for sabotaging logging expeditions, claims which it has denied. However, one of Greenpeace's more notorious splinter groups was set up by Paul Watson, a founding director of the movement and member number seven. Watson left Greenpeace in 1977, believing that its nonviolent direct action did not go far enough to protect the world's oceans (it is also alleged that he was expelled from the group for attacking seal hunters). Instead, he formed the Sea Shepherd Conservation Society. His new organization adopted an array of militant tactics, including the cutting of drift nets, ramming whaling ships, attacking commercial fishing operations, and even bombing fishing vessels.

It was also the London-based Greenpeace splinter group that, in 1986, waged a campaign against McDonald's, criticizing the restaurant chain on a number of issues, including the destruction of the Amazonian rain forests, cruelty to animals, and its labor policy. McDonald's sued the activists for defamation, leading to the so-called "McLibel" trial, the longest in British history. A judge awarded in McDonald's favor, but awarded only token damages after finding key elements of the activists' case correct.

As Mr Willcox called for everyone to get up on deck, there was a second explosion—a French mine detonated so close to Pereira's cabin that the photographer was probably knocked unconscious and drowned in the fast-rising water.

The Warrior listed grotesquely, held up on one side by its mooring ropes. Willcox gave the order to abandon ship and a stunned crew stood on the wharf watching the Rainbow Warrior spewing diesel oil and air bubbles.

CREW ARRESTED

The police arrested the Greenpeace crew, believing they must be behind the bombings. But at dawn, as soon as divers inspected the boat's hull, it was clear that mines had been attached externally.

Within days, fingers pointed at France and its desire to stop the planned "Pacific Peace Flotilla."

The Pacific Peace Flotilla was a fleet of protest boats to be led by Rainbow Warrior on a voyage to the Pacific island of Moruroa, to protest against French nuclear weapons tests.

France, who initially denied any involvement, later admitted responsibility.

Today, Greenpeace lobbies on many fronts—climate change, the oceans, ancient forests, genetic engineering, toxic chemicals, nuclear weapons, sustainable trade are all the focus of current campaigns.

Mr Willcox says he feels as strongly about these issues now as he did 24 years ago.

On bottom-trawling, he asserts: "Greenpeace is absolutely not anti-fishing—we want as much fish as it's sustainable to catch—we want our grandchildren to eat fish. But it's clear to me that we need to back off from the ocean and give it time to recover. History says fishing companies will fish a species to extinction if you let them."

Mr Willcox says he is proud to be captaining the Warrior as it takes a break from deep sea adventures to attend commemorations in Auckland.

In 1985, Fernando Pereira's body was laid to rest in New Zealand's Matauri Bay. It is there that the Rainbow Warrior will be on 10 July for a ceremony to honour Mr Pereira.

A benefit gig by New Zealand and Australian bands has also been organised for that night. It is expected the events will attract Greenpeace campaigners from all over the world.

Mic Dover

Source: BBC News, 2005

Whether these two examples could be regarded as the actions of "extremists" is purely subjective, but in both cases their methods went beyond what Greenpeace regarded as acceptable.

In recent years, Greenpeace has tried to make inroads in Southeast Asia and Latin America. Its recent campaigns have included opposition to the war in Iraq, President Bush's proposed Star Wars program, raising awareness of renewable sources of energy, opposition to nuclear energy, GM foods, and a renewed campaign to save the rain forests.

PHILOSOPHY AND TACTICS

Greenpeace is an international environmental organization that propagates nonviolent direct action to raise awareness and as a means of protest. It states in its 1983 pamphlet, the *Greenpeace Philosophy*: "Ecology teaches us that humankind is not the centre of life on the planet. Ecology has taught us that the whole earth is part of our 'body' and that we must learn to respect it as we respect ourselves." Its philosophy also draws on the Quaker tradition of bearing witness to raise awareness and bring public opinion to bear on decision-makers. It is naturally leftist, although it has never—in its recent history, at least—propagated any sort of Marxist interpretation of environmental issues.

Its direct action has manifested itself in a number of ways. Its most famous protests have been seaborne: intercepting whaling missions or disrupting nuclear tests, but these are generally exceptional and its activists are more prolific on a local basis. Its network of international, national, and regional offices means it can organize a protest on a micro level, yet also give global exposure to it.

Its huge "supporter" base, although currently forty percent down, gives it massive financial clout relative to other environmental organizations. At the same time, it refuses corporate donations, stating that it refuses to be compromised by such munificence, although it has accepted large sums from prominent business figures and celebrities.

OTHER PERSPECTIVES

In an article in *Forbes* in November 1991, entitled "The Not So Peaceful World of Greenpeace," published shortly after David McTaggart stepped down as Greenpeace boss, Leslie Spencer (with Jan Bollwerk and Richard C. Morais) criticized the organization's lack of accountability and accused it of cleverly manipulating the world's media. "Outfits like Greenpeace attack big business as being faceless and responsible to no one," the authors argued. "In fact, that description better fits Greenpeace than it does modern corporations that are regulated, patrolled and heavily taxed by governments, reported on by an adversarial press and carefully watched by their own shareholders. There's little accountability for outfits like Greenpeace. The media treat them with kid gloves. Press Greenpeace and it will reveal that McTaggart's salary was $60,000, but it won't say anything about any other forms of compensation—something a U.S. corporation would be compelled to reveal in its proxy statements...."

"Greenpeace campaigns, like the save-the-whale one, often seem open and almost spontaneous. But they are carefully orchestrated, beginning with a network of investigators who collect tips from government officials, truck drivers and sympathetic employees at corporate targets of Greenpeace antipollution campaigns.

... This much is clear: With its network of contacts, Greenpeace has turned itself into a vigilante group—vigilant in enforcing antipollution laws, but acting as judge and jury whenever it decides that government enforcers aren't forceful enough. That little of this is widely understood is not surprising. A sympathetic press has always been a Greenpeace ally...."

Although some environmentalists criticize Greenpeace for its relative conservatism, to many in the green movement they are heroes who brought the environmental cause into the political mainstream. Writing in *Satya*—a magazine of "vegetarianism, environmentalism, animal advocacy, and social justice"—Paul Clarke celebrated the organization for sticking to its nonviolent campaigning and for its enduring role.

"From it's [sic] very beginnings, Greenpeace has committed itself to a confrontational, no-compromise approach to dealing with international environmental problems in a strictly nonviolent manner," he wrote. "The way the organization dealt with issues such as nuclear testing and commercial whaling seemed unsettlingly non-conformist—even revolutionary—when compared with the activities of the more established conservation organizations, such as the Sierra Club and the Audobon Society... The conservation establishment, who had achieved much of their work through cautious compromises with large corporations and governments, worried that Greenpeace would bring the entire environmental movement down in disgrace with its crazy stunts; some of that uneasiness still lingers in the modern environmental movement. But, as the mainstream groups, corporations, and governments quickly learned, the use of high-profile actions and demonstrations coupled with taking international environmental issues to the streets seemed to produce results: the known annual harvest of whales dropped from 25,000 in 1975 to less than 300 in 1993, and in recent weeks an international agreement, heavily lobbied by Greenpeace and backed up by very successful boycotts in Europe, was passed by the International Whaling Commission, creating a whale sanctuary around Antarctica."

" ... [A]s Greenpeace continues to re-examine its approaches to accomplishing as much as possible in a rapidly changing world, there will always be one other constant: even if the research is ignored, the grassroots lobbying unsuccessful, the decision makers unsympathetic, there is always the certainty that Greenpeace activists will not give up. For after every other avenue is exhausted, there is still no building, smokestack, bridge, or boat that is completely impervious to the hanging of a colorful banner or the dramatics of nonviolent civil disobedience as Greenpeace activists work once more to bear witness to the world's most threatening international environmental dangers."

SUMMARY

As Greenpeace approaches its fourth decade, it has had a significant impact on a wide range of environmental issues from nuclear testing to whale hunting, and (in Europe, at least) genetically modified food. Greenpeace continues to employ direct actions and protests, but remains committed to nonviolence. Although it has suffered a considerable drop in supporters since 1991, this reflects a global decline in membership of political and pressure groups. Greenpeace still claims 2.8 million members.

SOURCES

Books

McTaggart, David. *Rainbow Warrior*. Munich: Goldmann, 2002.

Weyler, Rex. *Greenpeace: How a Group of Ecologists, Journalists and Visionairies Changed the World*. New York: Rodale, 2004.

Web sites

Guardian Unlimited. "Interview with Simon Tindale: What Happened Next?" < http://observer.guardian.-co.uk/magazine/story/0,,1118794,00.html > (accessed October 12, 2005).

SEE ALSO

Earth First!

Sea Shepherd Conservation Society

Gush Emunim

LEADERS: Rabbi Tzvi Yehuda Kook; Rabbi Moshe Levinger

USUAL AREA OF OPERATION: Israel; the West Bank; Gaza Strip

OVERVIEW

The *Gush Emunim*, which translates literally from Hebrew as "the bloc of the faithful," represents the right to extreme right in Israeli politics and society. The group most often is identified with settler groups and the mentality that territory that has fallen under Israeli control must never be seized because the land is sacred and had been given to the Jewish people by God.

Through this overriding philosophy, adherents of the Gush Emunim have been involved with settling land seized by Israel over the nation's numerous wars. Principally in the wake of the Six Day War in 1967, followers of the Gush Emunim settled in the area known as the West Bank, a region that remains hotly contested between Israel and the Palestinians and has been the site of many violent clashes between the Israeli army and local Palestinians.

HISTORY

The ideology of the Gush Emunim finds its roots in the teachings of Rabbi Zvi Yehuda Kook (1891–1982). The Kook family, reflecting a lineage of rabbinic figures, is directly associated with the advancement of religious Zionism in Palestine as well as in Israel after the state's independence in 1948. Religious Zionism refers to the movement

Jewish settlers in Hebron open fire on Palestinians on December 3, 1993. The attack was a response to the stoning of Rabbi Moshe Levinger's car earlier in the day. Levinger is one of the founders of the Gush Emunim movement. AP/Wide World Photos

to return Jews to their ancestral homeland out of the belief that they are religiously mandated to do so.

Even prior to the victory of Israeli forces over several Arab armies in June 1967, referred to as the Six Day War, Kook had been the leader in the movement to instill within Israeli society a sense that the state's creation was divinely inspired and it was the responsibility of its citizens to embrace that understanding. In the Six Day War, Israel took control over areas extending alongside the west bank of the Jordan River, commonly referred to as the West Bank or the "territories." Kook espoused that those areas, as part of the ancestral and religious homeland of the Jewish people, must be settled and to consider returning the lands following their capture by Jewish forces would be a violation of Jewish law.

In 1973, Israel was attacked on the holiest day of the Jewish calendar of Yom Kippur, leading to a Yom Kippur War, where Israel was very nearly destroyed. The religious right that adhered to the teachings of Rabbi Kook began

to organize itself, leading to the creation of the Gush Emunim.

From its inception, the primary practical goal of Gush Emunim was to expand the number of Jewish settlements in the West Bank. In the summer of 1974, Shimon Peres ascended to the position of defense minister and assumed control over these areas. With the encouragement of Gush Emunim, he began to supervise the settlements of the areas. The group was extremely successful in this venture and garnered the support of large segments of Israel's population, both religious and secular, as well as some key government and military officials. These settlements grew in number quickly and some remain flourishing today, albeit under difficult security arrangements.

PHILOSOPHY AND TACTICS

The underlying goals of the Gush Emunim are to expand the number of Jewish settlements in the area recognized as the territories by the international community. While dispute exists outside of Israel in regard to the Jewish state's legal claims to these areas, the position of adherents of the Gush Emunim has always been that these lands belong to the Jewish people as a result of their tradition and therefore can never be relinquished through diplomatic or any other means.

With governmental support for the settlement of these areas, the Gush Emunim movement gained considerable popularity in its early years with tens of thousands of Israelis joining the settlements in the West Bank and the Gaza Strip. In addition to their successes in the realm of populating these new areas, the Gush Emunim movement has made considerable inroads in the political arena. With their strong backing of the National Religious Party beginning in the early 1980s, the result was that the settlements began to receive increased funding.

The central philosophy that controls all activities of the Gush Emunim relies upon their belief that the modern land of Israel and her Jewish inhabitants are decedents of the ancient kingdoms of Israel where the Jewish people were brought following their exodus from Egypt, as is written in the Bible. The movement contends that modern Israel is a land that continues to maintain an unparalleled degree of holiness and

LEADERSHIP

RABBI TZVI YEHUDA KOOK

Rabbi Tzvi Yehuda Kook remained the leader of the Gush Emunim movement until his death in 1981. Recognized by many as the leading rabbinical figure in the modern Zionist movement, his teachings continue to serve as the philosophical basis for the Gush Emunim. As the head of the Mizrachi movement, which is the organizational center of religious Zionism with various entities and representations around the world, Rabbi Kook's leadership established him as one of the preeminent religious figures in the growth of the state of Israel. An institute of higher learning founded by Rabbi Kook, which continues to exist in Jerusalem by the name of Merkaz Harav (Center of the Rabbi), produces students who adhere closely to the philosophies of the Gush Emunim and serve as the core of the inhabitants of the settlements in the territories of the West Bank and the Gaza Strip.

RABBI MOSHE LEVINGER

The leading figure in the movement has been Rabbi Moshe Levinger, who was one of the original founders of the movement and is among the heads of the settlement of Kiryat Arba, located just outside of the city of Hebron. Levinger has been arrested several times for his pro-settlement activity and is regarded as one of the preeminent spiritual and activist leaders in the Jewish settlements located in the West Bank.

The movement, while remaining largely an ideological entity and less of a structured organization, appointed an executive secretary in 1984 as well as a spokesperson.

that situation is incumbent upon the land remaining whole and not ceding any of its territories to any non-Jewish authorities. A further philosophical tenet espoused by the Gush Emunim is that the state needs to be linked to the Jewish tradition in all of its manifestations.

Consequently, adherents of the movement are opposed to any secularization of governmental institutions and they believe that Israel needed to distinguish itself from other Western democracies by presenting itself first as a Jewish state. While other Zionist entities in Israel looked at Israel as a state with a Jewish identity, the philosophy of the Gush Emunim required that religious observance and not just identification with Judaism be the motivating force behind all state laws and traditions.

The movement contends that the return of a large Jewish presence to Israel serves as an indication of the imminent arrival of the Messiah and that the Jews, through divine assistance, will triumph over their non-Jewish adversaries. With this belief in mind, the Gush Emunim believe that all political and social decisions made by the Israeli government have the ability to either hasten the coming of the Messiah, or cause it to be postponed. The followers of the movement closely adhered to the teachings of the spiritual founder of the movement, Rabbi Zvi Yehuda Kook, who taught that all segments of the Jewish population are imbued with a level of sanctity. All citizens of Israel, whether observant of Jewish law or not, were to be recognized as emissaries of God in bringing about the coming of the Messiah.

With the Israeli victory in the Six Day War in June 1967, and the acquisition of new territories, the Gush Emunim taught that in order for the redemption to take place, these lands that had been promised to the Jewish people by Abraham four millennia earlier needed to be settled. Any loss of land would further delay the coming of the Messiah.

The relationship of the Gush Emunim with the primarily secular Israeli government has largely been one of accommodation and mutual respect, yet they have always preferred Jewish law and tradition over democratically reached decisions. When Israeli governments reached decisions perceived by the Gush Emunim as opposing the Jewish character of the state, they displayed their displeasure but primarily through legal means.

The central forces behind the movement are largely characterized as law-abiding citizens of Israel and, while protests and disobedience have been utilized as forms of expression by people associating with the Gush Emunim, violence is a rarity and is not the preferred mode of action for

KEY EVENTS

1967: The Israeli Defense Forces defeated the Arab armies of Egypt, Jordan, and Syria in Six Days and took control over large amounts of new territory.

1973: Gush Emunim movement was established.

1980: Gush Emunim oversaw the creation of the Yesha Council that represents Jewish communities in the West Bank areas of Judea and Samaria as well as the communities in the Gaza Strip region. This council has acted to offer a social and political voice for the communities in these regions.

the movement. At the same time, there have been fringe elements associated with the movement that have carried out acts of terrorism within Israeli society. Most notably was the creation of a Jewish Underground group that, in the wake of the Camp David peace accords signed in 1979, attempted to blow up the Dome of the Rock in Jerusalem, one of Islam's holiest sites.

OTHER PERSPECTIVES

In the global context, because of their fundamentalist views, the Gush Emunim movement is often perceived as a militant or even terrorist agency. Despite the actions of some fringe members of the movement, the Gush Emunim even by its critics is largely understood as a peaceful group that was neither created to foster violence nor does it thrive upon violence.

Within Israeli society, the group's most fierce opposition comes from the opposing left-wing political elements that view the actions of the Gush Emunim as serving as obstacles to the peace process. For those who believe that in order for Israel to secure a lasting peace with the Palestinians, it will require Israel to hand over lands that it acquired in previous wars. The

Gush Emunim's stance serves as counterproductive to achieving a lasting peace settlement.

Because of the traditionalist beliefs of the Gush Emunim as they apply to the land, the group stands in direct opposition to the effort for Palestinian statehood. Palestinians who live in the West Bank and the Gaza Strip see the settlement activity as an occupying element, and this position has led to a great deal of violence, particularly in the period of Palestinian uprisings, or intifada, which took place between 1987 and 1990, and then broke out again in September 2000.

SUMMARY

Despite the large amounts of criticism that has been directed towards Gush Emunim both from within Israel and the perception around the world that the movement is made up of militants, the group has had a strong impact upon Israeli society. Through the efforts of the movement, religion has become an increasingly central aspect of the Israeli society and has introduced important institutions into the nation's political, social, and educational environments.

In the area of settling the territories, the movement has been most successful and has lobbied the Israeli government both to allow these efforts to continue and to receive funding. Even as political and security conflicts continue to surround these areas, the movement has grown in recent years and are generally perceived within the broader Israeli society as an integral part of the State.

The Gush Emunim operates in a largely legal framework with the exception of some fringe elements that have been known to be involved with acts of violence against the Palestinian population, as well as in a small number of other acts of violent protest against the government of Israel. The movement has strong links to the political infrastructure and its accomplishments are attributed to those relationships.

The movement's philosophies are most evident in times of social and political discord surrounding the issue of the Jewish settlements in the West Bank and the Gaza Strip. The Gush Emunim and its adherents stood at the center of the debate over the Israeli withdrawal from the Sinai desert following the Camp David peace accords. When the Israeli government announced a withdrawal plan of approximately 8,000 Jewish settlers from the Gaza Strip in 2005, the Gush Emunim faced one of its most serious challenges and stood at the forefront of a bitter public campaign in opposition to the plan. Israel completed their disengagement from Gaza in 2005. The settlements of the West Bank today house more than 200,000 people and continue to play an important role in all decisions made by the Israeli government, pointing to the ongoing impact of the Gush Emunim. Israel plans to extend the disengagement process, evacuating to several large West Bank settlements in 2005 and 2006.

SOURCES

Books

Sprinzak, Ehud. *Brother Against Brother: Violence and Extremism in Israeli Politics from Altalena to the Rabin Assassination.* New York: The Free Press, 1999.

Web sites

The Jerusalem Quarterly. "Gush Emunim; The Tip of the Iceberg." < http://www.geocities.com/alabasters_archive/ gush_iceberg.html > (accessed October 18, 2005).

The Media Monitors Network. "Gush Emunim; The Twilight of Zionism?" < http://www.mediamonitors.net/ cantarow1.html > (accessed October 18, 2005).

HAMAS

ALTERNATE NAME: Harakat al-Muqawamah
al-Islamiyyah

LEADER: Mohammed Deif

YEAR ESTABLISHED OR BECAME ACTIVE: 1987

USUAL AREA OF OPERATION: Israel; Gaza Strip;
West Bank; Qatar; Syria; Lebanon; Jordan;
Iran

OVERVIEW

HAMAS (an acronym of *Harakat al-Muqawamah al-Islamiyyah*, which translates to Islamic Resistance Movement) is a Palestinian resistance movement that emerged during the first *intifada* (uprising) in 1987–1990. It regards the land of Palestine as an Islamic homeland that can never be surrendered to non-Muslims and believes that it is the religious duty of all Muslims to wage *jihad* (holy war) to wrest control of Palestine back from Israel. Since its formation, HAMAS has waged a violent campaign against Israel. It has carried out guerilla attacks against military installations, and shootings and suicide bombings against Israeli civilians. Although it is primarily based in the Gaza Strip, it carries out attacks on Israeli soil and also operates to a lesser extent from the West Bank.

HISTORY

The acronym HAMAS first appeared in a 1987 leaflet accusing Shin Bet (Israeli Secret Service) agents of undermining the morality of Palestinian youths by recruiting "collaborators." It emerged as a formally constituted organization the following year, but in reality its origins lay further back.

A Hamas leader, Nizar Rayen, speaks to a crowd at a Gaza City rally aimed at celebrating the killing of Israeli soldiers. © *Abbas | Magnum Photos*

Its roots lie with the Muslim Brotherhood in the late 1960s. The Brotherhood is an Egyptian charitable and educational organization that had formed in opposition to British colonial rule in the late 1920s, but been made illegal by Egyptian President Gamal Abdul Nasser after he came to power in 1954. At various stages, it was reformist and revolutionary, but by the time it had started establishing roots in Gaza following the Six Day War of 1967, it was in one of its reformist periods. Over the next fifteen years, it helped establish a variety of institutions in Gaza and the West Bank, including Gaza's Islamic University and various hospitals and schools.

The Muslim Brotherhood also operated as a kind of umbrella organization for a variety of professional societies, working men's groups, and charitable organizations in the occupied territories and also, to a degree, among the Arab population of Israel itself. Its constituency varied considerably between the two occupied territories, however, in Gaza it was more working class in makeup, while in the West Bank it

consisted largely of professional and merchant classes.

One of the most prominent charitable networks was al-Mujamma, headed by a quadriplegic Palestinian cleric, Sheik Ahmed Yassin. Ironically, given what was to follow, Israel's Likud government of the late 1970s and early 1980s had assisted Yassin in creating a network of social service and humanitarian projects as a way of building him up as a counterpoint to Yasser Arafat. Yassin disliked the attempts of Arafat to impose secularism on Palestinian politics and feared he may use his overwhelming position of power to sign away territories to Israel. The intention of the Israelis was to help assert a degree of control over the Palestinian populations of Israel and the occupied territories through their benevolence toward Yassin. What they in fact did was help build up a mass movement, which the cleric could tap into to recruit militants.

By the mid-1980s, however, the Israeli government had desisted from its benevolent attitude toward Yassin after they uncovered that he

Victims of a HAMAS suicide bomb on March 13, 1996, strewn amidst the wreckage of a downtown Jerusalem bus. AP/Wide World Photos. Reproduced by permission.

had been amassing arms under the cover of al-Mujamma. They briefly imprisoned him, but he was released in 1984 under a prisoner exchange. In Gaza, Yassin made his increasing militancy felt, setting up al-Majd in 1986, a vigilante group to hunt down Israeli collaborators in Gaza.

A year later, in October 1987, the first Palestinian intifada broke out. This was a largely spontaneous street revolution, consisting mostly of violent, but low-tech street protests and attacks on Israeli military personnel. It also saw Palestinian merchants in the occupied territories resisting the illegal taxes imposed on them by the Israeli government. There was also a spate of inter-Arab violence, with up to a thousand alleged informers killed by Palestinian death squads.

Against this backdrop, HAMAS was formed in December 1987, claiming to be the Muslim Brotherhood of Palestine, a misleading claim given that it represented only a minority of members of the relatively well-established organization. In its covenant published the following year, it stated that its aim was to "raise the banner of God over every inch of Israel" and replace it with an Islamic Republic. It explicitly rejected the prospect of a secular Palestinian state. The document is steeped in both Islamic rhetoric—it repeatedly states the primacy of Islam—but also long-discredited anti-Semitism, including citations from "The Protocols of the Elders of Zion." It also rejects a negotiated settlement stating that "there is no solution for the Palestinian question except through Jihad."

The fact that the Palestinian Liberation Organization (PLO) recognized Israel's right to exist in November 1988 helped add to HAMAS's preeminence. This was a first step toward the peace deal brokered in the Oslo Accords five years later in 1993, but was not universally welcomed among Palestinians in the thrall of an uprising.

By contrast to its brutal role in the second intifada, however, HAMAS's part in the first Palestinian uprising was comparatively minor. It organized the Izzedine al-Qassam Battalions, which carried out a number of shootings against Israelis in 1989, but was as active directing violence against its own people for alleged collaboration. At the same time, HAMAS continued its more benevolent activities through its network of schools, universities, and mosques at a time when civil life in the occupied territories was at a breaking point.

In 1989, Yassin was arrested by the Israeli authorities and convicted and sentenced for life for ordering the execution of two Israeli soldiers HAMAS had kidnapped. This came as part of a wider Israeli crackdown on the organization, and other militants were detained.

From prison, Yassin continued to direct HAMAS's policy and vigorously opposed the peace process initiated at Oslo in 1993. This opposition was grounded in the organization's covenant, but Yassin's group was the main beneficiary of the growing disenchantment with Arafat and astutely waged a campaign in which they portrayed themselves as the legitimate representatives of the Palestinian people. As leader of both the PLO and Palestinian National Authority, Yasser Arafat used his power to appoint various cronies to positions of authority in his top-heavy bureaucracy; HAMAS, by contrast, portrayed the PLO as "outsiders" (an allusion to the fact that Arafat and many within the PLO had spent years in exile in Lebanon and Tunisia) reaping the benefits of the homegrown

A fighter from the Izzedine Al-Qassam Brigades, the armed wing of the fundamentalist network Hamas, holds his AK-47 rifle in the Gaza Strip on October 11, 1994. AP/Wide World Photos. Reproduced by permission.

intifada HAMAS members had waged at huge sacrifice. HAMAS also emphasized its grass-roots social welfare activities, a direct contrast to the perceived venality and corruptness of the PLO, which was now "selling out" to the Israelis.

From spring in 1994, however, HAMAS used its influence in more insidious ways in an attempt to derail the peace process. First, as revenge for the slaughter of twenty-nine Muslim worshipers in Hebron in February by Baruch Goldstein, a fundamentalist Jewish terrorist, the group waged a series of bomb attacks against Israeli civilians, targeting public transport where masses of Israeli citizens would be gathered together. A car bomb next to a bus in the town of Afula on April 6, which killed eight, marked the opening chapter of a horrific catalog of slaughter. Five were killed by a suicide bomber in Hadera eight days later, twenty-two

were killed by a suicide bomber on a Tel Aviv bus on October 19, and so it went on. Even on Christmas Day, HAMAS would not desist, when a suicide bomber wounded thirteen at a bus stop in Jerusalem.

In part because of HAMAS's campaign and partly because of Jewish opposition—culminating in the assassination of the Israeli Prime Minister, Yitzhak Rabin, in November 1995—hopes for peace were all but over by late 1995. In spite of this, Israel continued its operations against HAMAS members, including its notorious strategy of targeted assassinations, which were frequently more potent in killing innocent bystanders than actual targets. Nevertheless, on January 5, 1996, the Israeli Defense Forces (IDF) succeeded in killing HAMAS chief bomb maker, Yahya Ayyash, by detonating explosives they had placed in his cell phone. Following this attack, HAMAS went on another campaign of bloodletting, killing more than sixty Israelis in a six-week period in February and March.

A year later, in September 1997, two Mossad agents were arrested in Jordan, following an aborted assassination attempt on Khaled Mishaal, political bureau chief of the HAMAS. As part of the deal to release the agents, Jordan demanded and got the release of Sheik Yassin. Yassin returned to Gaza where he resumed his leadership of HAMAS.

The breakdown of further moves toward peace at Camp David in the summer of 2000 helped prompt a second intifada. Israel used the insurgency to dismantle the existing civil structure of the occupied territories with a series of ferocious raids. When HAMAS or its fellow militants, Islamic Jihad and the secular al-Aqsa Martyrs Brigade, responded with a suicide bombing on Israeli territory, the Israeli government would accuse Yasser Arafat's Palestinian National Authority (PNA) of failing to control the militants and would strike with a reprisal attack, usually aimed at the ever-weakening government of Gaza or the West Bank. That HAMAS and Arafat were avowed enemies seemed to mean little to the Israeli government; nor did the fact that the destruction of Palestinian police stations and such merely increased the hold of HAMAS in an increasingly decimated Gaza Strip, where it was one of the few organizations that provided any sort of social welfare.

LEADERSHIP

MOHAMMED DEIF

Despite topping Israel's most wanted list for years, comparatively little was known about Mohammed Deif or where he stood in the HAMAS hierarchy until the summer of 2005. Leading up to Israel's withdrawal from Gaza, HAMAS confirmed that Deif was its "number one," confirming the long-held suspicions of Israeli intelligence.

Born in 1963, little is known about Deif's early life. He worked under the mentorship of HAMAS's chief bomb maker, Yahya Ayyash, and is thought to have replaced him following Ayyash's assassination in 1996. The Israeli government holds Deif personally responsible for the series of suicides in the late 1990s and during the al-Aqsa intifada. He was appointed the new commander of the HAMAS Izz al-Din al Qassam Brigades, following the killing of his predecessor, Salah Shehadeh, in an IAF bomb strike in July 2002.

Deif was seriously wounded in an attempted targeted killing by the IDF while in his vehicle in the Gaza Strip in September 2002.

Speaking about the Israeli withdrawal from Gaza in September 2005, Deif said: "You are leaving Gaza today in shame . . . Today you are leaving hell. But we promise you that tomorrow all Palestine will be hell for you, God willing.

"We did not achieve the liberation of the Gaza Strip without this holy war and this steadfastness," he said, adding that attacks should continue until Israel is "eradicated."

HAMAS, for its part, struck with brutality into the heart of Israeli society, meeting IDF attacks in Gaza with horrific reprisals of its own. These usually consisted of suicide bomb attacks in shopping malls, discotheques, and the public transport system, and were sometimes undertaken in partnership with other militant groups. Since 2000, around one hundred suicide bombings have taken place, with half involving HAMAS. Often, its logic has been confused: at times, it claims bombings are revenge for Israeli attacks on its people, while at others, they are reprisals for Israel's "disregard" of the Oslo accords, an agreement, which, ironically, HAMAS refused to recognize and has done its utmost to undermine.

On March 22, 2004, Sheik Yassin was assassinated, along with three others, by an Israeli missile attack. His murder prompted global outrage and was the subject of condemnatory UN Security Resolution (eventually blocked by the United States). In the week that followed, HAMAS launched two massive suicide bomb attacks, killing thirty-six Israelis and wounding nearly 200.

The following month, a senior HAMAS official, Abdel Aziz al-Rantissi, was assassinated by an Israeli air strike. This served as the prelude for another series of IDF raids in Gaza, with the apparent aim of severely weakening HAMAS forces ahead of the planned Israeli withdrawal from Gaza in September 2005.

In the weeks running up to Israel's final withdrawal from Gaza on September 12, 2005, a number of HAMAS leaders appeared in public and in the press vowing to fight on. Ismail Haniya, a senior figure in the movement, told reporters in Gaza City: "HAMAS confirms it is committed to armed resistance, it is our strategic choice until the end of the occupation of our land."

After the 2004 assassinations of HAMAS leaders Yassin and Adel-Aziz Rantissi, HAMAS formed a shared "collective leadership."

Immediately following the HAMAS upset victory in the January, 2006, Palestinian election, Mahmoud Zahhar (a surgeon and along with Yassin, a co-founder of HAMAS) and Ismail Haniya (a dean of Gaza's Islamic University also injured in an earlier Israeli assassination attempt on Yassin) publicly moved toward greater party leadership.

PHILOSOPHY AND TACTICS

HAMAS regards Palestine as an Islamic homeland that can never be surrendered to non-Muslims, and asserts that it is the religious duty of Palestinian Muslims to wage jihad in order to regain control of the lands from Israel. Its outlook is uncompromising and radical and it

KEY EVENTS

1987: HAMAS formed in Gaza, claiming to be the Muslim Brotherhood of Palestine.

1988: HAMAS issues its covenant.

1989: HAMAS involved in various attacks on Israeli military installations. Sheik Ahmed Yassin arrested and sentenced to life imprisonment.

1994: HAMAS begins its campaign of suicide bombings in an effort to derail the peace process.

1996: Israel assassinates HAMAS chief bomb maker, Yahya Ayyash. As a reprisal, HAMAS suicide bombings kill more than sixty Israelis.

1997: Ahmed Yassin released from jail following a Jordanian-brokered deal.

2000–2004: Al-Aqsa intifada; HAMAS launches countless attacks against Israel, including more than fifty suicide bombings.

2004: Sheik Yassin assassinated; in reprisal, HAMAS launched two massive suicide bomb attacks, killing thirty-six Israelis and wounding nearly 200.

2005: HAMAS admits that Mohammed Deif is its leader.

2005: Israeli withdrawal from Gaza.

2006: HAMAS gains clear majority of seats in the Palestinian parliament.

refuses to recognize the sovereignty of Israel, referring to it as the "Zionist entity."

The covenant of HAMAS, published in August 1988, is steeped in religious rhetoric: "The Islamic Resistance Movement is a distinguished Palestinian movement, whose allegiance is to Allah, and whose way of life is Islam," reads article six. "It strives to raise the banner of Allah over every inch of Palestine." It explicitly rejects a negotiated peace settlement and repeatedly affirms its commitment to jihad. It is also marked by a high degree of anti-Semitism.

HAMAS has sought to avert the possibility of a peace settlement between the Palestinian people and Israel with a calculated campaign of suicide bombings, designed to shock Israelis away from striking any further deal. Its roots as a community-based organization with popular support, particularly in Gaza, have seen its leaders portrayed as the true protectors of the Palestinian people. Just as the IDF has often launched reprisal attacks on Gaza, so HAMAS has felt obligated to do the same to Israeli targets.

OTHER PERSPECTIVES

Writing in *al-Ahram Weekly* following the assassination of Sheik Ahmed Yassin, Khaled Amayreh believed that the killing had created such anger that it virtually bred the next generation of HAMAS militants. Yassin's killing "has undoubtedly pushed most Palestinians to the edge, believing Israel has now gone too far," wrote Amayreh. "The murder is also likely to weaken moderate Palestinians and boost the popularity and strength of HAMAS and other resistance groups. It is very likely that HAMAS will now be able to recruit hundreds, if not thousands, of young men, who have been inspired by Yassin's glorious martyrdom. Hence, it is quite possible that the killing of Yassin may eventually prove a blessing in disguise for HAMAS, especially at a strategic level.

"The massive demonstrations throughout the Arab world protesting Yassin's assassination seem to have surprised even HAMAS's leaders. The movement will undoubtedly seek to utilize that massive support and sympathy in one way or the other in the hope of translating it into tangible results. The assassination of Yassin is also likely to serve as a setback to the so-called American war on terror, prompting millions of angry Arabs and Muslims to conclude that Osama bin Laden may have been right after all."

According to an editorial in the right-wing *Jerusalem Post*: "Ahmed Yassin's death is a signal victory for Israel and for the war against terrorism. He was the military and spiritual leader of the terror war against Israel, just as Osama bin Laden is, or was, the military and spiritual leader of the war against the West.

"The killing of Yassin by an IDF missile has spawned the usual flurry of claims that it was a futile and foolish act ... This is insanity ... Does

PRIMARY SOURCE

HAMAS a.k.a. Islamic Resistance Movement

DESCRIPTION

HAMAS was formed in late 1987 as an outgrowth of the Palestinian branch of the Muslim Brotherhood. Various HAMAS elements have used both violent and political means, including terrorism, to pursue the goal of establishing an Islamic Palestinian state in Israel. It is loosely structured, with some elements working clandestinely and others operating openly through mosques and social service institutions to recruit members, raise money, organize activities, and distribute propaganda. HAMAS' strength is concentrated in the Gaza Strip and the West Bank.

ACTIVITIES

HAMAS terrorists, especially those in the Izz al-Din al-Qassam Brigades, have conducted many attacks, including large-scale suicide bombings, against Israeli civilian and military targets. HAMAS maintained the pace of its operational activity in 2004, claiming numerous attacks against Israeli interests. HAMAS has not yet directly targeted U.S. interests, although the group makes little or no effort to avoid targets frequented by foreigners. HAMAS continues to confine its attacks to Israelis inside Israel and the occupied territories.

STRENGTH

Unknown number of official members; tens of thousands of supporters and sympathizers.

LOCATION/AREA OF OPERATION

HAMAS currently limits its terrorist operations to Israeli military and civilian targets in the West Bank, Gaza Strip, and Israel. Two of the group's most senior leaders in the Gaza Strip, Shaykh Ahmad Yasin and Abd al Aziz al Rantisi, were killed in Israeli air strikes in 2004. The group retains a cadre of senior leaders spread throughout the Gaza Strip, Syria, Lebanon, Iran, and the Gulf States.

EXTERNAL AID

Receives some funding from Iran but primarily relies on donations from Palestinian expatriates around the world and private benefactors in Saudi Arabia and other Arab states. Some fundraising and propaganda activities take place in Western Europe and North America.

Source: U.S. Department of State. *Country Reports on Terrorism.* Washington, D.C., 2004.

anyone really think that HAMAS needed further excuses to kill as many Israeli men, women, and children as possible? … Intent, as Americans learned on 9/11, is not a limiting factor for the jihadis the West faces today … The idea that by not fighting back we can limit the terrorists' appetite for death is exactly what they want us to believe. The engendering of such beliefs is precisely the jihadis' theory of victory, the tipping point at which terror has won and will only worsen in order to deepen the victory and the West's subjugation.

"[K]illing Ahmed Yassin will not end the war. No single battle ever does. Pay no attention to those who say that because a battle did not win the war, it was not worth fighting. It was not a counterproductive act, even though HAMAS will attempt to 'retaliate.' What is counterproductive is to allow leaders who organize and fuel terror and call for Israel's destruction to enjoy personal immunity."

SUMMARY

HAMAS in 2005 is arguably Gaza's preeminent political movement. To the outside world and particularly Israel, by contrast, the group that had formerly existed as a kind of humanitarian organization (and still, to an extent, does) is known almost wholly for the savagery of its suicide attacks.

Israel's withdrawal from the HAMAS stronghold of Gaza in September 2005 marked a victory of sorts for the group, just as Israel's retreat from south Lebanon five years earlier was characterized as a relative success for Palestinian interests. Yet, Israel left territory even more wracked by war, lacking in civil apparatus, and marked by want than the land that had originally given birth to HAMAS almost eighteen years earlier.

In January, 2006, HAMAS backed candidates achieved a political upset in Palestinian elections. HAMAS, holding a majority of parliamentary seats, immediately clashed with Fatah over control of security forces and foreign policy. U.S. and European governments (mutually designating HAMAS as a terrorist organization) vowed not to deal with HAMAS and threatened to withdraw aid to Palestine as long as HAMAS advocated armed struggle and refused to recognize Israel's right to exist.

Israel reasserted its right to assassinate militant HAMAS leaders.

SOURCES

Books

Cleveland, William L. *A History of the Modern Middle East*. New York: Westview, 2000.

Mishal, Shaul, and Avraham Sela. *The Palestinian HAMAS: Vision, Violence and Co-Existence*. New York: Columbia University Press, 2000.

Nusse, Andrea. *Muslim Palestine: Ideology of HAMAS*. London: Taylor & Francis, 1999.

SEE ALSO

Palestinian Liberation Organization (PLO)

Harakat ul-Jihad-I-Islami (HUJI)

OVERVIEW

Harkat ul-Jihad-al-Islami (HUJI, or Movement of Islamic Holy War) was reportedly conceived in Afghanistan in 1980, in the midst of the Afghanistan-Soviet Union war to support the Pakistan-based *Jihad* soldiers to fight the Soviet Union army. Reports indicate that the group has undergone a series of organizational and cosmetic changes and has expanded its operations in the Indian territories of Jammu and Kashmir, as well as in Bangladesh. Terrorism experts are of the opinion that HUJI is prominent among the various Pakistan-based terrorist organizations that are reportedly operational in the India-occupied Jammu and Kashmir (J&K).

As of 2004, the U.S. State Department has listed the group as a Foreign Terrorist Organization.

ALTERNATE NAME: Movement of Islamic Holy War

LEADERS: Qari Saifullah Akhtar

ESTIMATED SIZE: 300

USUAL AREA OF OPERATION: Initially Afghanistan, later Kashmir Valley region, in Indian-administered Kashmir and Pakistan, as well as in Central Asia, Chechnya, Burma, and Tajikistan

HISTORY

HUJI was reportedly set up in the 1980s by two Islamic extremist organizations based in Pakistan, the Jamaat-ul-Ulema-e-Islami (or Islamic Assembly, JuI) and the Tabligh-i-Jamaat (TiJ). The group was allegedly led by Maulvi Irshad Ahmed with the motive of providing relief services for the *Mujahideen* (holy

Detained suspected militants of the organization Harkat-Ul-Jehadi Islami escape from a police truck at Lakhanpur, south of Jammu, India, June 30, 2003. The four militants were arrested by Jammu Kashmir police two days earlier at Lakhanpur where authorities recovered arms, explosives and Indian currency worth $18,085. AP/Wide World Photos. Reproduced by permission.

warriors, the word is often used to describe various armed Islamic fundamentalist fighters) fighting for Afghanistan in their war against the Soviet Union. Eventually, the group also purportedly established contact with the principal intelligence body Inter-Services Intelligence (ISI) of Pakistan and went on to recruit and train the Mujahideen.

After the group leader Maulvi Irshad Ahmed was killed in the Afghan war in 1985, intelligence reports claim that the group split up into two factions, and one faction, Harakat ul-Mujahideen (HUM, or Movement of the Holy Warriors), was reportedly formed under the leadership of Fazalur Rehman Khalil. Terrorism experts pointed out that the new leader of HUJI was Qari Saifullah Akhtar, but reportedly the group further split and a new group, Jamait ul-Mujahideen (JUM), was formed under the leadership of Maulana Masood Kashmiri.

Reports indicate that in 1991, the three splinter groups reunited to form a combined force to fight aggressively in Kashmir. This united version, known as Harkat ul-Ansar (HUA, or Movement of the Islamic Patrons), was allegedly formed in Pakistan with Maulana Masood Azhar acting as the General Secretary and with Maulana Saadatullah as its leader. In 1992, the Bangladesh unit of HUJI, known as HUJI-B, was allegedly established under the patronage of Osama bin Laden. The group had Shouqat Osman, also known as Sheikh Farid, as its self-proclaimed leader.

In 1994, Masood Azhar and Sajjad Afghani, the HUA's J&K military chief, were arrested in Srinagar by the Indian government. The arrests, as well as various other attempts by the Indian government to curb the terrorist activities in J&K, have allegedly not led to a successful formation of the HUA alliance.

LEADERSHIP

QARI SAIFULLAH AKHTAR

Qari Saifullah Akhtar is one of the three mujahideens who allegedly founded the Harakat ul-Jihad-I-Islami. Intelligence reports suggest that he, along with his two companions, Maulana Irshad Ahmed and Maulana Abdus Samad Sial, studied at the Jamia Uloom-al-Islamia Madrassa at Karachi. In 1980, researchers indicate that he and his companions left for Afghanistan to participate in the jihad against the Soviet Union. Qari Saifullah Akhtar was born as Mohammad Akhtar, but reportedly his prowess in the Afghan war earned him the title of *Saifullah* (the sword of Allah).

The three-member group that they formed was reportedly known as Jamiat Ansar-ul-Afghaneen (Party of the Friends of the Afghanis) with Maulana Irshad Ahmed as their leader. Intelligence experts are of the opinion that after the group split up in the late 1980s, Maulana Fazlur Rehman Khalil and Maulana Masood Azhar formed the Harkatul Mujahideen.

During the mid 1990s, Qari Saifullah Akhtar was also accused by the Pakistani authorities of conspiring to form a military coup to overthrow the Benazir Bhutto government. There were published reports that he later escaped to Afghanistan and returned only after the Pervez Musharraf government came into existence in 1999. After the September 11 attacks in 2001, the HUJI activities were closely scrutinized by the world. It is alleged that Qari Saifullah Akhtar chose to be a part of the organization after the attacks.

However, experts indicate that HUJI has successfully committed various acts of communal violence and other acts of terrorism in J&K and other states in India. HUJI is reportedly a part of the Deobandi extremist network of Pakistan, and Indian authorities claim that it receives constant support from the ISI.

KEY EVENTS

1995: HUJI was found to be involved in a plot to assassinate Prime Minister Benazir Bhutto and General Abdul Waheed.

1999: HUJI was placed under Foreign Terrorist Organization category by the United States.

2001: Many members of HUJI perished in the Afghanistan war after the September 11 attacks. Qari Saifullah Akhtar is said to have escaped to Saudi Arabia and later to Dubai.

2002: HUJI was allegedly involved in the attack on the Kolkata office of the United States Information Service.

2004: Saifullah Akhtar was arrested by the Dubai authorities and handed over to the Pakistani authorities.

According to the Pakistani officials, HUJI, along with two other militant outfits, HUM and Jaish-e-Mohammad (JeM), was allegedly involved in the kidnapping and murder of *Wall Street Journal* reporter Daniel Pearl in 2002.

PHILOSOPHY AND TACTICS

The HUJI was originally formed in 1980 to support the jihad in Afghanistan against the Soviet Union. During this period, the group is said to have come in close contact with several Islamic extremist organizations in Afghanistan. After the war in Afghanistan ended, the group shifted its focus on the controversial Jammu and Kashmir issue. Intelligence authorities are of the opinion that the group believes in the liberation of Jammu and Kashmir from India, and plans on achieving this through violence. The Indian authorities also blame the group for targeted acts of violence in Bangladesh as well as in several parts of India. Reportedly, HUJI aims to spread terror and eventually jeopardize the

PRIMARY SOURCE

Harakat ul-Jihad-I-Islami (HUJI)
(Movement of Islamic Holy War)

DESCRIPTION

HUJI, a Sunni extremist group that follows the Deobandi tradition of Islam, was founded in 1980 in Afghanistan to fight in the jihad against the Soviets. It also is affiliated with the Jamiat Ulema-i-Islam's Fazlur Rehman faction (JUI-F) of the extremist religious party Jamiat Ulema-I-Is-lam (JUI). The group, led by Qari Saifullah Akhtar and chief commander Amin Rabbani, is made up primarily of Pakistanis and foreign Islamists who are fighting for the liberation of Jammu and Kashmir and its accession to Pakistan. The group has links to al-Qa'ida. At present, Akhtar remains in detention in Pakistan after his August 2004 arrest and extradition from Dubai.

ACTIVITIES

Has conducted a number of operations against Indian military targets in Jammu and Kashmir. Linked to the Kashmiri militant group al-Faran that kidnapped five Western tourists in Jammu and Kashmir in July 1995; one was killed in August 1995, and the other four reportedly were killed in December of the same year.

STRENGTH

Exact numbers are unknown, but there may be several hundred members in Kashmir.

LOCATION/AREA OF OPERATION

Pakistan and Kashmir. Trained members in Afghanistan until autumn of 2001.

EXTERNAL AID

Specific sources of external aid are unknown.

Source: U.S. Department of State. *Country Reports on Terrorism.* Washington, D.C., 2004.

---

internal security system of India by undertaking various acts of terrorism such as bomb blasts, shoot outs, communal riots, and so on. The Indian government argues that the group is also active in the state of Gujarat and that approximately eighty percent of the mosques in the state are run by Islamic extremists.

The HUJI allegedly uses its armed forces in conducting a series of attacks on the Indian military based in J&K. Allegedly, the Bangladesh branch of HUJI, known as HUJI-B, is responsible for spreading terror in Bangladesh and northeast frontier of India. Indian counter-terrorism analysts confer that several recruits are trained at militant camps in Afghanistan and Pakistan. The group reportedly obtains its funding through generous supporters based in Pakistan and elsewhere in the world, and by selling weapons to other militant organizations. The group also allegedly publishes a few journals known as *Al-Irshad* and *Sada-e-Mujahid.*

Several analysts also concur that the HUJI is supported by various religious leaders and organizations based in Pakistan and also the group receives financial support from the ISI. Published reports have indicated that a majority of HUJI recruits are Pakistanis and foreign Islamists. It is also speculated by the Indian authorities that it recruits its members from the Students Islamic Movement of India (SIMI) and perpetrates various acts of communal disharmony and beleaguered violence in India. There are several investigational reports indicating that the group also has associations with other terrorist outfits, including HUM and JUM.

After the fall of the Taliban government of Afghanistan in 2001, most Indian government officials agree that Harakat ul-Jihad-i-Islami ceased its training operations in Afghanistan. However, there are reports that indicate that HUJI has offices in over forty districts all over Pakistan.

OTHER PERSPECTIVES

In a testimony presented by Ambassador Michael A. Sheehan before the Senate Foreign Relations Committee Subcommittee on Near Eastern and South Asian Affairs in 1999, Mr. Sheehan discussed the newer challenges that are faced by South Asia. Mr. Sheehan said that other terrorist outfits, including Lashkar-i-Taiba, the Harakat ul-Jihad-i-Islami, and the Hizbul Mujahideen, continue to operate freely in Pakistan and also support various terrorist activities in India.

In a statement dated July 9, 2003, to the National Commission on Terrorist Attacks Upon the United States, Rohan Gunaratna (head, terrorism research, Institute for Defense and Strategic Studies, Singapore) condemned terrorist outfits by saying that, "in Pakistan, a dozen attacks have been conducted by Al Qaeda through individual members of Jaish-e-Mohommed, Lashkar-e-Jhangvi, Harakat-ul-Jihad-I-Islami, Lashkar-e-Tayyaba, and Harakat-ul Mujahidin."

SUMMARY

Several anti-terrorism analysts are of the opinion that HUJI is a much bigger organization than what most people believe it to be. HUJI has always kept a low profile, and not much is known about its members and other activities. Unlike other militant organizations such as Lashkar-e-Tayyiba and Jaish-e-Mohammad, HUJI has reportedly avoided most media and political attention. However, the fact that HUJI is relatively less known does not necessarily make it less dangerous in nature. There are several reports that indicate that HUJI has a widespread presence in many countries, including Pakistan, India, Chechnya, Tajikistan, Central Asia, and Burma. Published data suggest that more than 650 HUJI fighters have died in battles against the Indian army in the Kashmir region. HUJI has been allegedly receiving support of the affluent religious leaders as well as businessmen in Pakistan, including the ISI, which makes its position stronger in the Jammu and Kashmir terrorism chronicle.

SOURCES

Web sites

South Asia Terrorism Portal. "Harakat ul-Jihad-i-Islami." < http://www.satp.org/satporgtp/countries/india/states/jandk/terrorist_outfits/HuJI.htm > (accessed October 20, 2005).

Center for Defense Information. "Harakat ul-Jihad-i-Islami." < http://www.cdi.org/program/document.cfm?DocumentID = 2374&from_page = ../index.cfm > (accessed October 20, 2005).

The Middle East Forum. "Tablighi Jamaat: Jihad's Stealthy Legions." < http://www.meforum.org/article/686 > (accessed October 20, 2005).

National Commission on Terrorist Attacks upon the United States. "The Rise and Decline of Al Qaeda." < http://www.9-11commission.gov/hearings/hearing3/witness_gunaratna.htm > (accessed October 20, 2005).

SEE ALSO

Harakat ul-Mujahidin (HUM)

Harakat ul-Jihad-I-Islami/ Bangladesh

LEADER: Shauqat Osman
YEAR ESTABLISHED OR BECAME ACTIVE: 1992
ESTIMATED SIZE: 3,000
USUAL AREA OF OPERATION: Bangladesh

Harakat ul-Jihad-I-Islami/Bangladesh (HUJI-B) is headed by Shauqat Osman, and is a member of Osama bin Laden's International Islamic Front (IIF), and operates from Bangladesh. The U.S. State Department refers to it as HUJI-B or HUJI (B) to differentiate it from the Pakistan-based Harakat ul-Jihad-I-Islami (HUJI) led by Amin Rabbani.

HUJI-B seeks to ensure that Islamic rule prevails in Bangladesh. Of the many Islamic groups in Bangladesh, HUJI-B is considered by most analysts to be the most powerful and influential.

HISTORY

HUJI-B claims its history dates to establishment in 1992 as a faction of the more prominent Harakat ul-Jihad-I-Islami (HuJI) based in Pakistan. However, the group has been active only since 2000. According to published U.S. State Department reports, as of 2005, the group consists of approximately 15,000 members, possibly even more. The self-proclaimed leader of the group, Shauqat Osman, is also known as *Maulana*, or Sheikh Farid, and operates out of Chittagong, Bangladesh.

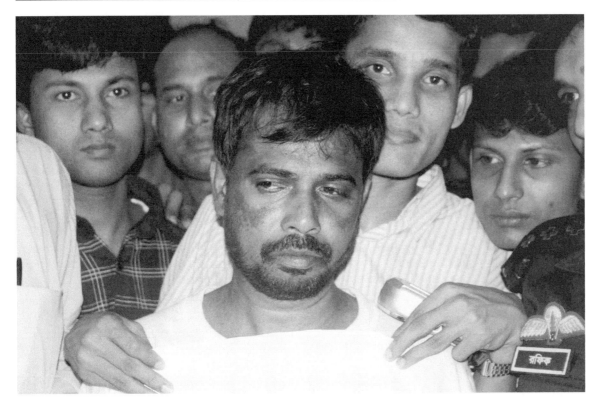

Mufti Mohammad Abdul Hannan stands under arrest, surrounded by officials from the Bangladesh Rapid Action Battalion on October 1, 2005. Hannan is suspected to be a key leader in the Harkat-ul-Jihad-al-Islam/Bangladesh terrorist group. Abir Abdullah/EPA/Landov

At its inception, primary funding for the group was allegedly provided by Osama bin Laden. The group is now thought to derive a majority of its additional funding from Bangladeshi *madrassas* (Islamic religious schools). Most of the members of the organization have been students in these schools . The group mainly recruits Bangladeshi natives as its members and trains them extensively at local camps. Many trainees are also reportedly sent to terrorist camps based in other countries.

In the past, the group referred to itself as the Bangladeshi Talibans (derived from the more well-known Taliban in Afghanistan). HUJI-B, since early 2000, is thought by Western intelligence services and monitoring groups to have close ties with Islamic extremist groups that operate in the neighboring Indian states of West Bengal and Assam. Analysts assert that they have deep links with Inter Services Intelligence (ISI), Pakistan's external

intelligence agency. Many experts argue that HUJI-B also encourages terrorist activities in the northeast frontier of India. The group is also reported to have helped in recruiting militants to conduct terrorist activities in the troubled territories of Indian-held Jammu and Kashmir.

Published reports provide evidence that HUJI-B has established and maintained at least six militant camps in Bangladesh, where it is actively conducting training sessions. Since its founding, HUJI-B members have consistently infiltrated into India through its eastern border. The prime reason for such activities, as alleged by the Indian government, is to maintain contacts and to conduct further illegal activities with the terrorist organizations operating within India.

In its short time of operation, HUJI-B has been the primary suspect of many extremist and terrorist activities in Bangladesh, and the group

LEADERSHIP

SHAUQAT OSMAN

Harakat ul-Jihad-I-Islami Bangladesh is headed by Shauqat Osman, who is also occasionally referred to as Maulana or Sheikh Farid. Osman, like many other members of the group, is thought to be greatly influenced by Osama bin Laden and the Taliban. He has reportedly, often, denounced non-Muslim religions in public. Analysts state that he has also frequently expressed vehement disregard for India and United States. However, most experts agree that Osman and other leaders of the HUJI-B are rather secretive about their mission and objectives.

The group's general secretary is Imtiaz Quddus. Very little is known about these two and other prominent members of this group.

has taken credit for multiple bombings, assassination attempts, and murders of prominent personalities. The group participated in the killing of noted Bangladeshi journalist, Shamsur Rahman, in 2000. He was murdered for making a documentary on the plight of Hindus (followers of the religion Hinduism) in Bangladesh. Ramman's writing was considered against the philosophies of HUJI-B, and so he was consequently "punished" for his action.

Following the arrest of several HUJI-B members, the Bangladeshi intelligence gathered and released reports that HUJI-B purported to murder at least twenty-eight influential academicians and scholars, including Professor Kabir Choudhury (a well-known national professor in Bangladesh), controversial writer, Taslima Nasreen, and the Director General of the Islamic Foundation, Maulana Abdul Awal, as the terrorist group claimed that these liberalist scholars were the "enemies of Islam."

In July 2000, an unsuccessful assassination attempt on Bangladeshi Prime Minister Sheikh Hasina was organized by the group. It has also claimed responsibility for conducting many other extremist and/or terrorist operations.

PHILOSOPHY AND TACTICS

HUJI-B aims at establishing Islamic rule in Bangladesh by eliminating opposing thinkers, journalists, and Bangladeshi politicians. Osama bin Laden and the Taliban regime are the key sources of inspiration for HUJI-B's ideology. In fact, the group is reported to have sent some of its members to Afghanistan to receive training under the patronage of seasoned al-Qaeda and Taliban members.

Every new recruit to this group is compelled to follow the hardcore Islamic doctrine of *jihad* (holy war). The group condemns all non-Muslim ideologies and propagates Islamic supremacy in Bangladesh. Analysts claim that the infrastructure at some of the militant camps of HUJI-B is said to be on a par with the best military training schools in the world.

To promote its philosophy, HUJI-B has in the past adopted violent tactics. The HUJI-B often spreads fear to enforce its philosophy. In November 2004, the HUJI-B issued an ultimatum to the Hindus in Bangladesh that they must convert to Islam in seven days or be prepared to die. Moreover, HUJI-B proclamations went on to declare that all non-Muslim individuals residing in Bangladesh should be prepared to be annihilated as they have no right to live in a Muslim country. For these reasons, HUJI-B is considered to be an Islamic extremist group aiming at coercing non-Muslims (especially Hindus and Christians) to embrace Islam and if they refuse to do so, the group members have not hesitated to commit gruesome murders, gang rapes, and other atrocities.

The HUJI-B borrows its philosophy from a number of other terrorist and extremist organizations. One such organization is the Jihad Movement of Bangladesh (JIB), led by Fazlur Rahman. Fazlur Rahman was one of the signatories of the Declaration of War on America, along with Osama bin Laden, Ayman Al Zawahiri, Abu-Yasir Rifa'i Ahmad Taha, both from Egypt, and Shaykh Mir Hamzah of Pakistan—as of 2005—some of the most wanted terrorists in the world.

KEY EVENTS

2000: HUJI-B is subsequently charged with a plot to assassinate Bangladeshi Prime Minister Sheikh Hasina.

2001: HUJI-B members involved in a series of blasts involving deaths of minorities at several locations.

2002: Sixty-three representatives of nine Islamic Extremist groups unite to form a council known as Bangladesh Islamic Manch, under the leadership of HUJI-B. The Asif Reza Commando Force (ARCF), an ally of HUJI-B strikes the American Centre at Kolkata, India.

2004: A HUJI-B camp is uncovered in the interior hilly region of Chittagong, Bangladesh. Several weapons and military paraphernalia are seized.

2004: Ties between *madrassas* and HUJI-B are confirmed when Maulana Mohammed Habibur Rahman, headmaster of a prominent madrassa, admits visiting the HUJI camps in Pakistan, in 1998, along with eight other Muslim leaders.

Apart from the JIB, HUJI-B is alleged to have strong links with other terrorist and extremist organizations including, but not limited to, the United Liberation Front of Assam (ULFA), the Asif Reza Commando Force (ARCF), the Jaish-e-Mohammed (JeM), Lashkar-e-Tayyiba (LeT), Roshingya Solidarity Organization (RSO), Harakat ul-Mudjahidin (HuM), as well as al-Qaeda.

The exchange of knowledge as well as personnel amongst HUJI-B and some of these groups is common practice. In July 1992, about 150 armed men belonging to the Taliban and al-Qaeda were reported to have been transported to Bangladesh from Afghanistan and Pakistan. After the fall of Kandahar (a major city in Afghanistan) in 2001, another fifty trained

terrorists shifted their base to Bangladesh. The ISI of Pakistan has also, allegedly, moved its base from Pakistan to Bangladesh to refocus its war against India. Analysts argue that HUJI-B with its power and influence supports anti-minorities activities undertaken by other Islamic extremist organizations.

OTHER PERSPECTIVES

Alex Perry, the South Asian bureau chief of the Time Magazine, mentioned in an article that, according to a HUJI-B insider, the ultimate dream of Islamic extremists is to create an Islamic land larger than Bangladesh, by taking over the Muslim-dominated areas of Assam, Bengal (states in India), and Myanmar.

In the article, "Is religious extremism on the rise in Bangladesh?" published by the *Jane's Intelligence Review* in May 2002, Bertil Lintner (cited as an expert on Southeast Asia), expressed concern over the present condition of Bangladesh and the Islamic extremist activities flourishing over there. He considered the activities of organizations, including that of HUJI-B, "worrisome," and pointed toward the alarming shift in the idea of a role model for the young men of Bangladesh. He states in the article that many young men in Bangladesh consider leaders of groups such as HUJI-B as their role models. According to them, these are "dedicated Islamic clerics."

SUMMARY

Militant activities emerging from Islamic extremist groups have seen exponential rise in Bangladesh during past few years. As of 2005, Harakat ul-Jihad-I-Islami Bangladesh is backed by various influential terrorist groups, and hence its power has been on the rise at a rapid alarming rate. Opponents of such policies argue that the fact that non-Muslims are in the minority and the Bangladesh government has declared Islam as the state religion has done nothing to help the plight of minorities in Bangladesh. HUJI-B actions evidence a disregard for human rights and civil liberties—evident from ever-increasing crimes against minorities. Governments around the world, including the U.S. government,

PRIMARY SOURCE
Harakat ul-Jihad-I-Islami/Bangladesh (HUJI-B)

The mission of HUJI-B, led by Shauqat Osman, is to establish Islamic rule in Bangladesh. HUJI-B has connections to the Pakistani militant groups Harakat ul-Jihad-I-Islami (HUJI) and Harakat ul-Mujahidin (HUM), which advocate similar objectives in Pakistan and Jammu and Kashmir. These groups all maintain contacts with the al-Qa'ida network in Afghanistan. The leaders of HUJIB and HUM both signed the February 1998 fatwa sponsored by Usama bin Ladin that declared American civilians to be legitimate targets for attack.

HUJI-B was accused of stabbing a senior Bangladeshi journalist in November 2000 for making a documentary on the plight of Hindus in Bangladesh. HUJI-B was suspected in the assassination attempt in July 2000 of Bangladeshi Prime Minister Sheikh Hasina. The group may also have been responsible for indiscriminate attacks using improvised explosive devices against cultural gatherings in Dhaka in January and April 2001.

Some estimates of HUJI-B cadre strength suggest several thousand members.

The group operates and trains members in Bangladesh, where it maintains at least six camps.

Funding of the HUJI-B comes primarily from *madrassas* in Bangladesh. The group also has ties to militants in Pakistan that may provide another funding source.

Source: U.S. Department of State. *Country Reports on Terrorism.* Washington, D.C., 2004.

strongly condemn such acts and have labeled HUJI-B as a terrorist organization.

SOURCES

Books
Kepel, Gilles. *Jihad: The Trail of Political Islam.* Cambridge, MA: Belknap, 2003.

Periodicals
Perry, Alex. "Deadly Cargo." *Time.* October 14, 2002.

Web sites
Asia Times Online. "Goons or Terrorists? Bangladesh Decides." < http://www.atimes.com/atimes/South_Asia/GC10Df04.html > (accessed October 16, 2005).

Central Intelligence Agency. "World Factbook, 2002." < http://www.cia.gov/cia/publications/factbook/ > (accessed October 16, 2005).

Federation of American Scientists. "Harakat ul-Jihad-I-Islami/Bangladesh (HUJI-B) (Movement of Islamic Holy War)." < http://www.fas.org/irp/world/para/huji-b.htm > (accessed October 16, 2005).

South Asia Analysis Group. "Bangladeshi < http://www.saag.org/papers9/paper887.html > (accessed October 16, 2005).

Harakat ul-Mujahidin (HUM)

OVERVIEW

The Harakat ul-Mujahidin (HUM), or the Movement of Holy Warriors, is a militant organization based in Muzaffarabad, Pakistan. The group is led by Farooq Kashmiri Khalil, an ex-military commander belonging to the disputed state of Kashmir. However, the main driving force behind this group is Fazlur Rehman Khalil, who served as the leader of the group since it was formed in 1985. The governments of India and the United States allege that both Kashmiri and Rehman have strong links with al-Qaeda leader, Osama bin Laden.

The HUM, in its early years, was involved in fighting against the Soviet Union in Afghanistan. However, subsequently it shifted its focus to the Indian state of Jammu and Kashmir (J&K), with the aim of liberating the state from India. The group is also referred to as Harakat ul-Ansar (HuA), Faran, Al Hadith, Al Hadid, and Jamiat-ul-Ansar.

LEADERS: Fazlur Rehman Khalil; Farooq Kashmiri Khalil

YEAR ESTABLISHED OR BECAME ACTIVE: 1985

USUAL AREA OF OPERATION: Kashmir (India)

HISTORY

The Harakat-ul-Mujahidin, as most analysts argue, has been in existence twice. It claims to be formed in Pakistan in 1985. Soon after its inception, members of the HUM reportedly were sent to Afghanistan for the *jihad* (holy war

Three Afghan Mujahidin ("holy warriors") stand on a mountain near the Afghan border in Pakistan.
© *Steve McCurry | Magnum Photos*

against those who do not believe in Islamist fundamentalism) against the Soviet forces protecting the communist regime in the country. The fight against the Soviet Union continued till 1989, when the Soviet forces withdrew from Afghanistan. However, the group did not disintegrate. Instead, it focused its effort on participating in the jihad against Indian forces fighting in Kashmir.

The group allegedly merged with other militant groups in the region. At this time, as reported by the Indian government, most of the group's funding was provided by Inter-Services intelligence (ISI)—Pakistan's secret service. It is even reported that the Clinton administration had asked the Pakistani government to sack numerous key members within the ISI who were allegedly involved with the HUM. Most experts argue that it was ISI that was responsible for merging HUM with another Pakistan-

based terrorist organization, Harakat-ul-Jihadi-i-Islami (HUJI), in 1993. The new group operated with the name Harakat ul-Ansar (HuA). During this period, the HUM conducted a number of operations against the Indian troops as well as civilians in Kashmir. Other leaders, including Maulana Masood Azhar and Ahmed Omar Sheikh, gained significant prominence within the group. They are thought to be the masterminds behind many of the killings and abductions organized by the group.

In 1997, the U.S. government labeled and banned HuA as a terrorist organization, issuing various reports stating that the group had strong links with Osama bin Laden's al-Qaeda, an already banned terrorist outfit that the government held responsible for a number of attacks on United States targets around the world. Although, the United States disagreed, Indian security forces and intelligence agencies claimed that the group was still operating under its earlier name, Harakat ul Mujahidin. In the subsequent years, the HUM was suspected to be the main driving force behind several killings in Kashmir. Analysts argued that the group had also started assisting in other jihad operations around the world, including those in Algeria, Egypt, Chechnya, and Bosnia.

Many members of the HUM were also involved in the infiltration into Kargil and Drass (parts of Indian-administered Kashmir) in 1999. Reports from the Indian Military and Intelligence agencies suggested that the infiltration was masterminded by leader of the Pakistani Army, Pervez Musharraf (as of 2005, the self-appointed president of Pakistan) and supported by the Pakistan government. After heavy fighting for days, the militants were driven back into Pakistan.

It was after the September 11, 2001, attacks in New York and Washington, D.C., that the U.S. government categorized the HUM as a terrorist organization and officially banned it. According to published U.S. State Department reports, as of 2005, the group also operates under the name Jamiat ul-Ansar (JUA) and has a few hundred members.

PHILOSOPHY AND TACTICS

HUM aims at establishing Islamic rule in the Indian-ruled state of Jammu & Kashmir by

LEADERSHIP

FAZLUR REHMAN KHALIL

Fazlur Rehman Khalil served as the leader of HUM right from its inception until the year 2000. As of 2005, Rehman is one of the most prominent terrorists in the world. He is reportedly hiding, especially since the U.S. government stepped up its efforts to capture him. He is thought to have close ties with Osama bin Laden and the former Taliban regime of Afghanistan. Many experts and monitor groups believe that he has mentored many Taliban members.

Reports suggest that Rehman was one of the signatories who signed Osama bin Laden's *fatwa* (declaration of war) against all Americans in 1998. Western and Indian intelligence agencies claim that Rehman has been responsible for setting up a large number of terrorist training camps across Afghanistan, Pakistan, and Pakistan-occupied Kashmir.

Other prominent leaders of HUM include Farooq Kashmiri Khalil (who took over as leader of HUM after Rehman stepped down), Maulana Saadatullah Khan, and Maulana Masood Azhar (founder of the terrorist organization Jaish-e-Mohammed).

---

liberating it from India. Osama bin Laden and other members of al-Qaeda are the key sources of inspiration for HUM's ideology. Although, the group was formed with the mission of fighting Soviet forces in Afghanistan in the mid-1980s, it quickly shifted focus to jihad against Indian security forces in Kashmir.

Every new recruit to this group is compelled to follow the hardcore Islamic doctrine of jihad. The group condemns all non-Muslim ideologies and propagates Islamic supremacy. It is also against secular influences from the Western world.

Soon after the Soviet withdrawal from Afghanistan in the late 1980s, the HUM set up

KEY EVENTS

1993: The ISI (Pakistan's intelligence agency), allegedly merges HUM with Harakat ul–i–Islami (HUJI) to form the Harakat ul-Ansar (HuA).

1994: Prominent leaders of HuA, including Pakistani national Maulana Masood Azhar, captured by Indian security forces.

1995: Five western tourists abducted and allegedly killed by Al-Faran (a splinter group of HUM).

1997: The U.S. Government declares HuA as a terrorist organization.

1998: HUM calls for a *fatwa* (holy war) against the United States.

1999: HUM members hijack an Indian Airlines flight and take it to Kandahar, Afghanistan. They demand the release of Azhar and other leaders in exchange for the hostages, which is eventually met by the Indian government.

2001: U.S. government declares the HUM as a terrorist organization.

---

training camps in Pakistan to assist other militant groups fighting the liberation of Indian-governed Kashmir. During this time, the group borrowed its ideology from a number of extremist organizations apart from al-Qaeda. These included other groups based in Pakistan such as the Harakal ul-Jihad-i-Islami, and the International Islamic Front for jihad.

The U.S. and Indian governments have alleged in the past that the ISI of Pakistan provided major funding to HUM until the Pakistani government cracked down on the operations of the outfit as a result of international pressure after the September 11 attacks in the United States. It is also suspected that other terrorist groups, *madrassas* (Islamic schools), and private donations supplement their funding.

Analysts suggest that the group, over the years, has also developed strong links with

PRIMARY SOURCE

Harakat ul-Mujahidin (HUM) a.k.a. Harakat ul-Ansar

DESCRIPTION

HUM is an Islamist militant group based in Pakistan that operates primarily in Kashmir. It is politically aligned with the radical political party Jamiat Ulema-i-Islam's Fazlur Rehman faction (JUI-F). The long-time leader of the group, Fazlur Rehman Khalil, in mid-February 2000 stepped down as HUM emir, turning the reins over to the popular Kashmiri commander and his second-in-com-mand, Farooqi Kashmiri. Khalil, who has been linked to Usama Bin Ladin and signed his fatwa in February 1998 calling for attacks on U.S. and Western interests, assumed the position of HUM Secretary General. HUM operated terrorist training camps in eastern Afghanistan until Coalition air strikes destroyed them during fall 2001. Khalil was detained by the Pakistanis in mid-2004 and subsequently released in late December. In 2003, HUM began using the name Jamiat ul-Ansar (JUA), and Pakistan banned JUA in November 2003.

ACTIVITIES

Has conducted a number of operations against Indian troops and civilian targets in Kashmir. Linked to the Kashmiri militant group al-Faran that kidnapped five Western tourists in Kashmir in July 1995; one was killed in August 1995, and the other four reportedly were killed in December of the same year. HUM was responsible for the hijacking of an Indian airliner on December 24, 1999, which resulted in the release of Masood Azhar. Azhar, an important leader in the former Harakat ul-Ansar, was imprisoned by the Indians in 1994 and founded Jaish-e-Muhammad after his release. Also released in 1999 was Ahmed Omar Sheik, who was convicted of the abduc-tion/murder in January-February 2002 of US journalist Daniel Pearl.

STRENGTH

Has several hundred armed supporters located in Azad Kashmir, Pakistan, and India's southern Kashmir and Doda regions and in the Kashmir valley. Supporters are mostly Pakistanis and Kashmiris and also include Afghans and Arab veterans of the Afghan war. Uses light and heavy machineguns, assault rifles, mortars, explosives, and rockets. HUM lost a significant share of its membership in defections to the Jaish-e-Mohammed (JEM) in 2000.

LOCATION/AREA OF OPERATION

Based in Muzaffarabad, Rawalpindi, and several other towns in Pakistan, but members conduct insurgent and terrorist activities primarily in Kashmir. HUM trained its militants in Afghanistan and Pakistan.

EXTERNAL AID

Collects donations from Saudi Arabia, other Gulf and Islamic states, Pakistanis and Kashmiris. HUM's financial collection methods also include soliciting donations in magazine ads and pamphlets. The sources and amount of HUM's military funding are unknown. In anticipation of asset seizures in 2001 by the Pakistani Government, the HUM withdrew funds from bank accounts and invested in legal businesses, such as commodity trading, real estate, and production of consumer goods. Its fundraising in Pakistan has been constrained since the Government clampdown on extremist groups and freezing of terrorist assets.

Source: U.S. Department of State. *Country Reports on Terrorism.* Washington, D.C., 2004.

Muslim insurgency groups in the other areas of the world. These include Abu Sayaff, the Bangsamoro Islamic Armed Forces (BIAF), and the Moro Islamic Liberation Front from the Philippines, as well as a few groups operating in the Middle East.

The HUM, as part of its strategy, has also changed names and combined with other militant outfits to avoid ramifications of the ban placed by the U.S., Indian, and Pakistani governments. The group stepped up its operations against Indian forces after the arrest of some of its key leaders such as Maulana Masood Azhar and Ahmed Omar Sheikh in 1994. Omar Sheikh was convicted of the kidnapping and murder, in 2002, of the *Wall Street Journal* reporter Daniel Pearl.

Since the arrest of the leaders in late 1999, the HUM's tactics were primarily aimed at kidnapping/killing Indian security force personnel and foreign tourists from Kashmir in a bid to release the captured leaders. Azhar, Omar Sheikh, and others were finally released in December 1999, when HUM members reportedly hijacked an Indian Airlines flight carrying more than 150 passengers from Katmandu, Nepal. The flight was taken to Kandahar, Afghanistan (then ruled by the Taliban regime).

Soon after his release, Azhar formed the Jaish-e-Mohammed (JeM) in Pakistan. Intelligence agencies and monitor groups report that the HUM's operations have been severely affected since most of its members joined the JeM in 2000. They also argue that due to the crack down by the Pakistani government, the group has allegedly removed its funds from bank accounts and invested them in legal businesses in Pakistan.

OTHER PERSPECTIVES

Harakat ul Mujahidin's leaders have often spoken about their enmity against India. It is also reportedly against the peace process between India and Pakistan. In 1999, Fazlur Rehman Khalil publicly opposed the visit of A.B. Vajpayee (Prime Minister of India, at the time) to Lahore, Pakistan. Before the visit, Rehman stated "Islam's enmity with India is ideological and not just territorial. More bodies of Indian officials would be sent in coffins from Kashmir on the days Vajpayee visits Lahore."

Indian authorities and leaders have consistently linked the HUM with al-Qaeda and the Taliban. In October 2001, soon after the terrorist attacks in the United States, the then Indian Foreign Minister Jaswant Singh stated in a press conference that, "The al-Qaeda network, it will be interesting to know for you, has a number of terrorist organisations that are operating in Jammu and Kashmir and in India. So, when al-Qaeda is targeted, these terrorist organisations

are all targeted. Amongst them is Harkat-ul-Mujahideen, Hizb-ul-Mujahideen, Jaish-e-Muhammad, Lashkar-e-Tayyaba and also there is one organisation that operates in Bangladesh called Harkat-ul-Jehad of Islam. These are organisations that are part of the al-Qaeda network that have already been announced."

At this time, Pakistani President Pervez Musharraf reportedly denied the existence of any of the militant groups in Pakistan. News reports have often quoted him comparing these organizations to "freedom fighters" fighting for the independence of Kashmir.

SUMMARY

The Harakat ul Mujahidin (a.k.a. Harakat ul Ansar) gained prominence among the various militant groups operating in Kashmir during the 1990s. They have reportedly carried out a number of terror operations against the Indian military and civilians in Kashmir (Jammu & Kashmir). However, Western and Indian intelligence agencies assert that since 2000, most of its members have joined the Jaish-e-Mohammed—another terrorist organization formed by Masood Azhar, a former leader of HUM.

The HUM has been designated a terrorist outfit by most governments in the world.

SOURCES

Web sites

CNN.com. "India Launches Major Ground Assault in Kashmir; Talks Set with Pakistan." < http://edition.cnn.com/WORLD/asiapcf/9905/29/india.pakistan.02 > (accessed October 19, 2005).

Embassy of India, Washington D.C. "Profile of the Terrorist Group Involved in Hijacking of Indian Airlines Flight IC-814." < http://www.indianembassy.org/pic/PR_1999/December_99/PR_Dec_27_1999.html > (accessed October 19, 2005).

Ministry of External Affairs, India. "Transcript of Press Conference by Shri Jaswant Singh, External Affairs and Defense Minister." < http://meaindia.nic.in/mediainter action/2001/10/11mi01.htm > (accessed October 19, 2005).

SAPRA India. "Indian Airlines Plane Hijack: Background Articles." < http://www.subcontinent.com/sapra/terrorism/harkat > (accessed October 19, 2005).

Hezbollah

ALTERNATE NAMES: Hizballah, Party of God

LEADER: Mohammed Hussein Fadlallah

USUAL AREA OF OPERATION: Lebanon; occasional incursions into northern Israel

Hezbollah (Party of God) is a Shi'ite political and military party in Lebanon, founded with extensive Iranian backing in 1982 to fight Israel in the country's south. Hezbollah is regarded by Israel and many Western states as an Islamist terrorist organization, and was designated a terrorist organization by the U.S. Department of State in October 1997. However, its political arm is an important part of Lebanon's democratically elected coalition government, and it maintains extensive civilian interests, including hospitals, schools, as well as television and radio stations and a newspaper.

HISTORY

The Lebanese Civil War (1975–1990) was not one war, but many. What began as a civil conflict between three of Lebanon's twenty-three ethnic communities, escalated beyond all recognition, ensnaring all of its minorities and several of its neighbors in what became one of the twentieth century's most prolonged and bitter wars. At various stages of the fighting, allies became enemies and enemies became allies; groups previously at peace with their neighbors became entangled, either through compulsion or necessity, with appalling results. Foreign powers also

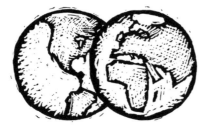

Lebanese posters depicting martyrs and religious leaders. © *Paolo Pellegrin | Magnum Photos*

became drawn in, usually to preserve their own regional position, or as a way of settling old scores.

Indeed, it was because of outside intervention that Lebanon's civil war became so bloody and prolonged and initial quarrels among Lebanese tended to become forgotten and distorted. This outside involvement extended to West Germany and Belgium arming Christian militias; the invasion of Syrian troops; the arrival of 1,500 Islamic Revolutionary Guards from Iran; Palestinian refugees based in south Lebanon organizing into militias; and latterly, Western peacekeepers.

Most incendiary of all, however, were attacks from Israel in 1978, followed by a full-scale invasion of south Lebanon in 1982. Comprehensively defeated by the Israeli army, a coalition of Shi'ite militias and other organizations united under the direction of Iran as the Lebanese National Resistance—which later became known as Hezbollah, or "Party of

God." It also received military and financial assistance from Syria.

This new movement comprised two main but quite different components of Lebanon's Shi'ite population. The first was from Shi'ite clans in Lebanon's Bekaa Valley, which had enjoyed increased prosperity through opium and marijuana cultivation and smuggling during the civil conflict. Encouraged by Iranian agents operating in their province, they saw it as an opportunity to create a populist Shi'ite movement and replicate the revolution in Iran three years earlier. Ba'labakk, the Bekaa Valley's capital, became a center for this emergent movement with its buildings plastered with posters depicting the Iranian leader, Ayatollah Khomeini, and draped with Iranian flags.

It also appealed to Shi'ite refugees forced to live in south Beirut's appalling slums. Many had ended up there following Phalangist (Christian-backed militias) attacks on Palestinians living in East Beirut in 1976, and were joined by refugees after Israel's invasions of south Lebanon in 1978 and 1982. For them, economically dispossessed and forced to live in horrific poverty and terror because of Phalangist and Israeli incursions, the call for a Shi'ite *jihad* (holy war) was particularly appealing.

In its early life, Hezbollah operated largely in the shadows, albeit with the capability of carrying out horrific acts of terror. It was not until 1985 that the movement emerged as a coherent organization propagating an open manifesto. In mosques, which became rallying points for Lebanon's Shi'ites, Hezbollah's spiritual leader, Mohammed Hussein Fadlallah, and his *uluma* preached a message of resistance to their enemies and loyalty to Khomeini. Iranian forces trained a semi-clandestine militia, the Islamic Resistance, which attacked Israeli forces in south Lebanon. This militia fought a guerilla-type war against the occupying force and was also responsible for a number of attacks across the Israeli border. Finally, the Organization of the Islamic Jihad emerged. This organization operated on a more covert basis with Syrian backing against Western targets after the introduction of a multinational peacekeeping force in August 1982.

In part because of who its targets were, but largely because of the particularly savage nature of its attacks, this group emerged as the most notorious part of the nascent Shi'ite resistance.

Hezbollah guerrillas holding their flag in the disputed Chebaa Farms region in south Lebanon on April 10, 2002. AP/Wide World Photos. Reproduced by permission.

Kidnappings and assassinations of individual foreigners quickly escalated into huge bombings against U.S., French, and Italian peacekeepers. The most brutal of these attacks were a truck bombing of the U.S. embassy on April 18, 1983, which killed sixty-three people; the Beirut barracks bombing of October 23, 1983, which killed 241 servicemen; and an identical attack on French barracks that same morning, which killed fifty-eight French peacekeepers; and a second bombing of the U.S. embassy on September 20, 1984, which killed twenty-three, including two military personnel.

The Beirut barracks bombing, which is the largest terrorist attack ever carried out against a U.S. military installation and was described by the FBI as the biggest non-nuclear bomb they had ever seen, resulted in the United States withdrawing its peacekeeping force from Lebanon. It also prompted the CIA to sponsor a mission by Elie Hobeika, a notorious Phalangist leader who

was responsible for the slaughter of 2,000 Palestinians in the refugee camps of Sabra and Shatila in 1982, to assassinate Fadlallah. In the failed attempt to kill him in a car bombing in March 1985, Hobeika claimed the lives of eighty innocent bystanders.

Hezbollah emerged as a coherent hierarchical organization in 1985 following the publication of an "open letter," which proclaimed its doctrine: "We are proceeding toward a battle with vice at its very roots," declared the letter, "and the first root of vice is America." The letter set out four objectives for the movement: the termination of all American and French influence in Lebanon; Israel's complete departure from Lebanon "as a prelude to its final obliteration"; submission of the Lebanese Phalangists to "just rule" and trial for their "crimes"; and granting the people the right to choose their own system of government, "keeping in mind that

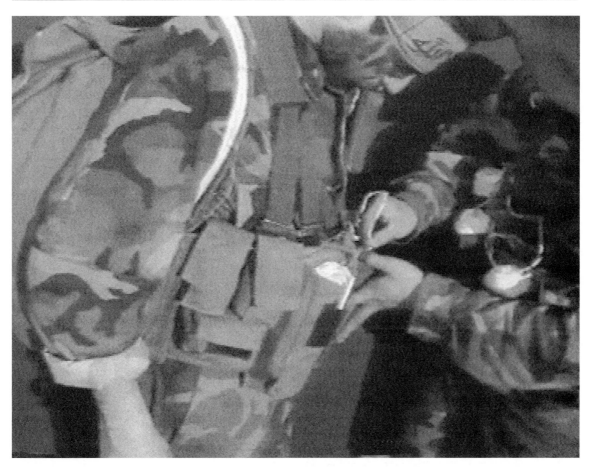

A Hezbollah suicide bomber in southern Lebanon has explosives strapped to him as another militant inserts a detonator in his vest in response to Hezbollah Secretary General Hassan Nasrallah's rally cry for "martyrdom fighters" to report for duty. AP/Wide World Photos. Reproduced by permission.

we do not hide our commitment to the rule of Islam."

In June 1985, the hijacking of TWA flight 847 by Islamic Jihad/Hezbollah operatives brought the organization further notoriety. Following protracted negotiations and the murder of a U.S. marine, the hostages on board were released in exchange for 700 Shi'ite militants held in Israeli jails since the invasion of south Lebanon in 1982. It also conducted hijackings of Kuwaiti airliners in 1984 and 1988 to win the freedom of Lebanese Shi'ites held in Kuwait.

Hezbollah also initiated a campaign of high-profile kidnapping. Its targets included U.S. Colonel William R. Higgins and the CIA Station Chief in Beirut, William Buckley (both of whom were killed); the journalists Terry

Anderson (held from March 1985 to November 1991) and John McCarthy (April 1986 to August 1991); the Archbishop of Canterbury's special envoy, Terry Waite (February 1987 to November 1991); and Brian Keenan, an Irish lecturer at Beirut's American University (April 1986 to August 1990). The taking of Western civilians seemed particularly senseless given the removal of outside forces from Lebanon and the lack of political demands that accompanied their kidnappings.

Hezbollah also did battle with other Shi'ite groups, notably the rival Amal militia, which was formed on more secular lines. Skirmishes for control of south Lebanon in 1988 erupted into full-scale civil war, at a cost of more than 1,000 lives until a peace deal was brokered by Syria and Iran.

LEADERSHIP

MOHAMMED HUSSEIN FADLALLAH

Just as a cleric, Ayatollah Ruhollah Khomeini had emerged to unite Iran's Shi'ite population and lead the country into a revolutionary era, so Mohammed Hussein Fadlallah led and united Lebanon's Shi'ite population after Israel's ruinous and comprehensive invasion in 1982. Fadlallah was born in the Iraqi city of Najaf in November 1935, moving to Lebanon as an Islamic scholar when he was sixteen. A poet and radical preacher, he railed against the failings of the Muslim people against a backdrop of a post-colonial era in which their homelands continued to be dominated by the West.

When, under Iranian direction, a populist Shi'ite movement emerged in the wake of Israel's occupation of Lebanon, and the intervention of Western peacekeepers, it was Fadlallah who emerged as its natural, if not titular, head. As the academic, Martin Kramer put it: "Obscure men carried out the acts of violence that made Hezbollah renowned . . . but it was the ubiquitous Fadlallah who processed the rage of Hezbollah into speech, in sermons and lectures, on tape and in print. Borne aloft on a wind of words, he made himself the voice of Hezbollah's conscience and its spokesman to the world. His very ubiquity suggested that he led the movement, a supposition that drew diplomats, mediators, and assassins to his door."

An alleged CIA-backed assassination failed in 1985, killing more than eighty bystanders, and Fadlallah was several times forced to retreat to Iran fearing for his safety.

Although the *fatwa* (struggle) he issued against any Muslim helping the United States occupy an Islamic country betrays a hardline instinct so common amongst ayatollahs, Fadlallah is relatively liberal in outlook, speaking out in favor of women's rights and against terrorism.

In essence, this formed the last stage of the Lebanese civil war. The Taif Agreement, which brought an end to the conflict in 1990, required all militias to disarm, but the Lebanese government made no attempt to disarm Hezbollah, given that it effectively controlled the frontier with Israel and prevented Israeli forces from making incursions further into Lebanon. Despite repeated promises that Israel would withdraw from south Lebanon, it continued to occupy a fifteen-kilometer strip until May 2000.

In this fractured nation, Hezbollah continued to operate as a militia, and in places was the only form of defense against Israeli attacks in south Lebanon. Hezbollah would respond to incursions with its own attacks on Israeli forces and also on Israeli citizens elsewhere in the world. Hezbollah was blamed for the 1992 bombing of the Israeli Embassy in Buenos Aires, which killed twenty-nine, and of a Jewish culture center in the same city two years later, killing eighty-five.

Israel, for its part, used its foothold in south Lebanon to launch sporadic attacks and sting operations to capture or assassinate militant leaders. This included the abduction of a pro-Hezbollah cleric, Sheik Abd al-Karim Ubayd, in 1989; and the killing with helicopter gunships of its secretary-general, Sayyid Abbas al-Musawi, and his family, in an attack on his motorcade in 1992. During "Operation Grapes of Wrath" in April 1996, an extended Israeli operation against south Lebanese militants, hundreds of civilians were killed, including 102 at the UN compound at Qana. An Amnesty International report into the operation gave equal blame to both the Israeli army and to Hezbollah for not respecting the laws of war.

The end of the Lebanese civil war also served as the prompt for Hezbollah to diverge into various other areas. Generously funded by the Iranian government and also with considerable funds from its own business and charitable ventures, Hezbollah came to exist as a wide-

KEY EVENTS

1982: Emerges as Lebanese National Resistance, an amalgamation of Shi'ite-based militia under Iranian influence following Israel's invasion of south Lebanon.

1983: Truck bombing of U.S. embassy in Beirut kills sixty-three.

1983: Simultaneous bombings of U.S. and French barracks kills 241 and fifty-eight servicemen, respectively.

1984: Kidnapping of CIA Beirut Chief, William Buckley, marks onset of Hezbollah campaign of kidnapping Western targets, both military and civilian.

1984: Second bombing of U.S. embassy kills twenty-three.

1985: Hezbollah issues its "open letter," declaring its doctrine.

1985: Hezbollah-offshoot Islamic Jihad blamed for the hijacking of TWA Flight 847.

1988–1990: Hezbollah involved in bloody dispute with rival Shi'ite militia, Amal.

1990: The Taif Agreement, which brings an end to the Lebanese Civil War, also marks Hezbollah's rebirth as a political movement. It also serves as Lebanon's *de facto* defense forces on its southern border, which Israel continued to occupy until 2000.

2005: After winning twenty-three seats to Lebanon's 128-seat Parliament, Hezbollah becomes part of a coalition government.

ranging movement, building and operating schools, hospitals, and orphanages. In 1992, it participated in free elections, winning twelve out of 128 seats in Lebanon's Parliament. By 2005, it had increased its electoral showing to twenty-three seats and formed part of a coalition government, this despite opposing the "Cedar Revolution," which had prompted the withdrawal of Syrian troops from Lebanon.

Nevertheless, Hezbollah continues to be tainted with accusations of extremism. It is still embroiled in border skirmishes with Israel in south Lebanon, although these have declined since Israel's withdrawal in 2000. Israel has accused Hezbollah of organizing suicide bombings during the al-Aqsa intifada, although there is no proof of this. Israel, for its part, however, continues to target Hezbollah officials in bombings and assassinations on Lebanese soil, a direct contravention of international law. Although it is fiercely anti-Zionist and anti-Western in many of its sentiments, Hezbollah is not overtly anti-Semitic (although its television station has been accused of anti-Semitic broadcasts), in contrast to many Islamist organizations. Its continued links with Iran and Syria, both regarded by the United States president George W. Bush as existing as an "axis of evil," remain a cause for concern among U.S. security officials, although accusations in the American media that Hezbollah has ties to al-Qaeda are almost certainly nonsense.

PHILOSOPHY AND TACTICS

Hezbollah is a Shi'ite political movement that favors the creation of an Islamic Republic in Lebanon modeled on that of Iran. However, it supports democratic measures to bring this about. In Hezbollah's view, Islam alone will redeem Lebanon from its troubled history of civil war and foreign intervention, which, it says, are the consequence of Lebanon's attempts to Westernize itself.

During the Lebanese Civil War, it adopted a two-pronged strategy to fight outside forces. Against Israel, primarily in the south of Lebanon, it waged a guerilla war, with "hit and run" assaults against defense installations, but also rocket attacks at Israeli settlements. This continued during Israel's prolonged occupation of south Lebanon until 2000. Against Western peacekeepers, it launched suicide bomb attacks of horrific intensity. Commonly, this would consist of a truck loaded with TNT driven into a military installation. In both instances, this "war" was fought by men who had accepted the call of Shi'ite clerics for jihad.

Hezbollah's campaign of jihad also included hijackings, kidnappings, and occasionally attacks against Jewish or Israeli interests on foreign soil. Often, the motivations for such attacks

PRIMARY SOURCE

Hizballah a.k.a. Party of God, Islamic Jihad, Islamic Jihad for the Liberation of Palestine

DESCRIPTION

Formed in 1982 in response to the Israeli invasion of Lebanon, this Lebanon-based radical Shia group takes its ideological inspiration from the Iranian revolution and the teachings of the late Ayatollah Khomeini. The Majlis al-Shura, or Consultative Council, is the group's highest governing body and is led by Secretary General Hasan Nasrallah. Hizballah is dedicated to liberating Jerusalem and eliminating Israel, and has formally advocated ultimate establishment of Islamic rule in Lebanon. Nonetheless, Hizballah has actively participated in Lebanon's political system since 1992. Hizballah is closely allied with, and often directed by, Iran but has the capability and willingness to act independently. Though Hizballah does not share the Syrian regime's secular orientation, the group has been a strong ally in helping Syria advance its political objectives in the region.

ACTIVITIES

Known or suspected to have been involved in numerous anti-U.S. and anti-Israeli terrorist attacks, including the suicide truck bombings of the U.S. Embassy and U.S. Marine barracks in Beirut in 1983 and the U.S. Embassy annex in Beirut in 1984. Three members of Hizballah, 'Imad Mughniyah, Hasan Izz-al-Din, and Ali Atwa, are on the FBI's list of 22 Most Wanted Terrorists for the 1985 hijacking of TWA Flight 847 during which a US Navy diver was murdered. Elements of the group were responsible for the kidnapping and detention of Americans and other Westerners in Lebanon in the 1980s. Hizballah also attacked the Israeli Embassy in Argentina in 1992 and the Israeli cultural center in Buenos Aires in 1994. In 2000, Hizballah operatives captured three Israeli soldiers in the Shab'a Farms and kidnapped an Israeli noncombatant.

Hizballah also provides guidance and financial and operational support for Palestinian

could appear as they were not always followed by a political statement or set of demands.

Since the end of the Lebanese Civil War, Hezbollah has merged into the mainstream and wide-ranging political movement. As well as contesting democratic elections with some success, it has been involved in implementing social policy in parts of the country, including schools, hospitals, orphanages, and clinics. At the same time, it has maintained a militia to protect Lebanon's southern border with Israel.

OTHER PERSPECTIVES

Robert Fisk is a veteran Middle East correspondent, whose book about the Lebanese Civil War, *Pity the Nation*, remains the classic account of the era. Terry Anderson, the U.S. journalist kidnapped by Hezbollah in 1985, is one of Fisk's closest friends, and for years Fisk lived in fear

that he too would suffer the same fate. Writing in 2002, at a time when another of his journalist friends, Daniel Pearl, had been kidnapped in Pakistan, he reflected that the kidnapping of journalists was the biggest goal such a movement could commit. "Back in the mid-to-late 1980s, journalists were culled by the hostage-takers of Beirut... and death threats were a regular occurrence," he wrote. "I remember spending an hour searching for my friend Terry Anderson's body on a garbage tip—a story I was thankfully able to tell him in person after his release almost seven years later. I met some of those kidnappers, tough, uncompromising men of ruthless determination.

"But they made one serious political error. Once foreigners were kidnapped, almost every Western journalist fled Beirut. Although *The Independent* kept operating... Lebanon's tragedy fell out of the news. No one read or heard of the great battles being fought between Hezbollah and the occupying Israeli army in

extremist groups engaged in terrorist operations in Israel and the occupied territories.

In 2004, Hizballah launched an unmanned aerial vehicle (UAV) that left Lebanese airspace and flew over the Israeli town of Nahariya before crashing into Lebanese territorial waters. Ten days prior to the event, the Hizballah Secretary General said Hizballah would come up with new measures to counter Israeli Air Force violations of Lebanese airspace. Hizballah also continued launching small scale attacks across the Israeli border, resulting in the deaths of several Israeli soldiers. In March 2004, Hizballah and HAMAS signed an agreement to increase joint efforts to perpetrate attacks against Israel. In late 2004, Hizballah's al-Manar television station, based in Beirut with an estimated ten million viewers worldwide, was prohibited from broadcasting in France. Al-Manar was placed on the Terrorist Exclusion List (TEL) in the United States, which led to its removal from the program offerings of its main cable service provider, and

made it more difficult for al-Manar associates and affiliates to operate in the United States.

STRENGTH

Several thousand supporters and a few hundred terrorist operatives.

LOCATION/AREA OF OPERATION

Operates in the southern suburbs of Beirut, the Beka'a Valley, and southern Lebanon. Has established cells in Europe, Africa, South America, North America, and Asia.

EXTERNAL AID

Receives financial, training, weapons, explosives, political, diplomatic, and organizational aid from Iran, and diplomatic, political, and logistical support from Syria. Hizballah also receives funding from charitable donations and business interests.

Source: U.S. Department of State. *Country Reports on Terrorism*. Washington, D.C., 2004.

the south of the country—save, of course, from Israel itself—and the terrible suffering of the Palestinian camps under siege by a Lebanese militia was a story largely untold. The Hezbollah, around which these kidnap groups floated like satellites, now acknowledges that hostage-taking was a major blunder, an own goal of the worst kind, quite apart from the inhumanity of imprisoning the innocent and threatening their lives. If Israel could not persuade the United States to put the Hezbollah on America's 'terrorist' list, the kidnappings would have done the trick. The argument that national resistance should not be confused with 'terrorism' was never heard—because the journalists who should have reported it were either locked up or running away."

The former *Jerusalem Post* editor and fierce defender of Israeli policy, David Bar-Illan, wrote in the wake of the TWA hijacking in 1985 that the kidnappers had waged an astute campaign to

garner global opinion, while at the same time portraying Israel as the *bete noire* of the piece.

"The hijackers and their supporters, whose sensitivity to media techniques and moods has been a source of wonder to communication experts, were quick to recognize a public-relations bonanza when they saw it," wrote Bar-Illan. "By sticking to this one demand alone, they had television networks throughout the West acting as their mouthpiece, and at their disposal the round-the-clock services of the world's most influential opinion-molders. Like the media, they themselves quickly dropped all their other demands and concentrated on Israel.

"So the familiar scene was set: on one side persecuted Arabs, 'understandably enraged' by horrible injustices, making 'reasonable' demands after all, they were entitled to the release of those prisoners, said American arbitration experts paraded before the cameras—and on the other side intransigent Israelis cold-bloodedly disregarding the fate of innocent people... Over and over again, television commentators, anchormen, and reporters, alternating hints with accusations, and assuming the roles of negotiators, arbiters, and moralizers, portrayed Israel as an ungrateful ally which had freed 1,150 convicted murderers in return for three Israeli soldiers, but would not free over 700 innocent Lebanese ('not charged with any crime') to save the lives of thirty-nine American tourists."

SUMMARY

Despite continuing to be tainted by accusations of extremism and terrorism, Hezbollah is carving a niche for itself as a political movement in post civil-war Lebanon. Its spiritual leader's disavowal of violence and support for women's rights, combined with an acknowledgement that some of its past actions were misguided, has prompted hopes that it can exist as a modern Islamist party. However, given the current concerns about Islamic extremism—particularly in light of its shadowy past—and the characterization of its two closest allies, Syria and Iran, as rogue nations mean it is unlikely to shake off its darker image.

SOURCES

Books

Fisk, Robert. *Pity the Nation.* Oxford: Oxford Press, 2001.

Tarik, Judith Palmer. *Hizbollah: The Changing Face of Terrorism.* London: I B Tauris, 2004.

Web sites

Martin Kramer on the Middle East. < http://www. martinkramer.org/pages/899526/index.htm > (accessed October 13, 2005).

US Memorial to Beirut Dead. "History: U.S. Embassy Bombing." < http://www.beirut—memorial.org/history/ embassy.html > (accessed October 13, 2005).

Institute for Historical Review

LEADER: Mark Weber

USUAL AREA OF OPERATION: United States

OVERVIEW

The Institute for Historical Review (IHR) claims to be an academic cooperative of independent scholars dedicated to historical revisionism, the critiquing mainstream historiography. IHR asserts that the Holocaust, or *Shoah*, was an elaborate hoax "concocted by world Jewry to gain support for the establishment of the Jewish state of Israel." IHR maintains that the Nazi government never embarked on the "Final Solution"; there were no death camps, no gas chambers, and no mass extermination of European Jews. The group further claims that the memory of the Holocaust, including the stories of survivors, is an elaborate—and conspiratorial—fabrication.

IHR maintains close ties to several neo-Nazi and anti-Semitic organizations, including the National Alliance and the Liberty Lobby. IHR continually employs rhetoric consistent with other anti-Semitic hate groups and is widely regarded by mainstream historians and watchdog groups, such as the Anti-Defamation League, as a leading force in the Holocaust denial movement.

HISTORY

Willis Carto founded the Institute for Historical Review in 1979. At that time, Carto spearheaded

Israeli Arab lawyer, Khaled Mahameed, left, sits in his private Holocaust institute in the northern Israeli Arab town of Nazareth. The institute hosts occasional lectures, provides informational brochures, and displays about 60 photos documenting the Holocaust. AP/Wide World Photos

the right-wing and anti-Semitic extremist group, Liberty Lobby. From the outset, IHR was dedicated to Holocaust denial. Carto organized IHR's founding convention. IHR's vigorous publishing arm began with the publication of conference materials. Within two years, Noontide Press published several pamphlets, booklets, articles, and IHR's flagship publication, the *Journal of Historical Review*.

IHR sought recognition from mainstream historians to legitimize its cause. When the first issue of *Journal of Historical Review* was published, IHR distributed the publication to members of the Organization of American Historians and the American Historical Association, as well as other prominent scholars. Both organizations, and most independent scholars, vehemently denounced the IHR's writings. The Organization of American Historians stated that the journal was "devoid of historical truth ... [and] nothing but a masquerade of scholarship."

Denounced by academia, the IHR and its *Journal of Historical Review* remained in relative public obscurity for several years. As a display of its devotion to "scholarship" and an affirmation to its members of its pursuit, IHR declared at its first conference that it would pay $50,000 to anyone "who could prove that the Nazis used gas chambers during World War II." IHR based much of its denial rhetoric on a perceived lack of concrete proof for the infamous death camp gas chambers. The group refuted the accepted historiography that substantiated the existence of gas chambers at camps like Auschwitz through coded Nazi communications, photographs, survivor testimony, (non-Jewish) concentration camp worker testimony, and archaeological evidence. IHR especially disavowed statements by Shoah survivors, claming that such stories were fictionalized accounts of life in "prison camps." IHR repeated its offer of reward in subsequent publications of its journal.

LEADERSHIP

MARK WEBER

Mark Weber has a lengthy history of association with numerous right-wing extremist, white supremacy, anti-Semitic groups. After receiving a master's degree in history from Indiana University, Weber accepted a position as news director for the National Alliance, a neo-Nazi organization. Weber's duties included overseeing publication of the group's magazine, the *National Vanguard*. During this time, Weber also contributed to *The Spotlight*, a tabloid produced by the Institute for Historical Review.

Weber rose quickly through the ranks of the IHR. He led the organization's annual conferences before joining the organization's editorial board. In 1992, he assumed editorship of the IHR's major publication, the *Journal of Historical Review*. Weber gained control of IHR in 1993 after the organization's board fired founder Willis Carto.

In 1981, Auschwitz survivor Mel Mermelstein came forward to challenge the IHR and claim the offered prize. Mermelstein submitted a formal, notarized statement to IHR detailing his arrival at Auschwitz. He survived selection, and was placed in a work detail. His sister and mother were separated from him and driven to the gas chambers. Mermelstein gave a detailed account of the layout of the camp, the selection of prisoners for work or immediate death, and the existence of the Krema, the gas chambers and crematoria. Mermelstein was denied the prize by IHR officials. He filed suit to recover the prize and seek redress for libel and the intentional infliction of emotional distress. In 1985, he prevailed in his claims against IHR, with the court noting that the events of the Holocaust were indisputable fact. After the Mermelstein trials, IHR could not avoid public label as a prominent denier organization. IHR continues to disclaim that it engages in Holocaust denial—

preferring instead to abuse the term "historical revisionism."

In 1993, Carto was replaced as leader of the IHR. The organization's board fired Carto for misusing organization finances (a battle that later was taken to court). Mark Weber, a long-time ranking member of IHR and one-time editor of the *Journal of Historical Review*, replaced Carto at the helm. Carto's Liberty Lobby then launched its own Holocaust denial publication, *The Barnes Review*.

In the 1990s, IHR become more outspoken. In the wake of the release of the film, *Schindler's List*, the IHR mailed denial propaganda to film critics, cinemas, and media. IHR provided written material used by other hate groups in their opposition to the film. The film went on to receive widespread public and critical acclaim, as well as spark a renewed interest in Holocaust history.

IHR members also covered the British libel trial of Emory University historian and professor of religious studies, Deborah Lipstadt. Lipstadt authored a book about the Holocaust denial movement. The book, *Denying the Holocaust*, frequently discussed the operation, tactics, and publications of self-styled "revisionist" groups, including IHR. British writer and IHR contributor, David Irving, sued Lipstadt in Britain for libel because she referred to Irving as a "Holocaust denier" and "racist." Organizations like IHR had shied away from the label "Holocaust denier," largely to help mask the underlying agenda of their writing—in other words, to deceive readers into thinking that they were reading mainstream, legitimate scholarship. Lipstadt eventually prevailed, but only after a long and embittered fight.

As of 2005, Mark Weber continues to lead the IHR. He has aligned the organization with other hate groups such as the National Alliance, Christian Identity Movement, and various neo-Nazi and skinhead organizations. In 2001, Weber attempted to organize an international conference on "Revisionism and Zionism" in Beruit, Lebanon. Weber wanted to broaden international support for Holocaust denial and anti-Israeli sentiment, especially among Arabs and other Muslims in the Middle East. The Lebanese government, bowing to pressure from the governments of Turkey, the United States, and Israel—as well as from international scholars—refused to permit the conference.

KEY EVENTS

1979: Willis A. Carto founds what eventually becomes the Institute for Historical Review. IHR publishes first pamphlet and conducts first radio broadcast on December 24.

1980: IHR begins publication of the *Journal of Historical Review*.

1985: Auschwitz survivor Mel Mermelstein attempts to collect a $50,000 reward offered by IHR for "concrete proof" of the use of gas chambers during the Holocaust. Mermelstein eventually prevails in court. The U.S. Superior Court in California declared in its ruling that the events of the Holocaust are "indisputable legal fact."

1993: Faction splits from Willis A. Carto and assumes leadership of IHR.

1996: IHR first publishes a collection of its materials on the Internet.

PHILOSOPHY AND TACTICS

Holocaust denial is perhaps the ultimate expression of anti-Semitic sentiment. Deniers seek to undermine the memory of the Shoah in order to glorify the Nazi regime of Adolf Hitler and the racist tenants of Nazism. Denial rhetoric often includes conspiracy theories on the abundance of Shoah survivor stories, the founding of Israel, and Jews in government.

IHR began disseminating its message through print materials such as pamphlets, tracts, and newsletters. Their initial recruitment tactic targeted members of white supremacist and neo-Nazi groups. However, IHR soon expanded its target audience, attempting to recruit academics and graduate students. With the publication of the first issue of the *Journal of Historical Review*, IHR launched

a new campaign to cast denial rhetoric as a legitimate vein of historical interpretation. IHR did manage to attract several core contributors, most of whom held master's or doctorate degrees in history. This group remained small; those who participated in IHR activities were rejected by the academic community and the *Journal of Historical Review* was roundly denounced as extremist.

As of 2005, IHR had returned to recruiting and disseminating materials within the sphere of English-speaking, international neo-Nazi, and right-wing extremist groups. Their primary means of publishing is via the Internet.

IHR continues to disavow the label of "Holocaust deniers." They maintain the position that their goal is to correct "false" and "pro-Jewish" mainstream histories that they claim are inaccurate. IHR has spread its tactics to other Holocaust denial groups, especially in Canada and Europe (where Holocaust denial is often prohibited by law). The sophistication of IHR's messages has increased. IHR produces scholarly looking web sites, articles, and documentaries, often featuring well-educated "revisionist authorities."

OTHER PERSPECTIVES

Historical revisionism, in the context of the Holocaust, is synonymous with Holocaust denial. There is no legitimate historiography that refutes the events of the Shoah. Historian Deborah Lipstadt stated during her libel trial that "merely to suggest the fact of the Holocaust ... is somehow open to debate is obscene." This view is echoed by every mainstream, legitimate historian, most of whom avow that scholars should never engage deniers in debate or public discussion.

Prominent Holocaust historians accuse Holocaust deniers of attempting to legitimize their agenda by cloaking it in the garb of methodical research: the ability to amass and cite publications and pore through archives. Richard Evans states that the duplicity of denial "scholarship" is what makes it so dangerous to the untrained eye. Denial propaganda can look seductively academic, but it is not legitimized by its mere appearance.

SUMMARY

The Anti-Defamation League asserts that the Institute for Historical Review is in decline. IHR has not published a new issue of its *Journal of Historical Review* since 2002, instead choosing to focus on publishing speeches, interviews, and articles on its main web site. IHR and members of several active neo-Nazi groups hosted a conference in California in 2004. As of 2005, that was the last public forum sponsored by IHR.

IHR remains active, though many of its members and most frequent contributors, including Ernst Zündel and David Irving, have increasingly chosen to publish works outside of the IHR's newsletters and journal.

SOURCES

Books

Evans, Richard J. *Lying about Hitler: History, Holocaust, and the David Irving Trial.* New York: Basic Books, 2002.

Lipstadt, Deborah E. *Denying the Holocaust: The Growing Assault on Truth and Memory.* New York: Plume (reprint edition), 1994.

Web sites

The Anti-Defamation League. "Institute for Historical Review (IHR): Outlet for Denial Propaganda" < http://www.adl.org/holocaust/ihr.asp > (accessed October 15, 2005).

SEE ALSO

National Alliance

Neo-Nazis

International Conspiratological Association

LEADER: Richard Masker
USUAL AREA OF OPERATION: Idaho

OVERVIEW

The International Conspiratological Association (ICA), sometimes known as the International Conspiratology Association, was created and is headed by Richard F. Masker. According to the Southern Poverty Law Center, the group is based in Idaho. The association's anti-Semitic rhetoric is centered on preventing the international Jewish population and their accomplices from destroying the "International White Race" and creating the "New World Order."

HISTORY

Richard Masker founded the ICA in 1982. His idea for the association grew from his realization of the existence of a communist conspiracy organized by the anti-white Jewish population while working at a drinking water facility in Pennsylvania. He decided to focus on ensuring the continued existence of the "White Racial People" for the remainder of his life, according to the organization's web site. He does this with the help of his wife Deon, as well as with other supporters of his cause. Masker appears to best reach possible sympathizers to his cause through the association's web site, where he sells merchandise with the phrase "White Pride World Wide" imprinted on it, suggests further readings

LEADERSHIP

RICHARD F. MASKER

Richard Masker founded the organization and continues to be its main leader as of August 2005. He worked in water facilities; first as executive manager of a drinking water facility in Pennsylvania, where he claims to have realized the presence of a Jewish communist conspiracy, and then he worked as a city water superintendent for Oregon. Since, he has been working on spreading the word about the "Conspiracy of the Jews," with a focus on making police agencies aware of this conspiracy, given that they have been main targets in the past of the Jewish population.

Masker also had a brief stint in politics when he ran for a minor position in Idaho in 2000. His goal in running was to spread his views on the Jewish conspiracy to the population and to promote awareness of its influence on the political arena. He did not succeed in obtaining the position, but he continued spreading his ideas through various paths. He supplies many articles, mainly through the association web site, expressing ways for potential members to learn more about the conspiracy as well as spread the word of its effects.

---

as well as provides his own articles for interested potential members, and offers to give lectures on his methodology.

financial domination." Masker intends to prevent Jews from dominating the lives of the American public fully and completely, in all aspects, according to their own agenda. Also explained on the web site is the necessity for political deprogramming, to secure the "history, culture and most of all...genetic existence" of the "White Racial People." Political deprogramming consists of talking to community members and making them aware of the conspiracy; undoing what the Jewish influence of the government has done to the population, in essence.

The introduction on the web site claims that the white race can destroy evil as well as "save and perfect every thing imaginable," while having "the infinite capacity for charity, love and compassion." The ICA does not see itself as a hate group, racist, white supremacist, or anti-Semitic. The group believes it is only realizing a great conspiracy, and trying to prevent the Jewish "World Government" from coming to power. Although the web site does not provide any specifics on how it plans to defeat the Jews, Masker claims in his article that "the tree of liberty is about to be heavily watered with the blood of Pro-NOW [New World Order] Marxist tyrants and their minions of Jewish World Congress secret societies and subversive groups." This suggests killing of some sort, but no further details are provided. Much of the group's aims are based on raising awareness about everything from the Jewish control of the political arena to their use of fluoridation in drinking water in order to create passiveness and servitude in the American public. Education surrounding the conspiracy is a central theme in many of the organization's reading materials, provided on its web site. Masker seems to suggest that before the group can take any further action, they must have a strong and knowledgeable membership base.

PHILOSOPHY AND TACTICS

The group uses Idaho as a home base, with Masker residing there. In an article by Masker himself, entitled "Vacation in Idaho: The Great Hate State," he claims Idaho is somewhere where "White Americans can safely visit their own Racial Family." The main goals of the group are to raise awareness of the so-called conspiracy of the Jews, and to ultimately, as stated on the association web site, "take the world back from International Jewish mental enslavement and

OTHER PERSPECTIVES

There is very limited coverage of the ICA, and most of the material that can be found on the group is provided by the group itself or by other extremist groups in accordance with the organization's teachings. One such web site, National Vanguard, is committed to breaking through censorship to provide hope to whites. This web site has an article from Richard Masker entitled "On the Road Again," which explains the

KEY EVENTS

1982: Richard Masker founded the International Conspiratological Association (ICA).

2000: Masker ran for a minor political position in Idaho.

intentions of the ICA to create signs that can be attached to vehicles that have messages like "Zionist Treason Rules America." Although there is not any commentary from the web site itself on the organization, its display of Masker's article suggests that it supports the group's mission. There are several other web sites that accomplish similar tasks, but most literature related to the group is written by Masker himself.

SUMMARY

The International Conspiratological Association continues to operate and carry out its vision of educating the white race about the Jewish Zionist forces at work in America, as of August 2005. News coverage of the group is few and far between, and can mainly be found in news sources closest to Idaho. The group continues to provide anti-Semitic articles and information on its web site covering the revelation of the Jewish influence in America and how to spread the word to others. Although there is no information provided about the membership of the group, or any other such statistics, Masker is still fighting for the cause so near and dear to him.

SOURCES

Web sites

Southern Poverty Law Center. "Active U.S. Hate Groups in 2004." < http://www.splcenter.org/intel/map/hate.jsp? T = 22&m = 3 > (accessed September 28, 2005).

The Spokesman-Review.com. "Our Cops Doing a Lot More Than Just Wingin' It." < http://www.spokesmanreview.com/news-story.asp?date = 011204&ID = s1470404 > (accessed September 28, 2005).

The Spokesman-Review.com. "Pischner Up against White Supremacist Foe." < http://www.spokesmanreview.com/pf.asp?date = 102100&ID = s868919 > (July 31, 2005).

International Revolutionary Action Group

OVERVIEW

The International Revolutionary Action Group was an extremist organization that operated in the early 1970s. The group was based in France and was known in French as *Groupes d'Action Révolutionnaire Internationaliste* (GARI).

GARI, as thought by most experts, operated only briefly during the 1970s. Although not much is know about its operations, reports do suggest that the group's main mission was the freedom of Spain and Europe in general from dictatorship. The group reportedly became inactive in 1975.

LEADER: Salavador Puig-Antich

USUAL AREA OF OPERATION: Spain, France, Belgium

HISTORY

From 1939 to his death in 1975, Francisco Franco Bahamonde served as the dictator of Spain. During his rule, Franco is thought to have suppressed many, including people belonging to the Basque community. This community has been primarily based in the Basque region of northern Spain, southern France, and Belgium. The International Revolutionary Action Group was reportedly formed in 1974, in France. Its primary objective, according to monitor groups, was to free the Basque people and create a separate Basque state.

LEADERSHIP

SALAVADOR PUIG-ANTICH

Not much is known about the leaders of the International Revolutionary Action Group. Most analysts and news reports suggest that Salavador Puig-Antich was the most prominent militant from GARI.

Salavador Puig-Antich was allegedly a Basque militant. His main objective was freedom of the Basque region from the dictatorship of Franco. Antich is thought to be the mastermind behind most terrorist operations carried out by GARI during its short existence.

Salavador Puig-Antich was executed by officials of the Spanish dictatorship. According to reports, the weapon that was used was a garotte, a common torture device used during that period.

The entire history of GARI is known to be very brief. Most analysts state the group operated for a short period from 1974–1975. During this period, group members mainly targeted government entities in Spain and Belgium (Spanish targets in Belgium). The first attacks were reported in Belgium soon after the group's inception.

In May 1974, Belgium authorities accused GARI of an attack on the office of Iberia Airlines (the official airlines of Spain) in Brussels. Although no one died in the attack, the office building reportedly suffered severe damage. In the same month, GARI also claimed responsibility for attacks on Spanish banks in Paris. Members of the group reportedly also kidnapped some bankers and later released them in exchange for a ransom. After a few days, GARI was allegedly involved in bomb explosions in some offices in Paris, including that of IBM.

According to analysts, GARI's intentions to attack Spanish targets were quite evident from all their operations, including bombings of many buses in Lourdes, France, in July 1974. The buses were reportedly part of the Tour de France. Allegedly, the attack was carried out because many Spanish bicyclists had taken part in the Tour de France.

Subsequently, later in 1974, the International Revolutionary Action Group claimed responsibility for a number of attacks on Spanish banks as well as, again, on offices of Iberia Airlines in Brussels. According to reports, there were no deaths. However, many people were injured and there was considerable property damage.

Similar attacks on businesses, transportation, and government buildings were reported throughout 1974 and 1975. Officials suspected GARI members behind most of these attacks. The last reported attack carried out by GARI was in May 1975. As thought by analysts and monitor groups, the group became inactive after 1975. Since then, there have been no reports of activities or operations carried out by the International Revolutionary Action Group.

Many French government officials, monitor groups, and anti-terrorism experts believe that the dissolution of GARI resulted in the formation of other terrorist organizations. *Action Directe* (AD) is the most prominent. AD, a terror organization that was formed in the late 1970s, is considered by many to be an extension of the International Revolutionary Action Group.

PHILOSOPHY AND TACTICS

The International Revolutionary Action Group was reportedly formed with a mission of separating the Basque region of Spain from the dictatorial regime of Francisco Franco. However, many analysts state that the GARI had broader objectives, which included their fight against fascism, and on the whole, the liberation of Spain and other countries of Europe.

GARI was thought to comprise a blend of Basque militants (whose sole purpose was the freedom of Basque) and French anarchists. The group claimed to be against any and all forms of government in European countries. According to experts on extremism, the objective of a free Basque region was mainly due to the group's alleged links with *Euzkadi Ta Askatasuna* (ETA), a terrorist organization based in Spain. The ETA was mainly comprised of Basque militants, and it is thought that many of GARI's operations were influenced by the ETA.

KEY EVENTS

1974: GARI was formed in May.

1974: The GARI members allegedly attacked the office of Iberia Airlines in Brussels, Belgium. The group members also claimed responsibility for kidnapping some bankers from a Spanish bank in Paris. The bankers were later freed in exchange of a ransom.

1974: Group members claimed responsibility for blowing up thirteen buses that were part of the Tour de France.

1975: The last attack by GARI; the group is thought to be inactive since.

To promote its philosophies, GARI reportedly used a number of violent tactics, including bombings and kidnappings. According to reports, the targets were mainly Spanish establishments in France and Belgium as well as in Spain itself. Throughout its history, GARI is known to have bombed Spanish banks, businesses, Spanish transportation agencies, Spanish airlines and airports, Spanish consulates in France, sporting events involving Spaniards, and so on. Analysts argue that most of the terrorist operations of the group resulted in major structural damage to these establishments, in addition to injuries to people. However, there were no deaths reported. This, as thought by most experts, shows that GARI mainly targeted the Spanish government, and not the people.

GARI reportedly also organized joint activities with the ETA. One of the most prominent joint operations was the bombing of the "Topo," trains running between Madrid (in Spain) and Paris. Apart from joint operations, exchange of personnel and arms between the groups was also thought to be common practice. Some anti-terrorism reports also allege that GARI, in association with ETA, had started smuggling arms to Belgium and other European countries.

The last attack reportedly carried out by GARI was in May 1975. The group is known to be inactive since. The reasons for the sudden inactivity are not known. Monitor groups claim that other factions that were extensions of GARI were formed after 1975.

OTHER PERSPECTIVES

The International Revolutionary Action Group claimed to be an organization working against the dictatorial regime in Spain. The group's proclaimed mission was to "struggle for direct action against the Franco-ist dictator, against capital, against the state, for the liberation of Spain, of Europe and of the world."

SUMMARY

The International Revolutionary Action group was known to target the regime of Francisco Franco (the dictator of Spain until 1975) and anarchism in general. GARI reportedly was operational for a very short period from 1974 to 1975. The group is known for a number of attacks (mainly bombings) against Spanish establishments.

There have been no reported operations by the GARI since mid-1975.

SOURCES

Web sites

MIPT Terrorism Knowledge Base. "International Revolutionary Action Group (GARI)." < http://www.tkb.org/Group.jsp?groupID = 4030 > (accessed October 20, 2005).

MIPT Terrorism Knowledge Base. "Basque Fatherland and Freedom." < http://www.tkb.org/Group.jsp?groupID = 31 > (accessed October 20, 2005).

Dr. Charles A. Russell, Air University Review. "Transnational Terrorism." < http://www.airpower.maxwell.af.mil/airchronicles/aureview/1976/jan-feb/russell.html > (accessed October 20, 2005).

Irish Republican Army (IRA)

LEADER: Gerry Adams

OVERVIEW

The IRA was Ireland's preeminent nationalist paramilitary organization for more than a century, until its apparent disbandment and the destruction of its arms in 2005. Because of its ubiquity and because a number of splinter organizations have taken its name, confusion has sometimes existed over its exact role.

HISTORY

In its nine-decades-long history, the IRA assumed four main guises. These can roughly be characterized as the pre-revolutionary IRA (to 1921); post-revolutionary IRA (1921–1969); the IRA of the Troubles era (1969–1998); and the post-Good Friday Agreement IRA (1998–2005). In the course of this timeline, the IRA has also suffered a number of splits with other groups taking its name.

The initial origins of the IRA lie within the Anglo-Irish War (1916–21), which resulted in the creation of the Irish Free State in 1921. Irish nationalism had long been marked by its violence, and rebellions had previously broken out in 1798, 1803, and 1865. The 1916 uprising, which had occurred at the height of World War I, had been instigated primarily by the Irish Republican Brotherhood (IRB) and Irish

Masked IRA members carry the casket of Bobby Sands, a Provisional IRA martyr who died in prison as a result of a hunger strike in 1981. © Peter Marlow | Magnum Photos

Volunteers. Although many of the events of the 1916 rising remain steeped in the lore of Irish history—namely, the Proclamation of the Irish Republic and declaration of independence—it was largely a political and military failure and failed to rouse the support of those who lived in and around its epicenter of Dublin. Moreover, many of the IRB and Irish Volunteer leaders were either executed or interned following the revolt.

In October 1917, Sinn Fein, a small republican political party led by Eamon De Valera, set about reorganizing the defeated Irish Volunteers. Sinn Fein had been wrongly blamed for organizing the 1916 rising and, as a consequence, emerged with an enhanced reputation in nationalist circles. Moreover, it was a genuinely national organization with a presence not just in Dublin, but in the nationalist heartlands of the south and across Ireland's remote rural west.

This new paramilitary group—the Irish Republican Army (IRA)—was organized into hundreds of companies across Ireland.

Following the end of World War I, Ireland exploded into full-scale insurrection, with a bloody war fought against the British authorities. This conflict was played out most viciously in Ireland's southern counties, where the British deployed a military police force known as the "Black and Tans," whose brutality saw large parts of the city of Cork burned, and even attracted the condemnation of King George V.

Indeed, it was partly due to the intervention of King George V that peace talks broke out in June 1921. These negotiations culminated in the Anglo-Irish Agreement of December 1921. Under the terms of this treaty, Ireland was partitioned between the twenty-six predominantly Catholic counties of the south, which became the Irish Free State and the six mostly Protestant counties of the north, which became Northern Ireland and remained part of the United Kingdom.

Yet, the treaty split the IRA. Those members who supported it, led by Michael Collins, became the regular Irish National Army;

A new mural showing a Provisional Irish Republican Army volunteer looms behind a Belfast, Northern Ireland resident on March 8, 2001. AP/Wide World Photos. Reproduced by permission.

however, many IRA members regarded the relinquishment of Northern Ireland as a betrayal of their cause and refused to recognize the Irish Free State, much less incorporate with its army. This marked the onset of the second phase of the IRA's history and the refusal to recognize the settlement created by Anglo-Irish Treaty would be its binding cause.

Because of this schism, the Irish Free State quickly descended into civil war, between the Irish National Army (i.e., pro-treaty IRA) and the IRA. During its year-long course, the Irish Civil War would claim more lives than the Anglo-Irish War had done and ended in defeat for the IRA.

Nevertheless, this defeat was never total and the remnants of the IRA still stubbornly insisted that the Irish Free State, which had been created by an "illegitimate" treaty, held no authority, and the group refused to recognize it or its institutions. Instead, it claimed that the IRA Army Executive was the real government of the still-existing Irish Republic proclaimed in 1918. These would remain important principles for the IRA for a further sixty years.

For nearly fifty years, this incarnation of the IRA would be a semi-dormant organization, manned by the principled and obstinate, and serving as a hindrance rather than a serious threat to both Irish and British governments. Its main extremist activities were a loose collaboration with Nazi Germany, which largely amounted to the passing on of intelligence during World War II, and border raids and sabotage during the 1950s and early 1960s.

By the late 1960s, the IRA was gripped by ideological splits and infighting. The third incarnation of the IRA came following a formal split in 1969 between the Marxist Official IRA and the Provisional IRA.

Despite its moniker, the Official IRA was a minor organization and played virtually no part in Northern Ireland's incipient "Troubles." It claimed responsibility for the bombing of British Army barracks in Aldershot, which killed six people, including a Catholic priest, and up to fifty other killings. But from 1973, the group adopted and stuck to a ceasefire, from which point it became almost completely dormant. A number of its members are known to have subsequently joined the Irish National Liberation Army (INLA), or reunited with the Provisional IRA.

It was the Provisional IRA that carried on the traditions of the "old" IRA. It continued the longstanding tradition of claiming that the IRA Army Council was the provisional government of a thirty-two-county Irish Republic, and refused to recognize the legitimacy of either the British or Irish governments. As Northern Ireland descended into fully blown civil insurrection by the early 1970s, the IRA dramatically increased in size, influence, and prestige. Although it retained and increased large-scale support in parts of the Republic of Ireland, the focus of the IRA increasingly centered on Northern Ireland.

The modern IRA's most deadly period lies in the 1970s, a time when it became a highly sophisticated paramilitary organization, capable of attracting financial and military support from

LEADERSHIP

GERRY ADAMS

Born in West Belfast in 1948, Gerry Adams is the individual most responsible for the evolution of the IRA over the last four decades, from a semi-dormant and ideologically split group, to hardened nationalist extremists, and then into a modern political organization. Despite its links to organized crime, Sinn Fein/IRA has, since 1998, carved out an important role in Irish politics on both sides of Ireland's north-south border.

Adams joined Sinn Fein at the age of sixteen, and despite repeated denials, was a member of the Provisional IRA from 1969. He was an important part of the IRA leadership throughout this third phase of the organization's history and was twice interned by the British authorities during the 1970s, eventually rising to Northern Ireland Commander in 1979. At the same time, he built up a political profile, rising to the rank of Sinn Fein Vice President (1978) and President (1983).

It was as President that he slowly switched the focus of the IRA from military to political struggle. The ending of abstentionism in 1986 was more than just an issue of principle: it paved the way for negotiations with the governments of Dublin and Belfast. Although the peace process was protracted and accompanied by continued violence, the culmination in the Good Friday Agreement of April 1998 marked a stunning breakthrough for Adams. Less than a decade earlier, the British media had not even been allowed to broadcast his voice by a government that regarded him a terrorist; now, he was regarded every bit a statesman as his fellow negotiators, which included Tony Blair and Bill Clinton.

The conviction that the Good Friday Agreement affords the necessary mechanisms to eventually bring a united Ireland, combined with Sinn Fein's role in the Northern Ireland Assembly, has seen the party grow as a mainstream political organization on both sides of the Irish border. The IRA's renunciation of violence in 2005 can surely only accentuate this progress.

---

both the Irish Diaspora and sympathetic regimes, including Libya.

Its strategy was initially twofold during this time: to disrupt the civil and economic life of Northern Ireland and to attack British military installations and rival loyalist paramilitary organizations as a way of "defending" its people. A third strategy emerged from 1974 with a bombing campaign in mainland Britain. This was designed to sap political will to hold onto the province within Westminster and among the British population. It occasionally made attacks in the Republic of Ireland also.

From 1983, when Gerry Adams was elected President of the IRA's political wing, Sinn Fein, there was a definite shift toward the seeking of a political—rather than military—solution to the future of Ireland. In 1986, Adams brought an end to the longstanding principle of abstentionism, allowing Sinn Fein to sit in the Irish Dáil (although not Westminster). In effect, this was recognition not just of the Irish government, but also a renunciation of the outmoded idea that the IRA was the "provisional government" of Ireland. The abandonment of abstentionism paved the way for negotiations—initially covert and highly tentative—with both Dublin and Westminster, and would eventually culminate in the Good Friday Agreement of April 1998, which afforded a political solution for Northern Ireland.

Nevertheless, Northern Ireland's peace process was both protracted and marked by violence. Only in 1994 would the IRA call a ceasefire—which broke down after seventeen months—before ending violence with a second, more lasting ceasefire in 1997.

The IRA's pursuit of a political process was also not universally welcomed by its members. Following the end of abstentionism in 1986, Adams' predecessor as Sinn Fein leader, Ruairi O'Bradaigh, a former president, and Daithi O'Conouill, a former chief of staff, led a breakaway organization, Republican Sinn Fein, which formed its own military wing, the Continuity IRA (CIRA). This group was based on the

PRIMARY SOURCE
IRA 'Has Destroyed All Its Arms'

The IRA has put all of its weapons beyond use, the head of the arms decommissioning body has said.

General John de Chastelain made the announcement at a news conference accompanied by the two churchmen who witnessed the process.

"We are satisfied that the arms decommissioned represent the totality of the IRA's arsenal."

Welcoming the move, Prime Minister Tony Blair said IRA decommissioning had been "finally accomplished."

The general said: "We have observed and verified events to put beyond use very large quantities of arms which we believe include all the arms in the IRA's possession."

He said they had handled every gun and made an inventory of the weapons.

The arms included a full range of ammunition, rifles, machine guns, mortars, missiles, handguns, explosives, explosive substances and other arms including all the categories described in the estimates provided by the U.K. and Irish security services, he said.

"Our new inventory is consistent with these estimates. We are satisfied that the arms decommissioning represents the totality of the IRA's arsenal."

The IRA announced an end to its armed campaign in July.

The republican organisation said it would follow a democratic path ending more than 30 years of violence.

General de Chastelain's report confirming that IRA decommissioning had been completed was given to the British and Irish governments earlier on Monday.

He described IRA decommissioning as "an important milestone towards the completion of its task to achieve decommissioning by all paramilitary groups."

The churchmen who witnessed the process were Catholic priest Father Alec Reid and ex-Methodist president Rev Harold Good.

Their statement said: "The experience of seeing this with our own eyes, on a minute-to-minute basis, provided us with evidence so clear and of its nature so incontrovertible that at the end of the process it demonstrated to us—and would have demonstrated to anyone who might have been with us—that beyond any shadow of doubt, the arms of the IRA have now been decommissioned."

The churchmen said they regarded IRA decommissioning as an "accomplished act."

General de Chastelain, Andrew Sens and Tauno Nieminen—the commissioners of the Independent International Commission on Decommissioning—have been in Ireland overseeing the latest round of decommissioning since the beginning of September.

Prime Minister Tony Blair said the completion of decommissioning was "an important step in the transition from conflict to peace in Northern Ireland."

---

principles of the IRA (i.e., refusal to acknowledge British and Irish governments; that it was the "true" government of a united Ireland, etc.) and linked to several terrorist acts in the run up to the Good Friday Agreement in 1997–1998. In July 2004, the U.S. State Department designated the CIRA as a foreign terrorist organization. It also estimated that the CIRA had just fifty remaining activists, a reflection of the fact that

it had barely been implicated in any extremist acts for nearly five years.

The CIRA had, however, long been outdone for notoriety by the Real IRA (RIRA). This was formed in late 1997 by several leading members of the Provisional IRA, and it adopted similar principles to those of the CIRA. Its aim to disrupt the emergent peace process reached an early and horrific denouement in the town of Omagh

"The true importance of today is that these weapons can never again be used to inflict suffering and create more victims," he added.

Irish Prime Minister Bertie Ahern said that it was a "landmark development" and appealed to unionists not to "underestimate the importance" of the move.

"The weapons of the IRA are gone, and are gone in a manner which has been verified and witnessed," he said.

Secretary of State Peter Hain said the announcement was the first step on the road to devolution being restored in Northern Ireland.

"After all the bitter agony of the victims who have suffered, deaths and families torn apart, people will want to be certain, not just for a few weeks but for some months that actually this is being delivered," he said.

"So far so good, today's statement was a landmark one which deals with the IRA's arsenal in a very credible way witnessed by independent people—but we have a long time to go to see whether we can actually get self government back on the road."

Sinn Fein President Gerry Adams admitted the announcement would be "difficult for many republicans" but it was a "very brave and bold leap."

Mr. Adams said the British and Irish governments must now implement the Good Friday Agreement, with progress needed on outstanding issues including equality, policing, human rights, victims and on-the-run prisoners.

However, unionists are unhappy there has been no photographic evidence of decommissioning and reacted with skepticism to the report.

Democratic Unionist leader Ian Paisley said there had been no transparent verification of IRA decommissioning in the announcement.

He said the church witnesses had been agreed by the IRA and as such could not be considered "independent."

Without a photographic proof, an inventory and details on how the weapons were destroyed questions remained, said Mr. Paisley.

"This afternoon the people of Northern Ireland watched a programme which illustrates more than ever the duplicity and dishonesty of the two governments and the IRA."

However, his deputy, east Belfast MP Peter Robinson said they accepted a significant amount of IRA weapons had been "put beyond use."

Mr. Robinson said they accepted it had been "a more substantial event than the previous events put together."

In a statement the Ulster Unionist Party said it regretted that the move had "failed to maximise public confidence."

"It is imperative that the movement's criminal empire be dismantled as well," it said.

Source: BBC News, 2005

in August 1998, when a massive car bomb killed twenty-nine people. The carnage created outrage and dissipated much of what little support it may have held among most Irish people and led to a huge crackdown by the British and Irish governments, leaving it an almost totally marginalized and ineffective organization.

Since the Good Friday Agreement of 1998, the IRA has assumed its fourth incarnation, acting as an organization that straddles the worlds of both politics and organized crime. Sinn Fein has taken up an important role within Northern Ireland's political institutions and it has also emerged as a mid-sized political force within the Irish Republic, where it had previously been a marginal political party. However, the IRA has continued to be linked to criminality, and former paramilitaries have divvied up Northern Ireland for control of drug-dealing, prostitution, and extortion rackets. It has also

KEY EVENTS

1917: Formation of the IRA out of the remnants of the Irish Volunteers.

1921: Anglo-Irish Agreement gives way to a split between the pro-treaty IRA (that became the regular Irish Army) and the anti-treaty IRA.

1969: Split between the Marxist Official IRA and the Provisional IRA. The latter group continue the IRA tradition, while the former quickly fade.

1986: The creation of Republican Sinn Fein, a splinter of the main political party, leads to the formation of the Continuity IRA.

1997: Split in IRA leadership over the peace process leads to the creation of the Real IRA, another splinter group.

1998: The Good Friday Agreement accentuates the evolution of Sinn Fein/IRA into a mainstream political organization, although the IRA continues to be dogged by claims of underworld involvement.

2005: IRA renounces violence and calls for its members to give up its arms.

2005: Northern Ireland's arms decommissioning body announces itself satisfied that the IRA has destroyed its arms.

---

been strongly implicated in bank robberies. The proceeds of a £25 million raid on Belfast's Northern Bank in December 2004 was believed to be for an IRA "retirement" fund.

There has also been a palpable sense that its members can still act with impunity. This manifested itself most notoriously in early 2005, when a Catholic man, Robert McCartney, was murdered by former paramilitaries in a Belfast bar, and the IRA both covered up the crime and obstructed the police investigation.

Nevertheless, overt sectarian violence has declined inexorably since the IRA assumed its

fourth incarnation. Its willingness to engage in politics saw it officially renounce violence in July 2005. Two months later, the head of Northern Ireland's arms decommissioning body announced himself satisfied that the IRA had put its entire arsenal beyond use, an act that seemingly brought an end to the group's long history as an armed organization.

PHILOSOPHY AND TACTICS

The IRA was a paramilitary organization committed to the creation of a united Ireland. For most of its history it existed on the premise that it was the legitimate government of a united Ireland and as such refused to recognize either the British or Irish governments. As such, it believed it would achieve its aims through armed struggle. Under the leadership of Gerry Adams (since 1983) it adopted a more political approach, resulting in a ceasefire (1994–96; and 1997–) and the Good Friday Agreement. This evolution into a political organization culminated in a renunciation of violence and the complete decommissioning of its weaponry in 2005.

OTHER PERSPECTIVES

The IRA's call for its members to lay down arms in July 2005 had been welcomed, but treated with skepticism by many commentators. The decommissioning of its weapons two months later was regarded as a welcome surprise, although most newspapers added a hint of caution. The *Guardian* wrote: "Not so long ago on the streets of the Bogside in Derry nationalist graffiti warned that the IRA would surrender 'not an ounce, not a bullet.' The slogan has been proved wrong and the optimists who believed the peace process meant something have been proved right. The IRA has delivered, if not peace—the Northern Bank raid, the killing of Robert McCartney and the harassment of his family and friends show peace has not arrived—then at least a sense that it may again be possible... Talks, and powersharing, must follow. But for all the monumental importance of yesterday's announcement, getting there will still require patience."

The right-wing *Daily Telegraph*, normally the most skeptical of Britain's national newspapers, declared the decommissioning of weapons a "welcome change in the nature of the IRA," but added its own slant on events. "No longer is it a revolutionary force, needing bombs and missiles to terrorise the British state into conceding a United Ireland," the newspaper declared. "Instead, it has become what most of its members always were a criminal gang of racketeers, for whose purposes light arms are enough."

SUMMARY

The IRA's decommissioning of arms in September 2005 apparently marked the last act in its violent, frequently sectarian armed struggle for a united Ireland, and the "throwing in" of its lot with the political process. Its supporters add that this marks the maturing of the terrorist organization, a realization that the ballot box is a more potent weapon than the barrel of a gun.

However, if nothing else, the IRA is an organization that has historically shown an appetite for change: first, an anti-imperial revolutionary organization; next, a small group of fanatical but disorganized republicans; thirdly, an insidious and potent terrorist organization; and finally, a mainstream political organization (albeit one with links to organized crime). Taking that view, skeptics might have good reason to fear that it could one day return to violence if its foray into politics fails to work out. Moreover, its failure to disavow its criminal links merely adds to the aura of suspicion that lingers over the organization. Only time will tell if the IRA's "doves" pervade over its more hawkish elements.

SOURCES

Books

McKittrick, David, and David McVeigh. *Making Sense of the Troubles.* London: Penguin, 2003.

Moloney, Ed. *Secret History of the IRA.* London: Penguin, 2003.

Taylor, Peter. *The Provos: The IRA and Sinn Fein.* London: Bloomsbury, 1998.

Web sites

Northern Ireland Office. "Homepage of the Decommissioning Commission." < http://www.nio.gov.uk/decommissioning > (accessed October 24, 2005).

SEE ALSO

Real Irish Republican Army

Provisional Irish Republican Army

Continuity Irish Republican Army

Islamic Army of Aden

LEADERS: Abu al-Hassan; Khaled Abdennabi

USUAL AREA OF OPERATION: Yemen

OVERVIEW

In 1998, the Islamic Army of Aden (IAA), also called the Islamic Army of Aden-Abyan, began to issue communiqués detailing its goals and objectives for Yemen and the rest of the world. Highest on its list was the removal of the members of the Yemeni government, to be tried under shari'a law and replaced by a government that would strictly adhere to the principles of Islamic law. The group voiced its support for Osama bin Laden and sought operations against U.S. and other Western powers' interests, which would force their withdrawal from the region. Since 1998, the group has engaged in both bombings and kidnappings to bring about their goals. As a result, they have been listed for sanctions as terrorists under United Nations Security Council Resolution 1333. In Arabic, the group is known as Jaysh Adan-Abiyan al-Islami.

Geographically, Yemen—particularly the Gulf of Aden—holds strategic value. The port operates as a refueling station and overlooks the westward flow of maritime traffic out of the Persian Gulf. All ships that travel from the Red Sea through the Suez Canal utilize Aden. This strategic importance was identified by Osama bin Laden in his "Declarations of War."

Sheikh Abu Hamza Al-Masri speaks at a 1999 Conference of the Islamic Revival Movement in Euston, London. Gerry Penny/AFP/Getty Images

HISTORY

The Republic of Yemen did not exist until 1990 when Northern Yemen, known as the Yemen Arab Republic (YAR), and the Southern People's Democratic Republic of Yemen agreed to unify. Northern Yemen had operated under Turkish rule until 1918. It was then controlled by Imam Yahya and later his son, Ahmad, until 1962. With the assistance of Egyptian President Nasser, the Imam was overthrown and the revolutionary forces declared the Yemen Arab Republic in 1970.

Southern Yemen operated under British control until 1965 when two rival groups sought to overthrow British rule. After two violent years, the British pulled out. By 1969, with assistance from the USSR, the radical wing of the Marxist movement in Yemen gained power and declared the People's Democratic Republic of Yemen (PDRY). Throughout the 1970s, the government of the PDRY maintained close ties with the Soviet Union and China and provided safe haven for Palestinian extremists.

By 1972, the governments of the YAR and the PDRY declared a desire to unify, although little progress was initially made toward that goal. In addition, beginning in 1979, the PDRY began to sponsor insurgency operations against the YAR. However, by 1989, after arbitration by the Arab League, the leaders of the YAR and the PDRY agree to unify under the terms drafted in 1981. On May 22, 1990, the Republic of Yemen (ROY) declared itself to international acceptance and was ratified by Yemenis by May 1991.

However, the celebration was short lived. By 1994, a group residing in the southern region declared the South's cessation from the ROY. Fighting in the civil war occurred mainly in the south and was quelled by July of that same year.

Although the Islamic Army of Aden did not officially appear until 1998, its history is intertwined with these aspects of Yemeni history. In 1998, the IAA issued its first communiqué expressing its goals. However, the group existed long before then. The leadership of the IAA is made up of individuals sent to Saudi Arabia for religious and military training in order to fight the Soviet Union in Afghanistan. In 1984, Yemen sent between 5,000 and 7,000 volunteers. These *mujahideen* (fighters) were trained in guerilla warfare tactics and many adopted the fundamentalist salafi sect of Sunni Islam.

Upon their return to Yemen, the mujahideen formed Jamiat al-Jihad and allied with the opposition to the socialists. During the 1994 civil war, these war veterans were used to suppress the cessationists residing in the south and undertook over 150 assassinations of Socialist Party members. As a reward for their success during the civil war, many of these religious fundamentalists were awarded ranking positions in the Education and Judicial branches of the Yemeni government. Many of the mujahideen saw this as an attempt to incorporate and control their religious movement. Individuals such as Zein al-Abidi Abu Bakr al-Mehdar, known as al-Hassan, were disillusioned by the government's choice to not strictly follow shari'a, or traditional Islamic law. Led by al-Hassan, like-minded salafi began to move away from the Yemeni government in 1996.

The Yemeni government denied the existence of the IAA until the group issued its first

LEADERSHIP

KHALED ABDENNABI (OR KHALID ABD AL-NABI AL-YAZIDI)

Little is known about Khaled Abdennabi. He was captured by Yemeni forces in 2003 after the attack on the medical convoy. Shortly thereafter, he was pardoned and released.

ZEIN AL-ABIDI ABU BAKR AL-MEHDAR (ABU AL-HASSAN)

Zein al-Abidi Abu Bakr al-Mehdar (Abu al-Hassan) was the founder of the IAA and a member of the salafi sect. He, along with other founding members of IAA, was trained in guerilla warfare tactics in preparation for fighting the Soviet forces in Afghanistan. In 1994, he assisted the Yemeni government to quell the civil war caused by the socialists in South Yemen, who had declared their intent to become independent from the Republic of Yemen. He was offered a position within the ruling party, but declined as it became clear that the government was not being run under strict adherence to Islamic law. In October 1999, al-Hassan was convicted of his participation in the December 1998 kidnapping of sixteen western tourists, which led to the death of four tourists. He was sentenced to death and executed by firing squad on October 17, 1999.

---

communiqué. The communiqué was issued in response to the U.S. strikes of Osama bin Laden's training camps in Afghanistan, which were in retaliation for the embassy bombings in Kenya and Tanzania. The IAA expressed its support for Osama bin Laden and praised the embassy bombings. It called for the overthrow of the Yemeni government, who, the IAA believed, should be tried under shari'a law. The government would then be replaced with leadership that strictly adhered to the fundamentals of Islamic law. The group also sought operations against U.S. and Western interests, which would force the withdrawal of these influences on

Yemen. In a subsequent communiqué, the IAA called for the resignation of the government.

In December 1998, the group initiated its operations against Western influences with the kidnapping of sixteen British, American, and Australian tourists, the largest incident of kidnapping in Yemen. The tourists were stopped at a roadblock in Mawdiyah. They were then taken to an IAA house where the IAA demanded the release of several comrades. Yemeni security forces surrounded the house. After negotiations failed, a firefight ensued. The IAA members used several of the hostages as human shields. As a result, four tourists were killed. Three of the kidnappers were also killed.

In October 1999, the leader of the operation and of the IAA, al-Hassan was convicted and sentenced to death by execution. Two other IAA members were sentenced to death and one was sentenced to twenty years in prison. Ten others were tried and acquitted. Despite threats that the IAA would retaliate, al-Hassan was executed by firing squad on October 17, 1999, within days of his conviction.

The IAA continued to operate after al-Hassan's death. The group claimed responsibility for the October 12, 2000, bombing of the U.S.S. Cole, a U.S. Naval vessel refueling in the port of Aden. A dinghy packed with explosives rammed the vessel, killing seventeen U.S. sailors and injuring thirty-nine. Both the U.S. and Australian intelligence services state that the bombings were orchestrated and acted out by al-Qaeda. Many believe that the bombing was organized and funded by al-Qaeda, but that the operatives came from the IAA.

In September 2001, the IAA was designated under Executive Order 13224 as a terrorist organization by the United States. In that same month, it was designated for sanctions under the United Nations Security Council Resolution 1333. Nevertheless, the group continued to operate. On October 6, 2002, the IAA claimed responsibility for the bombing of a French refueling tank, the Limburg. The group claimed that its target had actually been a U.S. Navy vessel. Days later, and on the third anniversary of al-Hassan's execution, the spiritual leader of the IAA, Abu-Hamzah al-Masri, announced that the group had joined the al-Qaeda organization.

The most recent activity by the IAA occurred on June 21, 2003, with an attack on a military medical convoy, which wounded seven

KEY EVENTS

1998: The IAA officially emerged with the issuance of several communiqués.

2002: The IAA claims responsibility for the attack on the French tanker, The Limburg.

2002: Three Yemenis were convicted of bombings at the Port of Aden.

2003: The IAA launches attack on military medical convoy, which injures seven people.

2003: Yemeni security forces engage IAA members at a base in Harat. During arrests for the attack on the medical convoy, security forces find cache of weapons.

2003: IAA led car bomb attacks planned for the U.S., British, and German embassies in capital of Sana'a are disrupted.

The strategic importance of Aden is not merely geographic. Al-Hassan believed in a literal interpretation of the teaching of Muhammad that 12,000 holy warriors would emerge from Aden-Abyan to restore Islam. This idea is voiced again by Osama bin Laden in his "Declarations of War," as he asserts the strategic importance of the Yemen.

As a result, the IAA has employed tactics such as bombings and kidnappings to seek the expulsion of Western influences in Yemen. The highest profile kidnapping occurred in December 1998 when sixteen tourists were kidnapped from a roadblock. After failed negotiations, four of the tourists were killed. In addition to kidnappings, the IAA has engaged in bombings. Although the group claims responsibility for the bombing of the U.S.S. Cole, blame is generally placed on the larger Islamic jihad organization, al-Qaeda. In addition, the IAA claimed responsibility for the bombing of a French oil tanker in 2003.

people. During arrests for the attack, Yemeni security forces discovered and seized cars packed with explosives, hand grenades, and rocket-propelled grenades.

Western intelligence services estimate that there are a hundred core members to the IAA, who are both Yemeni and Saudi. These members reside in the United Kingdom, Sudan, Pakistan, Jordan, and Eritrea. The current leader is Khaled Abdennabi, or Khalid Abd al-Nabi al-Yazidi.

PHILOSOPHY AND TACTICS

The philosophy of the IAA is rooted in the salafi sect of Sunni Islam and the belief that the Yemeni government should operate under strict adherence to Islamic law. Many of the members of the IAA were influenced toward salafi while in Saudi Arabia as they trained to fight the Soviet Union in Afghanistan. The philosophy is founded in the struggle to expel external influences from the Middle East.

OTHER PERSPECTIVES

The Yemeni government denied the existence of the IAA until after the 1998 release of communiqués and currently maintains that the group has been disbanded. However, Australian and U.S. intelligence organizations estimate that there are approximately one hundred core members of IAA residing in the United Kingdom, Sudan, Pakistan, Jordan, and Eritrea. Simon Kerr writes that, "Most Yemenis ridicule the Islamic Army." The attempt on the part of the Yemeni government to incorporate the salafi into its ranks reinforces its belief that those within the group are of little threat. As such, current leader, Khaled Abd al-Nabi was arrested after the 2003 attack on the military convoy. Shortly after his arrest, he was pardoned and released.

However, before his death, al-Hassan spoke of his involvement with the hostage taking in 1998, saying, "Dialogue between civilizations is useless. The only dialogue should be with bullets." As a result of comments like this and ties to the al-Qaeda network, the IAA has been renewed on both the U.S. and Australian terrorist watch-lists.

PRIMARY SOURCE

Islamic Army of Aden (IAA) a.k.a. Aden-Abyan Islamic Army (AAIA)

DESCRIPTION

The Islamic Army of Aden (IAA) emerged publicly in mid-1998 when the group released a series of communiqués that expressed support for Usama Bin Ladin, appealed for the overthrow of the Yemeni Government, and called for operations against U.S. and other Western interests in Yemen. IAA was first designated under EO 13224 in September 2001.

ACTIVITIES

IAA has engaged in small-scale operations such as bombings, kidnappings, and small arms attacks to promote its goals. The group reportedly was behind an attack in June 2003 against a medical assistance convoy in the Abyan Governorate. Yemeni authorities responded with a raid on a suspected IAA facility, killing several individuals and capturing others, including Khalid al-Nabi al-Yazidi, the group's leader. Before that attack, the group had not conducted operations since the bombing of the British Embassy in Sanaa in October 2000. In 2001, Yemeni authorities found an IAA member and three associates responsible for that attack. In December 1998, the group kidnapped 16 British, American, and Australian tourists near Mudiyah in southern Yemen. Although Yemeni officials previously have claimed that the group is operationally defunct, their recent attribution of the attack in 2003 against the medical convoy and reports that al-Yazidi was released from prison in mid-October 2003 suggest that the IAA, or at least elements of the group, have resumed activity. Speculation after the attack on the USS Cole pointed to the involvement of the IAA, and the group later claimed responsibility for the attack. The IAA has been affiliated with al-Qa'ida. IAA members are known to have trained and served in Afghanistan under the leadership of seasoned mujahedin.

STRENGTH

Not known.

LOCATION/AREA OF OPERATION

Operates in the southern governorates of Yemen—primarily Aden and Abyan.

EXTERNAL AID

Not known.

Source: U.S. Department of State. *Country Reports on Terrorism.* Washington, D.C., 2004.

SUMMARY

In 1998, the Islamic Army of Aden emerged with clear objectives: support of the international Islamic jihad led by Osama bin Laden, the removal and replacement of current Yemeni government to one based on strict adherence to Islamic law, and the expulsion of external influences on Yemen and the Middle East. These goals were founded in the original struggle of its leaders when they fought against the Soviet Union in Afghanistan. During their military training, many began to follow salafi, a fundamentalist sect of Sunni Islam, and sought to create Islamist governments. As a result, upon return from the Afghan war, some in the group were disillusioned by what they believed to be a lack of adherence to Islamic law on the part of the government. Consequently, they began in 1998 to move toward those goals.

Since 1998, the group has engaged in many bombings and kidnappings. The most famous kidnapping occurred in December 1998 and resulted in the death of four hostages. Another result of the hostage crisis was the arrest and subsequent execution of the IAA leader, al-Hassan. Several years after his death, the IAA officially allied itself with al-Qaeda. The last known activity of the group occurred in 2003, but U.S. and Australian intelligence agencies approximate that the group still has a hundred core members.

SOURCES

Periodicals

Karmon, Ely. "The Bombing of the U.S.S. Cole: An Analysis of the Principle Suspects." *International Policy Institute for Counter Terrorism.* October 24, 2000.

Kerr, Simon. "Yemen Cracks Down on Militants." *Middle East Journal.* December 1, 1999.

McGregor, Andrew. "Strike First." *The World Today.* December 1, 2002.

Web sites

FAS Intelligence Resource Program. "Islamic Army of Aden." < http://www.fas.org/irp/world/para/iaa.htm > (accessed October 18, 2005).

MIPT Terrorism Knowledge Database. "Aden Abyan Islamic Army (AAIA)." < http://www.tkb.org/Group. jsp?groupID = 4 > (accessed October 18, 2005).

National Security Australia. "Islamic Army of Aden (IAA)." < http://www.nationalsecurity.gov.au/agd/WWW/ nationalsecurityHome.nsf/Page/Listing_of_Terrorist_ Organisations_terrorist_listing_ Islamic_Army_of_Aden_-_ Listed_11_April_2003 > (accessed October 18, 2005).

Islamic Movement of Uzbekistan

LEADERS: Jumaboi Ahmadzhanovitch Khojaev; Tohir Abdouhalilovitch Yuldeshev

USUAL AREA OF OPERATION: Uzbekistan; Kyrgyzstan; Tajikistan; Kazakhstan; Turkmenistan; the Xinxiang province in China

In 1998, the Islamic Movement of Uzbekistan (IMU) officially announced its goal to overthrow the Uzbek government and replace it with an Islamic state. However, as the group continued its activities with financial assistance and training from Osama bin Laden and al-Qaeda, the IMU developed a larger goal. In 2001, the group issued its new goal and new name: the Islamic Party of Turkistan, which sought a pan-Islamic, Central Asian state that would include Uzbekistan, Kyrgyzstan, Tajikistan, Kazakhstan, Turkmenistan, and the Xinxiang province in China.

HISTORY

The primary goal of the IMU was the militant overthrow of the Uzbek government, which would be replaced by an Islamic state. This goal derives from the post-cold war history of Uzbekistan. Much of the group's initial activities were centered on the removal of President Islam Karimov's regime. In 1991, after the demise of the Soviet Union, Uzbekistan declared its independence. Islam Karimov, who was First Secretary of the Communist Party of Uzbekistan in 1989 and later appointed President of the Uzbek Soviet Socialist Republic in 1990, won

LEADERSHIP

JUMABOI AHMADZHANOVITCH KHOJAEV

Jumaboi Ahmadzhanovitch Khojaev served as a Soviet paratrooper fighting against the *mujahideen* (fighters) in Afghanistan during the Soviet-Afghan war. During this time, he developed respect for the mujahideen that he was fighting and this renewed his interest in his faith, Islam. Following his involvement in the war, Khojaev changed his name to Namangani to honor his hometown. Namangani returned to Uzbekistan after the war fully committed in his indoctrination to Wahabism, a fundamentalist view of Islam. After losing faith in the Islamic Renaissance Party (IRP) in Uzbekistan, Namangani co-founded a splinter movement called Adolat, dedicated to the creation of an Islamic state in Uzbekistan. In 1992, Adolat was declared illegal and Namangani fled to Tajikistan where he fought with the United Tajik Opposition in the Tajik civil war. Namangani remained in Tajikistan until coming to Afghanistan in 1998 where he and Yuldeshev founded the IMU.

During his fighting in the Tajik civil war and continuing with his activities with the IMU, Namangani developed a reputation as a charismatic leader and effective tactician. In August 1999, Namangani led 800 militants into southern villages in Kyrgyzstan and held residents hostage for a ransom. In August 2000, he led incursions into southern Uzbekistan. In November 2001, Namangani was sentenced to death for his involvement in the February 1999 bombing campaign in Tashkent, Uzbekistan that killed sixteen people. However, he is believed to have died during a U.S.-led bombing raid in Afghanistan in 2001.

TOHIR ABDOUHALILOVITCH YULDESHEV

Tohir Abdouhalilovitch Yuldeshev was an unemployed college dropout when he led a group of like-minded militant Islamists to storm the communist party headquarters of Uzbekistan in 1991. Following his disappointment with the IRP, he co-founded the group Adolat with Namangani, and he served as a mullah for the underground Islamic movement. When Adolat was banned from Uzbekistan, Yuldeshev traveled throughout Central Asia creating alliances and finding financial support for his Islamic revolution movement. After creating the IMU in 1998, Yuldeshev obtained Taliban permission to establish a training camp in northern Afghanistan, where he is believed to still reside. Yuldeshev is considered to be more of a religious and political leader than a military leader.

---

the presidency by popular vote in the country's first election. His first term was extended by a referendum and, in 2000 he was once again elected for his final term as President. However, in 2002 an additional referendum ensured his office until 2007. Human rights organizations question the validity of these elections.

In 1991, after Karimov's first election, the IMU began to organize, although it would take several more years to become an official organization. In December 1991, future IMU leaders, Tohir Abdouhalilovitch Yuldeshev and Jumaboi Ahmadzhanovitch Khojaev, led a group of unemployed Muslims to capture the communist party headquarters in the eastern city of Namangan. The men demanded land for a mosque to be built. Both Yuldeshev and Khojaev, who later changed his name to Namangani, were members of the Uzbekistan branch of the Islamic Renaissance Party (IRP). Feeling disillusioned by the IRP's refusal to demand an Islamic state in Uzbekistan, Yuldeshev and Namangani formed a splinter group called *Adolat* (Justice), and called for an Islamic revolution. By 1992, President Karimov had declared Adolat illegal, which resulted in the group fleeing to Tajikistan.

Tajikistan, in 1992, was on the brink of a civil war. As a result, Yuldeshev and Namangani parted paths. Yuldeshev moved to Afghanistan and began to establish ties throughout the Middle East. He visited Pakistan, Saudi Arabia, the United Arab Emirates, and Turkey, and received both sanctuary and funding from Islamic groups in these countries. During 1995–1998, Yuldeshev received assistance from the Pakistani intelligence service while residing in Peshawar. In addition, he met with Chechen rebel leaders during the 1994–1996 Chechen war. Yuldeshev's travels not only established alliances throughout the region, but also created underground cells of Adolat throughout Central Asia.

Namangani, on the other hand, fought in the Tajik civil war and created a reputation for himself as a fierce fighter and charismatic leader. In 1997, the civil war came to an end with a ceasefire, which Namangani initially refused to accept. With prodding, Namangani accepted the ceasefire and settled into life in the village of Hoit. There, he became involved in heroin trafficking. He also began to attract others who were unhappy with the Tajik ceasefire. The drug trade financed his group of growing supporters.

By 1998, Yuldeshev had settled in Kandahar as a guest of the Taliban and had made alliances with Osama bin Laden and Mullah Mohammad Omar, the Taliban's spiritual leader. Namangani relocated to Afghanistan with his supporters, and in 1998 the group announced the formation of the Islamic Movement of Uzbekistan. The group used Afghanistan as its base of operations for activities against the Uzbek government, and by 1999 the IMU began an orchestrated series of campaigns against the Karimov regime.

The aggressive campaign to overthrow the Uzbek government would include bombings and kidnappings, and be funded mainly through drug trafficking. In February 1999, an assassination attempt on President Karimov failed. However, a campaign of car bombings that same month in the Uzbek capital of Tashkent resulted in sixteen deaths. In August, the group kidnapped eight Kyrgyzstan soldiers and four Japanese geologists, who were held until a ransom was paid. In August 2000, four U.S. mountain climbers were taken hostage by the group. The mountain climbers were held for six days before finally escaping.

Prior to October 2001, the IMU aimed activity primarily at Uzbek targets. However, by mid-2001, the group began to broaden its goals. By June, the group renamed itself the Islamic Party of Turkistan and issued its new objective of a pan-Islamic state covering Central Asia. Following the events of September 11, 2001, the IMU fought alongside the Taliban against coalition forces in Afghanistan. In November, both Yuldeshev and Namangani were tried in absentia for their involvement in the 1999 Tashkent bombings, which killed sixteen people. They were both sentenced to death. However, Namangani was believed to have been killed in a U.S.-led bombing campaign of Afghanistan in late 2001.

In addition to fighting coalition forces in Afghanistan, IMU members began operations throughout Central Asia. The IMU claimed responsibility for explosions in the Kyrgyzstan city of Bishkek in December 2002 and in Osh in May 2003, which killed eight people. Also in May 2003, Kyrgyzstan security forces foiled an attempt by IMU operatives to detonate bombs at the U.S. Embassy and a U.S.-owned hotel in Bishkek, Kyrgyzstan. On July 29, 2004, the IMU executed a series of suicide car bombs in Tashkent, Uzbekistan, causing much damage and many deaths. The first car bomb exploded at the Prosecutor General's office, killing two and injuring four. The next suicide car bomber attacked at the Israeli embassy, killing three and injuring one. The final suicide bomber attempted to strike the U.S. Embassy, but failed and caused only minor damage to the building. However, the bomb killed two bystanders. The Uzbek government originally blamed the group, Hizb-ut-tahir, which was committed to the creation of an Islamic state in Uzbekistan through nonviolent methods. Hizb-ut-tahir denied involvement and the IMU claimed responsibility.

The IMU continues to operate under the leadership of Yuldeshev and with the guidance of al-Qaeda and Osama bin Laden. However, the group's use of militant activities has declined under the leadership of Yuldeshev, who is considered more of a political philosopher in contrast to the military leader, Namangani. The group continues to control drug trade and to traffic heroin to pay for its operations and is believed by U.S. intelligence to operate out of the Ferghan Valley—the region where Tajik, Kyrgyz, and Uzbek borders converge.

PHILOSOPHY AND TACTICS

In the beginning, Namangani and Yuldeshev were disillusioned by the lack of action on the part of the Islamic Renaissance Party. Both men ascribed to Wahabism, a fundamentalist sect of Islam that calls for strict adherence to Islamic law and seeks the creation of an Islamic state in Uzbekistan. As the group established itself and its alliances

KEY EVENTS

1998: IMU declared its goals.

1999: IMU attempted to assassinate President Karimov.

1999: Car bombing campaign in Tashkent, Uzbekistan, killed sixteen people.

1999: IMU kidnapped eight Kyrgyz soldiers and four Japanese geologists.

2000: IMU held four U.S. mountain climbers hostage for six days until they escaped.

2001: IMU announced its goal to create a pan-Islamic state in Central Asia.

2001: Leaders Namangani and Yuldeshev were convicted for their involvement in the February 1999 car bombing campaign in Tashkent and sentenced to death.

2002: IMU claimed responsibility for bombing that occurred in Bishkek, Kyrgyzstan.

2003: IMU claims responsibility for bombing that occurred in Osh, Kyrgyzstan.

2003: Kyrgyz security forces foiled a bombing attempt on U.S. interests in Kyrgyzstan.

2004: Three suicide car bombers in Tashkent, Uzbekistan, killed seven and injured eight.

---

throughout Central Asia, the IMU decided on a different goal, the creation of a pan-Islamic state that would include Uzbekistan, Kyrgyzstan, Tajikistan, Kazakhstan, Turkmenistan, and the Xinxiang province in China.

To reach these goals, the IMU used three tactics: creation of alliances, control of drug trade, and armed activities. Before the official creation of the IMU, both of its leaders, Namangani and Yuldeshev, developed alliances. While Namangani fought in the Tajik civil war, he developed a following of supporters. Yuldeshev, on the other hand, traveled throughout Central Asia and created alliances and underground cells of his group Adolat in areas

such as Pakistan, Saudi Arabia, the United Arab Emirates, and Turkey. However, the alliance with Osama bin Laden and al-Qaeda would define the group and help to establish its wider goal for Central Asia.

To fund its activities, the IMU relied on its involvement in the drug trade, as well as its alliances. Namangani established control of the heroin trade during his residence in Tajikistan. In 2001, the Kyrgyz director of the secret service revealed that the IMU controlled most of the drug trade in the region. The U.S. State Department also noted the IMU control of and participation in the trafficking of heroin from Central Asia.

From its inception, the IMU has advocated the militant overthrow of the Uzbek government. As such, it has claimed responsibility for a series of violent attacks in the region. It began its activities with a carefully orchestrated car bomb attack in the Uzbek capital of Tashkent. This attack killed sixteen people, which resulted in death sentences for both Namangani and Yuldeshev. In addition, the group arranged kidnapping operations, providing ransom funds to assist in funding other operations. Once the IMU established its pan-Islamic goal, it joined its activities to support al-Qaeda and its fight against the coalition forces in Afghanistan.

OTHER PERSPECTIVES

The IMU goal of a militant overthrow of the Karimov regime was enhanced by President Karimov's decision to help the United States in its fight against Osama bin Laden and al-Qaeda. However, a human rights watch group issued a report documenting the Karimov regime's oppressive activities. It alleges that under Karimov, over 7,000 prisoners, mostly Muslim, have been tortured and mistreated. As a result of these revelations, both the United States and the European Bank for Reconstruction have cut previously promised financial aid, citing slow progress toward democratic reforms. This has done little to quell the anti-Western sentiment in the region.

The IMU seeks more than the expulsion of Western interests from the region. It desires an Islamic state that would strictly adhere to a fundamentalist interpretation of Islamic law. According to Ahmed Rashid, the IMU, like the

PRIMARY SOURCE

Islamic Movement of Uzbekistan (IMU)

DESCRIPTION

The Islamic Movement of Uzbekistan (IMU) is a group of Islamic militants from Uzbekistan and other Central Asian states. The IMU is closely affiliated with al-Qa'ida and, under the leadership of Tohir Yoldashev, has embraced Usama Bin Ladin's anti-U.S., anti-Western agenda. The IMU also remains committed to its original goals of overthrowing Uzbekistani President Karimov and establishing an Islamic state in Uzbekistan.

ACTIVITIES

The IMU in recent years has participated in attacks on US and Coalition soldiers in Afghanistan and Pakistan, and plotted attacks on U.S. diplomatic facilities in Central Asia.

In November 2004, the IMU was blamed for an explosion in the southern Kyrgyzstani city of Osh that killed one police officer and one terrorist. In May 2003, Kyrgyzstani security forces disrupted an IMU cell that was seeking to bomb the U.S. Embassy and a nearby hotel in Bishkek, Kyrgyzstan. The IMU was also responsible for explosions in Bishkek in December 2002 and Osh in May 2003 that killed eight people.

The IMU primarily targeted Uzbekistani interests before October 2001 and is believed to have been responsible for five car bombs in Tashkent in February 1999. IMU militants also took foreigners hostage in 1999 and 2000, including four U.S. citizens who were mountain climbing in August 2000 and four Japanese geologists and eight Kyrgyzstani soldiers in August 1999.

STRENGTH

Probably fewer than 500.

LOCATION/AREA OF OPERATION

IMU militants are scattered throughout South Asia, Tajikistan, and Iran. The area of operations includes Afghanistan, Iran, Kyrgyzstan, Pakistan, Tajikistan, Kazakhstan, and Uzbekistan.

EXTERNAL AID

The IMU receives support from other Islamic extremist groups and patrons in the Middle East and Central and South Asia.

Source: U.S. Department of State. *Country Reports on Terrorism.* Washington, D.C., 2004.

Taliban and al-Qaeda, seeks an Islamic state "not as a way of creating just society but simply as a means to regulate personal behavior and dress code for Muslims—a concept that distorts centuries of tradition, culture, history, and even the religion of Islam itself."

SUMMARY

The IMU began as a group of militant Islamist seeking an Islamic state in Uzbekistan. As a result of its alliances with Osama bin Laden and al-Qaeda, the group has devised a larger goal of a pan-Islamic state covering Central Asia. The group engages in armed conflict and kidnappings in an effort to reach this goal. The IMU also controls much of the heroin trade

in the region to fund its activities. In 2001, the group fought alongside al-Qaeda in Afghanistan against coalition forces. During this time, one of its leaders, Namangani, is believed to have been killed. However, its armed activities have continued. The group is now believed to have 500 to 700 members throughout Central Asia. Its current leader, Yuldeshev, is believed to be in the Ferghan valley of Afghanistan.

SOURCES

Books

Rashid, Ahmed. *Jihad: The Rise of Militant Islam in Central Asia.* New Haven, Conn.: Yale University Press, 2002.

Periodicals

"IMU Controls Drug Traffic to Central Asia." *Pravada.* May 30, 2001.

Haven, Paul and Katherine Shrader. "U.S., Pakistan Exploit Rifts within Factions of al-Qaeda." *Ottawa Citizen.* May 11, 2005.

Web sites

Center for Defense Information. "In the Spotlight: IMU." <http://www.cdi.org/terrorism/imu.cfm> (accessed October 19, 2005).

Council on Foreign Relations. " Uzbekistan." <http:// cfrterrorism.org/coalition/uzbekistan.html> (accessed October 19, 2005).

Foreign and Commonwealth Offices. "Islamic Movement of Uzbekistan." <http://www.fco.gov.uk/servlet/Front? pagename = OpenMarket/Xcelerate/ShowPage&c = Page &cid = 1049909003533> (accessed October 19, 2005).

MIPT Terrorism Knowledge Base. "Islamic Movement of Uzbekistan." <http://www.tkb.org/Group.jsp?groupID = 4075> (accessed October 19, 2005).

Monterey Institute of International Studies. " Islamic Movement of Uzbeckistan." <http://cns.miis.edu/ research/wtc01/imu.htm> (accessed October 19, 2005).

Audio and Visual Media

Weekend Edition: NPR. "Interview: Martha Brill Olcot Discusses Terrorism in Uzbekistan." April 4, 2004.

Jaish-e-Mohammed (JEM)

LEADER: Maulana Masood Azhar

YEAR ESTABLISHED OR BECAME ACTIVE: 2000

USUAL AREA OF OPERATION: Jammu & Kashmir, India

Jaish-E-Mohammed (JEM) is a Pakistan-based Islamic extremist group formed by Maulana Masood Azhar, in 2000. Though it is relatively a newer terrorist outfit, it is rapidly gaining momentum in the terrorist activities arena in the Jammu and Kashmir (J&K) region of India. JEM is known by numerous other names, including Army of Mohammed, Army of the Prophet Mohammed, Jaish-e-Mohammad (Muhammed), Jaish-e-Mohammed Mujahideen E-Tanzeem, Jaish-i-Mohammed (Mohammed, Muhammad, Muhammed), Jeish-e-Mahammed, Khuddam-ul-Islam, Mohammed's Army, National Movement for the Restoration of Pakistani Sovereignty and Army of the Prophet, and Tehrik Ul-Furqaan.

In 2001, U.S. Secretary of State Colin Powell designated JEM as a foreign terrorist organization. In 2003, the JEM was re-designated as a foreign terrorist organization. Subsequently, Pakistani authorities banned the organization and froze its assets. However, the group allegedly continues to operate and is held responsible by Indian intelligence officials for various terrorist strikes against India.

HISTORY

In 1994, Maulana Masood Azhar, a prominent member of a terrorist group known as the

Sajad Bhat, a suspected regional leader of the Jaish-e-Mohammed movement, is escorted by Indian Border Security Force authorities shortly after his arrest on January 3, 2005. Fayaz Kabli/Reuters/ Landov

Harakat ul-Ansar (HUA), was arrested by the Indian authorities. Masood Azhar was allegedly involved with al-Qaeda and fought against the U.S. troops in Somalia. Several unsuccessful attempts were reportedly made by HUA to free Masood Azhar. In 1994, HUA kidnapped several American and British nationals in New Delhi, and in 1995 more Western tourists were kidnapped in Kashmir, to demand Masood Azhar's release from Indian authorities. The Indian government refused to give in to their demands. However, the authorities were forced to release him in 1999, when several HUA terrorists allegedly hijacked an Indian Airlines aircraft carrying 155 passengers and flew it to Kandahar, Afghanistan.

Soon after his release from jail, Azhar reportedly met with Osama bin Laden and obtained financial and tactical support from him to form his own militant organization, the Jaish-e-Mohammed, or Army of the Prophet (Mohammed). Meanwhile, the HUA was designated as a terrorist organization by the U.S. Department of State. According to published reports in the Indian media, the HUA changed its name to Harakat ul-Mujahidin (HUM) to avoid ramifications of the ban.

JEM was floated, in Pakistan, allegedly with the approval of three prominent scholars of religious schools (in Pakistan): Mufti Nizamuddin Shamzai of the Majlis-e-Tawan-e-Islami (MT),

Maulana Mufti Rashid Ahmed of the Dar-ul Ifta-e-wal-Irshad, and Maulana Sher Ali of the Sheikh-ul-Hadith Dar-ul Haqqania. Analysts state that Masood Azhar had garnered huge popularity and earned the respect of his colleagues after his coerced freedom from the Indian authorities. The Indian intelligence authority alleges that JEM was formed with the help of Pakistan's Inter-Services Intelligence (ISI), Osama bin Laden, the Taliban government of Afghanistan (at the time), and several Islamic extremists based in Pakistan. Analysts assert that when Masood Azhar formed JEM, he was planning on naming the group Lashkar-e-Mohammed, but decided against it as it could be easily confused with another existing Islamic extremist organization known as Lashkar-e-Jhangvi.

Some of the eminent HUM members were reportedly not too happy with Azhar's decision to form a new organization. The groups continued to coexist in spite of the fact that several top members from the HUM left the organization to join JEM. Even though the groups had similar ideologies, there were reportedly frequent clashes between them over matters such as financial allotments and other assets. Intelligence agencies and monitor groups claim that the HUM's operations were severely affected after most of its members joined the JEM, in 2000.

JEM members, since 2000, have organized a series of recruitment rallies all over Pakistan, allegedly motivating Islamic youths to wage *jihad* (a holy war against those who do not believe in Islamist fundamentalism). As thought by Indian intelligence, the outfit has grown significantly since its inception. According to published U.S. State Department reports, its cadre strength is estimated to be in the hundreds. The organization allegedly has members based in Pakistan, Azad Kashmir (Pakistan-occupied Kashmir, or PoK), and several Indian towns and villages in the Jammu and Kashmir (administered by India) region. According to analysts, most members of JEM are either Kashmiris or Pakistanis. However, a few Afghan war veterans, of Afghan and Arab descent, are also active members. The group is thought to recruit local people to act as guides or to partake in suicide bombing activities. The organization, allegedly, has centers in a few cities in Pakistan. Prior to the fall of the Taliban regime in Afghanistan, in

Maulana Massod Azhar, the leader of the terrorist group Jaish-e-Mohammed, attends a pro-Taliban conference in Islamabad, Pakistan, on August 26, 2001. Mian Khursheed/Reuters/Landov

2001, the outfit also reportedly maintained terrorist camps in Afghanistan.

The Indian Government claims that JEM has been involved in several terrorist operations against Indian civilians and armed forces in Kashmir, killing hundreds. The government also claims that the group is responsible for a few terrorist attacks in other parts of the country—the most prominent being the attack on the Indian Parliament in New Delhi, in 2001. This, as alleged by the government, was a joint operation conducted by the JEM and another Pakistan-based terrorist outfit, Lashkar-e-Tayyiba (LT), though both groups have denied responsibility for the operation. The Indian authorities, in the past, have also arrested or killed several terrorists who were allegedly working for the JEM in other states of India, apart from Jammu and Kashmir.

Because of pressure from India and other foreign countries after the Indian Parliament attack, Masood Azhar was arrested by Pakistani security forces on December 29, 2001. However, the Lahore High Court passed an order on December 14, 2002, to release Azhar, citing unlawful arrest.

There reportedly have been numerous other terrorist activities carried out by the JEM. In

October 2001, four JEM terrorists attacked the J&K Legislative building in Srinagar, India, killing more than thirty people. Following the reports that the United States considered declaring JEM as a foreign terrorist organization, JEM reportedly renamed itself as Tehrik-al-Furqan. Experts claim that JEM also transferred money from bank accounts to the names of their low-profile supporters. Indian intelligence officials as well as monitor groups assert that most of the money was invested in commodity trading, real estate, and production of consumer goods—in a bid to legalize the funds.

In late 2001, the U.S. Department of State announced the addition of JEM to the U.S. Treasury Department's Office of Foreign Asset Control (OFAC) list. This list includes organizations that allegedly support terrorist groups and have assets in U.S. jurisdiction that can be frozen or controlled. Toward the end of 2001, the U.S. Department of State did place JEM on its list of foreign terrorist organizations. Eventually, the Pakistan government banned a number of Islamic terrorist organizations, including JEM, and detained several of its members. Their assets were also reportedly frozen.

Another leading JEM member (also a close associate of Masood Azhar), Sheikh Omar Saeed, was involved in the kidnapping and murder of *Wall Street Journal* reporter Daniel Pearl, in 2002. Omar Saeed and his accomplices were later arrested by Pakistani police and found guilty of kidnapping and murdering Daniel Pearl. Around the same time, Pakistani authorities claimed that JEM terrorists were involved in fierce anti-Christian attacks in the Pakistani cities of Islamabad, Murree, and Taxila.

In 2003, reports indicated that the JEM was renamed as Khuddam-ul-Islam, and was divided after Azhar expelled the outfit's Karachi unit chief, Abdullah Shah Mazhar. Other members were also expelled. It is thought by many experts that the expelled members formed their own organizations.

The group, as thought by intelligence agencies and monitor groups, during this time, started claiming to propagate religion and undertake social welfare. In the same year, Jaish-e-Mohammed reportedly split into two factions; the splinter group was known as Jamaat ul-Furqaan.

LEADERSHIP

MAULANA MASOOD AZHAR

Maulana Masood Azhar was born in Bahawalpur, Pakistan, on July 10, 1968. He joined the Jamia Islamia *madrassa* (Islamic religious school) at the Binori Mosque in Karachi, Pakistan, and learned about the jihadi movement. Leaders of several radical Islamic organizations, including Harakat ul-Ansar (HUA), had an influence over the operations of the madrassa and recruited several students to join the Afghan war. Azhar reportedly participated in the Afghan war and also developed close contacts with other prominent members of the Harakat, as well as the head of another militant group, Jamiat-e-Ulemai Islam organization, Maulana Fuzlur Rahman. Analysts state that he eventually rose to power in HUA, and was appointed the general secretary.

Azhar traveled extensively to propagate Islamism and to allegedly encourage Muslims to join the jihad movement. In 1994, while on a mission to meet top HUA commanders in Kashmir, he was arrested by the Indian authorities. HUA reportedly made numerous unsuccessful attempts to get Masood Azhar released from the Indian authorities. On December 24, 1999, an Indian Airlines aircraft flying from Kathmandu, Nepal, to New Delhi, India, was hijacked by five Pakistani nationals purportedly belonging to HUA and taken off to Kandahar, Afghanistan. The crisis ended after eight days when the Indian authorities agreed to meet with the hijackers' demand of releasing the hostages in exchange for the release of three top Pakistani militant leaders, including Maulana Masood Azhar, Sheikh Ahmed Omar Saeed, and Mushtaq Ahmed Zargar. Soon after his release from jail, Masood Azhar and his accomplices reportedly formed Jaish-e-Mohammed.

PHILOSOPHY AND TACTICS

Terrorism experts are of the opinion that Jaish-e-Mohammed is ideologically and organizationally an extension of the militant group Harakat ul-Mujahideen, also based in Pakistan. The primary goal of JEM is to establish the independent state of Kashmir by forcing a withdrawal of Indian military from the region. Analysts and intelligence officials state that, like other leading Islamic terrorist organizations, JEM has a goal of "freeing" Kashmir by using violence and spreading terror in Jammu and Kashmir (J&K), and other parts of India. It is allegedly politically associated with the radical political party, Jamiat Ulema-i-Islam Fazlur Rehman faction.

JEM claims that each of its offices in Pakistan serves as training centers of jihad. During his period of detainment in the Indian jail (1994–1999), Masood Azhar allegedly wrote for a pro-Taliban journal commending the anti-minorities acts committed by Islamic fundamentalists in J&K.

Jaish-e-Mohammed employs suicide bombing as its main technique of attack. Additionally published reports suggest that rocket grenades, kidnappings, bombings, and shoot outs are also extensively used for targeted acts of terrorism against the Indian security forces and civilians. As thought by Western intelligence and monitor groups, the JEM borrows much of its ideology from al-Qaeda and the Taliban. The exchange of knowledge as well as personnel among JEM and some of the other militant groups is common practice.

Intelligence analysts and terrorism experts have described most Jaish-e-Mohammed attacks as *fidayeen* (an Arabic word meaning "one who is ready to sacrifice his life for the cause"—more commonly known as suicide fighters) attacks. In simpler terms, fidayeen attacks refer to the strategy of the terrorists to storm a high-security target, including army bases, camps, and public places, and kill as many military personnel/civilians as possible before getting killed in the attack.

Analysts claim that one such major attack was carried out purportedly by JEM terrorists, in 2000, when a teenage operative of JEM drove a car laden with explosives into the gates of the Badamibagh Army headquarters in J&K. This was allegedly the first known suicide attack carried out by the JEM.

JEM is based in the Pakistani cities of Peshawar and Muzaffarabad, and reportedly maintains terrorist camps in Afghanistan. Terrorism analysts generally agree that JEM,

KEY EVENTS

1999: Maulana Masood Azhar and two other terrorists released by the Indian government in exchange for hostages aboard a hijacked Indian Airlines aircraft.

2000: A JEM operative drives an explosive-laden car onto an army base in Kashmir, killing himself and several others.

2000: Four terrorists attack the Jammu and Kashmir legislative assembly building in Srinagar, India, killing more than 30 people. The JEM claims responsibility for the attack, but later denies the claim.

2001: The Indian government publicly implicates the JEM and Lashkar-e-Tayyiba for the December 13, 2001, attack on the Indian Parliament that kills nine and injures eighteen.

2002: Top JEM operative, Omar Saeed Sheikh, claims to be involved in the kidnapping and murder of *Wall Street Journal* reporter Daniel Pearl. Saeed and his accomplices are later charged and sentenced.

---

like other Islamic terrorist organizations operating in the Kashmir valley region, has received assistance from the madrassas in Pakistan. The Indian government has also repeatedly claimed that JEM and other terrorist outfits receive financial and operational help from Pakistan's ISI. The outfit reportedly has a close association with the Binoria Mosque in Karachi, Pakistan. According to analysts, it is through the mosque that the group is also closely associated with the Taliban regime and Osama bin Laden's al-Qaeda.

Indian and Pakistani authorities state that Masood Azhar has met with top al-Qaeda leaders, including bin Laden and Mullah Omar on several occasions. Most members of JEM are also thought to be deeply influenced by the ideology of Sipah-e-Sahaba organization founder Maulana Haq Nawaz Jhangvi, another prominent religious leader. In fact, Masood Azhar has reportedly declared in public that the Sipah-e-Sahaba and JEM have common goals of waging jihad in Kashmir. The JEM is also reported to have close ties with Sunni sectarian outfits like Lashkar-e-Jhangvi.

The JEM is thought to receive funding from Osama bin Laden and the Taliban (in addition to the madrassas). News reports suggest that the outfit raises funds for its operations by using various other means. This includes donation from businessmen and others through newsletters, magazines, and pamphlets. The group, allegedly, also propagates their ideology and collects donation through the Internet.

OTHER PERSPECTIVES

According to a report published in *The Guardian*, after his release from an Indian jail in 1999, Maulana Masood Azhar addressed a rally of more than 10,000 followers and declared, "I have come here because this is my duty to tell you that Muslims should not rest in peace until we have destroyed America and India." He went on to say that he will not rest until Kashmir is "liberated."

The government of India has often spoken about the terrorist activities conducted by Jaish-e-Mohammed, and the support it allegedly receives from the ISI of Pakistan. *The Hindu*, a national daily in India, in one of its reports stated that JEM claimed responsibility for a suicide attack on the Jammu and Kashmir legislative assembly building in Srinagar (capital of J&K) on October 1, 2000, that killed at least thirty-one persons—a claim the group denied after a few days. Reacting to the incident, the then-Union Home Minister of India, L.K. Advani, while visiting Srinagar, said, "Pakistan cannot deny that Maulana Azhar is there (in Pakistan). If they (Pakistan) are honest about fighting terrorism, let them hand over the JEM leader to India so that he is brought to justice." Mr. Advani further stated, "We believe that international terrorism is a global menace . . . It needs a global response and we have endorsed the stand taken by the U.S. in this regard."

According to the Indian Ministry of External Affair, after the terrorist attack on

PRIMARY SOURCE

Jaish-e-Mohammed (JEM) a.k.a. Army of Mohammed Tehrik ul-Furqaan, Khuddam-ul-Islam

DESCRIPTION

The Jaish-e-Mohammed is an Islamic extremist group based in Pakistan that was formed in early 2000 by Masood Azhar upon his release from prison in India. The group's aim is to unite Kashmir with Pakistan. It is politically aligned with the radical political party Jamiat Ulema-i-Islam's Fazlur Rehman faction (JUI-F). By 2003, JEM had splintered into Khuddam ul-Islam (KUI), headed by Azhar, and Jamaat ul-Furqan (JUF), led by Abdul Jabbar, who was released in August 2004 from Pakistani custody after being detained for suspected involvement in the December 2003 assassination attempts against President Musharraf. Pakistan banned KUI and JUF in November 2003. Elements of JEM and Lashkar e-Tayyiba combined with other groups to mount attacks as "The Save Kashmir Movement."

ACTIVITIES

The JEM's leader, Masood Azhar, was released from Indian imprisonment in December 1999 in exchange for 155 hijacked Indian Airlines hostages. The Harakat-ul-Ansar (HUA) kidnappings in 1994 of US and British nationals by Omar Sheik in New Delhi and the HUA/al-Faran kidnappings in July 1995 of Westerners in Kashmir were two of several previous HUA efforts to free Azhar. On October 1, 2001, JEM claimed responsibility for a suicide attack on the Jammu and Kashmir legislative assembly building in Srinagar that killed at least thirty-one persons but later denied the claim. The Indian Government has publicly implicated JEM, along with Lashkar e-Tayyiba, for the December 13, 2001, attack on the Indian Parliament that killed nine and injured

eighteen. Pakistani authorities suspect that perpetrators of fatal anti-Christian attacks in Islamabad, Murree, and Taxila during 2002 were affiliated with JEM. The Pakistanis have implicated elements of JEM in the assassination attempts against President Musharraf in December 2003.

STRENGTH

Has several hundred armed supporters located in Pakistan and in India's southern Kashmir and Doda regions and in the Kashmir valley, including a large cadre of former HUM members. Supporters are mostly Pakistanis and Kashmiris and also include Afghans and Arab veterans of the Afghan war.

LOCATION/AREA OF OPERATION

Pakistan. JEM maintained training camps in Afghanistan until the fall of 2001.

EXTERNAL AID

Most of JEM's cadre and material resources have been drawn from the militant groups Harakat ul-Jihad-i-Islami (HUJI) and the Harakat ul-Mujahidin (HUM). JEM had close ties to Afghan Arabs and the Taliban. Usama bin Ladin is suspected of giving funding to JEM. JEM also collects funds through donation requests in magazines and pamphlets. In anticipation of asset seizures by the Pakistani Government, JEM withdrew funds from bank accounts and invested in legal businesses, such as commodity trading, real estate, and production of consumer goods.

Source: U.S. Department of State. *Country Reports on Terrorism.* Washington, D.C., 2004.

---

the Indian Parliament in New Delhi on December 13, 2001, L. K. Advani in a statement from the government of India said, "It is now evident that the terrorist assault on the Parliament House was executed jointly by Pakistan based and supported terrorist outfits, namely, Lashkar-e-Taiba and Jaish-e-Mohammed. These two organizations are known to derive their support and patronage

from Pak ISI." He went on to say that during interrogation, one of the accomplices revealed that the attack was masterminded by Gazi Baba, a top leader of the Jaish-e-Mohammed organization. He further said that "Lashkar-e-Taiba and Jaish-e-Mohammed in particular have been in the forefront in organizing terrorist violence in our country."

At the time, the Pakistani President Pervez Musharraf reportedly denied the presence of JEM in Pakistan. However, in the aftermath of the September 11 attacks in the United States, there was reportedly mounting pressure (from the United States and other countries) on his government to ban several militant outfits, including Jaish-e-Mohammed.

In a nation-wide televised speech, in 2002, President Musharraf asserted that his government intends to impart severe punishment to those responsible for extremism in Indian-administered region of Jammu and Kashmir or anyone who is involved in anti-minorities activities inside Pakistan. The President mentioned that the two militant groups Lashkar-e-Tayyiba and Jaish-e-Mohammed that were implicated by the Indian government, to be involved in the attacks on the legislative building in Kashmir, and on the Indian Parliament were banned. According to a report published by the Center for Contemporary Conflict, this move of President Musharraf was commended by world leaders.

SUMMARY

The Indian government, until the early 2000s, had a long-standing ban on militant outfits operating in the Jammu & Kashmir region. These militant outfits have been accused (by the government) of performing targeted acts of terror against innocent civilians in J&K and other places in the country. Jaish-e-Mohammed is one of the more prominent militant outfits held responsible by the government for numerous acts of terror.

The Jaish-e-Mohammed, since 2001, has been recognized as a terrorist organization by most governments worldwide. Following the September 11 attacks, the U.S. government froze the assets of several militant organizations, including JEM, allegedly for their links with al-Qaeda and the Taliban. Soon after the terror strikes on the Kashmir Legislative Assembly

building in Srinagar, India, and the Indian Parliament in New Delhi, the U.S. Department of State formally designated Jaish as a Foreign Terrorist Organization.

Subsequently, President Pervez Musharraf of Pakistan banned JEM, and reportedly launched an operation against the organization by arresting members and conducting interrogations. It has been alleged that JEM has stated publicly that they will not succumb to the pressure of the ban imposed on them and will continue with their jihad in Kashmir.

Most analysts argue that the lack of comprehensive ceasefire (in the Kashmir region) implies that neither the JEM militants nor the government authorities would lower their guard. As of 2005, the JEM allegedly continues to carry out terrorist operations in J&K.

SOURCES

Web sites

GlobalSecurity.org. "Jaish-e-Mohammed." < http:// www.globalsecurity.org/military/world/para/jem.htm > (accessed October 20, 2005).

Kashmir Herald. "Jaish-e-Mohammed." < http:// www.kashmirherald.com/profiles/jaisheMohammed.html > (accessed October 20, 2005).

Ministry of External Affairs, India. "L.K. Advani's Speech after Terrorist Attack on Indian Parliament." < http://meaindia.nic.in/speech/2001/12/18spc01.htm > (accessed October 20, 2005).

South Asia Terrorism Portal. "Jaish-e-Mohammed Mujahideen e Tanzim." < http://www.satp.org/sat-porgtp/countries/india/states/jandk/terrorist_outfits/ jaish_e_Mohammed_mujahideen_e_tanzeem.htm > (accessed October 20, 2005).

South Asia Analysis Group. "Paper No. 376 Jaish-e-Mohammed." < http://saag.org/papers4/papers376.html > (accessed October 20, 2005).

SEE ALSO

Sipah-e-Sahaba Pakistan (SSP)

Japanese Red Army

LEADER: Fusako Shigenobu

YEAR ESTABLISHED OR BECAME ACTIVE: 1971

ESTIMATED SIZE: 25–40

USUAL AREA OF OPERATION: Asia and the Middle East, headquartered in Lebanon

OVERVIEW

One of the most feared terrorist organizations in the world, the Japanese Red Army (JRA, *Nippon Sekigun*) was a small, extremely violent group of Japanese anarchists intent on beginning a world-wide communist revolution. JRA grew out of a merger between the Red Army Faction (*Sekigun-ha*), a breakaway group from the Japanese Communist League, and the Keihin Anti-Treaty Joint Struggle (*Keihin Ampo Kyoto*). In 1986, the JRA changed its name to the Anti-Imperialist International Brigades.

The JRA began in 1971 and remains under the leadership of its founder, Fusako Shigenobu. Sponsored by Syria, Libya, and North Korea, it is closely linked to the Popular Front for the Liberation of Palestine (PFLP). The JRA had its heyday in the 1970s. With most of its leaders in jail or dead, the JRA has been quiet since the 1980s. It is now believed to be defunct.

HISTORY

There have been three Japanese Red Armies, all of them linked. The Red Army Faction, the first JRA, was a radical extremist group that began in the late 1960s during a period of violent student unrest. For its first large-scale public activity, the group planned to capture the residence of the

Fusako Shigenobu, founder of the Japanese Red Army. © Corbis

KEY EVENTS

1972: The best known JRA attack was the massacre of travelers in the terminal at LOD Airport in Tel Aviv, Israel.

1974: The JRA invaded the French Embassy at The Hague and held the ambassador and 10 other people captive for five days.

1975: JRA members attempted to take over the U.S. Embassy in Kuala Lumpur, Malaysia.

1986: JRA detonated a car bomb outside of the Canadian Embassy and launched rockets against the U.S. and Japanese embassies in Djakarta.

1987: JRA launched a rocket attack and car bombing against the U.S. and British embassies in Rome.

1988: JRA bombed a USO in Naples, Italy, that killed five people.

1990: The last confirmed JRA attack was a homemade rocket attack on the Imperial palaces in Kyoto and Tokyo.

Japanese Prime Minister, but this effort failed miserably. The Red Army Faction then captured international headlines in March 1970 when it carried out Japan's first airline hijacking. This Red Army action proved more peaceful than the ones that succeeded it. Some of the 155 passengers on board the hijacked Japan Air Lines claimed that the Red Army Faction terrorists provided better service than the flight attendants. The Red Army Faction members directed the plane to North Korea and remained there for guidance in carrying out world revolution.

With the Red Army Faction leadership expected to be out of action for years, some members of the group who had remained behind in Japan merged with another extremist group, Keihin Anti-Treaty Joint Struggle. (The treaty in the title refers to the U.S.-Japan Security Treaty.) Whereas the Red Army Faction had money but no weapons, the Keihin group had weapons but no money. The two groups formed the United Red Army (*Rengo Sekigun*). The aims of the new group, commonly known as the JRA, were to overthrow the Japanese government, end the Japanese monarchy, and foment world revolution.

The JRA was a marriage of convenience that ended in disaster. The groups united for logistical and tactical purposes, but differed too much in philosophy. The Red Army Faction insisted that the members of the new band prepare themselves for combat by thoroughly examining their motives to ensure that they were tough enough to create revolution. In December 1971, the members gathered in an isolated cabin in the Japanese mountains. A member of the Keihin group, Mitsuo Ozaki, was accused of having discussed the location of the JRA's weapons with unauthorized persons as well as failing to demonstrate true revolutionary spirit. It was decided that he needed to engage in fistfights with other members to toughen him up. When Ozaki thanked the group for this opportunity to prove himself, his comments were viewed as attempts to curry favor and signs of additional weakness. He was

Kozo Okamoto stands trial for being one of the Red Army terrorists who killed passengers at the Ben Gurion Airport in Tel Aviv in 1972. © *Micha Bar Am/Magnum Photos*

beaten, tied to a stake, and beaten some more before being left overnight. The next day, following additional beatings, Ozaki died. The JRA then decided that he chose to die when he realized he was weak. Another member was then beaten to death in a similar manner for flirting with women, conduct which was unbecoming for a true revolutionary. Eight more United Red Army members, most of them former Keihin revolutionaries, died from beatings before the attacks ceased in February 1972. Once the remains of the deceased revolutionaries were discovered, the murders shocked and repulsed the Japanese public.

Once it began to target people outside of the JRA, the organization accomplished seventeen noteworthy actions and attempted at least nine others that failed. The JRA's most infamous attack occurred on May 30, 1972, in Israel. Three JRA members, including leader Kozo Okamoto, used machine-guns and grenades to kill twenty-six people and wound eighty others at the LOD airport in Tel Aviv. Recognizing that

their capture was imminent, two of the terrorists participated in a murder-suicide pact. One shot the other, and the survivor blew himself up with a grenade. Okamoto, the only JRA survivor of the attack, was imprisoned in Israel until 1985 when he was released in exchange for Israeli prisoners and allowed to fly to Libya. Mentally ill as the result of purported torture in Israel, he has converted to Islam and remains in Libya.

The next major JRA attack occurred in Singapore. On January 31, 1974, the JRA united with the PFLP to take hostages and plant bombs at a Shell oil refinery on the island of Singapore. The attack resulted in minimal damage, no loss of life, and the escape of the JRA activists to South Yemen.

On September 12, 1974, three JRA members seized eleven hostages, including the French ambassador at the French Embassy in The Hague. They demanded the release of a JRA member, Yoshiabi Yamada, being held in France for attempting to bring counterfeit money and false passports into the country. To

LEADERSHIP

FUSAKO SHIGENOBU

Known as the Red Queen, Fusako Shigenobu was the guiding force behind the JRA. Her father had belonged to the ultra-rightist Blood Brotherhood League, a pre-World War II organization that assassinated prominent Japanese business and political leaders. She was born in 1946. The family was poor, and Shigenobu attended a commercial high school that marked her as a second-class citizen in Japan. She obtained a job as an office worker in a Kikkoman soy sauce plant after leaving school in 1964, but became disenchanted with rampant classism and sexism in the workplace. In 1965, she entered Meiji University to become a science teacher. On her first day, she joined students protesting a tuition rise. She would subsequently leave school to devote herself to the revolution, while earning money as a hostess in a bar in the Ginza section of Tokyo.

Drawn to communist ideology, Shigenobu's involvement in the student movement inspired her to found the Japanese Red Army in 1971. She aligned the JRA with the Popular Front for Liberation of Palestine because the Palestinian revolutionary movement was more advanced than the Japanese one. She married Takeski Okudaira in 1971, and they went to a terrorist training camp in the Middle East for their honeymoon. He would die in the Tel Aviv airport attack. Shigenobu was placed on the international wanted list after leading an attack on the French Embassy in the Hague. After years of being on wanted lists, she was arrested in November 2000 after police discovered her living in Tatasuki, Osaka, Japan. Immediately following her arrest, she told reporters that she would fight until the last and that she retained the same goals that she held in her youth. In 2001, Shigenobu announced that she was disbanding the JRA and would, in the future, pursue her goals using peaceful political means.

---

help speed up negotiations, the notorious terrorist Carlos Jackal acted on his own initiative and threw a grenade into a crowd of young people as a warning to the French and Dutch authorities. The grenade killed two and injured thirty-four on September 15. The JRA member was soon released.

On August 4, 1975, the JRA embarked on a successful campaign to free all of its imprisoned members by taking hostages and using them as bargaining chips. Ten JRA terrorists seized the U.S. Consulate in Kuala Lumpur, Malaysia, and held fifty-two hostages. The JRA promised to kill the hostages if seven imprisoned JRA members in Japan were not released.

Only five JRA members chose to leave prison, with the others apparently fearing additional jail time if recaptured. Yukiko Ekita, convicted in Japan in 1975 for her part in a series of bombings of large companies during 1974 and 1975, was one of the members who chose take advantage of this new policy. She was released as part of a deal struck by JRA members who hijacked a Japanese plane bound for Baghdad. Some of the other JRA members who were freed would later turn up as participants in JRA terrorist actions, much to the embarrassment and dismay of the government of Japan.

The group went into hiatus from late 1977 to mid 1986. On May 14, 1986, JRA members detonated a car bomb outside of the Canadian Embassy and launched rockets against the U.S. and Japanese embassies in Jakarta, Indonesia. Fingerprints found in a hotel room, along with the rocket launcher, matched those of a known JRA member, although credit was taken in the name of the Anti-Imperialist International Brigade. The attack occurred after the United States bombed Libya in retaliation for Libya-led terrorist attacks. The JRA choice of Libya as a sanctuary implied Libyan state sponsorship of the Japanese group.

PRIMARY SOURCE

Japanese Red Army (JRA) a.k.a. Anti-Imperialist International Brigade (AIIB)

DESCRIPTION

The JRA is an international terrorist group formed around 1970 after breaking away from the Japanese Communist League-Red Army Faction. The JRA's historical goal has been to overthrow the Japanese Government and monarchy and to help foment world revolution. JRA's leader, Fusako Shigenobu, claimed that the forefront of the battle against international imperialism was in Palestine, so in the early 1970s she led her small group to the Middle East to support the Palestinian struggle against Israel and the West. After her arrest in November 2000, Shigenobu announced she intended to pursue her goals using a legitimate political party rather than revolutionary violence, and the group announced it would disband in April 2001.

ACTIVITIES

During the 1970s, JRA carried out a series of attacks around the world, including the massacre in 1972 at Lod Airport in Israel, two Japanese airliner hijackings, and an attempted takeover of the U.S. Embassy in Kuala Lumpur. During the late 1980s, JRA began to single out American targets and used car bombs and rockets in attempted attacks on US Embassies in Jakarta, Rome, and Madrid. In April 1988, JRA operative Yu Kikumura was arrested with explosives on the New Jersey Turnpike, apparently planning an attack to coincide with the bombing of a USO club in Naples, a suspected JRA operation that killed five, including a U.S. servicewoman. He was convicted of the charges and is serving a lengthy prison sentence in the United States. Tsutomu Shirosaki, captured in 1996, is also jailed in the United States. In 2000, Lebanon deported to Japan four members it arrested in 1997, but granted a fifth operative, Kozo Okamoto, political asylum. Longtime leader Shigenobu was arrested in November 2000 and faces charges of terrorism and passport fraud. Four JRA members remain in North Korea following their involvement in a hijacking in 1970; five of their family members returned to Japan in 2004.

STRENGTH

About six hard-core members; undetermined number of sympathizers. At its peak, the group claimed to have 30 to 40 members.

LOCATION/AREA OF OPERATION

Location unknown, but possibly in Asia and/or Syrian-controlled areas of Lebanon.

EXTERNAL AID

Unknown.

Source: U.S. Department of State. *Country Reports on Terrorism*. Washington, D.C., 2004.

Evidence of further continued activity by the JRA surfaced in 1988 with the capture of JRA member, Yu Kikumura, who was arrested after behaving suspiciously on the New Jersey Turnpike. Caught with explosives, Kikumura apparently planned an attack to coincide with the April 14, 1988, bombing of a United Service Organizations (USO) club in Naples, Italy. This Italian attack killed five people, including an American servicewoman. Kikumura is currently serving a prison sentence in the United States.

By 1990, the JRA appeared on the verge of collapse. The end of the Soviet Union and the demise of the Soviet satellites in Eastern Europe badly weakened the cause of international communism. Supplanted in the Middle East by Islamist terrorist organizations and unable to recruit new members in Japan, the JRA became a collection of out-of-date middle-aged terrorists.

Perhaps more detrimental to the group's well-being, the identities of the top JRA members had become well known to police organizations throughout the world. In 1987, the Japanese government made a special effort to locate and arrest the JRA's leadership.

Humiliated on the world stage by the JRA's success at forcing the release of its members from Japanese prisons, Japan had become determined to wipe out the organization.

The first JRA member captured was Osamu Maruko. He had participated in two 1970s hijackings of Japan Airlines planes, the first in cooperation with four Palestinian terrorists and the second with the aid of JRA colleagues. Maruko was arrested in 1987, and convicted in 1993. Ekita, freed in 1975 in exchange for hostages, was arrested in March of 1995 in Romania and subsequently deported to Japan. She stood trial and was sentenced to twenty years in jail. Tsutomu Shirosaki was captured in 1996 and extradited to the United States, where he stood trial for the attack on the U.S. Embassy in Jakarta. Shirosaki was convicted and sentenced to a lengthy prison sentence.

By 2000, the JRA had become an embarrassment to some moderates in the Middle East, although it still enjoyed strong support among the Arab public. Lebanon expelled four JRA members in March 2000.

In the biggest blow to the organization, Fusako Shigenobu was captured in November 2000. While imprisoned, she announced that she would disband the JRA and launch new legal fights. Terrorism experts believe Shigenobu's declaration to be genuine and the United States downgraded the JRA from a designated terrorist organization to a watched terrorist organization in 2001.

PHILOSOPHY AND TACTICS

The JRA's early emphasis on hand-held weapons like knives, samurai swords, small-arms, and automatic weapons as well as direct contact with its victims reflected Japanese cultural customs. Such tactics seemed legitimated by the martial Bushido tradition that emphasized personal valor in direct confrontation and helped boost the prestige of the JRA within Japan. The JRA abandoned such tactics in 1977.

When it resumed public activities in 1986, the JRA began relying on bombings and rocket firings in which the JRA members would be quite remote from the target and could escape more easily. This tactical change helped preserve an organization that, given its notorious history

of killing its own and its remoteness from Japan, had great difficulties in recruiting new members.

The JRA was a tightly structured, centralized organization. The leader directed events through a political committee. The military committee, the organizational committee, and the logistics committee all reported to the political committee. The orders dispersed by JRA leaders were absolute, and a soldier would only receive tactical information. This severe restriction of information occasionally led to problems, such as the one that occurred when the JRA hijacked a Japan Air Lines flight from Tokyo to Paris on July 20, 1973. The lead hijacker died in a grenade accident and the surviving soldiers did not know what had been planned for the plane and the people onboard. After some confusion, the JRA chose to land in Libya where they then blew up the 747 airplane after releasing the passengers and crew.

The JRA was one of the first terrorist organizations to have an international focus. It worked in conjunction with other international terrorist groups, including the Baader-Meinhof Gang in Germany and the Red Brigades in Italy. It was also very closely allied with the Popular Front for the Liberation of Palestine (PFLP). By 1973, the JRA had built up a diversified network with headquarters in Beirut and Baghdad, as well as a training camp in Aden, South Yemen. It had cells in Europe, Manila, and Singapore.

While the JRA claimed to focus on overthrowing the Japanese government, it spent much of its energy creating destruction overseas and targeting non-Japanese targets. For this reason, commentators have described the organization as anarchistic.

In the 1972 Tel Aviv airport attack, the JRA aimed to kill Jews, who are not a group with a substantial presence in Japan. Most of the airport dead were Christian tourists from Puerto Rico. The JRA subsequently insisted that the Puerto Ricans deserved to die because they had arrived in Israel on Israeli visas and thereby had tacitly recognized the state that was the declared enemy of the Palestinians. The Puerto Ricans therefore were guilty of oppressing the Palestinians.

The 1974 attack on the Shell refinery in Singapore also targeted a business and people with tenuous links to Japan. The JRA publicly stated that it took this terrorist action, after studying the oil crisis, in solidarity with the

Vietnamese people in efforts to promote world-wide revolution. The PFLP, JRA's collaborators in the attack, subsequently independently issued a statement that the mission had been carried out in retaliation for the aggressive role of oil companies and the government of Singapore against Arab people in general.

In 1981, the JRA publicly stated that it was considering the rejection of violence as a political tool. In 1983, Shigenobu told the Japanese press that the group had "left the way of absolute terror." Despite this, the JRA continued to plan and execute attacks during the 1980s, although they were on a much smaller scale than the group's previous activities.

OTHER PERSPECTIVES

The brutality of the JRA meant that few people were willing to publicly speak on its behalf. One of its defenders was a man known for turning his country into a training ground for terrorism. In the wake of the Tel Aviv airport attack, Colonel Muammar el-Qaddafi of Libya praised the JRA: "Why should a Palestinian not carry out such an operation? You will see them all writing books and magazines full of theories, but otherwise unable to carry out one daring operation like that carried out by the Japanese." Israeli Prime Minister Golda Meir categorized the same attack as a "dastardly crime," and declared, "We expect that this heinous crime will be denounced by governments throughout the world and that the Arab countries participating in this great glee for murder will bear full responsibility for these acts."

SUMMARY

The JRA provided a vivid illustration of the havoc that could be caused by a small band of ruthless and dedicated terrorists. The sheer violence of the group and the unpredictability of its targets made it very difficult for government authorities to halt the JRA.

Despite its tactical success, the impact of the JRA is minimal. It did not achieve its goals of disrupting capitalism, ending the Japanese monarchy, or achieving a homeland for the Palestinians.

SOURCES

Books

Combs, Cindy. *Terrorism in the Twenty-First Century.* Upper Saddle River, NJ: Prentice-Hall, 2000.

Farrell, William R. *Blood and Rage: The Story of the Japanese Red Army.* Lexington, Mass.: D.C. Heath, 1990.

SEE ALSO

Popular Front for the Liberation of Palestine (PFLP)

Red Brigades

Jemaah Islamiyah (JI)

LEADER: Riduan Isamuddin

USUAL AREA OF OPERATION: Indonesia, Malaysia, the Philippines, Thailand, Singapore; and Pakistan

U.S. TERRORIST EXCLUSION LIST DESIGNEE: The U.S. Department of State declared JI to be a terrorist organization in October 2002

OVERVIEW

Jemaah Islamiyah (JI; translation, Islamic Organization) is a militant Islamic separatist movement dedicated to the establishment of a fundamentalist Islamic state in Southeast Asia. Its influence sweeps across the region, although many of its activities have been centered in Indonesia, the most notorious of which was the night club bombing on the island of Bali in October 2002.

HISTORY

The origins of Jemaah Islamiyah lie in the aftermath of Indonesia's successful guerilla struggle against Dutch colonists in the 1940s. A conservative strain of Islam emerged during the uprising, named Darul, which propagated the creation of an Islamic state in Southeast Asia. A Darul rebellion broke out in parts of West Java and Aceh in 1948, lasting up to fourteen years in some parts. Darul insurgents—who were often only following the instructions of village elders as opposed to set ideological goals—were ruthlessly suppressed by the dictatorships of President Sukarno and later President Suharto.

Subsequently, radicals existed in exile or underground. In 1969, a renewed attempt to spread the influence of Darul emerged under

Police officers restrain photographers after a bomb exploded at the Marriott Hotel in Jakarta, Indonesia, on August 5, 2003. Jemaah Islamiyah, a terror group linked to al-Qaeda, claimed responsibility for the attacks. AP/Wide World Photos. Reproduced by permission.

the leadership of two Javanese clerics, Abu Bakar Bashir and Abdullah Sungkar. They set up a religious school near the city of Solo and a radio station to spread their beliefs, but were repeatedly imprisoned by Suharto and forced into semi-exile in Malaysia. By the early 1980s, their small group of followers had become known as Jemaah Islamiyah (JI).

At this stage, however, JI was barely active outside its religious schools and other such affiliated institutions, and could scarcely be recognized as a formal political entity. Nevertheless, Bashir and Sungkar were building a solid base of followers. Because of the crackdowns of the Suharto government, it was sometimes necessary for them to continue seeking exile not just in Malaysia, but also in Afghanistan, where hundreds of JI followers joined the *mujahideen*'s (fighters) war against the USSR throughout the 1980s.

All senior members—more than 200 of them—of JI's current central command trained and fought in Afghanistan. Following the end of

the Afghan conflict, in the mid-1990s, the Afghanistan veterans became trainers of a new generation of mujahideen when they set up a camp in Mindanao, the second largest island in the Philippines. This was in cooperation with the Philippine-based Moro Islamic Liberation Front (MILF), which trained other JI members, plus other unaffiliated Islamic militants from Indonesia, an array of guerilla skills.

The Mindanao camp was well organized and offered a variety of training programs. These included a three-year program for new instructors and six months for regular cadets, as well as programs lasting for one year for non-JI instructors and for four months for non-JI cadets. At both levels, they encompassed both military (weapons training, bombing, map reading, guerilla training, etc.) and religious (Islamic law, traditions of the prophet, *aqidah* [faith], *jihad* [holy war], etc.) elements.

Afghanistan had further served to radicalize followers of JI, none more so than Riduan

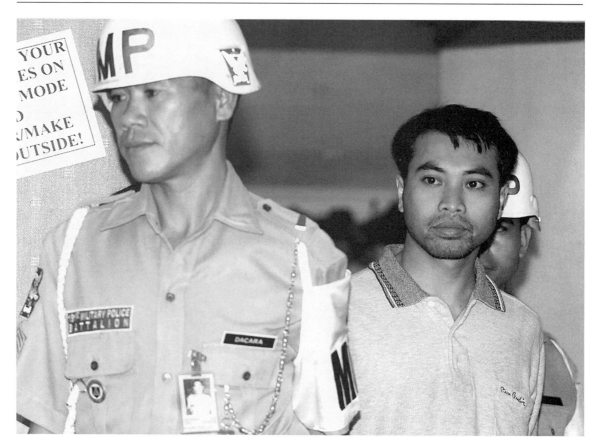

Fathur Rohman Al-Ghozi of the Jemaah Islamiya, is escorted by military police. AP/Wide World Photos

Isamuddin, currently known as Hambali. Reports have linked him to Bashir's religious school while he was a teenager; but his involvement with JI has also been dated back to a period when he lived in exile in Malaysia (c.1985–1987), or the period he spent fighting with mujahideen in Afghanistan in the late 1980s. He returned to Malaysia in 1990, setting up an import company that served as a conduit for al-Qaeda funds into Southeast Asia. Here, he was closely involved with the World Trade Center bomber, Ramzi Youseff, and his uncle, Khalid Sheik Mohammed, who between them concocted a variety of plots, including the assassinations of Pope John Paul and President Clinton when each visited Manila, and most audaciously, Operation Bojinka, a plot to blow up a dozen passenger jets flying between the United States and Asia. According to the 9/11 Commission Report, other conspiracies included, "conventional car bombing, political assassination, aircraft bombing, hijacking, reservoir poisoning,

and, ultimately, the use of aircraft as missiles guided by suicide operatives."

Quite where JI fit into this scheme of intrigue is unclear. Certainly, Hambali emerged as its leader of political and military operations in the mid-1990s, but whether plots like Bojinka were to be carried out in JI's name remain to be seen. JI never claimed any responsibility for any of the successful Islamist attacks in Malaysia and the Philippines at that time.

In 1998, Suharto was overthrown and JI followers started to return to Indonesia. Hambali is believed to have returned in October 2000. Around Christmas that year, JI carried out its first significant attack when a series of bombs went off in Indonesian cities, many in churches; eighteen people died in the attacks.

Around the same time, Indonesia's Moluccan Islands were undergoing a violent civil insurgency instigated by Islamic insurgents seeking to create a religious state. The conflict

LEADERSHIP

RIDUAN ISAMUDDIN (HAMBALI)

Described by *Time* magazine as "Asia's Own Osama," Riduan Isamuddin (known as Hambali) was the brains behind JI's bombing campaigns, and also linked to an array of ambitious terrorist plots in the mid-1990s. He is, wrote *Time* in April 2002, "a formidable figure, a meticulous, patient plotter, capable, when necessary, of taking massive risks when brewing commensurately destructive schemes."

He took charge of JI's military and political affairs in the 1990s and—following his arrest in Thailand in August 2003—admitted to being the chief Southeast Asian representative and logistical coordinator for al-Qaeda. Among the crimes he has been accused of include the organization of Operation Bojinka; plots to kill President Clinton and Pope John Paul; organizing travel itineraries, accommodation, and welcome dinners for two of the 9/11 hijackers and a suspect in the bombing of the U.S.S. Cole; and meeting with Zacarias Moussaoui, the so-called twentieth hijacker.

A pious child, Hambali had been drawn to radical Islam as a reaction to the attempts of the Suharto regime to promote nationalism by diluting the beliefs of Indonesia's Muslims. He met Abu Bakar Bashir at some point in the latter half of the 1980s. Either way, he helped make JI into a properly organized hierarchical group on his return to Malaysia in the early 1990s, while also tapping into the wider Islamic struggle through an array of ambitious plots, most notably Bojinka, for which investigators claimed he was the principal architect.

He returned to the country of his birth in October 2000, and soon began using his influence to deadly effect, first with the church bombings, then the Bali bomb attack. Following the bombing of the Marriott Hotel in Jakarta in August 2003, Hambali was captured by police in Thailand a week later. He was handed over to U.S. investigators and is reportedly being detained in Jordan.

---

was characterized by forced Islamicizations, attacks on Christian churches, and murders. When Molucca's Christian population formed into militias, full-scale civil insurgency broke out with between 5,000 and 20,000 deaths occurring. JI was strongly linked to the three main Islamist groups in the conflict and may have also sent over reinforcements.

This was, in many respects, a "secret war," although Western analysts and particularly the Indonesian government remained fearful that it could bubble over across the archipelago and beyond. In late 2001, police in Singapore arrested thirteen men that it claimed were plotting a huge bombing campaign and were in the process of assembling twenty-one tons of explosives. JI's military chief, Hambali, was said to be behind the plot.

Concern about Islamic militancy in Indonesia soon became worldwide, following devastating attacks in the resort of Kuta on the island of Bali in October 2002. A small, crude suicide

device went off in a bar, and as the panic-stricken and injured victims ran outside into the street, a second 1,000-kg bomb packed into the back of a van detonated, killing many more. The eventual death toll stood at 202, and included eighty-eight Australians, thirty-eight Indonesians, twenty-six Britons, and seven Americans. Simultaneously, a third bomb detonated outside the U.S. Consulate in Denpasar, Bali's capital, but caused minimal damage and no injuries.

A swift crackdown followed the Bali attacks, but Indonesia's security forces found JI's tightly knit ranks difficult to infiltrate. The price paid for that helplessness in the face of terror came on August 5, 2003, when a car bomb exploded in front of the Marriott Hotel in Jakarta, killing twelve and wounding some 150. In this case, the majority killed were Indonesians.

It is unknown if JI is part of the so-called al-Qaeda network. Certainly, it has many facets in

KEY EVENTS

1969: Renewed attempt to spread the influence of Darul emerges under the leadership of two Javanese clerics, Abu Bakar Bashir and Abdullah Sungkar; this has become known as Jemaah Islamiyah.

1985—1990: Many JI followers go and fight with the mujahideen in Afghanistan, further radicalizing the organization.

1990s: Hambali and Bashir establish JI as a cogent hierarchical organization.

1995: Hambali implicated in Operation Bojinka.

1998: President Suharto overthrown; many JI members return from exile.

2000: Church bombings.

2002: Bali nightclub bombing kills 202.

2003: Marriott Hotel in Jakarta bombed, killing twelve.

2003: Hambali captured in Thailand.

2005: Second bombing of Bali resort kills more than twenty.

---

common with al-Qaeda—a commitment to jihad; shared experience in Afghanistan—and has almost certainly received direct financial support from al-Qaeda. Moreover, individuals like Hambali are closely linked to some of al-Qaeda's most notorious followers, notably Khalid Sheikh Mohammed. Nevertheless, this liaison seems to have occurred before Mohammed moved into the bin Laden camp (he was with bin Laden in Afghanistan from around 1998; Hambali, by contrast, never followed him).

JI operates almost wholly on a local basis and, while its grand aim is the establishment of a Southeast Asian caliphate (something almost guaranteed to gain the approval of bin Laden), in practice its efforts have centered almost entirely on the creation of an Indonesian Islamic state. Nevertheless, at the trial of the Bali bombers, its ring leaders were unable or unwilling to state the origins of $35,500 that was transferred to the bombers' bank account. Similar large-scale money transfers preceding other attacks have often been linked back to al-Qaeda and its "sponsorship" of a jihadist attack.

On December 5, 2002, the last day of Ramadan, two bombs went off in Makassaron on the island of Sulawesi. One exploded at a McDonald's restaurant, killing the bomber and two patrons; the other wrecked a car showroom, but claimed no lives. With the Bali bombings still fresh in many minds, suspicion instantly turned to JI, but the reality of the situation was more complicated. The bombings had been carried out by two south Sulawesian-based organizations, Wahdah Islamiyah and Laskar Jundullah, with a largely local-based membership and a leadership entirely independent from JI. However, members of these two groups had received training from JI and cooperated extensively in the past with the larger organization. In this way, JI was emerging as a kind of "local" al-Qaeda, offering assistance towards the pursuit of jihad, but not necessarily knowing or instructing how this would be brought about.

PHILOSOPHY AND TACTICS

Followers of Jemaah Islamiyah (JI) believe in the establishment of a conservative Islamic state in Southeast Asia, although their activities have largely centered on Indonesia. Its followers are adherents to the Darul strain of Islam, which emerged in Indonesia in the 1940s. They believe that the West is seeking to destroy Islam through cultural, economic, and physical colonization and aim to eradicate Western influence by targeting its interests in the region.

JI's hierarchical structure is theoretically topped by an Amir, under whom four councils operate: *majelis qiyadah* (governing council), *majelis syuro* (religious council), a fatwa council, and *majelis hisbah* (disciplinary council). Nevertheless, most decisions come from the *Markaziyah* (Central command), which heads the governing council, and its members are seldom restricted by the formal hierarchy. It also maintains affiliations with like-minded organizations elsewhere in Southeast Asia, training individuals associated with other groups for jihadist attacks.

PRIMARY SOURCE
Jemaah Islamiya Organization (JI)

DESCRIPTION

Jemaah Islamiya Organization is responsible for numerous high-profile bombings, including the bombing of the J. W. Marriott Hotel in Jakarta on August 5, 2003, and the Bali bombings on October 12, 2002. Members of the group have also been implicated in the September 9, 2004, attack outside the Australian Embassy in Jakarta. The Bali attack, which left more than 200 dead, was reportedly the final outcome of meetings in early 2002 in Thailand, where attacks in Singapore and against soft targets such as tourist spots were also considered. In June 2003, authorities disrupted a JI plan to attack several Western embassies and tourist sites in Thailand. In December 2001, Singaporean authorities uncovered a JI plot to attack the U.S. and Israeli Embassies and British and Australian diplomatic buildings in Singapore. JI is also responsible for the coordinated bombings of numerous Christian churches in Indonesia on Christmas Eve 2000 and was involved in the bombings of several targets in Manila on December 31, 2000. The capture in August 2003 of Indonesian Riduan bin Isomoddin (a.k.a. Hambali), JI leader and al-Qa'ida Southeast Asia operations chief, damaged the JI, but the group maintains its ability to target Western interests in the region and to recruit new members through a network of radical Islamic schools based primarily in Indonesia. The emir, or spiritual leader, of JI, Abu Bakar Ba'asyir, was on trial at year's end on charges of conspiracy to commit terrorist acts, and for his links to the Bali and Jakarta Marriott bombings and to a cache of arms and explosives found in central Java.

STRENGTH

Exact numbers are unknown, but Southeast Asian authorities continue to uncover and arrest JI elements. Estimates of total JI members vary widely from the hundreds to the thousands.

LOCATION/AREA OF OPERATION

JI is believed to have cells spanning Indonesia, Malaysia, and the Philippines.

EXTERNAL AID

Investigations indicate that JI is fully capable of its own fundraising, although it also receives financial, ideological, and logistical support from Middle Eastern and South Asian contacts, non-governmental organizations, and other groups.

Source: U.S. Department of State. *Country Reports on Terrorism*. Washington, D.C., 2004.

As well as carrying out terrorist attacks on Indonesia's Christian population and Western targets, JI has also been involved in the practice of robbing "infidels" to secure funds to defend the faith. According to followers of Darul, this is permissible under Islamic law. JI has also been involved in people smuggling between Indonesia and Malaysia and the Philippines.

The JI network is held together not just by ideology, but also by an intricate network of marriages. According to the International Crisis Group (ICG), this "at times makes it seems [sic] like a giant extended family." Moreover the ICG believe that "insufficient attention has been applied to the role the women of JI play in cementing the network. In many cases, senior JI leaders arranged the marriages of their subordinates to their sisters or sisters-in-law to keep the network secure." Indeed, familial bonds and the strong ties built up in Afghanistan have helped stave off police infiltration.

It continues to recruit members from *pesantrens* (Muslim boarding schools), some of which it is closely affiliated to, although such institutions account for just a tiny fraction of the 14,000 or so Muslim boarding schools that exist in Indonesia.

OTHER PERSPECTIVES

In August 2003, the Belgian-based International Crisis Group (ICG) reported that "JI remains dangerous," adding that "The arrests that have taken place thus far—close to ninety people in Indonesia, ninety in Malaysia, and thirty in Singapore—almost certainly have put a crimp in the organization's activities, but they have not destroyed it. The markaziyah or central command of JI has lost a few of its members... but may well be still operational..."

Pointing to extensive research into JI's activities, the ICG stated: "The *wakalah* structure is probably far more extensive than previously thought, stretching across Malaysia to Sabah and Sarawak as well as across the Indonesian archipelago. The network of alliances, such as that between JI and the MILF in the Philippines or JI and Wahdah Islamiyah in South Sulawesi, means that even if some JI members lie low for the time being, others can work with the large pool of trained cadres that exists outside the JI organisation to undertake acts of violence. A new generation of *salafi* jihadists is also being raised among the children of JI members sent to study in the small circle of pesantrens that constitute the JI's educational circle.

"The good news is that internal dissension within JI appears to be growing. The Marriott bombing, in particular, generated a debate about appropriate targets, but there were apparently already divisions over the appropriateness of Indonesia as a venue for Jihad... The Marriott attack appears to have intensified that debate. Some JI members based in pesantrens have expressed concern that their ability to play the traditional outreach role in the local community is hampered by JI's clandestine nature. And with so many JI leaders in prison, some sympathisers are worried that individual JI members are going off on their own, without sufficient control from the centre. Internal rifts have destroyed more than one radical organisation; perhaps they will seriously weaken this one."

A special investigation carried out by *Time* magazine in December 2003 revealed that, despite a spate of arrests following the Bali and Marriott bombings, JI was still fully functioning. "As more and more senior JI members are arrested and questioned, and the organization's internal documents come to light, some of the veils of secrecy are being stripped away," the magazine reported. "Recent interrogation and intelligence reports... make it clear that one of JI's best-kept secrets is the ambitious scale of its training camps in Mindanao, which has replaced Afghanistan as the preferred location for learning how to wage terror. Even more alarming: more than a year after Bali, both the camps and the supply routes for recruits appear to be functioning normally."

SUMMARY

With the second bombing of the Bali resort of Kutu in October 2005, JI has shown that the strong familial and fraternal ties that bind it together have allowed a hard core to resist detection. While its threat beyond Indonesia has seemingly been nullified by security crackdowns, it remains a danger both to Indonesia's native population and to Western interests in the archipelago.

SOURCES

Books

Parry, Richard Lloyd. *In a Time of Madness*. New York: Random House, 2005.

Web sites

International Crisis Group. "Jemaah Islamiyah In South East Asia: Damaged But Still Dangerous." < http:// www.crisisgroup.org/library/documents/report_archive/ A401104_26082003.pdf > (accessed October 14, 2005).

Uterecht University. "Genealogies of Islamic Radicalism in Post-Suharto Indonesia." < http://www.let.uu.nl/~martin.vanbruinessen/personal/publications/genealogies_ islamic_radicalism.htm > (accessed October 14, 2005).

TimeAsia.com. "Asia's Own Osama." < http://www.-time.com/time/asia/features/malay_terror/hamba-li.html > (accessed October 14, 2005).

Jewish Defense League (JDL)

OVERVIEW

The Jewish Defense League (JDL) is a right-wing religious organization that aims to protect its members and fellow Jews from anti-Semitic attacks. When it was founded by Rabbi Meir Kahane in New York in 1968, this protection initially expressed itself as a kind of vigilantism, but the JDL's violence has, over the years, evolved and included the targeting of foreign government interests on U.S. soil, bombings, hijack attempts, and extortion.

HISTORY

The Jewish Defense League (JDL) was founded in 1968 by Rabbi Meir Kahane, an attorney and newspaper columnist. Concerned at the rising number of anti-Semitic attacks in America's cities, Kahane's initial idea was for a network of vigilante organizations to protect Jewish neighborhoods against African-American-instigated urban violence. Always an incendiary influence, however, Kahane soon oversaw a more radical reality before emigrating to Israel.

Kahane, in his mid-30s when he founded the JDL, had since boyhood been interested in ideas of radical Judaism. As a teenager, he had been a member of Betar—a quasi-military youth group—very loosely modeled on Irgun, that

LEADER: Ian Sigel

YEAR ESTABLISHED OR BECAME ACTIVE: 1968

USUAL AREA OF OPERATION: United States; Israel; Australia; South Africa; Europe

Hate graffiti on an Arab house in Hebron, West Bank. The message is signed by the militant Jewish Defense League. © *Larry Towell | Magnum Photos*

was then fighting for Jewish independence in Palestine. He was also profoundly influenced by the Jewish thinker, Ze'ev Jabotinsky, and his ideas of militant Zionism. One of his proudest boasts was that Jabotinsky had been a guest at his father's house when he was a boy.

Far from protecting Jews, however, the vigilantism of the JDL did much to exacerbate existing racial tensions, particularly in New York. Kahane's speeches often hinted at or advocated the use of violence, and when JDL members took credit for attacks, they would utter Kahane's slogan: "Never again"—a reference to the Holocaust. Kahane would invariably deny involvement with illegal activity, but usually gave his approval to a protagonist by suggesting that the respective target "had it coming."

His radicalism was rather like that of the Black Panthers, a radical black nationalist organization formed around the same time, using similar ideas of "self-defense" and "empowerment" before branching in other directions. (Ironically, the growth in African-American

anti-Semitism had largely been instigated by organizations like the Black Panthers). Kahane could be as incendiary as Malcolm X and his various protégés, frequently extolling a call to arms with catchphrases like "every Jew a .22" and "a .45 to survive." He believed strongly that the Jewish people had historically been too passive, and that the Holocaust had been the horrible denouement of this perceived weakness. The JDL argued fiercely that Jews would no longer passively suffer abuse.

At the time, Kahane was dismissed as an ideologue and a rabble rouser, and he grossly exaggerated the plight of Jews within American society, equating their status with those of Jews within Nazi Germany. To the majority of U.S. Jews, this was patent nonsense, but some of his ideas had relevance and effected lasting cultural change elsewhere. He highlighted, for instance, the plight of Jews within the USSR and Eastern Europe, first reminding American Jews of their passivity during the Holocaust, but also organizing demonstrations in front of and even inside Russian agencies. In November 1970, the JDL

Jewish hate graffiti on Abraham's Well in a Hebron, West Bank, Muslim cemetery. © *Larry Towell | Magnum Photos*

bombed Aeroflot's New York offices, causing extensive damage, and the following January, bombed a Soviet office in Washington, D.C. Other attacks included a shot fired into the USSR's UN offices, and pouring blood over the head of a Soviet diplomat at a Washington party. At the height of the cold war, these attacks were of a highly incendiary nature, but it cast global attention on the persecution of Soviet Jewry and indirectly led to huge numbers of Soviet-bloc Jews relocating to Israel during the 1970s and 1980s. At the time, virtually no one crossed the Iron Curtain, much less large-scale immigration.

The JDL also immersed itself in Arab-Israeli politics. Following crushing military defeats to Israel in 1948 and 1967 and without a democratic basis for government, many Arab regimes had been reduced to using anti-Semitic invective as a way of rallying support among their own populations. Just as the JDL targeted Soviet interests, so it targeted those of Arab regimes. In September 1969, for instance, the President of the United Nations Security Council revealed that six UN Missions of Arab states had received telegrams from the Jewish Defense League, which threatened each as a "legitimate target" in revenge for acts of terrorism committed by Arabs. Further attacks included the assault of workers at the offices of an Arab propaganda agency; a failed plot to hijack an Arab airliner; and death threats issued to the leader of the Palestinian Liberation Organization (PLO), Yasser Arafat.

Despite the JDL's exhortation for *Mishmaat* (discipline and unity), the group was not above attacking moderate Jews and Jewish organizations that usually had little time for the its extremism. This included several attempts at taking over the Park East Synagogue opposite the Soviet UN Mission, when fifty JDL members positioned themselves in the sanctuary, on the roof, and on scaffolding surrounding the building; they unfurled huge banners decrying the plight of Soviet Jews. On another occasion, a group of JDL members led by Kahane took over the executive offices of the Federation of Jewish Philanthropies in New York and occupied the offices for two hours, demanding $6 million for "Jewish education."

Kahane emigrated to Israel in 1971 where he established a JDL offshoot, Kach, although he retained close links to the United States, visiting regularly. Without his rabble-rousing invective, the JDL were less effective in gaining publicity (Kahane, at his peak, was rarely off the front pages), but continued to regularly engage in extremism. The campaign against the Soviet Union continued, with attacks including the sabotage of a performance by the Bolshoi Ballet and an abortive plot to kidnap a Soviet diplomat. Other incidents included the firebombing of part of JFK Airport; the targeting of evangelical Christian organizations, such as Jews For Jesus; and the bombing of an Iranian bank in San Francisco.

The JDL also carried out acts of violence against suspected Nazi war criminals living in

Rabbi Meir Kahane, leader of the Jewish Defense League, speaks to a supporter at a rally. AP/Wide World
Photos

the United States and against white supremacists. In a prerecorded telephone message in
February 1978, the JDL offered $500 for every
Nazi "lawfully killed during an attack on a
Jew." Calls to the New York headquarters of
the JDL activated the telephone message, which
also stated "We are calling for Jews to unite in
an all-out war against Nazis and other Jew-
haters... We are also advocating mass executions of Nazis in order to make their stay in this
country an unhealthy one." Attacks on suspects
included fire bombings, assassinations, and
intimidation.

As the 1980s progressed, however, the JDL
became increasingly marginalized by accusations that foul play was used to further the business interests of its leaders. Moreover, its claims
that American Jews were victimized in the same
way as German Jews in the 1930s rang hollow. In
1990, Meir Kahane was assassinated by a member of an Arab terrorist cell while speaking at a
meeting in New York. Although his U.S. presence had diminished since he left for Israel, his

death still represented the loss of the JDL's most
pivotal figure.

Distaste for the JDL peaked following the
1994 massacre in the Israeli town of Hebron,
when Baruch Goldstein, a Brooklyn-born Jew
(and former JDL member) and member of
JDL's Israeli offshoot, Kach, opened fire in a
mosque, killing twenty-nine worshippers. In the
United States, JDL's leaders vigorously
defended Goldstein, stating that they "understood" his "motivation,... grief, and his
actions" and that they were "not ashamed to
say that Goldstein was a charter member of the
Jewish Defense League."

The JDL was increasingly operating on the
margins of even right-wing opinion, and by the
turn of the year 2000 was essentially a two-man
operation backed by a handful of supporters.
Offshoots had opened up in Europe, Australia,
and South Africa, but the days when Meir
Kahane commanded front-page news seemed
to belong to a different bygone era.

The King Fahd Mosque in Culver City, California, was was targeted on December 12, 2001, in a bombing plot by the chairman and another member of the Jewish Defense League. AP/Wide World Photos. *Reproduced by permission*

KEY EVENTS

1968: JDL founded by Rabbi Meir Kahane.

1969: Kahane leads protests against Soviet targets in America against the plight of Russia's Jews.

1971: Kahane emigrates to Israel where he founds Kach.

1978: The JDL offers $500 to anyone who can kill or maim a Nazi.

1981: JDL bombs an Iranian bank in San Francisco.

1990: JDL founder Meir Kahane assassinated in New York.

1994: Following the Hebron massacre by a former member, Baruch Goldstein, the JDL causes consternation by defending him.

2001: JDL's Chairman, Irv Rubin, is arrested along with another member, Earl Krugel, in an FBI sting operation.

2002: Rubin commits suicide while awaiting trial.

2003: Krugel found guilty of conspiracy to commit terrorism.

The al-Qaeda attacks on New York and Washington in September 2001 prompted new fears that the JDL would reemerge as a serious force and carry out "reprisal" attacks on Muslims in the United States and elsewhere. Instead, it led to a federal crackdown on extremist groups operating within the United States, including the JDL. On December 12, 2001, JDL's International Chairman, Irv Rubin, and Earl Krugel, a leading member in the organization, were charged with conspiracy to commit acts of terrorism following an FBI sting operation.

While awaiting trial in November 2002, Rubin committed suicide. Krugel pleaded to the charges at his hearing three months later and was sentenced to twenty years imprisonment.

Following the FBI crackdown, the JDL in the United States went into a meltdown, with a series of factions emerging that claimed its title. Its former chairman, Moshe Finberg, has claimed that it remains a powerful militant force and is continuing to grow in size. Other chapters still exist elsewhere around the world. However, its opponents claim that it is down to less than a hundred, mostly elderly, members in the United States.

PHILOSOPHY AND TACTICS

Set up, as its name suggests, to protect Jews from rising anti-Semitism, particularly from African Americans, the Jewish Defense League operates

LEADERSHIP

IAN SIGEL

Ian Sigel became International Chairman of the Jewish Defense League in June 2005 after Moshe Finberg stepped down from the role. Sigel was born and raised in the Midwest and is of Russian-Jewish heritage. He previously worked in law enforcement and as a private contractor in conjunction with President Reagan's "Star Wars" program.

Only a member of the JDL since 1999, Siegel has held a variety of senior positions—which either reflects his ability, or the JDL's present lack of numbers—including the Chicago Chapter Chairman, Midwest Director, and National Vice-Chairman.

---

around five principles drawn from the Bible, Talmud and Rabbinical teachings. These include *Ahvat Yisroel* (love of Jewry); *Hadar* (dignity and pride); *Barzel* (iron); *Mishmaat* (discipline and unity); and *Bitachon* (the indestructibility of the Jewish people).

These articulate themselves in a variety of ways, but, in basic terms, they teach followers that faith should be the most important part of a Jew's life and identity, and that the historic weakness of the Jewish people should be confined to the past.

The JDL has aggressively followed its ideas of Jewish nationalism in both America and beyond. Nevertheless, it has always punched above its weight, and its membership has probably never numbered more than several thousand—and at present, is probably less than four figures in the United States.

In its heyday the JDL was heavily reliant on the charismatic and controversial Meir Kahane who, by stating invariably contentious and headline-grabbing opinions, brought attention to the perceived plight of Jews in America, and to the very real suffering of Jewry elsewhere in the world. Kahane was largely responsible

for initiating the large-scale emigration of Soviet and East European Jews to Israel and elsewhere.

Kahane's political aims for the JDL were initially twofold. He wanted to draw attention to the plight of Jews living in the USSR, but also to radicalize America's Jewish population, which he believed to be largely complacent. Writing in 1975 Kahane stated: "We wanted two things. One, the freedom of every Soviet Jew who wished to leave Russia. Two, to awaken the American Jew into a recognition that he had shamefully buried the Soviet Jewish problem while he himself enjoyed the freedoms of America, and to make him understand the pain of Jews anywhere is the pain of Jews everywhere. We wanted to force a world and a Jewish community that did not give a damn, to solve the problem or we would not give them peace. And finally we wanted to teach the American Jew who he was: first and last a Jew, and fated to struggle for or fall with all other Jews."

Publicity seeking was the least benign aspect of the JDL's make up, however. Overt violence against Soviet, Arab, and suspected Nazi targets included fire bombings, beatings, vandalism, and assassinations. The FBI estimates that the JDL was responsible for around fifty acts of terrorism.

Less quantifiable are the acts of vigilantism carried out in its name and encouraged by its leaders. Just as members of its Israeli offshoot, Kach, have committed hundreds of racially motivated attacks against Arabs, so did JDL followers carry out numerous assaults on gentiles, particularly African Americans. While the JDL currently denies the use of violence, its origins as a street-fighting organization and the blatant provocation of racial tensions by men like Meir Kahane point to a different reality in the past.

OTHER PERSPECTIVES

Writing in *Commentary* magazine in 1971, Milton Himmelfarb argued that the main reason the Jewish Defense League's campaign of protest and violence against the USSR was so successful was because it struck a chord among American Jews still harboring feelings of guilt about their compliance when faced with Hitler's Germany a generation earlier. As he muses, "how do you answer an eighteen-year-old son or daughter who asks you why the Jews of America were so well-behaved while the Nazis were murdering the Jews of Europe?"

By contrast, Meir Kahane, the Jewish Defense League's founder, believed that there was an awakening among Jews across the world of their need for solidarity in the face of oppression. "There are no boundaries when it comes to Jewish pain and oppression," he wrote in 1987 in *Uncomfortable Questions for Comfortable Jews*. "There are no Soviet Jews or Syrian Jews or American Jews. There are only Jews who live in the Soviet Union or in Syria or in America. There is one Jewish people, indivisible, that the Jewish State, which has the power and expertise and professionalism, is obligated to defend in every way, across and within any border."

SUMMARY

The arrest, and subsequent suicide, of JDL's Chairman, Irv Rubin, in 2001 was the latest chapter in a long-running story of decline for the JDL, which can be traced back almost to the day that its charismatic and controversial founder, Meir Kahane, emigrated to Israel in 1971. Though his speeches and writings were often laden with undertones of violence and overt racism, Kahane radicalized America's, then Israel's, Jewish populations, placing their perceived persecution on the front of every newspaper. Campaigns that mixed noisy demonstrations with violence—such as that waged against the USSR—were incredibly successful, despite usually being dismissed by more moderate Jews. Without Kahane, the JDL was half the organization it had once been, and although it continued its campaigning and violence, it seemed to lose the streak of populism that had once made it so potent.

SOURCES

Books

Kahane, Meir. *The Story of the Jewish Defense League.* Radnor, Penn.: Chilton, 1975.

Dolgin, Jane. *Jewish Identity and the JDL.* Princeton: Princeton University Press, 1977.

Web sites

Kahane.org. < http://www.kahane.org/ > (accessed October 14, 2005).

The Jewish Defense League.org. < http://www.jdl.org.il/ > (accessed October 14, 2005).

Jewish Virtual Library. "Rabbi Meir Kahane (1932–1990)." < http://www.jewishvirtuallibrary.org/jsource/biography/kahane.html > (accessed October 14, 2005).

Jewish Fighting Organization

LEADER: Avishai Raviv

USUAL AREA OF OPERATION: Israel

OVERVIEW

Jewish Fighting Organization (Eyal) was an obscure extreme right Jewish nationalist group that emerged in Israel following the 1993 Oslo Peace Accords. Its exact origins, goals, and fate remain murky and tainted by allegations that it was set up by a Shin Bet (Israeli Secret Service) agent provocateur. It was an extension of the Kach movement, which advocates the annexation of all disputed territories and the forced removal of Arabs from within them. It is most notorious for playing a part in the murder of the Israeli Prime Minister, Yitzhak Rabin.

HISTORY

On November 4, 1995, in Tel Aviv's King David Square, the Israeli Prime Minister, Yitzhak Rabin, was shot three times and died later in the hospital. His assassin, Yigal Amir, was an ultra-orthodox student, unhappy with the Arab-Israeli peace process, of which Rabin had been one of the principle architects.

During the course of the subsequent investigation, much emphasis was placed on whether Amir had been operating alone or under the orders of an extreme right-wing organization, the sort that had been among Rabin's most vociferous and potentially violent opponents.

The leader of the militant Irgun Party, Menahem Begin, delivering an anti-Ben Gurion speech during a Tel Aviv, Israel, rally in November 1950.
© Robert Capa © 2001 Cornell Capa | Magnum Photos

KEY EVENTS

1993: Oslo Peace Accords; Jewish Fighting Organization emerges in response.

1995: JFO plays a part in the murder of the Israeli Prime Minister, Yitzhak Rabin.

Two key facts emerged during Amir's trial and the inquiry into Rabin's death by the Shamagar Commission. The first was that he had apparently acted of his own volition when killing Rabin. More significant, however, was Amir's association with an extreme right-wing political activist and, as it would transpire, with Shin Bet (Israeli Secret Service) agent and informer, Avishai Raviv. Raviv had been involved in the creation of a number of militant groups, including Eyal, and the subsequent tangle of events created an impression that Amir, despite both men's protestations to the contrary, may have been operating under the orders of Eyal.

Raviv had been recruited to Shin Bet in December 1987. He was a right-wing militant with primitive views that would frequently teeter over into violence, and he was also obsessed with the idea of "Jewish traitors." Nevertheless, according to an interview with his Shin Bet supervisor, Raviv was a valuable agent "who provided hundreds of intelligence tips. His warnings prevented violent acts like attacks on Arab property, attempted attacks on Arabs, attacks on mosques, including the Temple Mount,

attempts to attack Jewish left-wing leaders and similar things."

Raviv is also credited with setting up a number of extreme right-wing groups, apparently under the direction of Shin Bet. According to Yossi Klein Havlei of *The Jerusalem Report*, many of these front groups—with names like Sword of David, Sword of Gideon, Fascist Zionist Youth, and Eyal—claimed acts of violence they had not actually committed, and put their name to incendiary leaflets inciting against Israeli "traitors." His recruits consisted of a "handful of teenagers who hung around him," and he conducted "a staged graveyard swearing-in ceremony . . . complete with blood oaths." All this received huge press coverage in Israel and created a false sense that a right-wing terrorist network existed.

Theories vary as to why Shin Bet would want to set up an extreme right-wing organization. It is likely that Eyal and similar groups were set up as a way of infiltrating the Israeli extreme right and as a way of recruiting young individuals who would progress to join groups like Kach. The British secret service, MI5, is widely rumored to have initiated a similar strategy in the 1990s, when it allegedly set up the neo-Nazi Combat 18 group as a way of infiltrating loyalist paramilitaries in Northern Ireland.

Eyal was set up on the campus of Bar-Ilan University in Ramat Gan around the time of the Oslo Accords in 1993. The extent of its activities remains unclear. Indeed, it is possible that it may have been nothing more than a "front group," literally a name that would be put on leaflets or graffiti, or claim responsibility for crimes that it did not commit. That was almost certainly the case on the only occasion the group actually

Young Jewish settler extremists, restrained by Israeli soldiers, try to force their way into the Kfar Darom settlement in Gush, Katif, Gaza Strip © Paolo Pellegin | Magnum Photos

claimed responsibility for an attack, after a Palestinian was shot dead in the town of Halhoul. That murder was later revealed to have been a robbery gone wrong that was actually carried out by other Palestinians.

One of the reasons Raviv has been so heavily implicated in Rabin's killing is because he and his various cover groups were among the most virulent and violent critics of the Prime Minister's role in the Oslo Accords and the peace process. Shortly before Rabin's murder, Raviv handed over a poster to a TV correspondent depicting Rabin in an SS uniform (which was widely shown in the Israeli media) and one of his fictitious front groups left a leaflet on the grave of the Hebron mass murderer, Baruch Goldstein, with the message: "A dictator traitor has arisen in our nation by the name of Yitzhak Rabin . . . His sentence is death."

Raviv was also a close associate of Yigal Amir, Rabin's assassin. The two had met at Bar-Ilan University and jointly led student protests and solidarity visits to West Bank settlements. Whether Amir was a formal member of Eyal or whether Eyal even had formal members remain the subject of intense dispute; however, the Shamagar Commission reported that "Raviv was connected to Amir more than to any other person in everything related to organizing student demonstrations, organizing weekends in West Bank settlements."

The Shamagar Commission found it likely that Raviv knew about Amir's intentions; but Amir's brother, Haggai, who was himself charged with involvement in the murder, testified that while Amir had considered involving Raviv, he had desisted because of rumors linking him to Shin Bet. It seems unlikely, therefore, that Yagil Amir killed Yitzhak Rabin under the orders of Eyal.

PHILOSOPHY AND TACTICS

Because of its shadowy roots and the fact that it probably only ever existed as a Shin Bet cover group with, at most, only a handful of members, Eyal never issued any sort of formal

LEADERSHIP

AVISHAI RAVIV

Avishai Raviv was a Shin Bet undercover agent credited with the formation of numerous small extreme-right groups. These groups essentially served as cover for extremists to be spied upon, but were sometimes so obscure they had no formal members.

Opinion is divided about the extent of the Israeli state's involvement with Raviv. Certainly his links to Yigal Amir have seen allegations exaggerated and conspiracy theories abound. The Shamagar Commission, which investigated the Rabin assassination, found that Raviv was merely a Shin Bet agent who was not properly controlled. On the other hand, a Likud deputy, Michael Eitan, insists that Raviv was the "biggest agent provocateur in the history of Israel," a view that many subscribe to.

A Shin Bet agent since 1987, Raviv not only received cash but also immunity from prosecution. Witnesses to the Shamagar Commission portrayed him as an unreconstructed thug with a visceral hatred of Arabs. He would tour Hebron, vandalizing Arab property and assaulting Arab shopkeepers. He was arrested sixteen times, but convicted only once—and on that occasion, received a suspended sentence.

Since Rabin's murder, Raviv has kept a low profile, apparently fearing reprisals either from right-wing extremists who feel he betrayed them by his involvement with Shin Bet, or from Shin Bet agents seeking to cover up further revelations.

---

manifesto. Nevertheless, it can be assumed from the involvement of Raviv and Yigal Amir that its philosophy would be in the tradition of Kach, with unyielding opposition to the secession of any Israeli territory. Moreover, it would have used halachic concepts to justify the use of violence. Terms such as *din rodef* (meaning, the duty to kill a Jew who imperils the life of another Jew) and *din moser* (meaning, the duty to eliminate a Jew who intends to turn another Jew into non-Jewish authorities) would have justified the assassination of Rabin in their eyes.

Tactically, Eyal was not a conventional extremist group. It seemed set on achieving notoriety by claiming crimes it never committed and by putting its name to leaflets denouncing its opponents in frequently obscene terms.

OTHER PERSPECTIVES

"Although most Israelis accept that Amir was alone when he pulled the trigger," wrote David B. Green in Middle Eastern Policy, "there are those who still ask if he wasn't decisively encouraged to act by the national-religious circles he moved in, and specifically if he didn't have rabbinical sanction to murder the Prime Minister. Others ask what responsibility Rabin bore for his own killing, in particular by treating his political enemies in the national-religious camp with a contempt that verged on provocation. That the Shin Bet security service, entrusted with protecting Rabin, failed at its job is a given, but many Israelis wonder whether the failure included advance knowledge of Amir's plans, and even his incitement by one of the service's operatives. Then there are those who have taken refuge in far-fetched conspiracy theories that see Rabin's No. 2, Shimon Peres, engineering the murder so that he could assume power."

Reviewing the Michael Karpin and Ina Friedman account of Rabin's assassination, *Murder in the Name of God*, Guilain Denouex, associate professor of government at Colby College, believes that, far from being a complicated conspiracy, Rabin's killing had a degree of inevitability. "Rabin's murder should have come as no surprise," she wrote. "Indeed, it was forecast by several leading commentators... Second, Amir was neither deranged nor isolated in his belief. Far from representing a 'lunatic fringe' living on the margins of Israeli society, he came out of a world and subculture that represent an important component of Israel and its body politic. Third, several individuals on the mainstream right, most notably Binyamin Netanyahu and Ariel Sharon, did not hesitate to rely on the religious and radical right to promote their own agendas. They repeatedly indulged and lent tacit support to zealots who called for violence to thwart the implementation of the Oslo agreements."

SUMMARY

Since the ending of the Shamagar Commission into Yitzhak Rabin's death, Eyal has disappeared into the shadows. If it ever existed as a conventional extremist organization—and there seems good reason to dispute that—its notoriety came by association, rather than for any acts it ever carried out.

SOURCES

Books

Karpin, Michael, and Ina Friedmann. *Murder in the Name of God, the Plot to Kill Yitzhak Rabin*. New York: Granta, 1999.

Web sites

Mideast Web. "The Last Speech of Yithak Rabin." < http://www.mideastweb.org/rabin1995.htm > (accessed October 10, 2005.)

Jewish Underground

LEADER: Rabbi Meir Kahane (The Jewish Defense League)

YEAR ESTABLISHED OR BECAME ACTIVE: early 1940s

USUAL AREA OF OPERATION: Worldwide

OVERVIEW

The Jewish Underground is a group of organizations that was first formed in the early 1940s. Ever since, there have been numerous organizations (with varying degrees of extremism) associated with the Jewish Underground. According to analysts, the objectives and founding philosophies of all the groups forming the Jewish Underground have been similar—fighting against the perceived "enemies" of Jews around the world.

Some of the most prominent groups allied with the Jewish Underground are Irgun, LEHI, Haganah, Jewish Direct Action, United Jewish Underground, and Jewish Defense League.

HISTORY

The Jewish Underground organizations were thought to be formed during the Warsaw Ghetto Uprising in 1942. According to published reports, Germany carried out deportations of thousands of Jews from Warsaw at that time. Many Jewish resistance organizations such as the Jewish Fighting Organization, the Revisionist Party, and the Jewish Fighting Union were formed to resist the deportation. All these organizations were later part of the greater Jewish Underground.

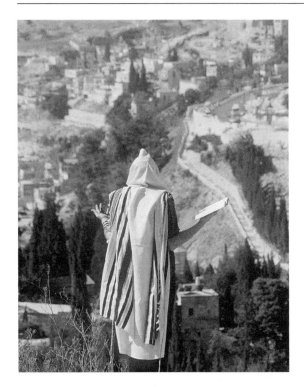

Yehuda Etzion, leader of the Jewish terrorist underground network, prays at Mount of Olives.

© Gueorgui Pinkhassov / Magnum Photos

Historians and analysts state that ever since the Warsaw Ghetto Uprising, many Jewish organizations claiming to be affiliated with Jewish Underground have been formed and disbanded. Each of these groups was formed around the world with the aim of protecting the rights of orthodox Jewish communities. One such prominent group during the 1970s and 1980s was the Jewish Defense League.

The Jewish Defense League (JDL) was reportedly formed in 1968 in New York. The group was thought to be a vigilante organization, protecting the Jewish population in the city. According to news reports, during the 1970s, it carried out various terrorist attacks against institutions that the group perceived as anti-Jew. The attacks were targeted mainly at Palestinian and Soviet organizations. In 1973, ten members of the JDL reportedly vandalized the offices of the World Council of Churches in New York. In April 1975, police authorities suspected the members of JDL to be responsible for a series of bombings in Los Angeles.

In January 1976, the members of JDL reportedly vandalized the Mexican consulate in Philadelphia. The JDL claimed that the incident was carried out to protest Mexico's anti-Jewish stance.

By the mid-1980s, reports suggested that the members of JDL, along with support from other Jewish Underground associations, had started attacking individuals perceived as anti-Semitics, in addition to the attacks on institutions. In 1985 and 1986, members of the JDL were suspected behind the car bombings of Soviet diplomats in New York. The attackers had used fire and pipe bombs.

In the late 1980s, the JDL was thought to be losing prominence. Many leaders, including its founder Rabbi Meir Kahane, were either killed, committed suicide, or were arrested. The last known attack by the JDL was reported in 1992. Police authorities claim that since then, the group has been inactive. However, a few incidents in the early 2000s have been linked to the JDL.

The Jewish Underground organizations comprised of many other small groups in the 1990s and early 2000s. However, none of these is thought to be of great prominence. As of 2005, a few groups associated with Jewish Underground were operating in Israel, the United States, and some other countries.

PHILOSOPHY AND TACTICS

The Jewish Underground organizations, ever since the 1940s, claim to have been formed to serve a common purpose: protecting the Jews around the world against perceived "enemies." Analysts state that the founding philosophy behind the first organizations formed in 1942 was to prevent deportation of Jews from Warsaw.

Similarly, the Jewish Defense League was reportedly formed to protect the Jews in New York and other parts of the United States against Soviet, Palestinian, and other authorities. Proclamations made by Rabbi Kahane, the leader of JDL, stated that the plight of Jews in America at the time was similar to those in Nazi Germany.

The Jewish Defense League and other similar Jewish Underground organizations reportedly

A demonstrator commemorates extremist Rabbi Meir Kahane on the anniversary of his death in 1995.
© *Abbas / Magnum Photos*

carried out aggressive tactics in order to propagate their ideology and mission. This included bombings, killings, and assassinations of prominent personalities who opposed the groups' tactics, vandalism, and robberies.

Analysts and monitor groups suggest that activities carried out by the Jewish Underground organizations, especially those since the 1970s, were mainly based on racism, violence, and political extremism. Analysts also claim that many Jewish Underground associations perceived the image of Jews worldwide as that of weak people who had been the target of violence for decades. These Jewish organizations allegedly aimed at changing such views by "fighting back."

Not much is known about alliances of the various Jewish Underground organizations with other terrorist groups. There have been reports of Jewish Underground associations providing support and training to members of other such

associations. Most organizations are also thought to be financially self-sustaining.

OTHER PERSPECTIVES

Terrorist acts carried out by the Jewish Underground organizations have often been criticized by officials around the world. In 2001, an alleged leader of JDL, Earl Krugel, was arrested and convicted of charges of plotting to blow up a mosque in California. U.S. District judge Ronald Lew said Krugel's crimes were "promoting hatred in the most vile way."

In the early 2000s, there have been some attacks on Palestinians in the West Bank region suspected to be carried out by members of various Jewish Underground organizations. Yesha, a prominent group representing Jewish settlers in this region, condemned such attacks in 2002, stating that "such acts are faulty and negative

LEADERSHIP

RABBI MEIR KAHANE

The Jewish Underground comprises several small organizations. One such organization is the Jewish Defense League—thought to be one of the more prominent associates of Jewish Underground. Rabbi Meir Kahane was the founder and leader of JDL for several years.

Kahane was the mastermind of several terrorist acts carried out by the Jewish Defense League. He was arrested several times during the 1970s and 1980s. Although, Kahane was thought to have migrated to Israel soon after the formation of JDL, he was reportedly the leader of the group, and monitored its activities from Israel.

According to published reports, Rabbi Kahane stepped down as JDL's leader in 1985. However, he was still thought to be a key figure in organizing many of the activities carried out by the group. Kahane was assassinated in 1990, reportedly by an Arab militant.

from every possible aspect, both legally and morally."

Ehud Sprinzak, dean of the School of Government at the Interdisciplinary Academic Center in Herzliya and an expert on Jewish terrorism, while referring to the reason for not being able to crack terrorist activities against the Palestinians since the early 2000s, states: "Jewish terrorism is marginal compared to other things [terrorist acts by extremists of other religions]." He goes on say, "I suppose that had there been a serious Jewish underground, the security forces would have invested more in dealing with it."

KEY EVENTS

1940s: Jewish Underground associations are formed during the Warsaw Ghetto Uprising.

1968: The Jewish Defense League is formed.

1990: Rabbi Kahane, former leader of the JDL, is killed in 1990 by an Egyptian militant.

SUMMARY

Jewish Underground organizations date back to the early 1940s. Throughout the twentieth century, there have been many organizations associated with Jewish Underground with similar ideologies and beliefs. As of 2005, reports suggest that a few associations are gaining prominence, especially in Israel.

SOURCES

Web sites

Anti Defamation League. "Backgrounder: The Jewish DefenseLeague." < http://www.adl.org/extremism/jdl_chron.asp > (accessed October 15, 2005).

BBC.com. "Jewish Bomb Plotter Jailed in US." < http://news.bbc.co.uk/2/hi/americas/4273790.stm > (accessed October 15, 2005).

Jewish Telegraphic Agency. "Fears of Jewish Underground Rise." < http://www.jewishaz.com/jewish-news/020517/fears.shtml > (accessed October 15, 2005).

MIPT Terrorism Knowledge Base. "Group Profile: Jewish Defense League." < http://www.tkb.org/Group.jsp?groupID=183 > (accessed October 15, 2005).

SEE ALSO

Jewish Defense League

Kach

OVERVIEW

Kach is an extreme-right Zionist extremist organization that uses terrorism to pursue its goals of
expanding Jewish rule across the biblical lands
of Israel. It resolutely opposes any concessions
that may give up part of Israel's territory. Its
most deadly attack came in February 1994,
shortly after the signing of the Oslo Peace
Accords between Israel and the Palestinian
Liberation Organization (PLO), when Baruch
Goldstein, a Brooklyn-born doctor and Kach
supporter, slaughtered 29 Palestinian worshipers
at the Ibrahimi Mosque in Hebron.

ALTERNATE NAME: Kahane Chai
LEADER: Meir Kahane

HISTORY

The origins and—arguably—inspiration for
Kach date back to the days when Israel was
part of Mandate Palestine. During the mid
1940s, Zionist extremist groups such as Irgun
and the Stern Gang waged a vicious war against
British forces in control of the Mandate—even
while the British were simultaneously at war
with Nazi Germany. The rationale was twofold:
that the Land of Israel is sacred and it was unacceptable that anyone else govern it; and that the
Jewish people use an armed struggle to realize
these beliefs.

Kach Party symbol on the remains of a burned-out Palestinian home in 2003. The Hebrew graffiti reads: "Kach were here" (left) and "Rape the women." © *Larry Towell | Magnum Photos*

When the state of Israel was born in 1948, these views became part of the Israeli mainstream. Irgun gave up their armed struggle and became part of the Likud political movement and, through war and territorial expansion, the state of Israel grew considerably in size. The view of an armed struggle evolved: from using such methods to create a political state of Israel, the imperative switched to protecting Zionism's gains and also the Jewish people. Of course, there were radically different views about how Israel defend itself: some merely advocated the defense of Israel's borders; others the forcible removal of all Gentiles (non-Jews) from the state—by violence if necessary.

One of the first manifestations of the latter view came via the extreme-right Jewish underground terror group, Machteret, in the early 1980s. This terror group carried out a number of attacks on Palestinian targets before being broken up by the Israeli authorities. Its actions included a failed plot to assassinate several Palestinian mayors and a plan to blow up the Al-Aqsa Mosque, an occurrence with the potential to thrust the region into war.

Machteret were merely inheritors of Zionist direct action, however. In 1971, Rabbi Meir Kahane, a 41-year-old lawyer from Brooklyn, emigrated to Israel. As a teenager, he had been a member of Betar, a quasi-military youth group modeled on the likes of Irgun. He had despised the image of Jews as weak or vulnerable and sought to transform them into "mighty fighters who strike back fiercely against tyrants." He had founded the Jewish Defense League (JDL) in 1968, the declared goal of which was to protect against black anti-Semitism.

In reality, the vigilantism of the JDL did much to exacerbate existing racial tensions, particularly in New York. Kahane's outpourings often hinted at or advocated the use of violence: one of his favorite mottos was "every Jew a .22"—indicating that Jews would no longer passively suffer abuse. He also highlighted the plight of Jews within the USSR, organizing demonstrations at Russian agencies in the U.S. Soviet diplomats were also attacked—a particularly incendiary tactic at the height of the cold war.

Kahane brought the JDL's militancy with him to Israel, founding its Israeli successor, Kach, within months of his arrival. Focusing the ire once reserved for Soviet dignitaries on Arabs, Kach made no secret of its desire to remove the Arab population from Israel nor did it make any distinction between Israeli Arabs or those living in the occupied territories. Among Kahane's stunts was the attempted show trial of the mayor of Hebron for the massacre of the town's Jewish population more than 50 years earlier. More violent was an aborted—and slightly farcical—plot to blow up the Libyan Embassy in Rome following the terrorist attack on Israeli Athletes at the 1972 Olympics.

Kach ran candidates in the 1973 Knesset elections, and again in 1977 and 1981, but each time failed to make any sort of impact. Many Israelis regarded Kahane as a publicity-hungry megalomaniac with views that bordered on extreme, while Kach's activities—both legal and illegal—had been low key and often poorly carried out.

However, following the Camp David Accords of 1979, which afforded a peace deal between Israel and Egypt, including the

Avishai Raviv, leader of the militant group Eyal, was one of several suspects arrested in connection with the assassination of Israeli Prime Minister Yitzhak Rabin on November 4, 1995.

AP/Wide World Photos. Reproduced by permission.

handover of some Israeli territory gained after the 1967 war, Kach intensified its activities. The Israeli Prime Minister and Camp David signatory, Menachem Begin, once an Irgun leader and hero of the Jewish resistance movement in Mandate Palestine, was depicted by Kach as a "traitor," sentiments which were shared by sections of the Israeli population. Kach intensified its efforts with a series of illicit acts in Judea, Jerusalem, and Samaria. These attacks were largely aimed at the Arab population in an effort to provoke the collapse of the peace deal, either through an Arab uprising or the protests of the Egyptian government. They included attacks on an Arab bus, pipe bombings, and shootings.

The most infamous of Kahane's stunts, however, came in April 1982 in the Yamit settlement, which was about to be handed back to the Egyptians. Kahane's followers described themselves as the "Movement Against the Retreat from Sinai" and fortified themselves in an underground bunker, declaring to the world's media that they intended to commit mass suicide. The Israeli government then rushed Kahane back from New York, where he was visiting, in order to convince his followers not to kill themselves. In fully televised negotiations, Kahane convinced them to end the drama peacefully.

The fame and infamy provided by these incidents saw Kach make an electoral breakthrough in 1984 when Meir Kahane was elected to the Knesset. Many Israelis, particularly those on the left, regarded this prospect with barely concealed horror. Kach was not yet regarded as a terrorist organization per se, but most Israelis were dismayed by the street violence and racially motivated attacks against Arabs that accompanied Kach's posturing as a legitimate political organization.

In view of this, one of the "Basic Laws" of Israel was amended a year later, prohibiting electoral candidates charged with "incitement to racism." Before the 1988 General Election, Israel's Central Elections Committee disqualified Kach, which unsuccessfully appealed against the ruling in the Israeli Supreme Court. This effectively ended Kach's existence as a political party.

Kahane had used his Knesset seat as a platform with which to spread his worldview. He had made several visits to Arab towns, baiting the local populations by publicly "inviting" them to leave Israel. On one occasion, 30,000 Arabs turned up to protest and only the presence of more than 1,000 police officers prevented a full-scale riot. His legislative proposals had focused on revoking Israeli citizenship from non-Jews and banning Jewish-Gentile marriages and sexual relationships. These were dubbed by the Israeli left as the "Nuremburg laws," and struck revulsion in a country where many had suffered horribly under similar legislation in Nazi Germany. Eventually, the rest of the Knesset boycotted the Parliament whenever Kahane spoke, leaving him to make his speeches to an empty chamber.

Banned from Israeli political life, but still with a wide following in Europe and North America as well as Israel, Kahane continued to travel widely. While speaking in Manhattan in November 1990, he was killed by an Arab terrorist, El Sayyid Nosair, who had links to the cell that blew up the World Trade Center.

LEADERSHIP

MEIR KAHANE

Meir Kahane was the founder and leader of Kach for most of its existence, and was also the abiding influence behind many of its offshoots. Born in Brooklyn, New York, in 1932, he was a member of various Jewish youth groups and profoundly influenced by Ze'ev Jabotinsky and his ideas of militant Zionism. He trained as a lawyer and was ordained a rabbi, and also worked as an editor on the influential *Jewish Press*.

In 1968, he formed the Jewish Defense League to combat the rising anti-Semitism in American cities, particularly that instigated by blacks. The JDL's vigilantism brought its founder fame and notoriety. Kahane emigrated to Israel in 1971, and Kach—essentially the JDL's Israeli cousin— emerged during the 1970s under his direction.

When Kahane made an electoral breakthrough in 1984, he used his Knesset seat as a platform to spread his views. He was adored by his followers, but despised by most Israelis. Nevertheless, although he had a reputation as an agitator and rabble rouser, it was Kahane, above most others, who brought attention to the plight of Soviet Jewry and to that of Jewish minorities in Ethiopia. Although his views were regarded as offensive in the 1970s and 1980s, they are reflected in mainstream Israeli politics by a variety of right-wing parties today.

Kahane was assassinated on November 5, 1990, while speaking in New York. His son, Binyamin, took up the mantle as leader of Kach's successor Kahane Chai until he too was murdered a decade later.

Kach, following Kahane's death, then split into two groups with somewhat overlapping ideologies: Kach and Kahane Chai ("Kahane Lives"). The latter was led by Meir Kahane's son Binyamin; the former, based in the ethnic melting pot of Hebron, by Baruch Marzel. The two groups publicly continued Kahane's tradition of longstanding racial agitation, while at the same illegally carrying out attacks on Arabs.

This was at a time of heightened tension. Moves towards an Arab-Israeli political solution had been initiated at U.S./Russian-sponsored talks held in Madrid in October 1991, and heightened after talks in Oslo throughout 1993, where a Declaration of Principles (DOP) was agreed between the Israeli and Palestinian parties. The DOP—also known as the Oslo Accords— outlined arrangements for interim government, elections of a Palestinian Council, and concessions in the West Bank, and was signed by Israeli Prime Minister Yitzhak Rabin, and the Palestinian leader, Yasser Arafat, at the White House on September 13, 1993.

The majority of Israelis was willing to give Rabin's vision for peace a chance. But to the religious right the plan was unacceptable. This was especially true for Kach, Kahane Chai, and other extremist organizations that believed in the restoration of the biblical state of Israel.

Part of the Israeli right's strategy to fight the Palestinian-Israeli peace process was to increase the number of Jewish settlements on occupied territory. The goals were twofold: in the short term, it would bring biblical lands into Jewish hands; in the long term, it threatened to complicate the handover of territories to the Palestinians.

Living in settlements, however, was fraught with danger and the regular attacks from Palestinians and physical isolation from the rest of Israel hardened the resolve and politics of many settlers. One man who apparently suffered at the hands of such attacks was Dr. Baruch Kappel Goldstein, a West Bank settler. Like Kahane, he was born in Brooklyn, and had emigrated to Israel and served as a physician in the Israeli Defense Force. He had formerly been a member of the JDL, and later became a member of Kach. A friend of Goldstein's and his son was murdered by Palestinians in December 1993, which apparently served as a prompt for Goldstein to bring his beliefs into action.

On Friday February 25, 1994, Goldstein entered the Cave of Patriarchs, a site in the city of Hebron holy to both Muslims and Jews. Friday marked the Muslim day of prayer, and around 500 men were praying. Armed with a submachine gun, Goldstein opened fire, killing 29 worshippers and injuring another hundred. He was eventually overcome by survivors and beaten to death.

KEY EVENTS

1971: Jewish Defense League founder Meir Kahane emigrates from the United States to Israel; Kach emerges over the subsequent 18 months.

1979–1981: Escalation in Kach activity during the Camp David peace process with Israel.

1982: Kahane talks Israeli settlers out of suicide pact.

1984: Kahane elected to the Knesset.

1988: Kach's political activity effectively ends following revisions to Israel's "Basic Laws" about racial incitement.

1990: Kahane murdered in New York; Kach splits into Kach and Kahane Chai.

1994: Hebron massacre.

1994: Kach/Kahane Chai outlawed by the Israeli government.

2000: Binyamin Kahane murdered.

Following the attack, Kach and Kahane Chai were both banned by the Israeli government and added to the U.S. Department of State's list of banned terrorist organizations. The majority of Kach's followers switched allegiance to other right-wing Israeli political parties, which had seen an explosion in popularity during the 1990s.

Meir's son, Binyamin Ze'ev Kahane, was murdered with his wife in an apparently random attack by Palestinians in December 2000. Kach supporters have pledged to avenge his death.

A number of Kahanist organizations have cropped up since 2000. These include the Kahane Movement, the New Kach Movement, and Noar Meir. Although they have usually been added to the U.S. State Department's list of terrorist organizations as—effectively—acting as Kach by proxy, none has been linked to significant extremist action.

PHILOSOPHY AND TACTICS

Kach's fundamental belief centers on the notion that the state of Israel is entitled to sovereignty over the biblical land of Israel. This is a core belief of most Orthodox Jews, but what sets Kach apart is the inadmissibility of withdrawing from any territories or compromising in any way the territorial integrity of these lands. Jews, according to Kach's founder Meir Kahane, should be ready to face death rather than surrender their land.

Tied to that belief is the notion that the world is inherently hostile to Jewry and it is therefore the duty of Jews to defend themselves, and even strike pre-emotively. This was the founding basis of the Jewish Defense League, and it articulated itself in similar ways with Kach and its splinter groups, particularly on the streets of towns like Hebron where "street fighting" between its members and Arab youths are not uncommon.

These beliefs make Kach an inherently racist organization and are behind the group's idea that Arabs must be expelled from Israel. Meir Kahane's teachings on eugenics and his proscription of Jewish-Gentile marriages have led to accusations of Facism.

Kach and its splinter organizations typically use violence to intimidate and provoke in order to disrupt the Palestinian-Israli peace process. While Kach is most commonly associated with the Hebron massacre of 1994, its violence is usually on a smaller scale. One of its followers described a typical operation to the author of *Patterns of Prejudice*, in 1985: "One day towards the end of July 1984, I agreed … to operate against the Arabs. We left Kiryat Arba in a hired car, headed towards Jerusalem… Around midnight, we saw an Arab in his twenties walking along the road. I said 'let's stop the car.' I went out and hit the Arab with my fist on the shoulder. I also kicked him. He escaped into the night. We continued to Hebron and it was decided—I don't remember by whom—to burn Arab cars. We had in our car two plastic bottles containing four and a half litres of gasoline. In Hebron Yehuda stopped the car. Mike took the gasoline and poured it under several cars, maybe three. Following the burning of the cars by Yehuda, we moved, not waiting to see what would happen."

In its early days, Kach's political activities were primarily aimed at attention seeking, to bringing the ideas of Meir Kahane into the political mainstream. Since his death, the huge influx of largely right-wing Russian Jews and the appalling effects of suicide bombings and the Al-Aqsa *intifada* (uprising) have helped achieve just that. Rather than engaging in terror, his supporters now seem focused on ensuring his memory remains.

OTHER PERSPECTIVES

Writing in 1985, when Meir Kahane was at the height of his notoriety, Ehud Sprinzak stated in an American Jewish Committee publication about Kach: "While a formal presentation of the background and ideology of Kach and its leader is helpful in identifying its place on the ideological map of Israel, only a closer examination of Kach's actual modus operandi, its imagery and symbolism, as well as some hidden undercurrents in its history, may locate it accurately on a general comparative political map. Having examined these facets of the Kach phenomenon, it would appear that, from a radical movement of minority self-defence with no comprehensive political ideology, it has gradually evolved into a radical right entity, with many similarities to historical fascist movements. Kach today is a quasi-fascist movement."

Gary Cooperberg was a friend of Kahane's and took over his long-running newspaper column in the *Jewish Press* after his assassination. He believed that Kahane and, in turn, Kach's, main problem was that they expressed commonly held beliefs that no one else dared articulate. "There are those who labeled him a racist, simply because he spoke the Jewish truth," Cooperberg wrote. "Every Jewish leader in Israel secretly agreed with all that he said, but none had the courage to speak what they believed. Rabbi Kahane faced the problems head on and came up with many brilliant ideas to solve them. The powers that be chose, and still choose not to recognize the war against the Jewish State and the Jewish people by 'our' Arabs, and today we are reaping the reward of that cowardice as we learn to live with Arab terror. And still they condemn the man, the only man, whose ideas would have ended the 'intifada' long before it began."

SUMMARY

Kach was instrumental in radicalizing the Israeli right in the 1970s and 1980s. Not all favored its hallmark racism or violence, especially not after the Hebron massacre of 1994, nor necessarily the aggressive way it articulated its views. Yet, Rabbi Kahane articulated the concerns of those on the Israeli right, particularly those living in Israel's settlements, at a time when it was considered politically incorrect to do so. Since his death in 1990, many of the views, ideas, and beliefs he expressed have become part of mainstream political debate in Israel. Moreover, while the organized violence of Kach itself may have diminished, in and around Israel's settlements in the occupied territories this violence has been taken up by others to the extent that attacks on Arab-Palestinians are now a daily occurrence.

SOURCES

Books

Kahane, Meir. *The Story of the Jewish Defense League.* Radnor, PA: Chilton Books, 1975.

Sprizak, Ehud. *Kach and Meir Kahane: The Emergence of Jewish Quasi-Fascism.* New York: The American-Jewish Committee, 1985.

Periodicals

Shragai, Nadav. "Yoztim lepeula (Going for the Action)." *Haaretz.* November 27, 1984.

Cooperberg, Gary. "In the Traditions of Rabbi Meir Kahane." *Jewish Press.* November 7, 1985.

Web sites

Kahane.org. "Shavuot and the Cultural War." < http://www.kahane.org/ > (accessed October 22, 2005).

Jewish Virtual Library. "Rabbi Meir Kahane (1932–1990)." < http://www.jewishvirtuallibrary.org/jsource/biography/kahane.html > (accessed October 22, 2005).

SEE ALSO

Jewish Defense League (JDL)

Kosovo Liberation Army

OVERVIEW

The Kosovo Liberation Army (KLA) was an Albanian guerilla group that operated in the late 1990s in the former Yugoslavian province of Kosovo, an ethically Albanian area then effectively under Serb control. It played an important part in the NATO war on Yugoslavia in 1999, and although it was meant to disband under the terms of the subsequent peace accords, its former members continue to exert a powerful role in Kosovo on both sides of the law.

LEADER: Hashim Thaci

YEAR ESTABLISHED OR BECAME ACTIVE: 1996

USUAL AREA OF OPERATION: Albania; Serb province of Kosovo; Macedonia

HISTORY

Modern Yugoslavia was created from the post-World War II wreckage of the Kingdom of Yugoslavia, by the wartime communist resistance leader, Josip Broz (better known as Tito). It comprised a federation of six republics—Slovenia, Croatia, Bosnia, Serbia, Montenegro, and Macedonia—and two autonomous regions within Serbia—Vojvodina and Kosovo. The federation was an ethnic patchwork, roughly split on religious lines. Slovenians and Croats are Roman Catholics; Serbs and Macedonians Orthodox Christians; and Muslims—generally descended from those Slavs who converted to Islam during the 500-year-long Ottoman occupation—were spread out across the federation,

A young soldier training for the Kosovo Liberation Army in a forest outside of Drenica in 1999.
© Corbis Sygma

particularly in Bosnia, parts of Macedonia, and the autonomous Serb province of Kosovo. Nevertheless, these splits were approximate and Muslims lived in Serbia just as Croats lived in Bosnia.

Tito maintained his policy of "brotherhood and unity" in Yugoslavia by suppressing overt signs of ethnic nationalism among the different Yugoslav peoples, and for the duration of his Presidency-for-life, his policy worked. When he died in 1980, however, Yugoslavia started to come apart. The key figure in the break up and the hostilities that followed was the Serbian politician, Slobodan Milosevic. He encouraged, and then exploited, Serb nationalism within Serbia and among Serb minorities in other republics to extend his influence. He also stripped Kosovo and Vojvodina of their autonomy, taking control of their votes in the rotating presidency that had replaced Tito's rule.

Deeply suspicious of Milosevic's growing power and the impact of his nationalism, Slovenia and Croatia seceded from the

Yugoslav federation in 1991. Slovenia gained its independence after a 10-day conflict, but Croatia became embroiled in a vicious war as the sizeable Serb minority, backed by Milosevic, carved out its own state and brutally cleansed it of Croat civilians. Croatian forces fought back, also expelling Serb citizens, in a struggle that would last until 1995. When Bosnia declared independence in 1992, a conflict there would play out along similar lines. That, too, would be fought until 1995.

In the middle of all this, Serbia had increased its repression of Kosovo amid fears that it too would secede. An unofficial referendum in September 1991 had seen 90% of the population turn out, and 98% back the creation of an independent "Republic of Kosovo." (The Serbian government declared the referendum illegal and the results null and void.)

Milosevic had already had Kosovo's President Azem Vllasi arrested in November 1989, and imposed a state of emergency from March 1989, but in 1990 he imposed a systemic

Kosovar Albanians protest against the indictment of former Kosovo Liberation Army soldiers by the United Nations on March 16, 2004. The soldiers were charged with war crimes. Valdrin Xhemaj/EPA/Landov

policy of economic and cultural apartheid on Kosovo's ethnic Albanian population. Most Kosovars worked in state-owned industry, but were replaced by Serbs; Pristina University, in the province's capital, was purged, with 22,500 of its 23,000 students expelled, and 800 lecturers sacked. With 80% of Kosovo's population unemployed, more than a third of adult males moved overseas in order to support their families back home.

Previously, Kosovo's leaders in exile had called for a campaign of peaceful resistance, having noted the brutal events in Bosnia and Croatia and the overwhelming power of Serb forces. But in April 1996, four simultaneous attacks in different parts of Kosovo were carried out on Serbian civilians and security forces by a previously unknown organization calling itself the Kosovo Liberation Army (KLA). Initially, it was suspected to be the work of Serb agent

provocateurs, who could then use the attacks as an excuse for further repression of the province. In actuality, it was a group of radicalized Albanians from western Kosovo. Their basic strategy was simple: to provoke Serb forces into committing reprisals on the Kosovan population. This, they hoped, would compel the wider international community—shamed by their belated intervention in the Bosnian conflict— into intervening in Kosovo.

Despite the initial ambivalence of the wider world, the nascent KLA's cause received a boost in June 1997 when Albania moved into a state of civil insurrection following the collapse of its economy. Arms dumps across the country were looted, and many weapons ended up over the border in Kosovo, particularly in the west. Over the course of the following year, a guerilla war broke out in western Kosovo, with the KLA launching a series of attacks against the Serbian

Ramush Haradinaj, a former leader in the Kosovo Liberation Army, shakes hands with the leader of the Kosovo Protection Corps, General Agim Ceku, on March 8, 2005. Haradinaj is on his way to stand trial for war crimes. Reuters/Landov

authorities. The Serbs responded by deploying the paramilitary police of the Serbian Interior Ministry, which had gained a reputation for brutality during the Bosnian war. A militia, under the control of Arkan, a notorious Serb warlord, also became embroiled in the emergening conflict.

By the summer of 1998, the KLA had effective control over Kosovo's western quarter and claimed a force of 30,000—although this was almost certainly an exaggeration. The Serbian government responded by launching an offensive against the KLA, and largely forced them back over the Albanian border. However, this was followed by indiscriminate violence against Kosovan Albanian villages that the Serbian forces claimed were harboring KLA rebels. In a reprise of the Bosnian and Croatian conflicts, Serb forces "ethnically cleansed" villages, burning people out of their homes and killing civilians.

This, to an extent, had been the KLA's intention. Serbian excesses were reported across the world, prompting international outrage while at the same time boosting the ranks and coffers of the KLA from Albanians overseas. The KLA, from being a rag-tag force of a few hundred radicals, came to number many thousands, with too many members for its training camps to cope. Its arsenal came to incorporate light artillery and anti-aircraft missiles, while the porous Albanian border enabled them to launch daring border raids.

Throughout late 1998 and early 1999, the guerilla conflict continued to escalate, with KLA forces attacking both Serb military and civilian targets, and Serb forces retaliating in kind. Incidents of brutality by the Serbs—such as the mass killing of 45 civilians in the village of Racak—increased pressure on the rest of the world to intervene. When full-scale war broke out in March 1999, NATO responded by

LEADERSHIP

HASHIM THACI

Hashim Thaci was a Kosovar student leader who returned from living in Switzerland in 1998 to fight with the KLA. Only 30 years old at the time of the NATO-led war, he attracted admiration for his articulation and uncompromising stance as political leader of the KLA.

After the war Thaci declared himself prime minister of a provisional Kosovan government. Thaci was accused of ordering the murders of at least half-a-dozen senior KLA members to consolidate his rise to power. These claims were refuted and were probably part of a campaign to discredit Thaci by his political oppoents. Thaci has also been accused of using his self-appointed government as a racketeering operation. When UN police raided his elder brother's apartment in January 2000, they found $250,000 in cash.

Moreover, in April 2001, Serbia asked the UN War Crimes Tribunal to file charges against Thaci for atrocities they allege he committed during the conflict. Thaci, as of 2005, has been investigated, but never indicted. Nevertheless, in January 2004, the Tribunal secretly indicted four former Kosovo Liberation Army (KLA) members, including Fatmir Limaj, a senior aide to Thaci.

As of 2005, Thaci was the leader of the Democratic Party of Kosovo.

---

launching air raids on Serb positions and, later, on its capital, Belgrade. The KLA, initially repelled by a strong Serb offensive, played a small part by attacking Serb positions and forcing them into the open to enable NATO planes to attack them. In 10 weeks of conflict, NATO flew 38,000 sorties.

NATO and the KLA allied to fight Serbian forces despite the previously stated position of the United States (a NATO member) that the KLA was a terrorist group. The United States reluctantly agreed to the air raids because of international pressure led by British Prime Minister Tony Blair, but refused to send in troops to fight on the ground.

Milosevic responded to the air attacks by dramatically increasing the Serb-led campaign of ethnic cleansing. Within a week of the conflict starting, 300,000 Kosovo Albanians had fled into Albania and Macedonia, and by April 1999, the UN reported that 850,000 had fled their homes.

Finally, in June 1999, completely isolated internationally and with the country scarred by bombing and global condemnation, Milosevic accepted a Finnish-Russian brokered peace deal, bringing an end to the KLA-instigated war. Kosovo was to be overseen by a UN force—KFOR—incorporating NATO troops.

International attention had been focused on Serbian attrocities before and during the war, a consequence of Serbia's brutality in earlier conflicts. Once peace was restored in Kosovo, however, the KLA was accused of a variety of crimes. This included the widespread burning and looting of homes belonging to Serbs, Roma, and other minorities; the destruction of Orthodox churches and monasteries; and harassment of remaining minorities after KFOR's intervention. Human Rights Watch estimates that up to 150,000 non-Kosovan minorities were forced out of the province and that, as of July 2001, 1,000 people still remained unaccounted for.

Under the terms of the peace deal, the KLA—which was not a signatory—was meant to disband, but to appease its members, a 3,000 strong Kosovo Protection Corps drawn from its ranks was established. Many KLA members were not pleased with this. Many became involved in Kosovo's extensive criminal network and their activities came to include racketeering, smuggling, people-trafficking, and drugs. Albanian immigrants also exert a powerful influence on organized crime in other countries, and KLA members have been accused of joining their ranks. In London and Milan, for instance, Albanian gangsters run the cities' vice trades, and Kosovar Albanian women—illegally smuggled into the country, and often against their will—make up large parts of the ranks of prostitutes.

Other former KLA members have sought to make their mark in politics. Its former political head, Hashim Thaci, is now the leader of the

KEY EVENTS

1996: Attacks on Serb military on civilians by group claiming to be the Kosovan Liberation Army.

1997: Collapse of Albanian government leads to extensive weaponry falling into KLA's hands.

1998: Upsurge in skirmishes between the KLA and Serb forces.

1999: Racak village massacre.

1999: NATO-led war on Serbia; KLA plays a minor role.

1999: KLA officially disbands under the terms of the peace agreement, but continues to assert a big influence within Kosovo.

Democratic Party of Kosovo. Nevertheless, in a region where unemployment still runs high, criminality remains an attractive option.

PHILOSOPHY AND TACTICS

The Kosovan Liberation Army was a nationalist irregular armed force, fighting for the secession of Kosovo from Serbia. Its aim, as set out by its political leader, Hashim Thaci, was to create "a liberated, independent Kosovo, and naturally, the democratization of Kosovo." Thaci maintained throughout that it was an army and not an "organization," and should be recognized as such. It never mixed its stated aims with any kind of political philosophy.

The group's tactics evolved over the KLA's short life. In its early stages, it set out to provoke Serb forces into action, which would draw attention to the situation within Kosovo to the outside world. As it grew in force and stature, it was able to launch intermittently successful attacks against Serb positions to force them out of large parts of western Kosovo.

However, the KLA was never a real match for Serb regular forces. When full-scale war broke out in March 1999, western Kosovo was soon overrun by the Serbs, leading to the creation of a huge refugee crisis. The KLA's role during the conflict was largely confined to "hit and run" tactics: striking hidden Serb military positions.

Post-war, the KLA's tactics came to resemble a brand of vigilantism: making reprisal attacks against Serb-civilians and forcing out the non-Kosovan minority.

OTHER PERSPECTIVES

"At the start of the crisis there were two main objectives," the playwright and peace campaigner Harold Pinter told Confederation of Analytical Psychologists in London on June 25, 1999. "To restore substantive autonomy to Kosovo and to ensure that the Yugoslav government respected the Kosovars' political, cultural, religious and linguistic freedoms... The Serbs had specifically agreed to grant Kosovo a large measure of autonomy. What they would not accept was NATO as the international peacekeeping force, or rather, an occupying force, a force whose presence would extend throughout Yugoslavia. They proposed a protectorate under United Nations auspices. NATO would not agree to this and the bombing started immediately."

Pinter believed that NATO had been duped into action, and intimated, as many on the left had done, that the KLA were CIA-backed provocateurs. He went on to say that America's intention was to "make Kosovo into a NATO—or rather American—colony."

"The KLA is the big winner in NATO's war against Milosevic," wrote Mark Almond, lecturer in modern History at Oxford University, in July 1999. "Its leaders are now determined not to lose the peace. Even as NATO troops moved into Kosovo, the KLA was rushing its forces ahead of them to seize the political initiative... A motley group of cheerleaders from State Department spokesman Jamie Rubin to the *Wall Street Journal*'s editorial writers has endorsed the KLA and especially its youthful self-proclaimed prime minister, Hashim Thaci, as the way forward for Kosovo. There can be little doubt that Thaci intends to lead Kosovo in the future and has a very good chance of doing so. Whether the West should rejoice at the prospect is another question." Almond went on to discuss the KLA's alleged role in drug-running and investigated its links to Albanian organized crime.

"Of course," he points out, "banditry and national liberation have gone hand in hand on all sides in the Balkans for as long as anyone can remember-and elsewhere as well.... In all likelihood, the fragile Balkans are witnessing the establishment of another mafia statelet. The Kosovo tragedy thus continues."

SUMMARY

Starting as a rag-tag irregular force to help bring the focus of the world onto the crimes of Serbia in the province of Kosovo, the KLA, within a matter of years, succeeded where Bosnian and Croat forces failed, namely bringing large-scale Western intervention into their conflict with Serbia. Although the KLA built a considerable force they were always outnumbered and outmatched by Serbian forces, and needed outside intervention to achieve victory over the Serbs. Its effective dissolution in September 1999 marked the entry of a number of its former members into organized crime or politics, in some cases both.

SOURCES

Books

Glenny, Misha. *The Balkans 1804–1999: Nationalism, War and the Great Powers.* New York and London: Granta, 2000.

Malcolm, Noel. *Kosovo: A Short History.* New York: Macmillan, 1998.

Parenti, Michael. *To Kill a Nation: The Attack on Yugoslavia.* New York and London: Verso, 2001.

Periodicals

Almond, Mark. "Our Gang: Kosovo Liberation Army." *National Review* July 26, 1999.

Web sites

HaroldPinter.org "Speech to Confederation of Analytical Psycologists." < http://www.haroldpinter.org/politics/ politics_serbia.shtml > (accessed December 14, 2005).

Ku Klux Klan

LEADERS: James Roesch, Ron Edwards, Jeff Berry

YEAR ESTABLISHED OR BECAME ACTIVE: 1866

USUAL AREA OF OPERATION: United States

OVERVIEW

The Ku Klux Klan, also known as the KKK or the Klan, is one of the oldest and best-known hate groups in America. Founded by a group of Confederate Civil War veterans in 1866, the group expanded throughout the South and beyond, attracting thousands of members unhappy with Reconstruction, the post-war period when the former Confederate states were occupied by Union troops and governed by northerners. The Klan eventually swelled to more than half a million members, though national leaders actually exercised little direct control over the local chapters. As the Klan became larger, it also grew more violent, prompting national leader Nathan Forrest to formally disband it in 1869. Despite his attempt to end the organization, local Klans continued their actions, and in 1871, federal legislation outlawing the Klan was passed. The resulting legal crackdown marked the end of the Klan's first incarnation.

In 1915, William J. Simmons reorganized the Klan in Georgia, focusing its attention on African-Americans, Catholics, immigrants, and various other groups. Membership swelled to 100,000 and money flooded in. This second incarnation of the KKK spread across the nation, and the group managed to recruit numerous political leaders into its ranks. A rising tide of violence, combined with a midwestern

In this 1978 photo, Ku Klux Klan leader David Duke, then 27, poses in front of the House of Parliament in London. AP/Wide World Photos

Klan leader's conviction for a grisly rape and murder, began the Klan's decline. An IRS tax lien finished the job by bankrupting the organization in 1944. While the formal Klan no longer exists as a unified organization, various splinter groups, estimated to have fewer than 10,000 members altogether, continue to employ the name and practices of the Ku Klux Klan.

HISTORY

The Ku Klux Klan was founded in 1866 in Pulaski, Tennessee, by six Confederate army veterans. In its earliest form, the group was largely social in nature, its members enjoying many of the rites and rituals often found in other fraternal organizations. But soon after its founding, the Klan's members became involved in racially motivated actions aimed at African-American families and organizations.

The Klan's 1867 convention created a formal structure for the group, as well as a three-item statement of purpose, called the "Prescript." This document defined the Klan's purposes: protecting the weak and defenseless, defending the U.S. Constitution, and enforcing the laws of the United States, particularly those dealing with unlawful seizure of property. While these objectives sound relatively benign to modern ears, they conveyed a clear message in the post Civil War South: the Klan existed to resist Reconstruction and impede the progress of freed slaves.

Leading the Klan in its new mission was a former Confederate general, Nathan Forrest, who was named the Klan's first Grand Wizard. Under his leadership, the Klan swiftly capitalized on Southern suffering, particularly in rural areas. The Klan was organized into various regions, with leaders creatively titled Grand Dragons, Titans, Giants, and Cyclopes. Across the rural South, Klansmen began a campaign of violence, including hundreds of lynchings. Klan violence was not restricted to freed slaves; Northern teachers, judges, and Republicans were all targeted for their perceived role in the

A Ku Klux Klan member responds to protesters at a 1997 Greensburg, Pennsylvania, rally.

AP/Wide World Photos

destruction of the South's traditional way of life. Despite ample evidence to the contrary, Klan leader George Gordon issued a proclamation in 1868 reaffirming the Klan's nonviolence and disavowing any connection with violent acts carried out in its name.

At its peak in 1868, the first Klan claimed more than half a million members nationwide. Despite its rapid numerical growth, the Klan's nominal leadership lacked any real control of its widely dispersed chapters. National leaders began to complain that local Klan groups were doing as they wished, and as violence escalated, reputable citizens began leaving the group. In 1869, in the face of growing unrest and infighting within the Klan's ranks, Grand Wizard Forrest ordered the organization disbanded. Whether this order was a legitimate effort to rein in the group's excessive violence or simply a form of legal self-protection for the group's leader, it had little effect and the violence continued to escalate.

In 1871, President Ulysses S. Grant signed legislation making the Klan illegal and authorizing law enforcement to use force in bringing the group under control. Hundreds of Klansmen were jailed or fined as a result of the new law, and while pockets of Klan membership remained throughout the South, the organization as a whole was largely destroyed.

Despite a court ruling in 1882, which struck down the original anti-Klan legislation, the Klan's reputation had been largely destroyed, and the Klan largely disappeared for more than 30 years. In 1915, D. W. Griffith's epic film *The Birth of a Nation* was released. This work of historical fiction depicted the post Civil War South as a noble society, African-Americans as uneducated and violent, and Northerners as wicked interlopers. The film's heroes were the hooded members of the Ku Klux Klan, who delivered Southern white virtue from the African-American menace.

The film was a box office smash, ultimately taking in more than $10 million to become the highest grossing movie to that date. While controversial, the movie played upon the fears of many Americans, particularly working class men who were nervously watching an enormous wave of immigrants enter the U.S. workforce. In Atlanta, newspapers carrying ads for the movie also carried a small advertisement soliciting interest in a new Klan. The response was overwhelming, and later that year, Methodist pastor William J. Simmons gathered with a group of followers to launch the second Ku Klux Klan, with Simmons as Grand Wizard.

Simmons' new Klan had much in common with the original Klan, opposing Jews, Catholics, African-Americans, and immigrants. It also took positions against various illegal and allegedly immoral acts, including bootlegging, prostitution, graft, and failure to observe the Sabbath. Simmons also is credited with adding the infamous burning cross to the Klan's repertoire.

Simmons was a consummate promoter, and in the years leading up to 1921, membership swelled to 100,000, as money flooded in. In 1924, 40,000 Klansmen marched through the streets of the nation's capital in support of the Democratic National Convention. And political leaders at all levels chose to join the Klan rather than risk incurring its opposition. Future president Harry Truman was briefly a member.

The second Klan was much better organized, and far more profitable, than the first. It also managed to extend its reach beyond the South to much of the United States. But like the first Klan, the second soon found itself swimming in a rapidly rising tide of violence. As Klan leaders battled for control of the group's coffers, local Klan groups became more and more violent. The conviction of Midwest Klan leader, D. C. Stephenson, for the gruesome kidnapping, rape, and murder of a young schoolteacher, played a major role in the Klan once again

Ku Klux Klan members at a ritual cross burning.
© Corbis

falling from public favor during the 1930s. Following an IRS tax lien filing in 1944, the Klan formally dissolved for the second time.

Although the Klan formally died in the 1940s, the name continued to be used by numerous independent groups. The rapid growth of the U.S. economy following World War II, combined with the nation's resulting prosperity, reduced support for these factions. Rising interest in civil rights and victims' increased willingness to fight back during the 1960s also reduced the Klan's influence, and Klan marches were frequently met by counter-protestors. Law enforcement officials also actively worked to monitor and disrupt Klan activities.

By the 1980s, three separate umbrella Klan groups were competing for members: the Imperial Klans of America, the American Knights of the Ku Klux Klan, and the Knights of the White Kamelia. A string of lawsuits has hurt these three groups; a civil suit following the 1981 lynching of Michael Donald pushed another group, the United Klans of America, into bankruptcy. The Southern Poverty Law Center and other civil rights groups have achieved some success in using high-dollar lawsuits to siphon off Klan resources.

While remaining one of the most widely known and most inflammatory of the nation's many hate groups, today's Ku Klux Klan is little more than a shadow of its former self, with an estimated 5,000–7,000 members scattered primarily across the South and Midwest. A 2002 report by the Jewish Anti-Defamation League concludes that, "Today, there is no such thing as the Ku Klux Klan. Fragmentation, decentralization, and decline have continued unabated."

PHILOSOPHY AND TACTICS

While the Ku Klux Klan has a lengthy history of bigotry, violence, and racism, the group's focus and tactics have proven remarkably malleable, often shifting in response to the current mood in the country. While the specific targets of Klan attacks have changed, a common theme runs throughout; in each of its incarnations, the Klan has targeted groups that are easily painted as a threat to working-class Americans. By blaming these groups for the struggles faced by blue-collar workers, the Klan has been able to tap into deep veins of frustration and paranoia, allowing it to attract new members and grow rapidly.

The original Ku Klux Klan, sprouting amid the rubble of the Reconstructionist South, quickly set its sights on those it saw as a threat to the South's way of life: freed slaves, Northern immigrants, and local judges who seized property and enforced federal equality laws. In addition, the original Klan offered defeated Confederate soldiers a second chance to battle the foes of the South. The tactics used by the first Klan were typically harassment, intimidation, and physical violence. Among the most violent acts was the practice of lynching.

Lynching, in its broadest sense, refers to any punishment administered outside the formal justice system. Lynching takes a variety of forms around the world; in the United States, the term most often refers to murder by hanging. During the late 1800s, lynchers often raided African-Americans' homes at night. In some cases, the attackers removed firearms, while in others they whipped or murdered the residents. Lynching was intended to intimidate African-Americans and prevent freed slaves from voting or owning weapons. The number of lynchings declined after the Klan was banned in 1871, but they continued to occur regularly well into the twentieth century. Thus the threat of lynching remained a potent weapon for Klan members for many years.

Hooded female Ku Klux Klan members are illuminated by a burning cross in North Carolina, 1964.
© *Black Star/Alamy*

The revived Klan of the early twentieth century was far broader in its geographic scope, moving beyond the South and into the Midwest and other regions of the country. As the group expanded, it found itself with new resources and new techniques at its disposal. The year 1915 saw the birth of the new Klan, and along with it, the arrival of a new technique, the placement of a burning cross on property in order to terrorize the owner. Along with the burning cross, the reorganized Klan also employed violence similar to that used in the group's first incarnation.

The Klan's rapid expansion in the 1920s also provided it with significant sums of money. Klan Grand Wizard William Simmons, a former pastor, used some of this income to hire publicists to assist the Klan with advertising and recruiting, and the group's numbers swelled. With both financial resources and a large membership, the group was now able to impact the political process in ways the original Klan never could. At its peak, the Klan had the resources to elect candidates of its choosing, most notably Ed Jackson,

whom the Klan aided in his successful bid for the Indiana governor's office.

Various national politicians were members or past members of the Klan. Edward White, Chief Justice of the U.S. Supreme Court in the early twentieth century, was one of two Supreme Court members known to have been Klansmen. While there remains some scholarly debate on the question, evidence suggests that President Warren Harding was a member of the Klan, having supposedly taken the oath of membership in the White House. Harry Truman was advised to join the Klan to help win re-election to a judgeship in Missouri, which he did, though he later distanced himself from the group. Hugo Black, Democratic Senator and Supreme Court Justice, was a Klan member in the 1920s, but later repudiated the group. West Virginia Senator Robert Byrd was a Klansman for many years. Byrd later called his membership a mistake.

In its second incarnation, the Klan once again identified groups that it blamed for the

KEY EVENTS

1866: Six middle-class Confederate veterans in Pulaski, Tennessee, form the original Ku Klux Klan, a social club focusing on fraternity-like rituals and hazing. The group soon begins racist activities.

1867: The Klan is formalized at a convention in Nashville. Former slave trader and Confederate general, Nathan Forrest, is named its first Grand Wizard, or national leader.

1868: Grand Wizard Forrest claims 550,000 members of the KKK, though most local groups remain autonomous.

1871: Amid rising violence, President U.S. Grant signs legislation banning the Klan and authorizing the use of force against its members, marking the end of the first Ku Klux Klan.

1915: D. W. Griffith's film, *The Birth of a Nation*, is released; the film glorifies the Klan as protectors of the South.

1915: William J. Simmons leads the creation of the second Ku Klux Klan, which espouses anti-Jewish, anti-Catholic, and anti-immigrant beliefs. The Klan grows to more than 100,000 members.

1924: More than 40,000 uniformed Klansmen march in Washington D.C.

1930s: Growing violence and scandals within the Klan turn the public against the group; membership declines.

1944: The Internal Revenue Service files a lien for $685,000 in back taxes against the Klan, leading to its dissolution. Various independent groups begin using the name.

1963: Klan members bomb a church used by civil rights leaders in Atlanta.

1964: The FBI begins efforts to infiltrate the Ku Klux Klan.

1981: Michael Donald is lynched by two Klansmen in Mobile, Alabama. The resulting civil suit bankrupts the United Klans of America, one of several Klan groups.

2002: The Anti-Defamation League issues a report on extremism, in which it declares that the Ku Klux Klan no longer exists as an organized group.

2005: Robed Klan members distribute literature following a fire at a Hispanic man's house in Ohio. The man had been accused of sexually assaulting a white girl.

---

struggles of working-class Americans. While the original Klan was largely a product of Southern frustration and had chosen its targets accordingly, the second Klan quickly spread beyond the South. Consequently, its list of targets was correspondingly longer and more diverse. The second Klan's enemy list formally included African-Americans, Jews, Catholics, and various lawbreakers, including drug dealers and prostitutes; informally, local Klan organizations were frequently willing to target anyone they perceived as threatening their chosen values. Given the general distrust of foreigners and "outsiders" prevalent in the United States at the time, the Klan's focus on opposition to these groups led to rapid growth.

The Klan's tactics against these new groups once again included traditional practices such as lynching, which became more frequent as the Klan grew. In addition, the new Klan began using the burning cross, a graphic threat that, by itself, was sometimes adequate to force victims to relocate. Klan leader Simmons also began to employ the tactics of marketing, hiring publicists to help him advertise and recruit new Klan members. The Klan's high point came in 1924, when 40,000 Klansmen converged to march in Washington, D.C. as a demonstration of the organization's growing political clout. Membership in the Klan approached 100,000 at its peak, and several top Klan leaders became wealthy.

As the Klan grew, it began to face a growing incompatibility between its public image of law and order and its private addiction to violence. With violent acts becoming more common and more extreme, the Klan's leadership found itself repeating the struggles of the first Klan's leaders, who had also tried to corral the group's increasingly radical fringe segments. This inability to exert control, combined with intense infighting over the group's profits, began to shake the Klan apart. By the late 1920s, the Klan was once again largely discredited among the general public, and its membership dissolved into dozens of competing factions, most with dwindling membership roles.

The Klan continued to decline throughout the Great Depression and World War II. With the U.S. economy rolling rapidly ahead following the war, the Klan's recruiting pleas were largely ineffective. While local Klan groups remained throughout America, efforts to reunite them into a monolithic Klan during the 1950s and 1960s failed. The coming of civil rights legislation in the 1960s did provide some new fuel for Klan fires, and membership nudged upward in response. However, the FBI and other law enforcement groups also became far more active in policing the Klan during this era, often using informants and infiltrators within the Klan to monitor and at times disrupt the group's operations. In one of the more bizarre episodes of this era, author Stetson Kennedy infiltrated the Georgia Klan and began stealing Klan passwords, which were then broadcast on the weekly Superman radio show. These episodes, in which Superman battled and defeated the Klan, revealed the group's mysterious secret rituals to actually be sophomoric passwords and signs, leaving the Klan publicly humiliated.

While the Ku Klux Klan has little political influence today, Klan members have attempted to enter the political arena. David Duke joined the Klan at the age of 17, and was eventually elected Grand Wizard of the Knights of the Ku Klux Klan, a title he later changed to "national director." Duke ran for the Louisiana State Senate in 1976. While he later left the Klan to create the National Association for the Advancement of White People, he maintained his white supremacist position and never repudiated his involvement with the Klan. Duke later ran for statewide office as a Republican,

prompting both Ronald Reagan and George H. W. Bush to visit the state and campaign for his opponent. Duke was imprisoned in 2002 for tax and mail fraud. He was reportedly considering a new run for office following his release in 2004.

OTHER PERSPECTIVES

While the Ku Klux Klan has found its popularity dwindling in recent years, it does still have allies, primarily other white supremacist organizations which share the Klan's views.

The ACLU, whose stated purpose is to defend American individual rights from government interference, is frequently criticized for their work on behalf of groups such as the KKK. In 2002, Klan members reserved a Riverside Country, California public facility. Upon learning of the Klan's connection to the event, state officials attempted to cancel the contract. The ACLU of Southern California obtained a court order permitting the event to take place, citing First Amendment freedom of speech protection for the Klan's activities.

The ACLU often serves as a legal advocate for the Klan, not based upon the merits of Klan philosophy and thought, but rather for their Constitutional right to express their views. In a statement on the ACLU of Southern California's website, Ramona Ripston, ACLU/SC Executive Director, offered this perspective: "We defend the free speech rights of individuals and groups no matter where they fall on the political spectrum, from left to right and no matter how repugnant we find their message."

SUMMARY

In the twenty-first century, the Ku Klux Klan is in disarray. Living in an increasingly diverse America, most U.S. citizens have become more comfortable with interpersonal differences, making them less receptive to white supremacist claims. Further, the generally healthy economic climate of the recent past has left fewer Americans out of work, further limiting the Klan's appeal. Today, the Klan exists only as around 100 independent Klaverns, whose influence is largely local and, in most cases, extremely limited. The

PRIMARY SOURCE

Ku Klutz Klan: KKK Initiation Ceremony Goes Astray

"Oh my God, I shot little brother!" was the first thing police say America's Invisible Empire Knights of the Ku Klux Klan member Gregory Allen Freeman said after he accidentally shot a fellow Klansman in the head during a Nov. 23 initiation in Johnson City, Tenn.

The ritual began to go awry after Klan initiate Karl Mitchell III, 27, was strung to a tree with a noose and made to stand on tiptoe while being pelted with paintballs.

According to Chief Deputy Patrick Littleton of Washington County, Freeman apparently meant to scare Mitchell with the sound of real gunfire by firing his handgun near Mitchell's ear.

But one of the paintballs apparently struck Freeman, causing him to buckle and squeeze off a round in the direction of Klan brother Jeffrey S. Murr, 24, who may have leaned forward after being hit with a paintball as well. A 9mm bullet entered the top of Murr's head and exited the bottom of his skull.

Freeman's reaction wasn't very helpful to his brother Klansman. A 45-year-old who goes by the nickname "Rebel," Freeman reportedly paced back and forth, hitting himself in the head with his handgun over and over, before he fled the scene.

Only Mitchell, the initiate, seemed to have his wits about him after the accidental shooting. After telling the Klansmen to cut him down from the tree, Mitchell rushed to Murr's side and applied pressure to the wound until help arrived.

Three months later Murr remained in serious condition, unable to speak.

Freeman was later found near his home and charged with reckless endangerment and aggravated assault. Released on $7,500 bail, he was scheduled to face a judge in mid-March.

Source: Southern Poverty Law Center, 2004

---

emergence of numerous other white supremacist organizations has also provided new options to potential Klan members, making recruiting even more difficult for the aging KKK.

SOURCES

Books

B'nai B'rith. *Extremism in America*. New York: Anti-Defamation League, 2002.

Wade, Wyn C. *The Fiery Cross: The Ku Klux Klan in America*. Oxford, England: Oxford University Press, 1998.

Web sites

Anti-Defamation League. " Ku Klux Klan." < http://www. adl.org/learn/ext_us/kkk.asp > (accessed October 18, 2005).

Bartleby.com. "The Columbia Encyclopedia: Ku Klux Klan." < http://www.bartleby.com/65/ku/KuKluxKl.html > (accessed October 18, 2005).

SEE ALSO

National Association for the Advancement of White People

Kumpulan Mujahidin Malaysia

LEADERS: Zainon Ismail; Nik Adli Datuk Nik
Abdul Aziz

USUAL AREA OF OPERATION: Malaysia; Indonesia;
southern Philippines

OVERVIEW

Kumpulan Mujahidin Malaysia (KMM) appeared in 1995 with the goal of overthrowing the presiding Malaysian government and replacing it with an Islamic state. The state that the group seeks to create would include Indonesia and southern Philippines. The group has established ties with other Islamist extremist groups in the region to expand its message and activities. The group continues to operate despite a series of measures by the Malaysian government to impede the organization's growth and development.

HISTORY

Malaysia represents a mix of cultures and religions, and since its independence, has enjoyed decades of relative racial calm. In 1957, Malaysia gained its independence from Great Britain. The territories encompassed by Malaysia included the eastern states in Borneo of Sabah and Sarawah, Singapore, which opted out of the union in 1965, and Malaysia. The new nation adopted a flag based on the flag of the United States, with stripes representing the 14 Malaysian states and a square in the upper left-hand corner, which contains the moon and sun of Islam.

LEADERSHIP

ZAINON ISMAIL

Zainon Ismail is the founder of the KMM and served as its leader until 1999 when he was replaced by Nik Adli Datuk Nik Abdul Aziz. Ismail is a former mujahedin who trained in guerilla warfare and fought in Afghanistan against Soviet forces. He was inspired by the successes in Afghanistan and returned to Malaysia with the goal of a pan-Islamic state. Ismail was detained under the Internal Security Act in 2001 for suspected activities in connection with the KMM.

NIK ADLI DATUK NIK ABDUL AZIZ

Nik Adli Datuk Nik Abdul Aziz is the current leader of the KMM. He was detained by the Malaysian government under the Internal Security Act in 2001 for planning jihad, possession of weapons, and membership in the KMM. His father is PAS opposition party leader Kelantan Mentri Besar Datuk Nik Abdul Aziz Nit Mat.

Malays were the majority population, resulting in a constitutionally guaranteed place in the government, Malay named as the national language, and Islam named as the national religion. The nation operates under a constitutional monarchy, allowing for a democratically elected government. In 1969, a series of initiatives was passed by the Malay-controlled government to provide increased economic opportunities for Malays. The action resulted in two years of violence after the opposition party won a significant number of seats in the government. Since then, race relations as well as economic growth have progressed. Much of the success is attributed to the leadership of the former prime minister, Mahathir bin Mohammed. However, the Kumpulan Mujahidin Malaysia (KMM) and other pan-Islamic groups in the region, seek to over throw the politician's continued ruling coalition, the United Malays National Organization (UMNO).

Mahathir ruled the Malaysian government and his party, UMNO, from 1981 until his resignation in October 2003. His authoritarian rule and varied cooperation with the Western powers facilitated the development of the opposition party, the Pan-Malaysian Islamic Party (PAS)—a group seeking the implementation of Islamic law into Malaysian governance. Other factors also fostered a political environment in which groups such as the KMM could develop. Approximately 1,000 mujahedin traveled from Southeast Asia to Afghanistan during the mid 1980s. Once there, the group received guerilla warfare training and religious schooling, focusing on Wahhabism—a fundamentalist sect of Islam that calls for strict adherence to Islamic law. Upon returning to Southeast Asia, these mujahedin began to establish schools called madrasses. These schools provided religious training for young Muslims in the region and began to promote the idea of a pan-Islamic state in Southeast Asia.

The financial growth of Malaysia, as well as its decline in the mid 1990s, also contributed to the development of organizations such as KMM. Malaysia's economy was one of the fastest growing economies in Southeast Asia. However, the majority of the wealth held in Malaysia belonged to the ethnic Chinese population. In 1995, when the economies of Asia began to fail, the opposition led by the PAS capitalized on the disproportionate distribution of wealth. Many Muslims turned to the PAS for leadership during the time of economic crisis, as apparent in the rise in enrollment of students at the madrasses. This breakdown of secular institutions and the growth of the PAS marked the weakening of the UMNO.

One of the most important factors in Southeast Asia that has allowed for the growth of groups such as the KMM is the porous borders and financial institutions. Prior to the September 11, 2001, attacks on the United States, Malaysia had no visa requirement for nationals of Organization of the Islamic Confederation member states. This allowed the mujahedin from various Southeast Asian nations to move freely, train, and recruit new members virtually unnoticed.

As a member of the mujahedin returning from Afghanistan, Zainon Ismail had been inspired by the religious and military training he had received. Upon his return, Ismail founded the

KEY EVENTS

1995: KMM founded by Zainon Ismail.

1998: Killing of Lunas state assemblyman Dr. Joe Fernandez considered unsolved until arrest of KMM members in 2001.

1998: Attempted murder of couple in Jalan Klang Lama also considered unsolved until links are made after the 2001 arrest of 10 members of KMM.

1999: Nik Adli Datuk Nik Abdul Aziz assumes leadership of the KMM.

2000: KMM believed to be involved in explosion near a temple in Jalan Padu Lama on Deepavali eve.

2001: Activities of the KMM are hampered as KMM members are detained as national security threats under the Internal Security Act. KMM members detained include Zainon Ismail and Nik Adli Datuk Nik Abdul Aziz, as well as several teachers from madrasses schools.

KMM with the goal to overthrow the Mahathir coalition and replace the Malaysian government with an Islamic state. The goal of the KMM, as well as other like-minded groups forming in Southeast Asia by returning mujahedin, was a pan-Islamic state that would include Malaysia, Indonesia, and southern Philippines. Ismail served as leader of the KMM until 1999 when Nik Adli Datuk Nik Abdul Aziz became leader.

The attacks on the United States on September 11, 2001, provided the Mahathir government the ammunition to attempt a marginalization of the PAS and Islamic fundamentalist groups, such as the KMM. The Mahathir government began its crackdown in mid 2001, but the attacks on the United States allowed an expansion of the government action. In August 2001, police arrested 10 men believed to be members of the KMM. The men's arrests occurred after a failed robbery attempt in Petaling Jaya. Investigations

linked the men to robberies and the murder of Lunas state assemblyman, Dr. Joe Fernandez. Other activities the men were arrested for included a February 2001 raid on the Guar Chempedak police station and an October 1998 attempted murder of a couple in Jalan Klang Lama.

Since 2001, over 80 alleged KMM members have been detained under the Internal Security Act (ISA). The act allows for the two-year detention of anyone deemed a threat to national security, with a provision for the additional two-year extension. The members of the KMM have been detained under the charges of possession of weapons and planning *jihad* (holy war). Present leader Nik Adli Datuk Nik Abdul Aziz has also been detained under the ISA. Nik Adli is the son of PAS opposition leader, Kelantan Mentri Besar Datuk Nik Aziz Nik Mat, causing many to believe that his incarceration is a political move.

Since 2001 and the detention of many of its members under the ISA, KMM activities have tapered off. However, the group's alliances with other pan-Islamic groups in the region have aided its continued existence.

PHILOSOPHY AND TACTICS

The KMM seeks the establishment of a pan-Islamic state to include Malaysia, Indonesia, and southern Philippines. In order to reach this goal, the group seeks to overthrow the presiding Malaysian government. In addition, the KMM has determined its enemies to be the secular governments within the region, as well as Western governments, namely the United States. The KMM has fostered alliances with other regional Islamic fundamentalist groups such as Jemaah Islamiyah (JI). JI religious leader Abu Bakar Bashir and operational leader Hambali have provided logistical and financial assistance to the KMM. In addition, the KMM has operational networks within Perak, Johor, Kedah, Selager, Terangganu, Kelantan, and the capital district of Wilayah Persukutuan. The KMM is believed to be self-financing, providing for its activities through robberies and kidnappings. The KMM and other regional groups recruit members from the madrasses schools established by mujahedin upon their return from Afghanistan. At least six of the men arrested under the Internal Security Act for connections to the KMM were instructors

PRIMARY SOURCE
Kumpulan Mujahidin Malaysia (KMM)

DESCRIPTION

Kumpulan Mujahidin Malaysia (KMM) favors the overthrow of the Malaysian Government and the creation of an Islamic state comprising Malaysia, Indonesia, and the southern Philippines. Malaysian authorities believe an extremist wing of the KMM has engaged in terrorist acts and has close ties to the regional terrorist organization Jemaah Islamiya (JI). Key JI leaders, including the group's spiritual head, Abu Bakar Ba'asyir, and JI operational leader Hambali, reportedly had great influence over KMM members. The Government of Singapore asserts that a Singaporean JI member assisted the KMM in buying a boat to support jihad activities in Indonesia.

ACTIVITIES

Malaysia is holding a number of KMM members under the Internal Security Act (ISA) for activities deemed threatening to Malaysia's national security, including planning to wage jihad, possession of weaponry, bombings and robberies, the murder of a former state assemblyman, and planning attacks on foreigners, including US citizens. A number of those detained are also believed to be members of Jemaah Islamiya. Several of the arrested KMM militants have reportedly undergone military training in Afghanistan, and some fought with the Afghan mujahedin during the war against the former Soviet Union. Some members are alleged to have ties to Islamic extremist organizations in Indonesia and the Philippines. In September 2003, alleged KMM leader Nik Adli Nik Abdul Aziz's detention was extended for another two years. In March 2004, Aziz and other suspected KMM members went on a hunger strike as part of an unsuccessful bid for freedom, but the Malaysian court rejected their applications for a writ of habeas corpus in September. One alleged KMM member was sentenced to 10 years in prison for unlawful possession of firearms, explosives, and ammunition, but eight other alleged members in detention since 2001 were released in July and in November. The Malaysian Government is confident that the arrests of KMM leaders have crippled the organization and rendered it incapable of engaging in militant activities. Malaysian officials in May 2004 denied Thailand's charge that the KMM was involved in the Muslim separatist movement in southern Thailand.

STRENGTH

KMM's current membership is unknown.

LOCATION/AREA OF OPERATION

The KMM is reported to have networks in the Malaysian states of Perak, Johor, Kedah, Selangor, Terengganu, and Kelantan. They also operate in Kuala Lumpur. According to press reports, the KMM has ties to radical Indonesian Islamic groups and has sent members to Ambon, Indonesia, to fight against Christians and to the southern Philippines for operational training.

EXTERNAL AID

Largely unknown, probably self-financing.

Source: U.S. Department of State. *Country Reports on Terrorism.* Washington, D.C., 2004.

---

at such schools. Recruits are sent to Thailand for paramilitary training and are organized into cells.

OTHER PERSPECTIVES

The Malaysian government has come under pressure by human rights groups, such as Amnesty International, for its detention of KMM members. Since 2001, over 80 alleged members of KMM have been detained, many of them without trial or formal charges. The Internal Security Act allows for a two-year detention of anyone deemed a threat to national security. The detention can be extended, as in the case of Zainon Ismail, who was arrested in 1999 and was still under detention in September 2005.

Opponents of the Internal Security Act state that the Malaysian government's "first duty is to prove the existence of the KMM." These human rights watch groups believe that the detention of KMM members is a political plot to weaken the Islamic fundamentalist opposition party, PAS. Amnesty International states, "The authorities claimed that both groups [KMM and JI] were planning to use violent means to set up a pan-Islamic state in southeast Asia. No evidence to support these allegations was made public, and none of the detainees was brought to trial." The detention of Nik Adli Datuk Nik Abdul Aziz, the son of opposition party leader, Kelantan Mentri Besar Datuk Nik Abdul Aziz Nit Mat, adds fuel to this argument.

SUMMARY

The KMM was established in 1995 by former mujahedin, Zainon Ismail, with the expressed goal to overthrow the Malaysian government. Upon accomplishing this goal, the KMM seeks the creation of a pan-Islamic state covering Indonesia, Malaysia, and the southern Philippines. The group is believed to be self-financing through robberies and its alliances with like-minded groups such as Jemaah Islamiyah. Since the Malaysian government began to detain suspected KMM members in 2001, the activities of KMM have been hampered. However, the connections and support from alliances such as JI have allowed the group's continued existence.

SOURCES

Periodicals

Abuza, Zachary. "The War on Terrorism in South East Asia." *Strategic Asia*. 2003–2004: pp. 321–364.

Aziz, A.A. "The Burden of Terrorism in Malaysia." *Prehospital Disaster Medicine*. 2003: no. 18(2), pp. 115–119.

Web sites

Amnesty International. "Malaysia." < http://web.amnesty.org/web/web.nsf/print/ AE8AB1DFBF598CA680256D3A0046B443 > (accessed October 11, 2005).

Center for Strategic and International Studies. "The Nexus Between Counterterrorism, Counter-proliferation, and Maritime Security in Southeast Asia." < http://www.csis.org/pacfor/issues/v04n04_ch3.cfm > (accessed October 11, 2005).

CNN.com/World. "South East Asia's Crackdown." < http://edition.cnn.com/2002/WORLD/asiapcf/southeast/01/07/terror.factbox/ > (accessed October 11, 2005).

Global Security. "Kumpulan Mujahidin Malaysia." < http://www.globalsecurity.org/military/world/para/kmm.htm > (accessed October 11, 2005).

National Library of Medicine, National Institutes of Health. "The Story of NLM Historical Collections." < http://www.nlm.nih.gov/hmd/about/collectionhistory.html > (accessed October 11, 2005).

Terrorism Knowledge Base. "Kumpulan Mujahidin Malaysia." < http://www.tkb.org/Group.jsp?groupID=4401 > (accessed October 11, 2005).

Time: Asia. "Untangling the Web." < http://www.time.com/time/asia/news/magazine/0,9754,197713,00.html > (accessed October 11, 2005).

U.S. Department of State. "Patterns of Global Terrorism, 2003, April 2004." < http://www.state.gov/documents/organization/31947.pdf > (accessed October 11, 2005).

SEE ALSO

Jemaah Islamiyah (JI)

Kurdistan Workers' Party (PKK)

LEADER: Abdullah Ocalan
YEAR ESTABLISHED OR BECAME ACTIVE: 1974
ESTIMATED SIZE: 4,000–5,000
USUAL AREA OF OPERATION: Turkey

OVERVIEW

The Kurdistan Workers' Party (PKK; its Kurdish name, *Partiya Karkeran Kurdistan*) is an extreme-left, nationalist/separatist group. Its goal—as part of a communist revolutionary movement—is to establish an independent Kurdish state in areas where Kurds reside, mostly in southeastern Turkey and adjoining countries of northern Iraq, western Iran, and in small parts of Armenia and Syria. (Kurds also live in Europe, mainly Germany, as exiles or migrants.) The Kurdistan Workers' Party is also identified by such aliases as Kurdistan Freedom and Democracy Congress (KADEK), Kurdistan People's Conference (KHK), and Kingra-Gel (KGK, or the Kurdistan People's Congress).

To reclaim Kurdish lands its leader, Abdullah Ocalan, used guerrilla warfare and terrorism against Turkey from 1984–1999. With PKK's defeat by the Turkish military and the February 1999 capture of Ocalan, most PKK soldiers have scattered to northern Iraq. The PKK leadership has established a political party, but Ocalan remains a Turkish prisoner.

HISTORY

Relations between Kurds and the Turkish government have been strained since the 1920

Abdullah Ocalan, a Kurdistan Workers' Party leader. Archive Photos/Getty

Treaty of Sevres (a result of World War I), which provided for an autonomous Kurdistan. However, Turkey forced modifications in the treaty and the plan was never implemented. Since then, the minority Kurds have not been given full rights from the Turkish government.

Kurds have many times attempted reclamation of their rights in Turkey. One such organized attempt was begun in 1973 when Abdullah Ocalan and several Turkish-Kurdish students formed the PKK to establish an independent Kurdistan. For the next five years, the PKK operated without any formal agenda. But, in 1978, Ocalan stated the PKK's heavily communist-influenced agenda and organized a revolt to free the Kurdish people.

Beginning in the early 1980s, the PKK left Turkey for Syrian-occupied Lebanon (because of a shared leftist philosophy) in order to receive professional training by Syrian terrorist groups. The group maintained Syria as its base of operations for almost two decades.

In 1984, the PKK began attacks against Turkish forces. The PKK attacked Turkish government and security facilities and personnel, along with civilians who assisted the Turkish government. Turkish experts verified PKK involvement when they linked the group with suicide bombs intended for governors and police stations. These initial attacks in the mid 1980s were reported to have killed thousands of civilians. During this time PKK membership increased drastically. The Turkish government eliminated all legal Kurdish organizations, making it popular to join the rebel PKK.

During the late 1980s and early 1990s, the PKK changed its strategy by eliminating attacks on civilians (including its own Kurdish people) in order to gain their support. It continued to attack Turkish domestic government sites, sabotage and firebomb Turkish diplomatic and commercial buildings in Europe, bomb tourist sites in Istanbul and at Turkish seaside resorts, and kidnap Western tourists in order to gain publicity. With its leftist strategy modified, the PKK attracted members and supporters of the Islamic faith.

By 1992, the PKK had grown considerably stronger. As a result, the Turkish government employed specially trained teams of soldiers specifically to fight against the rebel group. The rebellion intensified dramatically by March 1995 so that Turkish soldiers were forced to retaliate against the PKK by attacking them while in northern Iraq. The Turkish government repeated this successful tactic numerous times, often times with help from Masood Barzani's Democratic Party of Kurdistan, a rival Kurdish group.

In 1998, the PKK claimed that it possessed about 10,000 soldiers as part of its military unit, the Popular Army for the Liberation of Kurdistan. The PKK also professed a political branch based in Brussels called the National Liberation Front of Kurdistan.

Ocalan and his rebel troops were forced to leave Syria in October 1998 when the Syrian government cowered to international pressure—especially from Turkey, which threatened to attack Syria. Ocalan searched for political asylum throughout Europe and Africa.

On February 15, 1999, Ocalan was arrested in Nairobi, Kenya, by a coalition of U.S./Turkish special-forces personnel and sent back to Turkey. His arrest caused mass protests across Europe and the Middle East. The largest protest

Two female guerrilla members of the Kurdish Workers' Party on August 1, 1991, in northern Iraq. AP/Wide World Photos. Reproduced by permission.

LEADERSHIP

ABDULLAH OCALAN

Abdullah Ocalan became a student activist (with a Marxism philosophy) while a political science student at the University of Ankara, Turkey. He later became involved with the problems of his Kurdish people while in civil service at Diyarbakir, Turkey. During this time, Ocalan participated in the Kurdish rights activities of the Democratic Cultural Associations of the East. In 1973, Ocalan organized a Maoist group for socialist revolution. Five years later, in 1978, Ocalan founded the Kurdistan Workers' Party.

For the next two decades, Ocalan, under the name of Serok Apo, fought to restore Turkish rights of the Kurdish people. He was captured in Kenya on February 15, 1999, and returned to Turkey for trial. He was convicted in a Turkish court of treason and sentenced to death. Ocalan appealed the decision before the European Court of Human Rights. On May 12, 2005, the European Court agreed with his appeal, stating that his trial was unfair. Ocalan remains held under solitary confinement on Imrali Island in the Turkish Sea of Marmara.

came from Berlin, Germany, where three Kurdish militants were killed and 16 others wounded when they attempted to overrun the Israeli Consulate. Ocalan was convicted on terrorism charges and sentenced to death. However, Ocalan made an appeal to the European Court of Human Rights.

Without its leader, the PKK were severely weakened, so much that Ocalan agreed to stop fighting after Turkey agreed to reform its Kurdish policies. In August 1999, Ocalan declared a ceasefire and requested a peace plan. In 2000, the PKK stated that it had ended its revolution—promising it would work within Turkish law to improve the status of its Kurdish people.

In April 2002, the PKK changed its name to the Kurdistan Freedom and Democracy Congress (KADEK), supposedly to distance itself from its violent past and to promote its nonviolent future as a political party. In August 2002, Turkey abolished the death penalty and Ocalan's sentence was altered to lifelong aggravated imprisonment. Then, in 2003, the KADEK announced a three-part strategy for instituting Kurdish autonomy. However, the group continued to train its members for fighting.

Later in 2003, the KADEK announced that it was again changing its name, this time to the Kurdistan People's Conference (KHK). The Turkish government did not believe the group's violent ways had changed. Then, in November 2003, the KHK changed its name again. It now

called itself Kongra-Gel (KGK, or the Kurdistan People's Congress). The group continued to publicly state its peaceful intentions while conducting further attacks. In early 2004, the ceasefire ended and violence by the group's armed section (the HPG, or People's Forces of Defense) returned to Turkey. As of April 2005, the KHK had reverted back to its original name: the Kurdistan Workers' Party.

In all, between 30,000 and 40,000 people are thought to have been killed due to PKK actions from 1984–1999. Estimates vary, depending on the source, as to the number forcibly evacuated from their homes.

PRIMARY SOURCE

Kongra-Gel (KGK) a.k.a. Kurdistan Workers' Party, PKK

DESCRIPTION

The Kongra-Gel was founded by Abdullah Ocalan in 1974 as a Marxist-Leninist separatist organization and formally named the Kurdistan Workers' Party in 1978. The group, composed primarily of Turkish Kurds, began its campaign of armed violence in 1984, which has resulted in some 30,000 casualties. The PKK's goal has been to establish an independent, democratic Kurdish state in southeast Turkey, northern Iraq, and parts of Iran and Syria. In the early 1990s, the PKK moved beyond rural-based insurgent activities to include urban terrorism. Turkish authorities captured Ocalan in Kenya in early 1999, and the Turkish State Security Court subsequently sentenced him to death. In August 1999, Ocalan announced a "peace initiative," ordering members to refrain from violence and requesting dialogue with Ankara on Kurdish issues. At a PKK Congress in January 2000, members supported Ocalan's initiative and claimed the group now would use only political means to achieve its public goal of improved rights for Kurds in Turkey. In April 2002 at its 8th Party Congress, the PKK changed its name to the Kurdistan Freedom and Democracy Congress (KADEK) and proclaimed a commitment to non-violent activities in support of Kurdish rights. In late 2003, the group sought to engineer another political face-lift, renaming itself Kongra-Gel (KGK) and promoting its "peaceful" intentions while continuing to conduct attacks in "self-defense" and to refuse disarmament. After five years, the group's hard-line militant wing, the People's Defense Force (HPG), renounced its self-imposed cease-fire on June 1, 2004. Over the course of the cease-fire, the group had divided into two factions—politically-minded reformists, and hardliners who advocated a return to violence. The hardliners took control of the group in February 2004.

PHILOSOPHY AND TACTICS

When first formed from a radical Kurd youth movement in Turkey in the 1970s, the PKK declared itself a revolutionary socialist national liberation movement that followed Marxist-Leninist doctrine. Its leader, Ocalan, was heavily influenced by Maoism, a combination of orthodox Marxism-Leninism, and Confucianism.

According to the Federation of American Scientists, in 1977, the PKK published several public reports that demanded the separation of Kurdistan from Iran, Iraq, Turkey, and Syria. Its demands were based on the Turkish abuse of Kurds and on the denial by the Turkish government of the Kurd educational and cultural heritage. Throughout the 15-year rebellion against Turkey, the PKK maintained its original objectives: to form a federation system within the Middle East in which Kurd rights would be granted and preserved and to fight for the independence of Kurdistan in response to wrongdoings by Turkish authorities against the Kurdish population.

The armed tactics primarily used by the PKK included attacks against civilian Turkish citizens (including those of Kurdish ethnicity) whenever such people did not support its cause or were cooperating with the Turkish government; attacks and kidnappings of foreign tourists (especially those with large sums of foreign monies); attacks on Turkish government officials such as military leaders, teachers, scientists, and technicians; attacks on the Turkish military; and attacks on Turkish diplomatic offices and other interests in Europe. The PKK has used suicide bombing attacks on various occasions.

Ocalan employed guerilla tactics in his war against Turkish troops during the 1980s, primarily using hit-and-run methods to attack the enemy and then to quickly retreat into

ACTIVITIES

Primary targets have been Turkish Government security forces, local Turkish officials, and villagers who oppose the organization in Turkey. It conducted attacks on Turkish diplomatic and commercial facilities in dozens of West European cities in 1993 and again in spring 1995. In an attempt to damage Turkey's tourist industry, the then-PKK bombed tourist sites and hotels and kidnapped foreign tourists in the early-to-mid–1990s. While most of the group's violence in 2004 was directed toward Turkish security forces, KGK was likely responsible for an unsuccessful July car bomb attack against the governor of Van Province, although it publicly denied responsibility, and may have played a role in the August bombings of two Istanbul hotels and a gas complex in which two people died.

STRENGTH

Approximately 4,000 to 5,000, 3,000 to 3,500 of whom currently are located in northern Iraq. The group has thousands of sympathizers in Turkey and Europe. In November, Dutch police raided a suspected KGK training camp in The Netherlands, arresting roughly 30 suspected members.

LOCATION/AREA OF OPERATION

Operates primarily in Turkey, Iraq, Europe, and the Middle East.

EXTERNAL AID

Has received safe haven and modest aid from Syria, Iraq, and Iran. Syria and Iran appear to cooperate with Turkey against KGK in a limited fashion when it serves their immediate interests. KGK uses Europe for fundraising and conducting political propaganda.

Source: U.S. Department of State. *Country Reports on Terrorism.* Washington, D.C., 2004.

mountainous areas where they could hide. However, in the 1990s the Turkish government brought in specially trained commando units and special police forces with sophisticated equipment that removed the PKK advantages in these areas.

During its reign of violent activities, the PKK received its largest funding through drug smuggling and extortion. The U.S. Department of State's Bureau of International Narcotic Matters, according to the Federation of American Scientists, published the 1992 report "International Narcotics Control Strategy," which stated that the European drug cartel was controlled by PKK members. The amount of money generated from this illegal activity amounted to hundreds of millions of dollars. The PKK also received modest financial support from charities, commercial businesses, and the governments of Greece, Iran, Iraq, Syria, and several European countries.

OTHER PERSPECTIVES

According to CNN Interactive reporter Beat Witschi, Abdullah Ocalan is considered by the majority of Kurds to be a murderer, terrorist, and tyrant who used arson, assassination, robbery, extortion and blackmail, money laundering, and drug trafficking to promote his goals and undermine Turkish society. However, some Kurds, along with his supporters and PKK members, consider him a hero for valiantly battling the Turkish government to regain Kurdish culture, independence, and basic rights.

At the time of Ocalan's capture in 1999, many Turkish journalists interviewed him. According to the CNN article by Witschi, most of those reporters saw Ocalan as a "megalomaniac" and "sick man." In the same article, several human rights organizations had held Ocalan to be in the same class as Chilean dictator General Augusto Pinochet, who was condemned by the United

KEY EVENTS

1973: Abdullah Ocalan and other Turkish/Kurdish students form the PKK.

1973–1978: The PKK operates without structure.

1978: Its operations and agenda are formalized by Ocalan.

1980s: The PKK leaves Turkey for Syrian-occupied Lebanon to be trained.

1984: The PKK begins its fight against the Turkish government.

1992: The Turkish government establish a special unit to fight the PKK.

1993: PKK attacks take on a new character with the firebombing and vandalizing of Turkish/European diplomatic and commercial offices, tourist sites in Turkey, and the kidnapping of Western tourists.

1998: Ocalan and the PKK are forced to leave Syria.

1999: Ocalan is arrested in Kenya and sent back to Turkey. Later, Ocalan is convicted and sentenced to death. He declares a ceasefire.

2002: The PKK changes its name to the Kurdistan Freedom and Democracy Congress (KADEK).

2003: The KADEK announces a Kurdish strategy for resolving Kurdish rights.

2003: The KADEK announces it is changing its name to Kurdistan People's Conference (KHK).

2003: The KHK changes its name again, to Kongra-Gel (KGK, or the Kurdistan People's Congress).

2004: The ceasefire is ended and violence returns to Turkey.

2005: The KHK reverts to its original name: PKK.

2005: The European Court declares Ocalan's trial to be unfair. He remains in prison on an island near Istanbul.

Nations for torturing thousands of his enemies, and war crimes suspect Radovan Karadzic in Bosnia-Herzegovina, who was accused of killing thousands of Bosnian Muslims and Croats. It was also reported that Ocalan destroyed other Kurdish separatist organizations and rivals when they conflicted with him.

According to the article by the Council on Foreign Relations (CFR) that described the Kurdistan Workers' Party, the PKK does not, as of 2004, have any operational connections to other terrorist groups. According to the same CFR article, the country of Turkey continues to consider Kurds to be second-class citizens, calling them Mountain Turks, and denies them the rights given to its other citizens. The Turkish government continues to consider the PKK a terrorist group. It also considers Kurdish separatism and nationalism as threats to its security and the safety of its citizens.

According to the CFR, the European Union added the PKK to its list of terrorist organizations in May 2002. Likewise, Iran also agreed to make the PKK a terrorist organization in March 2002. As of 2005, according to the MIPT, England, Australia, Canada, and the United States continue to consider the PKK a terrorist organization. Most European countries are more tolerant of the PKK—viewing its members as freedom fighters, rather than terrorists—because they do not want to antagonize the group after experiencing riots when Ocalan was arrested.

SUMMARY

According to a *Time* article, the Kurds are the largest ethnic community in the world without its own nation. With about half of all Kurds residing in Turkey, they continue to be in conflict with the Turkish government. For several generations, the Kurds have tried to both peacefully and violently persuade Turkey to grant its people the same rights as its other citizens. The PKK— with its violent efforts to establish an independent Kurdistan incorporating territory that is part of Turkey—is an extreme element of this movement.

Since the beginning of their rebellion in the mid 1980s, the PKK is believed to have killed about 35,000 people, drawing condemnation from many nations and organizations as a terrorist group. The PKK has not achieved its goals, and has seen its leader captured and imprisoned, but it continues to stage attacks. Its efforts have drawn attention to often-troubling human rights issues that exist in Turkey. Human rights organizations continue to claim that the Turkish government has violated the basic rights of those that take even peaceful action against its policies. These Kurdish individuals—according to Amnesty International—have often been imprisoned or have disappeared.

Turkey has been an associate member of the European Union (EU) since 1963. It has been denied full membership due to what the EU considers a problematic human rights record. One of the main reasons for its continued denial as a full EU member has been Turkey's anti-Kurd policies.

SOURCES

Books

White, Paul J. *Primitive Rebels or Revolutionary Modernisers?*. London and New York: Zed, 2000.

Web sites

Council on Foreign Relations. "Kurdistan Workers' Party." < http://cfrterrorism.org/groups/kurdistan.html > (accessed October 20, 2005).

Ergil, Dogu. *CNN/Time In-Depth Special, CNN.com, and Time.com.* "The Kurdish Question after Ocalan." < http://www.cnn.com/SPECIALS/1999/ocalan/stories/kurdish.question/ > (accessed October 20, 2005).

Intelligence Resource Program, Federation of American Scientists. "Kurdistan Workers' Party (PKK)." < http://www.fas.org/irp/world/para/pkk.htm > (accessed October 20, 2005).

Kelly, Suzanne. *Time Interactive, CNN.com.* "Ocalan Trial Casts Light on Turkey's Human Rights Record." < http://cnn.com/SPECIALS/1999/ocalan/stories/turkey.human.rights/ > (accessed October 20, 2005).

MIPT Terrorism Knowledge Base, National Memorial Institute for the Prevention of Terrorism. "Kurdistan Workers' Party." < http://www.tkb.org/Group.jsp?groupID=63 > (accessed October 20, 2005).

Sanction, Thomas. *Time.com.* "A Terrorist's Bitter End." < http://www.time.com/time/daily/special/ocalan/bitter-end.html > (accessed October 20, 2005).

Usher, Rod. *Time International, Time.com.* "Nationalists Without a Nation." < http://www.time.com/time/daily/special/ocalan/nationalists.html > (accessed October 20, 2005).

Witschi, Beat. *CNN.com and Time.com.* "Who Is Abdullah Ocalan? (Ocalan: Key Moments of His Life)." < http://edition.cnn.com/SPECIALS/1999/ocalan/stories/ocalan.profile/ > (accessed October 20, 2005).

SEE ALSO

Al-Qaeda

Sources Consulted

BOOKS

Abanes, Richard. *American Militias*. Downers Grove, IL: InterVarsity Press, 1996.

Aburish, Said. *Arafat: From Defender to Dictator*. London and New York: Bloomsbury, 1998.

Abuza, Zachary. "The War on Terrorism in South East Asia." *Strategic Asia* (2003–2004): 321–364.

Africa, C., J. Christie, R. Mattes, M. Roefs, and H. Taylor. *Crime and Community Action: Pagad and the Cape Flats, 1996–1997*. Cape Town: Public Opinion Service, Institute for Democracy in South Africa, 1998.

Alexander, John K. *Samuel Adams: America's Revolutionary Politician*. Lanham, MD: Rowman & Littlefield, 2002.

American Nazi Party. *Official Stormtrooper's Manual*. Arlington, VA: American Nazi Party, 1962.

Anderson, Chris. *The Billy Boy: The Life and Times of Billy Wright*. Edinburgh: Mainstream, 2003.

Anderson, Sean, and Stephen Sloan. *Historical Dictionary of Terrorism, 2nd Edition*. Lanham, MD: Scarecrow Press, 2002.

Baird, Robert M., and Stuart E. Rosenbau, eds. *The Ethics of Abortion: Pro-Life vs. Pro-Choice*. Amhurst, NY: Prometheus Books, 2001.

Balasingham, Anton. *The Politics of Duplicity: Revisiting the Jaffna Talks*. Mitcham, England: Fairmax Publishing, 2000.

Ball, Phil. *Morbo: A History of Spanish Football*. London: WSC Books, 2003.

Barkun, Michael. *Religion and the Racist Right: The Origins of the Christian Identity Movement*. Chapel Hill, NC: The University of North Carolina Press, 1997.

Best, Steven, and Anthony J. Nocella (eds.). *Terrorists or Freedom Fighters: Reflections on the Liberation of Animals*. New York: Lantern Books, 2004.

Blee, Kathleen M. *Inside Organized Racism: Women in the Hate Movement*. Los Angeles: University of California Press, 2003.

B'nai B'rith. Anti-defamation League. *The Church of the Creator: Creed of Hate*. New York: Anti-Defamation League, 1993.

B'nai B'rith. *Extremism in America*. New York: Anti-Defamation League, 2002.

Brown, Adam (ed.). *Fanatics! Power, Identity and Fandom in FOOTBALL*. Oxford: Routledge, 1998.

Burke, Jason. *Al-Qaeda*. New York: Penguin, 2004.

Burnett, Christina Duffy, and Burke Marshall, editors. *Foreign in a Domestic Sense: Puerto Rico, American Expansion, and the Constitution*. Durham, NC: Duke University Press, 2001.

Byrnes, Rita M. "A Country Study: South Africa." *Library of Congress, Federal Research Division* May 1996.

Chapman, William. *Inside the Philippine Revolution*. New York: W.W. Norton, 1987.

Cleveland, William L. *A History of the Modern Middle East*. New York: Westview, 2000.

Combs, Cindy. *Terrorism in the Twenty-First Century*. Upper Saddle River, NJ: Prentice-Hall, 2000.

Conaghan, Catherine M. *Fujimori's Peru: Deception In The Public Sphere*. Pittsburgh: University of Pittsburgh Press, 2005.

Congressional Testimony. "Iran: Weapons Proliferations, Terrorism and Democracy." May 19, 2005.

Cook, David. *Understanding Jihad*. Berkeley: University of California Press, 2005.

Copeland, David A. *Debating the Issues in Colonial Newspapers: Primary Documents on Events of the Period*. Westport, CT: Greenwood Press, 2000.

Copesy, Nigel. *Contemporary British Fascism: The British National Party and the Quest for Legitimacy*. NY: Palgrave Macmillan, 2004.

Corbett, James. *England Expects*. London: Aurum, 2006.

Corpus, Victor N. *Silent War*. Zuezon City, Philippines: VNC Enterprises, 1989.

Courtemanche, Gils. *A Sunday at the Pool in Kigali*. Edinburgh: Canongate Books, 2004.

Cozic, Charles P., editor. *The Militia Movement*. Farmington Hills, MI: Greenhaven Press, 1997.

Cummings, Bruce. *Inventing the Axis: The Truth about North Korea, Syria and Iran*. New York: New Press, 2004.

Dailaire, Romeo. *Shake Hands With the Devil*. New York: Arrow, 1995.

Dawson, Henry B. *The Sons of Liberty in New York*. New York: Arno Press and the New York Times, 1969.

Deeb, Marius (ed.). *Syria's Terrorist War on Lebanon and the Peace Process*. New York: Macmillan, 2004.

Dill, Martin. *The Shankhill Butchers: A Case Study of Mass Murder*. London: Hutchinson, 1989.

Dixon, B. and L. Johns. *Gangs, PAGAD & the State: Vigilantism and Revenge Violence in the Western Cape*. Cape Town: Center for the Study of Violence and Reconciliation, 2001.

Dolgin, Jane. *Jewish Identity and the JDL*. Princeton: Princeton University Press, 1977.

Duke, Vic, and Liz Crolley. *Football, Nationality and the State*. New York: Longman, 1996.

Edwards, Ruth Dudley. *The Faithful Tribe*. New York: Harper Collins, 2000.

Ellingwood, Ken. *Hard Line: Life and Death on the U.S.-Mexican Border*. New York: Pantheon, 2004.

Evans, Richard J. *Lying about Hitler: History, Holocaust, and the David Irving Trial*. New York: Basic Books, 2002.

Farrell, William R. *Blood and Rage: The Story of the Japanese Red Army*. Lexington, MA: D.C. Heath, 1990.

Fisk, Robert. *Pity the Nation*. Oxford: Oxford Press, 2001.

Gardell, Mattias. *Gods of the Blood: The Pagan Revival and White Separatism*. NC: Duke University Press, 2003.

George, John, and Laird Wilcox. *American Extremists: Militias, Supremacists, Klansmen, Communists & Others*. NY: Prometheus Books, 1996.

Giulianotti, Richard, Norman Bonney and Mike Hepworth (eds.). *Football, Violence and Social Identity*. Oxford: Routledge, 1994.

Glenny, Misha. *The Balkans 1804—1999: Nationalism, War and the Great Powers*. London and New York: Granta, 2000.

Goritti, Gustavo. *The Shining Path: A History of the Millenarian War in Peru*. Durham, North Carolina: University of North Carolina Press, 1999.

Gourevitch, Philip. *We Wish to Inform You That Tomorrow We Will Be Killed With Our Families*. London: Picador, 2000.

Griffin, D. *Radical Common Law Movement and Paper Terrorism: The State Response*. National Conference of State, 2000.

Hellmann-Rajanayagam, Dagmar. *The Tamil Tigers: Armed Struggle for Identity*. Stuttgart: Franz Steiner Verlag, 1994.

Hitler's Apologists: The Anti-Semitic Propaganda of Holocaust Revisionism. New York: Anti-Defamation League, 1993.

Hoerder, Dirk. *Crowd Action in Revolutionary Massachusetts, 1765–1780*. New York: Academic Press, 1977.

Hutton, Joseph B. *The Subverters*. New York: Arlington House, 1972.

Ibrahim, Abdullah, editor. *Between Democracy and Terror: The Sierra Leone Civil War*. Dakar, Senegal: Council for the Development of Social Science Research in Africa, 2004.

Ignatieff, Michael. *Blood and Belonging: Journeys into the New Nationalism*. New York: Farrar, Straus and Giroux, 1995.

Jacquard, Roland. *In the Name of Osama bin Laden: Global Terrorism and the bin Laden Brotherhood, Revised and Updated Edition*. Durham, NC : Duke University Press, 2002.

Jakes, Dale, Connie Jakes, and Clint Richmond. *False Prophets: The Firsthand Account of a Husband-Wife Team Working for the FBI and Living in Deepest Cover with the Montana Freemen*. Allen Park, MI: Dove Books, 1998.

Jordan, Hugh, and David Lister. *Mad Dog: The Rise and Fall of Johnny Adair*. Edinburgh: Mainstream, 2003.

Kahane, Meir. *The Story of the Jewish Defense League*. Radnor, PA: Chilton Books, 1975.

Karpin, Michael, and Ina Friedmann. *Murder in the Name of God, the Plot to Kill Yitzhak Rabin*. New York: Granta, 1999.

Kepel, Gilles. *Jihad: The Trail of Political Islam*. Cambridge, MA: Belknap, 2003.

Kepel, Gilles. *Muslim Extremism in Egypt.* Los Angeles: University of California Press, 2003.

Khaled, Leila. *My People Shall Live: The Autobiography of a Revolutionary.* London: Hodder and Stoughton, 1973.

Kinzer, Stephen. *All the Shah's Men: An American Coup and the Roots of Middle East Terror.* Hoboken, NJ: John Wiley and Sons, 2004.

Leahy, Michael. *Against Liberation: Putting Animals in Perspective.* Oxford: Routledge, 1993.

Lee, Martin A. *The Beast Reawakens.* New York: Little, Brown, 1997.

Levitas, Daniel. *The Terrorist Next Door: The Militia Movement and the Radical Right.* New York: St. Martin's Press, 2002.

Lifton, Robert Jay. *Destroying the World to Save It: Aum Shinrikyo, Apocalyptic Violence, and the New Global Terrorism.* New York: Owl Books, 2000.

Lipstadt, Deborah E. *Denying the Holocaust: The Growing Assault on Truth and Memory.* New York: Plume (reprint edition), 1994.

Loader, B., and D. Thomas. *Cybercrime: Law, Security And Privacy in the Information Age.* New York: Routledge, 2000.

Lowles, Nick. *White Riot: The Rise and Violent Fall of Combat 18.* London: Milo Books, 2001.

Maier, Pauline. *From Resistance to Revolution: Colonial Radicals and the Development of American Opposition to Britain, 1765–1776.* New York: Knopf, 1972.

Malcolm, Noel. *Kosovo: A Short History.* New York: Macmillan, 1998.

Maloney, Ed. *Secret History of the IRA.* London: Penguin, 2003.

Marsden, Peter. *The Taliban: War and Religion in Afghanistan.* London: Zed Books, 2002.

Martin, Ian. *Self Determination in East Timor,* International Peace Academy Occasional Paper Series. Boulder, CO: Lynne Rienner Publishers, 2001.

Mason, Carol. *Killing for Life: The Apocalyptic Narrative of Pro-Life Politics.* Ithaca, NY: Cornell University Press, 2002.

Matthiessen, Peter. *In The Spirit of Crazy Horse.* New York: Viking Press, 1983.

McDonald, Henry, and Jim Cussack. *The UDA.* New York: Penguin, 2004.

McDonough, Frank. *Hitler and the Rise of the NSDAP.* London and New York: Pearson/Longman, 2003.

McKittrick, David, and David McVeigh. *Making Sense of the Troubles.* London: Penguin, 2003.

McTaggart, David. *Rainbow Warrior.* Munich: Goldmann, 2002.

Merkl, Peter H. and Leonard Weinberg, editors. *Right-wing Extremism in the Twenty-first Century.* London and Portland, OR: Frank Cass, 2003.

Mishal, Shaul, and Avraham Sela. *The Palestinian HAMAS: Vision, Violence and Co-Existence.* New York: Columbia University Press, 2000.

Moloney, Ed. *Secret History of the IRA.* London: Penguin, 2003.

Mooney, John, and Michael O'Toole. *Black Operations: The Secret War against the Real IRA.* County Meath, Ireland: Maverick House, 2003.

Moore, Robin. *The Hunt for bin Laden.* New York: Random House, Inc., 2003.

Morris, David B. *Earth Warrior: Overboard With Paul Watson and the Sea Shepherd Conservation Society.* Golden, Colorado: Fulcrum Publishing, 1995.

Mukarji, Apratim. *Sri Lanka: A Dangerous Interlude.* Chicago: New Dawn Press, 2005.

Murillo, Mario Alfonso, and Jesus Rey Avirama. *Colombia and the United States: War, Terrorism, and Destabilization.* New York: Seven Stories Press, 2003.

Murphy, Patrick, et al. *Football on Trial: Spectator Violence and Development in the Football World.* Oxford: Routledge, 1990.

Núñez Astrain, Luis. *The Basques: Their Struggle for Independence.* Cardiff: Welsh Academic Press, 1997.

Nantulya, Paul. "Exclusion, Identity and Armed Conflict: A Historical Survey of the Politics of Confrontation in Uganda with Specific Reference to the Independence Era."

Nusse, Andrea. *Muslim Palestine: Ideology of HAMAS.* London: Taylor & Francis, 1999.

Parenti, Michael. *To Kill a Nation: The Attack on Yugoslavia.* New York and London: Verso, 2001.

Parry, Richard Lloyd. *In a Time of Madness.* New York: Random House, 2005.

Pearce, Jenny. *Inside Colombia: Drugs, Democracy, and War.* New Brunswick, NJ: Rutgers University Press, 2004.

Ponce de León, Juana. *Our Word Is Our Weapon: Selected Writings of Subcomandante Marcos.* New York: Seven Stories Press, 2001.

Preston, Paul. *A Concise History of the Spanish Civil War.* New York: HarperCollins, 1996.

Quarles, Chester L. *Christian Identity: The Aryan American Bloodline Religion.* Jefferson, NC: McFarland & Company, 2004.

Rashid, Ahmed. *Jihad: The Rise of Militant Islam in Central Asia.* New Haven, CT: Yale University Press, 2002.

Rashid, Ahmed. *Taliban: Militant Islam, Oil and Fundamentalism in Central Asia.* New Haven: Yale University Press, 2001.

Reader, Ian. *Religious Violence in Contemporary Japan: Case of Aum Shinrikyo.* Honolulu: University of Hawaii Press, 2000.

Rochlin, James F. *Vanguard Revolutionaries in Latin America: Peru, Colombia, Mexico.* Boulder, CO: Lynne Rienner Publishers, 2003.

Rosenthal, David. *Racism on the Internet.* Geneva: World Conference Against Racism, Racial Discrimination, Xenophobia, and Related Intolerance, 2000.

Ross, John. *Rebellion from the Roots: Indian Uprising in Chiapas.* Monroe, ME: Common Courage, 1995.

Rus, Jan, et al. *Mayan Lives, Mayan Utopias: The Indigenous Peoples of Chiapas and the Zapatista Rebellion.* Lanham, MD: Rowman & Littlefield, 2003.

Ryan, Nick. *Homeland: Into a World of Hate.* Edinburgh, Scotland: Mainstream, 2004.

Safford, Frank, and Marco Palacios. *Colombia: Fragmented Land, Divided Society.* England: Oxford University Press, 2001.

Savigh, Yezid. *Armed Struggle and the Search for State: The Palestinian National Movement, 1949—1993.* England: Oxford University Press, 1999.

Scully, Matthew. *Dominion: The Power of Man, the Suffering of Animals, and the Call to Mercy.* New York: St. Martin's Press, 2002.

Seale, Patrick. *Abu Nidal: A Gun For Hire.* New York: Random House, 1992.

Seale, Patrick. *Assad of Syria: The Struggle for the Middle East.* Berkeley, CA: University of California Press, 1989.

Singer, Peter. *Animal Liberation, (3rd Edition).* New York: Harper Collins, 2002.

Sison, Jose Maria. *The Philippine Revolution: The Leader's View.* New York: Crane Russak, 1989.

Smith, Barbara. "Heaven or Hell?: Terrorism Hurts Revenue from Tourism." *The Economist* no. 350 (1999): 14–15.

Solinger, Rick (ed). *Abortion Wars: A Half Century of Struggle, 1950–2000.* Berkeley, CA: University of California Press, 2001.

Spielvogel, Jackson J. *Hitler and Nazi Germany.* Upper Saddle River, NJ: Prentice-Hall, 2001.

Sprinzak, Ehud. *Brother Against Brother: Violence and Extremism in Israeli Politics from Altalena to the Rabin Assassination.* New York: The Free Press, 1999.

Sprinzak, Ehud. *Kach and Meir Kahane: The Emergence of Jewish Quasi-Fascism.* New York: The American-Jewish Committee, 1985.

Stern, Kenneth S. *A Force upon the Plain: The American Militia Movement and the Politics of Hate.* New York: Simon and Schuster, 1995.

Strum, Philippa. *When the Nazis Came to Skokie; Freedom for Speech We Hate.* Lawrence, Kansas: University Press of Kansas, 2000.

Sykes, Andrew. *The Radical Right in Britain.* NY: Palgrave Macmillan, 2004.

Tarik, Judith Palmer. *Hizbollah:The Changing Face of Terrorism.* London: I B Tauris, 2004.

Taylor, Peter. *Loyalists.* London: Bloomsbury, 2000.

Taylor, Peter. *Loyalists: War and Peace in Northern Ireland.* New York: TV Books, 2004.

Taylor, Peter. *The Provos: The IRA and Sinn Fein.* London: Bloomsbury, 1998.

Tonge, Jonathan. *Northern Ireland: Conflict & Change.* New York: Longman, 2002.

Toolid, Kevin. *Rebel Hearts, Journeys in the Republican Movement.* NY: Picador, 1995.

Tsoukalas, Steven Malcolm. *The Nation of Islam; Understanding the Black Muslims.* Phillipsburg, New Jersey: P&R Publishing, 2001.

Tucker, Jonathan, editor. *Toxic Terror: Assessing Terrorist Use of Chemical and Biological Weapons (BCSIA Studies in International Security).* Cambridge, Massachusetts: MIT Press: Bantam, 2000.

Wade, Wyn C. *The Fiery Cross: The Ku Klux Klan in America.* Oxford, England: Oxford University Press, 1998.

Wallach, Janet. *Arafat: In the Eyes of the Beholder.* Amsterdam: Citadel, 2001.

Walvin, James. *Football and the Decline of Britain.* London and New York: Macmillan, 1986.

Wessinger, Catherine. *How the Millennium Comes Violently: From Jonestown to Heaven's Gate.* New York: Chatham House Publishers, 2000.

Weyler, Rex. *Greenpeace: How a Group of Ecologists, Journalists and Visionaries Changed the World.* New York: Rodale, 2004.

White, Paul J. *Primitive Rebels or Revolutionary Modernisers?* London and New York: Zed, 2000.

Woodworth, Paddy. *Dirty Wars, Clean Hands: ETA, the GAL, and Spanish Democracy.* Ireland: Cork University Press, 2001.

Wright, Richard T. *Environmental Science: Toward a Sustainable Future (9th edition).* NY: Prentice Hall, 2004.

X, Malcolm. *The Autobiography of Malcolm X (As Told to Alex Haley).* New York: Balantine Publishing Group, 1964.

PERIODICALS

Aras, Bulent, and Gokhan Bacik. "Hezbollah Horror: A National Shame." *The Middle East Quarterly* (June 2000) v9 i2 p147.

"As He Lay Dying." *The Village Voice* September 4–10, 2002.

Aydintasbas, Asli. "Murder on the Bosporus." *Middle East Quarterly* (June 2000) v7 i2 p15.

Aziz, A.A. "The Burden of Terrorism in Malaysia." *Prehospital Disaster Medicine* no. 18(2) (2003): 115–119.

Barsky, Yehudit. "Terrorism Briefing Islamic Jihad Movement in Palestine." *American Jewish Committee* July 18, 2002.

Brennan, Charlie. "Al-Fuqra Tied To Colorado Crimes: Leader Owned Land In Buena Vista; Followers Convicted In Bombing Of Krishna Temple." *The Rocky Mountain News* February 12, 2002.

Bridges, T. "Duke Brewed Hatred in a Potion of Lies." *Times-Picayune* (March 16, 2003: 7).

Calabres, Massimo. "My Tea with Arkan the Henchman." *Time* (April 12, 1999).

Carassave, Anthee. "Arrest Destroys Noble Image of Guerilla Group in Greece." *New York Times* (July 29, 2005).

"Central Europe's Skinheads: Nasty, Ubiquitous, and Unloved." *The Economist* (March 20, 1999).

Charney, Marc. "Word for Word / The Skinhead International; Some Music, It Turns Out, Inflames the Savage Breast." *The Economist* (July 2, 1995).

"Communist Terrorists Bomb Police Offices." *United Press International* May 6, 1985.

Daly, Sara. "The Algerian Salafist Group for Call and Combat: A Dossier." *The Jamestown Foundation* Volume 3, Issue 5 (March 11, 2005).

Davenport, Coral, M. "Elusive Terrorist Group Takes a Hit Finally." *Christian Science Monitor* July 5, 2005.

Desmond, Edward, W. "The Spirit of the Age Is in Favor of Equality, through Practice." *Time International* (April 13, 1992).

Dickey, Christopher, Mark Hosenball, and Michael Hirsh. "Looking for a Few Good Spies." *Newsweek* (February 14, 2005).

Feinstein, Adam. "People Will Not Take This Lying Down." *IPI Report* (February–March 1994, v.43).

"Fighters on the ropes." *Time International* (May 26), 2003 v161 i21 p46.

"Four Accused of Terror Group Links." *United Press International* (December 16, 1985).

"Germans Outlaw Neo-Nazi Group." *Evening Standard (London)* (February 24, 1995).

"Germany Bans Two Neo-Nazi Groups, Police Carry Out Raids." *Deutsche Press-Agentur* (February 24, 1995).

"Germany to Ask Court to Ban Neo-Nazi Party." *Agence France Presse* (September 15, 1993).

"Germany: Far Right Organization Banned." *U.S. News and World Report* (September 28, 2000).

Gorvett, Jon. "The Mystery of Turkish Hizballah." *Middle East Policy* March 2000.

Graham, Fred P. "Rockwell's Nazis Lost Without Him." *New York Times* (April 8, 1968, p. 21).

"Group Claims Bombings As Protest of U.S. Missiles." *United Press International* (October 4, 1984).

Haven, Paul and Katherine Shrader. "U.S., Pakistan Exploit Rifts within Factions of Al-Qaeda." *Ottawa Citizen* (May 11, 2005).

Hawthorne, Peter. "No Laughing Matter. A Shadowy Group of Racist Afrikaners Is Plotting to Bring Down the Government." *Time International* (October 21, 2001).

Henrard, Kristin. "Post-apartheid South Africa: Transformation and Reconciliation." *World Affairs* Vol. 6 No. 1 (July 1, 2003).

Hosenball, Mark. "Mixed Signals on MEK." *Newsweek* (April 11, 2005).

"IMU Controls Drug Traffic to Central Asia." *Pravada* (May 30, 2001).

"In Search of Uganda's Lost Youth." *Time International* v162 i4 p42, July 28, 2003.

"India: The Politics of Extremism." *The Economist* (October 2, 1999).

"India: Untouchable Bihar." *The Economist* June 24, 2000.

"Italian Northeast Seen as Fertile Recruitment Ground for Terrorism." *BBC* (March 24, 2002).

Ivaldi, Gilles. "Conservation, Revolution and Protest: A Case Study in the Political Cultures of the French National Front's Members and Sympathizers." *Electoral Studies* Vol. 15, No. 3, pp. MO-362, 1996.

Japan Economic Newswire. "Chukakuha Claims Series of Attacks." *Kyoto News International Inc* (November 1990).

Japan Economic Newswire. "Nineteen Activists Given Sentences over Airport Clash." *Kyoto News International Inc* (October 1989).

Japan Economic Newswire. "Radical Leader Held over Narita Threats." *Kyoto News International Inc* (September 1989).

"Jewish Cemetery Desecrated by Neo-Nazis in Eastern Germany." *United Press International* (September 8, 1993).

Karmon, Ely. "The Bombing of the U.S.S. Cole: An Analysis of the Principle Suspects." *International Policy Institute for Counter Terrorism* (October 24, 2000).

Kefner, John. "Lott, and Shadow of a Pro-White Group." *The New York Times* (January 14, 1999).

Kerr, Simon. "Yemen Cracks Down on Militants." *Middle East Journal* (December 1, 1999).

Kohen, Arnold S. "Making an Issue of East." *The Nation* (Feb 10, 1992) v254 n5 p162(2).

Koon, David. "A Young Skinhead Makes a Conversion—Of Sorts." *The Arkansas Times* (May 27, 2005).

Mahoney, Edmund. "A Rocket Attack, an FBI Revelation." *Hartford Courant* (November 12, 1999).

McCaffery, Jen. "Muslim Terrorists Convicted on Firearms Charges in the U.S." *The Roanoke Times* (December 1, 2001).

McCutcheon, Chuck. "Right-Wing Extremist Groups Becoming More Active After Post 9/11 Lull." *Newhouse News Service* (July 13, 2004).

McGregor, Andrew. "Strike First." *The World Today* (December 1, 2002).

Ojeda-Rios, Filberto. "The Boricua-Macheteros Popular Army, Origins, Program, and Struggle." *Latin American Perspectives* Issue 127, Vol. 29 No. 6 (2002): 104–116.

Ottey, Michael A.W. "Many Hondurans Say Guerillas, Not Gangs, Were Behind Massacre." *The Miami Herald* (December 29, 2004).

Perry, Alex. "Deadly Cargo." *Time Magazine* (October 14, 2002).

"Police Say White Revolution Racist Flyers 'Not Illegal.'" *Monroe Courier* (November 24, 2004).

Radmacher, D. "Most Whites in U.S. Not Exactly Oppressed, Earn More than Minorities." *The Charleston Gazette* (August 25, 2000: 4A).

Ruiz, Albor. "No Room at Inn for This Flock." *New York Daily News* (February 24, 2004).

Sabella, Bryan. "Hate Group Leaflets Turn Up in Metuchen: Community Leaders, Police Describe Distribution as Limited." *Sentinel.* May 12, 2004.

Sale, Richard. "Pakistan ISI Link to Pearl Kidnap Probed." *United Press International* (January 29, 2002).

Schanzer, Jonathan. "Lurking in Lebanon." *Washington Institute for Near East Policy.* June 4, 2003.

Schanzer, Jonathan. "Algeria's GSPC and America's War on Terror." *Washington Institute.* October 15, 2002.

Seper, Jerry, and Steve Miller. "Militant Muslims Seek Virginia Base." *The Washington Times* (July 1, 2002).

Sheean, Thomas. "Italy: Terror on the Right." *The New York Review of Books* Volume 27, Number 21 & 22, 1981.

Shepardson, David, Gary Heinlein, and Oralandar Brand-Williams. "White Supremacist Record Company in Oakland (Michigan) Raided in Tax-Fraud Probe." *The Detroit News.* April 11, 1997.

Southern Poverty Law Center. "A League of Their Own." *Intelligence Report* (Summer 2000).

Southern Poverty Law Center. "Against the Wall." *Intelligence Report* (Fall 2003).

Southern Poverty Law Center. "From Push to Shove." *Intelligence Report* (Fall 2002).

Staff writer. "Bigotry Racism Lingers." *The Charleston Gazette* (August 26, 2000: 4A).

Stanley, Alessandra. "Rome Journal; Agony Lingers, 20 Years After the Moro Killing." *New York Times* (May 9, 1998).

Suarez, Manny. "Possible Macheteros Office Contained FBI Information." *The San Juan Star* (April 5, 1984).

Taghavi, Seyed Mohammad Ali. "Fadaeeyan-i Islam: The Prototype of Islamic Hard-liners in Iran." *Middle Eastern Studies* (January 2004).

Tamayo, Juan O. "Attacks Put Puerto Rican Separatists Back in the Limelight." *The Miami Herald* (August 28, 1998).

"Terrorist Bombings Knock Out NATO Supply Lines." *United Press International* (December 12, 1984).

Thomas, Jo, and Ralph Blumenthal. "Rural Muslims Draw New, Unwanted Attention." *The New York Times* (January 3, 2002).

Thompson, Ginger. "Gunmen Kills 28 on Streets of Honduras; Street Gangs Blamed." *New York Times International* (December 25, 2004).

Trendle, Giles. "Splintered Loyalties, Shattered Lives." *Middle East.* February 1, 2003.

Turbiville, Graham H. Jr. "Naxalite Insurgency Draws Indian Concerns." *J.F.K. Special Warfare Center and School.* February 21, 2005.

Turner, Harry. "Macheteros Suspects May Face '79, '81 Raps." *The San Juan Star.* October 8, 1987.

"UGANDA: Museveni offers to Negotiate with LRA Rebels, Kampala." *IRIN News.* 16 April 2004.

"Uganda the Horror." *Smithsonian* v35 i11 p90 (February 2005).

"U.S. Senator Orrin Hatch (R-UT) holds hearing on Judiciary and FALN." *Wire Transcription Service.* October 10, 1999.

Wolin, Richard. "Mussolini's Ghost; Europe and the Specter of Fascism." *Tikkun* Vol. 9, No. 4, p.13, 1994.

"World: South Africa, The Wind Rises in Welkom in Defense of Apartheid." *Time* (May 28, 1990).

Wright, Lawrence. "The Man Behind Bin Laden: How an Egyptian Doctor Became a Master of Terror." *The New Yorker* (September 16, 2002).

WEB RESOURCES

ABC Asia Pacific. "Cause and Effect—Profiles of Terrorist Groups." < http://abcasiapacific.com/cause/network/sayyaf.htm > (accessed September 14, 2005).

Abortion facts.com. "U.S. Statistics." < http://www.abortionfacts.com/statistics/us_stats_ abortion.asp > (accessed October 16, 2005).

Activist Cash.com. "Norway to the USA: Stop Sea Shepherd." < http://www.activistcash.com/organization_overview.cfm/oid/347 > (accessed September 30, 2005).

Activist Cash.com. "People for the Ethical Treatment of Animals." < http://www.activistcash.com/organization_overview.cfm/oid/21 > (accessed October 19, 2005).

Activist.com. "Earth First!" < http://www.activistcash. com/organization_overview.cfm/oid/271 > (accessed September 29, 2005).

Activist.com. "At ActivistCash.com, We Follow the Money—for You." < http://www.activistcash.com/ aboutUs.cfm > (accessed October 21, 2005).

ADL.org. "National Alliance." < http://www.adl.org/ learn/ext_us/N_Alliance.asp > (accessed October 15, 2005).

African National Congress. "I am Prepared to Die: Nelson Mandela's Statement." < http://www.anc.org. za/ancdocs/history/rivonia.html > (accessed October 11, 2005).

African Studies Quarterly. "Conventional Wisdom and Rwanda's Genocide." < http://web.africa.ufl.edu/asq/ v1/3/10.htm > (accessed October 12, 2005).

African Terrorism Bulletin. "Renewed Threat from Defeated Ugandan Rebel Group?" < http://www.iss. org.za/Pubs/Newsletters/Terrorism/0305.htm > (accessed September 22, 2005).

Albion Monitor. "McVeigh Conviction Won't Deter Extremists." < http://www.monitor.net/monitor/9706a/ mcvdeter.html > (accessed October 17, 2005).

American Civil Liberties Union. "Planned Parenthood of the Columbia/Willamette Inc. v American Coalition of Life Activists (1999 decision)." < http://www.aclu.org/ ReproductiveRights/ReproductiveRights.cfm?ID= 13583&c=227 > (accessed October 21, 2005).

American Forces Information Service. "Tenent Briefs Senate on Terror Threats." < http://www.globalsecurity. org/intell/library/news/2004/intell-040224-afps01. htm > (accessed October 18, 2005).

American Religion.com. "The Identity Movement." < http://www.americanreligion.org/cultwtch/identity. html > (accessed September 29, 2005).

Amnesty International. "Colombia, A Laboratory of War: Repression and Violence in Arauca." < http:// web.amnesty.org/library/index/engamr230042004 > (accessed October 21, 2005).

Amnesty International. "Report into al-Aqsa Intifada." < http://www.stoptorture.org.il/eng/images/uploaded/ publications/43.pdf > (accessed October 21, 2005).

Amnesty International. "Algeria: A Human Rights Crisis: Civilians Caught in a Spiral of Violence." < http:// web.amnesty.org/library/Index/ENGMDE280361997? open&of=ENG-313 > (accessed July 28, 2005).

Amnesty International. "Colombia, A Laboratory of War: Repression and Violence in Arauca." < http:// web.amnesty.org/library/index/engamr230042004 > (accessed September 30, 2005).

Amnesty International. "Colombia: Report 2005." < http://web.amnesty.org/report2005/col-summary- eng > (accessed September 30, 2005).

Amnesty International. "PERU: Summary of Amnesty Internationals concerns 1980–1995." < http://web. amnesty.org/library/Index/ENGAMR460041996?open &of=ENG-PER > (accessed October 5, 2005).

Andrew Mueller. "A Brush With Death." < http:// www.andrewmueller.net/scroll.lasso?ID=56&story= A%20BRUSH%20WITH%20DEATH_full_story > (accessed October 3, 2005).

Anti Terrorism Force Protection 1st Marine Aircraft Wing. "Chukakuh-ha." < http://www.1maw.usmc.mil/ ATFP/News/02-3.pdf#search='MiddleCore%20 Faction' > (accessed September 27, 2005).

Anti-Defamation League "Farrakhan Reaches Out to Anti-Semitic Black Panther Party." < http://www.adl. org/main_Anti_Semitism_Domestic/farrakhan_black_ panther_party.htm > (accessed October 18, 2005).

Anti-Defamation League. "Border Disputes: Armed Vigilantes in Arizona." < http://www.adl.org/PresRele/ Extremism_72/4255_72 > (accessed October 17, 2005).

Anti-Defamation League. "Council of Conservative Citizens: December 21, 1998." < http://www.adl.org/ backgrounders/ccc.asp > (accessed October 23, 2005).

Anti-Defamation League. "Don Black: White Pride World Wide." < http://www.adl.org/poisoning_web/ black.asp > (accessed October 2, 2005).

Anti-Defamation League. "Extremism in America: Council of Conservative Citizens." < http://www. adl.org/learn/ext_us/CCCitizens.asp?xpicked=3 &item=12 > (accessed October 23, 2005).

Anti-Defamation League. "FBI Hate Crime Statistics 1991–2002." < http://www.adl.org/99hatecrime/ comp_fbi.asp > (accessed October 17, 2005).

Anti-defamation League. "Feminism Perverted: Extremist Women on the World Wide Web." < http:// www.adl.org/special_reports/extremist_women_on_ web/feminism_intro.asp > (accessed October 1, 2005).

Anti-Defamation League. "How to Combat Hate Crime." < http://www.adl.org/blueprint.pdf > (accessed October 17, 2005).

Anti-Defamation League. "James 'Bo' Gritz." < http:// www.adl.org/learn/ext_us/gritz.asp?xpicked=2&item= 5 > (accessed September 29, 2005).

Anti-Defamation League. "Michigan Community Unites Against Hate." < http://www.adl.org/PresRele/ Extremism_72/4255_72.asp > (accessed October 17, 2005).

Anti-Defamation League. "Muslims of the Americas: In Their Own Words." < http://www.adl.org/extremism/ moa/default.asp > (September 21, 2005).

Anti-Defamation League. "NAAWP." < http://www.adl. org/hate_symbols/groups_naawp.asp > (accessed October 18, 2005).

Anti-Defamation League. "Patriot Profiles #2: Patriot Purgatory: Bo Gritz and Almost Heaven." < http:// www.militia-watchdog.org/gritz.asp > (accessed September 29, 2005).

Anti-Defamation League. "Peter J. 'Pete' Peters." < http://www.adl.org/learn/ext_us/Peters.asp?LEARN_Cat = Extremism&LEARN_SubCat = Extremism_in_America&xpicked = 2&item = 8 > (accessed September 30, 2005).

Anti-Defamation League. "Still Howling." < http://www.adl.org/learn/extremism_in_america_updates/individuals/tom_metzger/metzger_update_020801.htm > (accessed October 17, 2005).

Anti-Defamation League. "The Growing Cost of Combating Hate Crimes." < http://www.adl.org/learn/news/cost_of_hate.asp > (accessed October 17, 2005).

Anti-Defamation League. "Ku Klux Klan." < http://www.adl.org/learn/ext_us/kkk.asp > (accessed October 18, 2005).

Anti-Defamation League. "Al-Fuqra: Holy Warriors of Terrorism." < http://www.adl.org/extremism/moa/al-fuqra.pdf > (September 21, 2005).

Apologetics Index. "Aum Shinrikyo." < http://www.apologeticsindex.org/a06.html > (accessed October 10, 2005).

Asia Times Online. "A New Dimension in India's Northeast Woes." < http://www.atimes.com/atimes/South_Asia/FJ23Df02.html > (accessed October 1, 2005).

Asia Times Online. "Goons or Terrorists? Bangladesh Decides." < http://www.atimes.com/atimes/South_Asia/GC10Df04.html > (accessed October 16, 2005).

Associated Press. "Hundreds of Villagers Killed in Algeria's Worst Massacre." < http://www.southcoasttoday.com/daily/08-97/08-30-97/a03wn016.htm > (accessed September 25, 2005).

Australian Broadcasting Corporation. "The Salafist Group for Call and Combat." < http://abcasiapacific.com/cause/network/salafist.htm > (accessed October 16, 2005).

BBC News Online. "Profile: Algeria's Salafist Group." < http://news.bbc.co.uk/1/hi/world/africa/3027621.stm > (accessed October 16, 2005).

BBC News Online. "Profile: Eugene Terreblanche." < http://news.bbc.co.uk/2/hi/africa/3797797.stm > (accessed October 10, 2005).

BBC News Online. "South Africa's Terreblanche Freed from Jail." < http://news.bbc.co.uk/2/hi/africa/3796467.stm > (accessed October 10, 2005).

BBC News UK Edition, British Broadcasting Corporation. "Profile: Turkey's Marxist DHKP-C." < http://news.bbc.co.uk/1/hi/world/europe/3591119.stm > (accessed October 19, 2005).

BBC News UK Edition. "Italy's Andreotti Cleared of Murder." < http://news.bbc.co.uk/1/hi/world/europe/3228917.stm > (accessed October 20, 2005).

BBC News UK Edition. "Profile: Jean-Marie Le Pen." < http://news.bbc.co.uk/1/hi/world/europe/3658399.stm > (accessed September 29, 2005).

BBC News World Edition "Victory for Timor Freedom Party." < http://news.bbc.co.uk/2/hi/asia-pacific/1526725.stm > (accessed October 1, 2005).

BBC News World Edition. "Italy's History of Terror." < http://news.bbc.co.uk/2/hi/europe/3372239.htm > (accessed October 20, 2005).

BBC News World Edition. "Profile: Uganda's LRA Rebels." < http://news.bbc.co.uk/1/hi/world/africa/3462901.stm > (accessed October 20, 2005).

BBC News World Edition. "Profile: Xanana Gusmao." < http://news.bbc.co.uk/1/hi/world/asia-pacific/342145.stm > (accessed October 1, 2005).

BBC News World Edition. "Timeline: East Timor." < http://news.bbc.co.uk/2/hi/asia-pacific/country_profiles/1504243.stm > (accessed October 1, 2005).

BBC News World Edition. "Turkey Charges 'Key Bomb Suspect.'" < http://news.bbc.co.uk/2/hi/europe/3333501.stm > (accessed October 5, 2005).

BBC News World Europe. "Turkish Hezbollah: 'No State Links.'" < http://news.bbc.co.uk/1/hi/world/europe/615785.stm > (accessed October 5, 2005).

BBC News, British Broadcasting Corporation. "Can UN Force Restore Peace?" < http://news.bbc.co.uk/1/hi/world/africa/742196.stm > (accessed October 3, 2005).

BBC News, South East Asia. "Profile: Bombay's Militant Voice." < http://news.bbc.co.uk/1/hi/world/south_asia/841488.stm > (accessed October 4, 2005).

BBC News, South East Asia. "Shiv Sena: Profile." < http://news.bbc.co.uk/1/hi/world/south_asia/3551067.stm > (accessed October 4, 2005).

BBC News. "Animal Rights, Terror Tactics." < http://news.bbc.co.uk/1/hi/uk/902751.stm > (accessed September 14, 2005).

BBC News. "Battling Online Hate." < http://news.bbc.co.uk/1/hi/world/americas/1516271.stm > (accessed October 2, 2005).

BBC News. "Cyber-racists 'Safe in US.'" < http://news.bbc.co.uk/1/hi/world/americas/645262.stm > (accessed October 2, 2005).

BBC News. "Egypt: The New Spectre of Terror." < http://news.bbc.co.uk/1/hi/world/analysis/32048.stm > (accessed September 21, 2005).

BBC News. "Loyalist Splinter Threat." < http://news.bbc.co.uk/hi/english/static/northern_ireland/understanding/themes/loyalist_splinter.stm/ > (accessed October 19, 2005).

BBC News. "Loyalists 'Aim to Create Peace Crisis.'" < http://news.bbc.co.uk/1/hi/events/northern_ireland/latest_news/276539.stm > (accessed October 19, 2005).

BBC News. "PAGAD: Vigilantes or Terrorists?" < http://news.bbc.co.uk/1/hi/world/africa/923701.stm > (accessed October 19, 2005).

BBC News. "Police Seize 'Red Brigades' Cache.'" < http://news.bbc.co.uk/go/pr/fr/-/2/hi/europe/3337809.stm > (accessed October 20, 2005).

BBC.co.uk "Paramilitaries: Loyalist Volunteer Force." < http://www.bbc.co.uk/history/war/troubles/factfiles/lvf.shtml > (accessed October 14, 2005).

BBC.co.uk. "Adolf Hitler (1889–1945)." < http://www.bbc.co.uk/history/historic_figures/hitler_adolf.shtml > (assessed October 20, 2005).

BBC.com. "Full Circle for German Revolutionaries." < http://news.bbc.co.uk/1/hi/world/europe/1250944.stm > (accessed October 15, 2005).

BBC.com. "German Red Army Faction Disbands." < http://news.bbc.co.uk/1/hi/world/europe/80960.stm > (accessed October 15, 2005).

BBC.com. "Germany Recalls Its 'Autumn of Terror.'" < http://news.bbc.co.uk/1/hi/world/europe/2340095.stm > (accessed October 15, 2005).

BBC.com. "Jewish Bomb Plotter Jailed in US." < http://news.bbc.co.uk/2/hi/americas/4273790.stm > (accessed October 15, 2005).

BBCNews.com. "Meeting Taleban's Foreign Fighters." < http://news.bbc.co.uk/1/hi/world/south_asia/1669996.stm > (accessed October 16, 2005).

BBCNews.com. "Profile: Mullah Mohammed Omar." < http://news.bbc.co.uk/2/hi/south_asia/1550419.stm > (accessed October 16, 2005).

Beat Witschi, CNN.com, and Time.com. "Who Is Abdullah Ocalan? (Ocalan: Key Moments of His Life)." < http://edition.cnn.com/SPECIALS/1999/ocalan/stories/ocalan.profile/ > (accessed October 20, 2005).

Black Press USA. "Blacks and Jews Split—again—over Farrakhan (New Black Panther Party Will Attend MMM)." < http://freerepublic.com/focus/f-news/1404429/posts > (accessed October 18, 2005).

Bobby Seale's Homepage, Black Panther Party Founder. "From the Sixties...to the Future." < http://publicenemy-seale.com/ > (accessed October 18, 2005).

Boston.com. "Last of the Confederates." < http://www.boston.com/news/globe/editorial_opinion/oped/articles/2005/02/21/last_of_the_confederates/ > (accessed October 18, 2005).

Brickman. "The Involvement of Arafat, PA Senior Officials and Apparatuses in Terrorism against Israel, Corruption and Crime." < http://www.brickman.dircon.co.uk/naveh.html > (accessed October 21, 2005).

CAIN Web Service "Speech by Ruairi O'Bradaigh." < http://cain.ulst.ac.uk/issues/politics/docs/sf/rob021186.htm > (accessed September 28, 2005).

Camera One Public Interest News and Culture. "Inaugural Protests Biggest Since Vietnam." < http://www.cameraone.org/inaguration.html > (accessed October 18, 2005).

Canadian National Security. "Mujahedine-e Khalq Organization." < http://www.psepc-sppcc.gc.ca/national_security/counter-terrorism/Entities_e.asp#38 > (accessed October 14, 2005).

Canadian Security Intelligence Service. "Perspectives: Trends in Terrorism." < http://www.csis-scrs.gc.ca/eng/miscdocs/200001_e.html > (accessed October 19, 2005).

CBC Archives. "The Hijacking of Achille Lauro." < http://archives.cbc.ca/IDC-1-71-1153-6340-11/that_was_then/conflict_war/achille_lauro > (accessed October 22, 2005).

CBS NEWS.com/U.S. "'Army of God' Anthrax Threats." < http://www.cbsnews.com/stories/2001/11/09/national/main317573.shtml > (accessed September 25, 2005).

Center for Contemporary Conflicts. "Libya's Return to the Fold?" < http://www.ccc.nps.navy.mil/si/2004/mar/boucekMar04.asp > (accessed October 18, 2005).

Center for Defense Information. "In the Spotlight: The Salafist Group for Call and Combat." < http://www.cdi.org/terrorism/gspc-pr.cfm > (accessed October 16, 2005).

Center for Defense Information. "Harakat ul-Jihad-i-Islami." < http://www.cdi.org/program/document.cfm?DocumentID = 2374&from_page = ./index.cfm > (accessed October 20, 2005).

Center for Defense Information. "In the Spotlight: Alex Boncayao Brigade (ABB)." < http://www.cdi.org/friendlyversion/printversion.cfm?documentID = 2052&from_page = ./program/document.cfm > (accessed September 15, 2005).

Center for Defense Information. "In the Spotlight: Al-Ittihad al-Islami (AIAI)." < http://www.cdi.org/program/document.cfm?DocumentID = 3026&from_page = ./index.cfm > (accessed September 21, 2005).

Center for Defense Information. "In the Spotlight: Asbat al-Ansar." < http://www.cdi.org/terrorism/asbat.cfm > (accessed October 15, 2005).

Center for Defense Information. "In the Spotlight: First of October Anti-Fascist Resistance Group." < http://www.cdi.org/program/document.cfm?DocumentID = 2873&from_page = ./index.cfm > (accessed October 15, 2005).

Center for Defense Information. "In the Spotlight: IMU." < http://www.cdi.org/terrorism/imu.cfm > (accessed October 19, 2005).

Center for Defense Information. "In the Spotlight: Islamic Army of Aden." < http://www.cdi.org/program/document.cfm?DocumentID = 2679&from_page = ./index.cfm > (accessed October 16, 2005).

Center for Defense Information. "Palestine Islamic Jihad." < http://www.cdi.org/program/document.cfm?DocumentID = 1176&StartRow = 1&ListRows = 10&appendURL = &Orderby = D.DateLastUpdated%20deSC&programID = 39&IssueID = 0&Issue = &Date_From = &Date_To = &Keywords = PIJ&ContentType = &Author = &from_page = documents.cfm > (accessed October 20, 2005).

Center for Strategic and International Studies. "The Nexus Between Counterterrorism, Counterproliferation, and Maritime Security in Southeast Asia." < http://www.csis.org/pacfor/issues/v04n04_ch3.cfm > (accessed October 11, 2005).

Center for Studies on New Religions. "Project Megiddo." < http://www.cesnur.org/testi/FBI_004.htm > (accessed September 30, 2005).

Center for the Defense of Free Enterprise. "Earth Liberation Front." < http://www.cdfe.org/elf.htm > (accessed October 21, 2005).

Center for the Defense of Free Enterprise. "Ecoterror Response Network." < http://www.cdfe.org/ern.htm > (accessed October 21, 2005).

Center for the Defense of Free Enterprise. "Ecoterrorism Top Stories." < http://www.cdfe.org/top_stories.htm > (accessed September 29, 2005).

Center for the Defense of Free Enterprise. "The Center View: Profiles in Ecoterror Advocacy." < http://www.cdfe.org/rosebraughs%20degree.htm > (accessed October 21, 2005).

Christian Science Monitor. "A Band of Maoist Rebels Terrorizes an Indian Region." < http://www.csmonitor.com/2002/0813/p07s02-wosc.html > (accessed October 11, 2005).

CIA Government Factbook. "Tunisia." < http://www.cia.gov/cia/publications/factbook/geos/ts.html > (accessed October 15, 2005).

CNN World Edition Online. "Spanish Terror Suspects Arrested." < http://edition.cnn.com/2000/WORLD/europe/11/09/france.grapo/ > (accessed October 15, 2005).

CNN.com/U.S. "Army of God Letters Support Accused Bomber Eric Rudolph." < http://archives.cnn.com/2002/US/03/18/army.god.letters/index.html > (accessed September 25, 2005).

CNN.com/U.S. "Atlanta Olympic Bombing Suspect Arrested." < http://www.cnn.com/2003/US/05/31/rudolph.main/ > (accessed September 25, 2005).

CNN.com/World. "South East Asia's Crackdown." < http://edition.cnn.com/2002/WORLD/asiapcf/southeast/01/07/terror.factbox/ > (accessed October 11, 2005).

CNN.com. "India Launches Major Ground Assault in Kashmir; Talks Set with Pakistan." < http://edition.cnn.com/WORLD/asiapcf/9905/29/india.pakistan.02 > (accessed October 19, 2005).

CNN.com. "Islamic Group Suspected in Kenya Attacks." < http://cnnstudentnews.cnn.com/2002/WORLD/africa/11/29/somali.group/ > (accessed September 21, 2005).

CNN.com. "Islamic Terrorists Slaughter Algerian Villagers." < http://edition.cnn.com/WORLD/9708/29/algeria.new/ > (accessed September 25, 2005).

CNN.com. "Special Report, War Against Terror: Osama bin Laden." < http://www.cnn.com/SPECIALS/2001/trade.center/binladen.section.html > (accessed September 22, 2005).

CNN. "The Death of Richard Klinghoffer." < http://www.cnn.com/resources/video.almanac/1985/achille.lauro/klinghoffer.dead.45.mov > (accessed October 22, 2005).

Colombia Journal Online. "The Hypocrisy of the Peace Process." < http://www.colombiajournal.org/colombia103.htm > (accessed September 30, 2005).

Colombia Report. "Good Terrorists, Bad Terrorists: How Washington Decides Who's Who." < http://www.colombiajournal.org/colombia62.htm > (accessed Octo 21, 2005).

Council on Foreign Relations. "Irish Loyalist Paramilitary Groups." < http://cfrterrorism.org/groups/uvf_print.html > (accessed October 19, 2005).

Council on Foreign Relations. "Kurdistan Workers' Party." < http://cfrterrorism.org/groups/kurdistan.html > (accessed October 20, 2005).

Council on Foreign Relations. "Terrorism: Questions and Answers: Mujahedine-e Khalq Organization." < http://cfrterrorism.org/groups/mujahedeen.html > (accessed October 14, 2005).

Council on Foreign Relations. "Uzbekistan." < http://cfrterrorism.org/coalition/uzbekistan.html > (accessed October 19, 2005).

Countercurrents.org. "Shiv Sena On The Threshold Of Disintegration." < http://www.countercurrents.org/comm-ketkar011104.htm > (accessed October 4, 2005).

Dennis Roddy, Post-Gazette. "Jared Taylor, a Racist in the Guise of 'Expert,'" < http://www.post-gazette.com/pg/05023/446341.stm > (accessed October 23, 2005).

Detroit Free Press. "Homegrown Hate: Ten years after Oklahoma City, anti-government and hate groups are weaker—but testing new tools." < http://www.freep.com/voices/sunday/ehate10e_20050410.htm > (accessed October 17, 2005).

Dogu Ergil, CNN/Time In-Depth Special, CNN.com, and Time.com. "The Kurdish Question after Ocalan." < http://www.cnn.com/SPECIALS/1999/ocalan/stories/kurdish.question/ > (accessed October 20, 2005).

Domestic Terrorist Group Profiles—MILNET. "Sword and Arm of the Lord (SAL)." < http://www.milnet.com/domestic/data/sal.htm > (accessed October 3, 2005).

Dr. Charles A. Russell, Air University Review. "Transnational Terrorism." < http://www.airpower.maxwell.af.mil/airchronicles/aureview/1976/jan-feb/russell.html > (accessed October 20, 2005).

Embassy of India, Washington D.C. "Profile of the Terrorist Group Involved in Hijacking of Indian Airlines Flight IC-814." < http://www.indianembassy.org/pic/PR_1999/December_99/PR_Dec_27_1999.html > (accessed October 19, 2005).

Embassy of the Philippines. "History of the Philippines." < http://www.philembassy.au.com/phi-hist.htm > (accessed October 21, 2005).

Enzo Di Matteo, NOW Magazine, NOW Communications. "A Racist No Longer: Ex-White Rights Fan Just Wants to be a Rock Star." < http://www.nowtoronto.com/issues/2001-01-25/news.html > (accessed October 15, 2005).

Ernie B. Esconde, The Manila Times. "A Former Rebel Town: A Case in Perspective." < http://www.manilatimes.net/national/2004/aug/11/yehey/prov/20040811pro12.html > (accessed October 21, 2005).

Eye on Hate, Seeking a Kinder and Gentler World. "Martyrs, Heroes, & Prisoners of War: The Order." < http://eyeonhate.com/pows/pows3.html > (accessed October 5, 2005).

FAS Intelligence Resource Program. "Islamic Army of Aden." < http://www.fas.org/irp/world/para/iaa.htm > (accessed October 16, 2005).

FAS Intelligence Resource Program. "Macheteros." < http://www.fas.org/irp/world/para/faln.htm > (accessed October 14, 2005).

FAS Intelligence Resource Program. "People's War Group (PWG)." < http://www.fas.org/irp/world/para/pwg.htm > (accessed October 11, 2005).

FAS Intelligence Resource Program. "Revolutionary Organization 17 November." < http://www.fas.org/irp/world/para/17_nov.htm > (accessed July 29, 2005).

Federal Bureau of Investigation "The Threat of Eco-Terrorism." < http://www.fbi.gov/congress/congress02/jarboe021202.htm > (accessed September 29, 2005).

Federal Bureau of Investigation. "Testimony of J. T. Caruso, Acting Assistant Director, Counter Terrorism Division, FBI." < http://www.fbi.gov/congress/congress01/caruso121801.htm > (accessed September 21, 2005).

Federal Bureau of Investigation. "Wanted Poster for al-Zawahiri." < http://www.fbi.gov/mostwant/terrorists/teralzawahiri.htm > (accessed October 10, 2005).

Federation of American Scientists. "Abu Sayyaf Group (ASG)." < http://www.fas.org/irp/world/para/asg.htm > (accessed September 14, 2005).

Federation of American Scientists. "Anti-Imperialist Territorial Nuclei (NTA)." < http://www.fas.org/irp/world/para/nta.htm > (accessed August 1, 2005).

Federation of American Scientists. "Harakat ul-Jihad-I-Islami/Bangladesh (HUJI-B) (Movement of Islamic Holy War)." < http://www.fas.org/irp/world/para/huji-b.htm > (accessed October 16, 2005).

Federation of American Scientists. "Patterns of Global Terrorism: 1992, Asia Overview." < http://www.fas.org/irp/threat/terror_92/asia.html > (accessed September 27, 2005).

Federation of American Scientists. "Revolutionary United Front (RUF)." < http://www.fas.org/main/home.jsp > (assessed October 3, 2005).

Flemish Republic. "Brussels: Europe's Hub of Terror." < http://www.flemishrepublic.org/extra.php?id = 1&jaargang = 1&nr = 1 > (accessed October 16, 2005).

Florida Center for Instructional Technology, University of South Florida. "Victims." < http://www.spartacus.schoolnet.co.uk/GERnazi.htm > (assessed October 20, 2005).

Foreign and Commonwealth Office. "Asbat al-Ansar." < http://www.fco.gov.uk/servlet/Front?pagename = OpenMarket/Xcelerate/ShowPage&c = Page&cid = 1049909003789 > (accessed October 15, 2005).

Foreign and Commonwealth Offices. "Islamic Movement of Uzbekistan." < http://www.fco.gov.uk/servlet/Front?pagename = OpenMarket/Xcelerate/ShowPage&c = Page&cid = 1049909003533 > (accessed October 19, 2005).

Foreign Policy Research Institute. "E-Notes: Terrorism in Colombia." < http://www.fpri.org/enotes/latin.20020121.posada.terrorismincolombia.html > (accessed September 30, 2005).

Fox News Channel. "ELF Suspected in California Eco-Terror." < http://www.foxnews.com/printer_friendly_story/0,3566,146927,00.html > (accessed October 21, 2005).

Fox News Channel. "Fire May Be Connected to 'Eco-Terrorism' Group." < http://www.foxnews.com/printer_friendly_story/0,3566,122902,00.html > (accessed October 21, 2005).

FOXNews.com—U.S. & World. "Abortion Doctor's Murderer Dies by Lethal Injection." < http://www.foxnews.com/story/0,2933,96286,00.html > (accessed September 25, 2005).

freebarghouti.org. "Supporters of Marwan Barghouti." < http://www.freebarghouti.org/index.html > (accessed October 21, 2005).

Frontline. "A Parochial Project." < http://www.flonnet.com/fl2010/stories/20030523004803200.htm > (accessed October 4, 2005).

Frontpagemag.com. "New Black Panther Mouthpiece." < http://www.frontpagemag.com/Articles/ReadArticle.asp?ID = 12053 > (accessed October 18, 2005).

Fur Commission USA. "In Their Own Words." < http://www.furcommission.com/debate/words6.htm?FACT Net > (accessed October 21, 2005).

GlobalSecurity.org. "Algerian Insurgency." < http://www.globalsecurity.org/military/world/war/algeria-90s.htm > (accessed October 16, 2005).

GlobalSecurity.org. "Kumpulan Mujahidin Malaysia." < http://www.globalsecurity.org/military/world/para/kmm.htm > (accessed October 11, 2005).

GlobalSecurity.org. "Alex Boncayao Brigade (ABB)." < http://www.globalsecurity.org/military/world/para/abb.htm > (accessed September 15, 2005).

GlobalSecurity.org. "Allied Democratic Forces: National Army for the Liberation of Uganda (NALU)." < http://www.globalsecurity.org/military/world/para/adf.htm > (accessed September 22, 2005).

GlobalSecurity.org. "Jaish-e-Mohammed." < http://www.globalsecurity.org/military/world/para/jem.htm > (accessed October 20, 2005).

GlobalSecurity.org. "Revolutionary United Front (RUF)." < http://www.globalsecurity.org/military/world/para/ruf.htm > (accessed October 3, 2005).

GlobalSecurity.org. "Sikh Terrorists." < http://www.globalsecurity.org/military/world/para/sikh.htm > (accessed October 11, 2005).

Government of Sierra Leone. "Bio Data of The President of Sierra Leone." < http://www.statehouse-sl.org/biodata.html > (accessed October 3, 2005).

Guardian Unlimited. "Interview with Simon Tindale: What Happened Next?" < http://observer.guardian.co.uk/magazine/story/0,,1118794,00.html > (accessed October 12, 2005).

Guardian Unlimited. "The Downfall of Mad Dog Adair." < http://books.guardian.co.uk/extracts/story/0,,1055999,00.html > (accessed October 3, 2005).

Guardian Unlimited. "Who is Foday Sankoh?" < http://www.guardian.co.uk/sierra/article/0,2763,221853,00.html > (accessed October 3, 2005).

Guardian.com "$4.4m for Environmentalists Framed by FBI." < http://www.guardian.co.uk/print/0,3858,4431940-103681,00.html > (accessed September 29, 2005).

Heidi Beirich and Bob Moser, Intelligence Report, Southern Poverty Law Center. "Communing with the Council." < http://www.splcenter.org/intel/intelreport/article.jsp?pid = 804 > (accessed October 23, 2005).

Houston Chronicle.com. "Still True Today: 'The Republic of Texas' Is No More." < http://www.chron.com/content/chronicle/editorial/97/05/01/brock.0-1.html > (accessed October 16, 2005).

Human Rights News. "Nepal: Government Forces, Maoist Rebels Target Civilians." < http://hrw.org/english/docs/2004/10/07/nepal9452.htm > (accessed October 21, 2005).

Human Rights Watch Group. "Algeria: Human Rights Development." < http://www.hrw.org/worldreport99/mideast/algeria.html > (accessed September 25, 2005).

Human Rights Watch. "Bosnia and Hercegovina Unfinished Business: The Return of Refugees and Displaced Persons to Bijeljin." < http://www.hrw.org/reports/2000/bosnia/index.htm#TopOfPage > (accessed October 17, 2005).

Human Rights Watch. "Colombia and the "War." on Terror: Rhetoric and Reality." < http://hrw.org/english/docs/2004/03/04/colomb7932.htm > (accessed October 21, 2005).

Human Rights Watch. "Egypt: Human Rights Background." < http://www.hrw.org/backgrounder/mena/egypt-bck-1001.htm > (accessed September 21, 2005).

Human Rights Watch. "Human Rights Developments, India." < http://www.hrw.org/worldreport99/asia/india.html > (accessed October 4, 2005).

Human Rights Watch. "Leave None to Tell the Story." < http://www.hrw.org/reports/1999/rwanda/ > (accessed October 12, 2005).

Human Rights Watch. "Peru." < http://hrw.org/english/docs/2004/01/21/peru6988.htm > (accessed October 4, 2005).

Human Rights Watch. "War without Quarter: Colombia and International Humanitarian Law." < http://www.hrw.org/reports98/colombia/ > (accessed October 21, 2005).

Institute for Security Studies. "Uganda." < http://www.iss.co.za/AF/profiles/Uganda/SecInfo.html > (accessed September 22, 2005).

Institute for the Study of Academic Racism. "Council of Conservative Citizens." < http://www.ferris.edu/isar/Institut/CCC/homepage.htm > (accessed October 23, 2005).

Institute for War and Peace Reporting. "New Danger from Ugandan Rebel Group?" < http://www.reliefweb.int/rw/RWB.NSF/db900SID/RMOI-6D53DW?OpenDocument > (accessed September 22, 2005).

Intelligence and Terrorism Information Center at the Center for Special Studies (C.S.S). "Profile of the Palestinian Islamic Jihad, Perpetrator of a Suicide Bombing Attack in Tel Aviv, February 25, 2005." < http://www.intelligence.org.il/eng/sib/3_05/pji.htm > (accessed October 20, 2005).

Intelligence Report, Southern Poverty Law Center. "A Group Is Born: Billy Roper, a Fired National Alliance Official, Has Formed His Own Group Called White Revolution." < http://www.splcenter.org/intel/intelreport/article.jsp?sid = 53 > (accessed October 3, 2005).

Intelligence Report, Southern Poverty Law Center. "Resisting Arrest: Racist Resistance Records Isn't Slowing Down." < http://www.splcenter.org/intel/intelreport/article.jsp?aid = 452 > (accessed October 15, 2005).

Intelligence Report, Southern Poverty Law Center. "Revolting in Arkansas." < http://www.splcenter.org/intel/intelreport/article.jsp?pid = 214 > (assessed October 3, 2005).

Intelligence Resource Program, Federation of American Scientists. "Kurdistan Workers' Party (PKK)." < http://www.fas.org/irp/world/para/pkk.htm > (accessed October 20, 2005).

International Crisis Group. "Jemaah Islamiyah In South East Asia: Damaged But Still Dangerous." < http://www.crisisgroup.org/library/documents/report_archive/A401104_26082003.pdf > (accessed October 14, 2005).

International Network of Prison Ministries. < http://prisonministry.net/ > (accessed October 3, 2005).

International Policy Institute for Counter-Terrorism. "Red Brigades." < http://www.ict.org.il/inter_ter/orgdet.cfm?orgid = 36 > (accessed October 20, 2005).

International Policy Institute for Counter-Terrorism. "Revolutionary Organization 17 November." < http://www.ict.org.il/organizations/orgattack.cfm?orgid = 38 > (accessed July 29, 2005).

International Policy Institute for Counter-Terrorism. "Revolutionary People's Liberation Party/Front Attacks: from 1988–the present." < http://www.ict.org.il/organizations/orgattack.cfm?orgid = 39 > (accessed October 19, 2005).

International Policy Institute for Counter-Terrorism. "The Red Brigades: Cooperation with the Palestinian Terrorist Organizations." < http://www.ict.org.il/articles/red_brigades-palestinians.htm > (accessed October 20, 2005).

International Policy of Counter-Terrorism. "Chukakuh-ha." < http://www.ict.org.il/inter_ter/orgdet.cfm?orgid = 9 > (accessed September 27, 2005).

International Relations Center. "Council of Conservative Citizens." < http://rightweb.irc-online.org/org/cofcc.php > (accessed October 23, 2005).

International Strategic Research Organization—Journal of Turkish Weekly. "Turkish Hizballah: A Case Study of Radical Terrorism." < http://www.turkishweekly.net/articles.php?id = 28 > (accessed October 5, 2005).

Islamic Republic of Iran Broadcasting. "Navab Safavi's Martyrdom." < http://www.irib.ir/occasions/Navab-e-Safavi/Navab-e-Safavi-En.htm > (accessed October 7, 2005).

Islamist Watch. "Jihad: The Absent Obligation." < http://www.islamistwatch.org/texts/faraj/obligation/oblig.html > (accessed October 10, 2005).

Jewish Telegraphic Agency. "Fears of Jewish Underground Rise." < http://www.jewishaz.com/jewishnews/020517/fears.shtml > (accessed October 15, 2005).

Jewish Virtual Library, The American-Israeli Cooperative Enterprise. "Holocaust Denial." < http://www.jewishvirtuallibrary.org/jsource/Holocaust/denial.html > (assessed October 20, 2005).

Jewish Virtual Library. "Rabbi Meir Kahane (1932–1990)." < http://www.jewishvirtuallibrary.org/jsource/biography/kahane.html > (accessed October 22, 2005).

Jonathan Marcus, BBC News, British Broadcasting Corporation. "Brutal Child Army Grows Up." < http://news.bbc.co.uk/1/hi/world/africa/743684.stm > (accessed October 3, 2005).

Kahane.org. "Shavuot and the Cultural War." < http://www.kahane.org/ > (accessed October 22, 2005).

Latin American Studies. "Los Macheteros." < http://www.latinamericanstudies.org/epb-macheteros.htm > (accessed October 14, 2005).

Law Enforcement Agency Resource Network, Anti-Defamation League. "White Revolution/Billy Roper." < http://www.adl.org/learn/ext_us/w_revolution.asp?print = true > (assessed October 3, 2005).

Law Enforcement Agency Resource Network. "Volksfront." < http://www.adl.org/hate_symbols/groups_volksfront.asp > (accessed October 3, 2005).

Major Rodney S. Azama, GlobalSecurity.org. "The Huks and the New People's Army: Comparing Two Postwar Filipino Insurgencies." < http://www.globalsecurity.org/military/library/report/1985/ARS.htm > (accessed October 21, 2005).

Mark Potok, Intelligence Report, Southern Poverty Law Center. "The Year in Hate: A Period of Realignment and Rebuilding Follows a Tumultuous Year on the American Radical Right." < http://www.splcenter.org/intel/intelreport/article.jsp?aid = 374&printable = 1 > (accessed October 15, 2005).

Martin Kramer on the Middle East. < http://www.martinkramer.org/pages/899526/index.htm > (accessed October 13, 2005).

Media Matters for America.org. "Who is Randall Terry?" < http://mediamatters.org/items/200503220001 > (accessed October 16, 2005).

Middle East Intelligence Bulletin. "Intelligence Briefs: Lebanon." < http://www.meib.org/articles/0110_lb.htm#lb1 > (accessed October 15, 2005).

Middle East Policy Council Journal. "Qadhafi's Libya and the Prospect of Islamic Succession." < http://www.mepc.org/public_asp/journal_vol7/0002_takeyh.asp > (accessed October 18, 2005).

Mike Doughney's Page. "People Eating Tasty Animals." < http://mtd.com/tasty/ > (accessed October 19, 2005).

Ministry for Safety and Security, South African Government. "Media Statement by Mr. Sydney Mufamadi, Minister for Safety and Security, Pretoria, 11 December 1996." < http://www.info.gov.za/speeches/1996/12170x86496.htm > (accessed October 19, 2005).

Ministry of External Affairs, India. "L.K. Advani's Speech after Terrorist Attack on Indian Parliament." < http://meaindia.nic.in/speech/2001/12/18spc01.htm > (accessed October 20, 2005).

Ministry of External Affairs, India. "Transcript of Press Conference by Shri Jaswant Singh, External Affairs and Defense Minister." < http://meaindia.nic.in/mediainteraction/2001/10/11mi01.htm > (accessed October 19, 2005).

Ministry of Home Affairs, Government of India. "Ministry of Home Affairs Reviews Security Scenario in Assam."

< http://mha.nic.in/pr052001.htm > (accessed October 1, 2005).

MIPT Terrorism Knowledge Base. "Republic of Texas (ROT)." < http://www.tkb.org/Group.jsp?groupID = 95 > (accessed October 16, 2005).

MIPT Terrorism Knowledge Base, National Memorial Institute for the Prevention of Terrorism (MIPT). "Anti-Imperialist Territorial Nuclei for the Construction of the Fighting Communist Party." < http://tkb.org/Group.jsp?groupID = 16 > (accessed August 1, 2005).

MIPT Terrorism Knowledge Base, National Memorial Institute for the Prevention of Terrorism. "DHKP-C." < http://www.tkb.org/Group.jsp?groupID = 38 > (accessed October 19, 2005).

MIPT Terrorism Knowledge Base, National Memorial Institute for the Prevention of Terrorism. "Group Profile: New People's Army (NPA)." < http://www.tkb.org/Group.jsp?groupID = 203 > (accessed October 21, 2005).

MIPT Terrorism Knowledge Base, National Memorial Institute for the Prevention of Terrorism. "Kurdistan Workers' Party." < http://www.tkb.org/Group.jsp?groupID = 63 > (accessed October 20, 2005).

MIPT Terrorism Knowledge Base, National Memorial Institute for the Prevention of Terrorism. "Revolutionary United Front (RUF)." < http://www.tkb.org/Group.jsp?groupID = 4247 > (accessed October 3, 2005).

MIPT Terrorism Knowledge Base, National Memorial Institute for the Prevention of Terrorism. "Terrorist Group Profile: Al-Fuqra." < http://www.tkb.org/Group.jsp?groupID = 3426 > (September 21, 2005).

MIPT Terrorism Knowledge Base. "African National Congress." < http://www.tkb.org/Group.jsp?groupID = 305 > (accessed October 11, 2005).

MIPT Terrorism Knowledge Base. "Alex Boncayao Brigade (ABB)." < http://www.tkb.org/Group.jsp?groupID = 3011 > (accessed September 15, 2005).

MIPT Terrorism Knowledge Base. "Basque Fatherland and Freedom." < http://www.tkb.org/Group.jsp?groupID = 31 > (accessed October 20, 2005).

MIPT Terrorism Knowledge Base. "Breton Revolutionary Army." < http://www.tkp.org/Group.jsp?groupID = 3548 > (accessed July 20 2005).

MIPT Terrorism Knowledge Base. "Group Profile—Covenant, Sword, and Arm of the Lord (CSA)." < http://www.tkb.org/Group.jsp?groupID = 3226 > (accessed October 3, 2005).

MIPT Terrorism Knowledge Base. "Group Profile: Red Army Faction." < http://www.tkb.org/Group.jsp?groupID = 163 > (accessed October 15, 2005).

MIPT Terrorism Knowledge Base. "Group Profile: United Liberation Front of Assam (ULFA)." < http://www.tkb.org/Group.jsp?groupID = 3686 > (accessed October 1, 2005).

MIPT Terrorism Knowledge Base. "Islamic Movement of Uzbekistan." < http://www.tkb.org/Group.jsp?groupID = 4075 > (accessed October 19, 2005).

MIPT Terrorism Knowledge Base. "Ku Klux Klan, Key Leader Profile: Berry, Jeff." < http://www.tkb.org/KeyLeader.jsp?memID = 109 > (accessed September 29, 2005).

MIPT Terrorism Knowledge Base. "Macheteros." < http://www.tkb.org/Group.jsp?groupID = 3227 > (accessed October 14, 2005).

MIPT Terrorism Knowledge Base. "Montana Freemen." < http://www.tkb.org/Group.jsp?groupID = 3406 > (accessed October 18, 2005).

MIPT Terrorism Knowledge Base. "Mujahedine-e Khalq Organization." < http://tkb.org/Group.jsp?groupID = 3632 > (accessed October 14, 2005).

MIPT Terrorism Knowledge Base. "National Army for the Liberation of Uganda (NALU)." < http://www.tkb.org/Group.jsp?groupID = 3515 > (accessed September 22, 2005).

MIPT Terrorism Knowledge Base. "Palestinian Islamic Jihad." < http://www.tkb.org/Group.jsp?groupID = 82 > (accessed October 20, 2005).

MIPT Terrorism Knowledge Base. "Salafist Group for Call and Combat." < http://www.tkb.org/Group.jsp?groupID = 3777 > (accessed October 16, 2005).

MIPT Terrorism Knowledge Base. "Terrorist Group Profile: Armed Forces of National Liberation." < http://www.tkb.org/Group.jsp?groupID = 3229 > (accessed October 18, 2005).

MIPT Terrorism Knowledge Base. "Terrorist Group Profile: Orange Volunteers (OV)." < http://www.tkb.org/Group.jsp?groupID = 79 > (accessed October 19, 2005).

MIPT Terrorism Knowledge Base. "The People's War Group (PWG)." < http://www.tkb.org/Group.jsp?groupID = 3658 > (accessed October 11, 2005).

MIPT Terrorism Knowledge Base. "Tunisian Combatant Group." < http://www.tkb.org/Group.jsp?groupID = 4346 > (accessed October 16, 2005).

MIPT Terrorism Knowledge Database. "The Libyan Islamic Fighting Group (LIFG)." < http://www.tkb.org/Group.jsp?groupID = 4400 > (October 18, 2005).

MIPT Terrorism Knowledge Database. "Revolutionary Organization 17 November." < http://www.tkb.org/Group.jsp?groupID = 101 > (accessed September 14, 2005).

MIPT Terrorism Knowledge Database. "First of October Antifascist Resistance Group." < http://www.tkb.org/Incident.jsp?incID = 13139 > (accessed October 15, 2005).

Monterey Institute of International Studies. "Islamic Movement of Uzbeckistan." < http://cns.miis.edu/research/wtc01/imu.htm > (accessed October 19, 2005).

MosNews.com. "Moscow Court Bans Russia's Radical National Bolshevik Party." < http://www.mosnews.com/news/2005/06/29/nbpliquidated.shtml > (accessed October 15, 2005).

MSNBC.com. "Poll Finds Muslim Support for bin Laden Waning." < http://www.msnbc.msn.com/id/8569229/ > (accessed September 22, 2005).

MSNBC.com. "Time & Again—Wounded Knee—Siege of 1973." < http://msnbc.com/onair/msnbc/TimeandAgain/archive/wknee/1973.asp > (accessed October 15, 2005).

MSNBC.com. "U.N. Seeks First Political Definition of Terrorism." < http://www.msnbc.msn.com/id/8676132/ > (accessed September 22, 2005).

MSNBC. "Former Spy to Testify about Cuban Support for Los Macheteros." < http://www.cubanet.org/CNews/y99/dec99/30e3.htm > (accessed October 14, 2005).

National Commission on Terrorist Attacks upon the United States. "The Rise and Decline of Al Qaeda." < http://www.9-11commission.gov/hearings/hearing3/witness_gunaratna.htm > (accessed October 20, 2005).

National Institute of Justice. "The American Terrorism Study: Patterns of Behavior, Investigation and Prosecution of American Terrorists." < http://www.ncjrs.org/pdffiles1/nij/grants/193420.pdf > (accessed October 18, 2005).

National Library of Medicine, National Institutes of Health. "The Story of NLM Historical Collections." < http://www.nlm.nih.gov/hmd/about/collectionhistory.html > (accessed October 11, 2005).

National Memorial Institute for the Prevention of Terrorism—Terrorism Knowledge Base. "Chukakuha." < http://tkb.org/Group.jsp?groupID = 3578 > (accessed September 27, 2005).

National Memorial Institute for the Prevention of Terrorism—Terrorism Knowledge Base. "Cinchoneros Popular Liberation Movement." < http://www.tkb.org/Group.jsp?groupID = 3987 > (accessed September 28, 2005).

National Memorial Institute for the Prevention of Terrorism—Terrorism Knowledge Base. "Turkish Hezbollah." < http://www.tkb.org/KeyLeader.jsp?memID = 5922 > (accessed October 5, 2005).

National Public Radio's Weekend Edition (audio clip). "FARC." < http://www.npr.org/templates/story/story.php?storyId = 1127278 > (accessed September 30, 2005).

National Public Radio. "Afghanistan Takes Steps to Reconcile with Taliban Fighters." < http://www.npr.org/templates/story/story.php?storyId = 4469449 > (accessed October 16, 2005).

National Security Australia. "Islamic Army of Aden (IAA)." < http://www.nationalsecurity.gov.au/agd/WWW/nationalsecurityHome.nsf/Page/Listing_of_Terrorist_Organisations_terrorist_listing_Islamic_Army_of_Aden_-_Listed_11_April_2003 > (accessed October 18, 2005).

NBC5i.com. "New Black Panther Party Emerges, Voices Demands." < http://www.nbc5i.com/news/3277640/detail.html > (accessed October 18, 2005).

Nobel Prize. "José Ramos-Horta—Curriculum Vitae." < http://nobelprize.org/peace/laureates/1996/ramos-horta-cv.html > (accessed October 1, 2005).

Northern Ireland Office. "Homepage of the Decommissioning Commission." < http://www.nio.gov.uk/decommissioning > (accessed October 24, 2005).

Observer Sports Monthly. "Lost Lives That Saved A Sport." < http://football.guardian.co.uk/News_Story/0,1563,1448505,00.html > (accessed October 20, 2005).

Observer. "Equality in Death." < http://observer.guardian.co.uk/magazine/story/0,11913,1200794,00.html > (accessed October 21, 2005).

Office of the Press Secretary, Malacanang, Philippines. "President George W. Bush's Speech during the Joint Session of Congress." < http://www.ops.gov.ph/pgwbvisit2003/speeches.htm > (accessed September 14, 2005).

Office of the Press Secretary, The White House. " President Bush Calls for New Palestinian Leadership." < http://www.whitehouse.gov/news/releases/2002/06/20020624-3.html > (accessed October 20, 2005).

Overseas Security Advisory Council (OSAC). "Anti-Imperialist Territorial Nuclei (NTA) a.k.a. Anti-Imperialist Territorial Units." < http://www.ds-osac.org/Groups/group.cfm?contentID = 1306 > (accessed September 25, 2005).

Overseas Security Advisory Council. "Asbat al-Ansar." < http://www.ds-osac.org/Groups/group.cfm?contentID = 1275 > (accessed October 15, 2005).

Overseas Security Advisory Council. "First of October Antifascist Resistance Group (GRAPO)." < http://www.ds-osac.org/Groups/group.cfm?contentID = 1312 > (accessed October 15, 2005).

Overseas Security Advisory Council. "Revolutionary People's Liberation Party/Front (DHKP/C)." < http://www.ds-osac.org/Groups/group.cfm?contentID = 1296 > (accessed October 19, 2005).

Overseas Security Advisory Council. "Tunisian Combatant Group." < http://www.ds-osac.org/Groups/group.cfm?contentID = 1335 > (accessed October 16, 2005).

PBS.org. "Alcatraz Is Not an Island." < http://www.pbs.org/itvs/alcatrazisnotanisland/activism.html > (accessed October 15, 2005).

PBS.org. "Hostage Crisis." < http://www.pbs.org/newshour/bb/latin_america/december96/peru_12–19.html > (accessed October 5, 2005).

PBS.org. "Inside al-Qaeda." < http://www.pbs.org/wgbh/pages/frontline/shows/network/alqaeda/ > (accessed September 22, 2005).

Peter C. Andersen's Sierra-Leone.org. "Footpaths to Democracy: Toward a New Sierra Leone." < http://www.sierra-leone.org/footpaths.html > (accessed October 3, 2005).

Public Broadcasting Service (PBS). "Profile: Abu Sayyaf." < http://www.pbs.org/newshour/terrorism/international/abu_sayyaf.html > (accessed September 14, 2005).

RAHOWA.com. " Klassen's Teachings." < http://www.rahowa.com > (accessed October 1, 2005).

ReasonOnline. "David Foreman vs. the Cornucopians." < http://www.reason.com/rb/rb082901.html > (accessed September 29, 2005).

Red Pepper Magazine. "Interview with Leila Khaled." < http://www.redpepper.org.uk/intarch/x-khaled.html > (accessed October 19, 2005).

Religious Tolerance.org. "Christian Identity Movement." < http://www.religioustolerance.org/cr_ident.htm > (accessed September 29, 2005).

Religious Tolerance.org. "How Christians View Non-Christian Religions." < http://www.religioustolerance.org/chr_othe2.htm > (accessed October 16, 2005).

Religious Tolerance.org. "The Creativity Movement."." < http://www.religioustolerance.org/wcotc.htm > (accessed October 1, 2005).

Resource Center of the Americas.org. "28 Killed in Bus Attack—Weekly News Update on the Americas #778." < http://www.americas.org/item_17213 > (accessed September 28, 2005).

Rick A Ross Institute. "Christian Identity." < http://www.rickross.com/groups/christian_identity.html > (accessed September 25, 2005).

Rod Usher, Time International, Time.com. "Nationalists Without a Nation." < http://www.time.com/time/daily/special/ocalan/nationalists.html > (accessed October 20, 2005).

Salon.com. "Brand New War for the Army of God? Parts 1 and 2." < http://www.salon.com/news/feature/2002/02/19/gays/index_np.html > (accessed September 25, 2005).

Salon.com. "The Angry Patriot " < http://www.salon.com/news/feature/2005/05/11/minuteman/ > (accessed October 23, 2005).

San Francisco Chronicle (March 6, 2005). "A Web of White Power." < http://www.rickross.com/reference/hate_groups/hategroups391.html > (accessed October 17, 2005).

SAPRA India. "Indian Airlines Plane Hijack: Background Articles." < http://www.subcontinent.com/sapra/terrorism/harkat > (accessed October 19, 2005).

Seattle Weekly. "Violence and Protest." < http://www.seattleweekly.com/features/0315/news-dawdy.php > (accessed October 21, 2005).

SHAC. "News Index." < http://www.shac.net/ > (accessed October 22, 2005).

Slate.com. "The Republic of Texas." < http://www.slate.com/id/1057 > (accessed October 16, 2005).

South Asia Analysis Group. "ABU SAYYAF: The Cause for the Return of U.S. Troops to Philippines?" < http://www.saag.org/papers5/paper417.html > (accessed September 14, 2005).

South Asia Analysis Group. "Bangladeshi & Jihadi Terrorism, An Update." < http://www.saag.org/papers9/paper887.html > (accessed October 16, 2005).

South Asia Analysis Group. "Paper No. 376 Jaish-e-Mohammed." < http://saag.org/papers4/papers376.html > (accessed October 20, 2005).

South Asia Analysis Group. "Students Islamic Movement of India (SIMI)." < http://www.saag.org/papers9/paper825.html > (accessed October 21, 2005).

South Asia Terrorism Portal. "Harakat ul-Jihad-i-Islami." < http://www.satp.org/satporgtp/countries/india/states/jandk/terrorist_outfits/HuJI.htm > (accessed October 20, 2005).

South Asia Terrorism Portal. "Jaish-e-Mohammed Mujahideen e Tanzim." < http://www.satp.org/satporgtp/countries/india/states/jandk/terrorist_outfits/jaish_e_Mohammed_mujahideen_e_tanzeem.htm > (accessed October 20, 2005).

South Asia Terrorism Portal. "Jamaat ul-Fuqra." < http://www.satp.org/satporgtp/countries/pakistan/terroristoutfits/jamaat-ul-fuqra.htm > (September 21, 2005).

South Asia Terrorism Portal. "The People's War Group (PWG)." < http://www.satp.org/satporgtp/countries/india/terroristoutfits/pwg.htm > (accessed October 11, 2005).

South Asian Terrorism Portal. "Sipah-e-Sahaba Pakistan, Terrorist Group of Pakistan." < http://www.satp.org/satporgtp/countries/pakistan/terroristoutfits/ssp.htm > (accessed October 1, 2005).

South Asian Terrorism Portal. "Students Islamic Movement of India (SIMI)." < http://www.satp.org/satporgtp/countries/india/terroristoutfits/simi.htm > (accessed October 21, 2005).

South Asian Terrorism Portal. "United Liberation Front of Asom (ULFA)—Terrorist Group of Assam." < http://www.satp.org/satporgtp/countries/india/states/assam/terrorist_outfits/ulfa.htm > (accessed October 1, 2005).

Southern Poverty Law Center. "A Soldier's Ransom." < http://www.splcenter.org/intel/intelreport/article.jsp?aid = 71&printable = 1 > (accessed October 17, 2005).

Southern Poverty Law Center. "Active U.S. Hate Groups in 2004." < http://www.splcenter.org/intel/map/hate.jsp?T = 22&m = 3 > (accessed September 28, 2005).

Southern Poverty Law Center. "Anti-Abortion Violence: Two Decades of Arson, Bombs, and Murder." < http://www.splcenter.org/intel/intelreport/article.jsp?aid = 411 > (accessed October 21, 2005).

Southern Poverty Law Center. "Anti-Semitism: 'Patriot' Publications Taking on Anti-Semitic Edge." < http://www.splcenter.org/intel/intelreport/article.jsp?aid = 68 > (accessed October 1, 2005).

Southern Poverty Law Center. "Appeasing the Beast." < http://www.splcenter.org/intel/intelreport/article.jsp?aid = 66 > (accessed September 25, 2005).

Southern Poverty Law Center. "False Patriots." < http://www.splcenter.org/intel/intelreport/article.jsp?pid = 366 > (accessed October 18, 2005).

Southern Poverty Law Center. "Hate and Hypocrisy: What Is Behind the Rare-but-recurring Phenomenon of Jewish Anti-Semites?" < http://www.splcenter.org/intel/intelreport/article.jsp?aid = 73 > (accessed October 21, 2005).

Southern Poverty Law Center. "Hate Group Numbers Slightly Up in 2004." < http://www.splcenter.org/center/splcreport/article.jsp?aid = 135 > (accessed October 1, 2005).

Southern Poverty Law Center. "Intelligence Report: Anti-Immigration Groups." < http://www.splcenter.org/intel/intelreport/article.jsp?sid = 175 > (accessed September 24, 2005).

Southern Poverty Law Center. "Return of the Pastor." < http://www.splcenter.org/intel/intelreport/article.jsp?aid = 507&printable = 1 > (accessed October 17, 2005).

Southern Poverty Law Center. "Sharks in the Mainstream." < http://www.splcenter.org/intel/intelreport/article.jsp?aid = 360 > (accessed October 23, 2005).

Southern Poverty Law Center. "Street Fighter: An Anti-racist Organizer's View of Skinheads." < http://www.splcenter.org/intel/intelreport/article.jsp?aid = 397 > (accessed October 3, 2005).

Southern Poverty Law Center. "The Neo-Confederates." < http://www.splcenter.org/intel/intelreport/article.jsp?pid = 461 > (accessed October 23, 2005).

Southern Poverty Law Center. "The Other Half: Interview with Sociologist Kathleen M. Blee." < http://www.splcenter.org/intel/intelreport/article.jsp?aid = 134 > (accessed October 1, 2005).

Southern Poverty Law Center. "Two Faces of Volksfront: A Growing and Increasingly Important Neo-Nazi Group Claims It Opposes Any Kind of Political Violence. Could It Be True?" < http://www.splcenter.org/intel/intelreport/article.jsp?aid = 475 > (accessed October 3, 2005).

Spartacus Educational. "Nazi Party (NSDAP)" < http://www.spartacus.schoolnet.co.uk/GERnazi.htm > (assessed October 20, 2005).

Steven Alan Hassan's Freedom of Mind Center. "About Kerry Noble." < http://www.freedomofmind.com/resourcecenter/articles/noble.htm > (accessed October 3, 2005).

Suzanne Kelly, Time Interactive, CNN.com. "Ocalan Trial Casts Light on Turkey's Human Rights Record." < http://cnn.com/SPECIALS/1999/ocalan/stories/turkey.human.rights/ > (accessed October 20, 2005).

Tamil Tigers. "Southern Journalists on Goodwill Mission to Trincomalee." < http://www.tamilnet.com > (accessed October 10, 2005).

Terrorism Knowledge Base. "Kumpulan Mujahidin Malaysia." < http://www.tkb.org/Group.jsp?groupID = 4401 > (accessed October 11, 2005).

The Anti-Defamation League. "Fighting Anti-Semitism, Bigotry and Extremism." < http://www.adl.org/ > (accessed October 13, 2005).

The Anti-Defamation League. "Institute for Historical Review (IHR): Outlet for Denial Propaganda" < http://www.adl.org/holocaust/ihr.asp > (accessed October 15, 2005).

The Anti-Defamation League. "Neo-Nazi Hate Music, A Guide." < http://www.adl.org/main_Extremism/hate_music_in_the_21st_century.htm?Multi_page_sections = sHeading_1 > (accessed September 26, 2005).

The Avalon Project, Yale University. "Program of the National Socialist German Workers' Party." < http://www.yale.edu/lawweb/avalon/imt/nsdappro.htm > (assessed October 20, 2005).

The Bethune Institute for Anti-Fascist Studies. "Aryan Nations: Christian Identity and Fascist Terror." < http://bethuneinstitute.org/documents/cift.html > (accessed October 17, 2005).

The Center for Consumer Freedom. "GRRR... PETA Pitches Violence to Kids." < http://www. consumerfreedom.com/news_detail.cfm/headline/1904 > (accessed October 19, 2005).

The Dr. Huey P. Newton Foundation. "There is No New Black Panther Party: An Open Letter from the Dr. Huey P. Newton Foundation." < http://www.blackpanther.org/newsalert.htm > (accessed October 18, 2005).

The Fox News Channel. "FBI: Radical-activist Groups Are Major Threat." < http://www.foxnews.com/printer_friendly_story/0,3566,161825,00.html > (accessed October 21, 2005).

The Guardian. "Breton Separatists on Trial for Attacks." < http://www.guardian.co.uk/france/story/o.html > (accessed July 20, 2005).

The Guardian. "Ulster Braced for Week of Orange Unrest." < http://www.guardian.co.uk/uk_news/story/0,,339130,00.html > (accessed October 19, 2005).

The High North News. "Sea Shepherd Conservation Society." < http://www.highnorth.no/Library/Movements/Sea_Shepherd/st-se-sh.htm > (accessed September 30, 2005).

The Institute of Cetacean Research. "Sea Shepherd's Violent History." < http://www.icrwhale.org/eng/history.pdf > (accessed September 30, 2005).

The Jamestown Foundation. "The Libyan Islamic Fighting Group (LIFG)." < http://www.jamestown.org/publications_details.php?volume_id = 411&issue_

id = 3275&article_id = 2369477 > (accessed October 18, 2005).

The Jerusalem Quarterly. "Gush Emunim; The Tip of the Iceberg." < http://www.geocities.com/alabasters_archive/gush_iceberg.html > (accessed October 18, 2005).

The Mackenzie Institute. "Babbar Khalsa Banned at Last." < http://www.mackenzieinstitute.com/2003/terror060403.htm > (accessed October 11, 2005).

The Manila Times Internet Edition SPECIAL REPORT. "Struggle Continues for Rebels." < http://www.manilatimes.net/others/special/2003/dec/26/20031226spe1.html > (accessed September 15, 2005).

The Media Monitors Network. "Gush Emunim; The Twilight of Zionism?" < http://www.mediamonitors.net/cantarow1.html > (accessed October 18, 2005).

The Middle East Forum. "Tablighi Jamaat: Jihad's Stealthy Legions." < http://www.meforum.org/article/686 > (accessed October 20, 2005).

The National Post. "Al-Qaeda Targets Gaddafi." < http://209.157.64.200/focus/f-news/1046103/posts > (accessed October 18, 2005).

The Nizkor Project. "Paranoia as Patriotism: Far-Right Influences on the Militia Movement. Covenant, Sword, and Arm of the Lord." < http://www.nizkor.org/hweb/orgs/american/adl/paranoia-as-patriotism/covenant.html > (accessed October 3, 2005).

The Ontario Institute for Studies in Education of the University of Toronto (OISE/UT). "History of Education: Selected Moments of the 20th Century." < http://fcis.oise.utoronto.ca/~daniel_schugurensky/assignment1/1994stretz.html > (accessed September 24, 2005).

The Open University, British Broadcasting Corporation (BBC). "Adolf Hitler Timeline." < http://www.open2.net/oulecture2005/hitler_timeline.html > (assessed October 20, 2005).

The Pittsburgh Channel. "Group Claims Credit For Irvine, Pa., Lab Fire; < http://www.thepittsburghchannel.com/team4/1775308/detail.html > (accessed October 21, 2005).

The Somaliland Times. "Terrorists Use Somalia As Hub." < http://www.somalilandtimes.net/2003/63/6304.htm > (accessed September 21, 2005).

The Southern Poverty Law Center. "Intelligence Project; Monitoring Hate and Extremist Activity." < http://www.splcenter.org/intel/intpro.jsp > (accessed September 25, 2005).

The Spokesman-Review.com. "Our Cops Doing a Lot More Than Just Wingin' It." < http://www.spokesmanreview.com/news-story.asp?date = 011204&ID = s1470404 > (accessed September 28, 2005).

The Spokesman-Review.com. "Pischner Up against White Supremacist Foe." < http://www.spokesmanreview.com/pf.asp?date = 102100&ID = s868919 > (July 31, 2005).

The St. Petersburg Times. "Ban on National Bolshevik Party Overturned by Court." < http://www.sptimes.ru/story/483 > (accessed October 15, 2005).

The Time 100 (The Most Important People of the Century), Time, Inc. "Adolf Hitler." < http://www.time.com/time/time100/leaders/profile/hitler.htm > (assessed October 20, 2005).

The Tribune. "Organisation Had Links with Laden." < http://www.tribuneindia.com/2001/20010929/main2.htm > (accessed October 21, 2005).

The Turkish Times. "PKK and DHKP-C in U.S. Terrorism Report." < http://www.theturkishtimes.com/archive/02/06_01/ > (accessed October 19, 2005).

The Turkish Times. "Shaping a Common Security Agenda for Southeast Europe: New Approaches and Shared Responsibilities." < http://www.anticorruption.bg/eng/news/artShow.php?id = 1112 > (accessed October 19, 2005).

The U.S. Embassy at Manila. "U.S., Philippine Presidents Announce Boost to Bilateral Ties." < http://usembassy.state.gov/posts/rp1/wwwhr006.html > (accessed September 14, 2005).

The University of Arizona Press "Coyotes and Town Dogs: Earth First! and the Environmental Movement." < http://www.uapress.arizona.edu/books/bid1417.htm > (accessed September 29, 2005).

Thomas Sanction, Time.com. "A Terrorist's Bitter End." < http://www.time.com/time/daily/special/ocalan/bitterend.html > (accessed October 20, 2005).

Time Magazine Europe. "From Quaint to Bloodthirsty." < http://www.time.com/time/Europe/magazine/2000.0501/burgerbomb.html > (accessed July 20, 2005).

Time Magazine. "Habash: 'Israel Will Fall.'" < http://www.time.com/time/archive/preview/0,10987,945844,00.html > (accessed October 19, 2005).

Time.com. "All You Need Is Hate: White-power Music Is Thriving Abroad—And Also in the U.S." < http://www.time.com/time/musicgoesglobal/na/mnoise.html > (accessed October 15, 2005).

Time.com. "Loathing Abe Lincoln." < http://www.time.com/time/nation/article/0,8599,1077193,00.html > (accessed October 18, 2005).

Time.com. "Primer: The Taliban and Afghanistan." < http://www.time.com/time/nation/article/0,8599,175372,00.html > (accessed October 16, 2005).

Time: Asia. "Untangling the Web." < http://www.time.com/time/asia/news/magazine/0,9754,197713,00.html > (accessed October 11, 2005).

TimeAsia.com. "Asia's Own Osama." < http://www.time.com/time/asia/features/malay_terror/hambali.html > (accessed October 14, 2005).

Tribung Pinoy. "A Brief History of the Philippines from a Filipino Perspective." < http://www.tribo.org/history/history3.html > (accessed October 21, 2005).

Truth and Reconciliation Commission (in Spanish). "Final Report." < http://www.cverdad.org.pe/ifinal/index.php > (accessed October 4, 2005).

U.S. Court of Appeals for the Ninth Circuit. "Planned Parenthood of the Columbia/Willamette Inc. v American Coalition of Life Activists (2002 decision)." < http://www.ca9.uscourts.gov/ca9/newopinions.nsf/0F569EF00290007188256BC0005876E6/$file/9935320ebcorrected.pdf?openelement > (accessed October 21, 2005).

U.S. Court of Appeals, Third Circuit. "U.S. v. Wickstrom, 893 F.2d 30 (3d Cir. 1989)." < http://www.cs.cmu.edu/afs/cs.cmu.edu/user/wbardwel/public/nfalist/us_v_wickstrom.txt > (accessed October 17, 2005).

U.S. Department of Justice. "Eight Montana Skinheads Sentenced for Civil Rights Crimes." < http://www.usdoj.gov/opa/pr/2002/March/02_crt_114.htm > (accessed October 4, 2005).

U.S. Department of State. "Country Reports on Terrorism, 2004." < http://library.nps.navy.mil/home/tgp/mek.htm > (accessed October 14, 2005).

U.S. Department of State. "Patterns of Global Terrorism, 2003, April 2004." < http://www.state.gov/documents/organization/31947.pdf > (accessed October 11, 2005).

U.S. Department of State. "Remarks Secretary of State Condoleezza Rice To the National Conference of Editorial Writers." < http://www.ncew.org/member_services/State%20Department%20Briefing/C%20Rices%20Comments.pdf > (accessed October 4, 2005).

U.S. State Department. "Patterns of Global Terrorism." < http://www.state.gov/s/ct/rls/pgtrpt/2003/31638.htm > (accessed October 15, 2005).

U.S. State Department. "Patterns of Global Terrorism." < http://www.state.gov/s/ct/rls/pgtrpt/2003/31638.htm > (accessed October 16, 2005).

UMN.edu. "The Earth Liberation Front and Environmental Terrorism." < http://www.is.wayne.edu/mrichmon/earth_liberation_front.htm > (accessed October 21, 2005).

United Nations. "Conflict Diamonds: Sanctions and War." < http://www.un.org/peace/africa/Diamond.html > (accessed October 3, 2005).

University of Wisconsin at Madison. "Tom Metzger and WAR." < http://slisweb.lis.wisc.edu/~jcherney/osmond.html > (accessed October 17, 2005).

US Memorial to Beirut Dead. "History: U.S. Embassy Bombing." < http://www.beirut—memorial.org/history/embassy.html > (accessed October 13, 2005).

Uterecht University. "Genealogies of Islamic Radicalism in Post-Suharto Indonesia." < http://www.let.uu.nl/~martin.vanbruinessen/personal/publications/genealogies_islamic_radicalism.htm > (accessed October 14, 2005).

Glossary

A

17 November Organization: Revolutionary Organization 17 November (17 November).

AAIA: Aden-Abyan Islamic Army (AAIA).

ABB: Alex Boncayao Brigade (ABB).

ADF: Allied Democratic Forces (ADF).

Agent provocateur: An operative or agent who infiltrates a group or organization with the purpose of inciting its members to self-destructive acts.

AIAI: Al-Ittihad al-Islami (AIAI).

AIIB: Anti-Imperialist International Brigade (AIIB).

Air marshal: United States air marshals are the first police force of the federal government created solely to protect against air terrorism.

Aleph: Aum Supreme Truth (Aum) Aum Shinrikyo, Aleph.

ALIR: Army for the Liberation of Rwanda (ALIR).

Al-Qaeda: Responsible for the September 11, 2001, terrorist attacks upon the United States, Al-Qaeda (also known as Al-Qaida) was established by Osama bin Ladin (also spelled Usama Bin Ladin or Osama bin Laden) in the late 1980s to bring together Arabs who fought in Afghanistan against the Soviet Union. Al-Qaeda helped finance, recruit, transport, and train Sunni Islamic extremists for the Afghan resistance. Al-Qaeda's current goal is to establish a pan-Islamic Caliphate throughout the world and has declared the United States to be an enemy to be attacked by terrorist actions.

ANSIR: FBI Awareness of National Security Issues and Response Program.

Anthrax: Anthrax refers to a disease that is caused by the bacterium *Bacillus anthracis*. The bacterium can enter the body via a wound in the skin (cutaneous anthrax), via contaminated food or liquid (gastrointestinal anthrax), or can be inhaled (inhalation anthrax). Potentially fatal, anthrax has been developed for use as a biological weapon.

APF: Alliance of Palestinian Forces (APF).

Aryan: As used by white supremacist groups, the term Aryan refers to whites of Northern European descent who are supposedly a superior "master race."

ASG: Abu Sayyaf Group (ASG).

Assassination: A sudden, usually unexpected act of murder committed for impersonal reasons, typically with a political or military leader as its target.

Asset: Agents, sympathizers, or supporters that intelligence agencies can exploit to complete mission objectives.

ATF: In accordance with the Homeland Security Act of 2002, on January 24, 2003, the Bureau of Alcohol, Tobacco, and Firearms (ATF or BATF) was transferred from the Department of the Treasury to the Department of Justice. There it became the Bureau of Alcohol, Tobacco, Firearms, and Explosives, but retained the initials ATF.

AUC: United Self-Defense Forces/Group of Colombia (AUC).

Aum Shinrikyo, Aleph: Aum Supreme Truth (Aum) Aum Shinrikyo, Aleph.

B

Bacillus anthracis: The bacterium that causes anthrax.

Ballistic fingerprint: A ballistic fingerprint is the unique pattern of markings left by a specific firearm on ammunition as it is discharged.

Barrel (of oil): The traditional unit of measure by which crude oil is bought and sold on the world market. One barrel of oil is equivalent to 159 liters (42 U.S. gallons).

BCIS: U.S. Department of Homeland Security, Bureau of Citizenship and Immigration Services.

Biocontainment laboratories: A biocontainment laboratory is a laboratory that has been designed to lessen or completely prevent the escape of microorganisms.

Biodetectors: Biodetectors are analytical devices that combine the precision and selectivity of biological systems with the processing power of microelectronics.

Biological warfare: As defined by The United Nations, the use of any living organism (e.g. bacterium, virus) or an infective component (e.g., toxin), to cause disease or death in humans, animals, or plants. In contrast to bioterrorism, biological warfare is defined as the "state-sanctioned" use of biological weapons on an opposing military force or civilian population. Biological weapons include pathogenic viruses, bacteria, and biological toxins.

Biological weaponization: Putting a pathogen in a form or suspension to make it an effective military weapon.

Biometrics: An automated technique measuring physical characteristics (such as fingerprints, hand geometry, iris, retina, or facial features) of an individual for the purpose of identification or authentication of that individual.

Bioterrorism: Bioterrorism is the use of a biological weapon against a civilian or military population by a government, organization, or individual. As with any form of terrorism, its purposes include the undermining of morale, creating chaos, or achieving political goals. Biological weapons use microorganisms and toxins to produce disease and death in humans, livestock, and crops.

Black September: aka/see: Abu Nidal organization (ANO).

Blackmail: The threat to expose an individual's illegal or immoral acts if the individual does not comply with specific demands.

Bomb-grade nuclear materials: Uranium or plutonium that has been refined to the point that it can be used as fuel for a nuclear weapon.

Botulinum toxin: Botulinum toxin is among the most poisonous substances known. The toxin, which can be ingested or inhaled, disrupts transmission of nerve impulses to muscles. It is naturally produced by the bacterium *Clostridium botulinum.* Certain strains of *C. baratii* and *C. butyricum* can also be capable of producing the toxin. Botulinum toxin can be used as a biological weapon.

Brainwashing: An attempt to tear down an individual's former beliefs and replace them with new ones through an intense psychological and sometimes physical process.

C

CDC: CDC is an acronym for Centers for Disease Control and Prevention. Headquartered in Atlanta, Georgia, the CDC is one of the foremost public health institutions in the United States and in the world. The CDC serves United States national security by monitoring the incidence of infectious disease in the U.S. (and around the world), and through the development and implementation of disease control procedures.

CDIS: Counter Drug Intelligence System.

Cell: Most fundamental or basic unit of a network (e.g. terrorist network).

CFF: Cambodian Freedom Fighters (CFF).

Chemical warfare: Chemical warfare involves the aggressive use of bulk chemicals that cause death or grave injury. These chemicals are different from the lethal chemical compounds that are part of infectious bacteria or viruses.

Chlorine gas: Lung irritant generally mixed with phosgene when used as a chemical weapon.

CIA: United States Central Intelligence Agency.

CIRA: Continuity Irish Republican Army (CIRA).

CNC: Crime and Narcotics Center [CNC], United States.

Cold War: The Cold War was an ideological, political, economic, and military conflict primarily between the United States, United Kingdom and Western allies against the Union of Soviet Socialist Republics (U.S.S.R.) and Soviet dominated Eastern bloc nations that began in the aftermath of World War II and ended in 1989. From the outset, the Cold War was inextricably linked with the development of the atomic bomb and its use as military deterrent.

Counterintelligence: In the context of national security, the process of protecting national assets and secrets from covert threats, especially enemy spying.

D

DEA: Drug Enforcement Administration.

DHKP: Revolutionary People's Liberation Party/Front (DHKP/C).

Dirty Bomb: A conventional bomb packed with usually low-level radioactive debris. It cannot cause a massive nuclear chain reaction and explosion, but the conventional explosives in the bomb can spread the waste over a wide area, contaminating it.

DNA: Deoxyribonucleic Acid. The molecular composition of genetic material that is, in part, made up of nitrogenous bases that form a genetic code.

DNA fingerprinting: DNA fingerprinting is the term applied to a range of techniques that are used to show similarities and dissimilarities between the DNA present in different individuals.

DNA profile: Evaluation of an individual's DNA to establish a unique pattern of markers that can be used for identification purposes.

E

E-bomb: An e-bomb, or electronic bomb, is a non-explosive artillery shell or missile that sends out an electromagnetic pulse (EMP) of enormous power, capable of permanently disabling mechanical and electronic systems.

ELA: Revolutionary People's Struggle (ELA).

Electromagnetic pulse (EMP): A short burst of high-intensity electromagnetic energy (such as radio waves). An EMP can induce electrical currents in metal objects and damage or destroy electrical or electronic equipment, including computers, radios, and electrical grids.

ELN: National Liberation Army (ELN)-Colombia.

ETA: Basque Fatherland and Liberty (ETA).

EU: European Union.

EURATOM: European Atomic Energy Community.

Executive order: A guideline issued by the President of the United States, directed toward a particular issue, and possessing the status of a de facto law. Unlike presidential directives, executive orders are unclassified.

F

FARC: Revolutionary Armed Forces of Colombia (FARC).

Fatwa: A legal opinion or ruling issued by an Islamic scholar.

FBI: United States Federal Bureau of Investigation.

FBIS: CIA, Foreign Broadcast Information Service.

Fingerprints: Fingerprints are the patterns on the inside and the tips of fingers. The ridges of skin, also known as friction ridges, together with the valleys between them form unique patterns on the fingers. Fingerprint analysis is a biometric technique comparing scanned image of prints with a database of fingerprints.

FOIA: Freedom of Information Act. Sometimes known as the Freedom of Information-

Privacy Acts, a term referring to 1967 (FOIA) and 1974 (Privacy Act) statutes and their amendments, which greatly restrict government agencies' authority to collect information on individuals, and to withhold that information.

Forensic science: Forensic science is a multidisciplinary subject used for examining crime scenes and gathering evidence to be used in prosecution of offenders in a court of law. Forensic science techniques are also used to examine compliance with international agreements regarding weapons of mass destruction.

G

GAO: United States General Accounting Office.

GIA: Armed Islamic Group (GIA).

Globalization: The integration of economies and markets worldwide.

GRAPO: First of October Antifascist Resistance Group (GRAPO).

GSPC: Salafist Group for Call and Combat (GSPC).

GSS: Israeli General Security Service.

Guerilla warfare: In the modern era, guerilla warfare refers to armed resistance by paramilitary or irregular groups toward an occupying force. Guerilla warfare also describes a set of tactics employed by smaller forces against larger, better equipped, and better supplied forces.

H

Habeas Corpus: U.S. Constitutional right to avoid unlawful detention or imprisonment. Taken from the Latin phrase "You have the body."

Hacktivism: The use of computer hacking in the service of political activism.

HAMAS: Islamic Resistance Movement (HAMAS).

High-altitude electromagnetic pulse: Any nuclear explosion 25 miles (40 km) or higher above the ground produces a high-altitude electromagnetic pulse (HEMP), a short-lived, overlapping series of intense radio waves that blanket a large swath of ground. These radio waves can induce electrical currents in metallic objects and so cause damage to electrical and electronic equipment, including electrical power grids, telephone networks, radios, and computers.

HUJI: Harakat ul-Jihad-I-Islami (HUJI).

HUJI-B: Harakat ul-Jihad-I-Islami/Bangladesh (HUJI-B).

HUM: Harakat ul-Mujahidin (HUM) (Movement of Holy Warriors).

I

IAA: Islamic Army of Aden (IAA).

IAEA: International Atomic Energy Agency.

IBIS: The Interagency Border Inspection System (IBIS) is a database of names and other identifying information used to deter and append suspects—including suspected terrorists—as they attempt to pass through international border crossing checkpoints.

Identity theft: An identity thief typically may obtain access to a victim's social security number, driver's license information, bank account numbers, credit card numbers, etc. with the intent to opens accounts in the victim's name and make purchases or perform other transactions.

IG: Al-Gama'a al-Islamiyya (Islamic Group, IG).

Illegal immigrant: Someone who has entered into a country illegally.

IMF: International Monetary Fund.

IMU: Islamic Movement of Uzbekistan (IMU).

Infectious diseases: Infectious diseases are those diseases that are caused by microorganisms such as bacteria and viruses, many of which are spread from person to person. An intermittent host, or vector, aids the spread of some infectious diseases.

INL: International Narcotics and Law Enforcement Affairs (INL), United States Bureau for.

INS: As of March 1, 2003, the newly created United States Department of Homeland Security (DHS) absorbed the former Immigration and Naturalization Service (INS). All INS border patrol agents and investigators—along with agents from the U.S. Customs Service and Transportation Security Administration—were placed under the direction of the DHS Directorate of Border and Transportation Security (BTS). Responsibility for U.S. border security and the enforcement of immigration laws was transferred to BTS. Former INS immigration service functions are scheduled to be placed under the direction of the DHS Bureau of Citizenship and Immigration Services. Under the DHS reorganization plan, the INS formally ceases to exist on the date the last of its functions are transferred.

Intelligence: In the context of national security, information about the enemy or potential enemies. Also the act of gathering such information, through spying and other means.

Intelligence Community (IC): The group of U.S. government agencies that are collectively responsible for intelligence activities, including the CIA, NSA, FBI, military intelligence branches, and other federal government agencies.

INTERPOL: International Criminal Police Organization.

Intifada: Literally, "shaking off," a term applied to the Palestinian uprising against Israel's occupation of the West Bank and Gaza.

IRA: Irish Republican Army (IRA).

Isotope: A form of a chemical element distinguished by the number of neutrons in its nucleus. E.g., ^{233}U and ^{235}U are two isotopes of uranium; both have 92 protons, but ^{233}U has 141 neutrons and ^{235}U has 143 neutrons.

IT: Information technology, a term that encompasses computers and related materials, machines, and processes.

IW (Indications and warnings): Intelligence that relates to time-sensitive information involving potential threats.

J

JEM: Jaish-e-Mohammed (JEM) (Army of Mohammed).

JI: Jemaah Islamiya (JI).

Jihad: In Islam: A holy struggle or war.

JUI-F: Jamiat Ulema-I-Islam Fazlur Rehman faction (JUI-F).

L

LRA: Lord's Resistance Army (LRA).

LT: Lashkar-e-Tayyiba (LT) (Army of the Righteous).

LTTE: Liberation Tigers of Tamil Eelam (LTTE).

LVF: Loyalist Volunteer Force (LVF).

M

MKO: Mujahedin-e Khalq Organization (MKO).

Money laundering: Disguising the origins of money by transferring it through other organizations. Money laundering usually involves taking money gained through criminal activity and passing it through the hands of one or more legitimate businesses so it will then appear to have been generated legally.

MRTA: Tupac Amaru Revolutionary Movement (MRTA).

N

NACIC: National Counter Intelligence Center.

NALU: National Army for the Liberation of Uganda (NALU).

Narcoterrorism: Terrorism undertaken by groups directly or indirectly involved in producing, transporting, or distributing illegal drugs.

NCR: National Council of Resistance (NCR).

Network: A group of individuals or cells (subgroups) engaged in specific operations (e.g., espionage or terrorist operations).

NLA: The National Liberation Army of Iran (NLA).

NPA: New People's Army (NPA).

NSA: The United States National Security Agency. The NSA is the leading cryptologic organization in the United States intelligence community, responsible for codemaking, code-breaking, and monitoring communications systems.

NTA: Anti-Imperialist Territorial Nuclei (NTA).

Nuclear weapons: Nuclear weapons are devices that utilize the processes of nuclear fission and/or fusion to release nuclear energy in the form of a very powerful explosion.

O

OPEC: Organization of Petroleum Exporting Countries, a cartel (group) of oil-producing nations that controls much of the world's petroleum production.

OV: Orange Volunteers (OV).

P

PAGAD: People Against Gangsterism and Drugs (PAGAD).

PATRIOT Act: The Patriot Act, or Uniting and Strengthening America by Providing Appropriate Tools Required to Intercept and Obstruct Terrorism Act (Public Law 107-56), was signed into law on October 26, 2001, in the wake of terrorist attacks on the World Trade Center and Pentagon. The law grants law enforcement and intelligence agencies more power to detain and question suspects for longer periods of time, and increases their ability to conduct surveillance operations.

PFLP: Popular Front for the Liberation of Palestine (PFLP).

PFLP-GC: Popular Front for the Liberation of Palestine-General Command (PFLP-GC).

PIJ: Palestine Islamic Jihad (PIJ).

PIRA: Provisional Irish Republican Army (PIRA).

PLO: Palestine Liberation Organization (PLO).

PKK: Kurdistan Workers' Party (PKK).

PLF: Palestine Liberation Front (PLF).

PMOI: People's Mujahidin of Iran (PMOI).

POG: Hizballah (Party of God).

Profiling: The process of developing descriptions of the traits and characteristics of unknown offenders in specific criminal cases. Also, targeting someone for particular attention because they bear a resemblance ("fit the profile"), real or imagined, of a criminal or terrorist. For example, giving special scrutiny to people who appear to be of Middle Eastern background.

Propaganda: Propaganda is a form of communication that attempts to influence the behavior of people by affecting their perceptions, attitudes and opinions.

R

Ricin: Ricin is a highly toxic protein that is derived from the bean of the castor plant (*Ricinus communis*). The toxin causes cell death by inactivating ribosomes, which are responsible for protein synthesis. Ricin can be produced in a liquid, crystal or powdered forms and it can be inhaled, ingested, or injected. It causes fever, cough, weakness, abdominal pain, vomiting, diarrhea and dehydration and death. There is no cure for Ricin poisoning.

Ring: A group or network.

RIRA: Real IRA (RIRA).

RJO: Revolutionary Justice Organization.

RN: Revolutionary Nuclei.

RN group (Greece): Revolutionary Nuclei.

Rogue state: A nation that harbors terrorists and/or poses a serious security threat to its neighbors.

RPA: Revolutionary Proletarian Army (RPA).

RUF: Revolutionary United Front (RUF).

S

Sarin gas: Sarin gas (O-Isopropyl methylphosphonofluoridate), also called GB, is a dangerous and toxic chemical. It belongs to a class of chemical weapons known as nerve agents, all of which are organophosphates. The G nerve agents, including tabun, sarin and soman, are all extremely toxic, but not very persistent in the environment. Pure sarin is a colorless and odorless gas, is extremely volatile, and can spread quickly through the air.

Sendero Luminoso: Sendero Luminoso (Shining Path, or SL).

Shin Bet: The Israeli intelligence agency.

Shin Beth: Israeli counterintelligence service.

Shining Path: Sendero Luminoso (Shining Path, or SL).

SL: Sendero Luminoso (Shining Path, or SL).

Supreme truth: Aum Supreme Truth (Aum) Aum Shinrikyo, Aleph.

T–W

Terrorism: Terrorism is the systematic belief in the political, religious, or ideological efficacy of producing fear by attacking—or threatening to attack—unsuspecting or defenseless populations, usually civilians, and usually by surprise.

TIFG: Tunisian Islamic Fighting Group.

UDA/UVF: Ulster Defense Association/Ulster Freedom Fighters (UDA/UVF).

Vigilante: A private citizen who is acting to detect and/or punish violations of the law. These violations may be real or only perceived, and the tactics used by vigilantes may include violence, intimidation, and other tactics that are themselves illegal.

Virus: Viruses are essentially nonliving repositories of nucleic acid that require the presence of a living prokaryotic or eukaryotic cell for the replication of the nucleic acid. There are a number of different viruses that challenge the human immune system and that may produce disease in humans. In common, a virus is a small, infectious agent that consists of a core of genetic material (either deoxyribonucleic acid [DNA] or ribonucleic acid [RNA]) surrounded by a shell of protein.

VOA: Voice of America.

Weapons of mass destruction: Weapons of mass destruction are weapons that cause a high loss of life within a short time span. Nuclear, chemical, and biological weapons are classified as weapons of mass destruction.

Weapons-grade material: Weapon-grade (or "bomb-grade") uranium or plutonium is any alloy or oxide compound that contains enough of certain isotopes of these elements to serve as the active ingredient in a nuclear weapon.

White supremacy: The concept that people of European, especially northern European, descent are inherently superior to other peoples.

WHO: World Health Organization.

WMD: Weapons of mass destruction.

World Islamic Front for Jihad: A group absorbed by Al-Qaeda (also known as Al-Qaida).

Index

Page references appearing after "1:" are in volume 1. Page numbers after "2:" are in volume 2. Bold page numbers indicate an entry on the extremist group in question. Italicized page numbers indicate a reference to an illustration.